Lecture Notes in Computer Science 1785

Edited by G. Goos, J. Hartmanis and J. van Leeuwen

Lecture Notes in Computer Science 1785

Springer
Berlin
Heidelberg
New York
Barcelona
Hong Kong
London
Milan
Paris
Singapore
Tokyo

Susanne Graf   Michael Schwartzbach (Eds.)

Tools and Algorithms for the Construction and Analysis of Systems

6th International Conference, TACAS 2000
Held as Part of the Joint European Conferences
on Theory and Practice of Software, ETAPS 2000
Berlin, Germany, March 25 – April 2, 2000
Proceedings

Springer

Series Editors

Gerhard Goos, Karlsruhe University, Germany
Juris Hartmanis, Cornell University, NY, USA
Jan van Leeuwen, Utrecht University, The Netherlands

Volume Editors

Susanne Graf
VERIMAG
2, Avenue de la Vignate, 38240 Gières, France
E-mail: Susanne.Graf@imag.fr

Michael Schwartzbach
University of Aarhus
BRICS, Department of Computer Science
Ny Munkegade, 8000 Aarhus C, Denmark
E-mail: mis@daimi.aau.dk

Cataloging-in-Publication Data applied for

Die Deutsche Bibliothek - CIP-Einheitsaufnahme

Tools and algorithms for the construction and analysis of systems :
6th international conference ; proceedings / TACAS 2000, held as part
of the Joint European Conferences on Theory and Practice of Software,
ETAPS 2000, Berlin, Germany, March 25 - April 2, 2000. Susanne Graf ;
Michael Schwartzbach (ed.). - Berlin ; Heidelberg ; New York ;
Barcelona ; Hong Kong ; London ; Milan ; Paris ; Singapore ; Tokyo :
Springer, 2000
    (Lecture notes in computer science ; Vol. 1785)
    ISBN 3-540-67282-6

CR Subject Classification (1991): F.3, D.2.4, D.2.2, C.2.4, F.2.2

ISSN 0302-9743
ISBN 3-540-67282-6 Springer-Verlag Berlin Heidelberg New York

Springer-Verlag is a company in the BertelsmannSpringer publishing group.
© Springer-Verlag Berlin Heidelberg 2000
Printed in Germany

Typesetting: Camera-ready by author, data conversion by DA-TeX Gerd Blumenstein
Printed on acid-free paper   SPIN 10719978   06/3142   5 4 3 2 1 0

Foreword

ETAPS 2000 was the third instance of the European Joint Conferences on Theory and Practice of Software. ETAPS is an annual federated conference that was established in 1998 by combining a number of existing and new conferences. This year it comprised five conferences (FOSSACS, FASE, ESOP, CC, TACAS), five satellite workshops (CBS, CMCS, CoFI, GRATRA, INT), seven invited lectures, a panel discussion, and ten tutorials.

The events that comprise ETAPS address various aspects of the system development process, including specification, design, implementation, analysis, and improvement. The languages, methodologies, and tools which support these activities are all well within its scope. Different blends of theory and practice are represented, with an inclination towards theory with a practical motivation on one hand and soundly-based practice on the other. Many of the issues involved in software design apply to systems in general, including hardware systems, and the emphasis on software is not intended to be exclusive.

ETAPS is a loose confederation in which each event retains its own identity, with a separate program committee and independent proceedings. Its format is open-ended, allowing it to grow and evolve as time goes by. Contributed talks and system demonstrations are in synchronized parallel sessions, with invited lectures in plenary sessions. Two of the invited lectures are reserved for "unifying" talks on topics of interest to the whole range of ETAPS attendees. The aim of cramming all this activity into a single one-week meeting is to create a strong magnet for academic and industrial researchers working on topics within its scope, giving them the opportunity to learn about research in related areas, and thereby to foster new and existing links between work in areas that were formerly addressed in separate meetings. The program of ETAPS 2000 included a public business meeting where participants had the opportunity to learn about the present and future organization of ETAPS and to express their opinions about what is bad, what is good, and what might be improved.

ETAPS 2000 was hosted by the Technical University of Berlin and was efficiently organized by the following team:

Bernd Mahr (General Chair)
Hartmut Ehrig (Program Coordination)
Peter Pepper (Organization)
Stefan Jähnichen (Finances)
Radu Popescu-Zeletin (Industrial Relations)

with the assistance of BWO Marketing Service GmbH. The publicity was superbly handled by Doris Fähndrich of the TU Berlin with assistance from the ETAPS publicity chair, Andreas Podelski. Overall planning for ETAPS conferences is the responsibility of the ETAPS steering committee, whose current membership is:

Egidio Astesiano (Genova), Jan Bergstra (Amsterdam), Pierpaolo Degano (Pisa), Hartmut Ehrig (Berlin), José Fiadeiro (Lisbon), Marie-Claude Gaudel (Paris), Susanne Graf (Grenoble), Furio Honsell (Udine), Heinrich Hußmann (Dresden), Stefan Jähnichen (Berlin), Paul Klint (Amsterdam), Tom Maibaum (London), Tiziana Margaria (Dortmund), Ugo Montanari (Pisa), Hanne Riis Nielson (Aarhus), Fernando Orejas (Barcelona), Andreas Podelski (Saarbrücken), David Sands (Göteborg), Don Sannella (Edinburgh), Gert Smolka (Saarbrücken), Bernhard Steffen (Dortmund), Wolfgang Thomas (Aachen), Jerzy Tiuryn (Warsaw), David Watt (Glasgow), Reinhard Wilhelm (Saarbrücken)

ETAPS 2000 received generous sponsorship from:

the Institute for Communication and Software Technology of TU Berlin
the European Association for Programming Languages and Systems
the European Association for Theoretical Computer Science
the European Association for Software Development Science
the "High-Level Scientific Conferences" component of the European
    Commission's Fifth Framework Programme

I would like to express my sincere gratitude to all of these people and organizations, the program committee members of the ETAPS conferences, the organizers of the satellite events, the speakers themselves, and finally Springer-Verlag for agreeing to publish the ETAPS proceedings.

January 2000   Donald Sannella
                                   ETAPS Steering Committee Chairman

Preface

This volume contains the proceedings of the 6th TACAS, International Conference on Tools and Algorithms for the Construction and Analysis of Systems. TACAS took place at the Technical University of Berlin, March 27–31, 2000, as a part of the third European Joint Conferences on Theory and Practice of Software (ETAPS) whose aims and organization are detailed in a separate foreword by Don Sannella.

Previous TACAS meetings were held in 1999 (Amsterdam), 1998 (Lisbon), 1997 (Twente), 1996 (Passau), and 1995 (Aarhus). Since 1998 TACAS has been a conference and part of ETAPS. All previous TACAS proceedings have been published as volumes in Springerr-Verlag's Lecture Notes in Computer Science series.

It is the goal of TACAS to provide a forum for researchers, developers, and users interested in the development and application of tools for the specification, verification, analysis, and construction of software and hardware systems. In particular, it aims to promote the exchange of ideas between different communities of theoreticians, tool builders, tool users, and system designers of various specialized areas that traditionally had little interaction. In this respect, TACAS reflects the overall goal of ETAPS from a tool oriented perspective. In effect, the scope of TACAS intersects with those of all other ETAPS events, which address more traditional areas of interest.

As a consequence, in addition to the standard criteria for acceptability, contributions have also been selected on the basis of their conceptual significance in the neighbouring areas. This comprises the comparison of concepts and methods, their degree of support via interactive or fully automatic tools, and case studies revealing the application profiles of the considered methods and tools.

In order to emphasize the practical importance of tools, TACAS encourages tool presentations on equal footing with traditional scientific papers, treating them as "first class citizens". In practice, this means that they have the same space in the proceedings and a full slot in the plenary conference session. Of course, during the conference there were also demonstrations of tools not announced in the official program.
These proceedings contain

- **an invited lecture** by Pierre Wolper and Bernhard Boigelot from the University of Liège "*On the Construction of Automata from Linear Arithmetic Constraints*".
- 33 **regular contributions**, covering a wide range of topics and being all relevant to the development of tools. They have been selected from 107 submissions, which is the largest number of submission TACAS has had so far.
- the text of two **short tool demonstrations** which were reviewed by the ETAPS steering committee.

TACAS was hosted by the Technical University of Berlin, and being part of ETAPS, it shared the excellent organization described by Don Sannella in the foreword. TACAS will be continued next year as a part of ETAPS at Genova and in 2002 in Grenoble.

Finally, we would like to thank the program committee and all the referees for their assistance in selecting the papers, Don Sannella for mastering the coordination of the whole ETAPS, and last but not least, the local organizers in Berlin.

January 2000   Susanne Graf
                                                      Michael Schwartzbach

Steering Committee

Ed Brinksma (U. Twente)
Rance Cleaveland (SUNY at Stony Brook)
Kim G. Larsen (U. Aalborg)
Bernhard Steffen (U. Dortmund)

Program Committee

Chairs: Susanne Graf (VERIMAG, Grenoble)
          Michael Schwartzbach (BRICS, Aarhus)

Thomas Ball (Microsoft Reasearch)   Joost Kok (U. Leiden)
Ed Brinksma (U. Twente)   Kim Larsen (U. Aalborg)
Rance Cleaveland (Stony Brook)   Tiziana Margaria (U. Dortmund)
Matthew Dwyer (Kansas State U.)   Bernhard Steffen (U. Dortmund)
Fausto Giunchiglia (U. Trento)   Perdita Stevens (U. Edinburgh)
Constance Heitmeyer (Naval Research)   Wang Yi (U. Uppsala)
Gerard Holzmann (Bell Labs)
Claude Jard (IRISA, Rennes)

Reviewers

Parosh Abdulla
Rajeev Alur
Tobias Amnell
Stuart Anderson
Myla M. Archer
Mark Ardis
Eugène Asarin
David Aspinall
Gerd Behrmann
Johan Bengtsson
Saddek Bensalem
Ramesh Bharadwaj
Roland Bol
Marcello Bonsangue
Ahmed Bouajjani
Julian Bradfield
Volker Braun
Paul Caspi
Frederico Crazzolara
Pedro D'Argenio
Mads Dam
Achim Dannecker
Alexandre David
Rick Dewar
Rolf Drechsler
Jakob Engblom
Harald Ganzinger
Stephen Gilmore
Jens Chr. Godskesen
David Griffioen
Corin Gurr
Michael Hanus
John Hatcliff
Klaus Havelund
Loïc Hélouët
Jesper G. Henriksen

Holger Hermanns
Andreas Holzmann
Juraj Hromkovic
Frank Huch
Thomas Hune
Hardi Hungar
Purush Iyer
Paul Jackson
Ralph Jeffords
Henrik E. Jensen
Peter K. Jensen
Thierry Jeron
Mark Jerrum
Bengt Jonsson
Pim Kars
Joost-Pieter Katoen
Tim Kempster
Yonit Kesten
James Kirby
Nils Klarlund
Jens Knoop
Kaare J. Kristoffersen
Yassine Lakhnech
Rom Langerak
Elizabeth Leonard
Martin Leucker
Jorn Lind-Nielsen
Hans Henrik Løvengreen
Angelika Mader
Thomas Mailund
Oded Maler
Radu Mateescu
Michael Mendler
Faron Moller
Laurent Mounier
Anders Møller

Markus Müller-Olm
Gustaf Naeser
Kedar Namjoshi
Uwe Nestmann
Peter Niebert
Oliver Niese
Marcus Nilsson
Thomas Noll
Jan Nyström
Corina Pasareanu
Doron Peled
Paul Pettersson
Xu Qiwen
Sriram Rajamani
Arend Rensink
Marina Ribaudo
Søren Riis
Judi Romijn
Mauno Ronkko
Vlad Rusu
Oliver Rüthing
Theo Ruys
Konstantinos Sagonas
Wolfram Schulte
Joseph Sifakis
Mikael Sjodin
Arne Skou
Margaret H. Smith
Colin Stirling
Jan Tretmans
Stavros Tripakis
Judith Underwood
Glynn Winskel
Sergio Yovine
René de Vries

Table of Contents

Infinite and Parameterized Systems

Diagnostic and Test Generation

Efficient Model-Checking

Model-Checking Tools

Symbolic Model-Checking

Visual Tools

Verification of Critical Systems

On the Construction of Automata from Linear Arithmetic Constraints*

Pierre Wolper and Bernard Boigelot

Université de Liège, Institut Montefiore, B28
4000 Liège Sart-Tilman, Belgium
{pw,boigelot}@montefiore.ulg.ac.be

Abstract. This paper presents an overview of algorithms for constructing automata from linear arithmetic constraints. It identifies one case in which the special structure of the automata that are constructed allows a linear-time determinization procedure to be used. Furthermore, it shows through theoretical analysis and experiments that the special structure of the constructed automata does, in quite a general way, render the usual upper bounds on automata operations vastly overpessimistic.

1 Introduction

Model checking [CES86,QS81,VW86] is a now widespread technique for verifying temporal properties of reactive programs. There are several ways to develop the theory of model checking, a particularly attractive one being through the construction of automata from temporal logic formulas [VW86,BVW94]. As a result, there has been a fair amount of interest in the construction of automata from temporal logical formulas, the history of which is actually fairly interesting.

The starting point is clearly the work of Büchi on the decidability of the first and second-order monadic theories of one successor [Büc62]. These decidability results were obtained through a translation to infinite-word automata, for which Büchi had to prove a very nontrivial complementation lemma. The translation is nonelementary, but this is the best that can be done. It is quite obvious that linear-time temporal logic can be translated to the first-order theory of one successor and hence to infinite-word automata. From a logician's point of view, this could be seen as settling the question, but an interest in using temporal logic for computer science applications, in particular program synthesis [MW84,EC82] triggered a second look at the problem. Indeed, it was quite obvious that a nonelementary construction was not necessary to build an automaton from a temporal logic formula; it could be done within a single exponential by a direct construction [WVS83,VW94]. As originally presented, this construction was worst and best case exponential. Though it was fairly clear that it could be modified to operate more effectively on many instances, nothing

---

* This research was partially funded by a grant of the "Communauté française de Belgique - Direction de la recherche scientifique - Actions de recherche concertées".

S. Graf and M. Schwartzbach (Eds.): TACAS/ETAPS 2000, LNCS 1785, pp. 1–19, 2000.

was written about this, probably because the topic was thought to be rather trivial and had no bearing on general complexity results.

Nevertheless, the idea that doing model checking through the construction of automata was taken seriously, at least by some, and attempts were made to incorporate automata-theoretic model checking into tools, notably into SPIN [Hol91,Hol97]. Of course, this required an effective implementation of the logic to automaton translation algorithm and the pragmatics of doing this are not entirely obvious. A description of such an implementation was given in [GPVW95] and "improved" algorithms have been proposed since [DGV99]. Note that there are some questions about how to measure such "improvements" since the worst-case complexity of the algorithms stays the same. Nevertheless, experiments show that, for the temporal logic formulas most frequently used in verification, the automata can be kept quite small. Thus, even though it is an intrinsically exponential process, building an automaton from a temporal logic formula appears to be perfectly feasible in practice. What is surprising is that it took quite a long time for the details of a usable algorithmic solution to be developed and codified.

Since building automata from temporal logic formulas turns out to be feasible, one might wonder if the same approach could work for other logics. This has been tried for the second-order monadic logic of one successor ($S1S$) in the MONA tool [HJJ⁺95]. Here, one is confronted with nonelementary complexity, but careful algorithm selection and coding as well as the fact that the practically useful formulas are not arbitrary make the tool unquestionably usable. Motivated by the need to represent sets of integer vectors in the context of the verification of infinite-state systems [BW94], an automata-based approach is being developed for linear integer (Presburger) arithmetic [WB95,Boi98]. The idea that Presburger arithmetic formulas can be represented by automata goes back at least to Büchi [Büc60], and has lead to nice characterization results for the finite-state representable sets of integer vectors [Cob69,Sem77,BHMV94]. The attractiveness of the approach is not so much for single-shot arithmetic decision problems for which more traditional decision procedures perform well [Pug92], but for situations in which represented sets are repeatedly manipulated and compared, as is necessary in verification. Indeed, minimized deterministic finite automata are a convenient normal form for arithmetic formulas, in a way similar to BDDs [Bry92] being a normal form for Boolean formulas.

Nevertheless, attempts to make a pragmatic use of automata representing arithmetic formulas are fairly recent [WB95,BC96] and one now needs to delve into the details of the automata constructions. Indeed, a straightforward approach to building the automata is quite unworkable and a crude complexity analysis leads only to a nonelementary upper bound, which is unsatisfactory since Presburger arithmetic is know to be decidable in double exponential space. Fortunately, one can do better. In [WB95] it was suggested to use concurrent automata as a representation. This indeed reduces the size of the automata, but pushes up the complexity of manipulating them. An important step was made in [BC96] where it was showed that there is a simple construction for obtaining a deterministic automaton corresponding to an equation or an inequation. That paper even goes further and claims that a triple exponential deterministic automaton can be built for an arbitrary Presburger formula. Unfortunately, though the result itself might not be false, the argument used to substantiate this claim is intrinsically incorrect as we will discuss in this paper. In [TRS98] an encouraging experiment with an automaton-based Presburger implementation is described. Finally, the LASH tool [LASH] is a comprehensive implementation of arithmetic through automata.

This paper aims at presenting and improving on the basics of the pragmatics of constructing automata from Presburger formulas. It starts with a detailed exposition of the construction of automata for linear equations and inequations. The fundamental idea of the construction is that of [BC96], which we extend and improve. First, we deal with signed integers using 2's complement notation (see also [BBR97,BRW98]). Second, we aim at obtaining automata for both directions of reading number encodings. For equations, this is not problematic since the constructed automaton is immediately deterministic in both directions. For inequations, the construction of [BC96] gives an automaton that is deterministic in one direction, but nondeterministic in the other. However, we show that the automaton, taken in its nondeterministic direction, has a special structure that allows the use of a linear-time determinization procedure of possibly independent interest. Furthermore, this result shows that at least in this special case, the general exponential upper bound on determinization is vastly pessimistic.

Finally, we turn to the problem of building automata for arbitrary Presburger formulas. Here, the interesting question is whether an unbounded alternation of quantifiers leads or not to a nonelementary blowup in the size of the automaton. This of course can be the case for arbitrary automata, but we show, with the help of a logic-based argument, that it is not the case for the automata obtained from Presburger formulas. We further substantiate this by giving the results of a number of experiments done with the LASH tool.

2   Preliminaries

Presburger arithmetic is the first-order theory of the structure $\langle \mathbf{N}, 0, \leq, + \rangle$, i.e. the natural numbers with the $\leq$ predicate as well as the 0-ary function 0 and the binary function $+$, all interpreted in the standard way. A Presburger formula with free variables thus represents a set of natural number vectors. In what follows, we will also refer to the theory of the related structure $\langle \mathbf{Z}, 0, \leq, + \rangle$, i.e. the additive theory of the integers, as Presburger arithmetic. Context will remove any ambiguity.

When encoded in a base $r \geq 2$, a natural number is a word over the alphabet $\{0, \ldots r-1\}$. A language or set of words thus represents a set of natural numbers. An obvious question to ask then is which sets of natural numbers correspond to the regular languages under this representation. The question was answered by Cobham who showed that the sets representable in at least two relatively prime bases are exactly those definable in Presburger arithmetic [Cob69]. If one limits oneself to a specific base, say base 2, slightly more is representable. Precisely, one can add to Presburger arithmetic the function $V_r(n)$ giving the largest power of the base r dividing its argument n (see [BHMV94]).

Similar results exist for vectors of natural numbers. To encode an n-dimensional vector $\mathbf{x} = (x_1, \ldots, x_n)$, one encodes each of its components in base r. The length of the encoding of the components is then made uniform by adding leading 0s to the shorter components. The result is then viewed as a word over the alphabet r^n by considering together the first digits of all the vector components, then the second digits, and so on.

Example 1. The vector $(4, 3)$ is encoded in binary by $(100, 011)$, which is viewed as the word $(1, 0)(0, 1)(0, 1)$ over the alphabet 2^2.

Cobham's result on the sets representable by regular languages was extended to natural number vectors by Semenov [Sem77].

In many situations, it is useful to deal with integers rather than with natural numbers. There are several ways to extend the encoding we just introduced to integers. An obvious one is to add a sign bit, but this leads to the need to constantly distinguish the cases of positive and negative numbers. If one works in base 2, which will be our choice from now on, things can be made more uniform, exactly as is done in computer arithmetic, by using 2's complement notation as proposed in [WB95,BRW98,Boi98].

In this notation, a number $b_k b_{k-1} \ldots b_1 b_0$ of length $k+1$ written in base 2 is interpreted as $-b_k 2^k + \sum_{0 \le i \le k-1} b_i 2^i$. It is thus positive if b_k is 0 and negative if this bit is 1. There is one slight difficulty that comes from the fact that there is no bound on the size of the integers we consider and that thus we are dealing with variable-length encodings of integers, as opposed to the fixed length usually used in computer arithmetic. This is not problematic if we require that the leading bit of a number is always a sign bit, i.e. it is 0 is the number is positive and 1 if the number is negative[1]. Indeed, there is then no ambiguity on the interpretation of the first bit of a number and repeating the sign bit, whether it is 0 or 1, has no incidence on the value of the number interpreted according to 2's complement's rule since $-2^k + 2^{k-1} = -2^{k-1}$. We can thus still easily make the lengths of the encodings of the components of a vector equal.

Example 2. The vector $(-2, 12)$ can be encoded as $(11110, 01100)$ or as the word $(1, 0)(1, 1)(1, 1)(1, 0)(0, 0)$.

Our goal here is to use finite automata to represent Presburger definable sets of integers. The advantages of this representation are that it is easy to compute with and that it makes questions about the represented sets, for instance nonemptiness, easy to decide. Furthermore, by using minimal deterministic automata, one even obtains a convenient normal form for Presburger definable sets of integer vectors. We will thus consider the problem of building automata corresponding to Presburger formulas. There are however two questions we have to deal with before doing so.

---

[1] More formally, this means that to represent an integer x, we use a number of bits $k > 0$ large enough to satisfy $-2^{k-1} \le x < 2^{k-1}$.

Since sign bits can be repeated any number of times, an integer vector has an infinite number of representations. The question then is, which representations should the automata accept. It turns out that the most convenient answer is *all valid representations*, a representation of a vector being valid if its length is sufficient to allow its largest magnitude component to start with a sign bit. Indeed, representing an integer vector by all its encodings allows the Boolean operations on sets of vectors to correspond exactly with the matching language operation on the encodings. The same is unfortunately not true of projection, which is the automaton operation that allows us to handle existential quantification. Indeed, if for example one projects out the largest component of a vector by using language projection on the encodings, one can be left with an automaton that accepts only encodings beyond an unnecessarily long minimum inherited from the component that was eliminated. This problem can nevertheless be solved by using a specific projection operation that allows skipping the repetition of the initial symbol of a word.

The second question is whether our automata will read encodings starting with the most significant or with the least significant bit. One can see advantages to using either directions, and the constructions we give allow automata to be built for either direction. However, our default choice, and the one we will use in examples, is to start with the most significant bit, this order often making the search for a vector accepted by an automaton more effective.

3   Building Automata for Presburger Formulas

We now turn to the problem of building an automaton accepting all encodings of the elements of a set defined by a Presburger formula. We could begin with a construction of automata for addition, equality and inequality, but there are interesting constructions that can deal directly with linear equations and inequations. We thus start with these.

3.1   Building Automata for Equations

The construction we present here is in essentially the one given in [BC96] adapted to handle negative numbers represented using 2's complement, as well as to reading numbers starting with the most significant bit first. The construction is based on the following simple observation. Consider a representation of a vector $\mathbf{x} = (x_1, \ldots, x_n)$ that is k bits long, and imagine adding the bits[2] $(b_1, \ldots, b_n) = \mathbf{b}$ respectively to the encodings of $(x_1, \ldots, x_n)$. The value $\mathbf{x}'$ of the $(k + 1)$-bit long encoding thus obtained is given by $\mathbf{x}' = 2\mathbf{x} + \mathbf{b}$ where addition is component-wise. This rule holds for every bit-tuple added except for the

---

[2] Note that since there is a unique integer vector corresponding to an encoding, we will quite liberally talk about the vector defined by an encoding and, when appropriate use vector notation for encodings. In particular, we will always write elements $(b_1, \ldots, b_n)$ of 2^n as bit vectors $\mathbf{b}$.

first one, in which 1s have to be interpreted as -1. Thus, the value of a one bit long vector $(b_1, \ldots, b_n) = \mathbf{b}$ is simply $-\mathbf{b}$.

Given this, it is very simple to construct an automaton for a linear equation $a_1 x_1 + \cdots + a_n x_n = c$ which we write $\mathbf{a}.\mathbf{x} = c$. Indeed, the idea is to keep track of the value of the left-hand side of the equation as successive bits are read. Thus, except for a special initial state, each state of the automaton corresponds to an integer that represents the current value of the left-hand side. From a state corresponding to an integer $\gamma = \mathbf{a}.\mathbf{x}$ for the vector $\mathbf{x}$ that has been read so far, there is a single transition for each bit vector $\mathbf{b}$ leading to the state $\gamma' = \mathbf{a}.(2\mathbf{x} + \mathbf{b}) = 2\mathbf{a}.\mathbf{x} + \mathbf{a}.\mathbf{b} = 2\gamma + \mathbf{a}.\mathbf{b}$. From the special initial state, the transition labeled $\mathbf{b}$ simply leads to the state $\mathbf{a}.(-\mathbf{b})$. The only accepting state is the one whose value is c. Formally, the automaton corresponding to an n-variable equation $\mathbf{a}.\mathbf{x} = c$ is $A = (S, 2^n, \delta, s_i, c)$ where

- $S = \mathbf{Z} \cup \{s_i\}$, i.e. the states are the integers plus a special state s_i;
- the alphabet 2^n is the set of n-bit vectors;
- the transition function δ is defined by
  - $\delta(s_i, \mathbf{b}) = -\mathbf{a}.\mathbf{b}$ and
  - $\delta(\gamma, \mathbf{b}) = 2\gamma + \mathbf{a}.\mathbf{b}$, for $\gamma \neq s_i$;
- the initial state is the special state s_i;
- the only accepting state is c, the value of the right-hand side of the equation.

As defined, the automaton is infinite, but there are only a finite number of states from which the accepting state is reachable. Indeed, if $\|\mathbf{a}\|_1$ represents the norm of a vector $\mathbf{a} = (a_1, \ldots, a_n)$ defined by $\|\mathbf{a}\|_1 = \sum_{i=1}^{n} |a_i|$, we have that from any state γ such that $|\gamma| > \|\mathbf{a}\|_1$, any transition leads to a state γ' with $|\gamma'| > |\gamma|$. So, if furthermore $|\gamma| > |c|$, c can never be reached from such a state. Hence, all states γ such that $|\gamma| > \|\mathbf{a}\|_1$ and $|\gamma| > |c|$ can be collapsed into a single nonaccepting state.

Example 3. The automaton for the equation $x - y = 2$ is given in Figure 2. Note that, according to the criterion we have just given, the states beyond the solid line cannot be reached from the accepting state and thus can be collapsed into a single nonaccepting state. Furthermore, looking more carefully at this particular automaton, one sees that the states to be collapsed can in fact include those beyond the dotted line.

The rule we have given for identifying unnecessary states is only approximative. It can be refined, but a more effective approach of identifying the necessary states is actually to construct the automaton backwards, starting from the accepting state. If this construction is limited to reachable states, only necessary states will be constructed. The exact construction is given in Figure 2.

When limited to its reachable states, the automaton obtained by this construction is exactly the useful part of the automaton given by the forward construction. One can complete it by directing all missing transitions to a single nonaccepting sink state. It is deterministic since it is a part of the forward automaton we constructed initially and furthermore, it is minimal, since the sets

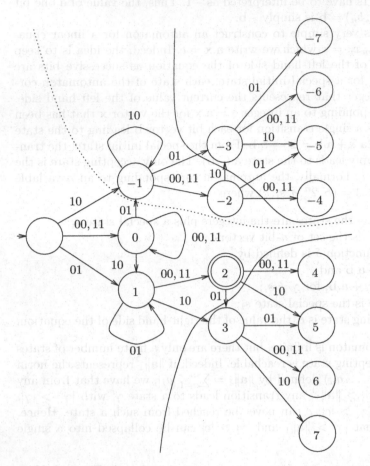

Fig. 1. The automaton for $x - y = 2$.

1. Create a table H of automata states and a list L of "active" states. Both are initialized to $\{c\}$.
2. Repeat the following step until $L = \emptyset$.
3. Remove a state γ from L, and for every $\mathbf{b} \in 2^n$:
   - If $\gamma_o = (\gamma - \mathbf{a}.\mathbf{b})/2$ is an integer, then
     - If γ_o is not in H, add it to H and L;
     - Add a transition labeled $\mathbf{b}$ from γ_o to γ;
   - If $\gamma = -\mathbf{a}.\mathbf{b}$, then
     - Add a transition labeled by $\mathbf{b}$ from the initial state s_i to γ.

Fig. 2. The automaton construction algorithm for an equation.

of words accepted from two distinct states cannot be identical. Indeed, the automaton is also deterministic when going backwards, except for transitions from the initial state, which is not a problem since the language accepted from the initial state is never equal to the one accepted from any other state. How many states does the automaton have? Clearly, any state (except for the initial one) is obtained from c by repeatedly applying the transformation $T(\gamma) = (\gamma - \mathbf{a}.\mathbf{b})/2$. The states obtained by applying this transformation i times, i.e. those in $T^i(c)$ are in the range

$$\left[\frac{c}{2^i} \pm \sum_{j=1}^{i} \frac{\|\mathbf{a}\|_1}{2^j}\right]$$

which is always included in

$$\left[\frac{c}{2^i} \pm \|\mathbf{a}\|_1\right]. \tag{1}$$

Equation (1), implies that for $i > \log_2 c$, the range reduces to $[-\|\mathbf{a}\|_1, \|\mathbf{a}\|_1]$. Thus the states can be found in at most $\log_2 c + 1$ ranges each of size bounded by $2\|\mathbf{a}\|_1 + 1$. The total number of constructed states is thus $O(\log_2 c \times \|\mathbf{a}\|_1)$, which is only logarithmic in the value of the additive constant c and hence linear in its number of bits.

3.2 Building Automata for Inequations

Consider now an inequation $\mathbf{a}.\mathbf{x} \leq c$. Note that since we are dealing with integers, a strict inequation $\mathbf{a}.\mathbf{x} < c$ is equivalent to the nonstrict inequation $\mathbf{a}.\mathbf{x} \leq c - 1$. The forward construction we gave in the previous section can still be used to build an automaton for the inequation, the only difference being that now the set of accepting states is the set $F = \{\gamma \mid \gamma \leq c\}$. Again, the automaton can be limited to a finite number of states. Indeed, starting with a positive γ such that $\gamma > \|\mathbf{a}\|_1$, all transitions will lead to a $\gamma' > \gamma$ and hence if $\gamma > c$, the equation will never be satisfied. Similarly, if γ is negative and $-\gamma > \|\mathbf{a}\|_1$, all transitions will always lead to a $\gamma' < \gamma$ and thus if $\gamma \leq c$, the inequation is satisfied.

Again, the analysis above is somewhat coarse and a backwards construction can yield an automaton with less states. However, we have to take into account the fact that we are dealing with an inequation and not an equation, which leads us to construct an automaton somewhat different from the forward automaton. The main point is that, when computing the transitions leading to a state γ, we can no longer dismiss transitions for which $\gamma_o = (\gamma - \mathbf{a}.\mathbf{b})/2$ is not an integer. Indeed, interpreting the fact that a state γ is reached to mean that the inequation $\mathbf{a}.\mathbf{x} \leq \gamma$ is satisfied by the word $\mathbf{x}$ read so far, the condition that has to be satisfied in a state γ_o from which γ is reached by a $\mathbf{b}$ transition is $\gamma_o \leq (\gamma - \mathbf{a}.\mathbf{b})/2$. An infinite number of states satisfy this condition, but it is sufficient to keep the largest since it corresponds to the weakest condition. Thus, as origin of a $\mathbf{b}$ transition to a state γ, we choose $\gamma_o = \lfloor(\gamma - \mathbf{a}.\mathbf{b})/2\rfloor$. Finally, we have to add the possibility of transitions originating in the initial state. Thus, if $-\mathbf{a}.\mathbf{b} \leq \gamma$, we also add a $\mathbf{b}$ transition from the initial state to γ.

The exact construction of the automaton is given in Figure 3, the initial state being s_i and the accepting state being c.

1. Create a table H of automata states and a list L of "active" states. Both are initialized to $\{c\}$;
2. Repeat the following step until $L = \emptyset$:
3. Remove a state γ from L, and for every $\mathbf{b} \in 2^n$:
   - Let $\gamma_o = \lfloor (\gamma - \mathbf{a}.\mathbf{b})/2 \rfloor$, then
     - If γ_o is not in H, add it to H and L;
     - Add a transition labeled $\mathbf{b}$ from γ_o to γ;
   - If $-\mathbf{a}.\mathbf{b} \le \gamma$, then
     - Add a transition labeled by $\mathbf{b}$ from the initial state s_i to γ.

Fig. 3. The automaton construction algorithm for an inequation

As opposed to the case of equations, the automaton we have just built is quite different from our initial forward automaton and is no longer deterministic. Indeed, clearly transitions from the initial state are not deterministic and, furthermore, $\lfloor (\gamma - \mathbf{a}.\mathbf{b})/2 \rfloor$ can be the same for two different values of γ, just think of $\gamma = 2$ and $\gamma = 3$ with $\mathbf{b} = \mathbf{0}$. The bound on the number of states we derived for the case equations still holds, but for a nondeterministic automaton. If a deterministic automaton is desired, one is now faced with a potentially exponential determinization cost. However, it would be quite surprising that the automaton for an inequation be so much bigger than the automaton for the corresponding equation. We show that this is not case since the automaton we have constructed has a special structure that allows it to be determinized without increasing its number of states.

The intuition behind the efficient determinization procedure is the following. Suppose that from a state γ, one has two $\mathbf{b}$ transitions leading respectively to states γ_1 and γ_2. One obviously has either $\gamma_1 < \gamma_2$ or $\gamma_2 < \gamma_1$ and one can assume without loss of generality that the former holds. If one reads being in a state γ as meaning that the inequation $\mathbf{a}.\mathbf{x} \le \gamma$ is satisfied by what has been read so far, it is immediate that any $\mathbf{x}$ that satisfies $\mathbf{a}.\mathbf{x} \le \gamma_1$ also satisfies $\mathbf{a}.\mathbf{x} \le \gamma_2$. Hence only the stronger of the two conditions, i.e. $\mathbf{a}.\mathbf{x} \le \gamma_1$ needs to be remembered in order to know if the word being read will end up being accepted, and the transition to the state γ_2 can be dropped. We now formalize this intuition.

Definition 1. *Given a nondeterministic finite automaton $A = (S, \Sigma, \delta, s_0, F)$, let A_s be the automaton $A = (S, \Sigma, \delta, s, F)$, i.e. A where the initial state is s. The automaton A is then said to be* ordered *if there is an explicitly given, i.e. constant-time decidable, strict total order $\prec$ on its set S (possibly excluding the initial state if no transitions lead to it) of states and if for any pair of states satisfying $s_1 \prec s_2$, we have that $L(A_{s_1}) \subset L(A_{s_2})$.*

Ordered automata can be determinized efficiently.

Lemma 1. *A nondeterministic ordered finite automaton can be determinized in linear time.*

Proof. Let $A = (S, \Sigma, \delta, s_0, F)$ be an ordered nondeterministic finite automaton, i.e its transition function is of the type $\delta : S \times \Sigma \rightarrow 2^S$. The corresponding deterministic automaton is $A' = (S, \Sigma, \delta', s_0, F)$, all components of which are identical to those of A, except for $\delta' : S \times \Sigma \rightarrow S$ which is defined by

$$\delta'(a, s) = \max(\delta(a, s)).$$

Thus, if several identically labeled transitions leave a state, they are replaced by a single transition to the largest of these states in the order defined on S. According to the definition of ordered automata, the language accepted from this largest state includes the language accepted from all smaller states and hence removing the transitions to smaller states does not change the language accepted by the automaton. Also note that if the initial state is not the target of any transition, it can safely be left out of the order. The determinization procedure just amounts to removing transitions and can be easily implemented in linear time.   □

We are aiming at applying Lemma 1 to the nondeterministic automata we have constructed for inequations. So we need to check if these automata are ordered. Let us look at the words accepted from a state γ of the automaton A constructed for an inequation $\mathbf{a}.\mathbf{x} \leq c$. These, will all be words w encoding a vector $\mathbf{x}_w$, which suffixed to any word w_0 encoding a vector $\mathbf{x}_{w_0}$ satisfying $\mathbf{a}.\mathbf{x}_{w_0} \leq \gamma$ form a word $w_0 w$ encoding a vector $\mathbf{x}_{w_0 w}$ that satisfies $\mathbf{a}.\mathbf{x}_{w_0 w} \leq c$. Thus all the words w accepted from a state γ are such that for all w_0 satisfying $\mathbf{a}.\mathbf{x}_{w_0} \leq \gamma$ one has

$$\mathbf{a}.\mathbf{x}_{w_0 w} = \mathbf{a}.\mathbf{x}_{w_0} 2^{length(w)} + \mathbf{a}.\mathbf{x}_w \leq c$$

and hence, since the above holds for any w_0 such that $\mathbf{a}.\mathbf{x}_{w_0} \leq \gamma$, w must satisfy

$$\gamma 2^{length(w)} + \mathbf{a}.\mathbf{x}_w \leq c. \tag{2}$$

So, one expects that, if $\gamma_1 < \gamma_2$, a word w accepted from γ_2 will also be accepted from γ_1. In other words, one expects that $L(A_{\gamma_2}) \subset L(A_{\gamma_1})$ and that the automaton is ordered with respect to the relation $\prec$ which is the inverse of the numerical order. However, this is not quite so. Indeed, even though all words accepted from a state γ satisfy the relation expressed by Equation (2), it is not the case that all words satisfying Equation (2) are accepted. Fortunately, it is possible to "complete" the automaton we have constructed in such a way that the words accepted from a state γ are exactly those defined by Equation (2), and this can be done without adding states to the automaton.

The completion procedure just adds transitions and accepting states. Given the automaton $A = (S, 2^n, \delta, s_i, c)$ constructed by the algorithm of Figure 3 for an inequation $\mathbf{a}.\mathbf{x} \leq c$, it constructs an automaton $A' = (S, 2^n, \delta', s_i, F')$ as described in Figure 4.

1. The set of accepting states is $F' = \{\gamma \in S \mid \gamma \leq c\}$;
2. For every state γ, and bit vector $\mathbf{b} \in 2^n$, $\delta'(\gamma, \mathbf{b}) = \delta(\gamma, \mathbf{b}) \cup \{\gamma' \in S \mid \gamma' \geq 2\gamma + \mathbf{a}.\mathbf{b}\}$.

Fig. 4. The completion algorithm.

The completion algorithm can add a number of transitions that is quadratic in the number of states and hence can require quadratic time. We will see how this can be improved, but first let us prove that the completion algorithm does produce an ordered automaton.

Lemma 2. *The completion algorithm of Figure 4 produces an ordered automaton that accepts the same language as the original automaton.*

Proof. The order with respect to which the completed automaton is ordered is the inverse of the numerical order. We thus have to prove that if $\gamma_1 < \gamma_2$ then $L(A_{\gamma_2}) \subset L(A_{\gamma_1})$. This is done by showing that the set of words accepted from any state γ is exactly the one satisfying the relation given in Equation (2), which at the same time shows that the language accepted by the completed automaton is unchanged since the original automaton already accepted all solutions of the inequation.

To show that any word satisfying Equation (2) in a state γ is accepted from that state, we proceed by induction on the length of words. For the induction to go through, we strengthen the property we are proving with the fact that for any word w of length k, the state $\gamma_w^{\max}$ which is the largest γ such that $\gamma 2^k + \mathbf{a}.\mathbf{x}_w \leq c$ is in S. If the word is of length 0 (the empty word ε), it must be accepted iff $\gamma \leq c$. This is guaranteed by the definition of the set of accepting states F'. Furthermore, $\gamma_\varepsilon^{\max}$ is simply c, which by construction is in S.

For the inductive step, let $w = \mathbf{b}_1 w_1$, where w_1 is of length $k-1$. By inductive hypothesis, the state $\gamma_{w_1}^{\max}$ is in S. By construction, the state $\lfloor (\gamma_{w_1}^{\max} - \mathbf{a}.\mathbf{b}_1)/2 \rfloor$ is in S and is the state $\gamma_w^{\max}$. Since w satisfies the relation of Equation (2) in γ, one must have that $\gamma \leq \gamma_w^{\max}$. Hence, the completion procedure adds from γ a transition to $\gamma_{w_1}^{\max}$ given that

$$\gamma_{w_1}^{\max} \geq 2\gamma_w^{\max} + \mathbf{a}.\mathbf{b}_1 \geq 2\gamma + \mathbf{a}.\mathbf{b}_1.$$

Hence w is accepted from γ. □

Note that the completion procedure adds transitions that will later be removed by the determinization procedure for the ordered automaton that is obtained. In fact from a state γ and for a bit vector $\mathbf{b}$, the determinization procedure only keeps the transition to the smallest γ' such that $\gamma' \geq \gamma + \mathbf{a}.\mathbf{b}$. Hence, in our completion procedure, we can add transitions according to the following rule:

1. For every state γ, and bit vector $\mathbf{b} \in 2^n$, $\delta'(\gamma, \mathbf{b}) = \delta(\gamma, \mathbf{b}) \cup \min\{\gamma' \in S \mid \gamma' \geq 2\gamma + \mathbf{a}.\mathbf{b}\}$.

This can be done in linear time and we have the following result.

Theorem 1. *The automaton constructed for an inequation by the algorithm of Figure 3 can be determinized in linear time.*

Example 4. The automaton produced by Algorithm 3 for the inequation $x - y \leq 2$ is given in Figure 5, with the elements added by the simplified completion procedure in boldface, and the transitions deleted by the determinization procedure underlined.

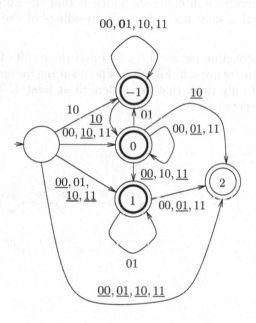

$00, 01, 10, 11$

Fig. 5. The automaton for $x - y \leq 2$.

3.3 Building Automata for Arbitrary Formulas

In an arbitrary Presburger formula, one can always move negations inwards and quantifications outwards. Doing so, one obtains a Boolean combination of linear (in)equations prefixed by a string of quantifiers, i.e. a formula of the form

$$Q_1 x_1 Q_2 x_2 \ldots Q_n x_n \phi(x_1, \ldots, x_n, y_1, \ldots, y_m) \tag{3}$$

where each Q_i is either $\forall$ or $\exists$, ϕ is quantifier free and $y_1, \ldots y_m$ are the free variables of the formula. The quantifier-free formula ϕ is a Boolean combination of linear equations and inequations ϕ_i. For each of the ϕ_i, we have seen how to build a deterministic automaton of size $O(2^{c|\phi_i|})$, where $|\phi_i|$ is the number of symbols needed to represent the (in)equation, coefficients being encoded in a base ≥ 2. The Boolean combination of these (in)equations can thus be represented by a deterministic automaton that is the product of the automata for the (in)equations, the accepting states being defined according to the given Boolean combination. This product is of size $O(\prod_i 2^{c|\phi_i|})$ or $O(2^{c\sum_i |\phi_i|})$, which is equal to $O(2^{c|\phi|})$. The size of this deterministic automaton is thus at most a single exponential in the size of the formula.

To handle quantification, one replaces $\forall$ by $\neg\exists\neg$, and uses projection as the automaton operation corresponding to existential quantification. There is however one slight problem in doing so, which is that the automaton obtained by standard projection does not accept all encodings of the projected set of integer vectors.

Example 5. The automaton for $x = 1 \wedge y = 4$ and the result of projecting out y from this automaton are given in Figure 6. The resulting automaton accepts the encodings of 1, but only those that are of length at least 4. The encodings 01 and 001 are not accepted.

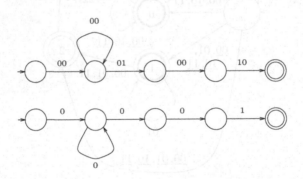

Fig. 6. Automata for $x = 1 \wedge y = 4$ and its projection.

The problem illustrated in Example 5 can be solved by modifying the automaton obtained from projection to ensure that when a word in $\mathbf{b}^+ w$ is accepted the word $\mathbf{b}w$ is also accepted. This is done by including in the set of states reachable from the initial state by $\mathbf{b}$ all states reachable from the initial state by $\mathbf{b}^+$.

The automaton obtained after a projection step is in general nondeterministic and one needs to determinize it in order to apply the complementation needed to handle universal quantification. One thus expects a exponential blowup in the size of the automaton for each quantifier alternation and thus an automaton whose size grows in a nonelementary way. In [BC96] it is argued that this is not the case, and that the size of the automaton is at most 3 exponentials in the size of the formula. Unfortunately, the argument used is false. Indeed, it essentially amounts to translating the string of alternating quantifiers to Boolean transitions, generalizing the translation to nondeterministic transitions done in the handling of projection. The result is thus an alternating automaton of size $O(2^{c|\phi|})$, which can be converted into a deterministic automaton two exponentials larger. The catch is that this implies that the quantifier prefix is handled bit-wise rather than number-wise. Explicitly, when moving from numbers to binary encodings, this implies that rather than translating (3) to

$$Q_1 b_{11} b_{12} \dots b_{1k} Q_2 b_{21} b_{22} \dots b_{2k} \dots Q_n b_{n1} b_{n2} \dots b_{nk} \phi,$$

one translates it to

$$Q_1 b_{11} Q_2 b_{21} \dots Q_n b_{n1} Q_1 b_{12} Q_2 b_{22} \dots Q_n b_{n2} \dots Q_1 b_{1k} Q_2 b_{2k} \dots Q_n b_{nk} \phi,$$

which has, of course, an entirely different meaning.

That the argument used in [BC96] is false does not mean that the size of the automaton for a Presburger formula will grow nonelementarily with respect to the number of quantifier alternations. Indeed, an analysis of the traditional quantifier elimination procedure for Presburger arithmetic [End72] shows the opposite. Looking at this procedure, one notices that the number of basic formulas that are generated stays elementary in the size of the initial formula. Whatever the quantifier prefix of the formula, the quantifier elimination procedure only generates a Boolean combination of this elementary number of formulas. Hence, the formula obtained by the quantifier elimination procedure is elementary and so will be the corresponding automaton.

3.4   Pragmatics

So far, we have tried to present in a fairly detailed way the algorithms used to build automata from Presburger formulas. However, there are still a a substantial number of "improvements" that can be added to what we have described in order to obtain a good implemented system. We discuss here one such important improvement. The reader is certainly aware of the fact that one of the drawbacks of the automata we are constructing is that their alphabet is exponential in the number of variables of the arithmetic formula. Thus, even very simple formulas involving many variables will lead to automata with a huge number of transitions. Fortunately, there is a way around this.

The idea is to sequentialize the reading of the bits of the vector components. That is, rather than reading a bit vector $\mathbf{b} = (b_1, b_2, \dots, b_n)$ as a single entity, one reads b_1, b_2, $\dots$, b_n one at a time in a fixed order. The size of the alphabet is now always 2, whatever the number of components of the integer vectors defined. Of course, the counterpart is that the number of states of the automaton is increased, but this increase can be more moderate than the explosion in the number of transitions that comes from a large number of variables. This can easily be understood by observing that using 2^n as alphabet amounts to representing the transitions from a state as a truth table, whereas sequentializing the reading of the bits corresponds to representing the transitions from a state as a decision diagram for a given bit order. Minimizing the automaton has the effect

of minimizing this diagram and one is in fact representing the transitions from
a state with a structure that is similar to an OBDD [Bry92]. This technique is
used in the LASH package [LASH] as well as in the MONA tool [HJJ+95]. The
construction algorithms presented in this paper can easily be adapted to the
sequentialized encoding of vectors.

4   Experimental Results

As discussed above, each application of a projection and determinization construction to an automaton representing arithmetic constraints is not going to
yield an exponential blowup in the size of the automaton. The question then is,
what blowup does in fact occur? To attempt to answer this question, we turned
to experiments performed with the help of the LASH tool.

The first experiment consists of applying an existential quantifier to the sets
of solutions of random systems of linear inequalities. The results obtained for
100 systems of 8 inequations of dimension 4 with coefficients in the interval
$[-5, \ldots, 5]$ are given in Figure 7. This figure depicts the number of states of the
quantified automata, which are made deterministic and minimal, with respect
to the size of the unquantified automata. Note that all the points fall below the
dotted equality line, which means that the number of states always decreases.

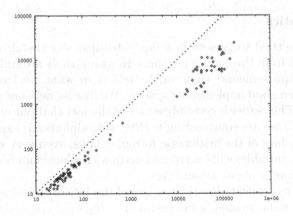

Fig. 7. Effect of quantification over systems of linear inequalities.

A second test consists of repeatedly applying an existential quantification
to the automata of the previous experiment, until only a single free variable
remains. Figure 8 gives the number of states of the automata obtained during,
and as a result of, this process, relative to the size of the automaton obtained
prior to the application of the last quantification operation.

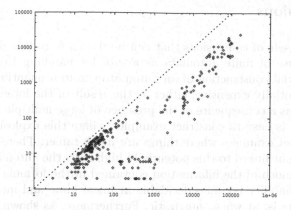

Fig. 8. Effect of repeated quantification over systems of linear inequalities.

Finally, Figure 9 illustrates the effect of applying existential quantification to non-convex sets obtained by joining together the sets of solutions of two random systems of linear inequalities.

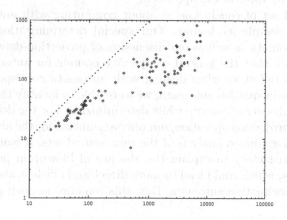

Fig. 9. Effect of quantification over non-convex sets.

It is rather surprising that these experiments show that every projection-determinization step in fact decreases the size of the automaton, whereas an exponential blowup could have been feared. This raises interesting questions, for instance, what exact bound can be proved on the size increase resulting from projecting and determinizing an arithmetic automaton? What structural properties of such automata explain this bound? These are still open questions.

5   Conclusions

There are two sets of conclusions that can be drawn from this paper. The first concerns the use of finite automata as a tool for handling Presburger arithmetic. The initial construction of an automaton from a quantifier-free formula can be exponentially expensive, either as the result of the interaction of many constraints or as a consequence of the presence of large multiplicative constants in formulas. It is easy to construct examples where this explosion occurs, but also to construct examples where things are much tamer. There is however, an important benefit linked to this potentially high cost: the automaton is a structure in which much of the information contained in the formula is explicit. For instance, satisfiability becomes decidable in linear time and inclusion between represented sets is, at worst, quadratic. Furthermore, as shown by our experiments, subsequent manipulation of the automaton need not be very costly. This indicates, that if one needs to repeatedly work with and transform a Presburger formula, as is often the case in verification applications, adopting the automata-based approach might very well be an excellent choice. On the other hand, if one is interested in a one shot satisfiability check, traditional approaches have the edge since building the automaton involves doing substantially more than just checking for the possibility of satisfying the given formula. Of course, only the accumulation of experiments coupled with the fine-tuning of tools will give the final word on the value of the approach.

The second set of conclusions is about computing with automata and the corresponding complexity bounds. Our special determinization procedure for inequation automata as well as our discussion of projection-determinization operations indicate that the general complexity bounds for automata operations do not tell the full story when dealing with automata corresponding to linear constraints. For inequation automata, we were able to identify the structure that explained the absence of blowup while determinizing. For the determinization of the result of a projection operation, our only arguments for the absence of blowup comes from a logic-based analysis of the represented sets. It would, however, be much more satisfactory to explain the absence of blowup in purely automata-theoretic terms, which could lead to more direct and efficient algorithms, just as in the case of inequation automata. But, this remains an open problem.

References

BBR97.   B. Boigelot, L. Bronne, and S. Rassart. An improved reachability analysis method for strongly linear hybrid systems. In *Proc. 9th Int. Conf.on Computer Aided Verification*, volume 1254 of *Lecture Notes in Computer Science*, pages 167–178, Haifa, June 1997. Springer-Verlag. 3

BC96.   A. Boudet and H. Comon. Diophantine equations, Presburger arithmetic and finite automata. In *Proceedings of CAAP'96*, number 1059 in Lecture Notes in Computer Science, pages 30–43. Springer-Verlag, 1996. 2, 3, 5, 13, 14

BHMV94.   V. Bruyère, G. Hansel, C. Michaux, and R. Villemaire. Logic and p-recognizable sets of integers. *Bulletin of the Belgian Mathematical Society,* 1(2):191–238, March 1994. 2, 4

Boi98.   B. Boigelot. *Symbolic Methods for Exploring Infinite State Spaces.* PhD thesis, Université de Liège, 1998. 2, 4

BRW98.   Bernard Boigelot, Stéphane Rassart, and Pierre Wolper. On the expressiveness of real and integer arithmetic automata. In *Proc. 25th Colloq. on Automata, Programming, and Languages (ICALP),* volume 1443 of *Lecture Notes in Computer Science,* pages 152–163. Springer-Verlag, July 1998. 3, 4

Bry92.   R.E. Bryant. Symbolic boolean manipulation with ordered binary-decision diagrams. *ACM Computing Surveys,* 24(3):293–318, 1992. 2, 15

Büc60.   J. R. Büchi. Weak second-order arithmetic and finite automata. *Zeitschrift Math. Logik und Grundlagen der Mathematik,* 6:66–92, 1960. 2

Büc62.   J.R. Büchi. On a decision method in restricted second order arithmetic. In *Proc. Internat. Congr. Logic, Method and Philos. Sci. 1960,* pages 1–12, Stanford, 1962. Stanford University Press. 1

BVW94.   Orna Bernholtz, Moshe Y. Vardi, and Pierre Wolper. An automata-theoretic approach to branching-time model checking. In *Computer Aided Verification, Proc. 6th Int. Workshop,* volume 818 of *Lecture Notes in Computer Science,* pages 142–155, Stanford, California, June 1994. Springer-Verlag. 1

BW94.   Bernard Boigelot and Pierre Wolper. Symbolic verification with periodic sets. In *Computer Aided Verification, Proc. 6th Int. Conference,* volume 818 of *Lecture Notes in Computer Science,* pages 55–67, Stanford, California, June 1994. Springer-Verlag. 2

CES86.   E.M. Clarke, E.A. Emerson, and A.P. Sistla. Automatic verification of finite-state concurrent systems using temporal logic specifications. *ACM Transactions on Programming Languages and Systems,* 8(2):244–263, January 1986. 1

Cob69.   A. Cobham. On the base-dependence of sets of numbers recognizable by finite automata. *Mathematical Systems Theory,* 3:186–192, 1969. 2, 3

DGV99.   M. Daniele, F. Giunchiglia, and M. Y. Vardi. Improved automata generation for linear temporal logic. In *Computer-Aided Verification, Proc. 11th Int. Conference,* volume 1633, pages 249–260, July 1999. 2

EC82.   E.A. Emerson and E.M. Clarke. Using branching time logic to synthesize synchronization skeletons. *Science of Computer Programming,* 2:241–266, 1982. 1

End72.   H. B. Enderton. *A mathematical introduction to logic.* Academic Press, 1972. 14

GPVW95.   Rob Gerth, Doron Peled, Moshe Y. Vardi, and Pierre Wolper. Simple on-the-fly automatic verification of linear temporal logic. In *Proc. 15th Work. Protocol Specification, Testing, and Verification,* Warsaw, June 1995. North-Holland. 2

HJJ$^+$95. Jesper G. Henriksen, Jakob L. Jensen, Michael E. Jørgensen, Nils Klarlund, Robert Paige, Theis Rauhe, and Anders Sandholm. Mona: Monadic second-order logic in practice. In Ed Brinksma, Rance Cleaveland, Kim Guldstrand Larsen, Tiziana Margaria, and Bernhard Steffen, editors, *Tools and Algorithms for the Construction and Analysis of Systems,* volume 1019 of *Lecture Notes in Computer Science,* pages 89–110. Springer-Verlag, 1995. 2, 15

Hol91.   G. Holzmann. *Design and Validation of Computer Protocols*. Prentice-Hall
            International Editions, 1991. 2
Hol97.   Gerard J. Holzmann. The model checker SPIN. *IEEE Transactions on Soft-
            ware Engineering*, 23(5):279–295, May 1997. Special Issue: Formal Methods
            in Software Practice. 2
LASH.   The Liège Automata-based Symbolic Handler (LASH). Available at
            http://www.montefiore.ulg.ac.be/~boigelot/research/lash/. 3, 15
MW84.   Zohar Manna and Pierre Wolper. Synthesis of communicating processes
            from temporal logic specifications. *ACM Transactions on Programming
            Languages and Systems*, 6(1):68–93, January 1984. 1
Pug92.   W. Pugh. A practical algorithm for exact array dependency analysis.
            Comm. of the ACM, 35(8):102, August 1992. 2
QS81.   J.P. Queille and J. Sifakis. Specification and verification of concurrent
            systems in Cesar. In *Proc. 5th Int'l Symp. on Programming*, volume 137,
            pages 337–351. Springer-Verlag, Lecture Notes in Computer Science, 1981.
            1
Sem77.   A. L. Semenov. Presburgerness of predicates regular in two number systems.
            Siberian Mathematical Journal, 18:289–299, 1977. 2, 4
TRS98.   R. K. Ranjan T. R. Shiple, J. H. Kukula. A comparison of Presburger
            engines for EFSM reachability. In *Proc. 10th Int. Conf. on Computer Aided
            Verification*, volume 1427 of *Lecture Notes in Computer Science*, pages 280–
            292, Vancouver, July 1998. Springer-Verlag. 3
VW86.   Moshe Y. Vardi and Pierre Wolper. An automata-theoretic approach to
            automatic program verification. In *Proceedings of the First Symposium on
            Logic in Computer Science*, pages 322–331, Cambridge, June 1986. 1
VW94.   Moshe Y. Vardi and Pierre Wolper. Reasoning about infinite computations.
            Information and Computation, 115(1):1–37, November 1994. 1
WB95.   Pierre Wolper and Bernard Boigelot. An automata-theoretic approach to
            Presburger arithmetic constraints. In *Proc. Static Analysis Symposium*,
            volume 983 of *Lecture Notes in Computer Science*, pages 21–32, Glasgow,
            September 1995. Springer-Verlag. 2, 4
WVS83.   Pierre Wolper, Moshe Y. Vardi, and A. Prasad Sistla. Reasoning about
            infinite computation paths. In *Proc. 24th IEEE Symposium on Foundations
            of Computer Science*, pages 185–194, Tucson, 1983. 1

An Extensible Type System for Component-Based Design

Yuhong Xiong and Edward A. Lee

{yuhong, eal}@eecs.berkeley.edu

Abstract. We present the design and implementation of the type system for
Ptolemy II, which is a tool for component-based heterogeneous modeling and
design. This type system combines static typing with run-time type checking. It
supports polymorphic typing of components, and allows automatic lossless type
conversion at run-time. To achieve this, we use a lattice to model the lossless
type conversion relation among types, and use inequalities defined over the type
lattice to specify type constraints in components and across components. The
system of inequalities can be solved efficiently, with existence and uniqueness
of a solution guaranteed by fixed-point theorems. This type system increases the
safety and flexibility of the design environment, promotes component reuse,
and helps simplify component development and optimization. The infrastructure
we have built is generic in that it is not bound to one particular type lattice. The
type system can be extended in two ways: by adding more types to the lattice,
or by using different lattices to model different system properties. Higher-order
function types and extended types can be accommodated in this way.

1 Introduction

Ptolemy II [5] is a system-level design environment that supports component-based
heterogeneous modeling and design. The focus is on embedded systems. In component-based design, each component has an interface, which includes the data type of
the messages sent or received by the component, and the communication protocols
used by the component to exchange information with others. In Ptolemy II, the interconnection of components is represented by hierarchical clustered graphs. Interconnections imply type constraints. In addition, components themselves may have
constraints on their interface and internal state variables.

A good type system is particularly important for embedded systems. A type
system can increase safety though type checking, promote component reuse through
polymorphic typing, provide services such as automatic type conversion, and help
optimize the design by finding low cost typing for polymorphic components.

Ptolemy II supports heterogeneous design by providing a variety of models of
computation (MoCs) [5]. It can be viewed as a coordination language where it man-

S. Graf and M. Schwartzbach (Eds.) TACAS/ETAPS 2000, LNCS 1785, pp. 20-37, 2000.

ages the communication among independent components without much knowledge about the computation they carry out. In this regard, it is similar to other coordination languages like Manifold [2]. In different MoCs, component interaction obeys different semantics. However, this level of detail can be ignored in data level type system design, and a general message passing semantics can be assumed. This abstraction enables the same type system to work with widely differing models. Fig.1 shows a simplified graph representation of a Ptolemy II model. In Ptolemy II terminology, each of the components A, B, and C is an *actor*, and actors contain *ports*, denoted by the small circles on the actors. Actors send and receive messages through ports. Messages are encapsulated in *tokens*, which are typed.

In general-purpose languages, there are two approaches for type system design: static typing and dynamic typing. Research in this area is driven to a large degree by the desire to combine the flexibility of dynamically typed languages with the security and early error-detection potential of statically typed languages. Polymorphic type systems of modern languages have achieved this goal to a large extent [14]. Since Ptolemy II is intended for large, complex, and possibly safety-critical system design, we choose static typing for its obvious advantages. To do this, we give each actor port a type. This type restricts the type of tokens that can pass though the port. Based on the port types and the graph topology, we can check the type consistency in the model statically, before it is executed. In Ptolemy II, static checking alone is not enough to ensure type safety at run-time because Ptolemy II is a coordination language, its type system does not have detailed information about the operation of each actor, except the declared types of the ports and the type constraints provided by the actors. In fact, Ptolemy II places no restriction on the implementation of an actor. So an actor may wrap a component implemented in a different language, or a model built by a foreign tool [11]. Therefore, even if a source actor declares its port type to be *Int*, no static structure prevents it from sending a token containing *Double* at run-time. The declared type *Int* in this case is only a promise from the actor, not a guarantee. Analogous to the run-time type checking in Java, the components are not trusted. Static type checking checks whether the components can work together as connected based on the information given by each component, but run-time type checking is also necessary for safety. With the help of static typing, run-time type checking can be done when a token is sent from a port. I.e., the run-time type checker checks the token type against the type of the port. This way, a type error is detected at the earliest possible time, and run-time type checking (as well as static type checking) can be performed by the system infrastructure instead of by the actors.

Another benefit of static typing is that it allows the system to perform lossless type conversion. For example, if a sending port with type *Int* is connected to a receiving port with type *Double*, the integer token sent from the sender can be converted to a double token before it is passed to the receiver. This kind of run-time type conversion is done transparently by the Ptolemy II system (actors are not aware it). So the actors can safely cast the received tokens to the type of the receiving port. This makes actor development easier. As a design principle of Ptolemy II, the system does not implicitly perform data type conversions that lose information. The lossless type conversion relation among different types is modeled as a partially ordered set, called the *type lattice*.

In Ptolemy II, polymorphic actors are actors that can accept multiple types on their ports. In general, the types on some or all of the ports of a polymorphic actor are not rigidly defined to specific types when the actor is written, so the actor can interact

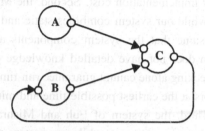

Fig. 1.   A simplified Ptolemy II model.

with other actors having different types. The acceptable types on polymorphic actors are described by a set of *type constraints*, which have the form of inequalities defined over the type lattice. The static type checker checks the applicability of a polymorphic actor in a topology (an interconnection of components) by finding specific types for them that satisfy the type constraints. This process, called *type resolution*, can be done by a very efficient algorithm.

In addition to maintaining type consistency for data transfer, our type system plays a larger role. In a component-based architecture, there are two ways to get data to components: static configuration (via parameters) and dynamic message passing (via ports). Our system allows constraints on the types of parameters, as well as the types of ports. In addition, Ptolemy II permits state variables that are local to a component to be typed, so type constraints between ports, parameters, and state variables can all be expressed.

Besides the models based on message passing, Ptolemy II also supports control oriented models, such as finite state machines (FSM), which represent a system as a sequence of state transitions in response to events. In this model, type constraints can link the transition guard and the event of the state machine. Hierarchical FSMs can be mixed with other concurrency models [7]. In these mixed models, type constraints can be propagated between the events of the control model and the data of the other concurrency models. Section 4.2 below shows an example of this.

Our type system is related to the work of Fuh and Mishra [6] that extended polymorphic type inference in ML [12] with subtypes. The lossless type conversion relation is a subtype relation. However, there are several key differences between our approach and the ML type system and the system of Fuh and Mishra. First, the ML type inference algorithm produces principal types. Principal types are the most general types for a program in that any other legal type assignment is a substitution instance of it. In our system, the type resolution algorithm finds the most specific type rather than the most general type. This specific type is the least fixed point solution for the type constraints rather than the greatest fixed point. As we will see, using the most specific type may help optimize the system under design, as the most specific type usually has a lower implementation cost. Second, the ML type system does all the checking statically, while our system combines static and run-time checking. As discussed above, we assume that the system components are opaque to the type system. The type system does not have detailed knowledge of the operation of the components, so static checking alone cannot guarantee run-time safety. Our combined approach can detect errors at the earliest possible time and minimize the computation of run-time checking. Third, the system of Fuh and Mishra allows arbitrary type conversion, represented by a coercion set, while our system concentrates on lossless conversion. This focus permits the conversion relation to form a lattice structure, and the type constraints to be expressed as inequalities on the lattice. As a result, the type constraints can be solved by a linear time algorithm, which is more efficient than the algorithm to check the consistency of a coercion set.

The advantage of a constraint-based approach, like ours, is that constraint resolution can be separated from constraint generation, and resolution can employ a sophisticated algorithm. Although the users need to understand the constraint formulation, they do not have to understand the details of the resolution algorithm in order to use the system. In addition, the constraint resolution algorithm can be built as a generic tool that can be used for other applications. Even more important in Ptolemy II, the types are not aware of the constraints, so more types can be added to the type lattice, resulting in an extensible type system.

2   Ptolemy II

Ptolemy II offers a unified infrastructure for implementation of a number of models of computation. It consists of a set of Java packages. The key packages relevant to the type system are the kernel, actor, data, and graph packages.

2.1   The Kernel Package

The kernel package defines a small set of Java classes that implement a data structure supporting a general form of uninterpreted clustered graphs, plus methods for accessing and manipulating such graphs. These graphs provide an abstract syntax for netlists, state transition diagrams, block diagrams, etc. A graph consists of *entities* and *relations*. Entities have *ports*. Relations connect entities through ports. Relations are multi-way associations. Hierarchical graphs can be constructed by encapsulating one graph inside the composite entity of another graph. This encapsulation can be nested arbitrarily.

2.2   The Actor Package

The actor package provides basic support for executable entities, or actors. It supports a general form of message passing between actors. Messages are passed between ports, which can be inputs, outputs or bidirectional ports. Actors can be typed, which means that their ports have a type. The type of the ports can be declared by the containing actor, or left undeclared on polymorphic actors; type resolution will resolve the types according to type constraints. Messages are encapsulated in tokens that are implemented in the data package or in user-defined classes extending those in the data package.

A subpackage of the actor package contains a library of (currently) about 40 polymorphic actors.

2.3   The Data Package

The data package provides data encapsulation, polymorphism, parameter handling, and an expression language. Data encapsulation is implemented by a set of token classes. For example, IntToken contains an integer, DoubleMatrixToken contains a two-dimensional array of doubles. The tokens can be transported via message passing between Ptolemy II objects. Alternatively, they can be used to parameterize Ptolemy II objects. Such encapsulation allows for a great degree of extensibility, permitting developers to extend the library of data types that Ptolemy II can handle.

One of the goals of the data package is to support polymorphic operations between tokens. For this, the base Token class defines methods for the primitive arithmetic operations, such as add(), multiply(), subtract(), divide(), modulo() and equals(). Derived classes override these methods to provide class specific operations where appropriate.

Parameter handling and an extensible expression language, including its interpreter, are supported by a subpackage inside the data package. A parameter contains a token as its value. This token can be set directly, or specified by an expression. An expression may refer to other parameters, and dependencies and type relationships between parameters are handled transparently.

2.4   The Graph Package

This package provides algorithms for manipulating and analyzing mathematical graphs. Mathematical graphs are simpler than Ptolemy II clustered graphs in that there is no hierarchy, and arcs link exactly two nodes. Both undirected and directed graphs are supported. Acyclic directed graphs, which can be used to model complete partial orders (CPOs) and lattices [4], are also supported with more specialized algorithms. This package provides the infrastructure to construct the type lattice and implement the type resolution algorithm. However, this package is not aware of the types; it supplies generic tools that can used in different applications.

3   Type System Formulation

3.1   The Type Lattice

A lattice is a partially ordered set in which every subset of elements has a least upper bound and a greatest lower bound [4]. This mathematical structure is used to represent the lossless type conversion relation in a type system. An example of a type lattice is shown in Fig.2. This particular lattice is constructed in the data package using the infrastructure of the graph package. In the diagram, type α is *greater than* type β if there is a path upwards from β to α. Thus, ComplexMatrix is greater than Int. Type α is *less than* type β if there is a path downwards from β to α. Thus, Int is less than ComplexMatrix. Otherwise, types α and β are *incomparable*. Complex and Long, for example, are incomparable. The top element, *General*, which is "the most general type," corresponds to the base token class; the bottom element, *NaT* (Not a Type), does not correspond to a token. Users can extend a type lattice by adding more types.

In the type lattice, a type can be losslessly converted to any type greater than it. For example, an integer can be losslessly converted to a double. Here, we assume an integer is 32 bits long and a double is 64 bits using the IEEE 754 floating point format, as in Java. This hierarchy is related to the inheritance hierarchy of the token classes in that a subclass is always less than its super class in the type lattice, but some adjacent types in the lattice are not related by inheritance. So this hierarchy is a combination of the subtyping relation in object oriented languages, and ad hoc subtyping rules, such as $Int \leq Double$ [13]. Organizing types in a hierarchy is fairly standard. For example, Abelson and Sussman [1] organized the coercion relation among types in a hierarchy. However, they did not deliberately model the hierarchy as a lattice. Long ago, Hext [9] experimented with using a lattice to model the type conversion relation, but he was not working with an object oriented language and did not intend to support polymorphic system components. This work predates the popular use of those concepts.

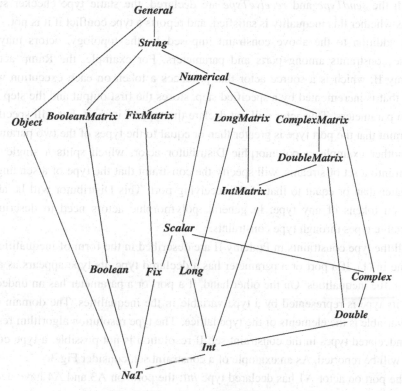

Fig. 2. An example of a type lattice.

Type conversion is done by a method convert() in the token classes. This method converts the argument into an instance of the class implementing this method. For example, DoubleToken.convert(Token token) converts the specified token into an instance of DoubleToken. The convert() method can convert any token immediately below it in the type hierarchy into an instance of its own class. If the argument is several levels down the type hierarchy, the convert() method recursively calls the convert() method one level below to do the conversion. If the argument is higher in the type hierarchy, or is incomparable with its own class, convert() throws an exception. If the argument to convert() is already an instance of its own class, it is returned without any change.

3.2   Type Constraints

In Ptolemy II, to guarantee that information is not lost during data transfer, we require the type of a port that sends tokens to be the same as or lower than the type of the receiving port:

$$sendType \leq receiveType \tag{1}$$

If both the *sendType* and *receiveType* are declared, the static type checker simply checks whether this inequality is satisfied, and reports a type conflict if it is not.

In addition to the above constraint imposed by the topology, actors may also impose constraints among ports and parameters. For example, the Ramp actor in Ptolemy II, which is a source actor that produces a token on each execution with a value that is incremented by a specified step, stores the first output and the step value in two parameters. This actor will not declare the type of its port, but will specify the constraint that the port type is greater than or equal to the types of the two parameters. As another example, a polymorphic Distributor actor, which splits a single token stream into a set of streams, will specify the constraint that the type of a sending port is greater than or equal to that of the receiving port. This Distributor will be able to work on tokens of any type. In general, polymorphic actors need to describe the acceptable types through type constraints.

All the type constraints in Ptolemy II are described in the form of inequalities like the one in (1). If a port or a parameter has a declared type, its type appears as a constant in the inequalities. On the other hand, if a port or a parameter has an undeclared type, its type is represented by a type variable in the inequalities. The domain of the type variable is the elements of the type lattice. The type resolution algorithm resolves the undeclared types in the constraint set. If resolution is not possible, a type conflict error will be reported. As an example of a constraint set, consider Fig.3.

The port on actor A1 has declared type *Int*; the ports on A3 and A4 have declared type *Double*; and the ports on A2 have their types undeclared. Let the type variables for the undeclared types be α, β, and γ; the type constraints from the topology are:

$Int \leq \alpha$
$Double \leq \beta$
$\gamma \leq Double$

Now, assume A2 is a polymorphic adder, capable of doing addition for integer, double, and complex numbers. Then the type constraints for the adder can be written as:

$Int \leq \alpha$
$Double \leq \beta$
$\gamma \leq Double$

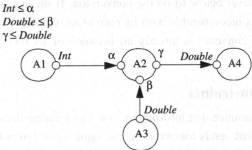

Fig. 3. A topology (interconnection of components) with types.

$$\alpha \le \gamma$$
$$\beta \le \gamma$$
$$\gamma \le Complex$$

The first two inequalities constrain the precision of the addition result to be no less than that of the summands, the last one requires that the data on the adder ports can be converted to *Complex* losslessly. These six inequalities form the complete set of constraints and are used by the type resolution algorithm to solve for α, β, and γ.

This inequality formulation is inspired by the type inference algorithm in ML [12]. There, type equations are used to represent type constraints. In Ptolemy II, the lossless type conversion hierarchy naturally implies inequality relations among the types instead of equalities. In ML, the type constraints are generated from program constructs. In a heterogeneous graphical programming environment like Ptolemy II, where details of the components are hidden, the system does not have enough information about the function of the actors, so the actors must present their type information by either declaring the type on their port, or by specifying a set of type constraints to describe the acceptable types on the undeclared ports. The Ptolemy II system also generates type constraints based on (1).

This formulation converts type resolution into a problem of solving a set of inequalities defined over a finite lattice. An efficient algorithm for doing this is given by Rehof and Mogensen [15]. The appendix of this paper describes this algorithm through an example. Essentially, the algorithm starts by assigning all the type variables the bottom element of the type hierarchy, *NaT*, then repeatedly updating the variables to a greater element until all the constraints are satisfied, or until the algorithm finds that the set of constraints are not satisfiable. This process can be formulated as the search for the least fixed point of a monotonic function on the lattice. The least fixed point is the set of most specific types. It is unique [4], and satisfies the constraints if it is possible to satisfy the constraints.

If the set of type constraints are not satisfiable, or some type variables are resolved to *NaT*, the static type checker flags a type conflict error. The former case can happen, for example, if the port on actor A1 in figure Fig.3 has declared type *Complex*. The latter can happen if an actor does not specify any type constraints on an undeclared sending port. If the type constraints do not restrict a type variable to be greater than *NaT*, it will stay at *NaT* after resolution. To avoid this, any sending port must either have a declared type, or some constraints to force its type to be greater than *NaT*.

A solution satisfying the constraints may not be unique. In fact, the algorithm given in [15] can be used to find either the most specific solution (least in the lattice) or the most general solution (greatest in the lattice). The ML type inference algorithm finds the most general types for a given program, which allows maximal reuse of compiled code. In our case, multiple occurrences of an actor in a topology are treated as different actors, even though they specify the same set of type constraints, so we do not need to use the most general type. In fact, our choice of using the most specific types has a key advantage: types lower in the type lattice usually have a lower implementation cost. For example, in embedded system design, hardware is often synthesized from a component-based description of a system. If a polymorphic adder is going be synthesized into hardware, and it receives *Int* tokens and sends the addition result to a *Double* port, our scheme will resolve the types of all the ports on the adder to *Int*, rather than *Double*. Using an integer adder will be more economical than a double adder. This is analogous to using types to generate more optimized code in compilers.

3.3   Run-Time Type Checking and Lossless Type Conversion

The declared type is a contract between an actor and the Ptolemy II system. If an actor declares that a sending port has a certain type, it asserts that it will only send tokens whose types are less than or equal to that type. If an actor declares a receiving port to have a certain type, it requires the system to only send tokens that are instances of the class of that type to that port. Run-time type checking is the component in the system that enforces this contract. When a token is sent from a sending port, the run-time type checker finds its type, and compares it with the declared type of the port. If the type of the token is not less than or equal to the declared type, a run-time type error will be reported.

As discussed before, type conversion is needed when a token sent to a receiving port has a type less than the type of that port but is not an instance of the class of that type. Since this kind of lossless conversion is done automatically, an actor can safely cast a received token to the declared type. On the other hand, when an actor sends tokens, the tokens being sent do not have to have the exact declared type of the sending port. Any type that is less than the declared type is acceptable. For example, if a sending port has declared type *Double*, the actor can send IntToken from that port without having to convert it to a DoubleToken, since the conversion will be done by the system. So the automatic type conversion simplifies the input/output handling of the actors.

Note that even with the convenience provided by the type conversion, actors should still declare the receiving types to be the most general that they can handle and the sending types to be the most specific that includes all tokens they will send. This maximizes their applications. In the previous example, if the actor only sends IntToken, it should declare the sending type to be *Int* to allow the port to be connected to a receiving port with type *Int*.

If an actor has ports with undeclared types, its type constraints can be viewed as both a requirement and an assertion from the actor. The actor requires the resolved types to satisfy the constraints. Once the resolved types are found, they serve the role of declared types at run time. I.e., the type checking and type conversion system guarantees to only put tokens that are instances of the class of the resolved type to receiving ports, and the actor asserts to only send tokens whose types are less than or equal to the resolved type from sending ports.

3.4   Discussion of Type Resolution and Polymorphism

Rehof and Mogensen proved that their algorithm for solving inequality constraints is linear time in the number of occurrences of symbols in the constraints, which in our case, can be translated into linear time in the number of constraints. This makes type resolution very efficient. On the other hand, one might be tempted to extend the formulation to achieve more flexibility in type specification. For example, it would be nice to introduce a *OR* relation among the constraints. This can be useful, in the case of a two-input adder, for specifying the constraint that the types of the two receiving ports are comparable. This constraint will prohibit tokens with incomparable types to be added. As shown in [15], this cannot be easily done. The inequality constraint problem belongs to the class of meet-closed problems. Meet-closed, in our case, means that if A and B are two solutions to the constraints, their greatest lower bound in the lattice is also a solution. This condition guarantees the existence of the least solution, if any solution exists at all. Introducing the OR relation would break the meet-closed property of the problem. Rehof and Mogensen also showed that any strict extension of the class of meet-closed problems solved by their algorithm will lead to an NP-complete problem. So far, the inequality formulation is generally sufficient for our purpose, but we are still exploring its limitations and workarounds.

We have been using the term polymorphic actor broadly to mean the actors that can work with multiple types on their ports. In [3], Cardelli and Wegner distinguished two broad kinds of polymorphism: universal and ad hoc polymorphism. Universal polymorphism is further divided into parametric and inclusion polymorphism. Parametric polymorphism is obtained when a function works uniformly on a range of types. Inclusion polymorphism appears in object oriented languages when a subclass can be used in place of a superclass. Ad hoc polymorphism is also further divided into overloading and coercion. In terms of implementation, a universally polymorphic function will usually execute the same code for different types, whereas an ad-hoc polymorphic functions will execute different code.

In an informal sense, Ptolemy II exhibits all of the above kinds of polymorphism. The Distributor actor, discussed in section 3.2 shows parametric polymorphism because it works with all types of tokens uniformly. If an actor declares its receiving type to be *General*, which is the type of the base token class, then that actor can accept any type of token since all the other token classes are derived from the base token class. This is inclusion polymorphism. The automatic type conversion during data transfer is a form of coercion; it allows an receiving port with type *Complex*, for example, to be connected to sending ports with type *Int, Double* or *Complex*. An interesting case is the arithmetic and logic operators, like the Add actor. In most languages, arithmetic operators are overloaded, but different languages handle overloading differently. In standard ML, overloading of arithmetic operators must be resolved at the point of appearance, but type variables ranging over equality types are allowed for the equality operator [16]. In Haskell, type classes are used to provide overloaded operations [8]. Ptolemy II takes advantage of data encapsulation. The token classes in Ptolemy II are not passive data containers, they are active data in the sense that they know how to do arithmetic operations with another token. This way, the Add actor can simply call the add() method of the tokens, and work consistently on tokens of different type. An advantage of this design is that users can develop new token types with their implementation for the add() method, achieving an effect similar to user defined operator overloading in C++.

4   Examples

This section provides two examples of type resolution in Ptolemy II.

4.1   Fork Connection

Consider two simple topologies in Fig.4. where a single sending port is connected to two receiving ports in Fig.4(a) and two sending ports are connected to a single receiving port in Fig.4(b). Denote the types of the ports by *a1, a2, a3, b1, b2, b3*, as indicated in the figure. Some possibilities for legal and illegal type assignments are:

- In Fig.4(a), if *a1 = Int, a2 = Double, a3 = Complex*. The topology is well typed. At run-time, the IntToken sent out from actor A1 will be converted to DoubleToken before transferred to A2, and converted to ComplexToken before transferred to A3. This shows that multiple ports with different types can be interconnected as long as the sender type can be losslessly converted to the receiver type.

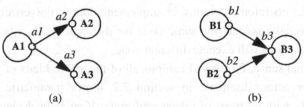

(a)   (b)

Fig. 4. Two simple topologies with types.

- In Fig.4(b), if *b1* = *Int*, b2 = *Double*, and *b3* is undeclared. The the resolved type for *b3* will be *Double*. If *b1* = *Int* and *b2* = *Boolean*, the resolved type for *b3* will be *String* since it is the lowest element in the type hierarchy that is higher than both *Int* and *Boolean*. In this case, if the actor B3 has some type constraints that require *b3* to be less than *String*, then type resolution is not possible, a type conflict will be signaled.

A Java applet that demonstrates the situation in Fig.4(b) and shows the type resolution process is available at the URL: *http://ptolemy.eecs.berkeley.edu/ ptolemyII/ ptII0.3/ptII0.3/ptolemy/domains/sdf/demo/Type/Type.htm*

4.2 Mixing FSM and SDF

In [7], Girault, Lee and Lee showed how to mix finite-state machines (FSMs) with other concurrency models. For example FSM can be mixed with synchronous dataflow (SDF) [10], as shown in Fig.5. In this figure, the top of the hierarchy is an SDF system. The middle actor B in this system is refined to a FSM with two states, each of which is further refined to a SDF subsystem. One type constraint on the receiving port of B is that its type must be less than or equal to the types of both of the receiving ports of the SDF subsystems D and E, because tokens may be transported from the receiving port of B to the receiving ports of D or E. Assuming the types of the receiving ports on D and E are *Int* and *Double*, respectively, type resolution will resolve the type of the receiving port of B to *Int*. Similarly, a type constraint for the sending port of B is that its type must be greater than or equal to the types of both of the sending ports of D and E, and its resolved type will be *Double*.

Note that this result is consistent with function subtyping [13]. If we consider the order in the type lattice as subtype relations, and the actors as functions, then D: *Int→Int*, E: *Double→Double*, and B: $\alpha \rightarrow \beta$ before type resolution. Since D and E can take the place of B during execution, their types should be considered as subtypes of the type of B. Since function subtyping is contravariant for function arguments and covariant for function results, the type α should be a subtype of *Int* and *Double* and β should be a super type of *Int* and *Double*. This is exactly what the type constraints specify, and the resulting type for B: *Int→Double* is indeed a supertype of both of the types of D and E.

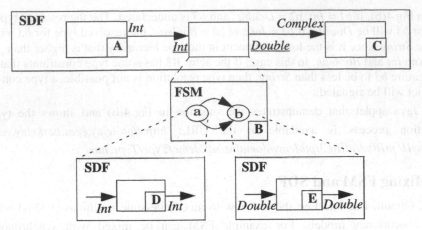

Fig. 5. Mixing FSM with SDF.

5   Conclusion and Future Work

In the design of the Ptolemy II type system, we have taken the approach of polymorphic static typing combined with run-time type checking. We use a lattice structure to model the lossless type conversion relation and provide automatic type conversion during data transfer. Polymorphism is supported by allowing the system components to specify type constraints, and a linear time algorithm is used for constraint resolution. This type system increases the safety and usability of the component-based design environment, promotes component reuse, and helps with design optimization. The infrastructure is built to operate on any type lattice, and so can be used to experiment with extended type systems.

Currently, we are working on extending this system to support structured types such as array and record types. The goal is to allow the elements of arrays and records to contain tokens of arbitrary types, including structured types, and to be able to specify type constraints on them. One of the major difficulty with this extension is that the type lattice will become infinite, which raises questions on the convergence of type resolution.

In the longer term, we will try to characterize the communication protocols used between system components, or some of the real-time properties of the system as types, and design a process-level type system to facilitate heterogeneous real-time modeling. This may potentially bring some of the benefit of data typing to the process level.

Acknowledgments

This work is part of the Ptolemy project, which is supported by the Defense Advanced Research Projects Agency (DARPA), the State of California MICRO program, and the following companies: The Cadence Design Systems, Hewlett Packard, Hitachi, Hughes Space and Communications, Motorola, NEC, and Philips.

Appendix   The Type Resolution Algorithm

The type resolution algorithm starts by assigning all the type variables the bottom element of the type hierarchy, *NaT*, then repeatedly updating the variables to a greater element until all the constraints are satisfied, or until the algorithm finds that the set of constraints are not satisfiable. This iteration can be viewed as repeated evaluation of a monotonic function, and the solution is the least fixed point of the function. The kind of inequality constraints for which the algorithm can determine satisfiability are the ones with the greater term being a variable or a constant. By convention, we write inequalities with the lesser term on the left and the greater term on the right, as in $\alpha \leq \beta$, not $\beta \geq \alpha$. The algorithm allows the left side of the inequality to contain monotonic functions of the type variables, but not the right side. The first step of the algorithm is to divide the inequalities into two categories, *Cvar* and *Ccnst*. The inequalities in *Cvar* have a variable on the right side, and the inequalities in *Ccnst* have a constant on the right side. In the example of Fig.3, *Cvar* consists of:

$Int < \alpha$

$Double \leq \beta$

$\alpha \leq \gamma$

$\beta \leq \gamma$

And *Ccnst* consists of:

$\gamma \leq Double$

$\gamma \leq Complex$

The repeated evaluations are only done on *Cvar*, *Ccnst* are used as checks after the iteration is finished, as we will see later. Before the iteration, all the variables are assigned the value *NaT*, and *Cvar* looks like:

$Int \leq \alpha(NaT)$

$Double \leq \beta(NaT)$

$\alpha(NaT) \leq \gamma(NaT)$

$\beta(NaT) \leq \gamma(NaT)$

Where the current value of the variables are inside the parenthesis next to the variable.

At this point, *Cvar* is further divided into two sets: those inequalities that are not currently satisfied, and those that are satisfied:

Not-satisfied	Satisfied
$Int \leq \alpha(NaT)$	$\alpha(NaT) \leq \gamma(NaT)$
$Double \leq \beta(NaT)$	$\beta(NaT) \leq \gamma(NaT)$

Now comes the update step. The algorithm selects an arbitrary inequality from the *Not-satisfied* set, and forces it to be satisfied by assigning the variable on the right side the least upper bound of the values of both sides of the inequality. Assuming the algorithm selects $Int \leq \alpha(NaT)$, then

$$(2) \alpha = Int \vee NaT = Int$$

After α is updated, all the inequalities in *Cvar* containing it are inspected and are switched to either the *Satisfied* or *Not-satisfied* set, if they are not already in the appropriate set. In this example, after this step, *Cvar* is:

Not-satisfied	Satisfied
$Double \leq \beta(NaT)$	$Int \leq \alpha(Int)$
$\alpha(Int) \leq \gamma(NaT)$	$\beta(NaT) \leq \gamma(NaT)$

The update step is repeated until all the inequalities in *Cvar* are satisfied. In this example, β and γ will be updated and the solution is:

$$\alpha = Int, \quad \beta = \gamma = Double$$

Note that there always exists a solution for *Cvar*. An obvious one is to assign all the variables to the top element, *General*, although this solution may not satisfy the constraints in *Ccnst*. The above iteration will find the least solution, or the set of most specific types.

After the iteration, the inequalities in *Ccnst* are checked based on the current value of the variables. If all of them are satisfied, a solution to the set of constraints is found.

As mentioned earlier, the iteration step can be seen as a search for the least fixed point of a monotonic function. In this view, the computation in (2) is the application of a monotonic function to type variables. Let L denote the type lattice. In an inequality $r \leq \alpha$, where α is a variable, and r is either a variable or a constant, the update function $f: L^2 \rightarrow L$ is $\alpha' = f(r, \alpha) = r \vee \alpha$. Here, α represents the value of the variable before the update, and α' represents the value after the update. f can easily be seen to be monotonic and non-decreasing. And, since L is finite, it satisfies the ascending chain condition, so f is also continuous. Let the variables in the constraint set be $\alpha_1, \alpha_2, \ldots, \alpha_N$, where N is the total number of variables, and define $A = (\alpha_1, \alpha_2, \ldots, \alpha_N)$. The complete iteration can be viewed as repeated evaluation of a function $F: L^N \rightarrow L^N$ of A, where F is the composition of the individual update functions. Clearly, F is also continuous. The iteration starts with the variables initialized to the bottom, A $= \perp^N$, and computes the sequence $F^i(\perp^N)$ ($i \geq 0$), which is a non-decreasing chain. By the fixed point theorem in [4], the least upper bound of this chain is the least fixed point of F, corresponding to the most specific types in our case.

Rehof and Mogensen [15] proved that the above algorithm is linear time in the number of occurrences of symbols in the constraints, and gave an upper bound on the number of basic computations. In our formulation, the symbols are type constants and type variables, and each constraint contains two symbols. So the type resolution algorithm is linear in the number of constraints.

References

1.   H. Abelson and G. J. Sussman, *Structure and Interpretation of Computer Programs*, The MIT Press, 1985.

2.   F. Arbab, *MANIFOLD Version 2.0*, CWI, Software Engineering Cluster, Kruislaan 413, 1098 SJ Amsterdam, The Netherlands, June, 1998.

3.   L. Cardelli and P. Wegner, "On Understanding Types, Data Abstraction, and Polymorphism," *ACM Computing Surveys*, Vol.17, No.4, Dec. 1985.

4.   B. A. Davey and H. A. Priestly, *Introduction to Lattices and Order*, Cambridge University Press, 1990.

5.   J. Davis II, M. Goel, C. Hylands, B. Kienhuis, E. A. Lee, J. Liu, X. Liu, L. Muliadi, S. Neuendorffer, J. Reekie, N. Smyth, J. Tsay and Y. Xiong, *Overview of the Ptolemy Project*, ERL Technical Report UCB/ERL No. M99/37, Dept. EECS, University of California, Berkeley, CA 94720, July 1999. (http://ptolemy.eecs.berkeley.edu/publications/papers/99/HMAD/)

6.   Y-C. Fuh and P. Mishra, "Type Inference with Subtypes," *Second European Symposium on Programming*, Nancy, France, 1988.

7.   A. Girault, B. Lee, and E. A. Lee, "Hierarchical Finite State Machines with Multiple Concurrency Models," *IEEE Transactions on Computer-Aided Design of Integrated Circuits and Systems*, Vol.18, No.6, June 1999.

8.   C. V. Hall, K. Hammond, S.L. Peyton Jones, and P. L. Wadler, "Type Classes in Haskell," *ACM Transactions on Programming Languages*, Vol.18, No.2, Mar. 1996.

9.   J. B. Hext, "Compile-Time Type-Matching," *Computer Journal*, 9, 1967.

10.   E. A. Lee and D. G. Messerschmitt, "Static Scheduling of Synchronous Data Flow Programs for Digital Signal Processing," *IEEE Transaction on Computer*, Jan. 1987.

11.   J. Liu, B. Wu, X. Liu, and E. A. Lee, "Interoperation of Heterogeneous CAD Tools in Ptolemy II," *Symposium on Design, Test, and Microfabrication of MEMS/MOEMS*, Paris, France, Mar. 1999.

12. R. Milner, "A Theory of Type Polymorphism in Programming," *Journal of Computer and System Sciences*, 17, pp. 384-375, 1978.

13. J. C. Mitchell, *Foundations for Programming Languages*, The MIT Press, 1998.

14. M. Odersky, "Challenges in Type Systems Research," *ACM Computing Surveys*, Vol.28, No.4es, 1996.

15. J. Rehof and T. Mogensen, "Tractable Constraints in Finite Semilattices," *Third International Static Analysis Symposium*, LNCS 1145, Springer, Sept., 1996.

16. J. D. Ullman, *Elements of ML Programming*, Prentice Hall, 1998.

Proof General:
A Generic
Tool for Proof Development

David Aspinall

LFCS, University of Edinburgh, U.K.
http://www.dcs.ed.ac.uk/home/da

Abstract. This note describes *Proof General*, a tool for developing machine proofs with an interactive proof assistant. Interaction is based around a *proof script*, which is the target of a proof development. Proof General provides a powerful user-interface with relatively little effort, alleviating the need for a proof assistant to provide its own GUI, and providing a uniform appearance for diverse proof assistants.

Proof General has a growing user base and is currently used for several interactive proof systems, including Coq, LEGO, and Isabelle. Support for others is on the way. Here we give a brief overview of what Proof General does and the philosophy behind it; technical details are available elsewhere. The program and user documentation are available on the web at http://www.dcs.ed.ac.uk/home/proofgen.

1 Background

Proof General is a generic interface for interactive proof assistants.

A *proof assistant* is a computerized helper for developing machine proofs. There are many uses for machine proofs, both during the specification, development, and verification of software and hardware systems, and in the development and teaching of mathematical proof and formal logic. Proof General helps with developing proof scripts.

A *proof script* is a sequence of commands sent to a proof assistant to construct a machine proof. A script is usually stored in a file. Roughly, a proof script is like a program written in a scripting programming language, and in particular, a language which has an interactive interpreter. Proof General uses a technique called *script management* to help the user write a proof script without using cut-and-paste or repeatedly typing "load file" commands. Proof General has a sophisticated implementation of script management which covers large developments spread across multiple files.

A guiding philosophy behind Proof General is to provide an interface which is useful to novices and expert-users alike. Some interfaces for theorem provers are aimed at novices and become infeasible for large developments; others are aimed at experts but have steep learning curves or require changes in work methods, discouraging their take-up. With this in mind, Proof General builds

S. Graf and M. Schwartzbach (Eds.): TACAS/ETAPS 2000, LNCS 1785, pp. 38–43, 2000.

on the programmable text editor *Emacs*, the powerful everyday editor of many computer scientists. Emacs brings many advantages. It is available on most platforms, including Unix, Linux, and NT. Although it once had a reputation for being hard to learn, modern versions of Emacs are very user-friendly, supporting the whole gamut of current GUI technologies and providing easy customization mechanisms.

Another important aspect of Proof General is that it is *generic*. It provides a uniform interface and interaction mechanism for different back-end proof assistants. It exploits the deep similarities between systems by hiding some of their superficial differences. This generic aspect is no empty claim or untested design goal; Proof General is already in use for three different proof assistants: Coq, LEGO, and Isabelle. Support for more is on the way.

The present implementation of Proof General is oriented towards proof assistants based on a single-threaded interactive command interpreter (or *shell*), where interaction consists of a dialogue between the user and the system. Several proof assistants have this kind of architecture, allowing more elaborate interfaces to be built on top. As a spin-off, building Proof General has suggested some useful design guidelines for the command protocol which should be implemented in a proof assistant shell.

To summarize, Proof General provides a fairly elaborate yet unobtrusive interface. It gives the proof assistant user many useful features, and allows the proof assistant implementor to concentrate on the proof engine.

2   Features of Proof General

Simplified communication. The proof assistant's shell is hidden from the user. Communication takes place via two or three buffers (Emacs text widgets). The *script buffer* holds input, the commands to construct a proof. The *goals buffer* displays the current list of subgoals to be solved. The *response buffer* displays other output from the proof assistant. The user sees only the output from the latest proof step, rather than a screen full of output. Nonetheless, the user can still access the shell to examine it or run commands.

Script management. Proof script editing is connected to the proof process, maintaining consistency between the edit window and the state of the proof assistant. Visual feedback on the state of the assistant is given by colouring the background of the text in the editing windows. Parts of a proof script that have been processed are displayed in blue and moreover can be *locked* to prevent accidental editing. Parts of the script currently being processed by the proof assistant are shown in red. The screenshot in Figure 1 shows script managament in action.

Multiple file handling. Script management also works across multiple files. When a script is loaded in the editor, it is coloured to reflect whether the proof assistant has processed it in this session. Proof General communicates with the assistant to discover dependencies between script files. If I want to edit a file which has been processed already, Proof General will *retract* the file and all the files which depend on it, unlocking them. Thus the editor is connected to the theory dependency or make system of the proof assistant.

Proof by Pointing. Clicking on a subterm of a goal can apply an appropriate rule or tactic automatically, or display a menu of choices. Proof General relies on support in the assistant to mark-up subterms and generate tactics for this feature, since it is specific to the prover's syntax and logic. Subterm mark-up also makes it easy to explore compilicated terms, and cut and paste from within them.

Syntax highlighting and symbol fonts. Proof scripts are decorated: proof commands are highlighted and different fonts can be used for definitions and assumptions, for example. Symbol fonts can be used to display proper glyphs for logical operators, Greek letters, etc, which occur throughout mathematical proofs.

Toolbar and menus. A toolbar includes buttons for examining the proof state, starting a proof, manoeuvring in the proof script, saving a proof, searching for a theorem, interrupting the assistant, and getting help. A menu gives access to further commands, and a useful collection of user preferences. Using the toolbar, you can replay proofs without knowing any low-level commands of the proof assistant or any Emacs short-cuts.

Tags and definitions menu. Using a TAGS file, one can quickly locate the definition and uses of an identifier, automatically searching many files. Using a definitions menu, one can quickly navigate within a proof script to find particular definitions, declarations and proofs.

Remote proof assistant. A proof assistant can be run remotely, perhaps across the internet, while Proof General and the proof script reside locally.

3   Proof General in Use

Figure 1 shows a screenshot of Proof General running in a single window on the screen. The window is split into two parts. The upper half displays the proof script Group.thy which is being processed. This is a script written for Isabelle using the new Isar proof language [4]. The lower half displays the current list of subgoals which are to be solved to complete the proof. Instead of this split window, it is perfectly possible to have separate windows on the screen, as the user likes. Proof General is even happy to run on a plain console, although graphical facilities will be reduced (e.g. no toolbar).

In the script file, the cursor appears at the end of the *locked* region, which has a blue background to indicate it has already been processed. The arrow buttons on the toolbar are used to manipulate the locked region, by sending commands to the proof assistant, or by issuing undo steps. In this manner, a user can *replay*

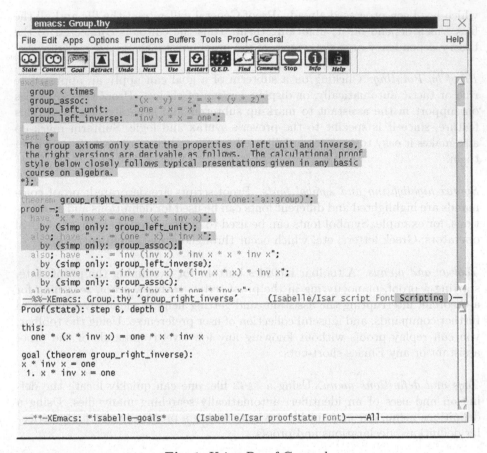

Fig. 1. Using Proof General

a proof interactively, without needing to know any low-level commands needed to start the proof assistant, or issue proof and undo steps. And without the extreme tedium of cut-and-paste.

4 Further Details

Technical references. Proof General has a detailed user manual [1] which also contains instructions for instantiating it to new proof assistants. The ideas of script management and proof by pointing were adapted from the CtCoq system [3]; proof by pointing in Proof General is described in an LFCS technical report [2]. (Proof General goes beyond CtCoq in some ways, but is less sophisticated in others; the biggest difference is that CtCoq provides its own GUI based on structure editing, which Proof General specifically avoids.) Future papers will describe the architecture of Proof General in more detail, including design guidelines for interactive proof development protocols, and plans for future directions.

Implementation. Proof General is implemented in Emacs Lisp. There is a generic core (about 7000 lines) which implements the toolbar, menus, script management, and process handling features. Each supported proof assistant has some additional Emacs Lisp (30 – 500 lines) for prover-specific configuration: setting regular expressions and command strings, and perhaps providing extra features. For robust operation and features like proof by pointing, the proof assistant may need modification to output special messages for Proof General.

Availability and System requirements. Proof General is easy to install, and is available free of charge (with sources and documentation) for research and educational use. The current release is Proof General 3.0. For best results, it requires a recent version of XEmacs (21.1 or later), alongside recent versions of one or more proof assistants: Coq (6.3 or later), Isabelle (version 99 or later), or Lego (version 1.3.1). Details of where to obtain these components can be found on the web page mentioned below. Success is guaranteed with a Unix (or Linux) environment, although XEmacs and some proof assistants are available for other operating systems, and there is nothing operating system specific in Proof General itself.

Acknowledgements

Many people have contributed to the design and code, both in the generic basis and for the prover-specific instances. For each instance of Proof General, we try to encourage somebody familiar with the proof assistant to develop and maintain the prover-specific code, perhaps also enhancing to the generic basis. In order of appearance, the main workers on Proof General have been: T. Kleymann, Y. Bertot, D. Sequeira, H. Goguen, D. Aspinall, P. Loiseleur, M. Wenzel, P. Callaghan. Many other people provided useful feedback, including: P. Brisset, R. Burstall, M. Hofmann, J. McKinna, and D. von Oheimb. Thomas Kleymann originated the Proof General project. David Aspinall is the present manager.

For more information about Proof General, please visit the home page at http://www.dcs.ed.ac.uk/home/proofgen.

References

1. D. Aspinall, H. Goguen, T. Kleymann, and D. Sequira. Proof General. System documentation, see http://www.dcs.ed.ac.uk/home/proofgen, 1999. 41
2. Yves Bertot, Thomas Kleymann, and Dilip Sequeira. Implementing proof by pointing without a structure editor. Technical Report ECS-LFCS-97-368, University of Edinburgh, 1997. 41
3. Yves Bertot and Laurent Théry. A generic approach to building user interfaces for theorem provers. *Journal of Symbolic Computation*, 25(7):161–194, February 1998. 41

4. Markus Wenzel. Isar — a generic interpretative approach to readable formal proof documents. In Y. Bertot, G. Dowek, A. Hirschowitz, C. Paulin, and L. Thery, editors, *Theorem Proving in Higher Order Logics, 12th International Conference, TPHOLs'99*, Lecture Notes in Computer Science 1690. Springer-Verlag, 1999. 40

ViewPoint-Oriented Software Development: Tool Support for Integrating Multiple Perspectives by Distributed Graph Transformation

Michael Goedicke[1], Bettina Enders[1], Torsten Meyer[1], and Gabriele Taentzer[2]

[1] Specification of Software Systems, Department of Mathematics and Computer Science,
University of Essen, Germany
{goedicke, enders, tmeyer}@informatik.uni-essen.de

[2] Theoretical Computer Science / Formal Specification Group, Department of Computing,
Technical University of Berlin, Germany
gabi@cs.tu-berlin.de

Abstract. Co-operative development of distributed software systems involves to address the multiple perspectives problem: many stakeholders with diverse domain knowledge and differing development strategies collaborate to construct heterogeneous development artifacts using different representation schemes. The ViewPoints framework has been developed for organizing multiple stakeholders, the development processes and notations they use, and the partial specifications they produce. In this contribution we present a tool environment supporting ViewPoint-oriented software development based on a formalization by distributed graph transformation.

1 Introduction and Related Work

In system design the various development stages are visited more than once and quite different notations and process models need to be integrated in order to satisfy the requirements of the different stakeholders' views and their processes. It is therefore highly desirable to provide flexible conceptual means and related tool support for representing the various cooperating stakeholders' views and process models. In this contribution we use the ViewPoints framework to represent such views and processes. In addition the ViewPoints framework involves to tolerate inconsistent information in related ViewPoints until it seems necessary or appropriate to check and (re)establish consistency -- at least in some parts of the system [1]. The ViewPoints framework has been used quite successfully and has been documented in the literature [2, 1, 4].

The question which is addressed here is how tool support can be constructed to effectively represent the loosely coupled approach: some local development within a ViewPoint is followed by interaction with related ViewPoints via consistency checks.

The approach of distributed graph transformation supports the idea of loosely coupled ViewPoints as outlined above quite naturally. It realizes the separation between

S. Graf and M. Schwartzbach (Eds.) TACAS/ETAPS 2000, LNCS 1785, pp. 43–47, 2000.

the independent development of single local ViewPoints and the configuration and connection of a set of related ViewPoints in a structured way.

Distributed graph transformation which is based on the double-pushout approach to algebraic graph transformation is introduced formally in [6]. Using AGG [7] as a computing platform an adequate level of tool support can easily be constructed. The manipulation of representation schemes is expressed as graph transformation rules and the interaction and cooperation of distributed ViewPoints is adequately formulated as distributed graph transformation rules. As a result we gain tool support for ViewPoints and a corresponding formal presentation [5, 4]. As such it provides the possibility for formal analysis and most importantly a great deal of flexibility for integrating new ViewPoints.

The ViewPoints framework was devised by A. Finkelstein et al. [2] to describe complex systems. An overview of other approaches related to multiple perspectives in software development can be found in [3]. In [1] a general overview wrt inconsistency management within the ViewPoints framework is given.

In the chapter *The ViewPoints Framework* we introduce briefly our approach to ViewPoint-oriented software development. Based upon this we present tool support for our approach in the chapter *The ViewPoint Tool*.

2   The ViewPoints Framework

A *ViewPoint* is defined to be a locally managed object or agent which encapsulates partial knowledge about the system and its domain. It contains partial knowledge of the design process [2]. The knowledge is specified in a particular, suitable representation scheme. An entire system is described by a set of related, distributable ViewPoints which are loosely coupled.

A single ViewPoint consists of five slots. The *style slot* contains a description of the scheme and notation which is used to describe the knowledge of the ViewPoint. The *domain slot* defines the area of concern addressed by the ViewPoint. *The specification slot* contains the actual specification of a particular part of the system which is described in the notation defined in the style slot. The fourth slot is called *work plan* and encapsulates the set of actions by which the specification can be built as well as a process model to guide application of these actions. Two classes of work plan actions are especially important: *In-ViewPoint check actions* and *Inter-ViewPoint check actions* are used for checking consistency within a single ViewPoint or between multiple ViewPoints, respectively. The last slot of a ViewPoint called *work record* contains the development history in terms of the actions given in the work plan slot.

A *ViewPoint template* is a kind of ViewPoint type. It is described as a ViewPoint in which only the style slot and the work plan slot are specified, i.e. the other slots are empty. When creating a new ViewPoint, the developer has the opportunity to use an existing ViewPoint template instead of designing the entire ViewPoint from scratch.

The ViewPoints framework is independent from any particular development method and actively encourages multiple representations. Software development methods and techniques are defined as sets of ViewPoint templates which encapsulate the notations provided as well as the rules how they are used. Integration of methods and views is realized by such rules referring to multiple ViewPoint templates.

A more detailed description of the ViewPoints framework and its formalization by distributed graph transformation is given in [4]. In the next section we now present a brief overview of tool support.

3 The *ViewPoint Tool*

The *ViewPoint Tool* comprises three main components: the *ViewPoint manager*, the *template editor* and *the ViewPoint editor*. While the *ViewPoint manager* serves as a central tool to coordinate all activities within using the ViewPoints framework, the *template editor* allows to design ViewPoint templates – i.e. styles combined with work plan actions – and the *ViewPoint editor* allows to work with specifications and work records of actual ViewPoints. All ViewPoints used in the *ViewPoint editor* have to be instantiated from existing ViewPoint templates developed by the *template editor*.

The *ViewPoint manager* serves to organize all developed ViewPoint templates and all actual ViewPoints (cf. Figure 1). It is used as a starting point to enter the *template editor* and the *ViewPoint editor*. First ViewPoint templates can be created which then can be developed further within the *template editor*. Then actual ViewPoints can be instantiated from a template which are usable within the *ViewPoint editor*.

The *template editor* allows to edit the work plan slot and the style slot of a View-Point template. All actions of the ViewPoint template's work plan have to be modeled as graph transformation rules (cf. Figure 2). The *ViewPoint editor* allows to edit a ViewPoint instantiated from a ViewPoint template developed by the *template editor*. All actions defined in the corresponding template's work plan can be applied to build an actual specification. Figure 3 depicts a *ViewPoint editor* window, the actual specification is displayed on the left and all work plan actions are listed on the right.

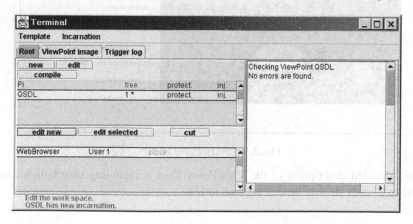

Fig. 1. *ViewPoint manager* window.

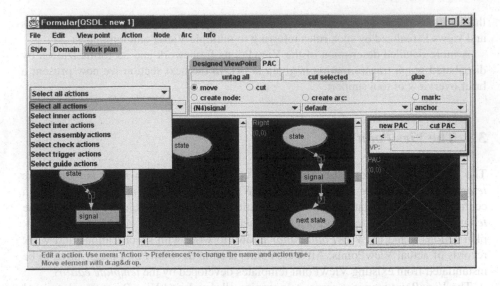

Fig. 2. The work plan window of the *template editor*.

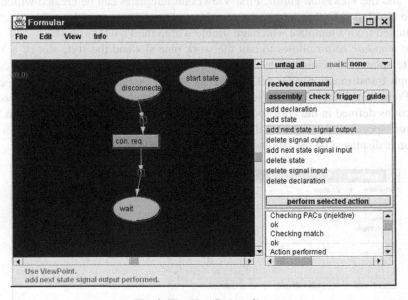

Fig. 3. The *ViewPoint editor*.

A more detailed description of the ViewPoint Tool – including distribution aspects and inconsistency management – is given in [7].

4   Conclusion and Further Work

In this contribution we have sketched a brief introduction to the ViewPoints framework and the *ViewPoint Tool* environment. Various case studies modeling non-trivial applications (e.g., integration of architecture design and performance evaluation views [5]) have shown that our implementation meets all the requirements for supporting the multiple perspectives problem in a flexible ViewPoint environmet. The present version of the *ViewPoint Tool* is based on the local version of AGG [9]. Currently we are working on integrating the features of a prototype AGG version realizing distributed graph transformation.

References

1. Easterbrook, S. and Nuseibeh, B., "Using ViewPoints for Inconsistency Management", *BCS/IEE Software Engineering Journal*, pp. 31-43, 1996.
2. Finkelstein, A., Kramer, J., Nuseibeh, B., Finkelstein, L., and Goedicke, M., "Viewpoints: A Framework for Integrating Multiple Perspectives in System Development", *Int. Journal of Software Engineering & Knowledge Engineering*, vol. 2(1), 1992.
3. Finkelstein, A. and Sommerville, I., "The Viewpoints FAQ", *Software Engineering Journal*, vol. 11 (1), pp. 2-4, 1996.
4. Goedicke, M., Meyer, T., and Taentzer, G., "ViewPoint-oriented Software Development by Distributed Graph Transformation: Towards a Basis for Living with Inconsistencies", *Proc. 4th IEEE International Symposium on Requirements Engineering*, Limerick, Ireland, 1999.
5. Goedicke, M., Enders, B., Meyer, T. and Taentzer, G., "Tool Support for ViewPoint-oriented Software Development", *Proc. International Workshop and Symposium AGTIVE*, Kerkrade, The Netherlands, 1999, Lecture Notes on Computer Science, Springer, to appear.
6. Taentzer, G., Fischer, I., , Koch, M., and Volle, V., "Distributed Graph Transformation with Application to Visual Design of Distributed Systems", in Rozenberg, G. (ed.), *Graph Grammar Handbook 3: Concurrency & Distribution*, World Scientific,1999.
7. Taentzer, G., Ermel, C., and Rudolf, C., "AGG-Approach: Language and Tool Environment", in Rozenberg, G. (ed.), *Graph Grammar Handbook 2: Specification & Programming*, World Scientific, 1999.

Consistent Integration of Formal Methods*

Peter Braun, Heiko Lötzbeyer, Bernhard Schätz, and Oscar Slotosch

Institut für Informatik, Technische Universität München
80290 München, Germany

Abstract. The usability of formal concepts for system design depends essentially on their integration in the design process. We discuss several possible levels of integration: *technical* integration of tools considering APIs and tool interfaces, *conceptual* integration of metamodels of description formalisms combined with hard and soft constraints, *semantical* integration of semantics of description techniques using a common semantic model, and finally *methodical* integration by an embedding in the development process. We show the feasibility of such an integrated approach and its advantages presenting AUTOFOCUS/Quest, a formal method CASE-Tool with its levels of integration. Parts of a banking system model are used as example.

1 Introduction

The need for development tools for the design of (embedded) systems has been widely accepted: several programs are available for their construction, often focusing on specific aspects of the design process like building a data-model, verifying system properties, or simulating a designed system. However, generally several of these aspects are important in a thorough design process.

An obvious way to obtain a more powerful tool is to combine existing tools and to integrate them. This approach has also been applied to description techniques like the UML. However, the result of the integration is not necessarily satisfying for the user: There can be redundancies (with the possibility to introduce inconsistencies while modeling overlapping aspects of the system), missing integration of concepts (with the need to bridge a gap between the design and the verification tool), or - as the most critical aspect - no integrated method for the user. These problems arise in conventional software development concepts as well as in formal method approaches.

In this paper we advocate a new multi-level integration concept. The most sophisticated level is the methodical integration, ideally based on the next level, the semantic integration of the used description techniques. The third level forms the conceptual integration of metamodels, followed by the lowest integration level, the technical integration of tools. Integration on all levels results into powerful

---

* This work was supported by the Bundesamt für Sicherheit im Informationswesen (BSI) within the project Quest, and the DFG within the Sonderforschungsbereich 342.

S. Graf and M. Schwartzbach (Eds.): TACAS/ETAPS 2000, LNCS 1785, pp. 48–62, 2000.

tools that provide a lot of features to the user. The layered integration hierarchy makes it easy to connect other programs, provided that the development methods fit together.

As an example for this new integration hierarchy we present the tool AUTO-FOCUS/Quest, offering many different features, ranging from different graphical description techniques to theorem proving, testing, code generation and model checking. AUTOFOCUS/Quest integrates the CASE tool prototype AUTOFOCUS with the formal tools VSE II, SMV, SATO, and CTE. This paper is structured as follows: after a short overview over the tool AUTOFOCUS/Quest in Section 2, we present (parts of) the banking system of the FM99 tool competition in Section 3 to introduce our description techniques. The main part of this paper (Section 4) describes the different levels of integration that are present in the AUTOFOCUS/Quest tool. We conclude with a comparison with other existing tools.

2   The AUTOFOCUS/Quest-Tool

AUTOFOCUS/Quest has been presented successfully at the Formal Method World Congress 1999[1]. In the following we briefly describe the features of the tool.

2.1   AUTOFOCUS

AUTOFOCUS [HMS+98] is a freely available CASE-Tool prototype for the development of correct embedded systems. Similar to other CASE-Tools it supports graphical description of the developed system using several different views. AUTOFOCUS builds upon formal methods concepts. The available views are:

- Interface and structure view: By using System Structure Diagrams (SSDs) users define structure and components of the developed system and the interfaces between components and the environment.
- Behavior view: State Transition Diagrams (STDs) describe the behavior of a component in the system.
- Interaction view: Extended Event Traces (EETs) capture the dynamic interactions between components (and the environment). EETs are used to specify test cases or example runs of the systems and have a Message Sequence Chart-like notation.
- Data view: (textual) Data Type Definitions (DTDs) define the data types for the description of structure, behavior and interaction diagrams. We use functional datatypes.

All views are hierarchic to support descriptions at different levels of detail. AUTOFOCUS can check the consistency between different views using an integrated consistency mechanism. AUTOFOCUS offers a simulation facility to validate the specifications based on rapid prototyping.

---

[1] AUTOFOCUS/Quest was acknowledged as the leading competitor in the tool competition of FM'99. See http://www.fmse.cs.reading.ac.uk/fm99/ for more information.

2.2 Quest

Within the project Quest several extensions to AUTOFOCUS were achieved.[2]
The aim of the project [Slo98] was to enrich the practical software development process by the coupling existing formal methods and tools to AUTOFOCUS
in order to ensure the correctness of critical parts of systems. The combination with traditional software engineering methods is achieved by specification-
based test methods which facilitate the selection of reasonable test-cases for
non-critical components. The tools developed within Quest translate the graphical concepts into other formalisms suitable for verification, model checking or
testing (VSE [RSW97], SMV [McM92], SATO [Zha97], CTE [GWG95]) and
support the systematic generation of test-cases. To provide an integrated, iterative development process (partial) retranslations from the connected tools were
implemented, supporting visualization of counterexamples, generation of test
sequences with input values, and the reimport of components that have been
corrected during verification. The translations were realized using an API and a
textual interface to AUTOFOCUS. This allows to easily connect other tools using
interfaces or generators.

3   The FM99-Banking System

In this section we briefly present parts of a model that was presented on the
Formal Methods World Conference 1999.[3] The banking system example was
used to compare different modeling methods and verification tools, presented at
FM'99, on a competitive basis.

The banking system contains a central (main host) and several tills (automated teller machines) that are communicating independently with the central
database. The connections from the central to the tills may be down. Among
other requirements it has to be ensured that the amount withdrawn within one
day does not exceed a maximum value.

We modeled the banking system with the graphical description techniques
from AUTOFOCUS/Quest. In the following sections we describe the main structure of the system, some of the datatypes used, the behavior of the connection,
and a possible interaction sequence from a connection and the central.

3.1 System Structure

We modeled the system with two tills and two connections. Since the connections
have a specific behavior (i.e. they can be down), we modelled connections as
components in the system. The structure of the system is described in the Fig. 1.
The connections pass transactions (of type Info) from the tills to the central, and
in the other direction connections report information to control the behavior of

---

[2] The project was carried out for the German "Bundesamt für Sicherheit in der Infor-
mationstechnik" (Information Security Agency) (BSI).

[3] See http://www4.in.tum.de/proj/quest/ for the full model.

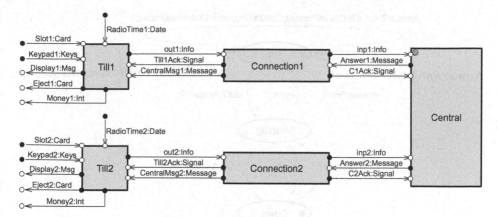

Fig. 1. SSD for Banking System

the till. The messages (of type `Message`) are defined in a DTD (see Section 3.2). Furthermore the connections have acknowledge channels to indicate the sender of a message that it has been sent successfully. The SSD shows the ports (little circles) of the components, the external ports, and the channels that connect these ports.

Reusing port names[4] in different components allows us to describe the behavior of each connection with the same state transition diagram. For example the channel `out1` connects to the port `out` of `Connection1`.

3.2 Datatypes

As simple examples, we show the definition of two datatypes and a function (defined using pattern matching) used within the graphical views:

```
data Message = Money(Int) | NoMoney | Balance | MailSent;
data Transaction = TA(Action,Account);
fun withdrawMoney(TA(Withdraw(x),acc))=Money(x);
```

3.3 Behavior

The behavioral description of the system refers to the ports of the components defined by the SSD in Section 3.1. The behavior of both connections are described in Fig. 2. If there are no values on both channels (expressed by the input patterns: `out?;Answer?`) the connection changes its state to reduce energy usage. This has been introduced to model the fact that connections sometime are down. If the connection is down and receives a value it moves to the state sleeping. If another value is received, then the connection is up, and ready to process the data.

---

[4] Port names are attributes of ports.

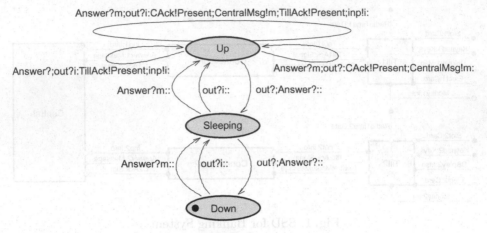

Fig. 2. STD for `Connection1`

3.4   Interaction Example

To illustrate the interaction from the connections and the central we use the EET in Fig. 3. This is only one example trace of the behavior of the system. All messages between two ticks (dashed lines) are considered to occur simultaneously.

4   Integration

In this section we describe the integrations within AUTOFOCUS/Quest. There are different integration layers:

- methodical integration (on the development process level)
- semantic integration (on the semantics level)
- conceptual integration (on the metamodel level)
- technical integration (on the tool level)

The quality of an integration depends on the reached level, and on the quality of the underlying levels, for example a complete semantic integration is not sufficiently helpful for a user without tool support.

4.1   Metamodel Integration

In our view, integrated metamodels are essential for further integration. Metamodels can be applied to define a modeling language [Met99] and are increasingly used, for instance to define UML [BJR97]. In the case of AUTOFOCUS the syntactic aspects of the modeling techniques, like SSDs and STDs, are described using a metamodel. We use class diagrams as defined by the UML for the description

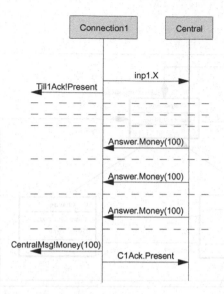

Fig. 3. Execution Example

of metamodels. We consider it essential that the metamodels of different concepts of a modeling language are integrated into one metamodel since otherwise different modeling concepts do not fit together. We show this for the example of SSDs and STDs.

Fig. 4 shows a simplified version of the integrated metamodel for SSDs and STDs. An SSD consists of components, ports, channels and relations between them. A component has a name, and can be decomposed in an arbitrary number of subcomponents, and can belong to a supercomponent. This is needed to model hierarchic components. A component is a composition of ports and channels. In the example of Fig. 1 the component `Connection1` has four output ports and two input ports and no channels. All channels in Fig. 1 belong to the component `Banking System`, the supercomponent of the shown components. Below the metamodel of SSDs is the metamodel of STDs. An automaton consists of one state, which may be hierarchic, as the component in the STD metamodel. Similar to the component a state has interface points and transition segments. A transition segment is a composition of a precondition, some input patterns, some actions and output patterns. See the example of Section 3 for an explanation of those elements.

We now have two concepts, the concept of system structure diagrams and the concept of automatons. But how do they fit together? In many other tools there will be only an association from components to automata: the dynamic behavior of a component can be described with an automaton. But there is more. In our case the input and output patterns that belong to a transition segment are connected to the ports of the component to which the automaton

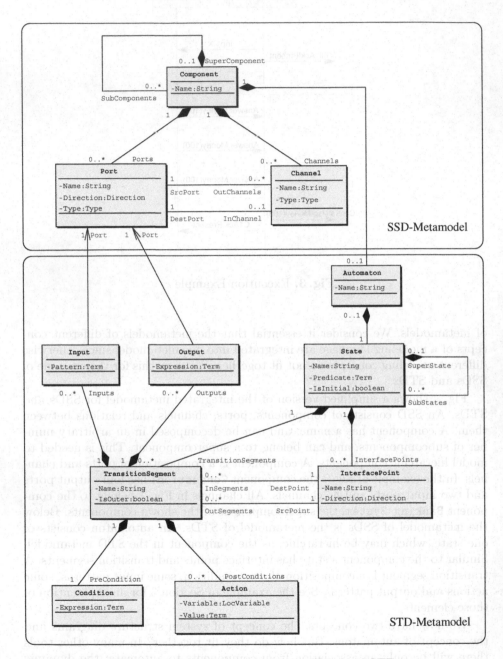

Fig. 4. Integrated Metamodel for SSDs and STDs

belongs. So an input to the automaton of component `Connection1` in Fig. 1 can only come from the ports `Answer` or `out` restricting what is considered a correct model. Thus for specifying a new input pattern one might want to only choose from ports of the related component or to create a new port, which then automatically belongs to the related component. Note that the constraint, that a port belongs to the right component, is not modelled in the class diagram of Fig. 4. There, only the fact is expressed, that every input has a relation to an arbitrary port. The constraint that the automaton belongs to the same component as the ports of the input and output patterns, is expressed in a logical constraint that belongs to the metamodel. Up to now AUTOFOCUS uses its own syntax for these expressions. However, a prototype exists using OCL [WK98], the constraint logic of UML [BJR97].

Beside the integration of the concepts of SSDs and STDs there are other concepts integrated in AUTOFOCUS/Quest. For instance, datatypes are modelled and used. In Fig. 4 attributes with types like term or type are shown. These are actually relations, like the ones from input and output to port, to classes in other parts of the integrated metamodel. So we do not only have different concepts, but we have merged them tightly together. But sometimes the user is handicapped by a very strict link between the different views of a system. So we tolerate the possibility that the model might be inconsistent at some stages of the development. For example, when specifying an SSD, it is sometimes desirable that datatypes can be used that are not yet defined. Thus, especially for the links between different concepts, we tolerate inconsistencies. Hard constraints like the need for a channel to have relations to a source-port and a destination-port may not be violated.

4.2   Semantic Integration

As with the conceptual level, where all system views are mapped onto a common metamodel, all description techniques are also mapped onto one semantic model. Thus, all descriptions are semantically integrated on the mathematical or the model level as sketched in the following subsection. However, this is a very low level of integration not suitable for system development. Instead we need to express the semantics of the described systems in terms of the techniques and actions performed by the user. The highest form of integration is achieved if the user can completely stay within the level of formalization used in the specification process so far, for instance, to SSDs, STDs, EETs, and DTDs, as described in the second subsection. However, this is not generally possible and thus other forms of integration adding new formalisms or techniques must be used as described in the last subsection.

Semantic Model As already suggested by the STD description formalism, we use a stepwise computation mechanism to model the behavior of a system or component. Each step consists of two substeps: reading the input ports of a component and processing the input, and generating the output. After each step the output of a component is transferred from its output ports along its channels to the input ports of the corresponding channels. The behavior of a component or a system is formalized by sequences of those steps.

One of the major incentives in choosing this semantic model is its simplicity. Furthermore, it is compliant with other approaches – both from the engineering and the formal methods domain – that are widely accepted. The concept of step-wise, cyclic computations with unbuffered variables (channels) is, for example found, in programming languages for PLCs (programable logical controllers) as well as in TLA (temporal logic of actions). This straight-forward yet expressive semantic model seems to be best suited for the domain of hardware oriented embedded systems compared to approaches using more complex concepts, for example state charts with the concept of OR- and AND-states. Nevertheless, other semantic models can be adapted to fit the basic principles of AUTOFO-CUS/Quest, adding concepts like buffering channels suitable for other domains like telecommunication.

Consistent Specifications As already mentioned on the conceptual level of the metamodel, during a development process inconsistencies in system spec-ifications may occur. This is especially the case using a view-based approach where the specification is simultaneously presented on different levels of abstrac-tion and spread over different aspects like structure (SSDs), behavior (STDs) or interactions (EETs). Then mechanisms must be offered to support the user in finding those inconsistencies. Those inconsistencies may occur on the conceptual level, for example if the type of a port does not meet the value sent on it. On the conceptual level those checks are comparably simple and can be carried out au-tomatically. However, even in the semantical level different inconsistencies may occur:

Abstract vs. concrete behavior: As mentioned in section 4.1, a component (or system) may be realized by a number of subcomponents using an SSD. Accordingly, the system designer can assign behavior to both the component and its subcomponents using STDs. In the AUTOFOCUS/Quest development methodology the assignment of behavior to the 'black box' and 'glass box' view of a system is considered as a refinement step performed by the de-signer. Thus, it should be checked that the abstract component including its behavior is refined by the concrete subcomponents and their behavior given by their STDs. Since this is a refinement step, the concrete behavior must fulfill the requirements of the abstract behavior, or - in other words - any behavior exhibited by the concrete system must also be possible in the abstract version.

Behavior vs. interaction: As mentioned in section 3 the views used in the AUTOFOCUS/Quest approach are not completely independent and may share common aspects. On the semantic level, both SSDs combined with STDs and EETs express behavior of a system (or component).

Again, support is needed to aid the user during the development process in detecting such inconsistencies. Again, those checks should be performed as automatic as possible. If the state space of the specified system is finite, in general model checking can be used to perform those checks. We used the model checker μcke [Bie97] to implement a prototype of such an automatic check ([SH99], [Bec99]. Naturally, the performability of such checks is heavily influenced by the size and the complexity of such a system. For the second check, i.e., verifying that an interaction described by EET corresponds with the behavior of a system characterized by SSDs and STDs, another proof method can be applied using a bounded model checking approach. Here, the model checker SATO is used to check that form of consistency (see [Wim00]).

Further Integration As mentioned above, automatic checks can not always be performed. In that case, other forms of integration must used.

One possible solution is to exchange the model checker by a theorem prover, as it was done with AUTOFOCUS/Quest using VSE. This integration adds a new description formalism, the logical formalism of the theorem prover, to the existing set of description techniques. Thus, this approach requires the user to get familiar with another formalism as well as an additional tool, the prover. While this results in a weaker integration from the user's point of view, it extends consistency checks to more general systems with an infinite state space.

Another possibility is to add another description formalism to express semantic properties of a component or system and integrate a suitable tool for this formalism. In AUTOFOCUS/Quest both SATO (see [Wim00]), and SMV (see [PS99]) were integrated. This approach adds a new description formalism, the temporal logic, and does not treat the inconsistencies mentioned in the previous subsection. However, it offers two advantages for easy integration in the tool environment:

- The checks can be performed automatically, thus - from the user's point of view - there is no need for another tool.
- The check either passes or results in a counter example expressed in form of an EET. Thus, besides the temporal logics, no other formalism is needed.

4.3 Methodical Integration

The last sections dealt with the integration of the semantical concepts behind the conceptual layer. Integrated and consistent semantics are not only a well founded basis but also a prerequisite for a continuous and straight-forward software development process. As a prime requisite to up-to-date system development, the AUTOFOCUS/Quest method covers the development process from the graphical description of the system over system verification using theorem proving to code generation. Beyond that, however, the methodical integration of different software development concepts is essential for a successful tool integration. An adequate integration of different methods will make any integrational tool worth more than the single parts from which it was made.

Generally, the development process is divided into phases like requirements, modeling, validation, prototyping, and test. In our approach, while each phase may use different techniques, they all work on the same metamodel with a common semantics. This enables the developer to switch between different phases like specification, verification, or testing, and the corresponding tasks without the need for complex manual transformations. Due to the versatility of the model based approach, there are no restrictions introduced by the model which complicate the combination of those tasks or integration of new methods in the process. The next paragraphs discuss the different phases in detail and show how they fit into the integrated metamodel and the given semantics.

The **requirements phase** generally deals with informal documents and fuzzy specifications. We provide extended event traces (EET, see Section 2.1) that allow the specification of use cases as exemplary interaction sequences. EETs, an AUTOFOCUS description technique, represent a first, generally incomplete, specification of the system.

In the next phase, the **modeling phase**, the skeleton of the system specification is enlarged and refined to get a more defined structure and behavior model. This is done by applying the AUTOFOCUS development method (See [HMS+98]). If one or more EETs already exist, it is also possible to derive the first version of the interface and the system structure from the axes and messages of the EETs.

In the **validation phase** the following tasks are supported:

- consistency checks (see Section 4.1),
- simulation (see [HMS+98]),
- model checking (see [PS99]), bounded model checking (see [Wim00]) and
- theorem proving.

AUTOFOCUS/Quest provides simulation of components. So, faults in the specifications can be detected and located directly while the simulation is running. Beyond that, the simulation also generates system traces which are displayed as EETs and can be later used for conformance testing.

In case of developing safety critical systems, validation by simulation is not sufficient. Often formal proofs are required to show the correctness of the specifications. With model checking it is possible to prove safety critical properties of components automatically. Therefore model checking became very popular. Model checking does not only check properties as valid, but also produces counter examples if the property does not hold. If the model checker finds a counter example, it is retranslated and displayed as an EET. Abstraction techniques are a further example for a method integration. They extend the power of model checking to large and infinite systems (we use [Mül98]). Simple proof obligations are generated (for VSE) to ensure that the model checked property in the abstract system also holds in the concrete systems. The design task, to find correct abstractions, is supported within AUTOFOCUS/Quest.

Besides the model checking approach, AUTOFOCUS/Quest also allows to translate the specification to a representation understood by the VSE system, a theorem prover for a temporal logic similar to TLA supporting hierarchic components like AUTOFOCUS/Quest [RSW97]. Within the VSE system a formal founded validation of the specification can be performed. It is also possible to make small changes of the specification in the VSE system and the re-import to AUTOFOCUS/Quest.

Beside system validation AUTOFOCUS/Quest supports the **test phase**. Testing in AUTOFOCUS/Quest focuses on conformance testing between a specification and its manually coded implementation. The most challenging task within software testing is a tool-supported test case generation. Therefore we have integrated the classification tree editor CTE [GWG95]. The CTE allows the classification of arbitrary datatypes with trees and the selection of certain combinations as test input classes. The construction of the classification trees is assisted by the classification tree assistant (CTA) which can be set up individually. In AUTOFOCUS/Quest we generate the CTA from datatype definitions, system structure, and automata. So the tester does not need to start from scratch, but can use the suggested standard classifications. The classification tree method is combined with a sophisticated test sequentialization which computes test cases, i.e. sequences of input/output data. Test cases are coded as EETs. A simple test driver allows the execution of the generated test cases with Java components.

The **implementation phase** is supported with Java and C code generators.

A well done methodical integration of different software development methods does not restrict the development process but gives more freedom. In AUTOFOCUS/Quest EETs play an important role in integration. EETs are a kind of multi-functional description technique. They serve as use cases, interaction description, counter examples, as well as test cases.

4.4   Tool Integration

In the previous section we have shown the methodical integration of the development process. Through the different phases of the development process we have to use different tools, like AUTOFOCUS, model checkers, theorem provers and test tools. So we designed AUTOFOCUS/Quest not to be one monolithic tool, but rather to be a collection of different specialized tools which are based on the same integrated metamodel. One big advantage of having many different tools is, that they are small, easier to understand and to replace. One example for this is the connection to the model checkers SMV and SATO. You can use each one or both for AUTOFOCUS/Quest or we can build another connection to a new model checker, which replaces the other two connections.

To link our tool-collection together we use a central repository with a conceptual schema, which is defined by the integrated metamodel. Every other tool can use the repository via an API. The API offers methods for e.g. importing or exporting a complete repository to a text file or to do some consistency checks on a model or a part of it. Note that the consistency checker bases on the core API, so that different tools to check the consistency of our models can be used.

Since we would like to integrate other tools, we want to have a flexible metamodel, and we want to be able to change things in the metamodel or to add new concepts to the metamodel without having to recode the central repository and without the need to touch every tool even if it is not affected by the change. So the core repository, which offers an API to create, modify or delete objects, is completely generated. As the core API the textual importer and exporter are generated [Mar98]. Thus we only have to change tools which are directly affected by the change. The generated core repository also ensures that our hard constraints are not violated. Every programmer using the API can rely on the fact that the hard constraints are not violated in any model, making programming considerably easier.

A common, well documented model is also important for integration of new tools. To connect a new tool to AUTOFOCUS/Quest directly the repository API or a translation from the model data in repository to the data needed by the tool can be used. Consistency checks can be used to ensure some constraints that are a prerequisite for the translation. Besides this a retranslation of results or model changes to AUTOFOCUS/Quest might be needed.

The spectrum of currently available tools in the field of embedded systems ranges from those tool focused on formal based design including verification techniques to tools concentrating on software engineering aspects including view-based system description, code generation and simulation. Consider, for example, Atelier B [Abr96] on the one hand, StateMate [Har90] or SDT [Tel96] on the other hand. Generally, those tools only partially integrate those aspects. An integrated combination of clearly defined but simple modeling concepts, an underlying well-defined semantic model for verification purposes, industrial-oriented notations supporting view-based development, prototyping for requirements validation, code generation for system implementation as well as test cases generation for system validation.

On the SW-engineering side, this is often due the fact that system modeling approaches like UML [BJR97] using different, graphical notation for the description of systems lack a sound conceptual and semantical basis. As a consequence, in many cases tools like Rational Rose [Rat98] and Rhapsody [i-L97] supporting this notation are missing a suitable formal semantics. Thus, while those notations and tools do offer support for checking syntactic consistency conditions, no such support is available on the semantic side. Those observations even hold for notations and tools based on more formally defined approaches like SDL and corresponding tools like SDT [Tel96].

On the other side, tools originating in formal approaches like STeP [BBC+95] or Atelier B [Abr96] often lack methodical or engineering functionality like the splitting of complete system descriptions into well-defined views of the system, combining these descriptions on different levels of abstraction as well as relating those views to form a consistent description.

The goal for developing AUTOFOCUS was not to build another tool but rather to investigate how the experiences gained in several basic research projects could be consequently applied to the development of embedded systems. Some aspects were considered as major topics: the use of well-defined description techniques, the modularity and expressiveness of those description techniques supporting different levels of abstractions and view-points, as well as the methodical integration of those techniques for integrated development approach. Those aspects also are the features distinguishing AUTOFOCUS from other tools in this area.

For example, approaches like StateMate mix different views (system structure and behavior by using AND- and OR-states). Furthermore, there a semantical basis is not applied to support model checking or theorem proofing. While other tools avoid those mixing of aspects, they are somewhat lax in the use of complete and clearly defined description techniques. Thus, for example, in ObjecTime, the diagrams for behavioral description are annotated with program code fragments to for a complete description. Since ROOM [SGW94] and ObjecTime were developed without a clear semantical model, in the end the meaning of diagrams is only described by the generated executable models, leaving the possibility for open questions concerning modeling concepts as well as lacking the requirements for formal support by theorem proofing or model checking.

The combination of the above mentioned aspects and the resulting methodical consequences are central incentives for the development of AUTOFOCUS. AUTOFOCUS supports a lean subset of description techniques based on a common mathematical model. These description techniques are independent of a specific method or a tool, while offering the essential aspects of similar description techniques, and can therefore be combined with a wide rage of methods and development processes.

5   Conclusion and Future Work

Integration of formal techniques is more than just integrating formal (and semiformal) tools; nevertheless, tool integration is one important step. Several tool platforms that can be readily connected to AUTOFOCUS/Quest, including NuSMV, Proovers, STeP, or Isabelle. Since the ultimate goal is the methodical integration, more steps have to be taken on this level: Code generators for C and Java are currently under development. Further work is needed in requirements phase, to support methods for requirements tracing (as found in the DOORS tool). Furthermore, in the modeling phase the use of graphical support for model based development steps (refinement, splitting of transitions, combining channels, etc.) in AUTOFOCUS must be investigated.

References

Abr96.   J.-R. Abrial. *The B-Book: Assigning Programs to Meanings*. Cambridge University Press, 1996. 60

BBC⁺95.   Nikolaj Bjorner, Anca Browne, Eddie Chang, Michael Colon, Arjun Kapur, Zohar Manna, Henny B. Sipma, and Tomas E. Uribe. STeP: The Stanford Temporal Prover (Educational Release) User's Manual. STAN-CS-TR 95-1562, Computer Science Department Stanford University, 1995. 60

Bec99.   Roland Bechtel. Einbettung des μ-Kalkül Model Checkers μ-cke in AUTOFOCUS. Master's thesis, Institut für Informatik, Technische Universität München, 1999. 57

Bie97.   Armin Biere. *Effiziente Modellprüfung des μ-Kalküls mit binären Entscheidungdiagrammen*. PhD thesis, Universität Karlsruhe, 1997. 57

BJR97.   G. Booch, I. Jacobson, and J. Rumbaugh. *UML Summary*. Rational Software Cooperation, January 1997. Version 1.0. 52, 55, 60

GWG95.   M. Grochtmann, J. Wegner, and K. Grimm. Test Case Design Using Classification Trees and the Classification-Tree Editor. In *Proceedings of 8th International Quality Week, San Francisco*, pages Paper 4–A–4, May 30–June 2 1995. 50, 59

Har90.   D. Harel. Statemate: A working environment for the development of complex reactive systems. *IEEE Transactions on Software Engineering*, 16(4):403–414, 1990. 60

HMS⁺98.   F. Huber, S. Molterer, B. Schätz, O. Slotosch, and A. Vilbig. Traffic Lights - An AutoFocus Case Study. In *1998 International Conference on Application of Concurrency to System Design*, pages 282–294. IEEE Computer Society, 1998. 49, 58

i-L97.   i-Logix. *Rhapsody Reference Version 1.0*, 1997. 60

Mar98.   Frank Marschall. Konzeption und Realisierung einer generischen Schnittstelle für metamodell-basierte Werkzeuge. Master's thesis, Institut für Informatik, Technische Universität München, 1998. 60

McM92.   K.L. McMillan. The SMV system, Symbolic Model Checking - an approach. Technical Report CMU-CS-92-131, Carnegie Mellon University, 1992. 50

Met99.   MetaModel. http://www.MetaModel.com/, 1999. 52

Mül98.   Olaf Müller. *A Verification Environment for I/O-Automata Based on Formalized Meta-Theory*. PhD thesis, Institut für Informatik, Techn. Univ. München, 1998. 58

PS99.   J. Philipps and O. Slotosch. The Quest for Correct Systems: Model Checking of Diagramms and Datatypes. In *Asia Pacific Software Engineering Conference 1999*, pages 449–458, 1999. 57, 58

Rat98.   Rational. Rational Rose 98 Product Overview. http://www.rational.com/products/rose/, 1998. 60

RSW97.   G. Rock, W. Stephan, and A. Wolpers. Tool Support for the Compositional Development of Distributed Systems. In *Proc. Formale Beschreibungstechniken für verteilte Systeme, GI/ITG-Fachgespräch*. GMD-Studien Nr. 315, ISBN: 3-88457-514-2, 1997. 50, 58

SGW94.   Bran Selic, Garth Gullekson, and Paul Ward. *Real-Time Object-Oriented Modeling*. John Wiley and Sons, 1994. 61

SH99.   Bernhard Schätz and Franz Huber. Integrating Formal Description Techniques. In Jeanette Wing, Jim Woodcock, and Jim Davies, editors, *FM'99 - Formal Methods*, pages 1206–1225. Springer, 1999. 57

Slo98.   O. Slotosch. Quest: Overview over the Project. In D. Hutter, W. Stephan, P Traverso, and M. Ullmann, editors, *Applied Formal Methods - FM-Trends 98*, pages 346–350. Springer LNCS 1641, 1998. 50

Tel96.   Telelogic AB. *Telelogic AB: SDT 3.1 Reference Manual*, 1996. 60

Wim00.   G. Wimmel. Using SATO for the Generation of Input Values for Test Sequences. Master's thesis, Technische Universität München, 2000. 57, 58

WK98.   Jos Warmer and Anneke Kleppe. *The Object Constraint Language*. Addison-Wesley, 1998. 55

Zha97.   H. Zhang. SATO: An efficient propositional prover. In William McCune, editor, *Proceedings of the 14th International Conference on Automated deduction*, volume 1249 of *LNAI*, pages 272–275, Berlin, July 13–17 1997. Springer. 50

An Architecture for Interactive Program Provers

Jörg Meyer and Arnd Poetzsch-Heffter

Fernuniversität Hagen, D-58084 Hagen, Germany
{Joerg.Meyer,Arnd.Poetzsch-Heffter}@fernuni-hagen.de

Abstract. Formal specification and verification techniques can improve the quality of programs by enabling the analysis and proof of semantic program properties. This paper describes the modular architecture of an interactive program prover that we are currently developing for a Java subset. In particular, it discusses the integration of a programming language-specific prover component with a general purpose theorem prover.

1 Introduction

Specification and verification techniques can improve the quality of programs by enabling the analysis and proof of semantic program properties. They can be used to show the absence of exceptions and to prove that a program satisfies certain interface properties or a complete interface specification. This is particularly interesting for the emerging market of software components. As we illustrate in Section 2, tool support is crucial for the application of such formal techniques.

The paper motivates and describes the modular architecture of an interactive program prover that we are currently developing for a Java subset. In particular, it discusses the integration of a programming language-specific prover component with a general purpose theorem prover. The goal of this research is to provide a powerful and flexible tool that

- supports complete a posteriori program verification;
- provides assistance in top-down program development, e.g. for deriving specifications of auxiliary procedures;
- allows one to specify and check certain simple, but in general undecidable properties, such as the absence of null pointer dereferencing and out-of-bounds access to arrays.

As illustrated by the last aspect, we are not only interested in algorithm verification, but as well in showing the absence of certain (language dependent) program errors. In particular, we have to deal with sharing and abstraction. We build on an object-oriented language, because it supports encapsulation on the level of types and because subtyping simplifies reuse.

Overview. The paper is organized as follows. Section 2 provides the technical background for specification and verification, motivates our approach, and discusses related work. Section 3 presents the overall architecture for the interactive verification environment. Section 4 focuses on the realization of the program prover component and describes its application by an example.

S. Graf and M. Schwartzbach (Eds.): TACAS/ETAPS 2000, LNCS 1785, pp. 63–77, 2000.

2 Verification of Realistic Programs

Verification of realistic programs is a fairly complex task. The goal of this section is to illustrate where this complexity comes from and to give an overview of tool-based approaches to cope with this complexity. The first subsection sketches state-of-the-art specification techniques and the involved formal background that has to be mastered by verification tools. The second subsection summarizes mechanical approaches to formal program verification from the literature.

2.1 Specifying Object-Oriented Programs

Program specifications should describe the behavior of program components in a *formal* and *abstract* way: Formality is a prerequisite for computer-aided verification. Abstraction is needed to achieve implementation independency and to simplify verification. In the following we summarize formal techniques to achieve abstraction in OO-languages.

We build on the Larch approach to program specification (cf. [GH93]) that uses type invariants and pre- and postconditions for procedures/methods. The following Java program fragment shows an interface type Set^1 and an implementation of this type based on arrays.

```
interface Set {                      class ArraySet implements Set {
   boolean add( Object o );             private Object[] elems;
   boolean contains( Object o );        private int setsize;
   int size();                          boolean add( Object o ){ ... }
   ... }                                ... }
```

Since the interface Set may have several implementations and since it should be possible to modify implementations without changing the specification, the specification of Set cannot refer to any implementation parts, i.e., it has to be given in abstract terms. We specify the behavior of type *Set* using an abstract data type with main sort SET and the usual operations, and an abstraction function *aSet*. *aSet* maps a Set object X and an object store to a value of sort SET. The object store is needed to capture the objects referenced by X. Method add can thus be specified as follows where $ is a variable denoting the current object store and the caret-operator yields the value of a variable in the prestate:

> boolean add(Object o)
> pre $o \neq null$
> post result $= (o \in aSet(\text{this}, \$\hat{\ })) \wedge aSet(\text{this}, \$) = \{o\} \cup aSet(\text{this}, \$\hat{\ })$
> $\wedge \ \forall \text{Object} \, X : \neg inRepSet(X, \text{this}, \$\hat{\ }) \ \Rightarrow \ unchanged(X, \$, \$\hat{\ })$

The first conjunct of the postcondition states that add yields true if and only if the object to be inserted is already contained in the set. The second conjunct specifies that after execution the implicit parameter **this** refers to the enlarged set. The third conjunct describes that the states of all objects not belonging to the representation of the input set remain unchanged. The representation of an

---

[1] A simplified version of the Set type as contained in the Java library.

abstract value comprises all objects that are used to represent the value in the object store. Since abstraction functions and the predicate *inRepSet* depend on implementations, they have to be explicitly defined. E.g., the provider of class **ArraySet** has to define an abstraction function and the predicate *inRepSet* for objects of type **ArraySet**. (For a set represented by an ArraySet-object Y, the representation consists of Y and the referenced array object.)

The above example illustrates the basic aspects needed in a realistic framework for formal program specification and verification. A more detailed presentation of the specification techniques can be found in [PH97b,MPH99]. In summary, such a framework has to provide the following features:

- To express abstraction, it is necessary to define and reason about abstract data types that are specified outside the programming language (e.g. SET).
- To specify modifications of the object store and to formulate properties on the program level (e.g. absence of null pointer dereferencing), a formalization of objects and the object store has to be provided by the framework.
- The abstract and program levels have to be integrated to be able to specify abstraction functions, representation predicates, and abstract data types that are based on types of the programming language (e.g. the abstract data type SET refers to elements of type **Object**).

The **Java** interactive verification environment JIVE that is described in this paper supports all of the above features (cf. Section 3 and 4).

2.2   Computer-Aided Program Verification

In the literature, we can essentially find three approaches to computer-aided program verification.

Verification Based on Language Semantics. This technique works as follows: Translate the program into a general specification framework (e.g. HOL) in which the semantics of the programming language is defined. Then state the program properties directly within this framework and use the rules of the language semantics for verification. This techniques is e.g. applied in [JvdBH+98].

The advantage of this approach is that existing frameworks equipped with powerful tools can be used without extensions (e.g., PVS [COR+95] or Isabelle [Pau94]). Only the translation process has to be implemented (and verified). The main disadvantage is that specification and verification on the semantics level is very tedious, because the abstraction step gained by an axiomatic language definition once has to be done in semantics level proofs again and again.

Verification Condition Generation. VCG was the classical approach to program verification. Based on a weakest precondition semantics, a program specification is transformed into a (weakest) precondition formula guaranteeing that a program satisfies its postcondition; i.e., program dependent aspects are eliminated by the wp-transformation. The precondition formula (verification condition) can be proved by a general theorem prover. This is the technique used in systems like e.g. the Standford Pascal Verifier [Com79].

The advantage of this approach is again that program dependent aspects are eliminated automatically and that the proper verification task can be done using standard tools. The disadvantage is that in realistic settings (cf. Section 2.1) the verification conditions become huge and very complex. There are essentially three reasons for that: (recursive) procedure/method calls, aliasing operations on the object store, and abstraction. As an example, consider an invocation site of method add of interface Set. If we use the specification of add to compute a weak precondition for a formula Q, the resulting precondition has about the size of the method specification plus the size of Q. The reason for this is that the postcondition of add does usually not match Q and that simplification is not trivial. Having several method invocations in a statement sequence easily leads to unmanagable preconditions.

Working with verification condition generation has two further disadvantages: a) If the generated condition cannot be proved, it is often difficult to find out why this is the case and which program statement causes to fail (cf. [GMP90] for a discussion of this issue). b) VCG is fairly inflexible and only applicable in an a-posteriori verification. E.g., in top-down program development, one would like derive the needed properties of a used method from the specification of the calling method.

Interactive Program Verification. Interactive program verification applies ideas from general tactical theorem proving to programming logics like e.g. to Hoare logic (see below) or dynamic logic (cf. [Rei95]). The main advantage of this approach is that program proofs can be developed around the program, i.e. as annotations to the program. The intuition about the program can be directly used for the proof. Strengthening and weakening steps can be applied where most appropriate. In particular, such steps can be done before and after method invocations to adapt method specifications to the needs at the invocation site. This way the described problem of VCG can be avoided. In addition to this, it is usually easy to detect program errors from failing proofs. Furthermore an advantage is that the interactive program prover "knows" the programming language and can provide appropriate views. On the other hand, a language dependent program prover has to be developed which is quite an engineering challenge.

Because of the described disadvantages of the first and second approach, we decided to construct an interactive, tactical prover for program verification. Within this prover, weakest precondition techniques can be implemented by tactics and used where appropriate without giving up flexibility. Depending on the goals, other combinations of the verification approaches sketched above are investigated in the literature. E.g. in [Gor89], Gordon demonstrates the development of programming logics based on a general HO-theorem prover showing the strength of HO-reasoning. However, he cannot exploit the specific relation between programs and program proofs. In the Extended Static Checker for Java (ESC/Java, cf. [DLNS98]), the translational approach is combinded with VCG for automatic checking of a restricted class of specifications.

3   An Architecture for Interactive Program Provers

This section presents our architecture for interactive program provers. The architecture is based on the following requirements: The functional properties as described in Section 2.1 have to be fulfilled. The newly implemented program prover component should only be responsible for proof tasks that are directly related to the program. General specification and verification aspects should be delegated and performed by state-of-the-art theorem provers. This comprises in particular the definition of the object store and abstraction functions. In the following, we first analyse the consequences of combining general provers with language-specific provers. Then, we explain the overall architecture.

Communicating Provers. There are two architectural alternatives for combining a general prover and a programming language specific prover component within a verification system: a) The general theorem prover is encapsualed by the system and hidden to users. b) Both prover components are accessible by users and the communication between them is visible. For the following reasons, we decided for the second alternative. It provides more flexiblity and is easier to react to new developments w.r.t. the general theorem prover. The implementation is less expensive. For third party users, the programming interfaces of existing theorem provers are not sufficiently powerful to control all prover operations by an external process. The disadvantage of this solution is that users of the resulting system have to handle two interactive components: the program prover component and the theorem prover component.

The communication between the two prover components is illustrated in Figure 1. The program prover sends type checking and proof requests to the general theorem prover. Type checking of pre- and postformulas is done in the general theorem prover, as

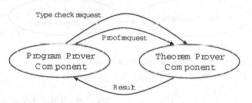

Fig. 1. Basic prover components.

these formulas contain logical variables and make use of abstract data types specified as theories in the syntax of the general theorem prover. Proof requests result from strengthening and weakening steps in program proofs. They are formulas not refering to a special program part and are verified online or offline in the theorem prover component. The information whether such proof obligations have been proven or not is sent back to the program proof component. This way, the program proof component can check whether program proofs are complete.

The communication between program prover and theorem prover is based on a communication interface that allows one to send formulas from the program prover to the theorem prover. Type check requests differ from proof requests in that they are usually[2] solved automatically whereas proof requests typically need user interaction.

---

[2] The subtyping of the used specification language (PVS) is in general undecidable.

The JIVE **Architecture.** This subsection describes the overall architecture of JIVE. JIVE supports the sequential kernel of the Java language including recursive methods, classes, abstract classes, interfaces, thus inheritance and subtyping, static and dynamic binding, aliasing via object references, and encapsulation constructs. Exception handling and some of the predefined data types (in particular float and char) are not yet supported (cf. [MPH99] for a precise description). In addition to the Java subset, JIVE supports annotations like that shown in Section 2.1. The common language for programs and annotations is called ANJA (annotated Java). In the following, we explain the architectural components and the input sources of proof sessions based on the overview given in Figure 2.

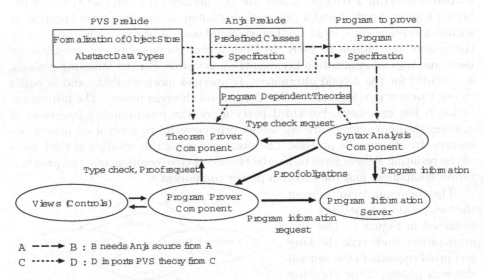

$$A \dashrightarrow B : B \text{ needs Anja source from } A$$
$$C \cdots\!\!\rightarrow D : D \text{ imports PVS theory from } C$$

Fig. 2. The JIVE architecture

System Components. The architecture is based on five components: 1.) The syntax analysis component that reads in and analyzes annotated programs and generates the program proof obligations. 2.) The program information server that makes the static program information gathered in the analysis phase available to other parts of the system. 3.) The program prover component managing the program proofs. 4.) Views to visualize program proofs and to control proof construction. 5.) The theorem prover to solve program independent proof obligations. In our current implementation, we use PVS for general theorem proving.

The program proof component encapsulates the construction of program proofs. It provides two things: (1.) A container which stores all information about program proofs and (2.) an interface which provides operations to create and modify proofs within this container. Since the content of the proof container represents the program proof state, it is strongly encapsulated to the rest of the system. Modifications of the proof state can only be achieved by operations of the container interface (see Section 4). Therefore correctness of proofs is ensured by the correctness of the basic container operations.

During program proof construction, various information about the underlying program is needed by the program proof component: The structure of the abstract syntax tree, results of binding and type analysis, and the program unparsing for visualization. This kind of information is provided by the program information server. In contrast to a compiler frontend, all information computed during static program analysis has to be available online after the analysis.

Proof Setup. The verification of a program is based on three formal texts: 1.) The PVS prelude containing two parts: (a) the formalization of the object-store; (b) the specification of abstract data types used in program annotations. Whereas the former part is program independent, the latter may be program dependent. 2.) The ANJA prelude containing the specifications of predefined and library classes and interfaces. 3.) An ANJA program, i.e. a program in our Java subset together with a suitable interface specification. Annotations are formulated in a language based on the specification language of the underlying theorem prover, i.e. PVS in our case. As illustrated in Section 2, they may refer to program variables and use abtract data types specified in the PVS prelude.

From the described sources, the syntax analysis component generates three things: 1. The program proof obligations which need to be proven to guarantee that the program fulfills its specification. They are entered into the proof container. 2. Program dependent theories formalizing some of the declaration information of the program for the theorem prover. 3. The abstract syntax tree decorated with information of the static analysis. It is managed by the program information server.

After syntax and static analysis, the system is set up for interactive proof construction. The user constructs program proofs using basic proof operations and tactics (see Section 4). The views and controllers provide access to the proof state. Program independent proof obligation are verified with the general theorem prover. The program prover monitors the overall proof process and signals the completion of proof tasks.

4   The Program Prover

Program proofs in JIVE are based on a Hoare logic for object-oriented programs (cf. [PHM99]). Hoare logic is sufficient for our purposes and enables us to visualize proof parts as program annotations. This section first describes how the basic proof operations of the proof container are derived from the logic and how tactics can be formulated. Then, it explains the user interface for proof construction and visualization and sketches a simple proof done within JIVE.

4.1   Mechanizing the Programming Logic

As the supported programming language provides recursive methods, the Hoare logic deals with *sequents* of the form $\mathcal{A} \vdash \{ \mathbf{P} \} \text{ comp } \{ \mathbf{Q} \}$ where $\mathcal{A}$ denotes a set of method specifications (the *assumptions*), $\mathbf{P}$ and $\mathbf{Q}$ are first-order formulas, and comp denotes a statement or a method, the so-called *program component* of the sequent. Program components are represented by references to the abstract program syntax tree. A rule in the logic consists of a finite number of antecedents and a sequent as conclusion. The antecedents are either sequents or first-order formulas. Rules without antecedents are called axioms. As examples, we show the rule to verify if-statements and the assumpt-intro-rule to introduce assumptions:

$$\frac{\mathcal{A} \vdash \{\, e \wedge \mathbf{P}\,\}\ \text{stmt1}\ \{\,\mathbf{Q}\,\}\,,\ \ \mathcal{A} \vdash \{\,\neg e \wedge \mathbf{P}\,\}\ \text{stm2}\ \{\,\mathbf{Q}\,\}}{\mathcal{A} \vdash \{\,\mathbf{P}\,\}\ \text{if (e)}\ \{\,\text{stm1}\,\}\ \text{else}\ \{\,\text{stm2}\,\}\ \ \{\,\mathbf{Q}\,\}} \qquad \frac{\mathcal{A} \vdash \mathbf{A}}{\mathbf{A_0}\,,\,\mathcal{A} \vdash \mathbf{A}}$$

Basic Proof Operations. As usual, proof trees are constructed from rule instances. A tree node has as many children as the rule has antecedents. There are two ways to construct proof trees. 1. A *forward proof step* takes several proof trees and combines them with a new root node. 2. A *backward proof step* adds a new node to one of the leaves. A proof tree is *closed* if all leaves are instances of axioms or first-order formulas that are proved by the theorem prover component.

To gain the flexibility explained in Section 2, JIVE supports operations for forward and backward proof steps. These operations have to be distinguished, because different directions require different context checks for formulas, program components, and parameters. The *if-rule* serves as an example: Forward proving combines two proof trees S_1 and S_2 to a new proof tree, backward proving refines a proof goal $\mathcal{G}$ of an if-statement into two subgoals for the then- and else-branch. The context conditions of the *if_forward* and *if_backward* operations are as follows:

Forward Proof:
1. S_1 and S_2 have to be roots of proof trees.
2. The assumptions of S_1 and S_2 have to be equal.
3. e has to be a conjunct of S_1.
4. $\neg e$ has to be a conjunct of S_2.
5. The preconditions of S_1 and S_2 have to be equal modulo the conjuncts e and $\neg e$ resp.
6. The postconditions of S_1 and S_2 have to be equal.
7. stmt1 and stmt2 have to be the then- and else-branch of the same if-statement.

Backward Proof:
1. $\mathcal{G}$ has to be the leaf of a proof tree.
2. The program component of $\mathcal{G}$ has to be an if-statement.

Proof operations are executed as follows: First, the context conditions are checked. If they are met, the proof operation is applied and leads to a new proof tree, and thus to a modified state in the proof container. Otherwise, an appropriate exception is raised that can be used in tactics (see below). Because operations first check all necessary context conditions, correctness of proofs is provided by the correctness of operations. The JIVE system is currently based on a Hoare logic with 26 rules and axioms. Thus, it provides 52 basic proof operations. In addition, JIVE provides a *cut* operation to remove, a *copy* operation to copy, a *paste* operation to combine proof tree parts, and operations to inspect parts of the proof tree or to navigate within proof trees. These operations allow for comfortable interactive work with program proof information, e.g., they enable one to cut off failing proof parts.

Tactics. Program proofs are constructed by successively using proof operations as described above. To simplify proof construction, sequences of proof operations, e.g. to apply a weakest precondition strategy, can be combined to form tactics. As an example, we show a tactic that eliminates the assumptions of an open leaf of the proof tree by iterating the *assumpt-intro-rule* unless all assumptions are eliminated[3]. Since the proof operations of JIVE are implemented in Java (see Section 4.4), tactics are formulated as Java programs invoking proof operations. The getPre(), getPost(), and getComp() operations return the precondition, the postcondition and the program component of the triple t:

```
public ProofTreeNode eliminate_assumptions(ProofContainer c,
                        ProofTreeNode ptn) throws ContextException {
  Enumeration e =  ptn.getAssumptions().elements();
  while(e.hasMoreElements()) {
    Triple t = (Triple)e.nextElement();
    ptn = c.assumpt_intro_backward(
                    ptn,t.getPre(), t.getCompRef(), t.getPost() );
  }
  return ptn;
}
```

4.2   User-Interfaces of the Program Prover

Interactive program proof construction with proof operations enforces users to work explicitly with several kinds of information like formulas, program structures, textual program representation, etc. A graphical user interface is required (1.) for an appropriate visualization of the proof state and of the related information as well as (2.) for convenient selection, input, and application of operations and tactics. Currently JIVE provides a so-called *tree view* and a *text view* to program proofs[4]. Of course, both views can be used together within one proof.

Tree View. The tree view (Figure 4 shows a screen shot) presents the information contained in the proof container in a graphical way. All parts of proof trees can be examined, selected, copied, combined, extended and deleted. Compared to the text view (see below), the tree view shows all details of proof trees. In particular, it enables the user to inspect proof steps that cannot be presented as proof outlines and shows the complete proof structure. It supports the structural operations on trees (*cut, copy, paste*) and proof operations that take several trees as arguments which are not related to one program component. Since proof trees are in general large structures, tree views enable to work with scalable clippings of trees, i.e., the user interface displays only relevant information.

---

[3] Applying the *assumpt-intro-rule* backward eliminates an assumption.
[4] At time of submission of this paper, the text view was still under construction.

Text View. To provide a more compact view to program proof information and to enable an embedding of program proof information into the program text, text views display selected proof information within a textual program representation (Figure 3 shows a screen shot). This technique is based on so called proof outlines (cf. [Owi75]). The text view allows the user to consider proofs (or at least most of the central proof steps) as annotations to the program text. This turns out to be very helpful for interactive program proofs as the program structure is well-known to the user and simpler to handle. In particular, it allows the direct selection of program components which is needed for forward proofs. In addition to this, well-designed proof outlines are a good means for program and proof documentation.

4.3   Using the Program Prover

In this section, we illustrate the use of the program prover by an example explaining in particular the interaction of automated and manual proof construction. Using an interface of a singly linked integer list, we want to prove a simple recursive sort method:

```
interface List {                    class Sort {
  public List rest()                  public static List sort(List l)
    pre  aL(this,$) = L;                 pre  l/=null AND L=aL(l,$);
    post aL(result,$) = rst(L)           post aL(result,$)=a_sort(L);
         AND result /= null;             {
    pre  $=OS;                             List lv,res;
    post $=OS;                             boolean bv; int ev;

  public int first()                      bv = l.isempty();
    pre  aL(this,$) = L;                   if(bv) res = l;
    post aI(result) = fst(L);              else {
    pre  $=OS;                               lv = l.rest();ev = l.first();
    post $=OS;                               lv = Sort.sort(lv);
                                             res = Sort.sortedIns(ev,lv);
  public boolean isempty()                }
    pre  aL(this,$)=L;                     return res;
    post aB(result)=isempt(L);          }
    pre  $=OS;                           static List sortedIns(int e, List l)
    post $=OS;                             pre  aL(l,$)=a_sort(L) AND aI(e)=E
}                                               AND l/=null;
                                          post aL(result,$) = a_sort(app(E,L));
                                          { ... }
                                        }
```

In the given ANJA source, we use logical variables (written with capital letters) to bind values in the precondition for use in the postcondition. Each list method is specified by two pre-post-pairs. The first pair expresses the functional behavior using the abstraction function aL mapping objects to an abstract list data type. The second pair states that each method does not change the object store. Method `sort` of class `Sort` implements insertion sort using `sortIns` as auxiliary method; `a_sort` sorts an abstract list. We sketch the proof of method `sort` assuming the correctness of the list interface. `sort` is a static method, i.e. behaves like procedures in imperative languages. The logical aspects of dynamic binding cannot be discussed here (cf. [PHM99]). Starting the JIVE system with the given example yields the following two proof obligations for methods `sort` and `sortedIns`:

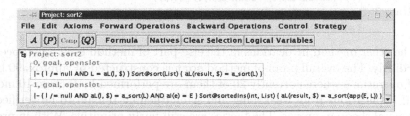

We start the verification of `sort` by applying the SWP-tactic to the goal 0. This tactic realizes a simple weakest-precondition-strategy. For the example, it reduces the method specification to a pre-post-pair for the statement sequence in the body. In our logic, this corresponds to two elementary proof steps that in particular conjoin "this ≠ null" to the precondition. Then, the SWP-tactic tries to verify the resulting pre-post-pair by forward proof steps starting with the rightmost innermost statement (according to the AST of the program), i.e., it starts at the end of the program text and works to the beginning. In our case, it automatically handles the return-statement and the then-branch of the if-statement. In the else-branch, it cannot procede because the postcondition of the if-statement does not match the postcondition of the specification for `sortedIns`. The corresponding proof state is illustrated by the screen shot of the text view in Figure 3. The system uses colors to distinguish program text from annotations and open proof slots (red) from verified triples (green). In the figure, this is indicated by brackets left to the screen shot. The red triple corresponds to the open leaf of the overall proof. The two green triples correspond to needed proof parts that have been constructed by the SWP-tactic.

The proof state after termination of a tactic can be interactively manipulated by the user. He or she can add further proof parts using other tactics or basic proof operations and then rerun the original tactic on the original goal. Typically, user interaction is necessary at method invocation sites, because there may be more than one specification for a method and it is not obvious which of them has to be used or how they have to be combined. How to handle such situations is demonstrated with the invocation of method `first` in the example. We show three states of a forward proof: 1. After instantiating the method specifications at the invocation site (one basic proof step). 2. After conjoining the resulting triple (one basic proof step). 3. After adding of an invariant term (one basic proof step) and eliminating the logical variable OS (several basic proof steps, done by a tactic). For space reasons, we leave out the surrounding window context:

- State 1:
  ```
  { I /= null AND aL(l, $) = L } 9
  { I /= null AND $ = OS } 10
      ev = 1.first();
  { $ = OS } 10
  { al(ev) = fst(L) } 9
  ```

- State 2:
  ```
  { I /= null AND aL(l, $) = L AND I /= null AND $ = OS } 11
      ev = 1.first();
  { al(ev) = fst(L) AND $ = OS } 11
  ```

- State 3:
  ```
  { I /= null AND aL(l, $) = L  AND aL(lv, $) = rst(L) } 20
      ev = 1.first();
  { al(ev) = fst(L)  AND aL(lv, $) = rst(L) } 20
  ```

The other method invocations in the else-part of method `sort` are processed accordingly. The overall proof of method `sort` is constructed by approx. 90 basic proof operations where currently 20 of them are performed by tactics; 10 mostly trivial implications from weakening and strengthening remain to be verified by the general theorem prover. The tactics are still fairly primitive. With improved tactics and a refined specification technique, we aim to drastically reduce the amount of needed user interaction.

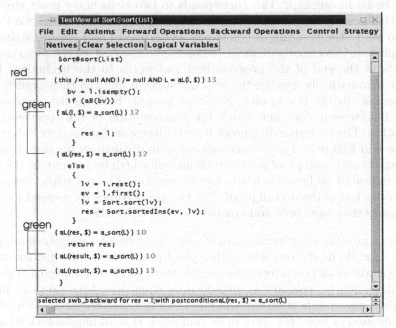

Fig. 3. The text view after applying the SWP-tactic.

The presented example shows three important aspects of the system: 1. Forward and backward proving is combined to gain the flexibility needed to encode typical proof strategies. 2. User-guided and automated proof construction by tactics can be freely mixed so that automation can be done where possible and user interaction can focus on the critical points. 3. Different views are needed that allow one to inspect the proof parts on different levels of abstraction. Even in the simple example, there exist up to 7 proof fragments at one time with 17 open proof slots and proof tree depth up to 20. This amount of information is conveniently abstracted by the text view. If detailed information is needed, the user can refer to the tree view (see Figure 4).

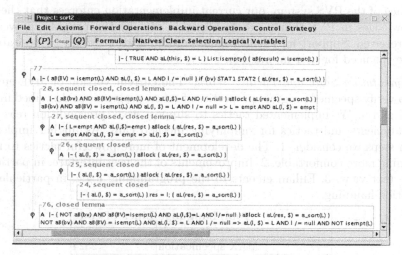

Fig. 4. A clipping of the proof tree view

4.4   Technical Issues

This section describes implementation issues concerning the JIVE system.

System Implementation. As shown in the table below, the JIVE system is implemented using a variety of tools and languages, mostly Java. Java combines several necessary properties, which are useful to implement heterogeneous tool environments. In particular, we make use of the Java Native Interface for C, of the API for TCP interfaces to connect to the theorem prover, and of the Swing library as graphical user interface. The central program proof component with the proof operations (as Java Methods) and auxiliary implementations parts such as formula handling is completely implemented in Java. Tactics are implemented as Java classes and can be dynamically loaded into the system. All other components are attached using the above mentioned interfaces.

Generative reuse techniques. One major design decision was to use as much as possible generative techniques to implement the system. This is possible because many subtasks to be solved are directly derived from compiler construction. 1. We use flex and bison for the syntax analysis of ANJA programs. 2. The program information server is based on attributed abstract syntax trees for programs and annotations. It is generated by the MAX tool (cf. [PH97a]). 3. ANTLR [PQ95] is a compiler generation tool for Java and is used to examine the structure of formulas given as arguments to proof operations. ANTLR is used as it can directly produce Java objects as output.

Integration of the PVS Theorem Prover. As explained above, JIVE uses PVS for type checking and for the verification of non-Hoare formulas. We use the techniques described in [But97] for the communication between PVS and the program prover. The connection to the proof system is implemented as a TCP connection with the PVS host system Emacs. Because of restrictions in the interface of the PVS system, our current implementation enforces that the user acknowledges in PVS that a proof obligation sent by the program prover has been received. Support for asynchronous communication would be desirable to reduce the need for user interaction.

Implementation State and Further Work. The current version of JIVE enables one to verify specified program properties of ANJA programs as described in Section 3 and 4. We implemented tactics to support weak precondition reasoning for statements and tactics for simplifying method calls. As further implementation steps we consider: 1. The development of more powerful tactics to make reasoning more comfortable. 2. Improvements of the user interface, in particular of the text view. 3. Enhancements to the programming logic, in particular for exception handling.

Tool/Language	Lines of code
Java code	13078
MAX specification	2524
C Code	1768
flex & bison specification	1218
ANTLR specification	854
Emacs lisp code	274
PVS standard prelude for JIVE	482
ANJA standard prelude for JIVE	158

5   Conclusion

Verification of program properties for object-oriented programming languages requires tool support, because the formal framework can hardly be handled by hand. In this paper, we presented the architecture of the interactive program verification environment JIVE. JIVE combines properties of different approaches to software verification. It divides program proving into a program proving and a theorem proving task. This enables the use of existing theorem provers for the proof steps that are not related to the program. For the program proving tasks, we described a technique to implement a given Hoare logic by basic proof operations supporting forward and backward proofs. Based on these proof operations, powerful tactics can be defined. We sketched the main user interface aspects of the system and described some implementation issues. (Current information about JIVE can be obtained at www.informatik.fernuni-hagen.de/pi5/jive.html)

Acknowledgments We thankfully acknowledge helpful comments from the reviewers and fruitful discussions with Peter Müller.

References

But97.   B. Buth.   An interface between Pamela and PVS.   Tech-
            nical report, Universität Bremen, 1997.   Available from
            http://www.informatik.uni-bremen.de/~bb/bb.html 76
Com79.   Computer Science Department, Stanford University. *Stanford PASCAL
            Verifier - User Manual*, 1979. 66
COR+95.   J. Crow, S. Owre, J. Rushby, N. Shankar, and M. Srivas. *A Tutorial
            Introduction to PVS*, April 1995. 65
DLNS98.   D. L. Detlefs, K. R. M. Leino, G. Nelson, and J. B. Saxe. Extended static
            checking. Research Report 159, Digital Systems Research Center, 1998.
            66
GH93.   J. V. Guttag and J. J. Horning. *Larch: Languages and Tools for For-
            mal Specification*. Texts and Monographs in Computer Science. Springer-
            Verlag, 1993. 64
GMP90.   D. Guaspari, C. Marceau, and W. Polak.   Formal verification of Ada
            programs. *IEEE Transactions on Software Engineering*, 16(9):1058–1075,
            September 1990. 66
Gor89.   M. J. C. Gordon. Mechanizing programming logics in higher order logic. In
            G. Birtwistle and P.A. Subrahmanyam, editors, *Current Trends in Hard-
            ware Verification and Automated Theorem Proving*. Springer-Verlag, 1989.
            Kopiensammlung. 66
JvdBH+98.   B. Jacobs, J. van den Berg, M. Huisman, M. van Berkum, U. Hensel,
            and H. Tews. Reasoning about Java classes. In *Proceedings of Object-
            Oriented Programming Systems, Languages and Applications (OOPSLA)*,
            1998. Also available as TR CSI-R9812, University of Nijmegen. 65
MPH99.   P. Müller and A. Poetzsch-Heffter. Modular specification and verification
            techniques for object-oriented software components. In G. Leavens and
            M. Sitaraman, editors, *Foundations of Component-Based Systems*. Cam-
            bridge University Press, 1999. 65, 68
Owi75.   S.S. Owicki. Axiomatic proof techniques for parallel programs. Technical
            report, Computer Science Dept., 1975. 72
Pau94.   Lawrence C. Paulson. *Isabelle: a generic theorem prover*, volume 828 of
            Lecture Notes in Computer Science. Springer-Verlag Inc., New York, NY,
            USA, 1994. 65
PH97a.   A. Poetzsch-Heffter. Prototyping realistic programming languages based
            on formal specifications. *Acta Informatica*, 34:737–772, 1997. 75
PH97b.   A. Poetzsch-Heffter. Specification and verification of object-oriented pro-
            grams. Habilitation thesis, Technical University of Munich, January 1997.
            65
PHM99.   A. Poetzsch-Heffter and P. Müller. A programming logic for sequential
            Java. In D. Swierstra, editor, *ESOP '99*, LNCS 1576. Springer-Verlag,
            1999. 69, 73
PQ95.   Terence J. Parr and Russell W. Quong. ANTLR: A predicated-LL(k)
            parser generator. *Software—Practice and Experience*, 25(7):789–810, July
            1995. 75
Rei95.   W. Reif. The KIV approach to software verification. In M. Broy and
            S. Jähnichen, editors, KORSO: *Methods, Languages, and Tools for the Con-
            struction of Correct Software*, volume 1009 of *Lecture Notes in Computer
            Science*. Springer-Verlag, 1995. 66

The PROSPER Toolkit*

Louise A. Dennis[1], Graham Collins[1], Michael Norrish[2], Richard Boulton[3], Konrad Slind[2], Graham Robinson[1], Mike Gordon[2], and Tom Melham[1]

[1] Department of Computing Science, University of Glasgow, G12 8QQ, UK
[2] Computer Laboratory, University of Cambridge, CB2 3QG, UK
[3] Division of Informatics, University of Edinburgh, EH1 1HN, UK

Abstract. The PROSPER (Proof and Specification Assisted Design Environments) project advocates the use of toolkits which allow existing verification tools to be adapted to a more flexible format so that they may be treated as components. A system incorporating such tools becomes another component that can be embedded in an application.
This paper describes the PROSPER *Toolkit* which enables this. The nature of communication between components is specified in a language-independent way. It is implemented in several common programming languages to allow a wide variety of tools to have access to the toolkit.

1 Introduction

Modern system design, both for hardware and software, must meet ever-increasing demands for dependable products of high quality, with shorter design times and early error detection. Incremental improvements to conventional design methods and tools are not enough. More powerful techniques of specification and analysis based on formal techniques are essential parts of new methods for design.

Formalisms provide specification and analysis at high levels of abstraction, so that designers can express and check a wider range of properties than with conventional techniques. This permits better structuring of complex systems, earlier detection of errors (leading to lower time to market), and higher quality.

Making effective use of formal techniques does *not* have to mean doing 'total verification' against 'complete formal specifications' or designing step-by-step with a formal refinement theory. This rather modernist Formal Methods programme has still to deliver significant benefits to large-scale design practice, and verification has, in consequence, remained largely an academic activity regarded sceptically by industry. Instead, one can view formal analysis (or 'property-checking') of systems as an advanced or more effective form of testing—whose objective is not necessarily to have a strong assurance of correctness, but rather to eliminate more bugs, earlier in the design process [10].

At present, a developer wishing to incorporate verification capabilities into a CAD or CASE tool, or any application, will face a difficult choice between

---

* Work funded by ESPRIT Framework IV Grant LTR 26241

S. Graf and M. Schwartzbach (Eds.): TACAS/ETAPS 2000, LNCS 1785, pp. 78–92, 2000.

creating a verification engine from scratch and adapting parts of one or more existing tools. Developing a verification engine from scratch is time-consuming and will usually involve re-implementing existing techniques. Existing tools, on the other hand, tend not to be suitable as components that can be patched into other programs. Furthermore, a design tool should embed verification in a way that is natural to a user, i.e. as an extension to the design process (much like debugging is an extension to the coding process). The verification engine must be customised to the application.

The PROSPER project[1] is addressing this issue by researching and developing a toolkit that allows an expert to easily and flexibly assemble *proof engines* to provide embedded formal reasoning support inside applications. The ultimate goal is to make the reasoning and proof support invisible to the end-user—or at least, more realistically, to incorporate it securely within the interface and style of interaction they are already accustomed to.

This paper describes the PROSPER toolkit and the methodology of building systems with it. §2 gives a high level view of the toolkit and what a resulting system may look like. While it is inappropriate to give much technical detail here,[2] §3 tries to give a flavour of the specification for communication. §4 discusses the methodology for building systems with the toolkit. §5 presents a case study. §6 gives an overview of related work.

2   Design Tools with Custom Proof Engines

A central part of PROSPER's vision is the idea of a proof engine—a custom built verification engine which can be operated by another program through an Application Programming Interface (API). A proof engine can be built by a system developer using the toolkit provided by the project. A proof engine is based upon the functionality of a theorem prover with additional capabilities provided by 'plugins' formed from existing, off-the-shelf, tools. The toolkit includes a set of libraries based on a language-independent specification for communication between components of a final system. The theorem prover's command language is treated as a kind of scripting or glue language for managing plugin components and orchestrating the proofs.

The central component is based on a theorem prover because this comes with ready made concepts of term, theorem, and goal, which are important for managing verifications. A side benefit is that all the functionality in the theorem prover (libraries of procedures, tactics, logical theories, etc.) becomes available to a developer for inclusion in their custom proof engine. This does not prevent theorem proving being very lightweight if desired.

A toolkit has been implemented based around HOL98, a modern descendent of the HOL theorem prover [11]. HOL98 is highly modular which suits the PROSPER approach of building up a proof engine from a set of components (be

---

[1] http://www.dcs.gla.ac.uk/prosper
[2] Technical documentation is available from the authors.

they HOL libraries or external plugins). It also contains a number of sophisticated automatic proof procedures. HOL's command language is ML [19] (a strict functional programming language) extended with HOL's own theorem proving functions which extend ML to include the language of higher order logic [6]. This allows a developer to have a full programming language available in which to develop custom verification procedures. Proof procedures programmed in the proof engine are offered to client applications in an API. This API can be accessed as a verification library in another programming language.

The toolkit provides several plugin components based on external tools which offer APIs to a proof engine. It also provides support to enable developers of other verification tools to offer them as PROSPER plugins.

The application, proof engine and plugins act as separate components in the final system (Figure 1). In the first prototype they are also separate processes.

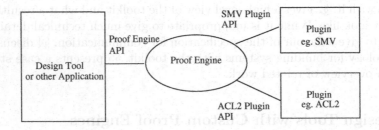

Fig. 1. A system built with the PROSPER toolkit

Communication between them is treated in a uniform manner specified by the PROSPER *Integration Interface.*

Work is currently underway to use this technology to add verification capabilities to IFAD's VDM-SL Toolbox [8]. The project is also building a *Hardware Verification Workbench.* This will allow specifications in Verilog and VHDL to be checked by a proof engine that incorporates a model checker.

Example 1. The IFAD VDM-SL Toolbox is a software design tool supporting the specification language, VDM-SL.

The proposed extensions to the Toolbox centre around the discharge of proof obligations generated by type invariants. Invariants are undecidable, so the automatic type checking functionality of IFAD's toolbox does not check their truth.

Many invariants can be discharged by first order logic decision procedures. To utilise these, the invariant condition needs to be translated from VDM-SL into first order logic. In particular, any user-defined functions must be simplified away. More complex simplification and theorem proving techniques can be used when the conditions fall outside the domain of first order logic. If an automatic proof attempt fails then a user must be able to intervene and guide a proof by hand.

This analysis suggests that the VDM-SL Toolbox requires a first order logic plugin; a proof engine with an embedding of the semantics of VDM-SL in higher order logic, specialised procedures for simplifying and translating VDM-SL expressions into first order logic (a subset of higher order logic) and some more complex proof techniques; procedures for the automatic generation of invariant proof obligations in the Toolbox itself, and a Toolbox specific interface to the proof guidance facilities provided by HOL. These elements can all be constructed together into the IFAD Toolbox using the PROSPER toolkit.

3   The Prosper Integration Interface

A major part of our methodology is the PROSPER Integration Interface (PII), a language-independent specification of communication for verification. This specification is currently implemented in several languages (C, ML, Java and Python) allowing components written in these languages to be used together.

The PII consists of several parts. The first is a datatype, called *interface data*, for all data transferred between an application and a proof engine and between a proof engine and its plugins. A major part of the datatype is the language of higher order logic used by HOL and so any formula expressible in higher order logic can be passed between components. Many plugins operate with logical data that is either already a subset of higher order logic (e.g. predicate calculus and propositional logic) or embeddable in it (e.g. CTL). The second part consists of a datatype for the results of remote function calls and support for installing and calling procedures in an API. There are also parts for managing low level communication, which are largely invisible to an application developer.

The PII distinguishes between clients and servers. An application is a client of a proof engine which is a client of any plugins it may have. Any server built using the toolkit offers an API to clients. This API describes its functionality in terms of interface data and a result type (which signals whether a function succeeded or failed and returns interface data). As far as an application or verification tool developer is concerned, all components talk the language of these datatypes; The details of translating calls made between components into and out of the raw communication format are entirely invisible.

The PII can be viewed as consisting of the layers in Figure 2. The lower layers deal with communication (handling interrupts and so on). The translation layer takes the raw data passed along the communication channel and translates it into the language's implementation of interface data. The application support layer supplies functions for working with interface data, starting and managing communication between components, and support for working with the API. On top of this sits the target application, proof engine or plugin. The application support layer is the highest specified by the PII.

3.1   Interface Data

Interface data is the high level language passed between components of the system. It can be used to represent a large number of types and expressions.

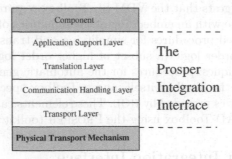

| Component |
| Application Support Layer |
| Translation Layer |
| Communication Handling Layer |
| Transport Layer |
| **Physical Transport Mechanism** |

The
Prosper
Integration
Interface

Fig. 2. The layers of the PII

The PII gives an abstract specification for interface data, but the exact form of the operations and their usage depends on the implementation language.

Each element of interface data has three operations, a constructor, a destructor, and a query (is_a) function which can be used to establish how an expression has been constructed.

Interface data consists of elements based on several standard types (booleans, integers, strings, etc.) and lists (allowing tree structures). It also contains special elements for handling proof concepts (logical terms, the types of logical terms and theorems).

Logical Terms and Types. Logical terms are central to the PROSPER toolkit and are not a standard feature of any programming language. Logical terms are based on the syntax of classical higher order logic [6] and are the basic expressions for communicating logical information (e.g. conjectures that need proving). As usual with Church-style formulation, there are four basic elements for variables, constants, function applications and lambda abstractions (with associated constructor, destructor and query operations). Higher order logic is typed so it is also possible to query a term for its logical type.

These four elements are too low level for everyday use. This is reflected in HOL which supplies *derived syntax* to provide a usable set of constructors for common term structures. This approach is also adopted by the interface data specification. The interface data derived syntax consists of the usual logical connectives and quantifiers plus a few other common constructs.

3.2 API Support

The PII application support layer provides functions to allow client and server components to handle remote procedure calls. It uses a datatype, *interface data result*, with constructors mk_succeeded:interface_data -> interface_data_result and mk_failed:interface_data -> interface_data_result to report back the results of calls.

A client can use the operation, `call_server`, which calls a function in another component's API, referenced by a string, and supplies it with interface data as arguments. It returns an interface data result.

A server has some database manipulation functions for using an *API database* containing functions of type `interface_data` -> `interface_data_result` referenced by strings. These are used to process calls from a client.

3.3 Connection Support and Lower Layers

The PII application support layer includes client side functions for connecting to and disconnecting from servers. At present a server has to be started and stopped manually, externally to the client. In future we intend to allow servers to be started and stopped by the client.

The low level details of communication handling are only relevant to those wishing to implement the PII in various languages. The underlying communication is currently based on Internet sockets.

4 Using the Toolkit

The basic PROSPER toolkit consists of relatively little: a small subset of HOL, called the *Core Proof Engine*. This consists of a theorem type, inference rules for higher order logic and an ML implementation of the PII. The Core Proof Engine forms the core of all proof engines built using the PROSPER Toolkit. A developer can write extensions to the Core Proof Engine and place them in an API to form a custom API.

Many applications will require a version of the PII in an implementation language other than ML. The toolkit currently includes PII implementations in several languages and a couple of pre-made plugins (the SMV model checker [17] and Prover Technology's proof tool [23,22]) which can be added into proof engines. Third party plugins are already also available for ACL2 [4][3] and Gandalf [25,14].

Developing an application using the toolkit is, potentially, a large task involving several languages and programs. We have identified three aspects of working with the toolkit which separate out the tasks involved. These partition the effort into the areas most likely to be undertaken by distinct groups of people. The three aspects also help identify which parts of a final system should be responsible for which tasks.

4.1 The Theorem Prover Aspect

The theorem prover aspect (Figure 3) mainly involves ML programming. This programming effort focuses on developing custom procedures and placing them in an API which extends the Core Proof Engine. A developer will have access to the entire command language of the theorem prover and a set of entrypoints into

---

[3] Currently unpublished, but available at http://www.cl.cam.ac.uk/users/ms204/

as many plugins and theories as they might wish and are available. They will
be able to develop custom verification procedures and theories within a strongly
typed, LCF-style, environment. The outcome will be a custom proof engine with
an API that can be passed on to the developer of an application as a verification
library.

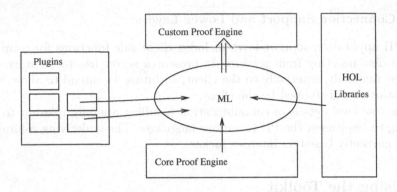

Fig. 3. The Theorem Prover Aspect

On the logical side, a custom proof engine will probably include an embedding
of the formalism used by the application into higher order logic. It will also include automated proof procedures tailored for the application. These procedures
may well use plugin decision procedures (e.g. for predicate or propositional logic)
or even include, as plugins, verification tools previously developed as support for
the application. Construction of such procedures may be a simple process of linking together highly-developed proof libraries and/or plugins or it may require
more complex development.

Although implementations of the PII provide basic functions for calling proof
engine APIs from clients, any serious application will want to wrap up the API
with language-specific bindings (e.g. In an object oriented language it would
be natural to present functions in a proof engine's API as methods in some
verification class, thus hiding all instances of `call_server` from the application
aspect developer). This can only be done if the implementation language of the
target application is known.

Example 2. In hardware verification there exist many decision procedures for
verifying designs. PROSPER sees its main application here as verification tasks
that can be handled automatically through combinations of plugin decision procedures and theorem proving (see §6). These combined procedures will be developed in the theorem prover aspect and presented as the API to a custom proof
engine.

4.2 The Application Aspect

The application aspect (Figure 4) focuses on the incorporation of a custom proof engine into an application so that it appears as a natural extension of the application's functionality. A developer will have access to an API offered by a proof engine already customised to their tool.

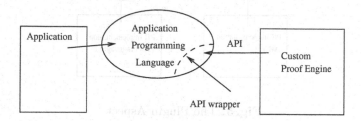

Fig. 4. The Application Aspect

The aim of PROSPER is that verification should fit as seamlessly as possible into the design flow. We envisage that most of the programming at this stage will focus on this task.

Example 3. The project is investigating the use of a natural language interface [13] to the Hardware Verification Workbench that will translate statements about circuits, in the normal technical language of engineers, into CTL propositions that a proof engine can verify. This will allow engineers to be largely unaware of the mathematical verification that is taking place.

4.3 The Plugin Aspect

The PROSPER toolkit supports a third aspect (Figure 5). The developer of a verification tool can adapt it so that it can be used as a PROSPER plugin. A plugin developer programs both in ML and in the plugin's own implementation language. The developer will place chosen entrypoints to the plugin into an API database. In the plugin's implementation language they will translate any arguments needed by these functions into interface data. In the theorem prover's command language they will need to unpackage these entrypoints again so they present themselves as language-specific bindings in that language (ML). In particular any additional theories required (i.e. an embedding of the logic used by the plugin into higher order logic) should be provided by the plugin developer. The plugin aspect is analogous to the theorem prover aspect except that it is assumed that the underlying functionality for the API is already implemented and provision of language-specific bindings is strongly recommended since the target language is known.

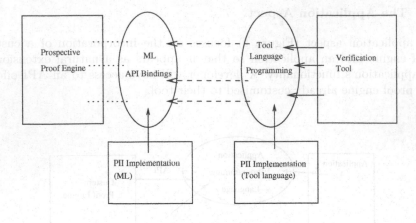

Fig. 5. The Plugin Aspect

It is also possible to run a verification tool in a 'harness' provided by the PROSPER toolkit. This talks to a tool's command line. This allows almost any tool to be used as a plugin, although the tool must be treated as a black box.

4.4   A Complete System

An application developer's view of a complete system should be something like Figure 6. Components are accessible to each other via their APIs. Communication is made possible by low-level functionality irrelevant to the developer. Components can be subdivided into those parts that provide important functionality, databases of functions in the component's API, and modules expressing the functionality of some other component's API.

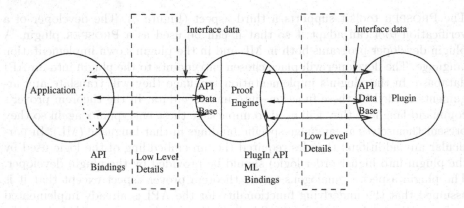

Fig. 6. A complete system

Someone working with such a system can issue an instruction which invokes verification. Such an instruction may arise automatically in response to certain actions they take in the process of design. This instruction states some conjecture which is translated into interface data and passed to a function in the API of the proof engine. This function may, by way of example, break the conjecture down into a number of sub-problems some of which are dealt with by procedures in the proof engine and some of which are passed on as interface data to a function in the API of a plugin. The plugin function executes and returns a result. The proof engine takes the result and may do some more processing on it before passing back its own result to the application. If this is successful and the verification arose automatically the user may not even be aware that anything has taken place. If it is unsuccessful then the user might receive a warning message about the actions they have just performed.

5   Case Study

We present a case study of the use of the PROSPER toolkit to embed some simple verification into a well known, existing application.

Excel is a spreadsheet package marketed by Microsoft [18]. Its basic constituents are rows and columns of cells into which either values or formulae may be entered. Formulae refer to other cells, which may contain either values or further formulae. Users of Excel are likely to have no interest in using or guiding mathematical proof, but they do want to know that they have entered formulae correctly. They therefore have an interest in 'sanity checking functions' that they can use to reassure themselves of correctness.

As a simple case study, the PROSPER toolkit developers undertook to incorporate a sanity checking function into Excel. We chose to implement an equality checking function which would take two cells containing formulae and attempt to determine whether these formulae were equal for all possible values of the cells to which they refer.

Simplifying assumptions were made for the case study. The most important were that cell values were only natural numbers or booleans and that only a small subset of the functions available in Excel (some simple arithmetical and logical functions) appeared in formulae. Given these assumptions, less than 150 lines of code were needed to produce a prototype. This prototype handled only a small range of formulae, but it demonstrated the basic functionality.

While the resulting program is clearly not marketable (requiring two machines using two different operating systems) it was pleasing to find it so easy to embed some verification into an existing program.

5.1   Architecture

The main difficulty in the case study was that Excel is Windows based, whereas the prototype toolkit had been developed for UNIX machines.[4] A subsidiary

---

[4] We intend to port a future version to Windows.

difficulty was that the PII was not implemented in Visual Basic, the macro language of Excel.

These problems were solved by using a Python implementation of the PII. Python has library support for COM (a middleware component standard which is also supported by Visual Basic and is a common way to add functionality to Excel). Python also has a freely available socket library, allowing a Python program on Windows to communicate via sockets with a proof engine on UNIX. The decision was taken not to implement the PII in Visual Basic but to call a Python COM server to handle the tasks in the application aspect and communicate both as a client to the proof engine running under Linux and as a server to an Excel COM client running under Windows. The easiest way to access Excel's formulae is as strings. It would have been necessary, whatever the approach taken, to parse these into interface data logical terms and it was unimportant whether this effort was made in Visual Basic or in Python. We hope that a Python based COM component implementing the PII will be of more general interest and use than a Visual Basic implementation of the PII would have been. A view of the architecture is shown in Figure 7.

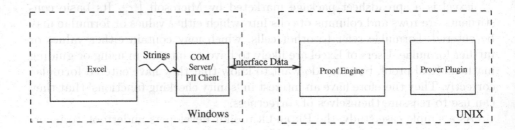

Fig. 7. The architecture of Excel with embedded verification

5.2   The Theorem Prover Aspect

The initial custom procedure is very simple-minded. It uses an arithmetic decision procedure provided by HOL98 and a propositional logic plugin decision procedure (based on Prover Technology's proof tool [23,22]) to decide the truth of formulae. While the approach is not especially robust, it is strong enough to handle many simple formulae.

This proved to be a very small piece of code (approx. 45 lines of ML were needed to write the function and place it in the API database). A more developed version of such a proof engine would require longer, more specialised code.

5.3   The Application Aspect

A function, ISEQUAL, was written using Excel's macro editor. Once written, it automatically appears in Excel's function list as a User Defined Function and can be used in a spreadsheet like any other function. ISEQUAL takes two cell references as arguments. It recursively extracts the formulae contained in the cells as strings (support for this already exists in Excel) and passes them on to the Python object.

The Python component parses the strings to interface data logical terms, which it passes on to the decision procedures in the proof engine. It returns the result of the proof attempt as true, false, or 'unable to decide', which is displayed in the cell containing the ISEQUAL formula.

The application aspect consisted of roughly 30 lines of Visual Basic code and 30 of Python code. We feel that the case study illustrated the relative speed and simplicity with which a prototype of embedded verification can be produced using the PROSPER toolkit.

6 Related Work

Combined Tools. There are many decision procedures available as verification tools, especially for use with hardware verification. They all have practical limits on the size of design with which they can cope. There has also been a great deal of recent work in combining decision procedures (in particular model checkers) with automated theorem proving to increase the size of design that can be dealt with [1,15,20,21]. The Hardware Verification Workbench, that the PROSPER project plans to produce, will hopefully make use of much of the knowledge and techniques developed for integrating model checkers and theorem proving.

In a slightly different vein the HOL/CLAM project [3] linked HOL to CLAM [5], a proof planning system which specialises in automating inductive proof. The HOL/CLAM project is, in some ways, a predecessor to PROSPER and much has been learned from it.

All this work has focused on producing one customised solution whereas PROSPER hopes to provide a framework in which many such interactions can be investigated.

Integration Architectures. There are several projects that provide a generic framework for the integration of tools.

ΩMEGA [2] is a system developed to act as a mathematical assistant. Like PROSPER, ΩMEGA makes use of other reasoning systems (e.g. resolution theorem provers and computer algebra systems). These are all incorporated into a distributed MathWeb [9] and there is work in progress to produce a standard interface for integrating components.

ETI [24], the Electronic Tool Integration platform, is an ambitious project aimed at allowing both the easy and rapid comparison of tools purporting to do similar jobs, and also the rapid prototyping of combinations of such tools (any software tool, not just verification tools). ETI has its own language, HLL, which acts much like PROSPER's combination of ML and interface data to provide a scripting language for tool integration. It is also possible to automatically generate glue code from easily written specifications. The ETI's implementation is based on C++, which allows all tools written in C++ to be treated in a glass box fashion, just as PROSPER allows all tools written in the languages which implement the PII to be treated as glass boxes.

The OMRS project aims to develop an *open* architecture for reasoning systems to be integrated together relatively easily. This architecture consists of three components: the logic of the system [12], the control strategies used by the system [7], and the interaction mechanisms supported by the system. Its framework forces systems to identify clearly what are the sequents, inference rules, control information, etc. and so makes them more open and extensible. The intention is that future reasoning systems will be developed using the OMRS architecture. At the same time work is underway to re-engineer popular existing tools, most notably ACL2 [4], so that they conform to the OMRS specifications.

These systems all allow the integration and combination of verification components ranging from an entirely black box treatment to an entirely glass box treatment in the case of OMRS. We prefer an easier and more flexible approach than OMRS allowing off-the-shelf integration rather than re-engineering. This means it is easier to build an unsound tool with our toolkit. We are not ignoring the logical issues but intend to solve them on an ad hoc basis. ETI is wider in scope but less specific than PROSPER. It is forced to treat some components as black boxes, which is inappropriate for many of the interactions PROSPER wishes to study. On the other hand, in many cases it is simple to experiment with coordination of several tools using ETI because of its automatic synthesis features.

Design Tools with Embedded Verification. The UniForM project aims to encourage the development of reliable software for industrially relevant tasks by enabling suitable tool-supported combinations of formal methods. The UniForM Workbench [16] is intended to be a generic framework, instantiated with specific tools. The project has produced a workbench for software design that gives access to the Isabelle theorem prover plus other verification tools through their command lines. The various components are held together by Concurrent Haskell, which is used as a sophisticated encapsulation and glue language.

The UniForM project is similar to PROSPER, with its focus on the integration of component based verification into design tools, its use of a functional language to manage the various components, and the provision of a theorem prover to perform logical tasks. But, the Workbench is a design tool in its own right rather than a toolkit for embedding verification into a design tool. The Workbench also treats plugin decision procedures as black boxes.

We are not aware of any project, other than PROSPER, which easily allows the integration of existing components with the view to producing an embeddable customised proof engine.

7   Conclusions

For embedded (possibly invisible) verification engines to gain widespread acceptance and use, verification tools must be customisable and combinable. We believe the way forward draws on many of the standard aspects of component technology but also requires dedicated support for building custom proof engines, such as language-independent datatypes for communicating logical concepts.

We hope that the work on PROSPER has been a significant step forward in establishing the nature of the support needed to encourage embedded verification. The focus of future work centres around three areas: basic improvements of the underlying implementation; case studies of the effectiveness of the toolkit (we are interested not only in the ease with which theorem proving can be embedded in an application but also in the benefits gained from the combination of theorem proving and decision procedures) and the development of generic proof support for integrated verification (procedures for handling certain classes of plugin effectively, methodologies for ensuring soundness, etc.).

Most importantly, we believe the way to encourage the incorporation of formal verification within design flows is not through the provision of some large *tool* that can perform a wide range of verification tasks but through the provision of a *toolkit* that allows the development of specialised proof engines.

References

1. M. D. Aagaard, R. B. Jones, and C.-J. H. Seger, Lifted-FL: A Pragmatic Implementation of Combined Model Checking and Theorem Proving. Y. Bertot, G. Dowek, A. Hirshowitz, C. Paulin and L. Théry (eds), *Theorem Proving in Higher Order Logics*, Lecture Notes in Computer Science 1690, Springer-Verlag, pp. 323–340, 1999. 89
2. C. Benzmüller, L. Cheikhrouhou, D. Fehrer, A. Fiedler, X. Huang, M. Kerber, M. Kohlhase, E. Meirer, E. Melis, W. Schaarschmidt, J. Siekmann, and V. Sorge, ΩMEGA, Towards a mathematical assistant. *14th Conference on Automated Deduction*, W. McCune (ed), Lecture Notes in Artificial Intelligence 1249, Springer-Verlag, pp. 252–255, 1997. 89
3. R. Boulton, K. Slind, A. Bundy, and M. Gordon, An interface between CLAM and HOL. J. Grundy and M. Newey (eds), *Proceedings of the 11th International Conference on Theorem Proving in Higher Order Logics*, Lecture Notes in Computer Science 1479, Springer-Verlag, pp. 87–104, 1998. 89
4. B. Brock, M. Kaufmann, and J Moore, ACL2 Theorems about Commercial Microprocessors. M. Srivas and A. Camilleri (eds), *Proceedings of Formal Methods in Computer-Aided Design (FMCAD'96)*, Springer-Verlag, pp. 275–293, 1996. 83, 90
5. A. Bundy, F. van Harmelen, C. Horn, and A. Smaill, The Oyster-Clam system. *10th International Conference on Automated Deduction*, M. E. Stickel (ed), Lecture Notes in Artificial Intelligence 449, Springer-Verlag, pp. 647–648, 1990. 89
6. A. Church, A Formulation of the Simple Theory of Types. *The Journal of Symbolic Logic*, vol. 5, pp. 56–68, 1940. 80, 82
7. A. Coglio, The Control Component of OMRS: NQTHM as a Case Study. Extended abstract in *Proceedings of the First Workshop on Abstraction, Analogy and Metareasoning*, IRST, Trento, Italy, pp. 65–71, 1996. 90
8. J. Fitzgerald and P. G. Larsen, *Modelling Systems: Practical Tools and Techniques in Software Development*, Cambridge University Press, 1998. 80
9. A. Franke, S. M. Hess, C. G. Jung, M. Kohlhase, and V. Sorge, Agent-Oriented Integration of Distributed Mathematical Services. *Journal of Universal Computer Science*, 5(3), pp. 156–187, 1999. 89

10. J. A. Goguen and Luqi, Formal methods and social context in software development. *Proceedings TAPSOFT'95*, Lecture Notes in Computer Science 915. Springer-Verlag, pp. 62–81, 1995. 78

11. M. J. C. Gordon and T. F. Melham (eds), *Introduction to HOL: A theorem proving environment for higher order logic*, Cambridge University Press, 1993. 79

12. F. Giunchiglia, P. Pecchiari, and C. Talcott, Reasoning Theories: Towards an Architecture for Open Mechanized Reasoning Systems. F. Baader and K. U. Schulz (eds), *Frontiers of Combining Systems—First International Workshop (FroCoS'96)*, Kluwer's Applied Logic Series (APLS), pp. 157–174, 1996. 90

13. A. Holt and E. Klein, A semantically-derived subset of English for hardware verification. *37th Annual Meeting of the Association for Computational Linguistics: Proceedings of the Conference*, Association for Computational Linguistics, pp. 451–456, 1999. 85

14. J. Hurd, Integrating Gandalf and HOL. Y. Bertot, G. Dowek, A. Hirshowitz, C. Paulin and L. Théry (eds). *Theorem Proving in Higher Order Logics*, Lecture Notes in Computer Science 1690, Springer-Verlag, pp. 311–321, 1999. 83

15. J. Joyce and C.-J. Seger, Linking BDD based symbolic evaluation to interactive theorem proving. *ACM/IEEE Design Automation Conference*, June 1993. 89

16. B. Kreig-Brükner, J. Peleska, E.-R. Olderog, and A. Baer, The UniForM WorkBench, a Universal Development Environment for Formal Methods. J. M. Wing, J. Woodcock and J. Davies (eds), *FM'99—Formal Methods*, vol. 2, Lecture Notes in Computer Science 1709, pp. 1186–1205, 1999. 90

17. K. L. McMillan, *Symbolic Model Checking*, Kluwer Academic Publishers. 1993. 83

18. Microsoft Corporation, *Microsoft Excel*, http://www.microsoft.com/excel. 87

19. R. Milner, M. Tofte, R. Harper and D. MacQueen, *The Definition of Standard ML (Revised)*, MIT Press, 1997. 80

20. J. O'Leary, X. Zhao, R. Gerth, and C.-J. H. Seger, Formally verifying IEEE compliance of floating-point hardware. *Intel Technology Journal*, First Quarter, 1999. Online at http://developer.intel.com/technology/itj/. 89

21. S. Rajan, N. Shankar, and M. Srivas, An integration of model checking and automated proof checking. *International Conference on Computer-Aided Verification*, Lecture Notes in Computer Science 939, Springer-Verlag, pp. 84–97, 1995. 89

22. M. Sheeran and G. Stålmarck, A tutorial on Stålmarck's proof procedure for propositional logic. *The Second International Conference on Formal Methods in Computer-Aided Design*, Lecture Notes in Computer Science 1522, Springer-Verlag, pp. 82–99, 1998. 83, 88

23. G. Stålmarck and M. Säflund, Modelling and Verifying Systems and Software in Propositional Logic. *Proceedings of SAFECOMP '90*, Pergamon Press, pp. 31–36, 1990. 83, 88

24. B. Steffen, T. Margaria, and V. Braun, The Electronic Tool Integration Platform: concepts and design. *International Journal on Software Tools for Technology Transfer*, $1(1 + 2)$, pp. 9–30, 1997. 89

25. T. Tammet, A resolution theorem prover for intuitionistic logic. *13th International Conference on Automated Deduction*, Lecture Notes in Computer Science 1104, Springer-Verlag, pp. 2–16, 1996. 83

CASL: From Semantics to Tools

Till Mossakowski

Department of Computer Science and Bremen Institute for Safe Systems,
Universität Bremen, P.O. Box 330440, D-28334 Bremen
till@informatik.uni-bremen.de

Abstract. CASL, the common algebraic specification language, has been developed as a language that subsumes many previous algebraic specification frameworks and also provides tool interoperability. CASL is a complex language with a complete formal semantics. It is therefore a challenge to build good tools for CASL. In this work, we present and discuss the Bremen HOL-CASL system, which provides parsing, static checking, conversion to LaTeX and theorem proving for CASL specifications. To make tool construction manageable, we have followed some guidelines: re-use of existing tools, interoperability of tools developed at different sites, and construction of generic tools that can be used for several languages. We describe the structure of and the experiences with our tool and discuss how the guidelines work in practice.

1 Introduction

During the past decades a large number of algebraic specification languages have been developed. Unfortunately, these languages are based on a diversity of basic algebraic specification concepts. The presence of so many similar specification languages with no common framework had hindered the dissemination and application of research results in algebraic specification. In particular, it had made it difficult to produce educational material, to re-use tools and to get algebraic methods adopted in industry. Therefore, in 1995, an initiative, CoFI[1], to design *a Common Framework for Algebraic Specification and Development* was started [18]. The goal of CoFI is to get a common agreement in the algebraic specification community about basic concepts, and to provide a family of specification languages at different levels, a development methodology and tool support. The family of specification languages comprises of a central, common language, called CASL[2], various restrictions of CASL, and various extensions of CASL (e.g. with facilities for particular programming paradigms).

The definition of CASL and some of its sublanguages has been finished [8]. Moreover, a complete formal semantics of CASL [9] has been developed in parallel with design of the language and indeed, the development of the semantics has given important feedback to the language design.

---

[1] CoFI is pronounced like 'coffee'.
[2] CASL is an acronym for *CoFI Algebraic (or* Axiomatic*) Specification Language* and is pronounced like 'castle'.

S. Graf and M. Schwartzbach (Eds.): TACAS/ETAPS 2000, LNCS 1785, pp. 93–108, 2000.

Now that design and semantics of CASL have been finished, it is essential to have a good tool support. Tools will be essential for the goal of CoFI to get CASL accepted in academic communities (in the short run), and, in the long run, in industry. This holds even stronger since CASL is a language with a formal semantics: many people believe that such a language cannot or will not be used in practice: "The best semantics will not win." [13]

Since CASL was designed with the goal to subsume many previous frameworks, it has become a powerful and quite complex language. This complexity makes it harder to build tools covering the whole language.

In this work, we will show that it is possible to build tools for a complex language with strong semantics in a reasonable time. In order to achieve this, we have followed several guidelines:

- As much as possible, re-use existing tools, instead of building new ones.
- Build tools in such a way that tools developed at different sites can be integrated; thus, not every site has to develop all the tools.
- Make tools as generic as possible. After all, CASL only is the central language in a whole family of languages, and it would be tedious to have to re-implement the same things for each language separately.

All these guidelines are even more important in a non-commercial environment as the CoFI initiative is, where only very limited (wo)man-power is available, and therefore collaborative effort is essential. Moreover, an explicit goal within the design of CASL was to provide a common language in order to achieve a better interoperability of (already existing) tools.

We will discuss these guidelines, reporting how well they work in practice and which difficulties arise with them.

The paper is organized as follows:

Section 2 gives a brief overview over CASL and its semantics. Section 3 explains the general architecture of the Bremen HOL-CASL tool. In section 4, tool interoperability using a common interchange format is discussed. Section 5 describes the problems with parsing CASL's mixfix syntax. Section 6 recalls the encoding of CASL in higher-order logic from [17], while section 7 reports our practical experiences when using this encoding to create an interface from CASL to Isabelle/HOL. In section 8, some difficulties of encoding CASL structured specifications into Isabelle are discussed. Section 9 describes several user interfaces for HOL-CASL. Finally, section 10 contains the discussion how the guidelines work in practice, and directions for future work.

This work is based on [17], but considerably extends the work begun there.

2   CASL

CASL is a specification language that can be used for formal development and verification of software. It covers both the level of requirement specifications, which are close to informal requirements, and of design specifications, which are close to implemented programs. CASL provides constructs for writing

- basic specifications (declarations, definitions, axioms),
- structured specifications (which are built from smaller specifications in a modular way),
- architectural specifications (prescribing the architecture of an implementation), and
- specification libraries, distributed over the Internet.

Basic CASL specifications consist of declarations and axioms representing theories of a first-order logic in which predicates, total as well as partial functions, and subsorts are allowed. Predicate and function symbols may be overloaded [4]. Datatype declarations allow to shortly describe the usual datatypes occurring in programming languages.

Structured specifications allow to rename or hide parts of specifications, unite, extend and name specifications. Moreover, generic specifications and views allow to abstract from particular parts of a specification, which makes the specification reusable in different context.

Architectural specifications allow to talk about implementation units and their composition to an implementation of a larger specification (or, vice versa, the decomposition of an implementation task into smaller sub-tasks).

Structured and architectural specifications together with libraries will be also referred to as CASL-in-the-large, while basic specifications will be referred to as CASL-in-the-small.

The semantics of CASL follows a natural semantics style and has both rules for static semantics (which are implemented by a static semantic checker) and model semantics (which are implemented by theorem-proving tools).

```
spec LIST [sort  Elem;] =
    free type  List[Elem]  ::=  nil  |  _ :: _(head :? Elem; tail :? List[Elem]);
    %list  [_], nil, _ :: _
    op  _++_  :  List[Elem] × List[Elem] → List[Elem];
    %prec  _ :: _ < _++_
    vars  e    :  Elem;
          K, L  :  List[Elem]
    •  %[concat_nil]  nil ++L  =  L
    •  %[concat_cons]  (e :: K) ++L  =  e :: K ++L
end
```

Fig. 1. Specification of lists over an arbitrary element sort in CASL

Consider the specification of lists over an arbitrary element sort in Fig. 1. The **free type** construct is a concise way to describe inductive datatypes. The semantic effect is the introduction of the corresponding constructor (here *nil* and _ :: _) and (partial) selector (here *head* and *tail*) functions, and of a number of axioms: a so-called sort generation constraint stating that the datatypes are inductively generated by the constructors and possibly by parameter sorts (here: the sort `Elem`), and first-order axioms expressing that the constructors are injective and have disjoint images and that the partial selectors are one-sided inverses of the corresponding constructors.

The annotation **%list** $[\_\_], nil, \_\_ :: \_\_$ allows to write lists in the form $[t_1, \ldots, t_n]$. This notation is not restricted to lists: with **%list**, one also can introduce abbreviating notations for sets, bags, etc.

3   Tool Architecture

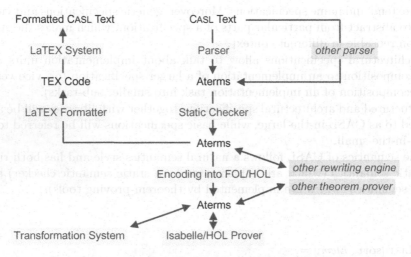

Fig. 2. Architecture of the HOL-CASL system

The Bremen HOL-CASL system consists of several parts, which are shown in Fig. 2. The *parser* checks the syntactic correctness of a specification (CASL Text) according to the CASL grammar and produces an abstract syntax tree (coded as ATerms). The *static checker* checks the static semantic correctness (according to the static semantics) and produces a global environment (also coded as ATerms) that associates specification names with specification-specific information such as the signature. The *LATEX formatter* allows to pretty print CASL specifications (which are input in ASCII format), using the CASL LATEX package from Peter Mosses [19]. For example, the specification in Fig. 1 has been generated from the ASCII input shown in Fig. 4.

Finally, the *encoding* is a bridge from CASL to first- or higher-order logic (FOL/HOL). It throws out subsorting and partiality by encoding it [17], and thus allows to re-use existing theorem proving tools and term rewriting engines for CASL. Typical applications of a *theorem prover* in the context of CASL are

- checking the model-semantic correctness of a specification (according to the model semantics) by discharging the proof obligations that have been generated during static semantic analysis,
- validate intended consequences, which can be added to a specification using an annotation. This allows a check for consistency with informal requirements,
- prove correctness of a development step (in a refinement).

4 Tool Interoperability

The are quite a number of existing specifications languages and tools for them. CASL was designed with the goal of providing a common language for better tool interoperability. This is reflected by having a common interchange format for CASL tools, the ATerm format [3]. ATerms are an easy-to-handle format with libraries in several languages (C, Java) available. The main reason for chosing ATerms was that the untyped term structures are very flexible, and their easy syntax makes it very easy to write parsers and printers for them (we needed to implement these in our implementation language, ML, which has been done very quickly).

Thus, ATerms are used as (untyped) low level tool format for data exchange between CASL tools. Based on this format, several (strongly typed) formats have been designed: the CasFix format [26] for abstract syntax trees, and a format for the global environment, containing the static semantic information.

A problem with ATerms is that the textual representation gets very large (the ATerm representation of the global environment for the CASL basic data types is about 10 MB). [3] have solved this problem by providing a compact binary format with full sharing of subterms. This format can deal efficiently even with Gigabyte-sized structures. However, parsers and printers for this format are more complex. Thus, we are using converters between the textual and the binary ATerm format written in C as a workaround, until an ML-based ATerm library dealing also with the binary format becomes available.

By providing conversions from and to ATerms at all intermediate points in the tool architecture, the Bremen HOL-CASL system can be used as a front-end or back-end in combination with other tools. Actually, it has been combined as a back-end with the Amsterdam CASL parser [27], and as a front-end with several theorem proving tools: ELAN [21], PVS [2] and Isabelle (see section 7). See also the CoFI Tools Group home page [10].

5 Parsing and Static Semantic Analysis

Apart from having a relatively complex grammar, CASL has several features that cause some difficulties for parsing and static analysis:

1. CASL's syntax allows user-defined mixfix syntax,
2. CASL allows mutually recursive subsort definitions, causing loops within a naive subsorting analysis, and
3. CASL allows overloading, and formulas which have a unique overload resolution up to semantical equivalence.

Concerning mixfix syntax, we separate parsing into two steps: The first pass of parsing produces an abstract syntax tree where formulas and terms (i.e. those parts of the specifications that may contain mixfix symbols) remain in their unparsed textual form.

Mixfix grouping analysis can be done only after a first phase of static semantic analysis has collected the operation and predicate symbols (among them the mixfix symbols). The CASL grammar is then extended dynamically according to the mixfix declarations, and formulas and terms are parsed with the generic Isabelle parser, which uses the well-known Cocke-Younger-Kasami algorithm for context-free recognition [11]. This grammar-parameterised algorithm has a complexity of $O(n^3)$, which is quite acceptable, since formulas and terms in CASL specifications are not that long. However, it turned out to be too slow to do the first pass of parsing with this approach. Therefore, we moved to ML-yacc for the first pass.

After having done the parsing of terms and formulas, those resulting parse trees are selected that are precedence correct with respect to the user-specified precedence relations. If more than one parse tree remains, the corresponding term or formula is ambiguous, and the possible disambiguations are output to the user. To obtain a concise output, not all pretty-printed forms of the parse trees are shown, but only the local places at which they actually differ.

The definition of precedence correctness follows the one of [1], generalized to CASL's pre-order based precedences ([1] uses number based precedences).

Concerning static semantic analysis, the treatment of subsorts and overload resolution needs a careful algorithmic design in order not to run into an exponential time trap. The details of this have already been worked out in [17].

6   Encoding CASL into HOL

In this section, we briefly recall the encoding from CASL into HOL from [17]:

At the level of CASL basic specifications, the encoding into higher-order logic proceeds in three steps:

1. The CASL logic, subsorted partial first-order logic with sort generation constraints (SubPCFOL), is translated to subsorted first-order logic with sort generation constraints (SubCFOL) by encoding partiality via error elements living in a supersort.
2. Subsorted first-order logic with sort generation constraints (SubCFOL) is translated to first-order logic with sort generation constraints (CFOL) by encoding subsorting via injections (actually, this is built-in into the CASL semantics [4]).

3. First-order logic with sort generation constraints (CFOL) is translated to higher-order logic (HOL) by expressing sort generation constraints via induction axioms.

These encodings are not only translations of syntax, but also have a model-theoretic counterpart[3], which provides an implicit soundness and completeness proof for the re-use of HOL-theorem provers for theorem proving in the CASL logic SubPCFOL. This is also known as the "borrowing" technique of Cerioli and Meseguer [5], which allows to borrow theorem provers across different logics.

7   The Interface to Isabelle/HOL

Using the encoding described in the previous section, we have built an interface from CASL to Isabelle/HOL. We have chosen Isabelle [20] because it has a very small core guaranteeing correctness. Furthermore, there is over ten years of experience with it (several mathematical textbooks have partially been verified with Isabelle). Last but not least, Isabelle is generic, i.e. it supports quite a number of logics, and it is possible to define your own logic within Isabelle. Despite the genericity of Isabelle, we have refrained from building the CASL logic directly into Isabelle – this would violate our guideline to re-use existing tools as much as possible: we would have to set up new proof rules, and instantiate the Isabelle simplifier (a rewriting engine) and tableau prover from scratch. Instead, we re-use the Isabelle logic HOL, for which already sophisticated support is available, with the help of the encoding described in section 6.

This encoding has a clear semantical basis due to the borrowing (most other encodings into Isabelle/HOL do not have an explicit model-theoretic counterpart). However, a good semantic basis does not imply that there are no practical problems:

First, the encoding of CASL in Isabelle/HOL as described in [17] produces too complex output. We had to fine-tune the output by suppressing superfluous parts (for example, trivial subsort injections), while retaining its mathematical correctness.

Another problem with borrowing is that the HOL-CASL user really works with the encoding of a CASL specification, and not with the CASL specification itself. In particular, goals and subgoals are displayed as HOL formulas, and the proof rules are of course the Isabelle/HOL proof rules. However, a typical user of the tool will probably be more familiar with CASL than with Isabelle/HOL. Therefore, we have decided to display goals and subgoals in a CASL-like syntax as much as possible. For example, an injection of a term t from a subsort $s1$ to a supersort $s2$ is displayed as $t : s2$, as in CASL, and not as $inj_{s1,s2}(t)$, as the encoding would yield. In this way, we get a CASL-like display syntax of Isabelle/HOL. Let us call this display syntax "CASLish Isabelle/HOL".

However, note that the CASLish Isabelle/HOL omits some information, e.g. the information that an injection $inj_{s1,s2}(t)$ starts from $s1$. In some practical example proofs, this turned out to be rather confusing (while in others, the longer

---

[3] Formally, they are institution representations in the sense of [16,24]

form $inj_{s1,s2}(t)$ is just tedious), and one would like to go back to the "pure Is-
abelle/HOL" view of the subgoals instead of using the "CASLish Isabelle/HOL".
Therefore, we plan to let the user choose among several pretty printing "views"
on his or her encoded CASL specification.

Another example for the mixture of CASL and Isabelle/HOL are Isabelle's
two different kinds of free variables, which may occur in CASL formulas during
a proof. Isabelle one one hand has object variables, which cannot be instantiated
during a proof. They are used for proofs of universally quantified sentences. The
other kind of variables are meta variables, which can be instantiated during a
proof. They are used for proofs of existentially quantified sentences (cf. Prolog,
narrowing). For example, when trying to prove

$$\exists\, x : Nat \;\bullet\; x + 9 = 12$$

by elimination of the existential quantifier, one gets

$$?x + 9 = 12$$

and then $?x$ is instantiated with 3 during the proof (while the goal $x + 9 = 12$
would not be provable, since $\forall\, x : Nat \;\bullet\; x + 9 = 12$ is false).

```
Level 0
((K ++ L) ++ M) = (K ++ (L ++ M))
 1. ((K ++ L) ++ M) = (K ++ (L ++ M))

Level 1
((K ++ L) ++ M) = (K ++ (L ++ M))
 1. !!x1 x2.
      ((x2 ++ L) ++ M) =
      (x2 ++ (L ++ M)) =>(((x1 :: x2) ++ L) ++ M) =
                            ((x1 :: x2) ++ (L ++ M))
 2. ((nil ++ L) ++ M) = (nil ++ (L ++ M))

Level 2
((K ++ L) ++ M) = (K ++ (L ++ M))
No subgoals!
```

Fig. 3. Proof of `forall K,L,M:List[Elem]` . `(K++L)++M=K++(L++M)`

Fig. 3 shows a proof of the associativity of the concatenation of lists, using
the specification from Fig. 1. Level 0 shows the original goal. In the first proof
step (level 1), the goal was resolved with the sort generation constraint for lists.
The two subgoals are the inductive arguments for `_::_` and `nil`, respectively.
In the second step, both subgoals can be proved feeding the axioms `concat_nil`
and `concat_cons` into Isabelle's simplifier (a rewriting engine).

Another problem is that of input of goals. Goals are of course *input* in the CASL syntax (only during a proof, they get redisplayed in CASLish Isabelle/HOL syntax). One would like also to be able to input goals in Isabelle/HOL, for example when one needs to prove a lemma that is formulated in Isabelle/HOL. We solve this by providing Isabelle/HOL as a theory within our interface, and we parse goals that are input for this theory always with the Isabelle/HOL parser, and not with the CASL parser.

8   Encoding of CASL Structured Specifications

The encoding of structured specifications is almost orthogonal to that of basic specifications and therefore can be done in a generic, logic-independent way.

When encoding CASL structured specification into Isabelle, the problem arises that the structuring mechanism of CASL and Isabelle are rather different. In particular, Isabelle's mechanisms are considerably weaker: Extensions and unions of specifications are available in Isabelle (though the union is defined is a slightly different way), while for CASL's renamings, hidings, and generic specifications, nothing similar is available in Isabelle.

Currently, we solve this problem by just flattening structured specifications to basic specifications, that is, we literally carry out all the renamings, unions etc. Hidings can be treated by renaming the symbol which shall be hidden with a unique name that cannot be input by the user.

However, this is not very satisfactory, since flattening destroys the structural information of a specification and thus makes theorem proving in the specification harder. In some cases, the loss of structural information makes it practically infeasible to do proofs which are doable when the structuring is kept. Therefore, we have asked the Isabelle implementors to improve Isabelle's structuring mechanisms, and they have promised to do something in this direction.

In principle, an alternative way would be to use a deep encoding of CASL, which means to directly describe the semantics of CASL within higher-order logic. However, this would not be very nice, since theorem proving in a deep encoding is relatively far away from proving in the encoded logic. In contrast, we use a shallow encoding, where proving in the encoding comes close to proving in the encoded logic. The advantage of a deep encoding would be that one can prove meta-properties about the semantics of CASL, but in our view, this does not outweigh the disadvantages.

An exceptional case are CASL's free specifications. One can hardly expect to implement them in a logic-independent way, since they depend on an involved construction in the model categories of the logic. All that one can expect here is to simulate the semantics of free specifications in a particular logic within higher-order logic, along the lines of [23].

Encoding of architectural specifications is beyond the scope of this paper – it will be dealt with elsewhere.

As described in the previous section, libraries are an orthogonal matter. However, there is one important incompatibility between CASL and Isabelle at this

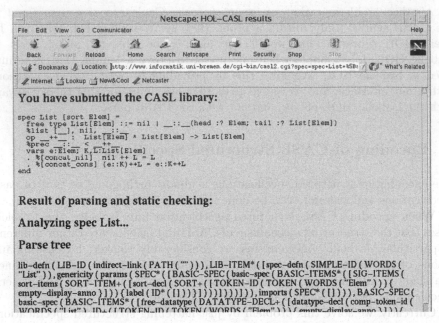

Fig. 4. The web interface of the HOL-CASL system

point: CASL text files may contain libraries consisting of several specifications, while Isabelle text files always consist of exactly one Isabelle theory. We solve this problem by just splitting a CASL library into small files containing one specification each, and feeding these files into Isabelle. Or course, we also have to maintain the information associating a CASL library with the split files.

9   User Interface

We provide several user interfaces to the Bremen HOL-CASL system. Actually, it has turned out that for the first contact with our tool, the most important user interface is the web-based interface[4], where the user can just type in a specification, and parse it, perform the static analysis and/or conversion to LaTeX. Most users want to try out this easy-to-use interface before taking the effort to download the stand-alone version (even if the latter effort is very small). The web-interface has even been used as a front-end in a prototype translation to PVS [2] (although it is much more convenient to use the stand-alone version in this case).

---

[4] You can play around with it: http://www.informatik.uni-bremen.de/cgi-bin/casl2.cgi.

The small stand-alone version of our tool[5] provides the full functionality shown in Fig. 2, except the Isabelle theorem proving environment. It has been quite crucial to exclude Isabelle here, since Isabelle is quite large, and users who want to use the tool as a front-end or back-end do not want to download the whole Isabelle system. The stand-alone tool can be called as a Unix command, and the different entry points and phases of analysis and encodings of the tool (cf. Fig. 2) can be selected with optional flags. In particular, it is also possible to select the encoding into FOL/HOL without having to use Isabelle (this is useful when combining our tool with theorem provers for first- or higher-order logic). We also plan to make the different steps of the encoding (see section 6) separately available, so that one can choose to "encode out" just partiality and keep the subsorting (this will be useful, for example, in connection with Maude [6] which supports subsorting). The Unix interface works quite well when using the tool in combination with other tools, although we plan to provide a fully-fledged applications programmer interface (API) in the future.

The full stand-alone version of the tool[6] also provides the Isabelle theorem prover, and the generic graphical user interface IsaWin [15,14], which has been built on top of Isabelle. We have instantiated IsaWin with our HOL-CASL encoding of CASL into Isabelle/HOL. In Fig. 5, you can see a typical IsaWin window. The icons labelled with (Σ, E) are CASL specifications (more precisely, their encodings in HOL). Note that the theory HOL itself also is available at this level. The icon labelled with a tree is an open proof goal. By double-clicking on it, you can perform proof steps with this goal. This is done by dragging either already proven theorems (those icons marked with $\vdash A$) or simplifier sets (icons marked with $\{l \rightarrow r\}$) onto the goal. The effect is the resolution of the goal with the theorem thrown onto it, or the rewriting of the goal with the chosen simplifier set. After the proof of a goal is finished, it turns into a theorem. You can then use it in the proof of other theorems, or, if it has the form of a rewrite rule, add it to a simplifier set.

Actually, some users explicitly told us that they feared to have to install Isabelle to run our tool. However, even the full version including Isabelle and IsaWin is completely stand-alone (apart from the need to install Tcl/Tk, which has already been installed on many sites).

10   Conclusion and Future Work

We have shown that it is possible to write tools for a complex language with strong semantical bias (though it turns out to be a complex task). We could reduce the amount of work by re-using existing tools as much as possible. Moreover, by using a common tool interchange format, we have created a tool which can be used in connection with other tools as a front end or back end. Cur-

---

[5] Available at http://www.informatik.uni-bremen.de/~cofi/CASL/parser/parser.html.

[6] Available at http://www.informatik.uni-bremen.de/~cofi/CASL/.

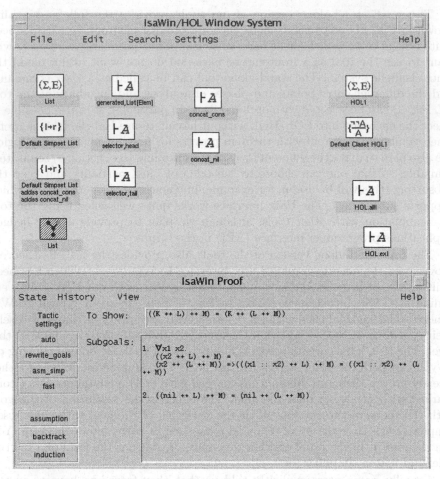

Fig. 5. The HOL-CASL instantiation of the IsaWin system

rently, our tool has been used in connection with two theorem provers (PVS and Isabelle) and one rewriting engine (ELAN).

We have followed three guidelines when implementing the HOL-CASL system. The first guideline was to re-use existing tools, rather than create a new tools. In practice, this has turned out to be very hard: Building an interface from CASL to an existing tool is quite a complex task, which not only deals with an input-output-transformation, but also has to take the interactive behaviour and the display of intermediate results into account.

Nevertheless, we think that it is worth the effort to re-use existing tools, since these tools have evolved and improved over time, and in a sense we borrow this maturity from other tools, which otherwise would only have been achieved through a long process of testing, use and maintenance. Of course, our bridges to other tools also have to become mature, but since the target of the bridging tools are already mature, the whole effort can start from a higher level.

Currently, we have re-used Isabelle/HOL for having a quick prototype of theorem proving environment for CASL, at the price to get a very HOLish CASL. In future work, we will develop derived rules and tactics for CASL (especially for the computation of normal forms w.r.t. the overloading axioms that state coincidence of overloaded functions on sub- and supersorts). With this, we will try to make the encoding to look more CASL-like by eliminating the need to work with HOL rules and instead provide a complete set of rules for CASL. Perhaps in a further step, we will even encode CASL directly in the generic Isabelle meta logic. Anyway, this step would probably have been too complicated in the first place, and working with Isabelle/HOL has the advantage of faster having a prototype.

Concerning the guideline of genericity, we have made the experience that the *use* of generic tools at some points can lead to inefficiencies: we had to replace the generic Isabelle parser by ML-yacc to obtain an efficient parsing. Yet, we have to use the generic parser for parsing user-defined mixfix syntax. Another experience was with the IsaWin system: it has been designed as a generic window-based interface to Isabelle, but when instantiating it to HOL-CASL, several changes to IsaWin were needed to make it actually useful. Nevertheless, the genericity was a great help in comparison to implementation from scratch.

Regarding genericity of our own tool, we have made the encoding of structured specifications independent of the underlying logic. One important future point will be to make also the static analysis of CASL structured and architectural specifications truly generic, i.e. also parameterized over a logic (this is possible because the semantics is already parameterized over a logic). This would allow to re-use the tool also for other logics than the logic underlying CASL (for example, higher-order CASL, reactive CASL, temporal logic, or just your own favourite logic).

Concerning interoperability, the use of ATerms helped a lot to interconnect our parser and static analysis with several theorem proving and rewriting tools at different other sites. Here, it was essential to use the very easy-to-handle textual ATerm representation to get quick prototypes of such interconnections, although for larger applications, the more complex binary format is needed.

Another use of the ATerm format will be the comparison of outputs of different tools for the same purposes that have been developed at different sites.

We hope that also tools developed by others will be integrated to work with our tools in the future. Currently, we have ATerm-based formats for parse trees and global static environments. For the integration of different theorem proving and rewriting tools, on would also need ATerm-based formats for proofs, proof states and possibly also transformations.

An even better integration can be achieved with the UniForM workbench [12], which also provides library management and access to a generic transformation application system [15,14] that will be instantiated to CASL.

Future work will turn our tool into a theorem proving environment that can be used for practical problems. On the way to this goal, we have to implement proof management, dealing with proof obligations, intended consequences and refinement. Moreover, special simplifiers and proof tactics for CASL will have to be developed an tested. A first case study will be the verification of proof obligations and intended consequences for the libraries of CASL basic datatypes [22].

Another direction of research will further exploit the possibility of the generic analysis of CASL-in-the-large. It is possible to extend CASL to a heterogeneous specification language, where one can combine specifications written in several different logics, see [25] for some first ideas. Tool support for such a language would extend the generic analysis of CASL-in-the-large with an analysis of structuring mechanisms for moving specifications between different logics.

Acknowledgements

I would like to thank Kolyang for an intensive cooperation lasting for several years. Christoph Lüth and Burkhart Wolff patiently helped with all kinds of questions about Isabelle and IsaWin. Pascal Schmidt did the implementation of the conversion from and to ATerms and of the LaTeX pretty printer. Markus Roggenbach wrote the first larger specifications in CASL, which were extensively used and tested with the tools. Bernd Krieg-Brückner provided a good working environment and discussions about the general directions of this work.

References

1. A. Aasa. Precedences in specifications and implementations of programming languages. *Theoretical Computer Science*, 142(1):3–26, May 1995. 98

2. D. Baillie. Proving theorems about CASL specifications. Talk at the 14th Workshop on Algebraic Development Techniques, Bonas, France, September 1999. 97, 102

3. M. Brand, H. Jong, P. Klint, and P. Olivier. Efficient Annotated Terms. Technical report, CWI, 1999. Accepted by SPE. 97

4. M. Cerioli, A. Haxthausen, B. Krieg-Brückner, and T. Mossakowski. Permissive subsorted partial logic in CASL. In M. Johnson, editor, *Algebraic methodology and software technology: 6th international conference, AMAST 97*, volume 1349 of *Lecture Notes in Computer Science*, pages 91–107. Springer-Verlag, 1997. 95, 98

5. M. Cerioli and J. Meseguer. May I borrow your logic? (transporting logical structures along maps). *Theoretical Computer Science*, 173:311–347, 1997. 99

6. M. Clavel, F. Durán, S. Eker, P. Lincoln, N. Martí-Oliet, J. Meseguer, and J. F. Quesada. The Maude system. In P. Narendran and M. Rusinowitch, editors, *Proceedings of the 10th International Conference on Rewriting Techniques and Applications (RTA-99)*, pages 240–243, Trento, Italy, July 1999. Springer-Verlag LNCS 1631. System Description. 103

7. CoFI. The Common Framework Initiative for algebraic specification and development, electronic archives. Notes and Documents accessible by WWW[7] and FTP[8]. 107

8. CoFI Language Design Task Group. CASL – The CoFI Algebraic Specification Language – Summary. Documents/CASL/Summary, in [7], Oct. 1998. 93

9. CoFI Semantics Task Group. CASL – The CoFI Algebraic Specification Language – Semantics. Note S-9 (version 0.95), in [7], Mar. 1999. 93

10. CoFI Task Group on Tools. The CoFI-Tools group home page. http://www.loria.fr/~hkirchne/CoFI/Tools/index.html. 97

11. J. Hopcroft and J. D. Ullman. *Introduction to Automata Theory, Language, and Computation.* Addison–Wesley, Reading, MA, 1979. 98

12. B. Krieg-Brückner, J. Peleska, E.-R. Olderog, D. Balzer, and A. Baer. The UniForM Workbench, a universal development environment for formal methods. In *FM99: World Congress on Formal Methods*, volume 1709 of *Lecture Notes in Computer Science*, pages 1186–1205. Springer-Verlag, 1999. 105

13. P. G. Larsen. VDM and proof rules for underdetermined functions. Talk at the IFIP WG 1.3 meeting, Bonas, France, September 1999. 94

14. C. Lüth, H. Tej, Kolyang, and B. Krieg-Brückner. TAS and IsaWin: Tools for transformational program developkment and theorem proving. In J.-P. Finance, editor, *Fundamental Approaches to Software Engineering FASE'99. Joint European Conferences on Theory and Practice of Software ETAPS'99*, number 1577 in LNCS, pages 239–243. Springer Verlag, 1999. 103, 105

15. C. Lüth and B. Wolff. Functional design and implementation of graphical user interfaces for theorem provers. *Journal of Functional Programming*, 9(2):167–189, Mar. 1999. 103, 105

16. J. Meseguer. General logics. In *Logic Colloquium 87*, pages 275–329. North Holland, 1989. 99

17. T. Mossakowski, Kolyang, and B. Krieg-Brückner. Static semantic analysis and theorem proving for CASL. In F. Parisi Presicce, editor, *Recent trends in algebraic development techniques. Proc. 12th International Workshop*, volume 1376 of *Lecture Notes in Computer Science*, pages 333–348. Springer, 1998. 94, 96, 98, 99

18. P. D. Mosses. CoFI: The Common Framework Initiative for Algebraic Specification and Development. In *TAPSOFT '97: Theory and Practice of Software Development*, volume 1214 of *LNCS*, pages 115–137. Springer-Verlag, 1997. Documents/Tentative/Mosses97TAPSOFT, in [7]. 93

19. P. D. Mosses. Formatting CASL specifications using LaTeX. Note C-2, in [7], June 1998. 96

20. L. C. Paulson. *Isabelle - A Generic Theorem Prover.* Number 828 in LNCS. Springer Verlag, 1994. 99

21. C. Ringeissen. Demonstration of ELAN for rewriting in CASL specifications. Talk at the 14th Workshop on Algebraic Development Techniques, Bonas, France, September 1999. 97

22. M. Roggenbach and T. Mossakowski. Basic datatypes in CASL. Note M-6, in [7], Mar. 1999. 106

23. P. Y. Schobbens. Second-order proof systems for algebraic specification languages. In H. Ehrig and F. Orejas, editors, *Recent Trends in Data Type Specification*, volume 785 of *Lecture Notes in Computer Science*, pages 321–336, 1994. 101

---

24. A. Tarlecki. Moving between logical systems. In M. Haveraaen, O. Owe, and O.-J. Dahl, editors, *Recent Trends in Data Type Specifications. 11th Workshop on Specification of Abstract Data Types*, volume 1130 of *Lecture Notes in Computer Science*, pages 478–502. Springer Verlag, 1996. 99

25. A. Tarlecki. Towards heterogeneous specifications. In D. Gabbay and M. van Rijke, editors, *Frontiers of Combining Systems, 2nd International Workshop*. Research Studies Press, 1999. To appear. 106

26. M. van den Brand. CasFix – mapping from the concrete CASL to the abstract syntax in ATerms format. http://adam.wins.uva.nl/~markvdb/cofi/casl.html, 1998. 97

27. M. G. J. van den Brand and J. Scheerder. Development of parsing tools for CASL using generic language technology. Talk at the 14th Workshop on Algebraic Development Techniques, Bonas, France, September 1999. 97

On the Construction of Live Timed Systems

Sébastien Bornot, Gregor Gößler, and Joseph Sifakis

VERIMAG, 2 rue Vignate, 38610 Gières, France

Abstract. We present a method that allows to guarantee liveness by
construction of a class of timed systems. The method is based on the use
of a set of structural properties which can be checked locally at low cost.
We provide sufficient conditions for liveness preservation by parallel composition and priority choice operators. The latter allow to restrict a system's behavior according to a given priority order on its actions.
We present several examples illustrating the use of the results, in particular for the construction of live controllers.

1 Introduction

Building systems which satisfy given specifications is a central problem in systems engineering. Standard engineering practice consists in decomposing the
system to be designed into a set of cooperating components or processes. A
key problem is the coordination of the components so that the global behavior satisfies given specifications. Usually, ad hoc design methodologies are used
leading to solutions that must be validated by verification and testing. In some
cases, it is possible to solve the coordination problem by synthesizing a controller
or supervisor that restricts the behavior of the components [3,1]. Both validation and synthesis techniques have well-known limitations due to their inherent
complexity or undecidability, and cannot be applied to complex systems. As an
alternative to cope with complexity, compositional description techniques have
been studied. However, the results obtained so far for reactive systems are in
general difficult to exploit. They boil down either to heuristics of limited application or to general methods formulated as systems of rules with undecidable
premises.

Timed systems are models of real-time systems consisting of a discrete control structure (automaton) extended with clocks, variables measuring the time
elapsed since their initialization. At semantic level, they can be considered as
transition systems that can perform either discrete timeless actions or time steps
of some real-valued duration. For a timed system to model a real-time system, it
is necessary that it is *timelock-free* that is, in any maximal run time diverges. Another essential property for timed systems modeling real-time applications such
as controllers, schedulers, etc. is that any maximal run contains infinitely many
actions. We call this property *livelock-freedom* as it implies deadlock-freedom
and excludes indefinite waiting.

We call *live* a timed system which is both timelock-free and livelock-free. We
propose a method for building live systems as the composition of live components
by using parallel composition and priorities.

S. Graf and M. Schwartzbach (Eds.): TACAS/ETAPS 2000, LNCS 1785, pp. 109–126, 2000.
© Springer-Verlag Berlin Heidelberg 2000

The method is based on a key idea that motivated several papers on the compositional description of timed systems [6,7,8]. It consists in enforcing the satisfaction of properties by appropriate structural restrictions preserved by composition operations. This leads to consider structural properties, intrinsic properties of the system which can be checked locally at low cost. We define a structural property called *structural liveness* which implies liveness and can be easily checked on components as the conjunction of three more elementary structural properties. We combine two kinds of constructs to build structurally live systems from structurally live components.

- Parallel composition operators defined in [6,7,8]. We provide sufficient structural liveness preservation conditions for and-synchronization.
- Priorities allowing to restrict the behavior of a timed system according to a given order relation on its actions. We consider timed systems with priority orders defined in [6,7,8] and show that priority orders preserve structural liveness. This is a basic result used to build live timed systems, as priority orders play a central role in our approach. They are used to achieve coordination in a system by appropriately restricting the behavior of its components. As an illustration of this idea, we show how priority orders can be used to specify mutual exclusion constraints by preserving structural liveness.

The use of the results for the design of live real-time controllers is illustrated by several examples.

The paper is organized as follows. Section 2 presents the properties of liveness and structural liveness, as well as sufficient conditions for guaranteeing this property. Section 3 presents priority orders, their properties and results about structural liveness preservation when priorities are applied. Section 4 presents compositionality results for systems of communicating processes. Section 5 presents a method for the compositional description of mutual exclusion properties by using priorities.

2 Timed Systems and Their Properties

2.1 Background

Let X be a set of real-valued variables called clocks. Clocks will be used as state variables measuring time progress. Their valuations will be denoted by the letter v. *true* (resp. *false*) denotes the predicate that is true (resp. false) for any valuation v. For any non-negative real t, we represent by $v + t$ the valuation obtained from v by increasing by t the values of all the clocks.

Definition 1 (Left- and right-closure). *A predicate p is called left-closed if*

$$\forall v \ . \ \neg p(v) \Rightarrow \exists \epsilon > 0 \ . \ \forall \epsilon' \leq \epsilon \ . \ \neg p(v + \epsilon')$$

It is called right-closed if it satisfies the previous expression where $p(v + \epsilon')$ is replaced by $p(v - \epsilon')$.

Notice that these two definitions correspond to the usual notions if we consider p as a function of time, where v is a clock valuation.

Definition 2 (Rising and falling edge). *Given a predicate p on clocks X, we define the rising edge of p, noted $p{\uparrow}$ by:*

$$p{\uparrow}(v) = p(v) \wedge \exists \epsilon > 0 \;.\; \forall \epsilon' \in (0, \epsilon] \;.\; \neg p(v - \epsilon') \vee$$
$$\neg p(v) \wedge \exists \epsilon > 0 \;.\; \forall \epsilon' \in (0, \epsilon] \;.\; p(v + \epsilon')$$

The falling edge of p, noted $p{\downarrow}$, is defined by the same formula where $v - \epsilon'$ and $v + \epsilon'$ are exchanged.

Definition 3 (Modal operators). *Given a predicate p on real-valued variables X, we define the modal operator $\Diamond_k \, p$ ("eventually p within k") for $k \in \mathbf{R}_+ \cup \{\infty\}$.*

$$\Diamond_k \, p \, (v) \text{ if } \exists t \in \mathbf{R}_+ \; 0 \le t \le k. \; p(v + t)$$

We write $\Diamond p$ for $\Diamond_\infty \, p$ and $\Box p$ for $\neg \Diamond \neg p$.

Notice that the operators $\Diamond_k$ are just a notation for existential quantifications over time and should not be confused with temporal logic operators. Expressions with modal or edge operators can be reduced to predicates on X whenever quantification over time can be eliminated e.g., when the operators are applied to linear constraints on X.

2.2 Timed Systems

Definition 4 (Timed systems). *A Timed System is:*

- *An untimed labeled transition system $(S, \to, A)$ where*
  - *S is a finite set of control states*
  - *A is a finite vocabulary of actions*
  - *$\to \,\subseteq S \times A \times S$ is an untimed transition relation*
- *A finite set X of clocks, real-valued variables defined on the set of non negative reals $\mathbf{R}_+$. The set of the valuations of X, isomorphic to $\mathbf{R}_+^n$ for some n, is denoted V.*
- *A labeling function h mapping untimed transitions of $\to$ into timed transitions: $h(s, a, s') = (s, (a, g, d, f), s')$, where*
  - *g and d are predicates on X called respectively the guard and the deadline of the transition. We require that $d \Rightarrow g$.*
  - *$f : V \to V$ is a jump.*

According to the above definition, a timed system can be obtained from an untimed one by associating with each action a, a *timed action* $b = (a, g, d, f)$.

Definition 5 (Semantics of timed systems). *A state of a timed system is a pair (s, v), where $s \in S$ is a control state and $v \in V$. We associate with a timed system a transition relation $\to \,\subseteq (S \times V) \times (A \cup \mathbf{R}_+) \times (S \times V)$. Transitions labeled by elements of A are discrete transitions while transitions labeled by non-negative reals are time steps.*

Given $s \in S$, if $\{(s, a_i, s_i)\}_{i \in I}$ is the set of all the untimed transitions issued from s and $h(s, a_i, s_i) = (s, (a_i, g_i, d_i, f_i), s_i)$ then:

$-\ \forall i \in I\ \forall v \in \mathbf{R}_{+}\ .\ (s,v) \xrightarrow{a_i} (s_i, f_i(v))\ if\ g_i(v).$

$-\ (s,v) \xrightarrow{t} (s, v+t)\ if\ \forall t' < t\ .\ c_s(v+t')\ where\ c_s = \neg \bigvee_{i \in I} d_i.$

For the state s, we denote by $guard_s$ and $deadline_s$ respectively the predicates $\bigvee_{i \in I} g_i$ and $\bigvee_{i \in I} d_i$.

Notice that for time steps we have the following *time additivity* property. If for some $t_1, t_2 \in \mathbf{R}_+$ and some state (s,v), $(s,v) \xrightarrow{t_1+t_2} (s, v+(t_1+t_2))$ then $(s,v) \xrightarrow{t_1} (s, v+t_1) \xrightarrow{t_2} (s, v+(t_1+t_2))$, and conversely. Due to this property any sequence of time steps can be reduced into a time step of cumulated duration. If from some state (s,v) indefinite waiting is allowed, we write $(s,v) \xrightarrow{\infty} (s, \infty)$.

Timed systems are a variant of TAD [6] with an additional relaxation of usual syntactical restrictions ensuring decidability. The simplest timed system is a single transition labeled with the timed action (a, g, d, f). The guard g characterizes the set of states from which the timed transition is possible, while the deadline d characterizes the subset of these states where the timed transition is enforced by stopping time progress. The relative position of d within g determines the urgency of the action. For a given g, the corresponding d may take two extreme values: $d = g$ meaning that the action is *eager*, and $d = false$, meaning that the action is *lazy*. A particularly interesting case is the one of a *delayable* action where $d = g\downarrow$ is the falling edge of a right-closed guard g (cannot be disabled without enforcing the action). The differences between these actions are illustrated in fig. 1.

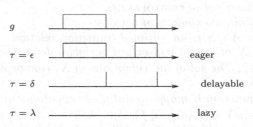

Fig. 1. Types for guards

It has been shown in [7] that any timed system can be described by a bisimilar system with only eager and lazy timed actions. In practice, we use the notation g^ϵ, g^δ and g^λ to denote a guard g of an action that is respectively eager $(d = g)$, delayable $(d = g\downarrow)$ and lazy $(d = false)$.

The containment of deadlines in guards $(d \Rightarrow g)$ is necessary for avoiding timelocks as it will be explained later.

Example 1. Consider the timed system of fig. 2 representing a process of period T and execution time E. The process has three control states s (sleep), w (wait) and e (execute). The clocks t and x are used to impose the period $T > 0$ and

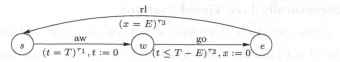

Fig. 2. A simple process

the execution time $E \leq T$, respectively. The guards $(t = T)$, $(t \leq T - E)$ and $(x = E)$ specify when discrete transitions can occur. According to the type of urgency for the actions (denoted by τ_1, τ_2, and τ_3 in the figure), the waiting times at control states may change. For instance, if all guards are lazy then it is possible for the system to remain stuck forever at one of the states s, w, or e. When all guards are eager, discrete transitions are taken as soon as they are enabled, which means in particular that the action *go* is always executed when $t = 0$ (no waiting allowed at w). On the contrary, when *go* is delayable, this action is possible at any time t, $0 \leq t \leq T - E$. Finally, notice that the behavior remains unchanged if eager punctual guards such as $x = E$ are considered as delayable.

Definition 6 (Initial clock valuations). *Let s be a control state of a timed system and $\{(s_i, b_i, s)\}_{i \in I}$ with $b_i = (a_i, g_i, d_i, f_i)$ the non-empty set of the in-going timed transitions. The set of the initial clock valuations at s is defined as the predicate*

$$in_s = \bigvee_{i \in I} post(b_i)$$

where $post(b_i)$ is the most liberal post-condition of the i-th transition defined by

$$post(b_i)(v) = \exists v', \ g_i(v') \wedge v = f_i(v')$$

When $I = \emptyset$, we take in_s to correspond to the valuation where all the clocks are set to zero.

Notice that in most practical cases where guards are linear constraints and jumps are linear functions, the quantifier in the expression of $post(b_i)$ can be eliminated. For the process of fig. 2, $in_s = (x = E)$, $in_w = (t = 0)$ and $in_e = (0 \leq t \leq T - E) \wedge (x = 0)$.

Definition 7 (Run). *A run of a timed system is a maximal sequence of alternating time steps and discrete transitions starting from (s_0, v_0) such that $in_{s_0}(v_0)$.*

$$(s_0, v_0) \xrightarrow{t_0} (s_0, v_0 + t_0) \xrightarrow{a_1} (s_1, v_1) \xrightarrow{t_1} \ldots (s_i, v_i) \xrightarrow{t_i} (s_i, v_i + t_i) \xrightarrow{a_{i+1}} (s_{i+1}, v_{i+1}) \ldots$$

Notice that due to time additivity of the transition system, any execution sequence of the model can be represented as a run (where some time steps may be of duration zero).

2.3   Structurally Live Timed Systems

In this section, we study three basic structural properties of timed systems.

Definition 8 (Timelock-freedom). *A timed system is timelock-free if in any run* $(s_0, v_0) \xrightarrow{t_0} (s_0, v_0 + t_0) \xrightarrow{a_1} \ldots \xrightarrow{t_i} (s_i, v_i + t_i) \xrightarrow{a_{i+1}} \ldots,$ $\sum_i t_i$ *diverges.*

Definition 9 (Livelock-freedom). *A timed system is livelock-free if in any run some action occurs infinitely often.*

Definition 10 (Liveness). *A timed system is called live if it is both timelock-free and livelock-free.*

Definition 11 (Structural non-Zenoness). *A timed system is structurally non-Zeno if in any circuit of the discrete transition graph at least one clock is reset, and it is tested against some positive lower bound.*

Structural non-Zenoness implies that there is a positive lower bound to the execution time of any circuit, and is the same as strong non-Zenoness in [16]. The periodic process of fig. 2 is structurally non-Zeno since $T > 0$.

Definition 12 (Local timelock-freedom). *A timed system is called locally timelock-free if for any state s, for any timed transition (a, g, d, f) exiting from s, $d{\uparrow} \Rightarrow guard_s$.*

Notice that timed systems with left-closed deadlines are locally timelock-free, as $d{\uparrow} \Rightarrow d \Rightarrow g$. Consequently, the timed system of fig. 2 is timelock-free independently of the type of urgency of the actions.

Lemma 1. *At any state (s, v) in a locally timelock-free timed system, time can progress or some action is enabled. (Proof omitted.)*

Lemma 2. *Any structurally non-Zeno and locally timelock-free timed system is timelock-free. (Proof omitted.)*

Definition 13 (Local livelock-freedom). *A timed system is called locally livelock-free if for any state s, $in_s \Rightarrow \Diamond deadline_s$, i.e., from any initial state some transition will be eventually taken.*

Proposition 1. *Any locally timelock-free and locally livelock-free timed system is livelock-free. (Proof omitted.)*

Definition 14 (Structural liveness). *A timed system is structurally live if it is locally timelock-free, locally livelock-free, and structurally non-Zeno.*

Clearly, structural liveness is a particular case of liveness that can be characterized by means of three properties easy to check.

Example 2. The process of fig. 2 is not locally livelock-free if one of the actions is lazy. Furthermore, even when the actions are delayable or eager, the requirement for local livelock-freedom fails for state s, since $in_s = (x = E)$, which does not imply $\Diamond(t = T) = (t \leq T)$. However, if the guard of rl is strengthened to $(x = E \wedge t \leq T)$, the behavior is not modified, and the system is locally livelock-free. So, the system is structurally live for $\tau_i \in \{\delta, \epsilon\}, i = 1, 2, 3$.

3   Timed Systems with Priorities

3.1   Motivation

In system specification, it is often convenient to consider that some priority is applied when from a state several actions are enabled. This amounts to restricting the guards of the action of lower priority to leave precedence to actions of higher priority.

Consider for example, two timed transitions $(s, (a_i, g_i, d_i, f_i), s_i)$, $i = 1, 2$ with common source state s. If a_1 has lower priority than a_2, then the transition labeled by a_1 becomes $(s, (a_1, g'_1, d'_1, f_1), s_1)$ with $g'_1 \Rightarrow g_1$ and $d'_1 \Rightarrow d_1$ while the other remains unchanged. Commonly, g'_1 is taken equal to $g_1 \wedge \neg g_2$ which means that when a_1 and a_2 are simultaneously enabled in the system without priorities only a_2 is enabled in the prioritized system. However, for timed systems it is possible to define priority relations leaving precedence to an action if it is known that it will be enabled within some finite time.

Coming back to the previous example, we can take $g'_1 = g_1 \wedge \neg \Diamond_k g_2$ for some finite k, or even $g'_1 = g_1 \wedge \neg \Diamond g_2$. In the former case a_1 gives priority up to a_2 if a_2 is eventually enabled within k time units. In the latter case, a_1 is enabled if a_2 is disabled forever.

This motivates a notion of priority within a given delay. As an example, consider that $g_1 = 0 \leq x \leq 3 \vee 5 \leq x \leq 8$ and $g_2 = 2 \leq x \leq 7$ for some clock x. We get the following decreasing values for g'_1 as the priority delay increases.

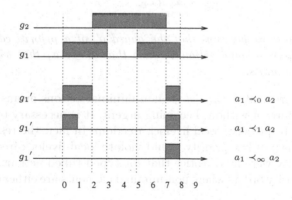

Fig. 3. Different priorities for a_2 over a_1

$g'_1 = g_1 \wedge \neg g_2 = 0 \leq x < 2 \vee 7 < x \leq 8$ (immediate priority)
$g'_1 = g_1 \wedge \neg \Diamond_1 g_2 = 0 \leq x < 1 \vee 7 < x \leq 8$ (priority within a delay of 1)
$g'_1 = g_1 \wedge \neg \Diamond g_2 = 7 < x \leq 8$ (priority within an unbounded delay).
Fig. 3 illustrates the above example.

The following definition of priority order has been introduced and studied in [7].

Definition 15 (Priority order). *Consider the relation* $\prec \subseteq A \times (\mathbf{R}_+ \cup \{\infty\}) \times A$. *We write* $a_1 \prec_k a_2$ *for* $(a_1, k, a_2) \in \prec$ *and suppose that* $\forall k \in \mathbf{R}_+ \cup \{\infty\}$:

- $\prec_k$ *is a partial order*
- $a_1 \prec_k a_2$ *implies* $\forall k' < k. \; a_1 \prec_{k'} a_2$
- $a_1 \prec_k a_2 \wedge a_2 \prec_l a_3$ *implies* $a_1 \prec_{k+l} a_3$ *for all* $l \in \mathbf{R}_+ \cup \{\infty\}$

Property: The relation $a_1 \prec\!\!\prec a_2 = \exists k \; a_1 \prec_k a_2$ is a partial order relation.

Definition 16 (Timed system with priorities). *A timed system with priorities is a timed system* $TS = (S, \rightarrow, A, X, h)$ *having all its guards and deadlines left- and right-closed, equipped with a priority function* pr. *The priority function* pr *associates with each state* $s \in S$ *a priority order* $pr(s)$ *such that if* $\{(a_i, g_i, d_i, f_i)\}_{i \in I}$ *is the set of the timed actions labeling transitions issued from* s, *then* $\Diamond g_i \Rightarrow \Diamond d_i$ *for any* a_i *which is not a minimal element of* $pr(s)$.

A timed system with priorities (TS, pr) *represents the timed system* $TS' = (S, \rightarrow, A, X, h')$ *with the same discrete transition structure and such that if* $h(s_1, a, s_2) = (s_1, (a, g, d, f), s_2)$ *then* $h'(s_1, a, s_2) = (s_1, (a, g', d', f), s_2)$ *where* g' *is defined in the following manner.*

For a given state s, *let* $\prec$ *denote the priority order* $pr(s)$, *and* $\{(a_i, g_i, d_i, f_i)\}_{i \in I}$ *be the set of the timed actions labeling transitions of* TS *exiting from* s. *The corresponding set of prioritized timed actions in* TS' *is then* $\{(a_i, g_i', d_i', f_i)\}_{i \in I}$ *defined by*

$$g_i' = g_i \wedge \bigwedge_{\substack{a_j \in I, \; k \in \mathbf{R}_+ \cup \{\infty\} \\ a_i \prec_k a_j}} \neg \Diamond_k g_j \qquad d_i' = d_i \wedge g_i'$$

This definition simply says that the guard g_i' *of a prioritized action* a_i *is not enabled if there is some action* a_j *such that* $a_i \prec_k a_j$ *that will become enabled within* k *time units.*

The requirement $\Diamond g \Rightarrow \Diamond d$ for non-minimal actions means that they cannot be disabled forever without becoming urgent. It is necessary to avoid overriding of deadlines to preserve local livelock-freedom. In fact, the restriction of guards (and deadlines) of low priority would violate local livelock-freedom if actions of higher priority were lazy. Notice that for typed timed actions, it is sufficient to consider priority orders where non-minimal elements are either eager or delayable actions.

We call TS' the *prioritized* timed system corresponding to (TS, pr). We denote by $guard_s'$ and $deadline_s'$ the restrictions of $guard_s$ and $deadline_s$ in TS'.

3.2   Preservation of the Structural Properties

Theorem 1. *If* TS *satisfies one of the structural properties local timelock-freedom, local livelock-freedom, or structural non-Zenoness, then* (TS, pr) *satisfies the same property. Thus, priority orders preserve structural liveness.*

Proof. – Local timelock-freedom: priority orders transform a left-closed guard g either into left-closed guards g' or into a guard g' such that another guard g_1 of higher priority is true at the rising edge of g' (see definition of timed system with priorities). Thus $d\uparrow \Rightarrow g \vee g_1$. By induction on the priority order it is then possible to show that local timelock-freedom is preserved.

– Local livelock-freedom: priority orders do not change the discrete transition structure of timed systems, and restrict guards of timed actions. Consequently, for each state s, the set of transitions entering s does not change, and in_s is restricted. If we note in'_s the set of initial clock values of s in the prioritized system, and as the non prioritized system is locally livelock-free, we have $in'_s \Rightarrow in_s \Rightarrow \Diamond deadline_s$.

If a deadline d of an action a is restricted to a deadline $d' \neq d$, then it is restricted by some transition (a_1, g_1, d_1, f_1) such that $a \prec_k a_1$, for some $k \in \mathbf{R}_+ \cup \{\infty\}$. This implies $d \wedge \neg d' \Rightarrow \Diamond_k g_1 \Rightarrow \Diamond g_1$. Since a_1 is not minimal, $\Diamond g_1 = \Diamond d_1$. Thus $d \Rightarrow d' \vee \Diamond d_1$. It follows that $\Diamond deadline_s = \Diamond deadline'_s$. Thus local livelock-freedom is preserved.

– Strong non-Zenoness: priority orders do not change the discrete transition structure of timed systems, and do not affect jumps. So any circuit in the prioritized system is a circuit in the initial one, and the clock resets are the same. Moreover, guards are restricted by priority orders, so a lower bound in a guard may only increase. Consequently, if the non prioritized system is structurally non-Zeno, then the prioritized one is structurally non-Zeno, too. ∎

It is often desirable to restrict a timed system TS with respect to several priority functions pr_i. At this end, we define a partial operation on priority orders.

Given $\prec^1$, $\prec^2$ priority orders on A, we represent by $\prec^1 \oplus \prec^2$ the least priority order, if it exists, that contains both $\prec^1$ and $\prec^2$, i.e.,

– $\prec^1 \cup \prec^2 \subseteq \prec^1 \oplus \prec^2$
– if $(a_1, k_1, a_2), (a_2, k_2, a_3) \in \prec^1 \oplus \prec^2$, then $(a_1, k_1 + k_2, a_3) \in \prec^1 \oplus \prec^2$.

The partially defined operator $\oplus$ is associative and commutative. We extend $\oplus$ on priority functions pr_i: $\forall s \in S.(pr_1 \oplus pr_2)(s) = pr_1(s) \oplus pr_2(s)$.

In order to simplify notations, we extend priority orders to sets of actions: $A^1 \prec_k A^2 :\Leftrightarrow \forall a_1 \in A^1 \forall a_2 \in A^2 . a_1 \prec_k a_2$.

In the rest of the paper, we show how to build live systems from live components.

4   Systems of Communicating Processes

We use the following general framework for the composition of timed systems studied in [6,7] and based on the use of an associative and commutative parallel composition operator $\|$.

Consider timed systems of the form $TS_i = (S_i, A_i, \rightarrow_i, X_i, h_i)$. For sake of simplicity, we assume that they have disjoint sets of control states S_i, disjoint sets of actions A_i, and disjoint sets of clocks X_i. Furthermore, we consider an action vocabulary A, $A_i \subseteq A$, with an operator $|$ such that $(A, |)$ is a commutative semi-group with a distinguished absorbing element $\perp$. The action $a_1|a_2$ represents the action resulting from the synchronization of a_1 and a_2 (if $a_1|a_2 \neq \perp$).

Definition 17 (Parallel composition). *The parallel composition* $(TS_1, pr_1)\|$ (TS_2, pr_s) *of two timed systems with priorities* (TS_1, pr_1) *and* (TS_2, pr_2) *is the timed system with priorities* (TS, pr) *defined by*

- $TS = (S_1 \times S_2, A, \rightarrow, X_1 \cup X_2, h)$ *where if* $s_i \xrightarrow{a_i}_i s'_i$ *and* $h_i(s_i, a_i, s'_i) = (s_i, b_i, s'_i)$ *with* $b_i = (a_i, g_i, d_i, f_i)$, $i = 1, 2$, *then*

  • $(s_1, s_2) \xrightarrow{a_1} (s'_1, s_2)$, $(s_1, s_2) \xrightarrow{a_2} (s_1, s'_2)$, *and* $(s_1, s_2) \xrightarrow{a_1|a_2} (s'_1, s'_2)$ *if* $a_1|a_2 \neq$ $\perp$. *That is, the transitions of* $\rightarrow$ *are obtained by interleaving or by synchronization.*

  • *If* $a_1|a_2 \neq \perp$, *then* $\Diamond g_i = \Diamond d_i, i = 1, 2$.

  • $h((s_1, s_2), a_1, (s'_1, s_2)) = ((s_1, s_2), b_1, (s'_1, s_2))$
    $h((s_1, s_2), a_2, (s_1, s'_2)) = ((s_1, s_2), b_2, (s_1, s'_2))$
    $h((s_1, s_2), a_1|a_2, (s'_1, s'_2)) = ((s_1, s_2), b_1|b_2, (s'_1, s'_2))$
    where $b_1|b_2$ *is an extension of* $|$ *on timed actions, defined later.*

- $pr = pr_1 \oplus pr_2 \oplus pr_{12}$, *where* $\forall (s_1, s_2) \in S_1 \times S_2$.
  $pr_{12}(s_1, s_2) = \{\{a_1, a_2\} \prec_\infty a_1|a_2 \mid a_1|a_2 \neq \perp \wedge \exists s'_1, s'_2 . s_1 \xrightarrow{a_1} s'_1 \wedge s_2 \xrightarrow{a_2} s'_2\}$
  if $pr_1 \oplus pr_2 \oplus pr_{12}$ *is defined.*

The composition principle is illustrated in fig. 4. Priorities are used to achieve

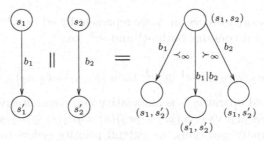

Fig. 4. Composition principle

maximal progress, that is, interleaving transitions will be taken only when synchronization is not possible.

In [6,7] a general method is provided to extend the operator $|$ on timed actions, preserving associativity and commutativity. We consider here a particular case of timed action synchronization, called *and-synchronization*, which is defined as follows:

For $b_i = (a_i, g_i, d_i, f_i), i = 1, 2$ if $a_1|a_2 \neq \perp$, then $b_1|b_2 = (a_1|a_2, g_1 \wedge g_2, (g_1 \wedge g_2) \wedge (d_1 \vee d_2), f_1 \cup f_2)$. This simply means that synchronization takes place only when both actions are enabled. The synchronization action becomes urgent whenever it is enabled, and one of the synchronizing actions becomes urgent. Finally, $f_1 \cup f_2$ denotes the composition of jumps (for disjoint state spaces of the components).

Notice that $\|$ is an associative and commutative partial operation on timed systems with priorities. We trivially consider a timed system TS as a timed system with priorities $(TS, pr_\emptyset)$, where $pr_\emptyset$ is the priority function associating the empty priority order with any state.

Theorem 2. *If TS_1 and TS_2 are structurally live, then $TS_1 \parallel TS_2$ is structurally live.*

Proof. If $(TS, pr) = TS_1 \| TS_2$, then it is sufficient to consider TS by application of Theorem 1, as for synchronizing actions (which are not minimal in $pr(s)$ for all s), $\Diamond g_i = \Diamond d_i$. We show that if TS_1 and TS_2 are structurally live, then TS is structurally live.

- Structural non-Zenoness: since each transition (interleaving or synchronization) corresponds to a transition in TS_1 or TS_2 or both, each circuit in the product contains a set of transitions forming a circuit in TS_1 or TS_2. If TS_1 and TS_2 are structurally non-Zeno, then in all these circuits some clock is reset and tested against a positive lower bound. Then this is the case for all the circuits of TS too. The bounds of a synchronization action may increase, but can not decrease.
- Local timelock-freedom: conjunction and disjunction preserve closure of guards and deadlines, so guards and deadlines of synchronizations are closed as well as those of interleaving actions. This guarantees local time-lock freedom.
- Local livelock-freedom: since interleaving transitions are transitions of the components, and synchronization guards are conjunctions of guards of the components, if TS_1 and TS_2 are locally livelock-free we have

$$in_{(s_1, s_2)} \Rightarrow in_{s_1} \vee in_{s_2} \Rightarrow \Diamond deadline_{s_1} \vee \Diamond deadline_{s_2}$$
$$\Rightarrow \Diamond deadline_{(s_1, s_2)}$$

Thus, the product system is locally livelock-free.   ∎

Example 3. Consider two structurally live processes P_1 and P_2 with execution times E_i and periods T_i, $i = 1, 2$, running in parallel, as shown in fig. 5. Each process P_i can procrastinate the go_i action, which models the start of its execution, as long as enough time remains for execution before the end of the period.

In order to let the processes exchange data, however, one wishes to coordinate them by a common $go_1 | go_2$ action whenever this is possible without violating the timing constraints of any of P_1 and P_2. This is done by synchronizing the go_1 and go_2 actions. Maximal progress is ensured in (w_1, w_2) by the priorities $go_1 \prec_\infty go_1 | go_2$ and $go_2 \prec_\infty go_1 | go_2$, and guarantees that the two processes will synchronize if they manage to be in (w_1, w_2) at the same time. The resulting

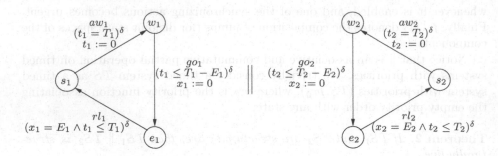

Fig. 5. Two processes with flexible synchronization

timed actions in the product system with priorities have typed guards g'_1, g'_2, and g_{12}, respectively, for go_1, go_2, and $go_1|go_2$:

$$g'_1 = ((x_1 \leq T_1 - E_1) \wedge \neg \Diamond (x_2 \leq T_2 - E_2))^\delta = ((x_1 \leq T_1 - E_1) \wedge (x_2 > T_2 - E_2))^\delta$$
$$g'_2 = ((x_2 \leq T_2 - E_2) \wedge \neg \Diamond (x_1 \leq T_1 - E_1))^\delta = ((x_2 \leq T_2 - E_2) \wedge (x_1 > T_1 - E_1))^\delta$$
$$g_{12} = ((x_1 \leq T_1 - E_1) \wedge (x_2 \leq T_2 - E_2))^\delta .$$

The product system is structurally live.

An important property in the previous example is individual livelock-freedom of the components in the product system. Liveness of the product does not imply that in any run, an action of some component occurs infinitely often. This remark motivates the following definition and theorem.

Definition 18 (Individual livelock-freedom). *A component (TS_i, pr_i) is livelock-free in a timed system $(TS, pr) = (TS_1, pr_1)\|(TS_2, pr_2)$ if in each run of (TS, pr), some action of (TS_i, pr_i) occurs infinitely often.*

Theorem 3. *If both (TS_1, pr_1) and (TS_2, pr_2) are structurally live and each synchronizing guard g is bounded (that is, $\Diamond \Box \neg g$), then both TS_1 and TS_2 are livelock-free in $(TS_1, pr_1)\|(TS_2, pr_2)$. (Proof omitted.)*

Example 4. Both processes of Example 3 are livelock-free in the product system.

Remark 1. Notice that for liveness preservation, the systematic use of "escape" actions (aborted communications) in the product system is instrumental. Our parallel composition operator allows a process to proceed unsynchronized on any action for which the communication will not be ready in its current state sometime in the future. This is different from usual "strong" parallel composition where synchronization is enforced by the use of restriction operators as in CCS [15] or by allowing interleaving only for internal (non communicating) actions as in CSP [12]. Such operators enforce synchronization at the risk of deadlock, particularly in the case of timed systems.

5   Mutual Exclusion

Consider a timed system initially composed of a set of interacting components. The goal is to restrict the behavior of the components by using priorities so that the global behavior satisfies a given mutual exclusion constraint. We study a method to obtain a structurally live system satisfying mutual exclusion from structurally live components.

The following notion of persistence will be central in this section.

Definition 19 (Persistence). *A control state s is called* persistent *if $in_s \Rightarrow \Diamond\Box guards_s$.*

This property means that at state s, maybe after some waiting, it is always possible to execute an action. It is instrumental for avoiding deadlocks when guards are restricted by using priorities.

Consider a timed system $(TS, pr) = TS_1\| \ldots \|TS_n$, where $TS_i = (S_i, A_i, \rightarrow_i, X_i, h_i)$, and $TS = (S, A, \rightarrow, X, h)$, as in section 4. We suppose that a mutual exclusion constraint is specified as a set $M \subseteq \bigcup_i S_i$ containing pairwise mutually exclusive states. We define two predicates on the product space S:

- $bad_M(s_1, \ldots, s_n) = \exists i, j, i \neq j.s_i \in M \wedge s_j \in M$
- $critical_M(s_1, \ldots, s_n) = \neg bad_M(s_1, \ldots, s_m) \wedge$
  $\exists a \in A, (s'_1, \ldots, s'_n) \in S . (s_1, \ldots, s_n) \xrightarrow{a} (s'_1, \ldots, s'_n) \wedge bad_M(s'_1, \ldots, s'_n).$

bad_M characterizes all the states violating the mutual exclusion constraint, whereas $critical_M$ characterizes all the legal states from which mutual exclusion can be violated by executing one transition.

For a given $M \subseteq \bigcup_i S_i$ we define $\bullet M$ and $M\circ$ as the set of actions entering M and the set of actions originating in M:

$$\bullet M = \{a \mid \exists i \exists s, s' \in S_i, s \notin M \wedge s' \in M \wedge s \xrightarrow{a}_i s'\}$$
$$M\circ = \{a \mid \exists i \exists s, s' \in S_i, s \in M \wedge s \xrightarrow{a}_i s'\}$$

The set of *waiting* states of component S_i with respect to M is the set of states from which some action entering M is issued: $\{s \in S_i - M | \exists a \in A_i, s' \in S_i \cap M \text{ s.t. } s \xrightarrow{a}_i s'\}$.

Theorem 4 (Mutual exclusion). *Let $TS_1 \ldots, TS_n$ be a set of structurally live timed systems with persistent waiting states w.r.t. a mutual exclusion constraint $M \subseteq \bigcup_i S_i$, and $(TS, pr) = TS_1\| \ldots \|TS_n$ be the parallel composition of the components with $\forall a_1 \in \bullet M \; \forall a_2 \in A.a_1|a_2 = \bot$. Then, the timed system with priorities $(TS, pr \oplus pr_M)$, where*

$$\forall s \in S . pr_M(s) = \begin{cases} \bullet M \prec_\infty M\circ & \text{if } critical_M(s) \\ \emptyset & \text{otherwise} \end{cases} \tag{1}$$

is structurally live, and satisfies the mutual exclusion constraint.

Proof (sketch).

- Structural liveness: Let us first show that $(pr \oplus pr_M)(s)$ is a partial order for all $s \in S.\neg bad_M(s)$. Suppose that $a_1 \prec_\infty a_2 \in pr$ (i.e., a_2 is a synchronizing action), and that $a_2 \prec_\infty a_1 \in pr_M$. This is not possible, since synchronizing actions are maximal in pr_M. Hence, $pr \oplus pr_M$ is a priority function. Structural liveness follows from Theorems 2 and 1.

- Mutual exclusion: No synchronization action can lead $(TS, pr \oplus pr_M)$ from a safe state $s \in S.\neg(critical_M(s) \vee bad_M(s))$ into a bad_M state violating mutual exclusion.

  Let $s = (s_1, \ldots, s_n)$ be a state of TS with $critical_M(s)$, such that there exist s_k, s_i, $s_k \in M$ and $\exists a \in A_i.s_i \xrightarrow{a} s_i'$ with $s_i' \in M$. Thus, a is an action leading (TS, pr) into a bad state. Since $a \in \bullet M$, we have $a_i \prec_\infty \{s_k\} \circ \subseteq pr_M(s)$. Let us show that from any initial clock valuation of s_k, some action issued from s_k will eventually be enabled, which means that a is disabled due to priority choice semantics.

  From the livelock-freedom assumption about TS_k, $in_{s_k} \Rightarrow \Diamond deadline_{s_k}$, one can deduce that in the product (TS, pr), for any state satisfying in_{s_k} there exists an action in $A_{s_k} = \{s_k\} \circ \cup \{a_1|a_2 \mid a_1 \in \{s_k\} \circ \wedge a_2 \in A \wedge a_1|a_2 \neq \bot\}$ with deadline d such that $\Diamond d$. This property remains true as long as TS_k is in state s_k in (TS, pr). The same argument can be applied for s_k in $(TS, pr \oplus pr_M)$, as the actions of A_{s_k} are not restricted by the priority function pr_M. ∎

Intuitively, equation (1) says that from critical states, M must be left before a new process can enter. The persistence of the waiting states makes sure that no process becomes deadlocked while waiting to enter M.

Remark 2. Notice that the above construction minimally restricts the untimed transition structure in the following manner: if from a state $s = (s_1, \ldots, s_n)$, $\neg bad_M(s)$ there exist transitions $s \xrightarrow{a_1} s'$ and $s \xrightarrow{a_2} s''$ with $a_1 \in \bullet M$ and $a_2 \in M\circ$, then $critical_M(s)$, and $bad_M(s')$.

Definition 20 (Individual deadlock-freedom). *A component TS_i of a timed system $(TS, pr) = TS_1\| \ldots \|TS_n$ is deadlock-free in TS if for each run of TS, some action of TS_i is enabled infinitely often.*

Theorem 5. *Let $TS_1 \ldots, TS_n$ be a set of structurally live timed systems, and $M \subseteq \bigcup_i S_i$ a mutual exclusion constraint, as in Theorem 4. If for each TS_i, any run of TS_i contains infinitely many occurrences of states in $S_i - M$, the actions in $M\circ$ do not synchronize, and TS_i is livelock-free in $(TS, pr) = TS_1\| \ldots \|TS_n$, then all components are deadlock-free in $(TS, pr \oplus pr_M)$. (Proof omitted.)*

Remark 3. Let TS_i be a structurally live timed system, and M a mutual exclusion constraint. A sufficient structural condition for the runs of TS_i to contain infinitely many occurrences of states in $S_i - M$ is that the untimed transition graph of TS_i has no cycles in M.

Theorem 6. *Let* $\{M_i\}_{i \in I}$ *be a set of mutual exclusion constraints on a structurally live timed system* (TS, pr). *If* pr_{M_i} *are the priority functions ensuring mutual exclusion according to Theorem 4, and* $\pi = pr \oplus \bigoplus_{i \in I} pr_{M_i}$ *is a priority function, then* (TS, π) *is structurally live and respects all mutual exclusion constraints* M_i. *(Proof omitted.)*

Example 5. Consider two processes of periods T_1, T_2 and execution times E_1, E_2 as in fig. 6. Each one of the processes is structurally live and remains livelock-

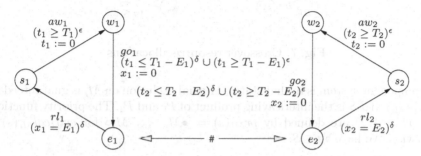

Fig. 6. Two processes with mutual exclusion between e_1 and e_2

free in the interleaving product of the two processes, which is structurally live. We apply the mutual exclusion constraint $M - \{e_1, e_2\}$ on the interleaving product and obtain $\bullet M \prec_\infty M\circ$, i.e., $\{go_1, go_2\} \prec_\infty \{rl_1, rl_2\}$ for the critical states (w_1, e_2), (e_1, w_2). This practically means that release-actions rl have higher priority than begin-actions go. According to Theorem 4, the product system with priorities is structurally live, and both processes are deadlock-free in it, due to the persistent waiting states w_1 and w_2.

Notice that in order to compute $(TS_1\| \dots \|TS_n, pr)$, it is not necessary to compute explicitly the product $T_1\| \dots \|T_n$. Priority choice can be applied "on the fly" to states of the product.

The construction of Theorem 4 can be generalized for mutual exclusion constraints of the type *m-out-of-n* for $m < n$, where $critical_M(s)$ $(bad_M(s))$ denotes the set of control states where exactly m (more than m) components are in M.

Example 6 (Resource allocation). Consider the well-known example of fig. 7, where two interleaving processes P_1 and P_2 use two shared resources R_1 and R_2. P_1 allocates resource R_1, then R_2, while it still holds R_1, before releasing both resources. P_2 tries to allocate the resources in the inverse order.

An action p_{ij} means that process P_i allocates resource R_j, and a v_i-action means that process P_i frees both resources. Mutual exclusion over R_1 is modeled by the set $M_1 = \{s_2, s_3, s_7\}$, and mutual exclusion over R_2 by $M_2 = \{s_3, s_6, s_7\}$, as indicated by arrows in the figure. Critical states are those characterized by $critical_{M_1} = (s_2 \vee s_3) \wedge s_6 \vee s_1 \wedge s_7$, and $critical_{M_2} = s_3 \wedge s_5 \vee s_2 \wedge (s_6 \vee s_7)$ (where the name of a component state is used as a proposition which is true if

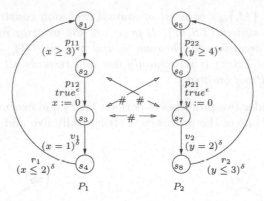

Fig. 7. Crossover resource allocations

the component system is in that state). Mutual exclusion on M_i is guaranteed for (TS, pr_{M_i}), if TS is the interleaving product of P_1 and P_2. The priority functions pr_{M_i} $(i = 1, 2)$ are defined by $pr_{M_i}(s) = \bullet M_i \prec_\infty M_i \circ$ for $critical_{M_i}(s)$, $\emptyset$ otherwise. We have $\forall s \in S$:

$$pr_{M_1}(s) = \begin{cases} \{p_{11}, p_{21}\} \prec_\infty \{p_{12}, v_1, v_2\} & \text{if } critical_{M_1}(s) \\ \emptyset & \text{otherwise} \end{cases}$$

$$pr_{M_2}(s) = \begin{cases} \{p_{12}, p_{22}\} \prec_\infty \{p_{21}, v_1, v_2\} & \text{if } critical_{M_2}(s) \\ \emptyset & \text{otherwise} \end{cases}$$

Both mutual exclusion constraints M_1 and M_2 are respected by $(TS, pr_{M_1} \oplus pr_{M_2})$, if $pr_{M_1} \oplus pr_{M_2}$ is defined. However, in state (s_2, s_6) — P_1 has allocated R_1 and waits for R_2, whereas P_2 has allocated R_2 and waits for R_1 —, one can see that priorities form a circuit with vertices p_{12} and p_{21}. This flaw in the specification (which means that the specification is intrinsically not deadlock-free) can be corrected by declaring states $\{s_2, s_6\}$ in mutual exclusion. The resulting mutual exclusion constraint is $M = \{s_2, s_3, s_6, s_7\}$, which means that the product state (s_2, s_6) is made unreachable. In practice, this means that the sequence consisting of the two resource allocations is atomic, and the obtained system is live.

Notice that each process eventually frees all resources, and the waiting states s_1 and s_5 are persistent, so that both processes remain individually deadlock-free after composition in this improved specification.

6   Discussion

We have presented a method for the construction of live timed systems based on the preservation of a set of structural properties by appropriately chosen composition operators. Structural properties verification can be done locally and does not require exploration of the global system's dynamic behavior. The set of initial states is also structurally determined.

An important question to be further investigated is applicability of the method. It concerns the expressivity of the class of structurally live systems as well as the possibility to apply in practice the liveness preservation theorems.

We believe that the two properties implying timelock-freedom correspond to completely natural common sense requirements of sanity. Structural non-Zenoness is a kind of "well-guardedness" property that is satisfied in practice. Local livelock-freedom is also a basic property to avoid problems in the interaction between time progress and discrete state changes. The main difficulty in the application of our method, is the satisfaction of the local livelock-freedom property. It may happen that the initial clock valuation at some state is too weak. In that case, the guards of the transitions entering this state must be strengthened in an appropriate manner (as in Example 2) and this is left to the user's ingenuity.

The proposed parallel composition operator can be enhanced by selective elimination of escape actions thanks to the use of additional priorities. If all non communicating actions are given infinitely higher priority than communicating actions then stronger interaction can be achieved and for this parallel composition operator Theorem 2 remains true. However, Theorem 3 does not hold and it is not easy to find conditions for individual liveness preservation.

The presented method uses a framework for the compositional description of timed systems [6,7,8]. This framework is based on "flexible" composition operations in the sense that composition allows only interaction resulting in a global behavior that preserves liveness. Priorities are essential for restricting appropriately the behavior of the cooperating components depending on their abilities to synchronize from their respective states. This contrasts with usual composition operations which are "constraint oriented" and consider parallel composition essentially as the intersection of "observable" behaviors. Such operations enforce action synchronization and respect components urgency at the risk of livelock or timelock. In the presence of timelock or livelock, the behavior of the components must be changed to get correct specifications. We prefer flexible composition, in spite of its deficiencies, because it is more appropriate for the "correct by construction" approach. To our knowledge, this approach has not been very much explored so far. [16] defines sufficient static conditions for deadlock- and timelock-freedom for the synchronized product of timed automata. Also, there exists some work about reactive systems such as [9,13].

Concerning the use of priorities, there exist many papers introducing priorities to process algebras, mainly for the untimed case [5,10,14]. Our notion of timed systems with priorities is closer to the work of [14] on the timed process algebra ACSR. However, this work does not tackle problems of property preservation.

This work is part of a more general project which aims at developing techniques and tools for modeling and analyzing real-time systems. We implemented priority choice, parallel composition as well as verification of structural properties, in a prototype tool, which we are currently using for the description of scheduling algorithms.

References

1. K. Altisen, G. Gößler, A. Pnueli, J. Sifakis, S. Tripakis, and S. Yovine. A Framework for Scheduler Synthesis. In IEEE *RTSS'99* proceedings, 1999. 109
2. R. Alur and D.L. Dill. A theory of timed automata. *TCS*, 126, pp. 183-235, 1994.
3. E. Asarin, O. Maler, and A. Pnueli. Symbolic Controller Synthesis for Discrete and Timed Systems. *Hybrid Systems II*, LNCS 999, Springer-Verlag, 1995. 109
4. P. C. Attie. Synthesis of Large Concurrent Programs via Pairwise Composition. In *CONCUR'99*.
5. J. C. M. Baeten, J. A. Bergstra, and J. W. Klop. Syntax and defining equations for an interrupt mechanism in process algebra. *Fundamenta Informaticae IX (2)*, pp. 127-168, 1986. 125
6. S. Bornot and J. Sifakis. On the composition of hybrid systems. In *International Workshop "Hybrid Systems: Computation and Control"*, LNCS, pp. 49–63. Springer-Verlag, April 1998. 110, 112, 117, 118, 125
7. S. Bornot and J. Sifakis. An Algebraic Framework for Urgency. In *Calculational System Design*, NATO Science Series, Computer and Systems Science 173, Marktoberdorf, July 1998. 110, 112, 115, 117, 118, 125
8. S. Bornot, J. Sifakis, and S. Tripakis. Modeling urgency in timed systems. In *COMPOS'97*, Malente, Germany. LNCS 1536, Springer-Verlag, 1998. 110, 125
9. L. P. Carloni, K. L. McMillan, and A. L. Sangiovanni-Vincentelli. Latency Insensitive Protocols. In *CAV'99*, Trento, Italy. LNCS 1633, Springer-Verlag, 1999. 125
10. R. Cleaveland, G. Lüttgen, V. Natarajan, and S. Sims. Priorities for Modeling and Verifying Distributed Systems. In *TACAS'96*, LNCS 1055, pp. 278-297. 125
11. T. A. Henzinger, X. Nicollin, J. Sifakis, and S. Yovine. Symbolic model checking for real-time systems. Proc. *7th Symp. on Logics in Computer Science (LICS'92)* and *Information and Computation* 111(2):193–244, 1994.
12. C. A. R. Hoare. Communicating Sequential Processes. Prentice Hall, 1985. 120
13. M. V. Iordache, J. O. Moody, and P. J. Antsaklis. A Method for Deadlock Prevention in Discrete Event Systems Using Petri Nets. Technical Report, University of Notre Dame, July 1999. 125
14. H. Kwak, I. Lee, A. Philippou, J. Choi, and O. Sokolsky. Symbolic schedulability analysis of real-time systems. In IEEE *RTSS'98*, Madrid, Spain, December 1998. 125
15. R. Milner. Communication and Concurrency. Prentice Hall, 1989. 120
16. S. Tripakis. Verifying Progress in Timed Systems. In *ARTS'99*, Bamberg, Germany, 1999 (to appear in LNCS series). 114, 125

On Memory-Block Traversal Problems
in Model-Checking Timed Systems

Fredrik Larsson[1], Paul Pettersson[2], and Wang Yi[1]

[1] Department of Computer Systems, Uppsala University, Sweden
{fredrikl,yi}@docs.uu.se
[2] BRICS*, Department of Computer Science, Aalborg University, Denmark
paupet@cs.auc.dk

Abstract. A major problem in model-checking timed systems is the huge memory requirement. In this paper, we study the memory-block traversal problems of using standard operating systems in exploring the state-space of timed automata. We report a case study which demonstrates that deallocating memory blocks (i.e. memory-block traversal) using standard memory management routines is extremely time-consuming. The phenomenon is demonstrated in a number of experiments by installing the UPPAAL tool on Windows95, SunOS 5 and Linux. It seems that the problem should be solved by implementing a memory manager for the model-checker, which is a troublesome task as it is involved in the underlining hardware and operating system. We present an alternative technique that allows the model-checker to control the memory-block traversal strategies of the operating systems without implementing an independent memory manager. The technique is implemented in the UPPAAL model-checker. Our experiments demonstrate that it results in significant improvement on the performance of UPPAAL. For example, it reduces the memory deallocation time in checking a start-up synchronisation protocol on Linux from 7 days to about 1 hour. We show that the technique can also be applied in speeding up re-traversals of explored state-space.

1 Introduction

During the past few years, a number of verification tools have been developed for real-time systems in the framework of timed automata (e.g. KRONOS and UPPAAL [HH95,DOTY95,LPY97,BLL+98]). One of the major problems in applying these tools to industrial-size systems is the huge memory-usage (e.g. [BGK+96]) for the exploration of the state-space of a network (or product) of timed automata. The main reason is that the model-checkers must store a large number of symbolic states each of which contains information not only on the control structure of the automata but also the clock values specified by clock constraints. To reduce memory usage, the model-checker must throw away parts of

---

* Basic Research In Computer Science, Centre of the Danish National Research Foundation.

S. Graf and M. Schwartzbach (Eds.): TACAS/ETAPS 2000, LNCS 1785, pp. 127–141, 2000.
© Springer-Verlag Berlin Heidelberg 2000

the state-space explored (resulting in memory deallocation), that are not needed for further analysis or re-traverse parts of the state-space explored and stored in (virtual) memory blocks to check a new property. In both cases, the underling operating system must traverse the memory blocks storing the state-space explored.

Unfortunately, using the standard memory management service for memory-block traversals e.g. memory deallocation is surprisingly time-consuming in particular when swapping is involved during state-space exploration. A problem we discovered in a very recent case study when UPPAAL was applied to check two correctness properties of the start-up algorithm for a time division multiple access protocol [LP97]. The first property was verified using 5 hours of CPU time and 335MB of memory[1] but the memory deallocation process, after verifying the first property, did not terminate until 7 days!

The phenomenon described above is caused by the so-called *thrashing*, which occurs occasionally in common-purpose operating systems, but much more often in the context of state-space exploration due to the large memory consumption. Unfortunately, this is a phenomenon not only occurring on Linux, but most of the existing operating systems. The fact has been demonstrated by our experiments on UPPAAL installed on Linux, Windows 95 and SunOS 5. Furthermore, we notice that as UPPAAL is based on the so-called symbolic reachability analysis which is the basis for several other model-checkers e.g. KRONOS and HYTECH, this should be a common problem for verification tools in the domain of real-time systems.

More intuitively, the problem can be described as follows: When throwing away parts of the state-space, the states are deallocated one by one. Note that the size of a state could be a number of bytes. To deallocate the amount of memory for a particular state, the memory page containing that state must be in the main memory. When swapping is involved, this means that the particular page must be loaded from disc. If the next state we want to throw away is in another page, and memory is almost full, the newly loaded page must be swapped out, even if it needs to be swapped in later when another state shall be removed. If the deallocation order is independent of how the allocated states are mapped to memory, unnecessary swapping will occur. Therefore, it is crucial to store information on the allocation order of memory blocks, but this will introduce extra overhead for the model-checker. It is not obvious how much information that should be collected during the verification process and used later for deallocating. The more information collected, the more overhead in the verification but the better the deallocation performance obtained. We need to find the best trade-off.

As our first experiment, we have simulated the allocation order of memory blocks in UPPAAL and experimented with three different deallocation orders. The first

---

[1] The experiment was performed on a 200 MHz Pentium Pro equipped with 256MB of primary memory running Red Hat Linux 5.

simply traverses the allocated structure without taking into account how blocks were allocated. This was the one used in UPPAAL when the start-up protocol was verified. The second strategy deallocates memory blocks in the same order as they were allocated. The third one deallocates them in the reverse allocation order. According to our experiments, the last strategy is clearly the best choice, which has been implemented in UPPAAL. It results in significant performance improvements on UPPAAL. For example, it reduces the memory deallocation time on Linux from 7 days to about 1 hour for the start-up protocol. The technique is also implemented to speed up re-traversing of the explored state-space to check new properties when the model-checker is used in an interactive manner. Our experiments demonstrate similar performance improvement.

The rest of the paper is organised as follows: In Section 2, we briefly introduce the notion of timed automata and symbolic reachability analysis for networks of timed automata. In Section 3, we describe and study the memory deallocation problem in more details. Several experiments are presented to illustrate that it is a common phenomenon for all the common-purpose operation systems. In Section 4, we present a solution to the problem and experimental results showing that our solution does result in a significant performance improvement for the UPPAAL tool. Section 5 concludes the paper by summarising our contributions and future work.

2   Preliminaries

2.1   Timed Automata

Timed automata was first introduced in [AD90] and has since then established itself as a standard model for real–time systems. For the reader not familiar with the notion of timed automata we give a short informal description.

A timed automaton is a standard finite–state automaton extended with a finite collection C of real–valued clocks ranged over by x, y etc. A clock constraint is a conjunction of atomic constraints of the form: $x \sim n$ or $x - y \sim n$ for $x, y \in C$, $\sim \in \{\leq, <, \geq\}$ and n being a natural number. We shall use $\mathcal{B}(C)$ ranged over by g (and later by D) to stand for the set of clock constraints.

Definition 1. *A timed automaton A over clocks C is a tuple $\langle N, l_0, E, I \rangle$ where N is a finite set of nodes (control-nodes), l_0 is the initial node, $E \subseteq N \times \mathcal{B}(C) \times 2^C \times N$ corresponds to the set of edges, and finally, $I : N \to \mathcal{B}(C)$ assigns invariants to nodes. In the case, $\langle l, g, r, l' \rangle \in E$, we write $l \xrightarrow{g,r} l'$.*   □

Formally, we represent the values of clocks as functions (called clock assignments) from C to the non–negative reals $\mathbf{R}$. We denote by $\mathbf{R}^C$ the set of clock assignments for C. A semantical *state* of an automaton A is now a pair (l, u), where l is a node of A and u is a clock assignment for C, and the semantics of A is given by a transition system with the following two types of transitions (corresponding to delay–transitions and edge–transitions):

- $(l, u) \rightarrow (l, u + d)$ if $I(u)$ and $I(u + d)$
- $(l, u) \rightarrow (l', u')$ if there exist g and r such that $l \xrightarrow{g,r} l'$, $u \in g$ and $u' = [r \mapsto 0]u$

where for $d \in \mathbf{R}$, $u + d$ denotes the time assignment which maps each clock x in C to the value $u(x) + d$, and for $r \subseteq C$, $[r \mapsto 0]u$ denotes the assignment for C which maps each clock in r to the value 0 and agrees with u over $C \backslash r$. By $u \in g$ we denote that the clock assignment u satisfies the constraint g (in the obvious manner).

Clearly, the semantics of a timed automaton yields an infinite transition system, and is thus not an appropriate basis for decision algorithms. However, efficient algorithms may be obtained using a *symbolic* semantics based on *symbolic states* of the form (l, D), where $D \in \mathcal{B}(C)$ [HNSY94,YPD94]. The symbolic counterpart to the standard semantics is given by the following two (fairly obvious) types of symbolic transitions:

- $(l, D) \rightsquigarrow \left(l, (D \wedge I(l))^\uparrow \wedge I(l) \right)$
- $(l, D) \rightsquigarrow \left(l', r(g \wedge D) \right)$ if $l \xrightarrow{g,r} l'$

where $D^\uparrow = \{u + d \mid u \in D \wedge d \in \mathbf{R}\}$ and $r(D) = \{[r \to 0]u \mid u \in D\}$. It may be shown that $\mathcal{B}(C)$ (the set of constraint systems) is closed under these two operations ensuring that the semantics is well–defined. Moreover, the symbolic semantics corresponds closely to the standard semantics in the sense that, whenever $u \in D$ and $(l, D) \rightsquigarrow (l', D')$ then $(l, u) \rightarrow (l', u')$ for some $u' \in D'$.

It should be noticed that the symbolic semantics above is by no means finite because clock values are unbounded. However, the following reachability problem can be solved in terms of a finite symbolic semantics based on the so-called k-normalisation on clock constraints [Pet99,Rok93].

2.2   Reachability Analysis

Given an automaton with initial symbolic state (l_0, D_0), we say that a symbolic state (l, D) is reachable if $(l_0, D_0) \rightsquigarrow^* (l_n, D_n)$ and $D_n \wedge D \neq \emptyset$. The problem can be solved by a standard graph reachability algorithm; but termination may not be guaranteed because the number of clock constraints generated may be infinite. The standard solution to this problem is by introducing a k-normalised version of the infinite symbolic semantics. The idea is to utilise the maximal constants

```
PASSED:= {}
WAITING:= {(l_0, D_0)}
repeat
        begin
        get (l, D) from WAITING
        if (l, D) ⊨ φ then return "YES"
        else if D ⊄ D' for all (l, D') ∈ PASSED then
                begin
                add (l, D) to PASSED
                SUCC:={(l_s, D_s) : (l, D) ⤳_k (l_s, D_s) ∧ D_s ≠ ∅}
                for all (l_{s'}, D_{s'}) in SUCC do
                        put (l_{s'}, D_{s'}) to WAITING
                end
        end
until WAITING={}
return "NO"
```

Fig. 1. An Algorithm for Symbolic Reachability Analysis

appearing in the clock constraints of the automaton under analysis and D of the final symbolic state to develop a finite symbolic transition system. For details we refer the reader to [Pet99]. The main fact about the k-normalisation is as follows:

Assume that k is the maximal constant appearing in an automaton A with initial state (l_0, D_0). Then (l, D) is reachable from (l_0, D_0) iff there exists a sequence of k-normalised transitions: $(l_0, D'_0) \leadsto_k (L_1, D'_1)...(l_{n-1}, D'_{n-1}) \leadsto_k (l_n, D'_n)$ such that $D \wedge D'_n \neq \emptyset$ where D'_i is the so-called normalised constraints with all constants being less than k.

Figure 1 shows the pseudo-code of a reachability algorithm to check if the automaton satisfies a given reachability formula e.g. a final symbolic state of the form (l, D)[2]. It is basically a standard graph-searching algorithm. The algorithm use two important data structures: WAITING and PASSED. WAITING contains the state-space awaiting to be explored. If this data structure is a queue the search order is breath-first; if it is organised as a stack, the search becomes depth-first. At start, the initial state is placed in the WAITING structure. PASSED contains the parts of the state-space explored so far. It is implemented as a hash table so that it can be searched and updated efficiently. Initially, it is empty. Due to the size of state-space, these structures may consume a huge amount of main memory.

---

[2] We define that $(l', D') \models (l, D)$ if $l' = l$ and $D' \wedge D \neq \emptyset$.

Table 1. Memory Deallocation Example

Memory	Disc	Operation
{s2,s4}	{s1,s3}	deallocReq(s1) SWAP
{s1,s3}	{s2,s4}	dealloc(s1)
{-,s3}	{s2,s4}	
{-,s3}	{s2,s4}	deallocReq(s2) SWAP
{s2,s4}	{-,s3}	dealloc(s2)
{-,s4}	{-,s3}	
{-,s4}	{-,s3}	deallocReq(s3) SWAP
{-,s3}	{-,s4}	dealloc(s3)
{-,-}	{-,s4}	
{-,-}	{-,s4}	deallocReq(s4) SWAP
{-,s4}	{-,-}	dealloc(s4)
{-,-}	{-,-}	

3   The Problem and Solutions

The algorithm (or its equivalent) presented in the previous section has been implemented in several verification tools e.g. UPPAAL for timed systems. Such tools are either used in an *interactive* manner, when the users interactively enters reachability properties given as symbolic states, or in a *non-interactive* manner, where the sequence of properties are known a priori.

When used interactively, the tool may in the worst case construct a huge date structure PASSED (storing the explored state-space) for each symbolic state when it contains a different maximal clock constant. Therefore, before each check, the model-checker must traverse and deallocate states (i.e. memory blocks) used for previous checks. Note that this is not the only reason why memory deallocation is required during the verification process. For example, for each separate reachability check, parts of the explored state-space may be thrown away when they are not needed for further analysis, which also requires memory deallocation. In the special case where the whole state-space must be deallocated, and this is known before the actual verification starts, it is possible to avoid traversing memory blocks by creating a separate process that does the verification. It is then possible to deallocate all states just by "killing" the dedicated process and have the operating system reclaiming all pages at once. However, this is not applicable when only parts of the state-space are deallocated.

When the tool is used non-interactively, the maximal constant of the whole sequence may be determined before the first property is checked, as all symbolic states to be checked are known. Thus, the PASSED structure does not have to be deallocated between two consecutive checks. In fact, the state-space generated in the previous checks is often reused to avoid unnecessary re-computation. A new check then amounts to determine if the symbolic state is already in the previously generated state-space and, if necessary, continue to generate new symbolic states. Note that, independent of how the tool is used, each check requires the previously generated state-space to be accessed, either during memory deallocation or when reusing the state-space[3]. Both cases result in memory-block traversals.

Surprisingly, the time spent on traversing states in PASSED consumes a very large part of the execution time. The reason is that standard operating-system services for memory management requires that the page containing the state to access resides in main memory. This is ensured by swapping out other memory pages to disc; pages that later may have to be swapped in again because they contain other states to access. It is clear that when swapping is involved, it is important how the memory is accessed, i.e. in what order the states are accessed. Ideally, we would like to localise memory accesses for states as much as possible.

To improve the presentation, the remainder of this section focuses on techniques for more efficient memory deallocation when swapping is involved. However, the presented techniques apply also to the case when a large portion of the memory is accessed, as when the state-space is reused when several properties are checked. We shall study the case of reuse further in the next section.

3.1   An Example

To illustrate the problem we study an example where memory is deallocated. We assume two memory pages, each containing two states. Initially one page is in main memory and one is in a part of the virtual memory currently on disc. Tables 2 and 3.1 show the page layout in main memory and on disc together with the operations an operating system may perform when the application requests deallocation of the states. The strategies illustrated is deallocation of the states when they are traversed in an order independent of memory layout and reverse allocation order respectively.

In Table 2 the allocation order is s1, s3, s2, s4 and the deallocation order is s1, s2, s3, s4. SWAP is a very expensive operation and the deallocation strategy in Table 2 requires four such operations in order to deallocate all states. In Table 3.1 the allocation order is the same as in Table 2 but the deallocation order is different; s4, s2, s3, s1 i.e. reverse allocation order. By using this deallocation strategy the number of SWAP operations can be reduced to one. The dealloc() can be performed immediately after the request in most cases.

---

[3] In the latter case the search may terminate before the whole state-space has been accessed.

Table 2. Memory Deallocation Example

Memory	Disc	Operation
{s2,s4}	{s1,s3}	deallocReq(s4)
{s2,s4}	{s1,s3}	dealloc(s4)
{s2,-}	{s1,s3}	
{s2,-}	{s1,s3}	deallocReq(s2)
{s2,-}	{s1,s3}	dealloc(s2)
{-,-}	{s1,s3}	
{-,-}	{s1,s3}	deallocReq(s3)
		SWAP
{s1,s3}	{-,-}	dealloc(s3)
{s1,-}	{-,-}	
{s1,-}	{-,-}	deallocReq(s1)
{s1,-}	{-,-}	dealloc(s1)
{-,-}	{-,-}	

Table 3. Deallocation time (in seconds) for hashtable order

Blocks	Linux	Solaris	Windows
32 768	169	845	469
65 536	387	1 795	1 038
131 072	1 029	4 272	2 487
262 144	2 709	9 779	6 250
524 288	7 691	25 193	12 288
1 048 576	27 790	22 082	43 227

3.2 Deallocation Strategies

A common way to represent state-spaces is to use data structures based on hash tables for efficient analysis. A convenient way to deallocate such data structures is to go through the table in consecutive hash value order and deallocate the symbolic states one by one. This is not by far the most efficient strategy even if it is convenient to implement. Table 3.1 shows deallocation times when blocks are deallocated in a hash-value order, an order totally ignoring how blocks are layed-out on pages and whether requested pages are on disc or in main memory. To further emphasise the fact that deallocation order affects the amount of swapping see example 3.1. The example in Table 2 and Table 3.1 illustrates the operations involved when deallocating memory according to two different strategies.

A much better strategy would be to first deallocate blocks on pages already in main memory and when a page is swapped in from disc deallocate all blocks on that page before swapping it out. This strategy would suit most common memory-management strategies used in operating systems. However this type of

Table 4. Deallocation time (in seconds) for allocation order

Blocks	Linux	Solaris	Windows
32 768	122	124	179
65 536	124	125	193
131 072	127	135	200
262 144	128	151	240
524 288	145	198	198
1 048 576	176	242	300

low-level information is generally not available to an application program like the UPPAAL model-checker. Most standard programming languages and portable operating system libraries only allow the application programs to request deallocation of a previously allocated block. It is up to the application program to perform the requests in a suitable order. Information that an application program may maintain is in what order memory blocks have been allocated.

It is also possible to collect information on how often a memory block is accessed. While this may give some hints on whether a block resides on a page in main memory or on a page on disc, it is not enough to decide what blocks reside on the same page thus leading to the same bad performance with heavy swapping.

To test if a successful deallocation strategy could be based only on information about allocation order, we had an experiment in which 32MB of memory were allocated in a number of equally sized blocks on three machines with 32MB of physical memory running the operating systems Linux, SunOS 5 and Windows 95. The blocks were placed randomly in a hash table with place for each allocated block. The blocks were then deallocated according to three different strategies: We call the first one hash table order. It is used to illustrate a commonly used order, easy to implement but independent of memory layout. The second is deallocation in the same order as allocation. The third order is deallocation in reverse allocation order.

Table 3.1, 3.2 and 4 show the deallocation times for the three chosen strategies implemented on the three operating systems: Linux, SunOS 5 and Windows 95. The experimental results clearly indicate that memory deallocation time really matters when swapping is involved. Both strategies that utilise the information about allocation order are superior to the first one i.e. the table order [4]. Note that the strategy using reverse allocation order demonstrates the best performance on all three operating systems. The reason may be that newly allocated blocks are used more recently and hence are more likely to reside in main memory.

---

[4] Note that this may be the most common strategy adopted by the existing verification tools e.g. UPPAAL.

Table 5. Deallocation time (in seconds) for reverse allocation order

Blocks	Linux	Solaris	Windows
32 768	26	74	33
65 536	18	110	13
131 072	21	119	19
262 144	31	130	38
524 288	44	153	44
1 048 576	77	204	99

4   Implementation and Performance

The experimental results presented in the previous section indicate that the deallocation strategy currently implemented in UPPAAL, which corresponds to hash table order, should be modified to optimise the time-performance. Note that the problem we want to solve here is how to find a suitable traversal strategy that for example let us control memory deallocation efficiently, by localising memory accesses as much as possible, without writing our own memory manager. Thus, the question is how to keep track of the allocation order of memory blocks without getting involved in low-level operations. Certainly, it is not a good idea to keep track of the allocation order of all memory blocks, as this might be as hard as writing a completely new memory manager.

Our solution is based on the observation that memory deallocation is mainly performed in two different situations: between consecutive reachability checks performed on the same system description, and just before the program terminates. In these situations deallocating memory corresponds to throwing away parts of the symbolic state-space that are not needed for the next reachability check. Thus, to utilise the presented deallocation strategies we need to keep track of the allocation order of the symbolic states. This is realised by extending every symbolic state with two pointers that are used to store the symbolic states in a doubly-linked list, sorted in allocation order. The list structure is easy to maintain and allows the symbolic state-space to be traversed in allocation order and reverse allocation order, as required by the presented memory deallocation strategies, in linear time. It also enables deallocation of symbolic states close to each other in memory to occur close in time while a page is in main memory, i.e. to keep the deallocation as local as possible.

In fact, the solution is an approximation to the exact allocation order for the symbolic states. This is because some operations performed by the reachability algorithm change parts of a symbolic state and it cannot be guaranteed that all data belonging to a given symbolic state is allocated consecutively. Further, all data for a state may not fit together on a single page. These facts make the assumption that states allocated consecutively will have all its data collected on the same page weaker.

4.1 Performance of Deallocation Strategies

The presented deallocation strategies have been implemented and integrated in a new version of UPPAAL. In this section we present the results of an experiment where the new UPPAAL version was installed on Linux, Windows 95 and SunOS 5, and applied to verify three examples from the literature:

Bang and Olufsen Audio/Video Protocol (B&O) This example is a protocol developed by Bang and Olufsen that is highly dependent on real-time [HSLL97]. It is used in their audio and video equipments to exchange control information between components communicating on a single bus. In the experiment we have verified the correctness criteria of the protocol. For details we refer to section 5.1 of [HSLL97].
   The verification was performed using UPPAAL installed on a Pentium 75MHz PC machine equipped with 8MB of physical memory running Linux.

Dacapo start-up Algorithm (Dacapo) The Dacapo protocol is a time division multiple access (TDMA) based bus protocol [LP97]. It is intended for physically small safety-critical distributed real-time systems limited to tens of meters and less than 40 nodes, e.g. operating in modern vehicles. In the experiment we verify that the start-up algorithm of the protocol is correct in the sense that the protocol becomes operational within a certain time bound. To vary the amount of needed memory in the verifications it is possible to adjust the number of communicating nodes of the protocol.
   Four versions of the protocol were verified on four machines: the Pentium 75MHz described above, a Pentium MMX 150MHz with 32MB of physical memory running both Linux and Windows 95, a Pentium Pro 200MHz equipped with 256MB of memory running Linux, and a Sun SPARC Station 4 with 32MB of memory running SunOS 5.

Fischer's Mutual Exclusion Protocol (Fischer) This is the well-known Fischer's protocol previously studied in many experiments, e.g. [AL92,KLL+97]. It is to guarantee mutual exclusion among several processes competing for a critical section. In the experiment we verify that the protocol satisfies the mutual exclusion property, i.e. that there is never more than one process in the critical section. Two versions of the protocol were verified using UPPAAL installed on the Pentium 75MHz PC.

Table 4.1 presents the memory usage together with the verification time (check) and the time needed to deallocate the required memory (dealloc) in seconds. Each example is verified with UPPAAL versions deallocating memory using the original strategy, i.e. the hash table order, and the two new strategies, namely allocation order and reverse allocation order.

As shown in Table 4.1, memory deallocation in reverse allocation order outperforms both hash table order and allocation order in the tested examples. In UPPAAL, the reverse allocation order saves 82% to 99% of the deallocation time compared with the originally used hash table order. It can also be observed that

Table 6. Deallocation times (in seconds)

Memmory Usage		Machine		Hash table		Allocation		Reverse	
Example	MB	OS	MB	check	dealloc	check	dealloc	check	dealloc
B&O	13	Linux	8	1 400	31 978	1486	1127	1497	1067
Fischer	8	Linux	8	126	1 118	132	207	133	197
	9	Linux	8	135	1 995	138	290	143	245
Dacapo	16	Linux	8	4 654	37 363	5 031	8 095	5 046	1 999
	38	Linux	32	621	6 013	689	812	690	597
	38	Solaris	32	3 406	3 780	3 740	304	3 704	279
	38	Windows	32	754	11 850	797	1035	823	995
	56	Linux	32	4 413	164 328	4 743	2 781	4 819	2 647
	56	Solaris	32	8 764	5 969	10 271	384	10 333	375
	336	Linux	256	21 189	602 354	24 741	6 754	23 390	5 307

the overhead during verification associated with keeping track of the allocation order is relatively small, which varies between 6% and 19% in the experiment. Moreover, the space overhead, which is not shown in the table, is insignificant.

4.2   Performance of State-Space Traversals

Table 7. Verification times (in seconds)

Memmory Usage		Hash table		Allocation		Reverse	
Example	MB	check	re-use	check	re-use	check	re-use
Dacapo	42	652	1 169	772	106	781	107
Fischer	43	532	498	540	94	546	99

In section 3 it was mentioned that properties were often verified interactively, and that changes in the maximal constants may require deallocation of the whole state-space before verification of a new property. If the properties are known a priori the maximal constant for all properties can be determined thus eliminating the need to destroy the PASSED and WAITING structures for that reason. Another advantage with such an approach is that we can search through the state-space generated so far and check if their already exist states satisfying our reachability property and only generate successors of states on WAITING if no states exist in PASSED.

This approach would obviously increase the memory consumption and increase the possibility of swapping during traversal of the generated state-space since

PASSEDand WAITINGwill not be deallocated. In fact the same reasoning in finding a better deallocation order of states may be used here. Assume that we want to verify n reachability properties $p_1...p_n$. If we traverse the state-space in a manner that keeps accesses to states as local as possible we might reduce swapping and the verification time for properties p_2 to p_n.

Table 4.2 compares the verification times of traversing the state-space in the three different orders described earlier. All of them were implemented in UP-PAAL and tested on a 150 MHz Pentium running Linux. To guarantee that the same number of symbolic states were search through by all the different strategies we only verify properties not satisfied by the system. In this way the whole generated state-space is traversed in all the three cases. As shown in Table 4.2, we obtain reductions in time-usage in traversing the state-space for up to 80%.

In order to perform experiments involving swapping we have to use examples that consume more physical memory than what is available on the given hardware architecture. Also, we are forced to use existing configurations of processors, amount of physical memory and the possibilities to install the different operating systems. It turned out that most of our case-studies did not meet the imposed requirements. They were either too small or too large. This explains the rich variation of used hardware architectures and why the same examples were verified multiple times. We still think that the results are significant since the behaviour of all three heuristics was consistent for all examples.

5   Conclusion and Future Work

We have studied memory-block traversal behaviour of verification tools for real time systems. We discovered that deallocating memory blocks during state-space exploration using standard memory management routines in the existing operating systems is extremely time-consuming when swapping is involved. This common phenomenon is demonstrated by experiments on three common-purpose operating systems, Windows 95, SunOS 5 and Linux. It seems that the problem should be solved by implementing a memory manager for the model-checker. However this may be a troublesome task as it is involved in internal details of the underlining operating system.

As the second contribution of this paper, we present a technique that allows the model-checker to control how the operating system deallocates memory blocks without implementing an independent memory manager. The technique is implemented in the UPPAAL model-checker. Our experiments show that it results in significant improvements of the performance of UPPAAL. For example, it reduces the memory deallocation time on Linux from 7 days to about 1 hour for a start-up synchronisation protocol published in the literature. The proposed solution introduces very little overhead during the reachability analysis, and it guarantees that examples not involving swapping still perform well. The technique has been applied to speed up re-traversals (i.e. re-use) of the explored state-space in reachability analysis for timed automata when checking a sequence of properties with the same maximal clock constant.

We should point out that even though most of the experiments presented here focus on memory-block deallocation in model-checking timed systems, our results are applicable to any problem involving traversals of large amounts of memmory in model-checking not only for timed systems, but concurrent systems in general. For other work in the context of memory management for automated verification, see [Boe93,Wil92,SD98]. As future work, we plan to develop a special-purpose memory manager for verification tools, that keeps total control over the allocation order and memory layout.

References

AD90.   Rajeev Alur and David Dill. Automata for Modelling Real-Time Systems. In *Proc. of Int. Colloquium on Algorithms, Languages and Programming*, number 443 in Lecture Notes in Computer Science, pages 322–335, July 1990. 129

AL92.   Martin Abadi and Leslie Lamport. An Old-Fashioned Recipe for Real Time. In *Proc. of REX Workshop "Real-Time: Theory in Practice"*, number 600 in Lecture Notes in Computer Science, 1992. 137

BGK+96. Johan Bengtsson, W.O. David Griffioen, Kåre J. Kristoffersen, Kim G. Larsen, Fredrik Larsson, Paul Pettersson, and Wang Yi. Verification of an Audio Protocol with Bus Collision Using UPPAAL. In Rajeev Alur and Thomas A. Henzinger, editors, *Proc. of the 8th Int. Conf. on Computer Aided Verification*, number 1102 in Lecture Notes in Computer Science, pages 244–256. Springer–Verlag, July 1996. 127

BLL+98.   Johan Bengtsson, Kim G. Larsen, Fredrik Larsson, Paul Pettersson, Wang Yi, and Carsten Weise. New Generation of UPPAAL. In *Int. Workshop on Software Tools for Technology Transfer*, June 1998. 127

Boe93.   Hans-J. Boehm. Space Efficient Conservative Garbage Collection. In *Proc. of the ACM SIGPLAN '91 Conference on Programming Language Design and Implementation*, pages 197–206, 1993. 140

DOTY95. C. Daws, A. Olivero, S. Tripakis, and S. Yovine. The tool KRONOS. In Rajeev Alur, Thomas A. Henzinger, and Eduardo D. Sontag, editors, *Proc. of Workshop on Verification and Control of Hybrid Systems III*, number 1066 in Lecture Notes in Computer Science, pages 208–219. Springer–Verlag, October 1995. 127

HH95.   Thomas A. Henzinger and Pei-Hsin Ho. HyTech: The Cornell HYbrid TECHnology Tool. In *Proc. of TACAS, Workshop on Tools and Algorithms for the Construction and Analysis of Systems*, 1995. BRICS report series NS–95–2. 127

HNSY94. Thomas. A. Henzinger, Xavier Nicollin, Joseph Sifakis, and Sergio Yovine. Symbolic Model Checking for Real-Time Systems. *Information and Computation*, 111(2):193–244, 1994. 130

HSLL97.   Klaus Havelund, Arne Skou, Kim G. Larsen, and Kristian Lund. Formal Modeling and Analysis of an Audio/Video Protocol: An Industrial Case Study Using UPPAAL. In *Proc. of the 18th IEEE Real-Time Systems Symposium*. IEEE Computer Society Press, December 1997. 137

KLL+97.   Kåre J. Kristoffersen, Francois Laroussinie, Kim G. Larsen, Paul Pettersson, and Wang Yi. A Compositional Proof of a Real-Time Mutual Exclusion Protocol. In *Proc. of the 7th Int. Joint Conf. on the Theory and Practice of Software Development*, April 1997. 137

LP97.   Henrik Lönn and Paul Pettersson. Formal Verification of a TDMA Protocol Startup Mechanism. In *Proc. of the Pacific Rim Int. Symp. on Fault-Tolerant Systems*, pages 235–242, December 1997. 128, 137

LPY97.   Kim G. Larsen, Paul Pettersson, and Wang Yi. UPPAAL in a Nutshell. *Int. Journal on Software Tools for Technology Transfer*, 1(1–2):134–152, October 1997. 127

Pet99.   Paul Pettersson. *Modelling and Analysis of Real-Time Systems Using Timed Automata: Theory and Practice*. PhD thesis, Department of Computer Systems, Uppsala University, February 1999. 130, 131

Rok93.   Tomas Gerhard Rokicki. *Representing and Modeling Digital Circuits*. PhD thesis, Stanford University, 1993. 130

SD98.   Ulrich Stern and David L. Dill. Using Magnetic Disk instead of Main Memory in the Murphi Verifier. In *Proc. of the 10th Int. Conf. on Computer Aided Verification*, Lecture Notes in Computer Science. Springer–Verlag, June 1998. 140

Wil92.   Paul R. Wilson. Uniprocessor Garbage Collection Techniques. In *Proc. of the International Workshop on Memory Management*, number 637 in LNCS. Springer–Verlag, 1992. 140

YPD94.   Wang Yi, Paul Pettersson, and Mats Daniels. Automatic Verification of Real-Time Communicating Systems By Constraint-Solving. In Dieter Hogrefe and Stefan Leue, editors, *Proc. of the 7th Int. Conf. on Formal Description Techniques*, pages 223–238. North–Holland, 1994. 130

Symbolic Model Checking for Rectangular Hybrid Systems*

Thomas A. Henzinger and Rupak Majumdar

Department of Electrical Engineering and Computer Sciences
University of California at Berkeley, CA 94720
{tah,rupak}@eecs.berkeley.edu

Abstract. An important case of hybrid systems are the rectangular automata. First, rectangular dynamics can naturally and arbitrarily closely approximate more general, nonlinear dynamics. Second, rectangular automata are the most general type of hybrid systems for which model checking –in particular, LTL model checking– is decidable. However, on one hand, the original proofs of decidability did not suggest practical algorithms and, on the other hand, practical symbolic model-checking procedures –such as those implemented in HYTECH– were not known to terminate on rectangular automata. We remedy this unsatisfactory situation: we present a symbolic method for LTL model checking which can be performed by HYTECH and is guaranteed to terminate on all rectangular automata. We do so by proving that our method for symbolic LTL model checking terminates on an infinite-state transition system if the trace-equivalence relation of the system has finite index, which is the case for all rectangular automata.

1 Introduction

The *hybrid automaton* [1] is a mathematical model for dynamical systems with mixed discrete-continuous dynamics. Model checking has been successfully applied to hybrid automaton specifications in automotive [30,32], aerospace [28,29], consumer electronics [26], plant control [25], and robotics [11] applications.

The maximal class of hybrid automata with a decidable model-checking problem is the class of *rectangular automata*[1]: in [22] it is shown that linear temporal logic (LTL) requirements can be checked for rectangular automata, while various minor generalizations of rectangular automata have formally undecidable reachability problems. The rectangular-automaton case is of practical significance, as hybrid systems with very general dynamics can be locally approximated arbitrarily closely using rectangular dynamics [20], which has the form $\dot{x} \in \prod_{i=0}^{n} [a_i, b_i]$,

---

* This research was supported in part by the DARPA (NASA) grant NAG2-1214, the DARPA (Wright-Patterson AFB) grant F33615-C-98-3614, the MARCO grant 98-DT-660, the ARO MURI grant DAAH-04-96-1-0341, and the NSF CAREER award CCR-9501708.

[1] In this paper, we refer as "rectangular automata" to the *initialized* rectangular automata of [22].

S. Graf and M. Schwartzbach (Eds.): TACAS/ETAPS 2000, LNCS 1785, pp. 142–156, 2000.
© Springer-Verlag Berlin Heidelberg 2000

constraining the time derivative $\dot{x}$ of a state in $\mathbb{R}^n$ to the n-dimensional rectangle $\prod_{i=0}^n [a_i, b_i]$ with rational corner points. The decidability proof of [22], however, does not yield a practical LTL model-checking algorithm (and has never been implemented), because it involves a reduction from a rectangular automaton of dimension n to a timed automaton of dimension $2n$, and dimension (i.e., number of clocks) is the most common bottleneck in timed analysis [13].

For practical applications, the tool HYTECH [19] can be used for checking LTL requirements of rectangular automata. Instead of translating a given rectangular automaton H into a timed automaton, HYTECH performs a symbolic computation directly on the n-dimensional state space of H. However, the symbolic procedures employed by HYTECH may not terminate, and thus do not qualify as decision procedures. In this paper, we resolve the gap between theory ([22]) and practice (HYTECH) by showing how given a rectangular automaton H and an LTL formula φ, we can run a symbolic procedure on the state space of H (using the primitives of HYTECH) which is guaranteed to terminate and, upon termination, returns the states of H that satisfy φ. We thus obtain a *symbolic* (rather than reductive) model-checking *algorithm* (rather than semi-algorithm) for LTL requirements of rectangular automata.

We obtain our result by first studying symbolic procedures for LTL model checking in a very general setting (Section 2, 3 and 4), namely, for arbitrary (infinite-state) transition systems with a computable *Pre* operator, which given a set of states, returns the set of predecessor states. We identify a symbolic LTL model-checking procedure based on the *Pre* operator, and a structural (syntax-independent) condition for transition systems (finite trace equivalence) which guarantees termination of the procedure. Since trace equivalence has finite index for all rectangular automata [22], we conclude that symbolic LTL model-checking terminates for rectangular automata. We illustrate our algorithm as applied to a rectangular automaton specifying a physical scheduling problem (Section 5).

Our symbolic LTL model-checking procedure executes a μ-calculus expression which is obtained from a given LTL formula. It is well-known that LTL can be translated into the μ-calculus [6,12,16], and it has been observed that the resulting μ-calculus expressions have a special form [15]: each conjunction has at least one argument which is atomic and constant (i.e., contains no fixpoint operators or variables). This leads us to define the following procedure, called *observation refinement* ($\mathcal{A}_{OR}$): starting from a finite initial partition of the state space, iteratively compute new sets of states by applying either the *Pre* operator, or intersection with an initial set. We show that $\mathcal{A}_{OR}$ terminates on a transition system (i.e., finds only a *finite* number of sets) if and only if the system has a trace-equivalence relation of finite index. Moreover, $\mathcal{A}_{OR}$ termination is a sufficient condition for termination of the μ-calculus based symbolic model-checking algorithm for LTL. Finally, we show that the μ-calculus based algorithm is, in a strong sense, equivalent to the standard, product-automaton based algorithm for symbolic LTL model checking [9].

Thus, $\mathcal{A}_{OR}$ plays with respect to LTL a role that is similar to the role of partition refinement ($\mathcal{A}_{PR}$), which iterates *Pre*, (unrestricted) intersection, and set difference, with respect to branching-time logics: the termination of $\mathcal{A}_{PR}$ on a transition system guarantees that symbolic model checking for the full μ-calculus (or CTL, CTL*) also terminates. This is because $\mathcal{A}_{PR}$ computes the bisimilarity quotient [27]. While $\mathcal{A}_{PR}$ is known to terminate on timed automata [2], whose time-abstract bisimilarity quotients are finite, there are rectangular automata on which $\mathcal{A}_{PR}$ does not terminate [17]. However, since rectangular automata have finite trace-equivalence quotients, $\mathcal{A}_{OR}$ terminates on every rectangular automaton, thus enabling symbolic LTL model checking.

2 Symbolic Model Checking for Infinite-State Systems

2.1 Transition Structures

A *transition structure* $\mathcal{K} = (Q, \Pi, \langle\!\langle \cdot \rangle\!\rangle, \delta)$ consists of a (possibly infinite) set Q of states, a finite set Π of observables, an observation function $\langle\!\langle \cdot \rangle\!\rangle \colon Q \to 2^{\Pi}$ which maps each state to a set of observables, and a transition function $\delta \colon Q \to 2^{Q}$ which maps each state to a nonempty set of possible successor states. We say that an observable π *holds* at a state q if $\pi \in \langle\!\langle q \rangle\!\rangle$. A state q is a *successor* of a state p if $q \in \delta(p)$. A *source-q_0 run* of $\mathcal{K}$ is an infinite sequence $r = q_0 q_1 q_2 \ldots$ of states such that q_{i+1} is a successor of q_i for all $i \geq 0$. The run r induces a *trace*, denoted $\langle\!\langle r \rangle\!\rangle$, which is the infinite sequence $\langle\!\langle q_0 \rangle\!\rangle \langle\!\langle q_1 \rangle\!\rangle \langle\!\langle q_2 \rangle\!\rangle \ldots$ of observable sets. For a state $q \in Q$, the *outcome* L^q from q is the set of all runs of $\mathcal{K}$ with source q. For a set L of runs, we write $\langle\!\langle L \rangle\!\rangle$ for the set $\{\langle\!\langle r \rangle\!\rangle \mid r \in L\}$ of corresponding traces.

A binary relation $\preceq^l \subseteq Q \times Q$ is a *trace containment* if $p \preceq^l q$ implies $\langle\!\langle L^p \rangle\!\rangle \subseteq \langle\!\langle L^q \rangle\!\rangle$. Define $p \preceq^L q$ if there exists a trace containment $\preceq^l$ with $p \preceq^l q$. Define the *trace-equivalence* relation $\cong^L$ as $p \cong^L q$ if both $p \preceq^L q$ and $q \preceq^L p$. A binary relation $\preceq^s \subseteq Q \times Q$ is a *simulation* if $p \preceq^s q$ implies (1) $\langle\!\langle p \rangle\!\rangle = \langle\!\langle q \rangle\!\rangle$, and (2) for all states $p' \in \delta(p)$, there exists a state $q' \in \delta(q)$ such that $p' \preceq^s q'$. A binary relation $\cong^b$ on Q is a *bisimulation* if $\cong^b$ is a symmetric simulation. Define $p \cong^B q$ if there is a bisimulation $\cong^b$ with $p \cong^b q$. The equivalence relation $\cong^B$ is called *bisimilarity*.

The observables induce an equivalence relation $\cong^A$, called *atomic equivalence*, on the states Q, with $p \cong^A q$ iff $\langle\!\langle p \rangle\!\rangle = \langle\!\langle q \rangle\!\rangle$. The equivalence classes of $\cong^A$ are called *atomic regions*. Let A denote the set of atomic regions. For an equivalence $\cong$ on the states Q which refines $\cong^A$, define $\mathcal{K}/\!\cong = (Q/\!\cong, \Pi, \langle\!\langle \cdot \rangle\!\rangle_{\cong}, \delta_{\cong})$, the *quotient structure of $\mathcal{K}$ with respect to $\cong$*, as follows. The states in $Q/\!\cong$ are the equivalence classes of $\cong$. The observables are the same as those of $\mathcal{K}$. Define the observation function $\langle\!\langle \cdot \rangle\!\rangle_{\cong}$ as $\pi \in \langle\!\langle R \rangle\!\rangle_{\cong}$ if $\pi \in \langle\!\langle q \rangle\!\rangle$ for any/all states $q \in R$. Define the transition function $\delta_{\cong}$ as $R \in \delta_{\cong}(P)$ if there are a state $p \in P$ and a state $q \in R$ such that $q \in \delta(p)$.

2.2 Symbolic Semi-algorithms

Let $\mathcal{K}$ be a transition structure. A *region* is a (possibly infinite) set of states of $\mathcal{K}$. If the state space of $\mathcal{K}$ is infinite, any algorithm that traverses the state space must represent regions implicitly, as formulas in some constraint system. With a transition structure $\mathcal{K}$ we associate a *symbolic theory* [23], which consists of (1) a set Σ of *region representatives* containing finite representations of some regions of $\mathcal{K}$, and (2) an extension function $\ulcorner \cdot \urcorner : \Sigma \to 2^Q$ which maps each region representative to the region it represents, such that the following conditions are satisfied:

- For every atomic region $R \in A$, there is a region representative $\sigma_R \in \Sigma$ such that $\ulcorner \sigma_R \urcorner = R$. Let $\Sigma_A = \{\sigma_R \mid R \in A\}$ denote the set of region representatives for the atomic regions.
- For every region representative $\sigma \in \Sigma$, there is a region representative $Pre(\sigma) \in \Sigma$ such that $\ulcorner Pre(\sigma) \urcorner = \{q \in Q \mid \delta(q) \cap \ulcorner \sigma \urcorner \neq \emptyset\}$; furthermore, the function $Pre: \Sigma \to \Sigma$ can be computed algorithmically.
- For every pair of region representatives $\sigma, \tau \in \Sigma$, there are region representatives $And(\sigma, \tau), Diff(\sigma, \tau) \in \Sigma$ such that $\ulcorner And(\sigma, \tau) \urcorner = \ulcorner \sigma \urcorner \cap \ulcorner \tau \urcorner$ and $\ulcorner Diff(\sigma, \tau) \urcorner = \ulcorner \sigma \urcorner \setminus \ulcorner \tau \urcorner$; furthermore, the functions $And, Diff: \Sigma \times \Sigma \to \Sigma$ can be computed algorithmically.
- The emptiness of a region representative is decidable; that is, there is a computable function $Empty: \Sigma \to \mathbb{B}$ such that $Empty(\sigma)$ iff $\ulcorner \sigma \urcorner = \emptyset$.
- The membership problem for a state and a region representative is decidable; that is, given a state q and a region representative σ, it can be decided if $q \in \ulcorner \sigma \urcorner$.

A *symbolic semi-algorithm* takes as input the symbolic theory for a transition structure $\mathcal{K}$, and generates region representatives in Σ by applying the operations Pre, And, $Diff$, and $Empty$ to the atomic region representatives in Σ_A. The expression "semi-algorithm" indicates that, while each operation is computable, the iteration of operations may or may not terminate. Two examples of symbolic semi-algorithms are well-known. The first is *backward reachability*, denoted $\mathcal{A}_\diamond$. Given an atomic region representative $\alpha \in \Sigma_A$, the symbolic semi-algorithm $\mathcal{A}_\diamond$ starts from $\sigma_0 = \alpha$ and computes inductively the region representatives $\sigma_{i+1} = Pre(\sigma_i)$. The semi-algorithm terminates if there is a k such that $\bigcup_{0 \leq i \leq k+1} \ulcorner \sigma_i \urcorner \subseteq \bigcup_{0 \leq i \leq k} \ulcorner \sigma_i \urcorner$; that is, no new state is encountered. Termination can be detected using the operations $Diff$ and $Empty$ [23]. Upon termination, a state q can reach the atomic region $\ulcorner \alpha \urcorner$ iff $q \in \ulcorner \sigma_i \urcorner$ for some $1 \leq i \leq k$.

The second example is *partition refinement* [7,27], denoted $\mathcal{A}_{PR}$. The symbolic semi-algorithm $\mathcal{A}_{PR}$ starts from the finite set $\mathcal{S}_0 = \Sigma_A$ of atomic region representatives and computes inductively the finite sets

$$\mathcal{S}_{i+1} = \mathcal{S}_i \cup \{Pre(\sigma), And(\sigma, \tau), Diff(\sigma, \tau) \mid \sigma, \tau \in \mathcal{S}_i\}$$

of region representatives. The semi-algorithm terminates if there is a k such that $\{\ulcorner \sigma \urcorner \mid \sigma \in \mathcal{S}_{k+1}\} \subseteq \{\ulcorner \sigma \urcorner \mid \sigma \in \mathcal{S}_k\}$; that is, no new region is encountered. Termination can be detected using the operations $Diff$ and $Empty$: for each region representative $\sigma \in \mathcal{S}_{k+1}$ check that there is a region representative $\tau \in \mathcal{S}_k$ such that both $Empty(Diff(\sigma, \tau))$ and $Empty(Diff(\tau, \sigma))$. Upon termination, two states p and q are bisimilar iff for all region representatives $\sigma \in \mathcal{S}_k$, we have

$p \in \ulcorner \sigma \urcorner$ iff $q \in \ulcorner \sigma \urcorner$. Thus, the symbolic semi-algorithm $\mathcal{A}_{PR}$ terminates iff the bisimilarity relation $\cong^B$ has finite index [18], as is the case, for instance, for timed automata [2].

2.3 Symbolic Model Checking

A *state logic* $\mathcal{L}$ is a logic whose formulas are interpreted over the states of transition structures. For a formula φ of $\mathcal{L}$ and a transition structure $\mathcal{K}$, let $[\![\varphi]\!]_{\mathcal{K}}$ be the set of states of $\mathcal{K}$ that satisfy φ. The $\mathcal{L}$ *model-checking problem* asks, given an $\mathcal{L}$-formula φ, a transition structure $\mathcal{K}$, and a state q of $\mathcal{K}$, whether $q \in [\![\varphi]\!]_{\mathcal{K}}$. A logic $\mathcal{L}$ induces an equivalence relation $\cong^{\mathcal{L}}$ on states: for all states p and q of a transition structure $\mathcal{K}$, define $p \cong^{\mathcal{L}} q$ if for all $\mathcal{L}$-formulas φ, we have $p \in [\![\varphi]\!]_{\mathcal{K}}$ iff $q \in [\![\varphi]\!]_{\mathcal{K}}$. Thus, two states p and q of a transition structure $\mathcal{K}$ are equivalent with respect to $\cong^{\mathcal{L}}$ iff there is no formula in the logic $\mathcal{L}$ that can distinguish p from q. Two formulas φ and ψ of state logics are *equivalent* if $[\![\varphi]\!]_{\mathcal{K}} = [\![\psi]\!]_{\mathcal{K}}$ for all transition structures $\mathcal{K}$. The logic $\mathcal{L}_1$ is *as expressive as* the logic $\mathcal{L}_2$ if for every formula ψ of $\mathcal{L}_2$, there exists a formula φ of $\mathcal{L}_1$ equivalent to ψ. The logics $\mathcal{L}_1$ and $\mathcal{L}_2$ are *equally expressive* if $\mathcal{L}_1$ is as expressive as $\mathcal{L}_2$, and $\mathcal{L}_2$ is as expressive as $\mathcal{L}_1$.

A state logic $\mathcal{L}$ *admits abstraction* if for every equivalence relation $\cong$ that refines $\cong^{\mathcal{L}}$, for every $\mathcal{L}$-formula φ, and for every transition structure $\mathcal{K}$, the region $[\![\varphi]\!]_{\mathcal{K}}$ is $\bigcup [\![\varphi]\!]_{\mathcal{K}/\cong}$. If $\mathcal{L}$ admits abstraction, and $\cong$ refines $\cong^{\mathcal{L}}$, then $\cong$ is called an *abstract semantics* for $\mathcal{L}$; if $\mathcal{L}$ admits abstraction, then $\cong^{\mathcal{L}}$ is the *fully abstract* semantics for $\mathcal{L}$. Let $\mathcal{L}$ be a logic that admits abstraction, and let $\cong$ be an abstract semantics for $\mathcal{L}$. Then a state p of $\mathcal{K}$ satisfies an $\mathcal{L}$-formula φ iff the $\cong$-equivalence class containing p satisfies φ in the quotient structure $\mathcal{K}/\cong$. This means that instead of model checking the structure $\mathcal{K}$, we can model check the quotient structure $\mathcal{K}/\cong$. In case the equivalence relation $\cong$ has finite index, we can so reduce model-checking questions over an infinite-state structure to model-checking questions over a finite-state structure.

A simple state logic of interest is the logic EFL, which contains all formulas of the form $\exists \Diamond \varphi$, where φ is a boolean combination of observables. The formula $\exists \Diamond \varphi$ *holds* at a state q of a transition structure $\mathcal{K}$ if there exists a source-q run r of $\mathcal{K}$, and a state p in r, such that φ holds in p. A model-checking algorithm for the logic EFL is easily derived from the symbolic semi-algorithm $\mathcal{A}_{\Diamond}$ (backward reachability). In particular, if $\mathcal{A}_{\Diamond}$ terminates on every atomic region representative of $\mathcal{K}$, then EFL model checking can be decided over $\mathcal{K}$. The logic EFL can express reachability (or dually, safety) properties. To express more interesting properties, we define the μ-*calculus*, which can encode temporal logics such as LTL, CTL, and CTL* [14]. The formulas of the μ-calculus are given by the grammar

$$\varphi ::= \pi \mid \neg \pi \mid X \mid \varphi_1 \vee \varphi_2 \mid \varphi_1 \wedge \varphi_2 \mid \exists \bigcirc \varphi \mid \forall \bigcirc \varphi \mid \mu X. \varphi \mid \nu X. \varphi,$$

where π is an observable, X is a propositional variable, μ is the least-fixpoint operator, and ν is the greatest-fixpoint operator. We interpret closed formulas over states in the standard way [14]. For example, the EFL formula $\exists \Diamond \pi$ is equivalent to the μ-calculus formula $\mu X.(\pi \vee \exists \bigcirc X)$.

The μ-calculus admits abstraction, and bisimilarity $\cong^B$ is a fully abstract semantics for the μ-calculus. Thus, if an infinite-state transition structure $\mathcal{K}$ with a symbolic theory has a finite bisimilarity quotient $\mathcal{K}/\cong_B$, or equivalently, if the symbolic semi-algorithm $\mathcal{A}_{PR}$ (partition refinement) terminates on $\mathcal{K}$, then μ-calculus model checking can be decided over $\mathcal{K}$: first, use partition refinement to compute the finite-state structure $\mathcal{K}/\cong_B$; then, model check over $\mathcal{K}/\cong_B$. There is, however, also a more direct, more efficient way of μ-calculus model checking over infinite-state transition structures with symbolic theories: we can attempt to compute fixpoints by successive approximation [8], using the operations *Pre*, *And*, and *Diff* [18]. If the successive approximation of each fixpoint subformula of a μ-calculus formula φ terminates in a finite number of steps, then we arrive at the region $[\![\varphi]\!]_{\mathcal{K}}$ in a finite number of applications of *Pre*, *And*, and *Diff*. Clearly, a sufficient condition is the termination of $\mathcal{A}_{PR}$, which applies all possible combinations of the three operations. The symbolic semi-algorithm for μ-calculus model checking, which performs only the subset of operations of $\mathcal{A}_{PR}$ called for by the input formula, is denoted $\mathcal{A}_\mu$. For example, for the EFL formula $\exists \Diamond \pi$, the semi-algorithm $\mathcal{A}_\mu$ is identical to $\mathcal{A}_\Diamond$.

3   A Symbolic Characterization of Trace Equivalence

3.1   Observation Refinement

We define a symbolic semi-algorithm, called *observation refinement* and denoted $\mathcal{A}_{OR}$, which repeatedly applies the two operations *Pre* and intersection with atomic region representatives, until no new regions can be generated. The symbolic semi-algorithm $\mathcal{A}_{OR}$ starts from the finite set $\mathcal{S}_0 = \Sigma_A$ of atomic region representatives and computes inductively the finite sets

$$\mathcal{S}_{i+1} = \mathcal{S}_i \cup \{Pre(\sigma), And(\sigma, \tau) \mid \sigma \in \mathcal{S}_i \text{ and } \tau \in \Sigma_A\}$$

of region representatives. Note that only a restricted form of intersection (intersection with atomic regions) is allowed. The semi-algorithm terminates if there is a k such that $\{\lceil\sigma\rceil \mid \sigma \in \mathcal{S}_{k+1}\} \subseteq \{\lceil\sigma\rceil \mid \sigma \in \mathcal{S}_k\}$; this is checked as in the case of $\mathcal{A}_{PR}$ (partition refinement). Observation refinement will typically produce more region representatives than $\mathcal{A}_\Diamond$ (backward reachability), but fewer than $\mathcal{A}_{PR}$. In particular, there are infinite-state transition structures on which backward reachability terminates, but not observation refinement; and structures on which observation refinement terminates, but not partition refinement.

3.2   The Guarded Fragment of the μ-Calculus

For a logical characterization of the regions computed by observation refinement, we define $G\mu$, the *guarded fragment of the μ-calculus*, as the set of formulas given by the following rules:

1. All observables and propositional variables are formulas of $G\mu$.
2. If π is an observable, then $\neg\pi$ is a formula of $G\mu$.
3. If φ_1 and φ_2 are formulas of $G\mu$, then
   (a) $\varphi_1 \vee \varphi_2$, $\exists\bigcirc \varphi_1$, $\mu X. \varphi_1$, and $\nu X. \varphi_1$ are formulas of $G\mu$.
   (b) $\varphi_1 \wedge \varphi_2$ is a formula of $G\mu$ provided at least one of φ_1 and φ_2 is a boolean combination of observables.

This definition is similar to the definition of L_1 in [5,15].[2] Over finite-state transition structures, there is a fast, $O(mnk)$ model-checking algorithm for $G\mu$, where m is the size of the transition structure, n is the size of the formula, and k is the alternation depth of the formula [5].

Proposition 1. *The guarded fragment of the μ-calculus admits abstraction.*

The equivalence relation $\cong^{G\mu}$ induced by the guarded fragment of the μ-calculus is characterized operationally by observation refinement. By induction, each region computed in step i of the symbolic semi-algorithm $\mathcal{A}_{OR}$ is a block (i.e., a union of equivalence classes) of $\cong^{G\mu}$. Thus, if $\cong^{G\mu}$ has finite index, then $\mathcal{A}_{OR}$ terminates. Conversely, suppose that $\mathcal{A}_{OR}$ terminates with $\mathcal{S}_{k+1} = \mathcal{S}_k$. We can show that if two states are distinguished by a formula in $G\mu$, then there is a region constructed by $\mathcal{A}_{OR}$ that separates them. Define the state equivalence $\cong^{OR}$ as $p \cong^{OR} q$ iff for each region representative $\sigma \in \mathcal{S}_k$, we have $p \in \ulcorner\sigma\urcorner$ iff $q \in \ulcorner\sigma\urcorner$. It follows that $p \cong^{OR} q$ implies $p \cong^{G\mu} q$.

Proposition 2. *Observation refinement ($\mathcal{A}_{OR}$) terminates on the symbolic theory of a transition structure $\mathcal{K}$ iff the equivalence relation $\cong^{G\mu}$ induced by the guarded fragment of the μ-calculus on $\mathcal{K}$ has finite index.*

3.3 Expressiveness of the Guarded Fragment

We can alternatively characterize the expressiveness of $G\mu$ using a linear-time logic (without path quantifiers). A *Büchi automaton* $\mathcal{B}$ is a tuple $(S, \Phi, \rightarrow, s_0, F)$, where S is a finite set of states, Φ is a finite input alphabet, $\rightarrow \subseteq S \times \Phi \times S$ is the transition relation, $s_0 \in S$ is the start state, and $F \subseteq S$ is the set of Büchi accepting states. An *execution* of $\mathcal{B}$ on an ω-word $w = w_0w_1 \ldots \in \Phi^\omega$ is an infinite sequence $r = s_0s_1 \ldots$ of states in S, starting from the initial state s_0, such that $s_i \overset{w_i}{\rightarrow} s_{i+1}$ for all $i \geq 0$. The execution r is *accepting* if some state in F occurs infinitely often in r. The automaton $\mathcal{B}$ *accepts* the word w if it has an accepting execution on w. The *language* $L(\mathcal{B}) \subseteq \Phi^\omega$ is the set of ω-words accepted by $\mathcal{B}$.

Let EBL be the state logic whose formulas have the form $\exists\mathcal{B}$, where $\mathcal{B}$ is a Büchi automaton whose input alphabet are sets of observables; that is, $\Phi = 2^\Pi$.

---

[2] In [15], condition (2) of our definition is changed to "If φ is an L_1 formula that does not contain any variables, then $\neg\varphi$ is in L_1," and condition (3b) is changed to "If φ_1 and φ_2 are L_1 formulas such that at most one of them contains any variables, then $\varphi_1 \wedge \varphi_2$ is in L_1." It can be shown that L_1 and $G\mu$ are equally expressive.

The formula $[\![\exists\mathcal{B}]\!]_{\mathcal{K}}$ *holds* at a state q of a transition structure $\mathcal{K}$ if there exists a source-q run r of $\mathcal{K}$ such that $\langle\!\langle r \rangle\!\rangle \in L(\mathcal{B})$. The logic EBL admits abstraction, and trace equivalence is a fully abstract semantics for EBL. Now we show that EBL is as expressive as the guarded fragment of the μ-calculus. This result is implicit in a proof in [15], although it is never explicitly stated.

Lemma 1. *Given a* $\mathrm{G}\mu$ *formula* φ *(over the observables* Π*), we can construct a Büchi automaton* $\mathcal{B}_\varphi$ *(on the alphabet* 2^Π*) such that* $[\![\exists\mathcal{B}_\varphi]\!]_{\mathcal{K}} = [\![\varphi]\!]_{\mathcal{K}}$ *for all transition structures* $\mathcal{K}$*. Conversely, given an* EBL *formula* $\exists\mathcal{B}$ *(over the alphabet* 2^Π*), we can construct an* $\mathrm{G}\mu$ *formula* $\varphi_\mathcal{B}$ *(over the observables* Π*) so that* $[\![\varphi_\mathcal{B}]\!]_{\mathcal{K}} = [\![\exists\mathcal{B}]\!]_{\mathcal{K}}$ *for all transition structures* $\mathcal{K}$*.*

The proof of the first part of the lemma proceeds by induction on the structure of the $\mathrm{G}\mu$ formula. For the converse claim, let $\mathcal{B}$ be a Büchi automaton. We construct a guarded μ-calculus formula that is equivalent to the formula $\exists\mathcal{B}$. For notational convenience, we present the formula in equational form [10]; it can be easily converted to the standard representation by unrolling the equations, and binding variables with μ or ν-fixpoints. For each set $R \in 2^\Pi$, let ψ_R abbreviate the formula $\bigwedge R \wedge \bigwedge\{\neg\pi \mid \pi \in \Pi\setminus R\}$. For each state s of $\mathcal{B}$, we introduce a propositional variable X_s. The equation for X_s is

$$X_s =_\lambda \bigvee\{\psi_R \wedge \exists\bigcirc X_{s'} \mid s \xrightarrow{R} s'\},$$

where $\lambda = \nu$ if $s \in F$ is an accepting state, and $\lambda = \mu$ otherwise. The top-level variable is X_{s_0}, where s_0 is the initial state. The correctness of the procedure follows from [6]. An equivalent construction is given in [12].

Theorem 1. *The logics* $\mathrm{G}\mu$ *and* EBL *are equally expressive.*

From Proposition 2, and since the fully abstract semantics of EBL is trace equivalence, we conclude the following.

Corollary 1. *Observation refinement* $(\mathcal{A}_{OR})$ *terminates on the symbolic theory of a transition structure* $\mathcal{K}$ *iff the trace-equivalence relation* $\cong^L$ *of* $\mathcal{K}$ *has finite index.*

When the symbolic semi-algorithm $\mathcal{A}_\mu$ for μ-calculus model checking is applied to an input in guarded form, then it computes only regions also computed by observation refinement. It follows that symbolic model checking for the guarded fragment of the μ-calculus terminates on all transition structures with finite trace-equivalence quotients.

4   Symbolic LTL Model Checking

4.1   Mu-Calculus Based Symbolic Model Checking for LTL

The formulas of *linear temporal logic* (LTL) are generated inductively by the grammar

$$\varphi ::= \pi \mid \neg\varphi \mid \varphi_1 \vee \varphi_2 \mid \bigcirc\varphi \mid \varphi_1\mathcal{U}\varphi_2,$$

where π is an observable, $\bigcirc$ is the *next* operator, and $\mathcal{U}$ is the *until* operator. From these operators, additional operators such as $\Diamond\varphi \overset{\Delta}{=} (true\mathcal{U}\varphi)$ and $\Box\varphi \overset{\Delta}{=} \neg\Diamond\neg\varphi$ can be defined as usual. Formulas of LTL are interpreted over traces [14]. We extend the interpretation to states *existentially*: an LTL formula φ holds at a state q of a transition structure $\mathcal{K}$ if there is a source-q run r such that the trace $\langle\langle r \rangle\rangle$ satisfies the formula φ. The logic LTL admits abstraction, and trace equivalence is a fully abstract semantics for LTL. The expressiveness of LTL lies strictly between EBL and EFL. In particular, for every LTL formula φ, we can construct a Büchi automaton $\mathcal{B}_\varphi$ such that $[\![\varphi]\!]_\mathcal{K} = [\![\exists\mathcal{B}_\varphi]\!]_\mathcal{K}$ for all transition structures $\mathcal{K}$ [31]. We call $\mathcal{B}_\varphi$ the *tableau automaton* of φ.

This suggests the following symbolic semi-algorithm $\mathcal{A}^1_{\text{LTL}}$, the *$\mu$-calculus based algorithm for* LTL *model checking*: given an LTL formula φ, first construct the tableau automaton $\mathcal{B}_\varphi$, then convert $\exists\mathcal{B}_\varphi$ into the guarded fragment of the μ-calculus (using the procedure described above), and finally evaluate the resulting Gμ formula on the given transition structure (using $\mathcal{A}_\mu$). The final step requires only *Pre* operations and intersections with atomic regions.

Theorem 2. *For a transition structure $\mathcal{K}$ with a symbolic theory, and an* LTL *formula φ, the symbolic semi-algorithm $\mathcal{A}^1_{\text{LTL}}$ terminates and computes $[\![\varphi]\!]_\mathcal{K}$ if the trace-equivalence relation $\cong^L$ of $\mathcal{K}$ has finite index.*

4.2 Product-Automaton Based Symbolic Model Checking for LTL

Traditionally, a different method is used for symbolic model checking of LTL formulas [9]. Given a state q of a finite-state transition structure $\mathcal{K}$, and an LTL formula φ, the question if $q \in [\![\varphi]\!]_\mathcal{K}$ can be answered by constructing the product of $\mathcal{K}$ with the tableau automaton $\mathcal{B}_\varphi$, and then checking the nonemptiness of a Büchi condition on the product structure. A Büchi condition is an LTL formula of the form $\Box\Diamond\psi$, where ψ is a disjunction of observables; therefore nonemptiness can be checked symbolically by evaluating the equivalent formula

$$\chi = \nu X_1. \mu X_2. (\exists\bigcirc X_2 \vee (\psi \wedge \exists\bigcirc X_1))$$

of the guarded fragment of the μ-calculus.

To extend this method to infinite-state structures, we need to be more formal. Let $\mathcal{K} = (Q, \Pi, \langle\langle\cdot\rangle\rangle, \delta)$ be a transition structure and let $\mathcal{B}_\varphi = (S, 2^\Pi, \rightarrow, s_0, F)$ be a tableau automaton. The *product structure* $\mathcal{K}_\varphi = (S \times Q, S \times \Pi, \langle\langle\cdot\rangle\rangle_\varphi, \delta_\varphi)$ is defined as follows. Define $(s', \pi) \in \langle\langle s, q \rangle\rangle_\varphi$ iff $s' = s$ and $\pi \in \langle\langle q \rangle\rangle$; that is, the state of the tableau automaton is observable. Define $(s', q') \in \delta_\varphi(s, q)$ iff $s \overset{R}{\rightarrow} s'$ and $q' \in \delta(q)$ and $\langle\langle q \rangle\rangle = R$. Then $q \in [\![\varphi]\!]_\mathcal{K}$, for $q \in Q$, iff $(s_0, q) \in [\![\Box\Diamond\psi]\!]_{\mathcal{K}_\varphi}$, where $\psi = \bigvee_{s \in F, \pi \in \Pi}(s, \pi)$. To perform symbolic model checking on the product structure, we need to ensure that from a symbolic theory for $\mathcal{K}$ we can obtain a symbolic theory for $\mathcal{K}_\varphi$. Let $(\Sigma, \ulcorner\cdot\urcorner)$ be a symbolic theory for $\mathcal{K}$. We choose as region representatives for the product structure $\mathcal{K}_\varphi$ the pairs of the form (s, σ), where s is a state of $\mathcal{B}_\varphi$ and σ is a region representative for $\mathcal{K}$; that is, $\Sigma_\varphi = S \times \Sigma$. Define $\ulcorner s, \sigma \urcorner_\varphi = \{(s, q) \mid q \in \ulcorner\sigma\urcorner\}$. Since the tableau automaton

$\mathcal{B}_\varphi$ is finite, it is easy to check that $(\Sigma_\varphi, \ulcorner \cdot \urcorner_\varphi)$ is a symbolic theory for $\mathcal{K}_\varphi$. Let $\mathcal{A}^2_{\text{LTL}}$ be the *product-automaton based algorithm for* LTL *model checking* which, given an LTL formula φ and a transition structure $\mathcal{K}$, evaluates the $G\mu$ formula χ (representing a Büchi condition) on the product structure $\mathcal{K}_\varphi$ (using $\mathcal{A}_\mu$). It is not difficult to see that if observation refinement terminates on $\mathcal{K}$ in k steps, then it also terminates on $\mathcal{K}_\varphi$ in k steps (if $\mathcal{A}_{OR}$ generates m regions on $\mathcal{K}$, then it generates at most $m \cdot |S|$ regions on $\mathcal{K}_\varphi$).

Corollary 2. *For a transition structure $\mathcal{K}$ with a symbolic theory, and an* LTL *formula φ, the symbolic semi-algorithm $\mathcal{A}^2_{\text{LTL}}$ terminates and computes $[\![\varphi]\!]_\mathcal{K}$ if the trace-equivalence relation $\cong^L$ of $\mathcal{K}$ has finite index.*

Indeed, by induction on the construction of regions, one can show that for each region representative (s, σ) computed in the product-automaton based algorithm, the variable X_s in the μ-calculus based algorithm represents the region $\ulcorner \sigma \urcorner$ at some stage of the computation, and conversely, for each valuation R of the variable X_s in the μ-calculus based algorithm, a region representative of $\{s\} \times R$ is computed in the product-automaton based algorithm. Thus, the two methods are equivalent in the regions they generate.

5 Rectangular Hybrid Automata

5.1 Definitions

Let $\mathbb{R}^n$ be the n-dimensional Euclidean space. A *rectangle* $\mathfrak{r}$ *of dimension n* is a subset of $\mathbb{R}^n$ which is a cartesian product of (possibly unbounded) intervals, all of whose finite end-points are integral[3]. The projection of a rectangle $\mathfrak{r}$ on its ith coordinate is denoted $\mathfrak{r}_i$, so that $\mathfrak{r} = \prod_{i=1}^n \mathfrak{r}_i$. The set of all n-dimensional rectangles is denoted $\Re^n$.

An *n-dimensional rectangular automaton H* consists of a finite directed multi-graph (V, E), three vertex labeling functions *init*: $V \to \Re^n$, *inv*: $V \to \Re^n$, and *flow*: $V \to \Re^n$, and three edge labeling functions *pre*: $E \to \Re^n$, *post*: $E \to \Re^n$, and *jump*: $E \to 2^{\{1,\dots,n\}}$ [22]. The vertices $\ell \in V$ specify the discrete states of the automaton; the edges $e \in E$ specify the discrete transitions. The initialization function *init* specifies the possible initial states of the automaton. If the automaton starts in vertex ℓ, then its continuous state must be in *init*(ℓ). The invariant function *inv* and the flow function *flow* constrain the continuous time evolution of the automaton. In vertex ℓ, the continuous state nondeterministically follows a smooth trajectory within the invariant region *inv*(ℓ). At each point, the derivative of the trajectory must lie within the flow region *flow*(ℓ). The edges are constrained by the pre-guard function *pre*, the post-guard function *post*, and the jump function *jump*. The edge $e = (\ell, \ell')$ may be traversed when the current vertex is ℓ and the continuous state lies within *pre*(e). For each $i \in jump(e)$, the ith coordinate of the continuous state is nondeterministically assigned a new value in the postguard interval *post*$(e)_i$. For each coordinate $i \notin jump(e)$, the

---

[3] It is straightforward to permit intervals with rational end-points.

continuous state is not changed, and must lie within $post(e)_i$. We require that for every edge $e = (\ell, \ell')$, and every coordinate $i = 1, \ldots, n$, if $flow(\ell)_i \neq flow(\ell')_i$, then $i \in jump(e)$. This condition is called *initialization* in [22], and it is shown there that it is necessary for simple reachability questions to be decidable.

With a rectangular automaton H, we associate an infinite-state transition structure $\mathcal{K}_H = (Q, V, \langle\langle \cdot \rangle\rangle, \delta)$ as follows. The states in Q are pairs $(\ell, \mathbf{x})$ consisting of a discrete part $\ell \in V$ and a continuous part $\mathbf{x} \in \mathbb{R}^n$ such that $\mathbf{x} \in inv(v)$. The observables are the vertices, and $\langle\langle \ell, \mathbf{x} \rangle\rangle = \ell$. We have $(\ell', \mathbf{x}') \in \delta((\ell, \mathbf{x}))$ iff either (1) [time transition of duration t and slope $\mathbf{d}$] $\ell' = \ell$, and $\mathbf{x}' = \mathbf{x} + t \cdot \mathbf{d}$ for some real vector $\mathbf{d} \in flow(\ell)$ and some real $t \geq 0$ such that for all $0 \leq t' \leq t$, $(\mathbf{x} + t' \cdot \mathbf{d}) \in inv(\ell)$; or (2) [discrete transition along edge e] $e = (\ell, \ell') \in E$, and $(\ell, \mathbf{x}) \in pre(e)$, and $\mathbf{x}'_i \in post(e)_i$ for all $i \in jump(e)$, and $\mathbf{x}'_i = \mathbf{x}_i$ for all $i \notin jump(e)$. The runs and traces of H are inherited from the underlying transition structure $\mathcal{K}_H$.

A natural symbolic theory for the rectangular automaton H is the following. Regions are represented as sets $\Sigma = \{(\ell, f) \mid \ell \in V\}$ of pairs, where ℓ is a vertex and f is a quantifier-free formula in the theory of reals with addition, $Th(\mathbb{R}, 0, 1, +, \leq)$, over the n variables $x_1, \ldots, x_n$. The atomic sentences in this theory are the linear inequalities; thus the continuous part of a region is represented by a boolean combination of linear inequalities. The *Pre* operation can be described in the theory using quantifiers, and since the theory permits quantifier elimination, the quantifier-free formulas suffice as region representatives [4]. The emptiness and membership checks are also decidable. The tool HYTECH [19] implements symbolic semi-algorithms for analyzing rectangular (and more general hybrid) automata using this symbolic theory. In particular, the symbolic semi-algorithms $\mathcal{A}_{PR}$, $\mathcal{A}_{OR}$, and $\mathcal{A}_\mu$ are all readily programmable using the scripting facility of HYTECH.

The variable x_i of the rectangular automaton H is a *finite-slope variable* if for each vertex $\ell \in V$, the interval $flow(\ell)_i$ is a singleton. If $flow(\ell)_i = [1, 1]$ for all vertices ℓ, then x_i is called a *clock*. The rectangular automaton H has *deterministic jumps* if for each edge $e \in E$, and each coordinate $i \in jump(e)$, the interval $post(e)_i$ is a singleton. If H has deterministic jumps and $x_1, \ldots, x_n$ are all finite-slope variables, then H is a *singular automaton*. If H has deterministic jumps and $x_1, \ldots, x_n$ are all clocks, then H is called a *timed automaton* [2].

5.2   Symbolic Model Checking

It can be shown that the bisimilarity relation of the transition structure $\mathcal{K}_H$ has finite index for every singular automaton H [2,1]. This implies that we can check μ-calculus properties symbolically on timed and singular automata [24]. For rectangular automata, dimension 2 is enough to have bisimilarity degenerate into equality on states [17]. However, the results of [22] show that the trace-equivalence quotient of $\mathcal{K}_H$ is finite for every rectangular automaton H. From Corollary 1, we get the following result.

Theorem 3. *Observation refinement ($\mathcal{A}_{OR}$) terminates when applied to the symbolic theory of a rectangular automaton.*

Corollary 3. *Symbolic* Gμ *model checking,* μ-*calculus based symbolic* LTL *model checking, and product-automaton based symbolic* LTL *model checking all terminate for rectangular automata.*

In practice, we are interested in the *divergent runs* of a rectangular automaton, i.e., those runs on which time advances beyond any bound. Formally, a run $(\ell_0, \mathbf{x}_0)(\ell_1, \mathbf{x}_1)\dots$ of a rectangular automaton is *divergent* if the infinite sum

$$\sum\{t_i \mid i \geq 0 \text{ and } (\ell_{i+1}, \mathbf{x}_{i+1}) \in \delta(\ell_i, \mathbf{x}_i) \text{ is a time step of duration } t_i\}$$

diverges. To restrict our attention to divergent runs, we can modify an n-dimensional rectangular automaton H in a standard way [3]. We add an additional clock variable at coordinate $n+1$, so that the dimension becomes $n+1$. For each vertex $\ell \in V$, we introduce a new vertex ℓ_{tick} and two edges $e = (\ell, \ell_{tick})$ and $e' = (\ell_{tick}, \ell)$. Define $pre(e)_i = post(e) = pre(e')_i = post(e') = \mathbb{R}$ for $1 \leq i \leq n$; $pre(e)_{n+1} = post(e)_{n+1} = pre(e')_{n+1} = 1$, $jump(e)_{n+1} = \emptyset$, $jump(e') = \{n+1\}$, and $post(e')_{n+1} = 0$. This construction ensures that the added clock is reset to 0 every time its value reaches 1. Then, the divergent runs are those for which the formula $\psi = \bigvee_{\ell \in V} \ell_{tick}$ is true infinitely often. To check if an LTL formula φ holds on some divergent run of H, we instead check that the LTL formula $(\Box \Diamond \psi) \wedge \varphi$ holds on any run of the extended automaton.

In [22], the proof that the trace-equivalence relation has finite index for every rectangular automaton H proceeds in two steps. First, the authors construct a singular automaton H' which forward simulates H, and is backward simulated by H. This implies that the trace-equivalence quotient for *finite* traces has finite index. In a second, involved step, they prove that a finite trace-equivalence quotient for finite traces implies a finite trace-equivalence quotient for infinite traces as well. The results of this paper allow a more direct proof, which immediately gives the desired result for infinite traces. It suffices to show that observation refinement ($\mathcal{A}_{OR}$) terminates on the transition structure of H. As in [22], it can be argued that every *Pre* operation on $\mathcal{K}_H$ corresponds in a precise sense to a *Pre* operation on $\mathcal{K}_{H'}$. Since the bisimilarity quotient of $\mathcal{K}_{H'}$ is finite, this implies that *Pre* operations on $\mathcal{K}_H$ can also generate only a finite number of distinct regions. There is only a finite number of observables (corresponding to the vertices of H). So the intersection of a region with an atomic region is simply the projection of the region onto a discrete part. Thus, the restricted intersection operation of $\mathcal{A}_{OR}$ does not give rise to any new continuous parts of regions beyond the ones already computed. It follows that $\mathcal{A}_{OR}$ terminates on $\mathcal{K}_H$. This result is sharp: for simple extensions to the model of rectangular automata, even backward reachability ($\mathcal{A}_\Diamond$) may not terminate [22].

5.3   Example: Assembly Line Scheduler

We describe an assembly line scheduler that must assign elements from an incoming stream to one of two assembly lines [21]. The stream has an inter-arrival time of four minutes. The lines process the parts at different speeds: on the first

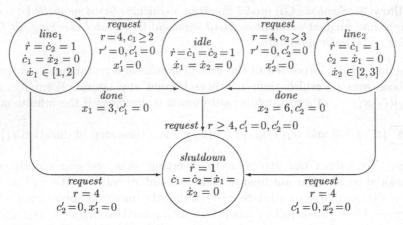

Fig. 1. Two assembly lines modeled as a rectangular automaton

line, jobs travel between one and two meters per minute, while on the second, jobs travel between two and three meters per minute. The first line is three meters long and the second line is six meters long. Once a line finishes processing a job, it enters a clean-up phase, and no jobs may be assigned to it while it cleans up. The clean-up time is two minutes for the first line and three minutes for the second line. The system may accept a job if both lines are free, and at most one is cleaning up. If the system is unable to accept a job, it shuts down.

The system is modeled by a rectangular automaton as shown in Figure 1. There are four discrete states: in *idle*, no jobs are being processed; in *line*$_1$ (*line*$_2$), line-1 (respectively, line-2) is processing a job, and in *shutdown*, the system is shut down. The variable x_1 (respectively, x_2) measures the distance a job has traveled along line-1 (respectively, line-2). The variable c_1 (c_2) tracks the amount of time line-1 (line-2) has spent cleaning up after its last job. Finally, the variable r measures the elapsed time since the last arrival of a job.

We modeled the system in HYTECH. Backward reachability ($\mathcal{A}_\Diamond$) terminates in set of states that can reach the unsafe vertex *shutdown*. We added a preprocessor to HYTECH which takes an LTL formula and generates a script to evaluate an equivalent $G\mu$ formula. We then considered the property that any feasible schedule must choose line-1 infinitely often. To establish this requirement, we checked that the formula $(\Diamond\Box\neg line_1) \wedge (\Box\neg shutdown)$ does not hold on any divergent run from the vertex *idle* (if this formula were to hold on some divergent run, then there would be a schedule that assigns jobs to *line*$_1$ only finitely many times, and still enforces that the system never shuts down). This required 0.39 seconds of CPU time on a DEC alpha with 2G RAM.

Acknowledgments

We thank Luca de Alfaro for several useful discussions.

References

1. R. Alur, C. Courcoubetis, N. Halbwachs, T.A. Henzinger, P.-H. Ho, X. Nicollin, A. Olivero, J. Sifakis, and S. Yovine. The algorithmic analysis of hybrid systems. *Theoretical Computer Science*, 138:3–34, 1995. 142, 152

2. R. Alur and D.L. Dill. A theory of timed automata. *Theoretical Computer Science*, 126:183–235, 1994. 144, 146, 152

3. R. Alur and T.A. Henzinger. Real-time system = discrete system + clock variables. *Software Tools for Technology Transfer*, 1:86–109, 1997. 153

4. R. Alur, T.A. Henzinger, and P.-H. Ho. Automatic symbolic verification of embedded systems. In *Proceedings of the 14th Annual Real-time Systems Symposium*, pages 2–11. IEEE Computer Society Press, 1993. 152

5. G. Bhat and R. Cleaveland. Efficient local model-checking for fragments of the modal μ-calculus. In *TACAS96: Tools and Algorithms for Construction and Analysis of Systems*, LNCS 1055, pages 107–126. Springer-Verlag, 1996. 148

6. G. Bhat and R. Cleaveland. Efficient model checking via the equational μ-calculus. In *Proceedings of the 11th Annual Symposium on Logic in Computer Science*, pages 304–312. IEEE Computer Society Press, 1996. 143, 149

7. A. Bouajjani, J.-C. Fernandez, and N. Halbwachs. Minimal model generation. In *CAV 90: Computer-aided Verification*, LNCS 663, pages 197–203. Springer-Verlag, 1990. 145

8. J.R. Burch, E.M. Clarke, K.L. McMillan, D.L. Dill and L.J. Hwang. Symbolic model checking: 10^{20} states and beyond. *Information and Computation*, 98(2):142–170, 1992. 147

9. E.M. Clarke, O. Grumberg, and D.E. Long. Verification tools for finite-state concurrent systems. In *A Decade of Concurrency: Reflections and Perspectives*, LNCS 803, pages. Springer-Verlag, 1994. 143, 150

10. R. Cleaveland, M. Klein, and B. Steffen. Faster model checking for the modal μ-calculus. In *CAV 92: Computer-aided Verification*, LNCS 663, pages 410–422. Springer-Verlag, 1993. 149

11. J.C. Corbett. Timing analysis of ADA tasking programs. *IEEE Transactions on Software Engineering*, 22:461–483, 1996. 142

12. M. Dam. CTL* and ECTL* as fragments of the modal μ-calculus. *Theoretical Computer Science*, 126:77–96, 1994. 143, 149

13. C. Daws and S. Tripakis. Model checking of real-time reachability properties using abstractions. In *TACAS98: Tools and Algorithms for the Construction and Analysis of Systems*, LNCS 1384, pages 313–329. Springer-Verlag, 1998. 143

14. E.A. Emerson. Temporal and modal logic. In *Handbook of Theoretical Computer Science*, volume B, pages 995–1072. Elsevier Science Publishers, 1990. 146, 147, 150

15. E.A. Emerson, C.S. Jutla, and A.P. Sistla. On model checking for fragments of μ-calculus. In *CAV 93: Computer-aided Verification*, LNCS 697, pages 385–396. Springer-Verlag, 1993. 143, 148, 149

16. E.A. Emerson and C. Lei. Efficient model checking in fragments of the propositional μ-calculus. In *Proceedings of the 1st Annual Symposium on Logic in Computer Science*, pages 267–278. IEEE Computer Society Press, 1986. 143

17. T.A. Henzinger. Hybrid automata with finite bisimulations. In *ICALP 95: Automata, Languages, and Programming*, LNCS 944, pages 324–335. Springer-Verlag, 1995. 144, 152

18. T.A. Henzinger. The theory of hybrid automata. In *Proceedings of the 11th Annual Symposium on Logic in Computer Science*, pages 278–292. IEEE Computer Society Press, 1996. 146, 147

19. T.A. Henzinger, P.-H. Ho, and H. Wong-Toi. HYTECH: a model checker for hybrid systems. *Software Tools for Technology Transfer*, 1:110–122, 1997. 143, 152

20. T.A. Henzinger, P.-H. Ho, and H. Wong-Toi. Algorithmic analysis of nonlinear hybrid systems. *IEEE Transactions on Automatic Control*, 43:540–554, 1998. 142

21. T.A. Henzinger, B. Horowitz, and R. Majumdar. Rectangular hybrid games. In *CONCUR 99: Concurrency Theory*, LNCS 1664, pages 320–335, 1999. 153

22. T.A. Henzinger, P.W. Kopke, A. Puri, and P. Varaiya. What's decidable about hybrid automata? *Journal of Computer and System Sciences*, 57:94–124, 1998. 142, 143, 151, 152, 153

23. T.A. Henzinger and R. Majumdar. A classification of symbolic transition systems. In *STACS 2000: Theoretical Aspects of Computer Science*, LNCS. Springer-Verlag, 2000. 145

24. T.A. Henzinger, X. Nicollin, J. Sifakis, and S. Yovine. Symbolic model checking for real-time systems. In *Proceedings of the 7th Annual Symposium on Logic in Computer Science*, pages 394–406. IEEE Computer Society Press, 1992. 152

25. T.A. Henzinger and H. Wong-Toi. Using HYTECH to synthesize control parameters for a steam boiler. In *Formal Methods for Industrial Applications: Specifying and Programming the Steam Boiler Control*, LNCS 1165, pages 265–282. Springer-Verlag, 1996. 142

26. P.-H. Ho and H. Wong-Toi. Automated analysis of an audio control protocol. In *CAV 95: Computer-aided Verification*, LNCS 939, pages 381–394. Springer-Verlag, 1995. 142

27. P.C. Kanellakis and S.A. Smolka. CCS expressions, finite-state processes, and three problems of equivalence. *Information and Computation*, 86:43–68, 1990. 144, 145

28. J. Kosecka, C.J. Tomlin, G. Pappas, and S. Sastry. Generation of conflict resolution manoeuvres for air traffic management. In *IROS 97: International Conference on Intelligent Robot and Systems*, volume 3, pages 1598–1603. IEEE Press, 1997. 142

29. S. Nadjm-Tehrani and J.-E. Strömberg. Proving dynamic properties in an aerospace application. In *Proceedings of the 16th Annual Real-time Systems Symposium*, pages 2–10. IEEE Computer Society Press, 1995. 142

30. T. Stauner, O. Müller, and M. Fuchs. Using HYTECH to verify an automotive control system. In *HART 97: Hybrid and Real-time Systems*, LNCS 1201, pages 139–153. Springer-Verlag, 1997. 142

31. W. Thomas. Automata on infinite objects. In *Handbook of Theoretical Computer Science*, volume B, pages 133–191. Elsevier Science Publishers, 1990. 150

32. T. Villa, H. Wong-Toi, A. Balluchi, J. Preußig, A. Sangiovanni-Vincentelli, and Y. Watanabe. Formal verification of an automotive engine controller in cutoff mode. In *Proceedings of the 37th Conference on Decision and Control*. IEEE Press, 1998. 142

Efficient Data Structure for Fully Symbolic Verification of Real-Time Software Systems*

Farn Wang

Institute of Information Science, Academia Sinica
Taipei, Taiwan 115, Republic of China
+886-2-27883799 ext. 1717; FAX +886-2-27824814
farn@iis.sinica.edu.tw
Tools available at: http://www.iis.sinica.edu.tw/~farn/red

Abstract. A new data-structure called RED (Region-Encoding Diagram) for the fully symbolic model-checking of real-time software systems is proposed. RED is a BDD-like data-structure for the encoding of regions [2]. Unlike DBM which records differences between pairs of clock readings, RED only uses one auxiliary binary variable for each clock. Thus the number of variables used in RED is always linear to the number of clocks declared in the input system description. Experiment has been carried out to compare RED with previous technologies.

1 Introduction

Fully symbolic verification of real-time systems is desirable with the promise of space and time efficiency through intense data-sharing in the manipulation of state space representations. We propose *Region-Encoding Diagram (RED)* as the new data-structure for such a purpose. RED is a BDD-like data-structure [5,8] for the encoding of regions [2]. The ordering among fractional parts of clock readings is explicitly encoded in the variable ordering of RED. To record sets of clock readings with the same fractional parts, we add one auxiliary binary variable per clock. Thus in RED, the number of variables used is linear to the number of clocks. Like BDD[8], RED is also a minimum canonical form with respect to a given variable ordering. It is also efficient for representing unions of zones. Experiments have shown better space efficiency against previous technologies like DBM (Difference-Bounded Matrix)[10].

We assume that system behavior is described as a set of m symmetric processes, identified with integers 1 to m, running different copies of the same program. Each process can use *global* and *local* variables of type *clock*, *discrete*, and *pointer*. Pointer variables either contain value NULL (0 in fact) or the identifiers of processes. Thus in our representation, we allow complicate dynamic networks to be constructed with pointers. We restrict that each process can declare at most one local clock and there is no global clock. The ordering of fractional parts of clock readings is encoded in RED with the following *normality condition*.

---

* The work is partially supported by NSC, Taiwan, ROC under grant NSC 89-2213-E-001-002.

S. Graf and M. Schwartzbach (Eds.): TACAS/ETAPS 2000, LNCS 1785, pp. 157–171, 2000.

"For any two local clocks $x[i], x[j]$, with $1 \leq i < j \leq m$, of processes i and j respectively, either $x[i]$ does not have a greater fractional part than $x[j]$ does or $x[j]$ is greater than the biggest timing constant used in the input system description and specification."

A state satisfying the normality condition is called a *normalized state*. With RED technology, we only work with the normalized images of states in runs. After a clock reading advancement or a clock reset operation, we may have to permute the process identifiers to maintain state normality. Thus our data-structure is perfect for symmetric systems with symmetric specifications.

Our innovation is that we use one bit for each clock to encode the ordering among the fractional parts of clock readings in the region construction [2]. Compared to the classic DBM [10], RED provides data-sharing capability of fully symbolic manipulation. In a DBM-based model-checker, since matrices and BDD are two different types of data-structure, we are forced to use a pair of BDD and matrix to represent a region. As a result, the set of regions are forced to be represented as an explicit directed graph which does not succinctly abstract out the interaction pattern in the pairs and whose size inevitably grows exponentially with timing constant magnitude and concurrency size. Moreover, to get region canonical representations, DBM-technology usually resorts to the processing of convex hulls which are equivalent to conjunctions of clock inequalities. Thus it may be necessary to break a big disjunction down to exponentially many conjunctions. Such breaking-down can be a source of inefficiency. But since the present RED algorithms derive time step next-state RED's at very tiny steps, DBM may have better verification performance with systems with big timing constants.

Newer technology of NDD[1] and CDD[7] use binary inequalities of the form $x[i] - x[j] \leq c$. NDD uses binary encoding for the possible values of c while CDD uses multiple value-ranges to record them. However, the number of variables in their data-structure is likely to be quadratic to the number of clocks used in the systems. The number of variables used in our RED technology, on the other hand, is always linear to the number of local clocks.

Here is our presentation plan. Section 2 defines the language for system behavior description. Section 3 formally presents our data-structure scheme. Section 4 shows how to maintain RED's after clock reading advancements and clock reset operations. Section 5 compares RED technology with previous ones by performing experiments on several benchmarks.

2   Real-Time Software Systems

We assume a real-time software system to be composed of a set of concurrent processes running different copies of the same program. Given a system of m processes, the processes are indexed with integers 1 through m which are called *process identifiers*. *NULL* is actually integer 0 and is used as the special null process identifier in data-structure construction. The program is presented as a

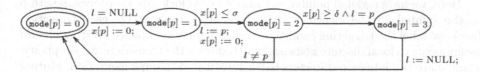

Fig. 1. Fischer's timed mutual exclusion algorithm

timed automaton[2] equiped with global and local variables of type clock, discrete variable, and pointer. A global variable can be accessed by all processes while a local variable can only be accessed by its declaring process. Clocks can hold reals, can be tested against integers, and can be reset to zero during transitions. Only one local clock per process is allowed and no global clock is allowed. Discrete variables can hold integer constants. Operations on discrete variables are comparisons and assignments with integer constants. A special local discrete variable *mode* is used to record the operation mode of the executing process. Pointer variables can hold NULL or process identifiers. Operations on pointers are comparisons and assignments with NULL or local process identifiers (the one of the executing process).

2.1 Syntax

Given a system of m processes with variable set X, we can define *global state predicates* and *local state predicates*. Global state predicates are used to specify initial conditions and safety properties and are presented with a process identifier attached to each local variable to distinguish which local references are for which processes. The syntax of a global state-predicate η is:

$$\eta ::= false \mid x \sim c \mid y = NULL \mid y = c$$
$$\mid x[i] \sim c \mid y[i] = NULL \mid y[i] = c \mid \neg\eta_1 \mid \eta_1 \vee \eta_2$$

Variables appended with square brackets are local variables while those not are global variables. x is either a clock variable or a discrete variable. y is a pointer variable. c is a natural constant. $\sim$ is an inequality operator in $\{\leq, <, =, >, \geq\}$. i is a process identifier constant in $[1, m]$. $\neg$ and $\vee$ are Boolean negation and disjunction respectively. Parentheses can be used to disambiguate the syntax. Standard shorthands are $true \equiv \neg false$, $\eta_1 \wedge \eta_2 \equiv \neg((\neg\eta_1) \vee (\neg\eta_2))$, and $\eta_1 \rightarrow \eta_2 \equiv (\neg\eta_1) \vee \eta_2$.

Local state-predicates are used to describe invariance and triggering conditions in the automata. Their syntax is very much like that of global state-predicates except that all occurrences of process identifier constants are replaced by the symbolic process identifier p which is to be interpreted as the process identifier of the executing process.

In figure 1, we have an example automaton for Fischer's timed mutual exclusion algorithm.

Here, we have a global pointer *lock* and a local clock $x[p]$ for process p with p as the symbol for the identifier of the executing process. On each transition (arc), we label the triggering condition and assignment sequence. Testing on and assignments to local discrete mode are omitted from the transitions for simplicity. σ and δ are two integer parameters to be substituted in implementation. Mutual exclusion to *mode* 3 is maintained when $\sigma < \delta$.

The formal syntax of a real-time software system S is given as a triple $\langle A, m, I \rangle$ where A is a timed automaton equiped with various variables as mentioned in the above, m is the number of processes in the system, and I is a global state-prediate for the initial condition. A is formally presented as a timed automaton $A = \langle X, \lambda, Q, \mu, E, \tau, \pi \rangle$ with the following restrictions. X is the set of variables. λ maps each variable in X into one of the following five types: local clock, global discrete, local discrete, global pointer, and local pointer. Q is the set of operation modes (or control locations). We assume that the elements in Q are indexed from 0 to $|Q| - 1$. μ is a function from $[0, |Q| - 1]$ such that for all $q \in [0, |Q| - 1]$, $\mu(q)$ is a local state-predicate describing the invariance condition at the q'th operation mode. Also we require that there is a special local discrete variable mode which always record the current operation mode index of a process.

$E \subseteq Q \times Q$ is the set of transitions. τ is a function from E such that for all $e \in E$, $\tau(e)$ is a local state-predicate describing the triggering condition of e. π is a function from E such that for all $e \in E$, $\pi(e)$ is a sequence of assignments α of the syntax form:

$$\alpha ::= L := R;$$
$$L ::= x \mid x[p] \mid y \mid y[p]$$
$$R ::= c \mid NULL \mid p \mid x \mid x[p] \mid y \mid y[p]$$

Such an assignment means that the value of R is assigned to variable L. The restriction is that constants or variables cannot be assigned to variables of different types. For example, if L is not of type pointer, then R cannot be $NULL$, p, or any pointer variables.

2.2   Semantics

Definition 1. <u>states</u> Suppose we are given a real-time software system $S = \langle A, m, I \rangle$ with $A = \langle X, \lambda, Q, \mu, E, \tau, \pi \rangle$. A state ν is a mapping from $X \times \{0, \ldots, m\}$ such that

- for every global pointer $x \in X$, $\nu(x, 0) \in \{NULL\} \cup \{1, \ldots, m\}$;
- for every global discrete $x \in X$, $\nu(x, 0) \in \mathcal{N}$;
- for every local clock $x \in X$ and $i \in \{1, \ldots, m\}$, $\nu(x, i) \in \mathcal{R}$;
- for every local pointer $x \in X$ and $i \in \{1, \ldots, m\}$, $\nu(x, i) \in \{NULL\} \cup \{1, \ldots, m\}$;
- for every local discrete $x \in X$ and $i \in \{1, \ldots, m\}$, $\nu(x, i) \in \mathcal{N}$.   ‖

For any $t \in \mathcal{R}$, $\nu + t$ is the state identical to ν except that for every local clock $x[i]$, $\nu(x, i) + t = (\nu + t)(x, i)$. For an atomic assignment $L := R$; and a process identifier i, $\nu[L := R; , i]$ is the new state obtained by letting process i executing $L := R$; in ν. It is identical to ν except that $(\nu[L := R; , i])(L, i) = \nu(R, i)$. Given a sequence β of assignments and a process identifier i, $\nu[\beta, i]$ is defined in the following inductive way.

- If β is empty, then $\nu[\beta, i] = \nu$.
- If $\beta = \alpha\beta'$, then $\nu[\beta, i] = (\nu[\alpha, i])[\beta', i]$.

Given a global state predicate η and a state ν, we say that ν satisfies η, in symbols $\nu \models \eta$, if and only if the following inductive restrictions hold.

- $\nu \not\models false$.
- $\nu \models x \sim c$ iff $\nu(x, 0) \sim c$.
- $\nu \models y = \text{NULL}$ iff $\nu(y, 0) = \text{NULL}$.
- $\nu \models y = c$ iff $\nu(y, 0) = c$.
- $\nu \models x[i] \sim c$ iff $\nu(x, i) \sim c$.
- $\nu \models y[i] = NULL$ iff $\nu(y, i) = \text{NULL}$.
- $\nu \models y[i] = c$ iff $\nu(y, i) = c$.
- $\nu \models \neg\eta_1$ iff it is not the case that $\nu \models \eta_1$.
- $\nu \models \eta_1 \vee \eta_2$ iff either $\nu \models \eta_1$ or $\nu \models \eta_2$.

The satisfaction relation between a local state predicate η and a state ν by process i, in symbols $\nu, i \models \eta$, can be similarly defined.

- $\nu, i \not\models false$.
- $\nu, i \models x \sim c$ iff $\nu(x, 0) \sim c$.
- $\nu, i \models y = \text{NULL}$ iff $\nu(y, 0) = \text{NULL}$.
- $\nu, i \models y = c$ iff $\nu(y, 0) = c$.
- $\nu, i \models x[p] \sim c$ iff $\nu(x, i) \sim c$.
- $\nu, i \models y[p] = NULL$ iff $\nu(y, i) = \text{NULL}$.
- $\nu, i \models y[p] = c$ iff $\nu(y, i) = c$.
- $\nu, i \models \neg\eta_1$ iff it is not the case that $\nu, i \models \eta_1$.
- $\nu, i \models \eta_1 \vee \eta_2$ iff either $\nu, i \models \eta_1$ or $\nu, i \models \eta_2$.

Definition 2. <u>runs</u> Given a real-time software system $S = \langle A, m, I \rangle$ with $A = \langle X, \lambda, Q, \mu, E, \tau, \pi \rangle$, a ν-run is an infinite sequence of state-time pair $(\nu_0, t_0)(\nu_1, t_1) \ldots (\nu_k, t_k) \ldots\ldots$ such that $\nu = \nu_0$, $t_0 t_1 \ldots t_k \ldots\ldots$ is a monotonically increasing real-number (time) divergent sequence, and for all $k \geq 0$,

- for all $t \in [0, t_{k+1} - t_k]$ and $1 \leq i \leq m$, $\nu_k + t, i \models \bigvee_{0 \leq q < |Q|}(\text{mode}[p] = q \wedge \mu(q))$; and
- either $\nu_k + (t_{k+1} - t_k) = \nu_{k+1}$; or there are $i \in \{1, \ldots, m\}$ and $e \in E$ such that $\nu_k + (t_{k+1} - t_k), i \models \tau(e)$ and $(\nu_k + (t_{k+1} - t_k))[\pi(e), i] = \nu_{k+1}$. ‖

A run $\rho = (\nu_0, t_0)(\nu_1, t_1) \ldots (\nu_k, t_k) \ldots\ldots$ of S satisfies *safety* global state predicate η, in symbols $\rho \models \eta$, iff for all $k \geq 0$ and $t_k \leq t \leq t_{k+1}$, $\nu_k + t \models \eta$. We say S satisfies η, in symbols $S \models \eta$, iff for all ν-runs ρ such that $\nu \models I$, $\rho \models \eta$. In case that $S \not\models \eta$, we say S *violates* η.

2.3   Normalized Runs and a Permutation Scheme

Given a constant $r \in \mathcal{R}$, $int(r)$ is the integer part of r while $frac(r)$ is the fractional part of r. Let C_S be the biggest integer constant used to compare with a local clock in the system description S. The normality condition is restated here:

> *"Suppose the local clock is x in a system $S = \langle A, m, I \rangle$. A state ν of S is normalized iff for any $1 \leq i < j \leq m$, either $\nu(x, j) > C_S$ or* $frac(\nu(x, i)) \leq frac(\nu(x, j))$."

Thus, in a normalized state, we can conceptually divide the process identifiers into several segments in the following pattern.

$$
\left.\begin{array}{l} 1, \\ \vdots \\ i_1, \end{array}\right\} \begin{array}{l} \nu(x, 1) \leq C_S \wedge \ldots \wedge \nu(x, i_1) \leq C_S \\ \wedge \, frac(\nu(x, 1)) = \ldots = frac(\nu(x, i_1)) \neq frac(\nu(x, i_1 + 1)) \end{array}
$$

$$
\left.\begin{array}{l} i_1 + 1, \\ \vdots \\ i_2, \end{array}\right\} \begin{array}{l} \nu(x, i_1 + 1) \leq C_S \wedge \ldots \wedge \nu(x, i_2) \leq C_S \\ \wedge \, frac(\nu(x, i_1 + 1)) = \ldots = frac(\nu(x, i_2)) \neq frac(\nu(x, i_2 + 1)) \end{array}
$$

$$\vdots \qquad\qquad\qquad\qquad \vdots$$

$$
\left.\begin{array}{l} i_k + 1, \\ \vdots \\ i_{k+1}, \end{array}\right\} \begin{array}{l} \nu(x, i_k + 1) \leq C_S \wedge \ldots \wedge \nu(x, i_{k+1}) \leq C_S \\ \wedge \, frac(\nu(x, i_k + 1)) = \ldots = frac(\nu(x, i_{k+1})) \end{array}
$$

$$
\left.\begin{array}{l} i_{k+1} + 1, \\ \vdots \\ m \end{array}\right\} \; \nu(x, i_{k+1} + 1) > C_S \wedge \ldots \wedge \nu(x, m) > C_S
$$

The last segment contains identifiers of those processes whose local clock readings are greater than C_S. The processes with identifiers in a segment other than the last one all have the same fractional part in their clock readings which are no greater than C_S.

Definition 3. normalized runs Given a run $\rho = (\nu_0, t_0)(\nu_1, t_1) \ldots (\nu_k, t_k) \ldots$ of a real-time software system $S = \langle A, m, I \rangle$, a *normalized run* $\bar{\rho}$ of ρ is a mapping from $\mathcal{N} \times \mathcal{R}$ such that for every $k \in \mathcal{N}$ and $0 \leq t \leq t_k$, $\bar{\rho}(k, t)$ is a normalized state of $\nu_k + t$. ‖

After each transition or clock readings advancement, a normalized state can be changed to an unnormalized one and there can be more than one identifier permutation whose application can maintain the normality of states. We propose the following permutation rules which can simplify our tool implementation.

1. When process i resets its local clock with a transition, we have to
   - change the identifier of process i to 1 (with global and local variables updated according to the transitions.); and

- for every $1 \leq j < i$, change the identifier of process j to $j + 1$; and
- for every $i < k \leq m$, keep the identifier of process k unchanged

in the destination state to make it normalized. The permutation can be viewed as an identifier movement from i to 1 with displacement $1 - i$.

2. When there is no integer clock readings $\leq C_S$ in the source state and some clocks will advance from noninteger readings $< C_S$ to integer readings, we first have to identify the segment of identifiers of those processes with such clocks. This is the segment right preceding the last segment which contains identifiers of processes with local clock readings $> C_S$. Suppose, we find out $x[j], \ldots, x[k]$ are such clocks. Then in the destination state,

    - for all $j \leq i \leq k$, the identifier of process i is changed to $i - j + 1$; and
    - for all $1 \leq i < j$, the identifier of process i is changed to $i + k - j + 1$; and
    - for all $k < i \leq m$, the identifier of process i is unchanged

    to make it normalized. The permutation can be viewed as an identifier segment movement from $[j, k]$ to $[1, k - j + 1]$ with displacement $1 - j$.

3. When some clocks advance from integer to noninteger readings. we first have to detect if some of those clocks advance their readings from C_S to beyond C_S. Suppose, we find out that $x[j], \ldots, x[k]$ are such clocks. Then in the destination state,

    - for all $j \leq i \leq k$, the identifier of process i is changed to $i + m - k$; and
    - for all $1 \leq i < j$, the identifier of process i is unchanged; and
    - for all $k < i < m$, the identifier of process i is changed to $i + j - k - 1$

    to make it normalized. The permutation can be viewed as an identifier segment movement from $[j, k]$ to $[j + m - k, m]$ with displacement $m - k$.

4. In all other cases, the identifiers of all processes stay unchanged to satisfy normality.

However, there is one thing unclear in the above-mention permutation scheme. That is, in the third item, how do we know that those processes with clock readings $= C_S$ will appear with consecutive process identifiers ? That is the good thing about this permutation scheme and can be established by the following lemma.

Lemma 1. *In the permutation scheme presented in the above, inside all segments of identifiers of processes whose clock readings are $\leq C_S$ and share the same fractional parts, the process identifiers are arranged according to monotonically increasing order of the local clock readings.*

Proof : True because every time when we reset a local clock, we change the identifier of the transiting process to 1. Thus the later a process resets its clock, the earlier its identifier appears in a segment.   ‖

Definition 4. Symmetric global state predicate Given a global state predicate η and a permutation θ of process identifier 1 through m, $\eta\theta$ is a new global state predicate obtained from η by renaming process identifiers according to θ. A global state predicate η for m processes is *symmetric* iff for any permutation

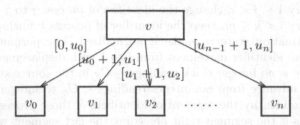

Fig. 2. Data structure implementation of a node in RED

θ of 1 through m, η equals to $\eta\theta$ according to commutation laws of Boolean algebra.   ‖

We want to establish the soundness of our RED technology with the following lemma.

Lemma 2. : *Given a state ν of a real-time software system $S = \langle A, m, I \rangle$ and a symmetric global state predicate η, for any normalized image ν' of ν, $\nu \models \eta$ iff $\nu' \models \eta$.*
Proof : Suppose the process identifier permutation that changes ν to ν' is θ. Then $\nu \models \eta$ has the same truth value as $\nu' \models (\eta\theta)$. But $\eta\theta$ is equal to η according to commutation laws of Boolean algebra. Thus the lemma is proven.   ‖

3   Region-Encoding Diagram

RED is a data-structure for representing set of normalized states. In the implementation aspect, it resembles CDD[7] and each node in RED has the structure shown in figure 2. Such a node is used to evaluate the truth value of a formula from variable v. The outgoing arcs are labeled with lower and upper bounds of **integer parts** (note, only integer parts) of values of variable v and direct to the RED's for the subformulae true in the corresponding ranges of v's values. For example, if the second arc from left in figure 2, is labeled with $[7, 9]$, then subformulus represented by the RED rooted at v_1 must be true when the integer part of v's value is in $[7, 9]$. The ranges labeled on arcs from a RED node are required to be disjoint.

The lower and upper bounds of outgoing arcs are chosen according to the following rules. For clock variables, we define constant $O_S = C_S + 1$ which symbolically denotes a clock reading greater than C_S. Thus the lower and upper bounds of outgoing arcs from RED nodes of clock variables are chosen from elements in $\{0, \ldots, C_S\} \cup \{O_S, \infty\}$ which is sufficient for the regions construction in [2]. For discrete variables, the lower and upper bounds of outgoing arcs are chosen from those constants assigned to and compared with the variable in both the automaton and the specification. For pointer variables, the lower and upper bounds of outgoing arcs are chosen from $NULL$ and integers 1 through m.

Given an automaton A with variable name set X, the variable set in the RED for an m process system is

$$\{x \mid x \in X; x \text{ is global}\} \cup \{x[i] \mid x \in X; x \text{ is local}; 1 \le i \le m\} \cup \{\kappa[i] \mid 1 \le i \le m\}$$

Here κ is the name for an auxiliary local binary discrete variable name used to encode the fractional part orderings among clock readings. According to Alur et al's region graph construction [2], the state-equivalence relation for model-checking is determined by the following three factors:
- the discrete information of each state,
- the integer parts of clock readings $\le C_S$.
- the ordering among the fractional parts of clock readings $\le C_S$.

Our innovation is that we use one bit (κ) for each clock to encode the ordering among the fractional parts of clock readings in normalized states. For each clock, say $x[i]$ of process i, $\kappa[i]$ is true in a normalized state s if and only if $s(x[i]) \le C_S$ and either
- $i = 1$ and $frac(s(x[i])) = 0$, i.e., $s(x[i])$ is an integer; or
- $i > 1$ and $frac(s(x[i-1])) = frac(s(x[i]))$, i.e., the fractional parts of $s(x[i-1])$ and $s(x[i])$ are the same.

With such definition of data-structure and appropriate permutations of process identifiers after clock reading advancements and clock reset operations, we are able to represent the regions of timed automata [2]. As for the other input variables, local or global, we simply copy them as the variables in our RED. Thus given a real-time software system $S = \langle A, m, I \rangle$ with $A - \langle X, \lambda, Q, \mu, E, \tau, \pi \rangle$, the number of variables used in our RED is $O(m|X| + m)$.

For example, we may have 8 processes in a normalized state with $x[1] = 0, x[2] = 3, x[3] = 1.3, \tau[4] = 1.456, x[5] - 9.456, x[6] = 20.7, x[7] - 38, x[8] - 10\pi$ while $C_S = 13$. The readings of clocks and values of $\kappa[i]$'s are shown in the following.

i	1	2	3	4	5	6	7	8
$x[i]$	0	3	1.3	1.456	9.456	20.7	38	10π
$\kappa[i]$	true	true	false	false	true	false	false	false

4 Manipulations on RED

4.1 Boolean Operations

The Boolean operations on RED's follow the same style in Bryant's BDD manipulations [5,7,8]. We present procedure $REDop(op, D_x, D_y)$ in table 4.1 to illustrate the idea in the implementation of such an operation. For convenience, we use $[l, u]D$ to denote an outgoing arc whose lower bound is l, upper bound is u, and the subformulus RED is D. Also, $D.v$ denotes the index, of D's variable, used in the variable-ordering of the RED.

We should point out that the algorithm shown in table 4.1 is for simplicity and clarity of algorithm presentation and is not for efficiency. Our implementation is more efficient in that it records which pairs of D_x, D_y have already

Table 1. Algorithm for computing $D_x op D_y$

$REDop(op, D_x, D_y)\{$
  (1) if $op=$ AND,
    (1) if D_x is *true*, return D_y;
    (2) else if D_y is *true*, return D_x;
    (3) else if either D_x or D_y is *false*, return *false*;
  (2) else if $op=$ OR,
    (1) if either D_x or D_y is *true*, return *true*;
    (2) else if D_x is *false*, return D_y;
    (3) else if D_y is *false*, return D_x;
  (3) else {
    (1) Construct a new RED node D with $D.v = \min(D_x.v, D_y.v)$;
    (2) if $D_x.v < D_y.v$, then for each outgoing arc $[l, u]D_c$ of D_x,
        add an outgoing arc $[l, u]REDop(op, D_c, D_y)$ to D.
    (3) else if $D_x.v > D_y.v$, then for each outgoing arc $[l, u]D_c$ of D_y,
        add an outgoing arc $[l, u]REDop(op, D_x, D_c)$ to D.
    (4) else for each outgoing arc $[l_x, u_x]D_x'$ of D_x and outgoing arc $[l_y, u_y]D_y'$ of D_y,
        if $[\max(l_x, l_y), \min(u_x, u_y)]$ is nonempty,
            add an outgoing arc $[\max(l_x, l_y), \min(u_x, u_y)]REDop(op, D_x', D_y')$ to D.
    (5) Merge any two outgoing arcs $[l, u]D_c, [u+1, u']D_c$ of D into one $[l, u']D_c$
        until no more merge can be done.
    (6) if D has more than one outgoing arcs, return D,
        else return the sole subformulus of D;
  }
$\}$

been processed. If a pair of D_x, D_y has already been processed with procedure $REDop()$ before, then we simply return the result recorded in the first time when such a pair was processed.

4.2 Preserving Normality after Transitions and Clock Reading Advancement

RED is a data-structure for normalized states of real-time software systems. Transitions and clock reading advancements may change normalized states into unnormalized states. This section tells us how to symbolically do necessary process identifier permutation to preserve the normality of states.

Given a local variable $v[i]$ of process i, we assume that $VarIndex(i, v)$ is the variable index of $v[i]$ in RED. For convenience, we use process identifier 0 (NULL) for those global variables. That is $VarIndex(0, v)$ returns a valid variable index in RED only when v is a global variable. As can be seen from the process identifier permutation scheme in subsection 2.3, segment movements are performed. We can thus define the following function which computes the new identifier of process i after such a segment movement.

NewProcId($i, j, k, disp$) /* process identifiers j through k are to be moved with displacement *disp.* */ {
    (1) if $i = 0$, return 0; /* Global is always global. */
    (2) else if $j \leq i \leq k$, return($i + disp$);
    (3) else if $i < j + disp$, return(i);
    (4) else if $j + disp \leq i < j$, return($i + k - j + 1$);
    (5) else if $k < i \leq k + disp$, return($i - (k - j + 1)$);
    (6) else /* $k + disp < i$ */ return(i);
}

Due to page-limit, we shall only describe the algorithm for symbolic manipulation of a procedure *ToInt*(R), in table 2 in page 168, which generates a new RED describing the set of states obtained from those in R by advancing those clocks with biggest fractional parts to integers. In the algorithm presentation, for simple clarity, we use Boolean operation symbols like $\vee, \wedge$ to represent our procedure REDop(). Also for an atom like $l \leq \chi \leq u$, it is implemented by constructing the following RED.

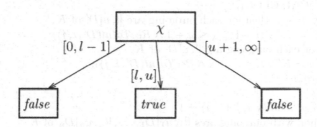

Of course, when $[0, l - 1]$ (or $[u + 1, \infty]$) is empty, the corresponding arc disappears. Symbolic manipulation procedures for next state set after transitions and clock reading advancement from integers to fractionals can all be defined similarly.

5   Experiments

We have experimented to compare RED technology with previously published performance data in two reports[4,6] that compared performances of various model-checkers respectively on two versions of Fischer's timed mutual exclusion algorithm as shown in Figure 3. The property to be verified is the safe property: *at any moment, no more than one process are allowed in* mode *3*.

UPPAAL's version has bigger timing constants while Balarin's version allows repetitions.

UPPAAL is based on DBM technology and has been well accepted as one of the most efficient model-checkers for real-time systems. It has been used to successfully verify many communication protocols. Recently, CDD technology was proposed to enhance the performance of UPPAAL[7]. However, further reports are yet to be seen. In [6], UPPAAL was compared with many other

ToInt(R) /* R describes the state set before advancing those clock readings with biggest fractional parts to integers. */ {

(1) $D := false$;

(2) For $1 \leq i \leq m$ and $i \leq j \leq m$, do {

    (1) Construct the condition K that
- there is no clock whose reading is an integer $\leq C_S$; and
- processes i to j are those with biggest fractional parts in their clock readings.

    (2) $D := D \vee RecToInt(K \wedge R, i, j)$;

}

(3) Return(D);

}

RecToInt(K, i, j) {

(1) If K is either *true* or *false*, return K;

(2) Get the process identifier k of $K.v$; /* $k = 0$ when v is global. */

(3) Generate the name χ of variable $K.v$ of process $NewProcId(k, i, j, 1 - i)$);

(4) $K' := false$;

(5) switch on type of $K.v$ {

(6) case LOCAL_CLOCK:

    (1) if $i \leq k \leq j$, then for each outgoing arc $[l, u]D'$ of K,
$$K' := K' \vee (l + 1 \leq \chi \leq u + 1 \wedge RecToInt(D', i, j));$$
    else for each outgoing arc $[l, u]D'$ of K,
$$K' := K' \vee (l \leq \chi \leq u \wedge RecToInt(D', i, j));$$

    (2) return(K');

(7) case $\kappa[k]$:

    (1) if $NewProcId(k, i, j, 1 - i) = 1$,

        (1) then with outgoing arcs $[l_1, u_1]D_1, \ldots, [l_n, u_n]D_n$ of K,
return($\kappa[1] = true \wedge \bigvee_{1 \leq h \leq n} RecToInt(D_h, i, j)$);

        (2) else for each outgoing arc $[l, u]D'$ of K,
$$K' := K' \vee (l \leq \kappa[NewProcId(k, i, j, 1 - i)] \leq u \wedge RecToInt(D', i, j));$$

    (2) return(K');

(8) case LOCAL_Discrete:

(9) case GLOBAL_Discrete:

    (1) for each outgoing arc $[l, u]D'$ of K,
$$K' := K' \vee (l \leq \chi \leq u \wedge RecToInt(D', i, j));$$

    (2) return(K');

(10) case LOCAL_POINTER:

(11) case GLOBAL_POINTER:

    (1) for each outgoing arc $[l, u]D'$ of K and each $l \leq h \leq u$, {

        (1) $g := NewProcId(h, i, j, 1 - i)$;

        (2) $K' := K' \vee (\chi = g \wedge RecToInt(D', i, j))$;

    }

    (2) return(K');

}

}

Table 2. Symbolic manipulation procedure for time-steps from regions with no integer clock readings $\leq C_S$ to those with ones

global pointer l;   local clock x;   local discrete mode;

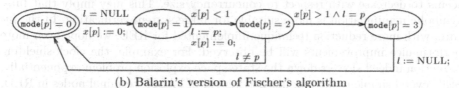

(a) UPPAAL's version of Fischer's algorithm

global pointer l;   local clock x;   local discrete mode;

(b) Balarin's version of Fischer's algorithm

Fig. 3. Two versions of Fischer's algorithm for experiments

model-checkers like HyTech's[3], Epsilon, and Kronos[13] on the automaton in figure 3(a). The experiments was reported to be performed on a Sparc-10 with 128 MB memory (real plus swap). All other tools fail when the number of processes reaches beyond 5 while UPPAAL can verify the algorithm on 8 processes.

We have implemented two version of RED on an Pentium II 366 MHz IBM notebook with 256 MB memory (real plus swap) running Linux. The tools are avaiable at:

http://www.iis.sinica.edu.tw/~farn/red

The first version is plain while the second version employs the clock shielding reduction technique reported in [12,14]. Reduction clock-shielding replaces clock readings with ∞ in a state when along any runs from the state, it is determined that such a reading will no longer be read unless the clock is reset. The performance is listed in the following table.

version	resources	2	3	4	5	6	7	8	9	10	11	12	13
no CS	time	0.19	1.22	6.5	27	105	320	888	2323	5556	N/A	N/A	N/A
	space	50	212	697	1959	4885	10966	22444	42858	77503	N/A	N/A	N/A
CS	time	0.17	0.98	4.4	16.5	50.3	134	325	724	1493	3002	5743	10152
	space	47	161	463	1134	2456	4810	8871	15726	26194	41930	64323	95389

"CS" means the version with clock-shielding reduction while "no CS" means the one without. The CPU time is measured in seconds. The space is measured in kilobytes and only includes those for the management of RED's and 2-3 trees. "N/A" means "not available" which indicates that the corresponding experiment has not been performed.

The time consumption is considerable bigger than that of UPPAAL[6] considering the CPU clock rate difference. This is due to our implementation philosophy. We believe time is an unbounded resource while space is not. As can be seen from procedure ToInt(), no RED for the relation between current state and next state is computed. In practice, such a relation in RED can occupy a great many bytes. The next-state set RED is computed by analysis on different situations of i and j. The sacrifice in CPU time pays off in the memory space efficiency. With twice the memory size used in [6], we are now able to verify the simplified Fischer's algorithm with 13 processes.

UPPAAL is a mature tool with a great arsenal of reduction technologies implemented. Our software at this moment only relies on minimal canonicality of RED to gain performance. Please note that the exponent base in our data seems to decrease with respect to concurrency size. This may imply that fully symbolic manipulation is more suitable for large system verification. In the future, with more reduction technique implemented for RED, we hope even more performance improvements will be observed. For example, the clock-shielding reduction indeed slowers down the state-space explosion problem exponentially. Still several simple reduction, like getting rid of FALSE terminal nodes in RED, can be implemented in the future version of RED to get constant factor of improvement.

In [4,15], weak and strong approximation technologies of symbolic verification are proposed and experiments are performed on algorithm in figure (b). We extend the performance data table in [4] to compare our tool with previous technologies.

#proc	strong	weak	KRONOS	Wong-Toi	RED(no CS)
6	155sec	18sec	1174sec	74sec	26sec/1374k
7	398sec	48sec	M/O	164sec	67sec/2488k
8	986sec	116sec	M/O	375sec	142sec/4242k
9	2220sec	247sec	M/O	891sec	303sec/6858k
10	M/O	576sec	N/A	N/A	558sec/10659k
11	N/A	N/A	N/A	N/A	1034sec/15673k
12	N/A	N/A	N/A	N/A	1724sec/22251k
13	N/A	N/A	N/A	N/A	2889sec/30593k
14	N/A	N/A	N/A	N/A	4492sec/41019k
15	N/A	N/A	N/A	N/A	7047sec/53737k
16	N/A	N/A	N/A	N/A	10782sec/69126k
17	N/A	N/A	N/A	N/A	15330sec/87431k

The original table consists of the firt five columns and only reports the CPU time in seconds used by various tools. "M/O" means "out of memory." KRONOS is also based on DBM technology while Wong-Toi's tool is based on approximation. In our extension, each entry is composed of both CPU time (in seconds) and space (in kilobytes) used. The column extension is for time/space consumed without clock-shielding reduction. Balarin's experiment is performed on Sparc 2 with 128 MB memory while ours is performed on IBM Thinkpads with PII 366 MHz and 256 MB memory. Be reminded that verification problems are of high space complexities in nature. The fact that RED-technology can handle much higher concurrency implies that it indeed control state-space explosion better. We believe that such performance is gained not only from utilization of system symmetry, but more importantly, from the data-sharing capability of RED.

6   Conclusion

We propose to use one auxiliary binary variable for each clock in our new data-structure for fully symbolic model-checking of real-time software systems. Since we now have fewer variables in the fully symbolic manipulation, theoretically we can expect better verification performance. With better implementation of reduction techniques borrowed from BDD technology, we are hoping for further performance improvement.

References

1. Asaraain, Bozga, Kerbrat, Maler, Pnueli, Rasse. Data-Structures for the Verification of Timed Automata. Proceedings, HART'97, LNCS 1201. 158
2. R. Alur, C. Courcoubetis, D.L. Dill. Model Checking for Real-Time Systems, IEEE LICS, 1990. 157, 158, 159, 164, 165
3. R. Alur, T.A. Henzinger, P.-H. Ho. Automatic Symbolic Verification of Embedded Systems. in Proceedings of 1993 IEEE Real-Time System Symposium. 169
4. F. Balarin. Approximate Reachability Analysis of Timed Automata. IEEE RTSS, 1996. 167, 170
5. J.R. Burch, E.M. Clarke, K.L. McMillan, D.L.Dill, L.J. Hwang. Symbolic Model Checking: 10^{20} States and Beyond, IEEE LICS, 1990. 157, 165
6. J. Bengtsson, K. Larsen, F. Larsson, P. Pettersson, Wang Yi. UPPAAL - a Tool Suite for Automatic Verification of Real-Time Systems. Hybrid Control System Symposium, 1996, LNCS, Springer-Verlag. 167, 169, 170
7. G. Behrmann, K.G. Larsen, J. Pearson, C. Weise, Wang Yi. Efficient Timed Reachability Analysis Using Clock Difference Diagrams. CAV'99, July, Trento, Italy, LNCS 1633, Springer-Verlag. 158, 164, 165, 167
8. R.E. Bryant. Graph-based Algorithms for Boolean Function Manipulation, IEEE Trans. Comput., C-35(8), 1986. 157, 165
9. E. Clarke and E.A. Emerson. Design and Synthesis of Synchronization Skeletons using Branching-Time Temporal Logic, Proceedings of Workshop on Logic of Programs, Lecture Notes in Computer Science 131, Springer-Verlag, 1981.
10. D.L. Dill. Timing Assumptions and Verification of Finite-state Concurrent Systems. CAV'89, LNCS 407, Springer-Verlag. 157, 158
11. T.A. Henzinger, X. Nicollin, J. Sifakis, S. Yovine. Symbolic Model Checking for Real-Time Systems, IEEE LICS 1992.
12. P.-A. Hsiung, F. Wang. User-Friendly Verification. Proceedings of 1999 FORTE/PSTV, October, 1999, Beijing. Formal Methods for Protocol Engineering and Distributed Systems, editors: J. Wu, S.T. Chanson, Q. Gao; Kluwer Academic Publishers. 169
13. X. Nicolin, J. Sifakis, S. Yovine. Compiling real-time specifications into extended automata. IEEE TSE Special Issue on Real-Time Systems, Sept. 1992. 169
14. F. Wang, P.-A. Hsiung. Automatic Verification on the Large. Proceedings of the 3rd IEEE HASE, November 1998. 169
15. H. Wong-Toi. Symbolic Approximations for Verifying Real-Time Systems. Ph.D. thesis, Stanford University, 1995. 170

Verification of Parameterized Systems Using Logic Program Transformations*

Abhik Roychoudhury[1], K. Narayan Kumar[2], C.R. Ramakrishnan[1],
I.V. Ramakrishnan[1], and Scott A. Smolka[1]

[1] Dept. of Computer Science, SUNY Stony Brook,
Stony Brook, NY 11794, USA
{abhik,cram,ram,sas}@cs.sunysb.edu
[2] Chennai Mathematical Institute
92 G.N. Chetty Road, Chennai, India
kumar@smi.ernet.in

Abstract. We show how the problem of verifying parameterized systems can be reduced to the problem of determining the equivalence of goals in a logic program. We further show how goal equivalences can be established using induction-based proofs. Such proofs rely on a powerful new theory of *logic program transformations* (encompassing unfold, fold and goal replacement over multiple recursive clauses), can be highly automated, and are applicable to a variety of network topologies, including uni- and bi-directional chains, rings, and trees of processes. Unfold transformations in our system correspond to algorithmic model-checking steps, fold and goal replacement correspond to deductive steps, and all three types of transformations can be arbitrarily interleaved within a proof. Our framework thus provides a seamless integration of algorithmic and deductive verification at fine levels of granularity.

1 Introduction

Advances in Logic Programming technology are beginning to influence the development of new tools and techniques for the specification and verification of concurrent systems. For example, constraint logic programming has been used for the analysis and verification of hybrid systems [Urb96] and more recently for model checking infinite-state systems [DP99]. Closer to home, we have used a tabled logic-programming system to develop XMC, an efficient and flexible model checker for finite-state systems [RRR+97]. XMC is written in under 200 lines of tabled Prolog code, which constitute a declarative specification of CCS and the modal mu-calculus at the level of semantic equations. Despite the high-level nature of XMC's implementation, its performance is comparable to that of highly optimized model checkers such as Spin [Hol97] and Murφ [Dil96] on examples selected from the benchmark suite in the standard Spin distribution.

* This work was partially supported by NSF grants CCR-9711386, CCR-9876242, CDA-9805735 and EIA-9705998.

S. Graf and M. Schwartzbach (Eds.): TACAS/ETAPS 2000, LNCS 1785, pp. 172–187, 2000.

More recently, we have been investigating how XMC's model-checking capabilities can be extended *beyond finite-state systems*. Essentially, this can be done by enhancing the underlying resolution strategy appropriately at the level of *meta-programming*, and without the undue performance penalties typically associated with the concept of meta-programming. In this sense, XMC can be viewed as a *programmable verification engine*. For example, we have shown in [DRS99] how an efficient model checker for real-time systems can be attained through the judicious use of a constraint package for the reals on top of tabled resolution.

In this paper, we expand on this theme even further. In particular, we examine how the tabled-resolution approach to model checking finite-state systems can be extended to the verification of *parameterized systems*. A parameterized system represents an *infinite* family of systems, each instance of which is finite state. For example, an n-bit shift register is a parameterized system, the parameter in question being n. In general, the verification of parameterized systems lies beyond the reach of traditional model checkers and it is not at all trivial (or even possible) to adapt them to verify parameterized systems.

The main idea underlying our approach is to reduce the problem of verifying parameterized systems to one of determining equivalence of goals in a logic program. We then establish goal equivalences by inducting on the size of proofs of ground instances of goals. To derive such induction proofs we were required to substantially generalize the well-established theory of *logic program transformations* encompassing unfold, fold and goal-replacement transformations. In particular, in a recent paper [RKRR99b] we developed a new transformation system that allows folding using multiple recursive clauses, which seems essential for proving properties of parameterized systems.

In our framework, unfold transformations, which replace instances of clause left-hand sides with corresponding instances of clause right-hand sides, represent resolution. They thereby represent a form of *algorithmic* model checking; viz. the kind of algorithmic, on-the-fly model checking performed in XMC. Unfold transformations are used to evaluate away the base case and the finite portions of the induction step in an induction proof. Fold transformations, which replace instances of clause right-hand sides with corresponding instances of clause left-hand sides, and goal replacement transformations, which replace a goal in a clause right-hand side with a semantically equivalent goal, represent *deductive* reasoning. They are used to simplify a given program so that applications of the induction hypothesis in the induction proof can be recognized.

Using our approach, we have been able to prove liveness and safety properties of a number of parameterized systems. Moreover, our approach does not seem limited to any particular kind of network topology, as the systems we considered have included uni- and bi-directional chains, rings, and trees of processes. The primary benefits can be summarized as follows.

- *Uniform framework.* Our research has shown that finite-state systems, real-time systems, and, now, parameterized systems can be uniformly specified and verified in the tabled logic programming framework.

- *Tighter integration of algorithmic and deductive model checking.* Unfold, fold, and goal-replacement steps can be arbitrarily interleaved within the verification proof of a parameterized system. Thus our approach allows algorithmic model checking computation (unfold) to be integrated with deductive reasoning (fold, goal replacement) at fine levels of granularity. Also, since deductive steps are applied lazily in our approach, finite-state model checking emerges as a special case of verifying parameterized systems.
- *High degree of automation.* Although a fully automated solution to verification of parameterized systems is not possible, for many cases of practical interest, we have identified certain heuristics that can be applied to our proof system in order to completely automate the deduction involved.

The idea of using logic program transformations for proving goal equivalences was first explored in [PP99] for logic program synthesis. Our work expands the existing body of work in logic program transformations with more powerful transformation rules and strategies that are central to verification of parameterized systems. Note that our transformation rules are also applicable for proving general program properties.

Regarding related work in the verification area, a myriad of techniques have been proposed during the past decade for verifying parameterized systems, and the related problem of verifying infinite-state systems. [BCG89,EN95,ID99] reduce the problem of verifying a parameterized system to the verification of an "equivalent" finite-state system. [WL89,KM95,LHR97] seek to identify a "network invariant" that is invariant with respect to the given notion of parallel composition and stronger than the property to be established. The network-invariant approach is applicable to parameterized systems consisting of a number of copies of identical components (or components drawn from some finite set) that are composed in parallel. Another approach [CGJ95] aims to *finitely* represent the state space and transition relation of the entire family of finite-state systems comprising a given parameterized system, and has been used in [KMM⁺97] to extend symbolic model checking [McM93] to the verification of parameterized systems. This method requires the construction of a uniform representation for each class of networks, and the property in question must have a proof that is uniform across the family of networks.

Perhaps the work most closely related to our own involves the use of theorem provers for verifying parameterized systems. Rajan et al. [RSS95] have incorporated a mu-calculus model checker as a decision procedure within the PVS theorem prover [OSR92]. Inductive proofs can be established by the prover via calls to the model checker to verify finite subparts. Graf and Saidi [GS96] combine a custom-built specification/deduction system with PVS to formalize and verify invariant properties of infinite-state systems.

The key difference between our approach and these is that we enhance model checking with deductive capabilities, rather than implement model checking as a decision procedure in a deductive system. In particular, the underlying evaluation mechanism for model checking in XMC is essentially unfolding, and we have enhanced this mechanism with folding and goal-replacement transformations. In our approach, deductive steps are deployed only on demand and hence do not affect the efficacy of the algorithmic model-checking. More importantly our framework demonstrates that a tabled constraint logic-programming system can form the core of a verification engine that can be programmed to verify properties of various flavors of concurrent systems including finite-state, real-time, and parameterized systems.

2   Parameterized System Verification as Goal Equivalence

In this section, we discuss how verification of temporal properties of parameterized systems can be reduced to checking equivalence of goals in a logic program.

```
gen([1]).
gen([0|X]) :- gen(X).
trans([0,1|T], [1,0|T]).
trans([H|T], [H|T1]) :- trans(T, T1).
```

```
thm(X) :- gen(X), live(X).
live(X) :- X = [1|_].
live(X) :- trans(X, Y), live(Y).
```

System description   Property description

Fig. 1. Example: Liveness in a unidirectional token-passing chain

Modeling Parameterized Systems: Consider the parameterized system consisting of a chain of n token-passing processes. In the system's initial state, the process in the right-most position of the chain has the token and no other process has a token. The system evolves by passing the token leftward. A logic program describing the system is given in Figure 1. The predicate **gen** generates the initial states of an n-process chain for all n. A global state is represented as an ordered list (a list in Prolog-like notation is of the form [Head|Tail]) of zeros and ones, each bit corresponding to a local state, and the head of the list corresponding to the local state of the left-most process in the chain. Each process in the chain is a two-state automaton: one with the token (an entry of 1 in the list) and the other without the token (an entry of 0). The set of bindings of variable S upon evaluation of the query gen(S) is { [1], [0,1], [0,0,1], ... }. The predicate **trans** in the program encodes a single transition of the global automaton. The first clause in the definition of **trans** captures the transfer of the token from right to left; the second clause recursively searches the state representation until the first clause can be applied.

Liveness Properties: The predicate **live** in Figure 1 encodes the temporal property we wish to verify: eventually the token reaches the left-most process. The first clause succeeds for global states where the token is already in the left-most process (a good state). The second (recursive) clause checks if a good state is reachable after a (finite) sequence of transitions. Thus, every member of the family satisfies the liveness property if and only if $\forall$ X gen(X) $\Rightarrow$ live(X). Moreover, this is the case if $\forall$ X thm(X) $\Leftrightarrow$ gen(X), i.e., if thm and gen are equivalent (have the same least model). Clearly, testing the equivalence of these goals is infeasible since the minimal model of the logic program is infinite. However, we present in Section 3 a proof methodology, based on program transformations, for proving equivalences between such goals.

Safety Properties: We can model safety properties by introducing negation into the above formulation for liveness properties, using the temporal-logic identity $G\ \phi \equiv \neg F\ \neg\phi$. Although our program transformation systems have been recently extended to handle programs with negation [RKRR99a], for simplicity of exposition we present here an alternative formulation without negation. In particular, we define a predicate bad to represent states that violate the safety property, show that the start states are not bad, and, finally, show that bad states are reachable only from other bad states. For instance, mutual exclusion in the n-process chain can be verified using the following program:

```
bad([1|Xs]) :- one_more(Xs).
bad([_|Xs]) :- bad(Xs).            bad_start(X) :- gen(X), bad(X).

one_more([1|_]).                    bad_src(X,Y) :- trans(X, Y), bad(X).
one_more([_|Xs]) :- one_more(Xs).   bad_dest(X,Y) :- trans(X, Y), bad(Y).
```

bad is true if and only if the given global state has more than one local state with a token. Showing bad_start(X) $\Leftrightarrow$ false establishes that the start states do not violate the safety property. Showing that bad_src(X) $\Leftrightarrow$ bad_dest(X) establishes that states that violate the safety property can be reached only from other states that violate the property. These two facts together imply that no reachable state in the infinite family is bad and thus establish the safety property.

A Note on the Model: XMC [RRR+97] provides a highly expressive process description language based on value-passing CCS [Mil89] for specifying parameterized systems (although XMC is guaranteed to terminate only for finite-state systems). The above simplified presentation (which we will continue to use in the rest of this paper) is used to prevent a proliferation of syntax.

3   Goal Equivalence Proofs Using Tableau

In this section we describe the basic framework to construct such equivalence proofs. We begin by defining the relevant notations.

Notations: We assume familiarity with the standard notions of terms, models, substitutions, unification, and most general unifier (mgu) [Llo93]. A term having no variables is called a *ground* term. *Atoms* are terms with a predicate symbol at the root (true and false are special atoms), and *goals* are conjunctions of atoms. Atoms whose subterms are distinct variables (i.e., atoms of the form $p(X_1, \ldots, X_n)$, where p is a predicate symbol of arity n) are called *open atoms*. We use the following notation (possibly with primes and subscripts): p, q for predicate symbols; X, Y for variables; t, s for terms; $\overline{X}, \overline{Y}$ for sequences of variables; $\overline{t}, \overline{s}$ for sequences of terms; A, B for atoms; σ, θ for substitutions; C, D for Horn clauses; α, β for goals; and P for a *definite logic program*, which is a set of Horn clauses. A Horn clause C is written as $A :- B_1, B_2, \ldots, B_n$. A, the consequent, is called the *head* of C and the antecedent $B_1, B_2, \ldots, B_n$ the *body* of C. Note that we can write Horn clauses as $A :- \alpha$. Semantics of a definite logic program P is given in terms of least Herbrand models, $M(P)$. Given a goal α and a program P, SLD resolution is used to prove whether instances of α are in $M(P)$. This proof is constructed recursively by replacing an atom B in α with $\beta\theta$ where $B' :- \beta \in P$ and $\theta = mgu(B, B')$. We use $P_0, P_1, \ldots, P_n$ to denote a program transformation sequence where P_{i+1} is obtained from P_i by applying a transformation. We call P_0 as the *original* program.

3.1   Tableau Construction

The *goal equivalence problem* is: given a logic program P and a pair of goals α, β, determine if α and β are semantically equivalent in P: i.e., whether for all ground substitutions θ, $\alpha\theta \in M(P) \Leftrightarrow \beta\theta \in M(P)$. This problem is undecidable in general and we attempt to provide a deductive system for identifying equivalence.

We now develop a tableau-based proof system for establishing goal equivalence. Our proof system is analogous to SLD resolution. Let $\Gamma = \langle P_0, P_1, \ldots, P_i \rangle$ be a sequence of logic programs such that P_{j+1} is obtained from P_j ($1 \leq j < i$) by the application of a rule in our tableau. Further let $M(P_0) = M(P_1) = M(P_2) = \ldots = M(P_i)$. An *e-atom* is of the form $\Gamma \vdash \alpha \equiv \beta$ where α and β are goals, and represents our proof obligation: that α and β are semantically equivalent in any program in Γ. An *e-goal* is a (possibly empty) sequence of e-atoms (e-atoms and e-goals correspond to atoms and goals in standard resolution).

$$(\mathbf{Ax}) \qquad \frac{\Gamma \vdash \alpha \equiv \beta}{\text{hline}} \qquad\qquad \text{where } \alpha \cong \beta$$

$$(\mathbf{Tx}) \qquad \frac{\Gamma \vdash \alpha \equiv \beta}{\Gamma, P_{i+1} \vdash \alpha \equiv \beta} \qquad\qquad \text{where } M(P_{i+1}) = M(P_i)$$

$$(\mathbf{Gen}) \qquad \frac{\Gamma \vdash \alpha \equiv \beta}{\text{hline } \Gamma, P_{i+1} \vdash \alpha \equiv \beta, \quad P_0 \vdash \alpha' \equiv \beta'} \quad \text{where } M(P_{i+1}) = M(P_i) \text{ if } \alpha' \equiv \beta'$$

Fig. 2. Rules for constructing equivalence tableau

The three rules used to construct equivalence tableau are shown in Figure 2. The *axiom elimination rule* (**Ax**) is applicable whenever the equivalence of goals α and β can be established by some automatic mechanism, denoted by $\alpha \cong \beta$. Axiom elimination is akin to the treatment of facts in SLD resolution. The *program transformation rule* (**Tx**) attempts to simplify a program in order to expose the equivalence of goals. We use this rule when we apply a (semantics-preserving) transformation that does not add any equivalence proof obligations *e.g.* unfolding, folding. The *sub-equivalence generation rule* (**Gen**) replaces an e-atom with new e-atoms which are (hopefully) simpler to establish. This step is akin to standard SLD resolution step. Note that the proof of $\alpha' \equiv \beta'$ may involve a transformation sequence different from, and not just an extension of, Γ. A *successful tableau* for an e-goal E_0 is a finite sequence $E_0, E_1, \ldots, E_n$ where E_{i+1} is obtained from E_i by applying **Ax/Tx/Gen** and E_n is empty.

Theorem 1 *Let $E_0, E_1 \ldots, E_n$ be a successful tableau, P_0 be a (definite) logic program and $E_0 = \langle P_0 \rangle \vdash \alpha \equiv \beta$. For all ground substitutions θ, $\alpha\theta \in M(P_0) \Leftrightarrow \beta\theta \in M(P_0)$, i.e. α and β are equivalent in the least Herbrand model of P_0.*

The tableau, however, is not complete. There can be no such complete tableau (which can be proved using a reduction in [AK86]).

Theorem 2 *The problem of determining equivalence of predicates described by logic programs is not recursively enumerable.*

3.2 Program Transformations

The **Tx** and **Gen** rules of our proof system require us to transform a program P_i into a program P_{i+1}. This is accomplished by applying logic program transformations that include unfolding, folding, goal replacement and definition introduction.

For a simple illustration of program transformations, consider Figure 3. There, program P_1 is derived from P_0 by *unfolding* the occurrence of r in the definition of q. P_2 is derived from P_1 by *folding* t,s in the definition of p using the definition of q. While unfolding is semantics preserving, indiscriminate fold-

```
p :- t, s.      p :- t, s .   p :- q.
q :-  r , s.    q :- t, s.     q :- t, s.
r :- t.         r :- t.        r :- t.
...             ...            ...

Program P₀   Program P₁   Program P₂
```

Fig. 3. Example of an unfold/fold transformation sequence

ing may introduce circularity, thereby removing finite proof paths. *e.g.* folding t,s in the definition of q in P_2 using the definition of p in P_0 results in a program p :- q. q :- p. r :- t. .... This removes p and q from the least model.

We now present the program transformations informally. For a formal description, the reader is referred to [RKRR99b]. With each clause C in program P_i of the transformation sequence, we associate a pair of integer counters that bound the size of a shortest proof of any ground atom A derived using C in program P_i relative to the size of a shortest proof of A in P_0. Thus the counters keep track of potential reductions in proof lengths. Conditions on counters are then used to determine if a given application of folding is semantics preserving.

$$B : -\beta, \boxed{A}, \beta'.$$

$$A_1 : -\alpha_1.$$
$$A_2 : -\alpha_2.$$
$$\vdots \quad\quad \Longrightarrow$$
$$A_n : -\alpha_n.$$

$$B\sigma_1 : -(\beta, \boxed{\alpha_1}, \beta')\sigma_1.$$
$$B\sigma_2 : -(\beta, \boxed{\alpha_2}, \beta')\sigma_2.$$
$$\vdots$$
$$B\sigma_n : -(\beta, \boxed{\alpha_n}, \beta')\sigma_n.$$
$$A_1 : -\alpha_1.$$
$$\vdots$$
$$A_n : -\alpha_n.$$

$$P_j: \quad \begin{array}{l} A_1 : -\alpha_1'. \\ \vdots \\ A_n : -\alpha_n'. \end{array}$$

$$P_i: \quad \begin{array}{l} B : -\beta, \boxed{\alpha_1}, \beta'. \\ B : -\beta, \boxed{\alpha_2}, \beta'. \\ \vdots \\ B : -\beta, \boxed{\alpha_n}, \beta'. \end{array} \Longrightarrow B : -\beta, \boxed{A}, \beta'.$$

(a) Unfolding   (b) Folding

Fig. 4. Schema for unfold/fold transformations

Unfolding of an atom A in the body of a clause in P_i is shown in Figure 4a. The conditions for applying the transformation are : (i) $A_1, \ldots, A_n$ are the only clause heads in P_i which unify with A, and (ii) σ_j is the mgu of A and A_j for all $1 \le j \le n$. Note that these conditions are taken directly from resolution, which means that unfolding is essentially a resolution step.

Folding replaces an occurrence of the body of a clause with its head. The clause where the replacement takes place is called the *folded* clause and the clauses used to perform the replacement are called the *folder* clauses. The folding schema is illustrated in in Figure 4b, where the clauses of B are the folded clauses, and the clauses of A are the folder clauses. The folder clauses may come from some earlier program $P_j (j \le i)$ in the transformation sequence. The conditions for applying the transformation are[1]: (i) α_l is an instance of α_l' with substitution σ_l for all $1 \le l \le n$ (ii) there is an atom A such that $\forall 1 \le l \le n \; A_l \sigma_l = A$ and the folder clauses are the only clauses in P_j whose heads unify with A.

Goal replacement replaces an atom B in a clause $A :- \alpha, B\beta$ in program P_i with a semantically equivalent atom B' to obtain the clause $A :- \alpha, B', \beta$. Note that such a replacement can change lengths of proofs of A arbitrarily. To obtain the counters associated with the new clause we need to estimate the changes in proof lengths. In practice, we do so by using techniques based on Integer Linear Programming. Details appear in [Roy99].

Theorem 3 ([RKRR99b]) *Let $P_0, P_1, \ldots, P_N$ be a sequence of definite logic programs where P_{i+1} is obtained from P_i by an application of unfolding, folding, or goal replacement. Then $M(P_i) = M(P_0)$, $1 \le i \le N$.*

Definition-introduction transformation adds clauses defining a new predicate to a program P_i. This transformation is used to generate "names" for goals. Note

---

[1] In addition, certain other conditions need to be imposed including conditions on the counters of the folder and folded clauses; we do not mention them here.

that after definition introduction, $M(P_{i+1}) \neq M(P_i)$ since a new predicate is added to P_{i+1}. But for every predicate p in P_i, and all ground terms $\bar{t}$, $p(\bar{t}) \in M(P_i) \Leftrightarrow p(\bar{t}) \in M(P_{i+1})$. The tableau presented earlier can be readily extended to include such transformations.

3.3   Checking Goal Equivalence from Syntax

Recall that the axiom elimination rule (**Ax**) is applicable whenever we can mechanically establish the equivalence of two goals. We now develop a *syntax-based* technique to establish the equivalence of two *open atoms*, i.e., atoms of the form $p(\overline{X})$ and $q(\overline{X})$.

```
p(X) :- r(X).           q(X) :- s(X).
p(X) :- e(X,Y), p(Y).   q(X) :- e(X,Y), q(Y).
r(X) :- b(X).           s(X) :- b(X).
```

Consider the example program given above. We can infer that $r(X) \equiv s(X)$ since r and s have identical definitions. Then, we can infer $q(X) \equiv p(X)$, since their definitions are "isomorphic". Formally:

Definition 1 (Syntactic Equivalence) *A syntactic equivalence relation, $\overset{P}{\sim}$, is an equivalence relation on the set of predicates of a program P such that for all predicates p, q in P, if $p \overset{P}{\sim} q$ then:*
1. p and q have same arity, and
2. Let the clauses defining p and q be $\{C_1, \dots, C_m\}$ and $\{D_1, \dots, D_n\}$, respectively. Let $\{C'_1, \dots, C'_m\}$ and $\{D'_1, \dots, D'_n\}$ be such that C'_l (D'_l) is obtained by replacing every predicate symbol r in C_l (D_l) by s, where s is the name of the equivalence class of r (w.r.t. $\overset{P}{\sim}$). Then there exist two functions $f : \{1, \dots, m\} \to \{1, \dots, n\}$ and $g : \{1, \dots, n\} \to \{1, \dots, m\}$ such that:
(a) $\forall 1 \leq i \leq m$ C'_i is an instance of $D'_{f(i)}$, and
(b) $\forall 1 \leq j \leq n$ D'_j is an instance of $C'_{g(j)}$.

The largest syntactic equivalence relation can be computed by starting with all predicates in the same class, and repeatedly splitting the classes until a fixed point is reached. Syntactic equivalence is sound w.r.t. semantic equivalence, *i.e.*

Lemma 4 *Let P be a program and $\overset{P}{\sim}$ be the syntactic equivalence relation. For all predicates p, q, if $p \overset{P}{\sim} q$, then $p(\overline{X}) \equiv q(\overline{X})$.*

4   Automated Construction of Equivalence Tableau

We describe an algorithmic framework for creating strategies to automate the construction of the tableau. The objective is to: (a) find equivalence proofs that arise in verification with limited user intervention, and (b) apply deduction rules lazily, i.e. a proof using the strategy is equivalent to algorithmic verification for finite-state systems.

> **algorithm** *Prove*(A, B: open atoms, Γ:prog. seq.)
> **begin**
>   **let** $\Gamma = \langle P_0, \ldots, P_i \rangle$
>   (* **Ax** rule *)
>   **if** $(A = p(\overline{X}) \wedge B = q(\overline{X}) \wedge p \overset{P_i}{\sim} q)$ **then**
>   **return** *true*
>   **else nondeterministic choice**
>   (* **Tx** rule *)
>   **case** $FIN(\langle \Gamma, unfold(P_i) \rangle)$: (* Unfolding *)
>   **return** $Prove(A, B, \langle \Gamma, unfold(P_i) \rangle)$
>   **case** Folding is possible in P_i:
>   **return** $Prove(A, B, \langle \Gamma, fold(P_i) \rangle)$
>   (* **Gen** rule *)
>   **case** Conditional folding is possible in P_i:
>   **let** $(A', B') = new\_atom\_equiv\_for\_fold(P_i)$
>   **return** $replace\_and\_prove(A, B, \langle A', B' \rangle, \Gamma)$
>   **case** Conditional equivalence is possible in P_i:
>   **let** $(\alpha, \beta) = new\_goal\_equiv\_for\_equiv(A, B, P_i)$
>   **return** $replace\_and\_prove(A, B, \langle \alpha, \beta \rangle, \Gamma)$
>   **end choices**
> **end**

Fig. 5. Algorithmic framework for automated construction of tableau

In our framework, the tableau rules and associated transformations are applied in the following order. Given an c-atom $\Gamma \vdash \alpha = \beta$, the proof is complete whenever the axiom elimination rule (**Ax**) is applicable. Hence, we first choose to apply **Ax**. When the choice is between the **Tx** and **Gen** rules, we choose the former since **Tx** allows unfolding, i.e. resolution. This will ensure that our strategies will perform algorithmic verification, a' la XMC, for finite-state systems. For infinite-state systems, however, uncontrolled unfolding will diverge. To create finite unfolding sequences we impose the finiteness condition *FIN* in Definition 2. If *FIN* prohibits any further unfolding we either apply the folding transformation associated with **Tx** or use the **Gen** rule. Care must be taken, however, when **Gen** is chosen. Recall from the definition of **Gen** that $\alpha \equiv \beta$ in P_{i+1} implies $\alpha \equiv \beta$ in P_i only if we can prove a new equivalence $\alpha' \equiv \beta'$ in P_0. Since **Gen** itself does not specify the goals in the new equivalence, its application is highly nondeterministic. We limit the nondeterminism by using **Gen** only to enable **Ax** or **Tx** rules.

Definition 2 (Finiteness condition) *An unfolding transformation sequence* $\Gamma = \langle P_0, \ldots, P_i, \ldots \rangle$ *satisfies FIN(Γ) if and only if for the clause C and atom A selected for unfolding at P_i: (i) A is distinct modulo variable renaming from any atom B which was selected in unfolding some clause $D \in P_j (j < i)$ where C is obtained by repeated unfolding of D (ii) the term size of A is bounded a-priori by a constant.*

Hence, when no further unfoldings are possible, we apply any possible folding. If no foldings are enabled, we check if there are new atom equivalences that will enable a folding step. We call this a *conditional folding* step. Note that atom equivalences may be of the form $p(\bar{t}) \equiv q(\bar{s})$, where t and s are sequences of arbitrary *terms*, whereas the test for syntactic equivalence is only done on open atoms. We therefore introduce new definitions to convert them into open atoms. Finally, we look for new goal equivalences, which, if valid, can lead to syntactic equivalence. This is called as a *conditional equivalence* step. In such a step, an equivalence proof on arbitrary goals is first converted into equivalence between open atoms by introducing new definitions.

The above intuitions are formalized in Algorithm *Prove* (see Figure 5). Given a program transformation sequence Γ, and a pair of open atoms A, B, algorithm *Prove* attempts to prove that $\Gamma \vdash A \equiv B$. Algorithm *Prove* uses the following functions. Function *replace_and_prove* constructs proofs for sub-equivalences created by applying the **Gen** rule. *replace_and_prove*$(A, B, \langle \alpha, \beta \rangle, \Gamma)$ first introduces definitions for α and β, then proves the equivalence $\langle P_0 \rangle \vdash \alpha \equiv \beta$ by invoking *Prove*, then replaces α by β and finally invokes *Prove* to complete the proof of $\Gamma \vdash A \equiv B$. Functions *unfold*(P) and *fold*(P) apply unfolding and folding transformations respectively to program P and return a new program. Whenever conditional folding is possible, the function *new_atom_equiv_for_fold*(P) finds the pair of atoms whose replacement is necessary to do the fold operation. Similarly, when conditional equivalence is possible, *new_goal_equiv_for_equiv*(A, B, P) finds a pair of goals α, β s.t. syntactic equivalence of A and B can be established after replacing α with β in P.

Note that *Prove* terminates as long as the number of definitions introduced (i.e., new predicate symbols added) is finite. If multiple cases of the nondeterministic choice are enabled, then *Prove* tries them in the order specified in Figure 5. If none of the cases apply, then evaluation fails, and backtracks to the most recent unexplored case. There may also be nondeterminism within a case; for instance, many fold transformations may be applicable at the same time. By providing selection functions to pick from the applicable transformations, one can implement concrete strategies from *Prove*. Details appear in [Roy99].

4.1   Example: Liveness Property in Chains

Recall the logic program of Figure 1 which formulates a liveness property about token-passing chains, namely, that the token eventually reaches the left-most process in any arbitrary length chain. To establish the liveness property, we prove thm(X) $\equiv$ gen(X) by invoking *Prove*(thm(X), gen(X), $\langle P_0 \rangle$). The proof tree is illustrated in Figure 6 (dashed arrows in the figure denote multiple applications of the transformation annotating the arrow). *Prove* first unfolds the clauses of thm to obtain:

```
thm([1]).
thm([0|X]) :- gen(X), X = [1|_].
thm([0|X]) :- gen(X), trans(X,Y), live([0|Y]).
```

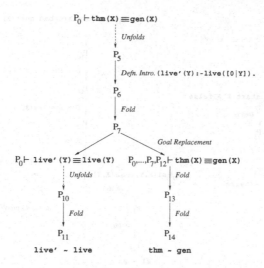

Fig. 6. Proof tree for liveness property in chains

Since no unfolding or folding is applicable, conditional folding is done giving rise to the (sub)-equivalence `live([0|Y]) ≡ live(Y)`. Since `live([0|Y])` is not an open atom, a new definition `live'(Y) :- live([0|Y])` is added to P_5 to yield P_6. Then *Prove* folds the third clause of `thm` using this definition and recursively invokes *Prove*(`live'(X)`, `live(X)`, $\langle P_0 \rangle$) to establish `live'(X) ≡ live(X)`. This subproof appears in the left branch of Figure 6. Finally, *Prove* replaces `live'(X)` with `live(X)` in the clauses of `thm` and completes the proof of `thm(X) ≡ gen(X)` by applying two folding steps.

It is interesting to observe in Figure 6 that the unfolding steps that transform P_0 to P_5 and P_7 to P_{10} are interleaved with folding steps. This illustrates how we interleave algorithmic model-checking steps with deduction steps.

4.2   Example: Mutual Exclusion in Token Rings

Algorithm *Prove* generates a proof for mutual exclusion in a n-process token ring. The token ring is described by the following logic program:

```
gen([0,1]).                        trans(X,Y) :- trans1(X,Y).
gen([0|X]) :- gen(X).              trans([1|X],[0|Y]) :- trans2(X,Y).
trans1([0,1|T],[1,0|T]).           trans2([0], [1]).
trans1([H|T],[H|T1]) :- trans1(T,T1). trans2([H|X],[H|Y]) :- trans2(X,Y).
```

As in the case of chains (see Section 2), we represent the global state of a ring as a list of local states. Processes with tokens are in local state 1 while processes without tokens are in state 0. `trans` is now divided into two parts: `trans1` which transfers the token to the left neighbor in the list, and `trans2` which transfers the token form the front of the list to the back, thereby completing the ring. Mutual

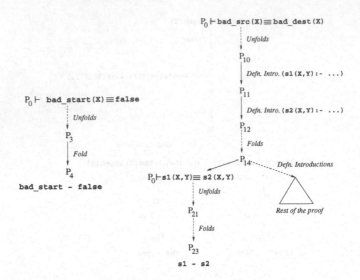

Fig. 7. Proof trees for mutual exclusion in token rings

exclusion, a safety property, is modeled using the predicates `bad`, `bad_start`, etc. as discussed in Section 2. These predicates, along with those listed above, form the initial program P_0. Recall that a safety proof can be completed by showing `bad_start` $\equiv$ `false` and `bad_src` $\equiv$ `bad_dest`. Figure 7 illustrates the proofs generated by *Prove* to demonstrate these equivalences.

Invocation of *Prove*(`bad_start(X)`, `false`, $\langle P_0 \rangle$) performs unfoldings to obtain program P_3 where `bad_start` is defined using a single clause, namely: `bad_start([0|X]) :- gen(X), bad(X)`. *Prove* now folds using the original definition of `bad_start` to obtain P_4 where `bad_start` is defined by the clause: `bad_start([0|X]) :- bad_start(X)`. Since `bad_start` is defined by a single self-recursive clause, it is detected as failed, and hence `bad_start` $\equiv$ `false`.

An invocation of *Prove*(`bad_src(X)`, `bad_dest(X)`, $\langle P_0 \rangle$) performs unfoldings, to get program P_{10} where the definitions of `bad_src` and `bad_dest` are:

```
bad_src([0,1,1|X], [1,0,1|X]).
bad_src([0,1,H|T], [1,0,H|T]) :- one_more(T).
bad_src([1|X],[1|Y]) :- trans1(X,Y), one_more(X).
bad_src([H|X],[H|Y]) :- trans1(X,Y), bad(X).
bad_src([1,1|X],[0,1|Y]) :- trans2(X,Y).
bad_src([1,H|X],[0,H|Y]) :- trans2(X,Y), one_more(X).
bad_dest([0,1,1|X], [1,0,1|X]).
bad_dest([0,1,H|T], [1,0,H|T]) :- one_more(T).
bad_dest([1|X],[1|Y]) :- trans1(X,Y), one_more(Y).
bad_dest([H|X],[H|Y]) :- trans1(X,Y), bad(Y).
bad_dest([1,1|X],[0,1|Y]) :- trans2(X,Y), one_more(Y).
bad_dest([1,H|X],[0,H|Y]) :- trans2(X,Y), bad(Y).
```

Now, to show bad_src ≡ bad_dest, *Prove* applies conditional equivalence
steps, generating the following (sub)-equivalences:

trans1(X,Y), one_more(X) ≡ trans1(X,Y), one_more(Y)
trans1(X,Y), bad(X) ≡ trans1(X,Y), bad(Y)
trans2(X,Y), one_more(Y) ≡ trans2(X,Y)
trans2(X,Y), one_more(X) ≡ trans2(X,Y), bad(Y)

We now show the proof of the first of the above. Proofs of the other three
(sub)-equivalences proceed similarly, and are omitted. Since the goals are not
open atoms, the following definitions are created to obtain program P_{12}.

    s1(X, Y) :- trans1(X,Y), one_more(X).
    s2(X, Y) :- trans1(X,Y), one_more(Y).

Since no new unfolding is applicable at P_{12}, the clauses of bad_src and bad_dest
are folded using the above two clauses to obtain P_{14}. $Prove(s1(X), s2(X), \langle P_0 \rangle)$
is then invoked by *Prove* as a subproof. This subproof is completed after a
sequence of unfoldings (to reach program P_{21}) and two foldings, yielding P_{23}:

    s1([0,1|X], [1,0|X]).   s2([0,1|X], [1,0|X]).
    s1([1|X],[1|Y]) :- trans1(X,Y).   s2([1|X],[1|Y]) :- trans1(X,Y).
    s1([H|X],[H|Y]) :- s1(X,Y).   s2([H|X],[H|Y]) :- s2(X,Y).

s1 $\overset{P_{23}}{\sim}$ s2 and hence s1(X) ≡ s2(X).

5 Concluding Remarks

A preliminary prototype implementation of our transformation system, built on
top of our XSB tabled logic-programming system [XSB99], has been completed.
So far we have been able to automatically verify a number of examples including
the ones described in this paper. Our plan now is to investigate the scalability
of our system on more complex problems such as parameterized versions of the
Rether protocol [DSC99] and the Java meta-locking protocol [BSW00].

References

AH96.   R. Alur and T. A. Henzinger, editors. *Computer Aided Verification (CAV '96)*, volume 1102 of *Lecture Notes in Computer Science*, New Brunswick, New Jersey, July 1996. Springer-Verlag. 186

AK86.   K. Apt and D. Kozen. Limits for automatic verification of finite-state systems. *Information Processing Letters*, 15:307–309, 1986. 178

BCG89.   M. Browne, E. Clarke, and O. Grumberg. Reasoning about networks with many identical finite-state processes. *Information and Computation*, 81(1):13–31, 1989. 174

BSW00.   S. Basu, S.A. Smolka, and O.R. Ward. Model checking the Java meta-locking algorithm. In *IEEE International Conference on the Engineering of Computer Based Systems*. IEEE Press, April 2000. 185

CGJ95.   E. Clarke, O. Grumberg, and S. Jha. Verifying parametrized networks using abstraction and regular languages. In *CONCUR, LNCS 962*, 1995. 174

Dil96.   D. L. Dill. The Murφ verification system. In Alur and Henzinger [AH96], pages 390–393. 172

DP99.   G. Delzanno and A. Podelski. Model checking in CLP. In *TACAS'99*, volume LNCS 1579, pages 74–88. Springer-Verlag, March 1999. 172

DRS99.   X. Du, C.R. Ramakrishnan, and S.A. Smolka.   Tabled resolution + constraints: A recipe for model checking real-time systems. Technical report, Dept. of Computer Science, SUNY Stony Brook, http://www.cs.sunysb.edu/~vicdu/papers, 1999. 173

DSC99.   X. Du, S. A. Smolka, and R. Cleaveland. Local model checking and protocol analysis. *Software Tools for Technology Transfer*, 1999. 185

EN95.   E. Emerson and K.S. Namjoshi. Reasoning about rings. In *POPL*, pages 85–94, 1995. 174

GS96.   S. Graf and H. Saidi. Verifying invariants using theorem proving. In Alur and Henzinger [AH96]. 174

Hol97.   G. J. Holzmann. The model checker SPIN. *IEEE Transactions on Software Engineering*, 23(5):279–295, May 1997. 172

ID99.   C. N. Ip and D. L. Dill. Verifying systems with replicated components in Murφ. *Formal Methods in System Design*, 14(3), May 1999. 174

KM95.   R.P. Kurshan and K. Mcmillan. A structural induction theorem for processes. *Information and Computation*, 117:1–11, 1995. 174

KMM$^+$97. Y. Kesten, O. Maler, M. Marcus, A. Pnueli, and E. Shahar. Symbolic model-checking with rich assertional languages. In *CAV, LNCS 1254*, 1997. 174

LHR97.   D. Lesens, N. Halbwachs, and P. Raymond. Automatic verification of parametrized linear networks of processes. In *POPL*, pages 346–357, 1997. 174

Llo93.   J.W. Lloyd. *Foundations of Logic Programming, Second Edition*. Springer-Verlag, 1993. 176

McM93.   K. L. McMillan. *Symbolic Model Checking*. Kluwer Academic, 1993. 174

Mil89.   R. Milner. *Communication and Concurrency*. International Series in Computer Science. Prentice Hall, 1989. 176

OSR92.   S. Owre, N. Shankar, and J. Rushby. PVS: A Prototype Verification System. *Proceedings of CADE*, 1992. 174

PP99.   A. Pettorossi and M. Proietti. Synthesis and transformation of logic programs using unfold/fold proofs. *Journal of Logic Programming*, 41, 1999. 174

RKRR99a.   A. Roychoudhury, K. Narayan Kumar, C.R. Ramakrishnan, and I.V. Ramakrishnan. Beyond Tamaki-Sato style unfold/fold transformations for normal logic programs. In *ASIAN, LNCS 1742*, pages 322–333, 1999. 176

RKRR99b.   A. Roychoudhury, K. Narayan Kumar, C.R. Ramakrishnan, and I.V. Ramakrishnan. A parameterized unfold/fold transformation framework for definite logic programs. In *PPDP, LNCS 1702*, pages 396–413, 1999. 173, 178, 179

Roy99.   A. Roychoudhury. Program transformations for automated verification of parameterized concurrent systems.   Technical report, Department of Computer Science, State University of New York at Stony Brook, http://www.cs.sunysb.edu/~abhik/papers, 1999. Dissertation proposal. 179, 182

RRR+97.   Y.S. Ramakrishna, C.R. Ramakrishnan, I.V. Ramakrishnan, S.A. Smolka,
           T. Swift, and D.S. Warren. Efficient model checking using tabled resolu-
           tion. In *CAV, LNCS 1254*, 1997. 172, 176
RSS95.   S. Rajan, N. Shankar, and M. K. Srivas. An integration of model checking
           with automated proof checking. In *CAV, LNCS 939*, 1995. 174
Urb96.   L. Urbina. Analysis of hybrid systems in CLP(R). In *Constraint Program-
           ming (CP'96)*, volume LNCS 1102. Springer-Verlag, 1996. 172
WL89.   P. Wolper and V. Lovinfosse. Verifying properties of large sets of processes
           with network invariants. In *Automatic Verification Methods for Finite
           State Systems, LNCS 407*, 1989. 174
XSB99.   The XSB logic programming system v2.01, 1999. Available by anonymous
           ftp from www.cs.sunysb.edu/~sbprolog. 185

Abstracting WS1S Systems to Verify
Parameterized Networks*

Kai Baukus[1]**, Saddek Bensalem[2], Yassine Lakhnech[2]**, and Karsten Stahl[1]

[1] Institute of Computer Science and Applied Mathematics, University of Kiel
Preusserstr. 1–9, D-24105 Kiel, Germany.
{kba,kst}@informatik.uni-kiel.de
[2] VERIMAG, Centre Equation
2 Av. de Vignate, 38610 Gières, France.
{bensalem,lakhnech}@imag.fr

Abstract. We present a method that allows to verify parameterized networks of finite state processes. Our method is based on three main ideas. The first one consists in modeling an infinite family of networks by a single WS1S transition system, that is, a transition system whose variables are set (2nd-order) variables and whose transitions are described in WS1S. Then, we present methods that allow to abstract a WS1S system into a finite state system that can be model-checked. Finally, in order to verify liveness properties, we present an algorithm that allows to enrich the abstract system with strong fairness conditions while preserving safety of the abstraction. We implemented our method in a tool, called PAX, and applied it to several examples.

1 Introduction

Recently there has been much interest in the automatic and semi-automatic verification of parameterized networks, i.e., verification of a family of systems $\{\mathcal{P}_i \mid i \in \omega\}$, where each $\mathcal{P}_i$ is a network consisting of i finite-state processes. Apt and Kozen show in [AK86] that the verification of parameterized networks is undecidable. Nevertheless, automated and semi-automated methods for the verification of restricted classes of parameterized networks have been developed. The methods presented in [GS92,EN95,EN96] show that for classes of ring networks of arbitrary size and client-server systems, there exists k such that the verification of the parameterized network can be reduced to the verification of networks of size up to k. Alternative methods presented in [KM89,WL89,BCG89,SG89,HLR92,LHR97] are based on induction on the number of processes. These methods require finding a network invariant that abstracts any arbitrary number of processes with respect to a pre-order that preserves the property to be verified. While this method has been originally presented for linear networks, it has been generalized in [CGJ95] to networks generated by context-free grammars. In [CGJ95], abstract transition systems were

---

* This work has been partially supported by the Esprit-LTR project Vires.
** Contact Author.

S. Graf and M. Schwartzbach (Eds.): TACAS/ETAPS 2000, LNCS 1785, pp. 188–203, 2000.
© Springer-Verlag Berlin Heidelberg 2000

used to specify the invariant. An abstract transition system consists of abstract states specified by regular expressions and transitions between abstract states. The idea of representing sets of states of parameterized networks by regular languages is applied in [KMM$^+$97], where additionally finite-state transducers are used to compute predecessors. These ideas are applied to linear networks as well as to processes arranged in a tree architecture and semi-automatic symbolic backward analysis methods for solving the reachability problem are given. The work presented in [ABJN99] extends the ideas in [KMM$^+$97] by considering the effect of applying infinitely often a transition that satisfies certain restrictions. These restrictions allow to characterize the effect of the repeated application of the transition by finite-state transducers. Moreover, the method presented in [ABJN99] allows to consider networks of processes guarded by both local and global conditions that restrict the context in which a transition can be taken. Global conditions are typically used in many mutual exclusion algorithms such as Szymanski's algorithm, the bakery and ticket algorithms by Lamport and Dijkstra's algorithm.

In this paper we present a method for the verification of parameterized networks that can deal with a larger class of networks than the methods presented in [KMM$^+$97,ABJN99] and that is applicable to verify *communal liveness* (also referred to as *weak liveness*) properties [MP94].

To verify parameterized protocols we first transform a given infinite family of networks of finite processes into a bisimilar single transition system whose variables are set variables and whose transitions are described in WS1S, the weak monadic second order logic of one successor. We call such systems WS1S transition systems. Then, we abstract the obtained WS1S transition system into a finite abstract system that can be analyzed using model-checking techniques. To obtain such a finite abstraction, one needs to come up with an appropriate abstraction relation and to construct a *correct* abstract system, i.e., a system which exhibits for every behavior of the WS1S system a corresponding abstract behavior. We present a method to construct an abstraction relation from the given WS1S transition system and three techniques that allow to *automatically* construct either a correct abstract system, the reachability state graph of a correct abstract system without constructing the system itself or, finally, an abstraction of such a graph. Our experience shows that our method for constructing an abstraction relation is useful for many examples and that it is useful to have the three techniques for constructing an abstract system.

It is well known that an obstacle to the verification of liveness properties using abstraction, e.g. [CGL94,LGS$^+$95,DGG94], is that often the abstract system contains cycles that do not correspond to paths in the concrete system. This is not surprising since the main goal of an abstraction relation is to identify and merge states together, which consequently introduces new cycles. A way to overcome this difficulty is to enrich the abstract system with fairness conditions or more generally ranking functions over well-founded sets that eliminate undesirable cycles, that is, cycles that do not correspond to concrete computations. The main problem is, however, to find such fairness conditions. To tackle this problem, we present an algorithm that given a reachability state graph of an abstraction of a WS1S system enriches the graph with strong fairness conditions while preserving the property that to each concrete computation corresponds an abstract *fair* one. Hence, we can use the enriched graph to prove liveness properties of the WS1S systems, and consequently, of the parameterized network.

We implemented our method in a tool, we call PAX, that uses the decision procedures of MONA [KM98,HJJ+96] to check the satisfiability of WS1S formulas. We then applied our method to several examples including Szymanski's mutual exclusion algorithm, a server-ring as well as a token passing protocol. The first results obtained using our method and PAX are very encouraging.

2 Preliminaries

In this, section, we briefly recall the definition of weak second order theory of one successor (WS1S for short) [Büc60,Tho90] and introduce the logic we use to describe the class of parameterized systems we are interested in.

Terms of WS1S are built up from the constant 0 and 1st-order variables by applying the successor function $succ(t)$ ("$t + 1$"). *Atomic formulae* are of the form b, $t = t'$, $t < t'$, $t \in X$, where b is a boolean variable, t and t' are terms, and X is a set variable (2nd-order variable). WS1S-formulae are built up from atomic formulae by applying the boolean connectives as well as quantification over both 1st-order and 2nd-order variables. *First-order monadic formulae* are WS1S-formulae in which no 2nd-order variables occur.

WS1S-formulae are interpreted in models that assign finite subsets of ω to 2nd-order variables and elements of ω to 1st-order variables. The interpretation is defined in the usual way.

Given a WS1S formula f, we denote by $[\![f]\!]$ the set of models of f. The set of free variables in f is denoted by $free(f)$. We say that f is (1st-order) *closed*, if it does not contain (1st-order) free variables. In addition to the usual abbreviations, given a 2nd-order variable P, we write $\forall_P i : f$ instead of $\forall i : i \in P \rightarrow f$ and $\exists_P i : f$ instead of $\exists i : i \in P \wedge f$.

Finally, we recall that by Büchi [Büc60] and Elgot [Elg61] the satisfiability problem for WS1S is decidable. Indeed, the set of all models of a WS1S-formula is representable by a finite automaton (see, e.g., [Tho90]).

Let n be a variable. To define parameterized systems, we introduce the set $AF(n)$ of formulae f defined by:

$$ f ::= b[x] \mid \neg f \mid f \wedge f \mid \forall_n x : f \mid \exists_n x : f \; , $$

where x is a *position variable*, b is a *boolean array variable*. Let $m \in \omega$. We denote by Σ_m the set of evaluations s such that $s(n) = m$, $s(x) \in \{0, \cdots, m - 1\}$ and $s(b) : \{0, \cdots, m - 1\} \rightarrow \{\text{true}, \text{false}\}$. Then, formulae in $AF(n)$ are interpreted over evaluations $s \in \bigcup_{m \in \omega} \Sigma_m$ in the usual way. In the sequel, we also assume the usual notion of free variables, closed formulae, etc., as known.

3   Parameterized Systems

We now introduce a class of parameterized systems for which we develop an abstraction-based verification technique.

Definition 1 (Boolean Transition Systems). *A boolean transition system $S(i, n)$, parameterized by n and i, where n and i are variables ranging over natural numbers, is described by the triple $(V, \Theta, \mathcal{T})$, where*

- *$V = \{b_1, \ldots, b_k\}$ and each b_j, $1 \leq j \leq k$, is a boolean array of length n.*
- *Θ is a formula in $\mathrm{AF}(n)$ with $\mathrm{free}(\Theta) \subseteq V \cup \{i\}$ and which describes the set of initial states.*
- *$\mathcal{T}$ is a finite set of transitions where each $\tau \in \mathcal{T}$ is given by a formula $\rho_\tau \in \mathrm{AF}(n)$ such that $\mathrm{free}(\rho_\tau) \subseteq V \cup V' \cup \{i\}$ and*

We denote by $\mathcal{P}_m$ the parallel composition $\|_{l=0}^{m-1} S(l, m)$, where $S(l, m)$ is obtained from $S(i, n)$ by substituting m for n and l for i and where $\|$ denotes the interleaving-based parallel composition (asynchronous product). Notice, that if we identify the boolean array variables b_j by the m boolean variables $b_j[1], \cdots, b_j[m]$, the formulae describing the initial states as well as the transitions of $\|_{l=0}^{m-1} S(l, m)$ are first-order WS1S formulae whose free variables are in V, respectively, $V \cup V'$. Thus, $\mathcal{P}_m$ is a transition system in the usual sense, i.e., it does not contain the parameters n and i. Hence, we assume the definition of a computation of $\mathcal{P}_m$ as known and we denote by $[\![\mathcal{P}_m]\!]$ the set of its computations. Then, a *monadic parameterized system* $\mathcal{P}$ (MPS for short) built from $S(i, n)$ is the set $\{\mathcal{P}_m \mid m \geq 1\}$.

To illustrate the above definitions we consider Szymanski's mutual exclusion algorithm [Szy88] as a boolean transition system.

Example 1 (Szymanski's mutual exclusion algorithm). Consider the following version of Szymanski's mutual exclusion algorithm (cf. [ABJN99]), where each process $S(i, n)$ is described as follows:

ℓ_1: **await** $\forall_n j : \mathrm{at\_}\ell_1[j] \vee \mathrm{at\_}\ell_2[j] \vee \mathrm{at\_}\ell_4[j]$
ℓ_2: **skip**
ℓ_3: **if** $\exists_n j : \mathrm{at\_}\ell_2[j] \vee \mathrm{at\_}\ell_5[j] \vee \mathrm{at\_}\ell_6[j] \vee \mathrm{at\_}\ell_7[j]$
          then goto ℓ_4
          else goto ℓ_5
ℓ_4: **await** $\exists_n j : \mathrm{at\_}\ell_5[j] \vee \mathrm{at\_}\ell_6[j] \vee \mathrm{at\_}\ell_7[j]$
ℓ_5: **await** $\forall_n j : \mathrm{at\_}\ell_1[j] \vee \mathrm{at\_}\ell_2[j] \vee \mathrm{at\_}\ell_5[j] \vee \mathrm{at\_}\ell_6[j] \vee \mathrm{at\_}\ell_7[j]$
ℓ_6: **await** $\forall_n j : j < i \rightarrow (\mathrm{at\_}\ell_1[j] \vee \mathrm{at\_}\ell_2[j] \vee \mathrm{at\_}\ell_4[j])$
ℓ_7: $\langle$ *critical section* $\rangle$;   goto ℓ_1

For the sake of presentation, the example is given in the style of [MP95]. The **await** statements express the guards for the transitions leading from one control location to the next one, i.e., the processes have to wait until the guard becomes true. In our formal model the control locations are modeled by a boolean array variable at_ℓ_k for each location ℓ_k, $1 \le k \le 7$. According to Definition 3 the transition from ℓ_1 to ℓ_2 is given by the $AF(n)$ formula:

$$(\forall_n j : at\_\ell_1[j] \lor at\_\ell_2[j] \lor at\_\ell_4[j]) \land \forall_n j : j \ne i \rightarrow \bigwedge_{l=1}^{7} at\_\ell_l[j] \leftrightarrow at\_\ell'_l[j]$$
$$\land at\_\ell_1[i] \land \neg at\_\ell'_1[i] \land at\_\ell'_2[i] \land \bigwedge_{l=3}^{7} at\_\ell_l[i] \leftrightarrow at\_\ell'_l[i] \ .$$

The initial condition states that each process starts in ℓ_1.

Our aim is to prove that this algorithm satisfies the mutual exclusion property, which can be expressed by $\Box \neg \exists_n i, j : i \ne j \land at\_\ell_7[i] \land at\_\ell_7[j]$.   ◇

4   WS1S Transition Systems

In this section, we introduce WS1S transition systems which are transition systems with variables ranging over finite sub-sets of ω and show how they can be used to represent infinite families of boolean transition systems.

Definition 2 (WS1S Transition Systems). *A WS1S transition system* $\mathcal{S} = (\mathcal{V}, \Theta, \mathcal{T})$ *is given by the following components:*

- $\mathcal{V} = \{X_1, \ldots, X_k\}$: *A finite set of second order variables where each variable is interpreted as a finite set of natural numbers.*
- Θ: *A WS1S formula with* $free(\Theta) \subseteq \mathcal{V}$ *describing the initial condition of the system.*
- $\mathcal{T}$: *A finite set of transitions where each* $\tau \in \mathcal{T}$ *is represented as a WS1S formula* $\rho_\tau(\mathcal{V}, \mathcal{V}')$, *i.e.,* $free(\rho_\tau) \subseteq \mathcal{V} \cup \mathcal{V}'$.   □

The computations of $\mathcal{S}$ are defined as usual. Moreover, let $[\![\mathcal{S}]\!]$ denote the set of computations of $\mathcal{S}$.

Relating parameterized and WS1S transition systems. We define a translation that maps an MPS to a bisimilar WS1S system.

We fix a 2nd-order variable P that is used to model the set of indices of the processes up to n. The translation from MPS to WS1S systems uses a function tr from $AF(n)$ into WS1S. This function replaces in an $AF(n)$-formula all occurrences of atomic sub-formulae of the form $b[i]$ by $i \in B$, all n by $max(P) + 1$[1], and λ_n by λ_P where λ is one of the quantifiers $\forall$ or $\exists$.

Definition 3 (Translation of Boolean to WS1S Systems). *Consider an MPS system* $\mathcal{P}$ *built from* $S(i, n)$ *where* $S(i, n) = (V, \Theta, \mathcal{T})$. *Define a WS1S system* $(\widetilde{V}, \widetilde{\Theta}, \widetilde{\mathcal{T}})$ *by constructing the variable set, the initial condition, and the transitions as follows:*

- *For each boolean array* b_k *in* V, $\widetilde{V}$ *contains the variable* B_k. *Additionally,* $\widetilde{V}$ *contains the set variable* P.
- *Let* $\widetilde{\Theta}$ *be* $\exists n : P = \{0, \ldots, n-1\} \land \bigcup_{l=1}^{k} B_l \subseteq P \land (\forall_P i : tr(\Theta))$.
- *Let* $\widetilde{\mathcal{T}}$ *be the set* $\{\exists_P i : tr(\rho_\tau) \land P = P' \land \bigcup_{l=1}^{k} B'_l \subseteq P' \mid \tau \in \mathcal{T}\}$.

---

[1] It is not difficult to check that $max(P)$ can be expressed in WS1S.

We denote the above transformation of an MPS system $\mathcal{P}$ by $Tr(\mathcal{P})$.   □

Example 2 (Szymanski cont'd). The translation of Example 1 into a WS1S system introduces a set variable P and set variables $At\_\ell_1, \ldots, At\_\ell_7$. According to the above definition of the translation we have as initial condition $\widetilde{\Theta}$

$$\exists n : P = \{0, \ldots, n-1\} \wedge \bigcup_{l=1}^{k} B_l \subseteq P \wedge \forall_P i : (i \in At\_\ell_1 \wedge \bigwedge_{l=2}^{7} i \notin At\_\ell_l) \ .$$

The translation of the $AF(n)$ formula characterizing the transition from ℓ_1 to ℓ_2 presented in Example 1 yields

$$(\forall_P j : j \in At\_\ell_1 \cup At\_\ell_2 \cup At\_\ell_4) \wedge \forall_P j : j \neq i \rightarrow \bigwedge_{l=1}^{7} j \in At\_\ell_l \leftrightarrow j \in At\_\ell'_l$$
$$\wedge\, i \in At\_\ell_1 \wedge i \notin At\_\ell'_1 \wedge i \in At\_\ell'_2 \wedge \bigwedge_{l=3}^{7} i \in At\_\ell_l \leftrightarrow i \in At\_\ell'_l$$

which, using the invariant $\bigcup_{l=1}^{k} B_l \subseteq P$, can be simplified to

$$(\forall_P j : j \in At\_\ell_1 \cup At\_\ell_2 \cup At\_\ell_4) \wedge \bigwedge_{l=3}^{7} At\_\ell_l = At\_\ell'_l$$
$$\wedge\, At\_\ell'_1 = At\_\ell_1 \setminus \{i\} \wedge At\_\ell'_2 = At\_\ell_2 \cup \{i\} \ .$$

◇

In order to state the relationship between an MPS $\mathcal{P}$ and its translation, we introduce a function h relating the states of both systems. Let $\mathcal{P}$ be an MPS built from $S(i,n) = (V, \Theta, \mathcal{T})$ with $V = \{b_1, \ldots, b_k\}$. Let m be a natural number. Let $\widetilde{\Sigma}$ denote the set of interpretations $\tilde{s}$ of $\widetilde{V}$ such that $\tilde{s}(X) \subseteq \tilde{s}(P)$, for each $X \in \widetilde{V}$. Then, define $h_m : \Sigma_m \rightarrow \widetilde{\Sigma}, s \mapsto \tilde{s}$ by $\tilde{s}(P) = \{0, \ldots, m-1\}$ and $\tilde{s}(B_j) = \{l < m \mid s(b_j[l]) = \text{true}\}$, for every $1 \leq j \leq k$. Then, we define $h = \bigcup_{m \in \omega} h_m$. Notice that h is a bijection.

The following lemma shows that h is consistent with the translation tr from $AF(n)$ into WS1S.

Lemma 1. *Let f be a formula in $AF(n)$ with $free(f) \subseteq V \cup V' \cup \{i\}$ and let all $m \in \omega$, for all $s, s' \in \Sigma_m$, we have:*

$$(s, s') \models f \quad \textit{iff} \quad (h(s), h(s')) \models tr(f) \ .$$

□

Using this lemma we can prove the following theorem that justifies our verification method given in Section 5. The theorem states that $\mathcal{P}_m$ is bisimilar to $Tr(\mathcal{P})$ when we initialize P to $\{0, \ldots, m-1\}$.

Theorem 1 (Relating Boolean and WS1S Systems). *Let $\mathcal{P}$ be an MPS built from $S(i,n)$ and $m \in \omega$. Then, h is a bisimulation between $\mathcal{P}_m$ and $Tr^*(\mathcal{P})$, where $Tr^*(\mathcal{P})$ is obtained from $Tr(\mathcal{P})$ by taking as initial condition $\widetilde{\Theta} \equiv P = \{0, \ldots, m-1\} \wedge \bigcup_{l=1}^{k} B_l \subseteq P \wedge \forall_P i : tr(\Theta)$.*

Proof: Consider s_0 to be an initial state of $\mathcal{P}_m$, i.e., $s_0 \models \Theta$. With Lemma 1 it follows that

$$h(s_0) \models P = \{0, \ldots, m-1\} \wedge \bigcup_{l=1}^{k} B_l \subseteq P \wedge (\forall_P i : tr(\Theta)) \ .$$

Vice versa, for any initial state $\tilde{s}_0$ of some computation in $[\![Tr^*(\mathcal{P})]\!]$ the state $h^{-1}(\tilde{s}_0)$ is an initial state of $\mathcal{P}$.

With the same argumentation we can show for $s, s' \in \Sigma_m$ and $\tilde{s}, \tilde{s}' \in \tilde{\Sigma}$ with $\tilde{s} = h(s)$ that for any $\tau \in \mathcal{T}$,

- if s' is a τ-successor of s then $h(s')$ is a $tr(\rho_\tau)$-successor of $\tilde{s}$, and
- if $\tilde{s}'$ is an $tr(\rho_\tau)$-successor of $\tilde{s}$ then $h^{-1}(\tilde{s}')$ is a τ-successor of s.

Hence, both systems are bisimilar.   □

Using Theorem 1, we can prove the following:

Corollary 1. *Let $\mathcal{P}$ be an MPS built from $S(i, n)$. Then, lifting h to computations, we have a bijection between $\bigcup_{m \in \omega} [\![\mathcal{P}_m]\!]$ and $[\![Tr(\mathcal{P})]\!]$.*   □

5   Abstracting WS1S Systems

In Section 4, we have shown how parameterized boolean transition systems can be translated into WS1S systems. This translation allows us to consider a single, though infinite-state, transition system instead of an infinite family of systems. In the following, we present a method to construct finite abstractions of WS1S systems.

To do so, we first present a heuristic that allows to construct for a given WS1S system an abstraction function such that the corresponding abstract system has a finite state space. Then, we present a method that, given such a function, constructs a finite transition system that is an abstraction of the given WS1S system. Model-checking techniques can then be used to construct a state graph of this abstract system.

The nodes of the constructed graph represent sets of abstract states and the edges correspond to abstract transitions. This graph contains all reachable abstract states. The nodes of the finest graph that can be constructed represent singleton sets, i.e., single abstract states. The coarsest graph has one node corresponding to the set of reachable states. In fact, the granularity of the computed graph depends on the techniques used during exploration.

While the previous method first constructs an abstract system from which a graph is computed, we also present two methods inspired by [GS97] for computing an abstract state graph, resp. an abstraction of it, without computing the abstract transition system at all. These methods are useful in case the abstract system is not computable for size reasons.

Finally, we describe our PAX tool which implements these techniques using MONA [KM98,HJJ+96].

We first recall some definitions and the idea of proving properties of systems by abstraction.

Given a transition system $\mathcal{S} = (\mathcal{V}, \Theta, \mathcal{T})$ and a total abstraction relation $\alpha \subseteq \Sigma \times \Sigma_A$, we say that $\mathcal{S}_A = (\mathcal{V}_A, \Theta_A, \mathcal{T}_A)$ is an *abstraction* of $\mathcal{S}$ w.r.t. α, denoted by $\mathcal{S} \sqsubseteq_\alpha \mathcal{S}_A$, if the following conditions are satisfied:

- $s_0 \models \Theta$ implies $\alpha(s_0) \models \Theta_A$
- $\tau \circ \alpha^{-1} \subseteq \alpha^{-1} \circ \tau_A$.

Let $\Box\varphi, \Box\varphi_A$ be invariance formulae, i.e., φ, φ_A are state formulae. Then, from $\mathcal{S} \sqsubseteq_\alpha \mathcal{S}_A$, $\alpha^{-1}(\llbracket \varphi_A \rrbracket) \subseteq \llbracket \varphi \rrbracket$, and $\mathcal{S}_A \models \Box\varphi_A$ we can conclude $\mathcal{S} \models \Box\varphi$. This statement, which is called preservation result, shows the interest of verification by abstraction: since if $\mathcal{S}_A$ is finite, it can automatically be checked whether $\mathcal{S}_A \models \Box\varphi_A$. In fact a similar preservation result holds for any temporal logic without existential quantification over paths, e.g., $\forall CTL^*$, LTL, or $\mu_\Box$ [CGL94,DGG94,LGS+95].

5.1   Constructing the Abstraction Function

Our heuristic to construct an abstraction function for WS1S systems assumes the transitions to have the following form:

$$\exists_P i : G \wedge L(i) \wedge C(i) \wedge \mathcal{V}' = exp(\mathcal{V}, \mathcal{V}') \ ,$$

where $G, L(i), C(i)$ are WS1S formulae whose free variables are in $\mathcal{V}$ and such that:

- G is a 1st-order closed WS1S formula. Intuitively, G describes a global condition. E.g., in the Szymanski example (see Example 2), the presented transition contains the global condition $\forall_P j : j \in \text{At\_}\ell_1 \cup \text{At\_}\ell_2 \cup \text{At\_}\ell_4$.
- $L(i)$ is a quantifier-free formula with i as the unique free 1st-order variable. Intuitively, if i models a process index then $L(i)$ is a condition on the local state of this process.
- $C(i)$ is a condition that as in the case of $L(i)$ has i as the unique free 1st-order variable but which contains 1st-order quantifiers. Intuitively, it imposes conditions on the context of process i.

Though, the above requirements restrict the set of considered WS1S systems, it still includes all translations of *MPS* systems.

Let $\mathcal{S} = (\mathcal{V}, \Theta, \mathcal{T})$ be a WS1S system whose transitions satisfy the restriction above.

We are now prepared to present our heuristic for constructing abstraction functions. The set $\mathcal{V}_A$ of abstract variables contains a boolean variable b_X for each variable $X \in \mathcal{V}$. Moreover, for each global guard G, resp. local guard L occurring in a transition, it contains a boolean variable b_G, resp. b_L. Since the context guards $C(i)$ describe a dependence between process i and the remaining processes, it turns out to be useful to combine them with the local guards. Indeed, this allows to check, for instance, whether some dependence is propagated over some transitions. Therefore, we introduce boolean variables b_{L_k,C_l} for some boolean combinations of local guards and context guards. Additionally, $\mathcal{V}_A$ contains a boolean variable for each state formula appearing in the property to be verified.

It remains now to present how we relate the concrete and abstract states, i.e., to describe an abstraction relation α. The abstraction relation α can be expressed on the syntactic level by a predicate $\widehat{\alpha}$ over $\mathcal{V}, \mathcal{V}_A$ which is defined as the conjunction of the following equivalences:

$$b_X \equiv X \neq \emptyset$$
$$b_G \equiv G$$
$$b_L \equiv \exists_P i : L(i)$$
$$b_{L_k,C_l} \equiv \exists_P i : L_k(i) \wedge C_l(i)$$
$$b_\xi \equiv \xi$$

Henceforth, we use $\widehat{\alpha}(\mathcal{V}', \mathcal{V}'_A)$ to denote the predicate obtained from $\widehat{\alpha}$ by substituting the unprimed variables with their primed versions.

Example 3 (Szymanski cont'd). Applying the above heuristic on Szymanski's algorithm (see Example 2) we get seven boolean variables:

$$\psi_i \equiv \text{At\_}\ell_i \neq \emptyset, \text{ for each } 1 \leq i \leq 7 .$$

The global guards not referring to i can be derived by the above variables and do not lead to a finer partitioning of the state space. All the local guards $i \in \text{At\_}\ell_l$ would introduce a boolean variable with meaning $\exists i : i \in \text{At\_}\ell_l$ which is equivalent to stating that $\text{At\_}\ell_l$ is not empty. In the transition leading from ℓ_6 to ℓ_7 we have a context $\forall j < i : j \in \text{At\_}\ell_1 \cup \text{At\_}\ell_2 \cup \text{At\_}\ell_4$ which we have to combine with the local guards $i \in \text{At\_}\ell_l$. For this example it turns out to be enough to take only one combination, namely

$$\varphi \equiv \exists i : i \in \text{At\_}\ell_7 \wedge \forall j < i : j \in \text{At\_}\ell_1 \cup \text{At\_}\ell_2 \cup \text{At\_}\ell_4 .$$

Moreover, for the property of interest we introduce

$$\xi \equiv \neg \exists l, j : l \neq j \wedge l \in \text{At\_}\ell_7 \wedge j \in \text{At\_}\ell_7 .$$

◇

5.2   Constructing the Abstract System

In Section 5.1, we presented a method that allows to construct an abstraction function from a given WS1S system. In this section, we show how to use this abstraction function to automatically construct a finite transition system that can be model-checked.

Let $\mathcal{S} = (\mathcal{V}, \Theta, \mathcal{T})$ be a given WS1S system that satisfies the restriction given in Section 5.1 and let α be the abstraction function constructed by the method given in the same section. Notice that since the abstract variables are booleans, the abstract system we construct is finite, and hence, can be subject to model-checking techniques. Moreover, we make use of the fact that both $\widehat{\alpha}(\mathcal{V}, \mathcal{V}_A)$ and the transitions in $\mathcal{T}$ are expressed in WS1S to give an effective construction of the abstract system.

Henceforth, given a set γ of abstract states, we denote by $\widehat{\gamma}(\mathcal{V}_A)$ a WS1S formula that characterizes this set.

The abstract system we construct contains for each concrete transition τ an abstract transition τ_A, which is characterized by the formula

$$\exists \mathcal{V}, \mathcal{V}' : \widehat{\alpha}(\mathcal{V}, \mathcal{V}_A) \wedge \rho_\tau(\mathcal{V}, \mathcal{V}') \wedge \widehat{\alpha}(\mathcal{V}', \mathcal{V}'_A)$$

with free variables $\mathcal{V}_A$ and $\mathcal{V}'_A$.

The initial states of the abstract system we construct can be described by the formula

$$\exists \mathcal{V} : \widehat{\alpha}(\mathcal{V}, \mathcal{V}_A) \ .$$

To compute them, one has to find all states fulfilling this formula, which is possible since this is a WS1S formula.

5.3   Constructing Abstract State Graphs

We first define state graphs of transition systems. Note that there is a whole set of state graphs for a given transition system.

Definition 4 (State Graphs). *Let $\mathcal{S} = (V, \Theta, \mathcal{T})$ be a transition system and Σ be the set of all reachable states of $\mathcal{S}$. A state graph $\mathcal{G}$ of $\mathcal{S}$ is a tuple $(\mathcal{N}, \mathcal{E}, \mathcal{N}_0, \mu)$, where $\mathcal{N}$ is a set of nodes, $\mathcal{N}_0 \subseteq \mathcal{N}$ is the set of initial nodes, $\mathcal{E} \subseteq \mathcal{N} \times \mathcal{T} \times \mathcal{N}$ is a set of labeled edges, and $\mu : \mathcal{N} \rightarrow 2^\Sigma$ is a labeling function, such that the following conditions are satisfied:*

1. *$[\![\Theta]\!] \subseteq \bigcup_{q \in \mathcal{N}_0} \mu(q)$.*
2. *$\forall q \in \mathcal{N}, \tau \in \mathcal{T} : post_\tau(\mu(q)) \subseteq \bigcup_{(q,\tau,q') \in \mathcal{E}} \mu(q')$, where $post_\tau(\mu(q))$ is the set of successors of $\mu(q)$ w.r.t. τ.*   □

There are several strategies to calculate a state graph for an abstract system. First of all, if one has previously computed the abstract system as explained in Section 5.2, one can use model-checking techniques, for example a forward state exploration, to construct a state graph. The actual graph obtained depends on the computation techniques used.

Another way is to compute such a graph without calculating the abstract system at all. The nodes of the graph are sets of abstract states. One starts with an initial node representing the set of abstract initial states, which are computed as shown in Section 5.2. Assume that a concrete transition τ and node q are given. The formula

$$\exists \mathcal{V}_A, \mathcal{V}, \mathcal{V}' : \widehat{\mu(q)}(\mathcal{V}_A) \wedge \widehat{\alpha}(\mathcal{V}, \mathcal{V}_A) \wedge \rho_\tau(\mathcal{V}, \mathcal{V}') \wedge \widehat{\alpha}(\mathcal{V}', \mathcal{V}'_A)$$

describes the set M of abstract post states w.r.t. τ_A. Then, a node q' with $\mu(q') = M$ and an edge (q, τ_A, q') are added to the graph. This process is repeated until no new nodes or edges can be added. The so obtained graph is a state graph of $\mathcal{S}_A$, we call this calculation *precise computation*.

Since we restrict ourselves to abstraction functions of the form

$$\widehat{\alpha}(\mathcal{V}, \mathcal{V}_A) \equiv \bigwedge_{1 \le i \le k} a_i \leftrightarrow \varphi_i(\mathcal{V}) \ ,$$

where $\mathcal{V}_A = \{a_1, \ldots, a_k\}$, we can also eliminate the abstract variables $\mathcal{V}_A$ by replacing each abstract variable a_i by $\varphi_i(\mathcal{V})$.

The decision procedure for WS1S is based on constructing a finite automaton over finite words that recognizes the set of models of the considered formula. In practice, however, it can happen that the automaton cannot be constructed because of its size. In this case, we propose to go on as follows to obtain an abstract state graph of $\mathcal{S}_A$.

We start with the same initial node as before. Given a node q and concrete transition τ, we construct new nodes by computing for each abstract variable a_i the set $M_i \subseteq \{\text{true}, \text{false}\}$ of fulfilling values for a_i' of

$$\exists \mathcal{V}_A, \mathcal{V}, \mathcal{V}' : \widehat{\mu(q)}(\mathcal{V}_A) \wedge \widehat{\alpha}(\mathcal{V}, \mathcal{V}_A) \wedge \rho_\tau(\mathcal{V}, \mathcal{V}') \wedge (a_i' \leftrightarrow \varphi_i(\mathcal{V}')) \ .$$

Again, the abstract variables $\mathcal{V}_A$ can be eliminated. In case M_i is empty for some i, then there does not exist any post state, and hence, the computation for the other variables can be omitted. Otherwise, instead of taking a node representing the set of abstract post states, one takes a new node q' with $\mu(q') = \{s \mid \forall i : s(a_i) \in M_i\}$ and a new edge (q, τ_A, q'). The set $\mu(q')$ contains at least all possible abstract post states w.r.t. τ_A. It is not difficult to see that this method computes an abstraction of $\mathcal{S}_A$, and hence, is also an abstraction of $\mathcal{S}$.

5.4   The Pax Tool

We use MONA [KM98,HJJ+96] to decide the predicates mentioned above. In fact, MONA is able to construct all models of a WS1S predicate.

Our system PAX constructs state graphs. It uses MONA to compute the abstract initial states, the abstract transitions, or the set of abstract post states represented by a state graph node. To do so, it creates from its input files input for MONA and interprets the MONA results. Once an abstract system (resp. abstract state graph) is constructed, a translation to SMV, alternatively to SPIN, can be used to model-check the obtained abstract system (resp. abstract state graph).

PAX allows the combination of the method of Section 5.2, which consists in computing abstractions of concrete transitions independently of any source abstract state, with the methods of Section 5.3. This is helpful in case MONA does not succeed in computing an abstract transition because of memory limitations.

In Table 1 we give run time results for the calculation of the abstract systems of some examples, one of it is the Szymanski mutual exclusion algorithm given in Example 3. The construction of the state graph from the abstract system does not require mentionable time. We used a Sun Ultra Sparc 5/10 with 768 MB of memory and 333 MHz processor.

Table 1. PAX construction of abstract transition systems

Example	Abstract Transitions System
Szymanski	7 min 28 sec
Server-ring	40 sec
Token passing	5 sec

The run time results for the construction of a state graph (resp. an abstraction) without previous computation of the abstract system of these examples is summarized in Table 2.

Table 2. PAX results for state graph construction

Example	Precise Computation	Abstraction
Szymanski	49 min 52 sec	56 sec
Server-ring	1 min 5 sec	13 sec
Token passing	1 min 40 sec	19 sec

Example 4 (Szymanski cont'd). For the Szymanski's algorithm and the abstraction function given in Example 3, we obtain using the last method of Section 5.3 the state graph presented in Figure 1. The labeling function μ is also given in Figure 1 in form of the predicates $\widehat{\mu(q)}$ for each node q. The initial states are marked by an edge without source node. It is not difficult to check that no state falsifying the mutual exclusion property is reachable in the obtained graph. ◇

6 Proving Liveness Properties

Let S be a WS1S transition system and $\mathcal{G} = (\mathcal{N}, \mathcal{E}, \mathcal{N}_0, \mu)$ be a state graph of S_A constructed from S and an abstraction function α. Let φ be an LTL formula. Let $\xi_1, \cdots, \xi_n$ be the atomic subformulae of φ such that, for every node $p \in \mathcal{G}$, either all states in $\mu(p)$ satisfy ξ_i or none does, i.e., we have either $\widehat{\mu(p)} \to \xi_i$ or $\widehat{\mu(p)} \to \neg\xi_i$ is valid. For each ξ_i, we introduce a proposition P_i. Then, let $\check{\mathcal{G}} = (\mathcal{N}, \mathcal{E}, \mathcal{N}_0, \nu)$ be a Kripke structure with the same nodes, edges, and initial nodes as $\mathcal{G}$ and such that $P_i \in \nu(p)$ iff $\widehat{\mu(p)} \to \xi_i$ is valid. Let also $\check{\varphi}$ be the formula obtained from φ by substituting P_i for ξ_i. Then, $S \models \varphi$, if $\check{\mathcal{G}} \models \check{\varphi}$.

Example 5 (Szymanski cont'd). Let $\mathcal{G} = (\mathcal{N}, \mathcal{E}, \mathcal{N}_0, \mu)$ be the state graph for Szymanski's algorithm given in Example 4. Let us now consider the liveness property $\varphi \equiv \Box\Diamond\psi_7$ expressing that the critical section is entered infinitely

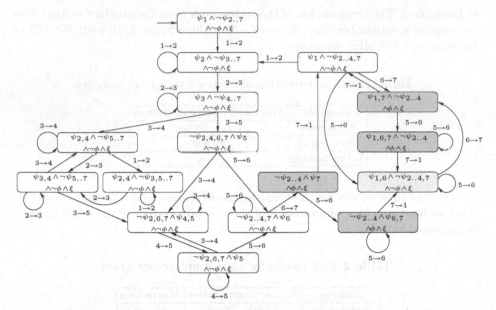

Fig. 1. Reachability graph for Szymanski's mutual exclusion algorithm

often. Clearly, we can define a Kripke structure $\check{\mathcal{G}} = (\mathcal{N}, \mathcal{E}, \mathcal{N}_0, \nu)$ with the same nodes and edges as $\mathcal{G}$ and with a proposition P such that $P \in \nu(p)$ iff $\models \widehat{\mu(p)} \rightarrow \psi_7$. Thus, all nodes labeled by P are shadowed in Figure 1. Moreover, we get $\check{\varphi} \equiv \Box\Diamond P$.   ◇

It is easy to see that $\check{\varphi}$ does not hold in the Kripke structure $\check{\mathcal{G}}$. This is due to the cycles which generate infinite traces in $\check{\mathcal{G}}$ without ever reaching a shadowed node. However, these traces have no corresponding computations in the concrete WS1S system. E.g., the loops labeled $1 \rightarrow 2$ are the abstraction of the transition taking an element out of At_ℓ_1 and adding it to At_ℓ_2. Clearly, since WS1S is interpreted over finite sets, it is impossible to infinitely execute transition $1 \rightarrow 2$ without taking a transition that adds elements to At_ℓ_1.

In this section we present a method that allows us to add fairness conditions to the Kripke structure $\check{\mathcal{G}}$ constructing a fair Kripke structure $\check{\mathcal{G}}^F$ such that we still have $\mathcal{S} \models \varphi$, if $\check{\mathcal{G}}^F \models \check{\varphi}$ and such that the added fairness conditions rule out infinite traces in $\check{\mathcal{G}}$ that have no counter-parts in $\mathcal{S}$.

The method uses a marking algorithm that labels each edge of the considered state graph with one of the symbols $\{+_X, -_X, =_X\}$ for each set variable X of the original WS1S system. Intuitively, the labels $-_X$ resp. $=_X$ express whether the transitions at the concrete level reduce resp. maintain the cardinality of a set X, the label $+_X$ represents all other cases.

For the sake of presentation, we use $\hat{p}(\mathcal{V}_A)$ instead of $\widehat{\mu(p)}$.

Marking Algorithm

Input: WS1S system $\mathcal{S} = (\mathcal{V}, \Theta, \mathcal{T})$, abstraction relation $\widehat{\alpha}$, state graph $\mathcal{G} = (\mathcal{N}, \mathcal{E}, \mathcal{N}_0, \mu)$ of $\mathcal{S}_A$

Output: Edge labeling of $\mathcal{G}$

Description: For each $X \in \mathcal{V}$, for each edge $e = (p, \tau_A, q) \in \mathcal{E}$, let τ be the concrete transition in $\mathcal{T}$ corresponding to τ_A. Moreover, let $\Delta(X, e, \prec)$, with $\prec \in \{\subset, =\}$, denote the WS1S formula:

$$\widehat{p}(\mathcal{V}_A) \wedge \widehat{\alpha}(\mathcal{V}, \mathcal{V}_A) \wedge \widehat{q}(\mathcal{V}'_A) \wedge \widehat{\alpha}(\mathcal{V}', \mathcal{V}'_A) \wedge \tau(\mathcal{V}, \mathcal{V}') \Rightarrow X' \prec X \ .$$

Then, mark e with $-_X$, if $\Delta(X, e, \subset)$ is valid, mark e with $=_X$, if $\Delta(X, e, =)$ is valid, and mark e with $+_X$ otherwise.

Now, for a set variable X we denote with $\mathcal{E}_X^+$ the set of edges labeled with $+_X$.

Then, the fair Kripke structure is defined as $\check{\mathcal{G}}^F = (\check{\mathcal{G}}, F)$ where F is the set of strong fairness conditions containing for each edge e and each of its labels $-_X$ the set $(e, \mathcal{E}_X^+)$. Each fairness condition states that e can only be taken infinitely often if one of the edges in $\mathcal{E}_X^+$ is taken infinitely often.

Example 6 (Szymanski cont'd). Figure 2 shows part of the abstract state graph after running the labeling algorithm. All $=_X$ symbols are left out and the labels $+\text{At}\_\ell_k$, $-\text{At}\_\ell_k$ are abbreviated with $+_k, -_k$. The figure shows a strongly con-

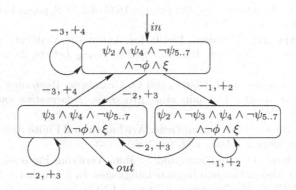

Fig. 2. Part of the labeled state graph

nected part of the graph with the only ingoing edge *in* and only outgoing edge *out*. To prove communal accessibility it is necessary to show that the system cannot cycle forever in this component.

It can be proved, e.g., using model-checking, that $\check{\mathcal{G}}^F \models \check{\varphi}$. Hence, Szymanski's algorithm satisfies $\square\lozenge \exists_p i : i \in \text{At}\_\ell_7$.   ◇

7 Conclusion

We have presented a method for the verification of parameterized networks of finite processes. Our method is based on the transformation of an infinite family of systems into a single WS1S transition system and applying abstraction techniques on this system. We also showed how our method can deal with liveness properties. We have applied this method, which has been implemented in our tool PAX, to a number of parameterized protocols. The obtained results are encouraging.

Closest to our work is [ABJN99]. Therefore, we give a short account of the main differences between this and our work. While the method in [ABJN99] aims at computing the exact set of reachable states, our method computes an over-approximation. On the other hand, their method may fail because of the divergence of the exploration algorithm, even when acceleration is applied. Moreover, our method can deal with a larger class of networks and with a class of liveness properties, often called communal accessibility.

We intend to extend our method to deal with a larger class of liveness properties. It is also clear that we can use WS2S instead of WS1S when we consider networks arranged in trees.

References

ABJN99.   P.A. Abdulla, A. Bouajjani, B. Jonsson, and M. Nilsson. Handling Global Conditions in Parameterized System Verification. In N. Halbwachs and D. Peled, editors, *CAV '99*, volume 1633 of *LNCS*, pages 134–145. Springer, 1999. 189, 191, 202

AK86.   K. Apt and D. Kozen. Limits for Automatic Verification of Finit-State Concurrent Systems. *Information Processing Letters*, 22(6):307–309, 1986. 188

BCG89.   M.C. Browne, E.M. Clarke, and O. Grumberg. Reasoning about networks with many identical finite state processes. *Information and Computation*, 1989. 188

Büc60.   J.R. Büchi. Weak Second-Order Arithmetic and Finite Automata. *Z. Math. Logik Grundl. Math.*, 6:66–92, 1960. 190

CGJ95.   E. Clarke, O. Grumberg, and S. Jha. Verifying Parameterized Networks using Abstraction and Regular Languages. In I. Lee and S. Smolka, editors, *CONCUR '95: Concurrency Theory*, LNCS. Springer, 1995. 188

CGL94.   E. M. Clarke, O. Grumberg, and D. E. Long. Model checking and abstraction. *ACM Transactions on Programming Languages and Systems*, 16(5), 1994. 189, 195

DGG94.   D. Dams, R. Gerth, and O. Grumberg. Abstract interpretation of reactive systems: Abstractions preserving ACTL*, ECTL* and CTL*. In E.-R. Olderog, editor, *Proceedings of PROCOMET '94*. North-Holland, 1994. 189, 195

Elg61.   C.C. Elgot. Decision problems of finite automata design and related arithmetics. *Trans. Amer. Math. Soc.*, 98:21–52, 1961. 190

EN95.   E. A. Emerson and K. S. Namjoshi. Reasoning about rings. In *22nd ACM Symposium on Principles of Programming Languages*, pages 85–94, 1995. 188

EN96.   E. A. Emerson and K. S. Namjoshi. Automatic verification of parameterized synchronous systems. In *8th Conference on Computer Aided Verification*, LNCS 1102, pages 87–98, 1996. 188

Gru97.   O. Grumberg, editor. *Proceedings of CAV '97*, volume 1256 of *LNCS*. Springer, 1997. 203

GS92.   S.M. German and A.P. Sistla. Reasoning about systems with many processes. *Journal of the ACM*, 39(3):675–735, 1992. 188

GS97.   S. Graf and H. Saidi. Construction of Abstract State Graphs with PVS. In Grumberg [Gru97]. 194

HJJ⁺96.   J.G. Henriksen, J. Jensen, M. Jørgensen, N. Klarlund, B. Paige, T. Rauhe, and A. Sandholm. Mona: Monadic Second-Order Logic in Practice. In *TACAS '95*, volume 1019 of *LNCS*. Springer, 1996. 190, 194, 198

HLR92.   N. Halbwachs, F. Lagnier, and C. Ratel. An experience in proving regular networks of processes by modular model checking. *Acta Informatica*, 22(6/7), 1992. 188

KM89.   R.P. Kurshan and K. McMillan. A structural induction theorem for processes. In *ACM Symp. on Principles of Distributed Computing, Canada*, pages 239–247, Edmonton, Alberta, 1989. 188

KM98.   N. Klarlund and A. Møller. MONA Version 1.3 User Manual. BRICS, 1998. 190, 194, 198

KMM⁺97.   Y. Kesten, O. Maler, M. Marcus, A. Pnueli, and E. Shahar. Symbolic Model Checking with Rich Assertional Languages. In Grumberg [Gru97], pages 424–435. 189

LGS⁺95.   C. Loiseaux, S. Graf, J. Sifakis, A. Bouajjani, and S. Bensalem. Property preserving abstractions for the verification of concurrent systems. *Formal Methods in System Design*, 6(1), 1995. 189, 195

LHR97.   D. Lesens, N. Halbwachs, and P. Raymond. Automatic verification of parameterized linear networks of processes. In *POPL '97*, Paris, 1997. 188

MP94.   Z. Manna and A. Pnueli. Verification of parameterized programs. In E. Borger, editor, *Specification and Validation Methods*, pages 167–230, Oxford University Press, 1994. 189

MP95.   Z. Manna and A. Pnueli. *Temporal Verification of Reactive Systems, Safety*. Springer Verlag, 1995. 191

SG89.   Z. Stadler and O. Grumberg. Network grammars, communication behaviours and automatic verification. In *Proc. Workshop on Automatic Verification Methods for Finite State Systems*, Lecture Notes in Computer Science, pages 151–165, Grenoble, France, 1989. Springer Verlag. 188

Szy88.   B.K. Szymanski. A simple solution to Lamport's concurrent programming problem with linear wait. In *Proceedings of International Conference on Supercomputing Systems 1988*, pages 621–626, St. Malo, France, July 1988. 191

Tho90.   W. Thomas. Automata on infinite objects. In *Handbook of Theoretical Computer Science, Volume B: Formal Methods and Semantics*, pages 134–191. Elsevier Science Publishers B. V., 1990. 190

WL89.   P. Wolper and V. Lovinfosse. Verifying properties of large sets of processes with network invariants (extended abstract). In Sifakis, editor, *Workshop on Computer Aided Verification*, LNCS 407, pages 68–80, 1989. 188

FMona: A Tool for Expressing Validation Techniques over Infinite State Systems

J.-P. Bodeveix and M. Filali

IRIT Université Paul Sabatier
118 route de Narbonne, F-31062 Toulouse
{bodeveix,filali}@irit.fr

Abstract. In this paper, we present a generic tool, called FMona, for expressing validation methods. we illustrate its use through the expression of the abstraction technique and its application to infinite or parameterized space problems. After a review of the basic results concerning transition systems, we show how abstraction can be expressed within FMona and used to build a reduced system with decidable properties. The FMona tool is used to express the validation steps leading to synthesis of a finite abstract system;then SMV and/or Mona validate its properties.

Keywords: abstraction, transition systems, model checker, monadic second order logic.

1 Introduction

In recent years, important work has been done in the design and implementation of general specification languages and validation systems. Usually, we distinguish three families of tools: model checkers (SMV [BCMD90], SPIN [Hol91]) to build a finite model and check its temporal properties; automatic proof tools (Mona [HJJ+95]) which offer a complete decision procedure if the underlying logic is decidable and proof assistants (Coq [BBC+97], HOL [GM94] and PVS [ORS92]) which offer an expressive higher order logic (and thus not decidable) and an assistance to the validation of formulas expressed in this logic.

Our experience in using these tools has led us to the following observations:

- model checkers are generally easy to use but their validation algorithm is "hardwired" and the available data structures are generally poor,
- automatic proof tools lack a specification language level to express methods
- and proof assistants lack powerful decision procedures and their integration is a delicate operation. Moreover their use is uneasy and require for instance the knowledge of the underlying type theory, the proof tactics, the tactic language and the underlying decision procedures.

In this paper, we relate an attempt to overcome these problems. We have chosen an intermediate approach combining an automatic proof tool and higher level

S. Graf and M. Schwartzbach (Eds.): TACAS/ETAPS 2000, LNCS 1785, pp. 204–219, 2000.

aspects so that the expression of validation methods becomes easy. Of course, unlike proof assistants, our tool FMona cannot be used to validate the methods themselves. Encoded methods can only be instantiated on given applications. As our automatic proof tool target, we have chosen Mona as the main proof tool. Actually, within its underlying logic (WS1S) we can express transition systems and most of their basic properties without restricting to finite state spaces. Indeed, we can consider parameterized transition systems. We have used FMona to express several validation techniques, e.g. iterative methods with convergence acceleration over parameterized state systems and abstraction methods. In the following, we focus on the use of FMona to express and apply the abstraction method.

The remainder of this paper is organized as follows: section 2 presents the logic underlying the studied validation techniques and its associated tools. Section 3 describes the transition system formalism and states the theorems underlying the abstraction technique. In section 4, we describe the use of the abstraction method to the validation of always true and simulation properties. Sections 5 and 6 illustrate the technique on two concrete examples. Section 7 considers some ongoing work.

2   Monadic Second Order Logic and Related Tools

We recall below the definition of the two variants (WS1S and S1S) of the monadic second order logic of one successor [Tho90]. Then, we present the Mona tool deciding WS1S formulas and its high level interface FMona.

Definition 1 (The S1S and WS1S logics) *Let* $\{x_1, \ldots, x_n\}$ *be a family of first order variables and* $\{X_1, \ldots, X_n\}$ *a family of second order monadic variables. A primitive grammar of this logic can be defined as follows:*

- *A term t is recursively defined as:* $t ::= 0 \mid x_i \mid s(t)$
- *A logic formula f is recursively defined as:* $f ::= X_i(t) \mid \neg f \mid f \wedge f \mid \exists x_i.\ f \mid \exists X_i.\ f$

Notice that the successor function s is the only function.

Validity of a formula A closed formula is valid in S1S or WS1S if it is valid in the interpretation on the set $\mathcal{N}$ of naturals, where s is the successor function, first order quantifiers relate to the naturals and second order quantifiers to the subsets (finite in the case of WS1S) of $\mathcal{N}$. These two logics are decidable [Tho90].

The monadic second order logic naturally supports the method presented since it makes it possible on the one hand to express the concept of sequence of execution on a finite state space and the temporal properties associated, and on the other hand the refinement relation between a parameterized concrete space and a finite abstract space.

The Mona Tool The Mona tool [HJJ+95] implements a decision procedure for WS1S, based on the automata theory. The Mona syntax accepts the constructions of the WS1S logic presented in the preceding section. Mona data types are thus limited to booleans, naturals and finite sets of naturals. Thus, propositional, first order and second order variables are respectively declared, existentially and universally quantified by var_i, ex_i and all_i where i is the order of the variable.

The FMona Tool The FMona tool [BF99b] is a high level interface for Mona. For instance, it is possible to declare enumerated and record with update types and quantify over them. Furthermore, FMona allows the definition of higher order macros parameterized by types and predicates. FMona source code is typechecked, macro expanded and translated to pure Mona. The following example defines the transition relation req1 between the states st and st'. The complete example is given in section 5.

```
type PC = {out,req,mutex}; type Sys = record{pc1,pc2: PC; y1,y2: nat;};
pred req1(var Sys st,st') =
  st.pc1=out & st'=st with {pc1:=req; y1:=st.y2+1;};
```

Note that the expression st'=st with { pc1 := req; y1 := st.y2 + 1;} expresses that st' is obtained by updating the fields pc1 and y1 of st.

We will use the FMona tool to express parameterized transition systems, abstraction relations, the synthesis of finite abstractions and the validation of their safety properties (mainly the so called always true properties).

3   The Formalism and the Basic Results

This section presents the formalism used: transition systems [Arn92]. We recall then the basic results concerning transition systems. The Coq proof assistant has been used to formalize the definitions and to validate the stated theorems.

Notations Given a set S, its complement is denoted $\overline{S}$. In the following, sets and predicates are identified. Given a relation $\varphi \subset A \times B$ and a subset $P \subset A$, we note $\varphi(P) = \{y \in B \mid \exists x : P(x) \wedge \varphi(x,y)\}$.

3.1   Transition Systems, Refinements, Simulations and Implementations

Definition 2 *A labeled transition system is defined by a quadruple $(E, I, L, \rightarrow)$, where E is a set of states, $I \subset E$ is the set of initial states, L is a set of labels and $\rightarrow \subset E \times L \times E$ is the transition relation. We will note $e \xrightarrow{l} e'$ instead of $(e, l, e') \in \rightarrow$.*

Definition 3 (Invariance) *A predicate P is **invariant** in the transition system S if: it is true over the initial states and is is preserved by each transition.*

*A state $s \in E$ is **reachable** in S if there exists a sequence $s_0, \ldots, s_n = s$ such that $s_0 \in I$ and $\forall i \in 0..n - 1 : s_i \rightarrow s_{i+1}$. The set of reachable states of a* *transition system S will be denoted $Acc(S)$. A predicate P is said to be* **always true** *in S if it holds in all reachable states of S. This is denoted $S \vdash \Box P$.*

Theorem 1 (Sufficient condition for validity) *An invariant property is always true.*

Within FMona, we define the macro `reachable` and `always_true` as follows:

```
pred reachable(type State,
   pred(var State s) init, pred(var State s,s') tr, var State s) =
      ex array nat of State A: ex nat i: A[i]=s & init(A[0]) &
         all nat j where j < i: tr(A[j],A[j+1]);

pred always_true(type State, pred(var State s) p,
                     pred(var State s) init, pred(var State s,s') tr) =
   all State s: reachable(init,tr,s) ⇒ p(s);
```

Definition 4 (Refinement) *Given two transition systems with the same set of labels L,*
$C = (E_c, I_c, L, \rightarrow_c)$ *and* $A = (E_a, I_a, L, \rightarrow_a)$, *and* $\varphi \subset E_c \times E_a$. *$C$ refines A through φ, denoted $C \sqsubseteq_\varphi A$, if:*

- *φ maps each initial state of C to an initial state of A.*
- *Given two states c and c' of E_c such that $c \xrightarrow{l} c'$ and a state $a \in E_a$ in relation with c through φ, there exists a state $a' \in E_a$ in relation with c' such that $a \xrightarrow{l} a'$.*

Definition 5 (Run) *Given a transition system $S - (E, I, L, \rightarrow)$. A run is a relation $\_ \Rightarrow \_ \in E \times L^* \times E$ inductively defined as:*

- *$e \xrightarrow{\epsilon} e$*
- *if $e \xrightarrow{l} e'$ and $e' \xrightarrow{a} e''$ then $e \xrightarrow{l.a} e''$*

We define the set of **finite traces** *$T(S)$ of the system S as follows:*
$$T(S) = \{l \in L^* \mid \exists i \in I, e \in E : i \xrightarrow{l} e\}.$$

Definition 6 (Simulation and implementation) *Given two transition systems C and A. C* **simulates** *A through φ if for every state c of C reachable by a trace t, c has a φ image reachable in A by t. C* **implements** *A if the set of traces of C is a subset of the set of traces of A.*

Theorem 2 (Sufficient conditions) *Refinement is a sufficient condition for simulation. Simulation is a sufficient condition for implementation.*

The validation of always true properties relies on the following theorems which state two equivalent sufficient conditions; the first one is expressed at the abstract level and the second one at the concrete level.

Theorem 3 (Always true properties preservation) *Given two transition systems C and A such that C simulates A through φ. If the abstraction of P by φ ($\overline{\varphi(\overline{P})}$) is always true over A, then P is always true over C. More formally, we have the two equivalent formulas:*

$$\frac{C\,simulates_\varphi\, A \quad A \vdash \Box\overline{\varphi(\overline{P})}}{C \vdash \Box P} \qquad \frac{C\,simulates_\varphi\, A \quad \varphi^{-1}(Acc(A)) \Rightarrow P}{C \vdash \Box P} \qquad (1)$$

3.2   Abstraction

The abstraction technique aims at verifying the properties of a transition system through the reduction of its state space: the original system is said concrete and the reduced one is said abstract. In fact, it can be considered as the reverse of the refinement technique where we derive a concrete system from an abstract one. The abstraction technique synthesizes an abstract system from the concrete one. Relevant properties are studied over the abstract system and inherited by the concrete one. This method has been used by [CGL94] to reduce the state explosion resulting from an exhaustive search over a finite state space. It is also used by [BLO98] for analyzing infinite state space systems. Given an abstraction function, they propose heuristics for the construction of the abstract system whereas in our approach the abstract system is built in an automatic way by the FMona tool.

In the following, we recall the basic definitions and results.

Definition 7 (Abstraction) *Let $C = (E_c, I_c, L, \to_c)$ be a transition system, E_a a set of so called abstract states and φ a relation over $E_c \times E_a$. The abstraction of C through φ is the transition system $(E_a, I_a, L, \to_a)$ where I_a is the image by φ of I_c and for each label l, $\overset{l}{\to}_a$ is the set of images through φ of the pairs connected by $\overset{l}{\to}_c$.*

It follows that the abstraction of a transition can be expressed by the generic and higher order FMona macro:

```
pred tr_a(type State_c, type State_a, pred(var State_c c, c') tr_c,
        pred(var State_c c, var State_a a) φ, var State_a a,a') =
  ex State_c c,c': φ(c,a) & φ(c',a') & tr_c(c,c');
```

Theorem 4 (Refinements and abstractions) *Let φ a total relation between two state spaces E_c and E_a. A transition system over E_c refines its abstraction through φ.*

4   Automatic Validation through Abstraction

Let us recall that the abstraction introduced in the paragraph 3.2 consists in defining a finite reduced system starting from a concrete system, a finite state space and a total relation known as the abstraction. It is the reverse of a refinement as the starting system is the concrete one. Moreover, for a refinement, the two transition systems are provided.

One generally considers two approaches for the expression of properties to be validated:

- the first one is based on states: a property is expressed as a temporal logic predicate over the state space (more exactly over the state variables defining the interface of the system).
- the second one is based on transitions: we are interested in a simulation property between a concrete system and an abstract system (also called the reference system).

In the following, we illustrate the abstraction method by considering the two approaches: to validate the mutual exclusion implemented by the bakery algorithm, we adopt a state based approach; to validate some classes of cache coherency protocols, we adopt the transition based approach.

4.1 Specification and Synthesis of the Abstract Transition System

The formulas defining the transitions of the abstract transition system, as introduced in definition 7, are quantified over the domain of the concrete space and thus are not propositional. It follows that the existence of a transition between two abstract states is not necessarily decidable. In order to be in a decidable context, we consider the framework of the WS1S logic for expressing:

- the infinite or parameterized concrete state space (with first and second order variables),
- the transitions of the concrete system,
- the abstraction relation between the concrete and abstract systems.

Thus, according to definition 7, an abstract transition is a WS1S predicate over two abstract variables. Consequently, the properties of an abstract system can

- either be studied within the WS1S logic, which assumes the encoding of temporal logic operators in this formalism [Tho90]. Then, safety properties (which are inherited) can be expressed and automatically decided [ABP97].
- or be studied using a model checker as SMV [BCMD90]. Such a use requires the synthesis of a propositional expression of abstract transitions. Since this alternative resorts to a dedicated tool, it seems to be more efficient on the considered examples. The synthesis of the propositional expression can be performed through two methods:
    - by an exhaustive exploration of the abstract state space: the existence of a transition between two abstract states is determined by the validity of a closed WS1S formula (definition 7).

- by a symbolic reduction to propositional logic of an abstract transition expressed in WS1S. This reduction is possible within the Mona tool where the set of solutions of a predicate with free variables is encoded by an transition system whose transitions are labeled by propositional formulas. In this context the free variables are booleans and the automaton generated by Mona contains a unique transition.

Let us illustrate the synthesis of the finite transition system over a trivial example. The state space of the concrete transition system is a finite set of naturals of unknown size, the concrete transition is defined by the predicate $\text{Init}_c(S) = (S = \{0\})$ and the transition $\text{Tr}_c(S, S') = \exists_1 x, y : y \in S \land S' = S \backslash \{y\} \cup \{x\}$. As an abstraction, we consider a state reduced to a unique boolean b, and the abstraction relation $\varphi(S, b) = (b \Leftrightarrow \forall_1 x, y : x \in S \land y \in S \Rightarrow x = y)$. The abstract transition system is defined by the predicate $\text{Init}_a(b) = \exists_2 S : \text{Init}_c(S) \land \varphi(S, b)$ and the transition $\text{Tr}_a(b, b') = \exists_2 S, S' : \varphi(S, b) \land \text{Tr}_c(S, S') \land \varphi(S', b')$. The Mona tool can automatically simplify the previous monadic second order logic formulas to propositional formulas. Actually, we have synthesized the finite transition system defined by: $\text{Init}_a(b) = b$ and $\text{Tr}_a(b, b') = b \Rightarrow b'$.

4.2 Verification of Always True Properties

Given a total abstraction relation φ, the validation of a formula on the concrete transition system relies on the deduction rules of theorem 3. In this theorem, the abstract system is the abstraction through φ of the concrete system. By theorem 4, φ being total, the concrete system simulates its abstraction. Then, the rules (1) can be simplified as follows:

$$\frac{\text{Abs}_\varphi(C) \vdash \Box\varphi(\overline{P})}{C \vdash \Box P} \qquad \frac{\varphi^{-1}(Acc(\text{Abs}_\varphi(C))) \Rightarrow P}{C \vdash \Box P}$$

Given these two rules, the validity of P is derived form the properties of the abstract transition system. Let us recall that the synthesis can be expressed in WS1S. Consequently, the two preceding rules give two decidable sufficient conditions. To summarize, given a user defined abstraction relation, we have two automatic verification methods:

Method 1

1. Construction of the abstract transition system.
2. Construction of the reachable states Acc of the abstract transition system.
3. Definition of a superset of the reachable states of the concrete transition system as the inverse image by φ of Acc.
4. At the concrete level, we show that $\varphi^{-1}(Acc) \Rightarrow P$.

Note that the term $\varphi^{-1}(Acc)$ can be interpreted as a lemma automatically proven through an exhaustive exploration of the abstract state space. This lemma helps in the validation of P.

Method 2

1. Construction of the abstract transition system.
2. Computation of the abstraction of P: $\varphi(\overline{P})$.
3. Verification of this abstraction over the reachable states of the abstract transition system.

Since the abstract state space is finite, this verification can be performed by a model checker like SMV. This second method uses a dedicated tool for the verification of always true properties.

4.3 Validation of Simulation Relations

The goal is to determine the existence of a simulation relation between a concrete system and a reference system. For that, we provide a projection of the concrete space to the state space of reference and a total abstraction relation. Then, we show that the restriction of the concrete system to some superset of its reachable states refines the reference system.

Thus, given a user defined projection π and a total abstraction relation φ_{abs}, the construction of the simulation relation automatically proceeds according to the following steps:

1. Construction of the abstract transition system (WS1S): the concrete system refines the abstract system.
2. Construction of the accessible states *Acc* of the abstract transition system (WS1S).
3. Restriction of the concrete transition system to the reverse image of the accessible states of its abstraction.
4. Validation of the refinement between the reduced concrete transition system and the reference system (WS1S formula).

4.4 Abstraction Heuristics

To reduce parameterized or infinite data structures, we apply the heuristics presented in the following paragraph. The abstraction function associates with a parameterized or infinite type a finite approximation. We consider three classes of types: integer types, arrays with opaque[1] index and finite values, arrays with natural index and finite value, and arrays with opaque index and values. We have considered the following abstractions which can be expressed in WS1S:

1. We associate with natural state space variables a family of boolean variables coding the comparisons between these variables or the variables and the constants of the problem. Notice that this heuristics is in fact the one used in an automatic way by [Les97].

---

[1] An opaque type supports only the assignment and comparison operations.

2. We associate with an array with opaque index and finite values within the set $\{x_1, \dots, x_n\}$ a family of bounded counters $\{c_1, \dots, c_n\}$ with value in the set $\{0, \dots, k, +\}$. A counter C_i indicates the number of indexes with value x_i. This enumeration being bounded by k, a higher number of occurrences is denoted $+$.

3. We associate with an array t with natural index and finite values the number of alternations $t(i) \neq t(i-1)$, counted in the finite set $\{0, \dots, k, +\}$.

4. We associate with an array with opaque index and values the number of different values in the array, counted in the finite set $\{0, \dots, k, +\}$.

Notice that the heuristics we present relate to the construction of an abstraction function, the abstract transition system being automatically built and validated by the FMona tool for the considered class of problems. On the other hand, [BLO98] supposes the existence of an abstraction function and proposes heuristics for the construction of the abstract system.

5   Application to the Bakery Mutual Exclusion Protocol

The transition system of the Bakery mutual exclusion algorithm over two processes is described in FMona by the following code. Its state space contains two finite-typed variables `pc1` and `pc2` and two naturals `y1` and `y2`. The state space is thus infinite.

```
type PC = {out,req,mutex}; type Sys = record{pc1,pc2: PC; y1,y2: nat;};

pred Init(var Sys st)= st.pc1=out & st.pc2=out & st.y1=0 & st.y2=0;
pred req1(var Sys st,st')= st.pc1=out &
     st'=st with {pc1:=req; y1:=st.y2+1;};
pred req2(var Sys st,st')= st.pc2=out &
     st'=st with {pc2:=req; y2:=st.y1+1;};
pred enter1(var Sys st,st')=
  st.pc1=req & (st.y2=0 | st.y1≤st.y2) & st'=st with{pc1:=mutex;};
pred enter2(var Sys st,st')=
  st.pc2=req & (st.y1=0 | st.y2<st.y1) & st'=st with{pc2:=mutex;};
pred leave1(var Sys st,st')= st.pc1=mutex &
     st'=st with {pc1:=out; y1:=0;};
pred leave2(var Sys st,st')= st.pc2=mutex &
     st'=st with {pc2:=out; y2:=0;};
```

We notice that it is not possible to bound the natural variables `y1` and `y2`. Actually, when considering the execution sequence $r_1(e_1 r_2 l_1 e_2 r_1 l_2)^*$, the sequence of (`y1`,`y2`) values is $(0,0) \xrightarrow{r_1(e_1 r_2 l_1 e_2 r_1 l_2)^k} (2k+1, 0)$ where r, e, l respectively abbreviate `req`,`enter`,`leave`.

We seek to establish that the mutual exclusion property is always true:

```
pred excl(var Sys st) = ~(st.pc1 = mutex & st.pc2 = mutex);
```

The predicate `excl` is *not* an invariant. Actually, it is not preserved by `enter1`. However, as shown in the following, it is always true, i.e., true in any reachable state. In order to get a finite state space, the fields `pc1` and `pc2` being finite, it is enough to abstract the fields `y1` and `y2`. We consider the abstraction which consists in coding the comparisons between these two fields. Then, we get the abstract system `Sys_a` and the abstraction relation φ defined as follows:

```
type Cmp = {z1z2,z1,z2,inf12,inf21,eq};
type Sys_a = record{pc1,pc2: PC; y1y2: Cmp;};
pred φ(var Sys st, var Sys_a a) =
  a.pc1 = st.pc1 & a.pc2 = st.pc2 &
    if st.y1 = 0 & st.y2 = 0 then a.y1y2 = z1z2
    elsif st.y1 = 0 then a.y1y2 = z1
    elsif st.y2 = 0 then a.y1y2 = z2
    elsif st.y1 < st.y2 then a.y1y2 = inf12
    elsif st.y2 < st.y1 then a.y1y2 = inf21
    else a.y1y2 = eq endif;
```

The relation φ being total, according to theorem 4, the `Bakery` transition system refines its abstraction through φ. The abstraction through φ of the `Bakery` system, computed by FMona, is a finite state system of which transitions can be expressed using WS1S and reduced to propositional logic using Mona. Consequently, the computation of the reachable states is possible. Mona validates that any state reachable by this transition system cannot be the image of a state where two processes would not be in mutual exclusion. The following logical formula (extracted from the transition system produced by Mona) encodes the set of reachable states of the abstract system:

st1 = idle	∧ st2 = idle	∧ cmp = z1z2	(* 0 = y1 = y2 *)
∨ st1 = idle	∧ st2 = req	∧ cmp = z2	(* 0 = y1 < y2 *)
∨ st1 = idle	∧ st2 = mutex	∧ cmp = z2	(* 0 = y1 < y2 *)
∨ st1 = req	∧ st2 = idle	∧ cmp = z1	(* 0 = y2 < y1 *)
∨ st1 = req	∧ st2 = req	∧ cmp = inf12	(* 0 < y1 < y2 *)
∨ st1 = req	∧ st2 = req	∧ cmp = inf21	(* 0 < y2 < y1 *)
∨ st1 = req	∧ st2 = mutex	∧ cmp = inf21	(* 0 < y2 < y1 *)
∨ st1 = mutex	∧ st2 = idle	∧ cmp = z1	(* 0 = y2 < y1 *)
∨ st1 = mutex	∧ st2 = req	∧ cmp = inf12	(* 0 < y1 < y2 *)

According to theorems 2 and 3, it follows that the mutual exclusion predicate `excl` is always true in the `Bakery` system.

Note that the validation of the abstract system can also be achieved by SMV after reducing abstract transitions to propositional logic. Such a reduction can be performed by Mona. The following FMona predicate defines the transitions of the abstract system according to the abstraction relation φ and the concrete transition relation `Trans`[2](`tr_a` has been defined in section (3.1)).

```
pred bakery_tr_a(var Sys_a a,a') = tr_a(Trans,φ,a,a');
```

---

[2] FMona automatically synthesizes type parameters.

214   J.-P. Bodeveix and M. Filali

The Mona tool produces a transition system representing the reduction of the relation **Trans_a**. Since the transitions of this system are labeled by *propositional formulas* relating the arguments of **Trans_a**, a SMV expression of the abstract transition can be extracted and analyzed.

It is interesting to note that since the abstraction did not modify the interface fields **pc1** and **pc2**, it also defines a mutual exclusion algorithm over a finite state space similar to Peterson's algorithm [PS85] comprising apart from the fields **pc1** and **pc2** a finite field y1y2 that can be encoded by three booleans.

6   Application to Cache Coherency Protocols

In this section we consider cache coherency protocols for shared memory multiprocessor machines [Ste90]. In such an architecture, each processor has a private cache where it stores copies of the shared memory data. The protocol ensures coherence between the multiple copies of a same data. Informally, atomic coherency means that the processors behave as if data were not duplicated. For this purpose, a *given* finite state is associated with each copy. For instance, in the Illinois protocol [AB86], the **State** type can be encoded as the enumeration {Inv, Excl, Shared, Dirty} where Inv marks an invalid copy, Excl an exclusively held copy, Shared a shared copy, and Dirty a modified copy. The data structures handled by such protocols are described by the following declarations, where **Proc** and **Word** are two opaque types. In the following, we denote by *control* the array **Ctr** and by *data* the array **C** and the memory **M**.

```
var nat NProc;
type Proc  = ... NProc; type State = {Inv, Shared, Excl, Dirty};
type Word  = record{b1:bool; b2:bool;}; #   see section 6.2
type Sys   =
record{Ctr:array Proc of State; C:array Proc of Word; M:Word;};
```

This protocol is parameterized by the number of processors, defined by the type **Proc**, and by the size of the words, defined by the type **Word**. The validity of such a protocol is expressed either by the satisfaction of an *always true* property, or by the simulation of a canonic atomic memory [BF99b]. The canonic atomic transition system (6.1) includes a register and the operations for reading and writing in this register.

6.1   Specification of the Transition System

The transition system defining atomic protocols establishes the interface of a memory access protocol comprising the **Init** predicate and three transitions: the reading of a value v by the processor p, the writing of a value v by the processor p. and the Skip transition which does nothing.

```
type Word = record{b1:bool; b2:bool;}; #   see section 6.2
pred Init_atomic(var Word r) = true;
```

```
pred Read_atomic(var Word v, var Word r,r') = (v = r) & (r' = r);
pred Write_atomic(var Word v, var Word r,r') = (r' = v);
pred Skip(var Word r,r') = (r' = r);
```

The transition system of an atomic coherency protocol must implement the preceding reference system.

6.2   Elimination of the Opaque Type Word

The expression of the abstract system in the WS1S logic requires to fix the size of Word. For this purpose, we use the result established in [BF99a]. It concerns the reduction of formulas where the comparisons between elements of some opaque type D only occurs in terms of the form $f(x) = g(x)$ or $f(x) = k$ where f, g and k are identically quantified at the top level of the formula. Let n be the number of such functions or variables. The validity of the formula over a domain D of size $\geq n$ is equivalent to its validity over a domain of size n.

Here, the opaque type Word must be eliminated from formulas expressing data abstraction and transition refinement. In both cases, variables of type Word are either global arrays or global variables (the array of words C, the memory M and the value to be read or written d). According to our result, we can restrict the type Word to a domain of size three. Consequently, we have chosen a record with two booleans.

6.3   Abstraction and Reduction

In this paragraph, we show how the abstract transition system is actually synthesized. The abstraction relation φ^{ca} can be structured as the conjunction of a control abstraction and a data abstraction.

Control abstraction associates to the (parameterized size) array Ctr a fixed family of counters, through the application of the second heuristic of §4.4. Thus, we introduce the abstraction data type as a record with three bounded counters, one for shared caches, one for exclusive caches and one for dirty caches. The abstraction relation φ_ctr maps the Illinois control array to these counters.

```
#    array abstraction through bounded counters
type B_Cpt = {Zero, One, More};
pred abstr_p(type State, pred(var State s) p, var B_Cpt f) =
 if all State s: ~p(s) then f=Zero
 elsif ex State s1: p(s1) & all State s: s≠s1⇒~p(s) then f=One
 else f=More endif;
type Sys_a_ctr = #    abstraction of Illinois control
      record{c_Shared: B_Cpt; c_Excl: B_Cpt; c_Dirty: B_Cpt;};
pred φ_ctr(var Ctr s, var Sys_a_ctr a) =
 abstr_p(pred(var Proc p):s[p]=Shared,a.c_Shared) &
 abstr_p(pred(var Proc p):s[p]=Excl,a.c_Excl) &
 abstr_p(pred(var Proc p):s[p]=Dirty,a.c_Dirty);
```

Data abstraction associates to the array C and the memory M the cardinal, counted over $\{1, 2, +\}$, of the set of valid data in the system.

```
type Sys_a_data = {One_d,Two_d,More_d};
pred φ_data(var Sys s, var Sys_a_data c) =
  if (all Proc p: s.Ctr[p]≠Inv ⇒ s.C[p]=s.M) then c = One_d
  elsif (ex Proc p,q: s.Ctr[p]≠Inv & s.Ctr[q]≠Inv & s.C[p]≠s.C[q]
               & s.C[p] ≠ s.M & s.C[q] ≠ s.M) then c = More_d
  else c = Two_d endif;
```

Consequently, the abstract domain consists in a fixed family of bounded counters $(B_i)_{i \leq K}$, defined here by the record Sys_a. The abstraction relation φ is then defined as the conjunction of the abstractions of the control and data parts. Note that for efficiency purposes, this conjunction has been restricted to the reachable states of the control part. Otherwise, the complexity of the computation is too high and the resulting formula cannot be decided by Mona.

```
type Sys_a = record{ ctr_a: Sys_a_ctr; data_a: Sys_a_data;};
pred φ(var Sys s, var Sys_a a) =
  is_abs_ctr_Acc(a.ctr_a) & φ_ctr(s.Ctr, a.ctr_a) & φ_data(s,a.data_a);
```

6.4 Validation of the Simulation Relation

In this section, we show the simulation of the canonic transition system, reduced to one register R (see §6.1) by the abstract one. Here, we are interested in the refinement approach. With this intention, one introduces a projection between the state space of the Illinois protocol and the space reduced to one register. The relation ill_atm expresses that the contents of the register R is either equal to the memory if the caches are all invalid, or equal to the common value of the non-invalid caches.

```
pred ill_atm(var Sys s, var Word r) =
  ((all Proc p:s.Ctr[p]=Inv)⇒s.M=r) & all Proc p:s.Ctr[p]≠Inv⇒s.C[p]=r;
```

It should be noted that this relation does not make it possible to define a refinement with the atomic model. In fact, the Illinois transition system must be restricted to some superset, called is_Acc of its reachable states. For this purpose, we consider the inverse image through φ of the reachable states of its abstraction.

```
pred is_Acc(var Sys c) = ex Sys_a a: φ(c,a) & is_abs_Acc(a);
```

Then, the validity of the Illinois protocol can be stated: we show that the relation ill_atm establishes a refinement between the reduced concrete transition system and the atomic one. More precisely, such a refinement is specified by the following conjunction which is transformed by FMona to pure Mona code and validated by Mona.

```
#    Illinois validation
refinement_init(restrict_init(Init,is_Acc),Init_atomic,ill_atm) &
(all Word v: refinement_tr(restrict_tr(Read_Miss(v),is_Acc)
                          ,Read_atomic(v),ill_atm)) &
(all Word v: refinement_tr(restrict_tr(Write_Miss(v),is_Acc)
                          ,Write_atomic(v),ill_atm)) &
refinement_tr(restrict_tr(Flush,is_Acc),Skip,ill_atm);
```

7 Other Validation Techniques

Apart from abstraction techniques, we have also expressed in FMona iteration based techniques. It should be stressed that we have applied them on parameterized systems. However, since the state spaces of the considered problems are not fixed, we have no decidability results. It follows that the user must provide an iteration bound to apply the proposed macros. Backward iteration techniques have been successfully applied to mutual exclusion algorithms on ring networks [Mar85]. However, forward and backward analysis fail for some well known problems (e.g. termination detection [DFvG83], dining philosophers, Szymanski mutual exclusion protocol [Szy90]). To overcome such problems, convergence acceleration techniques have been proposed [ABJN99]. The basic idea consists in approximating the transitive closure of the transition relation. We can express such techniques in FMona. In a forthcoming paper [BF00], we present some new acceleration techniques and their expression in FMona. These techniques allowed us to validate the above-mentioned problems.

8 Conclusion

In this paper, we have illustrated the use of FMona to express the abstraction technique and its applications. Thanks to the higher order features of FMona, the validation steps of the method could be expressed in a generic way and instantiated on specific problems.

FMona has also been used to express other well known methods such as iterative methods applied to parameterized systems. It should be stressed that these methods have been generically defined and have been applied to well know problems (mutual exclusion on parameterized rings, parameterized multiprocessor memory protocols, infinite space bakery algorithm).

For efficiency reasons, we have also connected FMona to propositional solvers. We also plan to consider the validation of the methods themselves and how to integrate them smoothly into FMona.

References

AB86.   J. Archibald and J.-L. Baer. Cache coherence protocols: Evaluation using a multiprocessor simulation model. *ACM Transactions on Computer Systems*, 4(4):273–298, November 1986. 214

ABJN99.   Parosh Aziz Abdulla, Ahmed Bouajjani, Bengt Jonsson, and Marcus Nilsson. Handling Global Conditions in Parameterized System Verification. In *Proc. 11th Int. Conf. on Computer Aided Verification*, volume 1633 of *Lecture Notes in Computer Science*, pages 134–145. Springer Verlag, 1999. 217

ABP97.   A. Ayari, D. Basin, and A. Podelski. Lisa: A specification language based on ws2s. In *11th International Conference of the European Association for Computer Science Logic (CSL '97)*, volume 1414 of *LNCS*, pages 18 – 34. Springer-Verlag, 1997. 209

Arn92.   A. Arnold. *Systèmes de transitions finis et sémantiques des processus communicants*. Etudes et recherches en informatique. MASSON, 1992. 206

BBC⁺97.   B. Barras, S. Boutin, C. Cornes, J. Courant, J.C. Filliatre, E. Giménez, H. Herbelin, G. Huet, C. Muñoz, C. Murthy, C. Parent, C. Paulin, A. Saïbi, and B. Werner. The Coq Proof Assistant Reference Manual – Version V6.1. Technical Report 0203, INRIA, August 1997. 204

BCMD90.   J.R. Burch, E.M. Clarke, K.L. McMillan, and D.L. Dill. Symbolic model checking: 10E20 states and beyond. In *5th Symposium on Logic in Computer Science*, June 1990. 204, 209

BF99a.   J.-P. Bodeveix and M. Filali. Reduction and quantifier elimination techniques for program validation. *Formal Methods in System Design*, to appear, 1999. 215

BF99b.   J.-P. Bodeveix and M. Filali. The FMONA tool. Technical Report http://www.irit.fr/ACTIVITES/EQ_COS/MF/FMONA, IRIT, may 1999. 206, 214

BF00.   J.-P. Bodeveix and M. Filali. Experimenting acceleration methods for the validation of infinite state systems. In Dr. Pao-Ann Hsiung, editor, *International Workshop on Distributed System Validation and Verification*, Institute of Information Science, Academia Sinica, Taiwan, R.O.C., april 2000. to appear. 217

BLO98.   S. Bensalem, Y. Lakhnech, and S. Owre. Computing abstractions of infinite state systems compositionnaly and automatically. In *Computer-Aided Verification (CAV'98)*, volume 1427 of *Lecture Notes in Computer Science*, pages 319–331, Vancouver, BC, Canada, june 1998. Springer-Verlag. http://www.csl.sri.com/~owre/cav98.html. 208, 212

CGL94.   E.M. Clarke, O. Grumber, and D.E. Long. Model checking and abstraction. *ACM Transactions on Programming Languages and Systems*, 16(5):1512–1542, september 1994. 208

DFvG83.   E. W. Dijkstra, W. H. J. Feijen, and A. J. M. van Gasteren. Derivation of a termination detection algorithm for distributed computations. *Information Processing Letters*, 16(5):217–219, june 1983. 217

GM94.   M.J.C. Gordon and T.F. Melham. *Introduction to HOL*. Cambridge University Press, 1994. 204

HJJ⁺95.   J.G. Henriksen, J.L. Jensen, M.S. Jorgensen, N. Klarlund, R. Paige, T. Rauhe, and A.B. Sandholm. Mona: Monadic second-order logic in practice. In *Workshop on Tools and Algorithms for the Construction and Analysis of Systems*, pages 58–73, Aarhus, May 1995. 204, 206

Hol91.   G.J. Holzmann. *Design and validation of computer protocols*. Prentice Hall, 1991. 204

Les97.   Lessens, D. and Saïdi, H.   Abstraction of parameterized networks. *Electronic notes in theoretical computer science*, 9:12, 1997. http://www.elsevier.nl/locate/entcs/volume9.html. 211

Mar85.   A.J. Martin. Distributed mutual exclusion on a ring of processes. *Science of Computer Programming*, 5(3):265–276, October 1985. 217

ORS92.   S. Owre, J.M. Rushby, and N. Shankar. PVS: A prototype verification system. *Lecture Notes in Computer Science*, 607, 1992. 204

PS85.   J.L. Peterson and A. Silberschatz. *Operating system concepts*. Addison-Wesley, 1985. 214

Ste90.   P. Stenstrom. A survey of cache coherence schemes for multiprocessors. *Computer*, 23(6):11–25, June 1990. 214

Szy90.   B.K. Szymanski. Mutual exclusion revisited. In *fifth Jerusalem conference on information technology*, pages 110–117. IEEE Computer Society Press, 1990. 217

Tho90.   W. Thomas. Automata on infinite objects. In J.v. Leeuwen, editor, *Handbook of Theoretical Computer Science*, pages 133–192. MIT Press, 1990. 205, 209

Transitive Closures of Regular Relations for Verifying Infinite-State Systems*

Bengt Jonsson and Marcus Nilsson

Dept. of Computer Systems, P.O. Box 325, S-751 05 Uppsala, Sweden
{bengt,marcusn}@docs.uu.se

Abstract. We consider a model for representing infinite-state and parameterized systems, in which states are represented as strings over a finite alphabet. Actions are transformations on strings, in which the change can be characterized by an arbitrary finite-state transducer. This program model is able to represent programs operating on a variety of data structures, such as queues, stacks, integers, and systems with a parameterized linear topology. The main contribution of this paper is an effective derivation of a general and powerful *transitive closure* operation for this model. The transitive closure of an action represents the effect of executing the action an arbitrary number of times. For example, the transitive closure of an action which transmits a single message to a buffer will be an action which sends an arbitrarily long sequence of messages to the buffer. Using this transitive closure operation, we show how to model and automatically verify safety properties for several types of infinite-state and parameterized systems.

1 Introduction

In recent years, substantial progress has been made regarding the automated verification of finite-state systems. Fully automated techniques have now been developed to the extent that they can routinely handle systems with millions of states. Partial order techniques and symbolic representations, such as Binary Decision Diagrams (BDDs) [BCM+90] have been important in this development. There is also progress in the development of verification algorithms for infinite-state systems (e.g., [ACD90,AH89,BS95,Sti96,Fin94,AJ96]), and for parameterized systems, i.e., systems consisting of an arbitrary number of homogeneous processes connected in a regular topology (e.g., [GS92,KMM+97,ABJN99]).

The problem of verifying that a system satisfies a certain correctness property is usually reduced to checking some form of reachability problem on a transition system model of the system. For example, verifying that a system never gets into an "unsafe" state consists in checking that no "unsafe" state can be reached (by a sequence of transitions) from the set of initial states. This problem is often analyzed by symbolic or enumerative state-space exploration, starting from

---

* support in part by the ASTEC competence center, and by the Swedish Board for Industrial and Technical Development (NUTEK)

S. Graf and M. Schwartzbach (Eds.): TACAS/ETAPS 2000, LNCS 1785, pp. 220–235, 2000.

the set of initial states. However, naive reachability analysis is guaranteed to terminate only when the reachable state-space has finite depth, meaning that there is a uniform bound on the number of transitions needed to get to any reachable state. Finite-state systems trivially have a state-space with finite depth (bounded by the number of states), but the depth of the state-space of an infinite-state system is in general infinite.

In this paper, we will consider infinite-state systems whose states can be represented as finite strings over a finite alphabet. This includes parameterized systems consisting of an arbitrary number of homogeneous finite-state processes connected in a linear or ring-formed topology: take the (finite) set of local states of each process as the alphabet, and let a string of process states represent a system state (the length of the string is equal to the number of processes). Our model also includes systems that operate on queues, stacks, integers, and other data structures that can be represented as sequences of symbols. We represent the transition relation of such a system by a finite set of actions; each action is a regular relation between strings, which can be represented, e.g., by a finite-state transducer.

For this class of systems, reachability analysis can be performed as follows. Assume that a set of initial states and a set of "unsafe" states are both given as regular sets. Using the transducer representation of actions, we can calculate the set of successors of a regular set of states as a regular set. Explore the reachable states by successive calculations of sets of successor states, starting from the set of initial states. If the set of reachable states has finite depth, this exploration is guaranteed to terminate. Dually, we can perform the exploration backwards, starting from the unsafe states and taking predecessors, with guaranteed termination if the "backwards depth" of the state-space is finite. This approach is pursued, e.g., by Kesten et al. [KMM+97], who illustrate their approach by some examples with finite backwards depth.

In general, however, an infinite-state or parameterized system need neither have a finite depth nor a finite backwards depth. To explore the entire state-space, one must then be able to calculate the effect of arbitrarily long sequences of transitions. This problem would be solved if we could calculate the transitive closure of an action, and then adding this transitive closure to set of actions that are explored during verification. Remember that an action can be seen as a relation on states: therefore the transitive closure of an action represents the effect of executing the action an arbitrary number of times. For example, the transitive closure of an action which transmits a single message to a buffer will be an action which sends an arbitrarily long sequence of messages to the buffer. The transitive closure of an action in which a process in a parameterized system passes a token to its neighbor, will be an action that passes the token through an arbitrary sequence of neighbors to another process.

The main contribution of this paper is a construction of the transitive closure for a large class of actions in the system model described above. This transitive closure is also representable as a finite-state transducer, and can therefore be used in the state-space exploration in the same way as the original actions. Furthermore, we show how this construction makes is possible to verify safety properties of many parameterized and infinite-state systems fully automatically. We reduce safety properties to reachability using standard techniques. To check reachability, we first calculate the transitive closure of each action, if possible, and thereafter perform reachability analysis with the extended set of actions. In many cases, this analysis terminates even when the state space does not have finite depth. We have implemented the technique, using the Mona package [HJJ+96a], and present some examples.

In order to characterize the class of actions for which our transitive-closure construction works, we define a notion of *local depth*. Intuitively, an action has local depth k if each position in the string is transformed at most k times in any sequence of executions of that action. For example, an action in a parameterized system, in which a process passes a token to its right neighbor has local depth 2, since in an arbitrary execution sequence, each process is affected at most twice: once when receiving the token, and once when sending the token. Similarly, if a queue is modeled by an unbounded array with a finite contiguous segment of positions filled by messages, then an action which sends a message to the channel, thus putting a message into an empty position, has local depth 1. The main theorem of the paper shows that we can calculate the transitive closure of any action with finite local depth, and represent it as a finite-state transducer. We can also approximate the transitive closure of an action which does not have finite local depth. For an arbitrary k, we can calculate, as a finite-state transducer, the action which corresponds to executing the action an arbitrary number of times, subject to the constraint that each position is transformed at most k times.

A special case of the present paper is our earlier work [ABJN99]. There we consider parameterized systems, whose state can be represented by a string, and where each action is allowed to change the string in only one position. By requiring this change to be idempotent, each action gets local depth 1, and we could give a construction of its transitive closure. The restrictions limited the applicability to certain classes of parameterized algorithms.

Related Work The use of regular sets as a symbolic state representation in the verification of infinite-state systems has been proposed by e.g., Boigelot and Wolper [WB98] and Kesten et al. [KMM+97]. Kesten et al. perform backwards reachability analysis on state spaces of finite depth or finite backward depth. The decidability results for systems with unbounded lossy FIFO channels [AJ96] and for well-structured systems [AČJYK96] follow from the fact that the considered verification problems have a finite backward depth. Other researchers, e.g., [FO97], use regular sets in a deductive framework, where basic manipulations on regular sets are performed automatically, e.g., using the Mona [HJJ+96a] or MoSel [KMMG97] packages. In [Sis97], parameterized systems are verified using induction on the number of processes, where the inductive invariant is specified using automata on two dimensional strings.

A related technique for analyzing unbounded sequences of executions of an action, called *acceleration*, has been developed for finite state processes that communicate via unbounded FIFO channels [BG96,BGWW97,BH97,ABJ98] and for systems that operate on integer variables [BW94]. An acceleration of an action can be seen as the application of the transitive closure to a particular set of states. By a suitable representation, we can model the operations considered in the work on QDDs [BG96] as actions with finite local depth. Bouajjani and Habermehl [BH97] also perform acceleration of actions with non-finite local depth, sometimes resulting in non-regular sets of states. The acceleration operation is related to the *widening* operation, used for computing fixpoints in abstract interpretation [CC77], but aims at computing an *exact* fixpoint of a sequence of approximations, each of which represents a bounded number of executions of an action.

Outline In the next section, we define our model of systems and illustrate it by modeling a parameterized termination detection algorithm intended for a ring topology. In Section 3, we review the principles of symbolic reachability analysis for verifying safety properties, and note that this analysis would be significantly improved by taking the transitive closure of actions. Section 4 presents the main result: a construction for computing the transitive closure of an action with local depth k, for arbitrary k. Section 5 discusses two extra composition operations which also augment the power of the analysis. In Section 6, we outline how our results can be used for modeling and analysis of programs that operate on unbounded FIFO channels and integers. An implementation of our method, and the modeling and automated analysis of several infinite-state algorithms is reported in Section 7. Section 8 contains conclusions.

2   Program Model

In this section, we introduce our model of programs. A global state (or a configuration) of a system is represented as a string over a finite alphabet C. As usual, C^* is the set of finite strings over C. The dynamic behavior of a system is defined through a finite set of *actions*. Each action rewrites a certain portion of the string that represents the state. The rewriting relation is given by a finite-state transducer. The rewriting may furthermore be conditioned on the sequence of symbols to the right and to the left of the rewritten portion of the string. We use subclasses of regular languages, called *left contexts* and *right contexts*, to represent such conditions.

Definition 1. A *left context* is a regular language which can be accepted by a deterministic finite-state automaton with a unique accepting state, and where all outgoing transitions from the accepting state are self-loops. (transitions with identical source and target states). A *right context* is a language such that the language of reversed strings is a left context. The *tail* of a left context is the set of symbols that label self-loops from the accepting state. The tail of a right context is the tail of the left context which is its reverse language.   □

Examples of left contexts are a^* (with tail $\{a\}$), and $(a+b)^*b(a+b)^*$ (with tail $\{a, b\}$). An example of a regular language which is not a left context is $(a+b)^*b$. This language is, however, a right context with tail $\{a, b\}$.

We will represent (length-preserving) relations on C^* by *finite-state transducers*. A finite-state transducer defines a regular language over $C \times C$. It represents the relation on C^* which contains the pair $(c_1 c_2 \cdots c_n , c_1' c_2' \cdots c_n')$ iff the transducer accepts the string (c_1, c_1') (c_2, c_2') $\cdots$ (c_n, c_n').

We are now ready to give the formal definition of our model.

Definition 2. A *program* is a triple $\mathcal{P} = \langle C, \phi_I, \mathcal{A} \rangle$ where

C is a finite alphabet, called the set of *colors*,

ϕ_I is a regular set over C, denoting a set of *initial configurations*, and

$\mathcal{A}$ is a finite set of *actions*. An *action* is a triple

$$\phi_L \;\boxed{\tau}\; \phi_R$$

where ϕ_L is a left context, ϕ_R is a right context, and τ is a regular set over $C \times C$.

A *configuration* γ of a program $\mathcal{P}$ is a string $\gamma[1]\, \gamma[2]\, \cdots\, \gamma[n]$ over C. For a regular expression ϕ, we use $\gamma \in \phi$ to denote that γ is a string in the language denoted by ϕ. For $i, j : 1 \leq i \leq j \leq n$, we use $\gamma[i\,..\,j]$ to denote the substring $\gamma[i]\, \gamma[i+1]\, \cdots\, \gamma[j]$. An action

$$\alpha = \phi_L \;\boxed{\tau}\; \phi_R$$

defines a relation α on configurations such that $(\gamma, \gamma') \in \alpha$ if γ and γ' are of equal length n, there are i, j with $1 \leq i \leq j \leq n$ such that

- $(\gamma[i], \gamma'[i])(\gamma[i+1], \gamma'[i+1]) \cdots (\gamma[j], \gamma'[j]) \in \tau$,
- $\gamma[1\,..\,i-1] = \gamma'[1\,..\,i-1] \in \phi_L$, and
- $\gamma[j+1\,..\,n] = \gamma'[j+1\,..\,n] \in \phi_R$.

If these conditions hold, we say that $\alpha(\gamma, \gamma')$ holds with *active index pair* (i, j). □

The above program model is a generalization of the one in our earlier work [ABJN99]. Our earlier model had the same structure, but the middle component τ in an action was constrained to be a relation on C, instead of a (regular) relation on C^*, implying that each action can only change one position in the string. With the new definition, a much wider class of systems can be modeled.

Example To illustrate our program model, we will model an algorithm for termination detection in a ring-shaped network, due to Dijkstra, Feijen, and van Gasteren [DFvG83]. The algorithm is intended to detect termination of an underlying computation among a ring of N processes, numbered from 1 to N. Each process can spontaneously change state from *computing* (non-idle) to *idle*, but process i can change from *idle* to *computing* only if process $i-1$ (or N if $i = 1$) is computing. The system is *terminated* when all processes are idle. The detection algorithm employs a token, which is sent around by process 1, when it is idle, in increasing order of indices until it reaches process 1 again. When the token is sent out, it is white. Each process passes the token on, and paints it black if it is non-idle. If it comes back to process 1 and is still white, then termination is signaled provided that process 1 was idle during the entire round. Otherwise another round of termination detection will be started at a later moment.

We model the state of the algorithm by a string, where the ith element represents the state of process i. The state of process i is defined by a boolean variable q_i which is true iff process i is idle, and a variable t_i ranging over {**black, white, none**}, which has value **none** when process i does *not* have the token, and otherwise denotes the color of the token. In addition, process 1 has a boolean variable *wasq* (w for short), which is true if it has stayed idle during the current round. Thus, the set of colors is the set of triples of form $\langle q, t, w \rangle$ where q and w are boolean, and $t \in \{\textbf{black, white, none}\}$. The value of w is relevant only in position 1.

The set of initial states of the system, in which process 1 has a black token, is described by the regular expression

$$(t = \textbf{black}) \quad (t = \textbf{none})^*$$

where we use predicates to denote sets of colors, e.g., $(t = \textbf{black})$ denotes the set of triples $\langle q, t, w \rangle$ such that $(t = \textbf{black})$. An undesired state, in which detection is signaled although the system is not terminated is given by the regular expression

$$[(t = \textbf{white} \wedge w) \;\; true^* \; \neg q \;\; true^*] \;\;\; \cup \;\;\; [(\neg q \wedge t = \textbf{white} \wedge w) \;\; true^*]$$

which states that the condition $t = \textbf{white} \wedge w$ for process 1 to signal detection is satisfied, but some process is not idle.

Let us then give examples of actions. An action in which some process i with $1 < i < N$ passes the token to its next neighbor, possibly after painting it black, is described by the action $(t = \textbf{none})^+ \;\boxed{\tau}\; (t = \textbf{none})^*$ where τ is the relation between strings of length two such that

$$\tau \;\; (\; \langle q_1, t_1, w_1 \rangle \; \langle q_2, t_2, w_2 \rangle \;\;\;, \;\;\; \langle q_1', t_1', w_1' \rangle \; \langle q_2', t_2', w_2' \rangle \;)$$

iff $q_1' = q_1$, $\;\; q_2' = q_2$, $\;\; t_2 = t_1' = \textbf{none}$, and $\;t2' = \textbf{if } q_1 \textbf{ then } t_1 \textbf{ else black}$. We also need an action which models the passing of the token from process N to process 1. This is the action $\{\epsilon\} \;\boxed{\tau}\; \{\epsilon\}$ where τ is the relation between strings of length at least two such that

$$\tau(\; \langle q_1, t_1, w_1 \rangle \; \gamma \; \langle q_2, t_2, w_2 \rangle \;\;\;, \;\;\; \langle q_1', t_1', w_1' \rangle \; \gamma \; \langle q_2', t_2', w_2' \rangle \;)$$

where γ is any string in $(t = \textbf{none})^*$, where $q_2' = q_2$, $\;\; q_1' = q_1$, $\;\; t_1 = t_2' = $ **none,**, and where $t_1' = \textbf{if } q_2 \textbf{ then } t_2 \textbf{ else black}$. In addition, we need an action for passing the token from process 1 to process 2, which is given in an analogous way. In Section 4, we will see that the first action has local depth 2, and that its transitive closure represents an action which passes the token from position i to position j for arbitrary $1 < i < j < N$. However, it is not meaningful to take the transitive closure of the second action, since it disables itself after being executed.

Summarizing, we see that the passing of a token from one process to the next is modeled by one action for the "standard" case $1 < i < N$ and by separate actions for special cases, such as passing from N to 1, and passing from 1 to 2. The changes to q, modeling the underlying computation, can be modeled in a similar way.

The above algorithm is an example of a parameterized distributed algorithm which assumes a linear or ring topology. In our earlier work [ABJN99], we were able to model a restricted class of parameterized algorithms where only one process changed its local state in each transition. In the above algorithm, two processes change their state simultaneously. In Section 6, we will describe how we can also model and analyze programs that operate on unbounded queues, and unbounded integers.

3   The Reachability Problem

We write $\gamma_1 \longrightarrow \gamma_2$ to denote that $\alpha(\gamma_1, \gamma_2)$ for some action $\alpha \in \mathcal{A}$. We use $\overset{*}{\longrightarrow}$ to denote the transitive closure of $\longrightarrow$. A configuration γ is said to be *reachable* if there is a configuration $\gamma_I \in \phi_I$ such that $\gamma_I \overset{*}{\longrightarrow} \gamma$.

The *reachability problem* is defined as follows.

Instance A program $\mathcal{P}$ and a set of configurations of $\mathcal{P}$ represented by a regular expression ϕ_F.

Question Is any $\gamma \in \phi_F$ reachable?

It is well-known (e.g., [VW86]) that the problem of verifying linear-time safety properties can be transformed into the problem of checking that a set of "bad" states is not reachable.

The reachability problem can be analyzed using standard *symbolic reachability analysis* to explore the state-space. The analysis maintains a set of reachable configurations, which is initially the set of initial configurations. At each step of the algorithm the set of reachable configurations is extended with the configurations that can be reached by executing some action in the program from a configuration in the current set

We use regular sets of strings to represent (in general infinite) sets of configurations. A regular set is represented by an automaton. The effect of executing an action, which is represented by a finite-state transducer, can be calculated by computing, in the usual way, the product of the automaton and the transducer, and then projecting on the second component in the alphabet of the transducer. This approach is proposed and described in more detail in [KMM+97].

A limitation of the above approach is that it can only explore state spaces of finite depth[1]. After k iterations, one can only explore configurations at a

---

[1] the depth of a state space is the maximal distance (measured in computation steps) from the set of initial states to any reachable state

distance at most k from the set of initial configurations. For instance, in the above algorithm one can only explore the effect of passing a token through a sequence of k processes. To explore the entire state-space, one must in general be able to calculate the effect of executing arbitrarily long sequences of computation steps. This can be done by augmenting verification by adding the transitive closure of an action, i.e., the effect of executing an action an arbitrary number of times. For example, the transitive closure of the first token-passing action in the previous example, is an action in which the token is passed through an arbitrary sequence of neighbors to another process. In the next section we show how to compute the transitive closure of a large class of actions.

4   Computing the Transitive Closure

In the previous section, we showed how to use actions in the symbolic reachability analysis by representing the effect of executing an action in terms of a finite-state transducer. For a subclass of actions, we will now show how to represent the effect of an unbounded number of executions in terms of a finite-state transducer. We will classify actions according to a *local depth*, which is the maximum number of rewritings of a symbol in a configuration, defined more precisely below.

As usual, let α^* denote the relation on strings, which is the reflexive and transitive closure of α. Let α^+ denote the transitive closure of α. For an action α, we say that a sequence of configurations $\gamma_0, \cdots, \gamma_m$ is a *configuration sequence* of α with active index pairs $(l_1, l_1') \cdots (l_m, l_m')$ iff for each p with $1 \leq p \leq m$ we have that $\alpha(\gamma_{p-1}, \gamma_p)$ holds with active index pair (l_p, l_p').

Definition 3. *A configuration sequence $\gamma_0, \cdots, \gamma_m$ of α has* local depth k *if each position $i \geq 1$ satisfies $|\{p : l_p \leq i \leq l_p'\}| \leq k$. An action α has* local depth k *if whenever $(\gamma, \gamma') \in \alpha^*$ then there is a configuration sequence $\gamma_0, \cdots, \gamma_m$ of α with local depth k such that $\gamma = \gamma_0$ and $\gamma_m = \gamma'$.*   □

For an action α with local depth k for some k, we can represent α^+ by a finite-state transducer, due to the following theorem.

Theorem 1. *Let $\alpha = \phi_L \boxed{\tau} \phi_R$ be an action with local depth k for some k. Then α^+ is a regular relation on strings, which can be represented by a finite-state transducer with no more than $7^{k+1} \cdot (|\tau| + 1)^k + |\phi_L| + |\phi_R|$ states, where $|R|$ is the number of states in the automaton representing R.*

Proof. (Sketch) Let $\alpha = \phi_L \boxed{\tau} \phi_R$ be an action as above. For each pair of configurations (γ, γ') in α^+, we can establish matrix of the form:

$$
\begin{array}{cccccccc}
t_0^1 & \xrightarrow{\langle c_1^0, c_1^1 \rangle} & t_1^1 & \xrightarrow{\langle c_2^0, c_2^1 \rangle} & t_2^1 & \cdots & t_{n-1}^1 & \xrightarrow{\langle c_n^0, c_n^1 \rangle} & t_n^1 \\
t_0^2 & \xrightarrow{\langle c_1^1, c_1^2 \rangle} & t_1^2 & \xrightarrow{\langle c_2^1, c_2^2 \rangle} & t_2^2 & \cdots & t_{n-1}^2 & \xrightarrow{\langle c_n^1, c_n^2 \rangle} & t_n^2 \\
& & & & \vdots & & & & \\
t_0^m & \xrightarrow{\langle c_1^{m-1}, c_1^m \rangle} & t_1^m & \xrightarrow{\langle c_2^{m-1}, c_2^m \rangle} & t_2^m & \cdots & t_{n-1}^m & \xrightarrow{\langle c_n^{m-1}, c_n^m \rangle} & t_n^m
\end{array}
$$

where

- t_i^j is a state in the transducer for α, for every i, j.
- t_0^j is a starting state and t_n^j is an accepting state of the transducer for α, for every j.
- $t \xrightarrow{\langle c, c' \rangle} t'$ iff the transducer for α can make a transition from t to t' on $\langle c, c' \rangle$.
- $c_i^0 = \gamma[i]$ and $c_i^m = \gamma'[i]$, for every i.

In the transducer for α, let q_L be the accepting state of ϕ_L and q_R be the starting state of ϕ_R. From the definition of contexts, it follows that each column in the above picture is either 1) a sequence of identical states in the transducer that copies ϕ_L, 2) a sequence of identical states in the transducer that copies ϕ_R, or 3) a sequence consisting of occurrences of q_L, q_R, and states inside the transducer for τ.

The main step of the proof is now to show that if we can construct a matrix as above, then we can construct a matrix in which all columns of the third form are sequences of form

$$w_0 \ r_1 \ w_1 \ r_2 \ w_2 \ \cdots \ w_{l-1} \ r_l \ w_l$$

where l is at most the local depth of α, where each r_j is a state in the transducer for τ, and where each w_j is in one of the seven sets (this is where the number 7 in the theorem comes from)

$$\{\varepsilon\} \quad q_L^+ \quad q_R^+ \quad q_L^+ q_R^+ \quad q_R^+ q_L^+ \quad q_R^+ q_L^+ q_R^+ \quad q_L^+ q_R^+ q_L^+$$

This can be proven by starting from an arbitrary matrix as above and permuting its rows when some column has too many consecutive alternations of q_R and q_L until it is on the just described regular form. If the permutation of rows is done carefully, the initial and final configurations (γ and γ') are not affected.

We finally observe that the number of consecutive q_L's in a column is unimportant for the effect to the left of that column, and vice versa for the number of consecutive q_R's. By disregarding the number of repetitions of q_L's and q_R's, we get a finite number of different possible columns. Each such column will be a state of the transducer for α^+, and we build a transition relation which emulates the effect of the above matrix.   □

As a corollary, we note that we can also approximate the transitive closure of an action which does not have a finite local depth. More precisely, for an action α, define the *approximation to local depth k of α^** as the set of pairs (γ, γ') such that there is a configuration sequence $\gamma_0, \cdots, \gamma_m$ of α with local depth k where $\gamma = \gamma_0$ and $\gamma_m = \gamma'$. From the construction in Theorem 1 it follows that we can compute the approximation to local depth k of the transitive closure of any action, represented as a transducer.

5   Compositions of Actions

For some algorithms, we need to add actions representing the composition of two or more actions. In combination with the transitive closure operation, this makes it possible to compute the effect of an unbounded number of executions of a sequence, e.g. a loop, or a choice, e.g. modeling an if-statement, consisting of the actions in the composition.

Let $\alpha = \phi_L \boxed{\tau} \phi_R$ and $\alpha' = \phi'_L \boxed{\tau'} \phi'_R$ be two actions. Their *sequential composition* can be defined as

$$\phi_L \cap \phi'_L \boxed{\tau \circ \tau'} \phi_R \cap \phi'_R$$

where $\tau \circ \tau'$ is the transducer corresponding to the relational composition of the relations given by τ and τ'. Their *union* can be similarly defined as

$$\phi_L \cap \phi'_L \boxed{\tau \cup \tau'} \phi_R \cap \phi'_R$$

where $\tau \cup \tau'$ is the union of τ and τ'. We note that the intersection of two left contexts is always a left context, and similarly for right contexts.

As an isolated operation, composition does not add to the power of reachability analysis. If, however, used in combination with the transitive closure operation, i.e., using the transitive closure of composed actions, it can often give extra power to the reachability algorithm.

An important observation is that, in an action which is the result of a composition operation, it is sometimes possible to extend the left or right context by including a part of the string which is transformed by τ, if τ leaves that part unchanged. As a concrete example, if τ_1 changes the first position from a to b and τ_2 changes the first position from b to a, then the left context of the sequential composition of these two actions may be extended by an extra symbol, which then has to be a. After having the context in this way, the local depth of the action may decrease, thus giving even more power to the transitive closure operation.

6   Modeling Different Classes of Infinite-State Algorithms

In Section 2, we showed how to model a parameterized algorithm in which each computation step changes the state of 2 processes. In this section, we will show how our framework can also be applied to programs operating on unbounded FIFO channels, and to certain programs that use unbounded sequence numbers. In Section 7, we show how algorithms in these classes can be verified automatically, thanks to our transitive closure operation.

6.1   Programs Operating on Unbounded FIFO Channels

In this subsection, we outline how our framework can model and analyze protocols in which a set of finite-state processes communicate by sending messages over a set of unbounded FIFO channels. The verification of such protocols has been considered by Boigelot and Godefroid, [BG96,BGWW97], who propose to use a representation called QDDs (Queue Decision Diagrams) to represent sets of states of such a system. QDDs are essentially automata which recognize the contents of the channels. In the paper [BG96] it is shown how to calculate the effect of exploring the acceleration of certain actions from a given set of states represented as a QDD. We will here show how transitive closure of corresponding operations can be calculated in our framework.

For this presentation, consider a system of two finite-state processes that communicate via one unbounded FIFO channel in each direction. Assume that the control state of each process belongs to a set Q of control states, and that each channel contains a sequence of messages in some finite set $\mathcal{M}$. A state of the system, where the processes are in control states q_1 and q_2, respectively, and the channels contain the sequences w_1 and w_2, respectively, can be represented by a string in the set given by the regular expression

$$q_1 \quad q_2 \quad \perp^* w_1 \perp^* \quad \| \quad \perp^* w_2 \perp^*$$

where the symbol $\perp$ represents an empty position in a channel, and $\|$ is used to separate the syntactic representations of the channels from each other. Thus, the representation of each channel is surrounded by "padding" with an arbitrary number of $\perp$ symbols. This allows each the contents of a channel to expand to the right when messages are inserted, and to shrink from the left when messages are removed. Of course, each particular representation of a system state allows only a finite number of insertions into a channel before all the $\perp$ symbols are "used up". However, since the padding can be arbitrarily long, we can capture the effect of arbitrarily long but finite sequences of insertions and removals, which is sufficient for analyzing safety properties.

An operation in which the first process changes control state from q_1 to q_1' and sends message m to the first channel, is modeled by an action which changes q_1 to q_1' and changes any sequence of form $\perp^{n_1} w_1 \perp^{n_2} \|$ with $n_2 \geq 1$ into $\perp^{n_1} w_1 m \perp^{n_2-1} \|$. If $q_1 \neq q_1'$, the action is idempotent, and it is thus not interesting to compute its transitive closure. If $q_1 = q_1'$, then we can calculate its transitive closure. We must then first represent the action with contexts as

$$q_1 \quad Q \perp^* \mathcal{M}^* \boxed{\tau} \perp^* \| \perp^* \mathcal{M}^* \perp^*$$

where τ changes the one-symbol string $\perp$ into m. This action has local depth 1, and we can compute its transitive closure. The transmission of a sequence of messages to a channel, or the reception of a sequence of messages from a channel, can be represented in an analogous way.

A more challenging operation is one in which the first process in control state q_1 receives message m from the second channel and transmits it to the first. For the special case that our state representation has no padding symbols $\perp$ around the separator $\|$, we can model the operation by the action

$$q_1 \quad Q \quad \perp^* \mathcal{M}^* \quad \boxed{\tau} \quad \mathcal{M}^* \perp^*$$

where τ transforms strings of length 2 of form $\| m$ into $m \|$. This action has local depth 2, and we can therefore calculate its transitive closure. However, this transitive closure results only in states without padding symbols $\bot$ around the separator $\|$. After applying the transitive closure, we must therefore "renormalize" the representation by a non length-preserving transformation which inserts an arbitrary amount of padding around the separator $\|$. This representation can be performed directly on the regular expression or automaton. As with the previous operation, we can generalize this treatment to operations that receive a sequence of message from one channel and transmit a sequence to another. In Section 7, we describe how the above method has been used to generate the set of reachable states of a version of the alternating-bit protocol with unbounded FIFO channels.

6.2   Programs Operating on Integers

We will also give a sketchy presentation of how systems that operate with integers, e.g., as counters or sequence numbers, can be modeled. The state of such a system can be modeled by letting the string represent the number line with the values "laid out" at the position corresponding to their value. Thus, the set of colors has a bit for each variable, which is true if the variable has the value corresponding to that position. The number line is infinite, but it suffices that we represent an arbitrary finite segment which contains the values of all variables. Thus, the predicate $x + 2 = y$ is modeled by the regular expression

$$(\neg x \ \wedge \ \neg y)^* \quad x \wedge \neg y \quad (\neg x \ \wedge \ \neg y) \quad \neg x \wedge y \quad (\neg x \ \wedge \ \neg y)^*$$

It should not be difficult to see that we can represent, e.g., incrementation of a variable by a constant under some conditions, and compute the transitive closure of such an action. In Section 7, we describe how the above method has been used to generate the set of reachable states of a version of a sliding window protocol with unbounded sequence numbers.

7   Experiments

We have implemented a special case of the method described in this paper, for actions that have a local depth of 2 and where the sequence of active index pairs in a configuration sequence is either increasing or decreasing. The implementation builds a transducer for the transitive closure of each action and converts the union of these transducers into the DFA library of MONA[KM98,HJJ$^+$96b] which is implemented using BDDs[Bry86] to represent the transitions. Using the implementation, we have modeled and generated the set of reachable states of the following algorithms:

Parameterized Mutual Exclusion Algorithms We have analyzed idealized versions of parameterized algorithms for mutual exclusion, including Szymanski's algorithm, Burns's and Dijkstra's mutual exclusion algorithms, and the bakery and ticket algorithms by Lamport. Several of these could be handled by the limited framework in our earlier work [ABJN99].

Parameterized Distributed Algorithms As an example of a parameterized distributed algorithm operating on a ring, we have considered the termination detection of Dijkstra, Feijen, and van Gasteren [DFvG83], presented in Section 2.

Algorithms operating on unbounded FIFO channels . We have modeled and analyzed the Alternating Bit Protocol with unbounded FIFO channels. We have used the model of [AJ96].

Algorithms with unbounded sequence numbers . We have modeled and analyzed a sliding window protocol, in which the maximal sequence number is a parameter n. The sender window has size n and the receiver window size 1. We use a version where the channel from the sender to receiver has a capacity of 3 messages, and the channel from the receiver to the sender is synchronous. The length of the channels can of course be changed. However, we have not figured out how to model and analyze the case where both the channels and the sequence numbers are unbounded

In Table 7, we show for each algorithm the domains of the variables that are infinite, the number of steps required to generate the set of reachable configurations, the size of the transducer, the maximum number of states among automata generated during analysis, and the maximum number of BDD nodes among automata generated during analysis. Note that all automata are deterministic.

8   Conclusions

We have presented techniques for reachability analysis of parameterized and infinite-state systems whose state can be represented as a string over a finite alphabet. Since naive symbolic reachability analysis does not in general converge for such systems, we propose to use acceleration of actions to obtain termination. The main contribution is the definition of a notion of local depth of an action, and the construction of the transitive closure of an action with finite local depth, in the form of a finite-state transducer. We have shown that with this framework, we are able to model and verify a variety parameterized algorithms, and

Table 1. Experiments

Algorithm	Domains	Steps	Size	Max states	Max BDD
Szymanski	process id	8	26	144	3574
Dijkstra	process id	15	22	2503	81487
Bakery	process id, integers	5	10	32	163
Ticket	process id, integers	3	12	30	338
Burns	process id	5	14	111	2445
Termination detection	process id	7	29	133	1497
Alternating bit protocol	queues	15	67	4000	66149
Sliding Window: queue length 3	integers	21	45	339	4788

infinite-state systems operating on queues and integers. In comparison with our earlier work [ABJN99], we are able to cover a much broader class of systems. For instance, we can model systems of finite-state processes that communicate over unbounded FIFO channels, and perform transitive closure operations that are analogous to the meta-transitions presented by Boigelot and Godefroid [BG96], using QDDs. Our work is not more powerful, but shows how the techniques can be seen as part of a uniform framework.

Future work includes the treatment of liveness properties.

Acknowledgments We are grateful to Parosh Abdulla and Ahmed Bouajjani for fruitful collaboration and to Amir Pnueli for fruitful discussions during this work. At the presentation of our earlier work at CAV 1999, Ken McMillan posed a question about generalizing that work which we hope to have partially answered in this paper.

References

ABJ98.   Parosh Aziz Abdulla, Ahmed Bouajjani, and Bengt Jonsson. On-the-fly analysis of systems with unbounded, lossy fifo channels. In *Proc. 10th CAV*, volume 1427 of *LNCS*, pages 305–318, 1998. 223

ABJN99.   Parosh Aziz Abdulla, Ahmed Bouajjani, Bengt Jonsson, and Marcus Nilsson. Handling global conditions in parameterized system verification. In *Proc. 11th CAV*, volume 1633 of *LNCS*, pages 134–145, 1999. 220, 222, 224, 226, 231, 233

ACD90.   R. Alur, C. Courcoubetis, and D. Dill. Model-checking for real-time systems. In *Proc. 5th LICS*, pages 414–425, Philadelphia, 1990. 220

AČJYK96. Parosh Aziz Abdulla, Karlis Čerāns, Bengt Jonsson, and Tsay Yih-Kuen. General decidability theorems for infinite-state systems. In *Proc. 11th LICS*, pages 313–321, 1996. 222

AH89.   R. Alur and T. Henzinger. A really temporal logic. In *Proc. 30th Annual Symp. Foundations of Computer Science*, pages 164–169, 1989. 220

AJ96.   Parosh Aziz Abdulla and Bengt Jonsson. Verifying programs with unreliable channels. *Information and Computation*, 127(2):91–101, 1996. 220, 222, 232

BCM+90.   J.R. Burch, E.M. Clarke, K.L. McMillan, D.L. Dill, and L.J. Hwang. Symbolic model checking: 10^{20} states and beyond. In *Proc. 5th LICS*, 1990. 220

BG96.   B. Boigelot and P. Godefroid. Symbolic verification of communication protocols with infinite state spaces using QDDs. In Alur and Henzinger, editors, *Proc. 8th CAV*, volume 1102 of *Lecture Notes in Computer Science*, pages 1–12. Springer Verlag, 1996. 223, 229, 230, 233

BGWW97. B. Boigelot, P. Godefroid, B. Willems, and P. Wolper. The power of QDDs. In *Proc. of the Fourth International Static Analysis Symposium*, LNCS. Springer Verlag, 1997. 223, 229

BH97.   A. Bouajjani and P. Habermehl. Symbolic reachability analysis of fifo-channel systems with nonregular sets of configurations. In *Proc. ICALP '97*, volume 1256 of *Lecture Notes in Computer Science*, 1997. 223

Bry86.   R.E. Bryant. Graph-based algorithms for boolean function manipulation.
            IEEE Trans. on Computers, C-35(8):677–691, Aug. 1986. 231
BS95.   O. Burkart and B. Steffen. Composition, decomposition, and model check-
            ing of pushdown processes. *Nordic Journal of Computing*, 2(2):89–125,
            1995. 220
BW94.   B. Boigelot and P. Wolper. Symbolic verification with periodic sets. In
            Proc. 6th CAV, volume 818 of *LNCS*, pages 55–67. Springer Verlag, 1994.
            223
CC77.   P. Cousot and R. Cousot. Abstract interpretation: A unified model for
            static analysis of programs by construction or approximation of fixpoints.
            In *Proc. 4th ACM Symp. on Principles of Programming Languages*, pages
            238–252, 1977. 223
DFvG83.   E.W. Dijkstra, W.H.J. Feijen, and A.J.M. van Gasteren. Derivation of a
            termination detection algorithm for distributed somputations. *Information
            Processing Letters*, 16(5):217–219, 1983. 224, 232
Fin94.   A. Finkel. Decidability of the termination problem for completely specified
            protocols. *Distributed Computing*, 7(3), 1994. 220
FO97.   L. Fribourg and H. Olsén. Reachability sets of parametrized rings as regu-
            lar languages. In *Proc. 2nd Int. Workshop on Verification of Infinite State
            Systems (INFINITY'97)*, volume 9 of *Electronical Notes in Theoretical
            Computer Science*. Elsevier Science Publishers, July 1997. 222
GS92.   S. M. German and A. P. Sistla. Reasoning about systems with many
            processes. *Journal of the ACM*, 39(3):675–735, 1992. 220
HJJ⁺96a.   J.G. Henriksen, J. Jensen, M. Jørgensen, N. Klarlund, B. Paige, T. Rauhe,
            and A. Sandholm. Mona: Monadic second-order logic in practice. In
            *Proc. TACAS '95, 1th Int. Conf. on Tools and Algorithms for the Con-
            struction and Analysis of Systems*, volume 1019 of *LNCS*, 1996. 222
HJJ⁺96b.   J.G. Henriksen, J. Jensen, M. Jørgensen, N. Klarlund, B. Paige, T. Rauhe,
            and A. Sandholm. Mona: Monadic second-order logic in practice. In *Tools
            and Algorithms for the Construction and Analysis of Systems, First Inter-
            national Workshop, TACAS '95, LNCS 1019*, 1996. Also available through
            http://www.brics.dk/k̃larlund/Mona/main.html. 231
KM98.   N. Klarlund and A. Møller. *MONA Version 1.3 User Manual*. BRICS
            Notes Series NS-98-3 (2.revision), Department of Computer Science, Uni-
            versity of Aarhus, October 1998. 231
KMM⁺97.   Y. Kesten, O. Maler, M. Marcus, A. Pnueli, and E. Shahar. Symbolic
            model checking with rich assertional languages. In O. Grumberg, editor,
            Proc. 9th CAV, volume 1254, pages 424–435, Haifa, Israel, 1997. Springer
            Verlag. 220, 221, 222, 226
KMMG97.   P. Kelb, T. Margaria, M. Mendler, and C. Gsottberger. Mosel: A flexi-
            ble toolset for monadic second–order logic. In *Proc. of the Int. Workshop
            on Tools and Algorithms for the Construction and Analysis of Systems
            (TACAS'97), Enschede (NL)*, volume 1217 of *LNCS*, pages 183–202, Hei-
            delberg, Germany, March 1997. Springer–Verlag. 222
Sis97.   A. Prasad Sistla. Parametrized verification of linear networks using au-
            tomata as invariants. In O. Grumberg, editor, *Proc. 9th CAV*, volume 1254
            of *LNCS*, pages 412–423, Haifa, Israel, 1997. Springer Verlag. 222
Sti96.   C. Stirling. Decidability of bisimulation equivalence for normed pushdown
            processes. In *Proc. CONCUR '96, 7th Int. Conf. on Concurrency Theory*,
            volume 1119 of *LNCS*, pages 217–232. Springer Verlag, 1996. 220

VW86.   M. Y. Vardi and P. Wolper. An automata-theoretic approach to automatic
         program verification. In *Proc. 1ˢᵗ LICS*, pages 332–344, June 1986.   226
WB98.   Pierre Wolper and Bernard Boigelot. Verifying systems with infinite but
         regular state spaces. In *Proc. 10th CAV*, volume 1427 of *LNCS*, pages
         88–97, Vancouver, July 1998. Springer Verlag.   222

Using Static Analysis to Improve Automatic Test Generation

Marius Bozga[1], Jean-Claude Fernandez[2], and Lucian Ghirvu[1]*

[1] VERIMAG – Joint Laboratory of CNRS, UJF and INPG Grenoble, Centre
Equation, 2 avenue de Vignate, F-38610 Gières
{Marius.Bozga,Lucian.Ghirvu}@imag.fr
[2] LSR/IMAG, BP 82, F-38402 Saint Martin d'Hères Cedex
tel: +(33) (0)4 76 82 72 14 fax: +(33) (0)4 76 82 72 87
Jean-Claude.Fernandez@imag.fr

Abstract. Conformance testing is still the main industrial validation technique for telecommunication protocols. The automatic
construction of test cases based on the model approach is hindered
by the state explosion problem. Our method reduces its magnitude
by reconsidering the test case generation at a higher level and by
taking advantage of some static analysis techniques, in particular
the slicing techniques. The specification is simplified by pipelining a
set of three modules, each one implementing a different slicing technique.

Keywords: conformance testing, asynchronous systems, static
analysis, slicing, bisimulation

1 Introduction

Conformance testing is a well-established technique for the validation of telecommunication protocols. Currently, it is still the main validation technique used
at an industrial scale, given the inherent complexity of more ambitious techniques such as formal verification. Moreover, in the case of protocols, the conformance testing was completely formalized by [22,7,15] and is also standardized
within [12]. Test cases can be automatically generated from formal specifications
and tools such as TGV [11], TVEDA [18], AUTOLINK [21] or TORX [2] concretely
implement this activity.

In the model-based approach, test cases are usually constructed by exploring
a synchronous product between the model of the specification and some test purpose, both represented as labeled transition systems. The central problem arising
here is the well known state explosion problem. To deal with it we propose to
reconsider the test generation at a higher level i.e., to work with specifications
and test purposes represented by some kind of extended automata and to perform relevant static simplifications before generating test cases. In this paper,
we consider specifications as asynchronously communicating extended automata

---

* Work partially supported by Région Rhône-Alpes, France

S. Graf and M. Schwartzbach (Eds.): TACAS/ETAPS 2000, LNCS 1785, pp. 235–250, 2000.
© Springer-Verlag Berlin Heidelberg 2000

and test purposes as acyclic automata with constraints. We want to generate tests describing a finite interaction between the tester and the implementation under test. Moreover, by the fact that the test purpose is an automaton with constraints, it is possible to generate symbolic tests.

We propose to simplify specifications by means of *slicing* [23]. A first slicing consists in taking into account the set of interactions between specification components, starting from inputs enabled in the test purpose, and regardless the signal parameters. We obtain a first reduction of the specification, consisting of the part of it which is reachable given the enabled inputs. Then, for the second slicing, we look at the set of variables and parameters which are relevant to outputs observed by the test purpose and safely discard the others. Finally, the specification is sliced with respect to constraints attached to the test purpose. These analyses transform specifications without loss of information with respect to the test purpose. They are independent of each other and can be implemented separately. Each of them inputs a specification, performs a slicing on it, and then outputs a new equivalent one. They can be applied in any order, until no more reduction can be obtained. Concerning the overall simplification on the initial specification, our experiments showed very good results.

The idea of using static analysis to improve model checking and test generation was already being investigated in different contexts. For instance, TVEDA [18] produces test cases from SDL specifications by performing simple syntactic transformations on them. Slicing is used in the context of automatic generation of test data for sequential programs. In [13], the authors present an approach to selective regression testing using slicing. Selective regression approach identifies the parts of the program that are affected by a change. In [14], slicing is used for verification purposes, to extract finite-state machines from multi-threaded programs.

The paper is structured as follows. Section 2 briefly remember the notions of conformance testing and presents the underlying model. In section 3 we propose and formalize three new slicing techniques of the specification with respect to the test purpose. Finally, we give some results in section 4 and we conclude in section 5.

2   Conformance Test Case Generation

This section reviews some notions of conformance testing and presents the underlying model, which is parallel asynchronous processes communicating via queues.

Conformance testing is a black-box testing method, which aims at validating that the implementations of protocols conform to their specifications. Conformance testing activity is standardized in [12] and work has been done to formalize it [22]. In this context, our purpose is to generate automatically conformance test cases for telecommunication protocols.

In the classification of testing architectures from [12,20], our method is a *local single-layer test method* with synchronous communication between the tester and the *implementation under test* (IUT). It is *local* because in the interactions between the tester and the IUT no event caused by the surrounding environment appears. It is *single-layer* because we test implementations of specifications organized in one layer. The tester interacts with the IUT via some *points of control and observation* (PCOs), which, in our case, are seen as external queues of the specification (see below). The communication at the PCOs is synchronous. This architecture is pictured in Figure 1.

In order to assure the feasibility of our method (correctness, compatibility with the industrial practice) we require that the tester, the IUT and the specification satisfy some conditions :

1. *controllability condition* : the tester always controls its outputs and can feed the specification only at one PCO at the time (therefore, for each state of the test purpose, whenever an input is enabled, it is the only transition starting in this state),
2. *consistency relation* : between the test purpose and the specification (which ensures that the set of behaviors described by the test purpose is included in the set of behaviors described by the specification)[1],
3. *conformance relation* : ensures that the outputs of the implementation must be produced also by the specification.

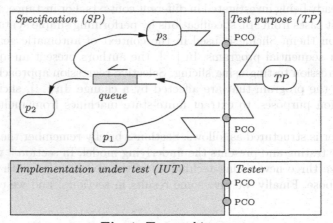

Fig. 1. Test architecture

2.1   The Specification

We consider specifications consisting of asynchronous parallel composition of a number of processes that communicate through parameterized signals passing via a set of unbounded fifo queues. We distinguish between internal queues (closed inside the specification) and external queues (opened to the environment). In the context of conformance testing with local tester, external queues contents are controlled by the tester. Then, we make explicit the assumption of synchronicity

---

[1] This assumption is strong, however it can be verified during the test generation process (as in TGV [10]).

between the tester and the IUT. Processes are extended finite-state automata. They perform actions on queues and local variables. For the sake of simplicity, the actions are simple guarded commands.

Definition 1 (specification syntax). *A specification SP is a tuple (S, C, P) where S is the set of signals, $C = C^{int} \cup C^{ext}$ is the set of queues (internal and external ones) and P is the set of processes. A process $p \in P$ is a tuple (X_p, Q_p, T_p, q_p^0) where X_p is a set of local variables, Q_p is a set of states, Σ_p is a set of actions which can be performed by p, and $T_p \subseteq Q_p \times \Sigma_p \times Q_p$ is a set of transitions. An action can be either a guarded assignment $[\, b \,]\ x := e$, a guarded input $[\, b \,]\ c?s(x)$, or a guarded output $[\, b \,]\ c!s(e)$. Above, b and e are expressions, $x \in X_p$ is a variable, $c \in C$ is a queue and $s \in S$ is a signal.*

We give the semantics of specifications in terms of labeled transition systems. We assume the existence of the universal domain D which contains the values of variables and signal parameters. We suppose that the boolean values $\{\mathbf{t}, \mathbf{f}\}$ and also the special undefined $\bot$ value are contained in D. We define variable contexts as being total mappings $\rho : \bigcup_{p \in P} X_p \to D$ which associate to each variable x a value v from the domain. We extend these mappings to expressions in the usual way. We define internal queue contexts as being also total mappings $\delta : C^{int} \to (S \times D)^*$ which associates to each internal queue c a sequence $(s_1, v_1), ..., (s_k, v_k)$ of messages, that is pairs (s, v) noted also by $s(v)$, where s is a signal and v is the carried parameter value. We assume also the existence of some special undefined message σ. The empty sequence is noted with ϵ.

Definition 2 (specification semantics). *The semantics of a specification SP is given by a labeled transition system $\widehat{SP} = (\widehat{Q}_{sp}, \widehat{T}_{sp}, \hat{q}_{sp}^0)$. States $\hat{q}_{sp}$ of this system are triples of the form (ρ, δ, θ), where ρ is a variable context, δ is a queue context and $\theta = \langle q_1, ... q_n \rangle \in \times_{p \in P} Q_p$ is a global control state. Transitions are either internal and labeled with τ, when derived from assignments or internal communication, either visible and labeled with the concrete action when derived from external communication. Transitions are constructed by the following rules:*

$$\frac{q_p \xrightarrow{[b]\ x:=e} q_p'\ \ \rho(b) = \mathbf{t}\ \ \rho(e) = v}{(\rho, \delta, \theta) \xrightarrow{\tau} (\rho[v/x], \delta, \theta')} \qquad \frac{q_p \xrightarrow{[b]\ c!s(e)} q_p'\ \ \rho(b) = \mathbf{t}\ \ \rho(e) = v\ \ c \in C^{ext}}{(\rho, \delta, \theta) \xrightarrow{c!s(v)} (\rho, \delta, \theta')}$$

$$\frac{q_p \xrightarrow{[b]\ c!s(e)} q_p'\ \ \rho(b) = \mathbf{t}\ \ \rho(e) = v\ \ c \in C^{int}\ \ \delta(c) = w}{(\rho, \delta, \theta) \xrightarrow{\tau} (\rho, \delta[w.s(v)/c], \theta')}$$

$$\frac{q_p \xrightarrow{[b]\ c?s(x)} q_p'\ \ \rho(b) = \mathbf{t}\ \ c \in C^{ext}}{(\rho, \delta, \theta) \xrightarrow{c?s(v)} (\rho[v/x], \delta, \theta')} \qquad \frac{q_p \xrightarrow{[b]\ c?s(x)} q_p'\ \ \rho(b) = \mathbf{t}\ \ c \in C^{int}\ \ \delta(c) = s(v).w}{(\rho, \delta, \theta) \xrightarrow{\tau} (\rho[v/x], \delta[w/c], \theta')}$$

where θ' was obtained from θ by considering one step in process p from q_p to q_p', and the initial state $\hat{q}_{sp}^0$ is obtained considering the default value of the variables, empty queues and processes initial states.

2.2   Test Purpose

The test purpose is an acyclic finite state automaton which describe a pattern of interactions between the tester and the IUT. It is described from the implementation side i.e., inputs and outputs in the test purpose means respectively inputs and outputs in the implementation. It contains both constrained signal inputs and unconstrained signal outputs.

A *constraint* C is a boolean combination of atoms, each of them being a particular restriction on the used value. For example, we can test the containment of an element to an interval or to a set of values. The notation $v \models C$ stands for the value v satisfies the constraint C. For a given input of the test purpose, there is a constraint related to the signal parameter [12]. There are no relational dependencies between constraints attached to different inputs.

This test purpose definition was inspired by TTCN and has the following intuition : if the tester provide a signal to the implementation with the value of its parameter satisfying a constraint then we would like to approximate the value of outputs parameters.

Definition 3 (test purpose). *A test purpose* TP *is a tuple* $(Q_{tp}, T_{tp}, q_{tp}^0, Q_{tp}^{acc})$ *where* Q_{tp} *is a set of states,* $T_{tp} \subseteq Q_{tp} \times \Sigma_{tp} \times Q_{tp}$ *is a set of transitions and* $Q_{tp}^{acc} \subseteq Q_{tp}$ *is a set of accepting states, without successors by* T_{tp}. Σ_{tp} *is the set of interactions* α_{tp} *which can be fixed within the test purpose. This set contains both constrained signal inputs of the form* $c?s(C)$ *and unconstrained signal outputs of the form* $c!s(*)$, *where* $c \in C^{ext}$ *is an external queue and* $s \in S$ *is a signal.* C *denotes a generic constraint e.g., interval constraint, on the received value and* $*$ *denotes any value.*

The feeds are the set of inputs we intend to supply to the IUT during the test. Feeds are a parameter completely controlled by the tester. They will be taken into account during the test case generation process. That is, any external input in the specification will be enabled if and only if it is contained in the set of feeds. Intuitively, the set of feeds must cover the set of inputs given in the test purpose.

Definition 4 (feeds). *The feeds* Σ_f *are a set of constrained signal inputs* $\{c?s(C) \mid c \in C^{ext}, s \in S\}$.

2.3   Synchronous Product

The tests are automatically derived by exploring a kind of synchronous product between the model of the specification $(\widehat{Q}_{sp}, \widehat{T}_{sp}, \hat{q}_{sp}^0)$, the test purpose $(Q_{tp}, T_{tp}, q_{tp}^0, Q_{tp}^{acc})$, and taking into account the set of feeds $\Sigma_f = \{c?s(C) \mid c \in C^{ext}, s \in S\}$.

Definition 5 (synchronous product). *We define the synchronous product* $\prod(\widehat{SP}, TP, \Sigma_f)$ *as the labeled transition system* (Q_π, T_π, q_π^0), *with* $Q_\pi \subseteq \widehat{Q}_{sp} \times Q_{tp}$, *where* Q_π *and* T_π *are the smallest sets obtained by the application of the following rules:*

$$\frac{-}{(\hat{q}_{sp}^0, q_{tp}^0) \in Q_\pi} \qquad \frac{(\hat{q}_{sp}, q_{tp}) \in Q_\pi \quad \hat{q}_{sp} \xrightarrow{\tau} \hat{q}'_{sp} \quad q_{tp} \notin Q_{tp}^{acc}}{(\hat{q}'_{sp}, q_{tp}) \in Q_\pi \quad (\hat{q}_{sp}, q_{tp}) \xrightarrow{\tau} (\hat{q}'_{sp}, q_{tp})}$$

$$\frac{(\hat{q}_{sp}, q_{tp}) \in Q_\pi \quad \hat{q}_{sp} \xrightarrow{c?s(v)} \hat{q}'_{sp} \quad q_{tp} \xrightarrow{c?s(C)} q'_{tp} \quad v \models C}{(\hat{q}'_{sp}, q'_{tp}) \in Q_\pi \quad (\hat{q}_{sp}, q_{tp}) \xrightarrow{c?s(v)} (\hat{q}'_{sp}, q'_{tp})}$$

$$\frac{(\hat{q}_{sp}, q_{tp}) \in Q_\pi \quad \hat{q}_{sp} \xrightarrow{c?s(v)} \hat{q}'_{sp} \quad c?s(C) \in \Sigma_f \quad v \models C}{(\hat{q}'_{sp}, q_{tp}) \in Q_\pi \quad (\hat{q}_{sp}, q_{tp}) \xrightarrow{c?s(v)} (\hat{q}'_{sp}, q_{tp})}$$

$$\frac{(\hat{q}_{sp}, q_{tp}) \in Q_\pi \quad \hat{q}_{sp} \xrightarrow{c!s(v)} \hat{q}'_{sp} \quad q_{tp} \xrightarrow{c!s(*)} q'_{tp}}{(\hat{q}'_{sp}, q'_{tp}) \in Q_\pi \quad (\hat{q}_{sp}, q_{tp}) \xrightarrow{c!s(v)} (\hat{q}'_{sp}, q'_{tp})} \qquad \frac{(\hat{q}_{sp}, q_{tp}) \in Q_\pi \quad \hat{q}_{sp} \xrightarrow{c!s(v)} \hat{q}'_{sp}}{(\hat{q}'_{sp}, q_{tp}) \in Q_\pi \quad (\hat{q}_{sp}, q_{tp}) \xrightarrow{c!s(v)} (\hat{q}'_{sp}, q_{tp})}$$

Example 1. The previous definitions are exemplified in Figure 2. The specification is composed of two processes which communicate through an internal queue $cl \in C^{int}$. The external queues of the specification are $ci, co \in C^{ext}$. The set of feeds are $\Sigma_f = \{ci?sr([1, 10])\}$. This example will be used throughout the paper in order to picture the changes of the specification induced by the following slicing algorithms.

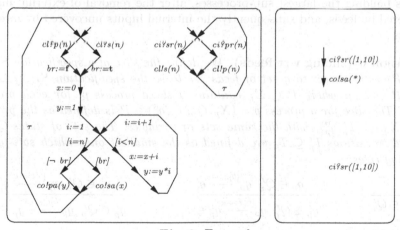

Fig. 2. Example

3   Static Analysis for Testing

The purpose of static analysis is to compute, given the test purpose and the feeds, the part of the specification which is relevant to them. We present three kinds of analyses :

1. *the relevant control analysis*: restricts the processes contained in the specification, to the sets of states and transitions which might be statically reached, given the set of feeds,
2. *the relevant variables analysis*: computes and simplifies processes, with respect to variables which might be used to compute values needed for outputs mentioned in the test purpose and
3. *the constraint propagation*: aims to further simplify processes, given the concrete constraints attached to feeds.

Each one of the analysis takes as input a specification and provides an equivalent one with respect to the test generation method presented below. They are completely independent and can be applied in any order. Furthermore, they could be applied iteratively as the code optimization techniques ([17]). The reduction obtained by one can be further exploited by another and so on, until no more reductions are possible.

We detail each one of these analysis below and illustrate them on the example presented before.

3.1 Relevant Control Analysis

A conservative approximation for the specification is computed, by taking into account the set of feeds. We restrict each process to the set of states and transitions that might be reached given the feeds. Intuitively, this analysis can be seen as building the largest sub-processes, after the removal of external inputs uncovered by feeds, and subsequently the internal inputs uncovered by internal outputs.

Definition 6 (slicing wrt feeds). *We define the slice of a specification $SP = (S, C, P)$ with respect to a set of feeds Σ_f to be the specification $SP \setminus_f \Sigma_f = (S, C, P \setminus_f \Sigma_f)$, where $P \setminus_f \Sigma_f$ contains a sliced process p' for each process $p \in P$. The slice for a process $p = (X_p, Q_p, T_p, q_p^0) \in P$ is defined as the process $p' = (X_p, Q'_p, T'_p, q_p^0)$, with the same sets of variables. The sets of states $Q'_p \subseteq Q_p$ and transitions $T'_p \subseteq T_p$ are defined as the smallest ones which satisfy the following rules:*

$$\frac{-}{q_p^0 \in Q'_p} \qquad \frac{q_p \in Q'_p \quad q_p \xrightarrow{[b]x:=e} q'_p}{q'_p \in Q'_p \quad q_p \xrightarrow{[b]x:=e} q'_p \in T'_p} \qquad \frac{q_p \in Q'_p \quad q_p \xrightarrow{[b]c!s(e)} q'_p}{q'_p \in Q'_p \quad q_p \xrightarrow{[b]c!s(e)} q'_p \in T'_p}$$

$$\frac{q_p \in Q'_p \quad q_p \xrightarrow{[b]c?s(x)} q'_p \quad c \in C^{ext} \quad c?s(C) \in \Sigma_f}{q'_p \in Q'_p \quad q_p \xrightarrow{[b]c?s(x)} q'_p \in T'_p}$$

$$\frac{q_p \in Q'_p \quad q_p \xrightarrow{[b]c?s(x)} q'_p \quad c \in C^{int} \quad \exists r. q_r \xrightarrow{[b']c!s(e)} q'_r \in T'_r}{q'_p \in Q'_p \quad q_p \xrightarrow{[b]c?s(x)} q'_p \in T'_p}$$

We must notice here the input/output propagation between processes. That is, we keep an input inside some process p if and only if there exists some dual output enabled in some other process r.

The algorithm computing the sliced system proceeds in an iterative manner. It maintains the sets of states and transitions reached for each process. Initially, the sets of states contain the initial state of the processes, and the sets of transitions are empty. Then, at each step, one of the rules before is applied until the least fixed point is reached and no more rule is applicable.

This algorithm is similar to reachability analysis but it is performed at the control level.

Example 2. If one applies the previous algorithm for the specification and the feeds from Figure 2, one obtains the specification shown in Figure 3. The external input $ci?pr(n)$ is uncovered by the feeds so its elimination induces the elimination of $cl!p(n)$ and thus $cl?p(n)$ is no more covered by an internal output so it is eliminated together with $br := f$.

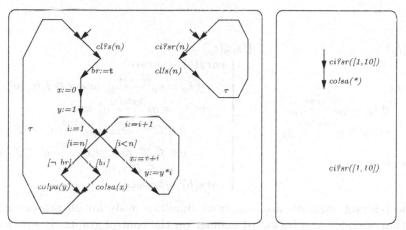

Fig. 3. Example slicing wrt feeds

The slicing with respect to feeds preserves the synchronous product, that is, the following proposition holds.

Proposition 1 (slicing wrt feeds correctness). *Let $SP = (S, C, P)$ be a specification, TP a test purpose and Σ_f a set of feeds which covers TP. The synchronous products between the models of SP and respectively $SP \setminus_f \Sigma_f$ with the test purpose TP, given the feeds Σ_f are strongly bisimilar. That is,*
$$\prod(\widehat{SP}, TP, \Sigma_f) \sim \prod(\widehat{SP \setminus_f \Sigma_f}, TP, \Sigma_f).$$

3.2   Relevant Variables Analysis

This calculus is an extension of live variable analysis [4]. It attempts to compute, for each process, the set of relevant variables in each state. The relevance is defined with respect to test purpose outputs: a variable will be relevant in a state if its value at that state might be used to compute the parameter value of some signal output occurring in the test purpose. Or, similar to the live variables definition, we consider a variable to be relevant in a state if and only if there exists a path starting at that state such that the variable is used before being redefined on the path. But, in our case, we consider a variable to be used only in external outputs mentioned by the test purpose, or in assignments (eventually via internal inputs) to relevant variables.

Definition 7 (relevant variables wrt outputs). *Let $SP = (S, C, P)$ be a specification and $TP = (Q_{tp}, T_{tp}, q^0_{tp}, Q^{acc}_{tp})$ be a test purpose. Let Σ_o be the set of signal outputs mentioned in the test purpose. The relevant variables are defined for each process $p = (X_p, Q_p, T_p, q^0_p) \in P$ by a function $Rlv_p : Q_p \to 2^{X_p}$ mapping states to subsets of variables. The sets $Rlv_p(q_p)$ for states $q_p \in Q_p$ are defined as the least fixed point of the following equation system:*

$$Rlv_p(q_p) = \bigcup\nolimits_{t_p : q_p \xrightarrow{\alpha} q'_p} Rlv(q'_p) \setminus Def_p(t_p) \cup Use_p(t_p)$$

where

$$Def_p(t_p) = \begin{cases} \{x\} \\ \quad if\ t_p = q_p \xrightarrow{[b]x:=e} q'_p \\ \quad or\ t_p = q_p \xrightarrow{[b]c?s(x)} q'_p \\ \emptyset\ otherwise \end{cases}$$

$$Use_p(t_p) = \begin{cases} vars(b) \cup vars(e) \\ \quad if\ t_p = q_p \xrightarrow{[b]x:=e} q'_p\ and\ x \in Rlv_p(q'_p) \\ \quad or\ t_p = q_p \xrightarrow{[b]c!s(e)} q'_p\ and \\ \quad c \in C^{ext}\ and\ \exists q_{tp} \xrightarrow{c!s(*)} q'_{tp} \in T_{tp}\ or \\ \quad c \in C^{int}\ and\ \exists r.q_r \xrightarrow{c?s(x)} q'_r \in T_r\ and \\ \quad\quad x \in Rlv_r(q'_r) \\ vars(b)\ otherwise \end{cases}$$

The relevant variables are computed simultaneously for all processes. The algorithm operates in a backward manner on the control graphs. It starts with empty sets of variables for each state, and at each step one transition is analyzed: the set of used variables is recomputed in the current context and then, the relevant variables set for the source state is updated. The algorithms ends when the least fixed point is reached and no more change in the relevance sets occurs for any of the transitions.

For this analysis too, we notice that the relevance of variables is propagated interprocesses. In fact, variables used in expressions sent through internal channels will become relevant only if, at the destination side their value is further relevant.

The slicing with respect to relevant variables attempts to reduce the number of variables used inside processes. Concretely, we cut off all the definitions assigning irrelevant variables. Irrelevant variables used in inputs are replaced by some special, don't care, variable $\top$. Finally, expressions occurring in unused outputs are replaced by the undefined value $\bot$. This transformation is formally described below.

Definition 8 (slicing wrt outputs). *Let $SP = (S, C, P)$ be a specification and TP be a test purpose. We define the slice of the specification SP given the relevant variables computed wrt outputs to be the specification $SP \setminus_o \Sigma_o = (S, C, P \setminus_o \Sigma_o)$, where $P \setminus_o \Sigma_o$ contains a sliced process p' for each process $p \in P$. The slice for a process $p = (X_p, Q_p, T_p, q_p^0)$ is defined as a process $p' = (X_p', Q_p, T_p', q_p^0)$ which has the same set of states and the same initial state, but operates only on relevant variables. We put $X_p' = \bigcup_{q_p \in Q_p} Rlv_p(q_p)$ and transitions T_p' are constructed from T_p such that they do not more define irrelevant variables :*

$$\frac{q_p \xrightarrow{[b]x:=e} q_p' \quad x \in Rlv_p(q_p')}{q_p \xrightarrow{[b]x:=e} q_p' \in T_p'} \qquad \frac{q_p \xrightarrow{[b]x:=e} q_p' \quad x \notin Rlv_p(q_p')}{q_p \xrightarrow{[b]\tau} q_p' \in T_p'}$$

$$\frac{q_p \xrightarrow{[b]c?s(x)} q_p' \quad x \in Rlv_p(q_p')}{q_p \xrightarrow{[b]c?s(x)} q_p' \in T_p'} \qquad \frac{q_p \xrightarrow{[b]c?s(x)} q_p' \quad x \notin Rlv_p(q_p')}{q_p \xrightarrow{[b]c?s(\top)} q_p' \in T_p'}$$

$$\frac{q_p \xrightarrow{[b]c!s(e)} q_p' \quad Use(c!s)}{q_p \xrightarrow{[b]c!s(e)} q_p' \in T_p'} \qquad \frac{q_p \xrightarrow{[b]c!s(e)} q_p' \quad \neg Use(c!s)}{q_p \xrightarrow{[b]c!s(\bot)} q_p' \in T_p'}$$

where $Use(c!s) = \exists q_{tp} \xrightarrow{c!s(*)} q_{tp}' \in T_{tp}$ or $\exists r.q_r \xrightarrow{c?a(x)} q_r' \in T_r$ and $x \in Rlv_r(q_r')$ denote the global utility of outputs of the form $c!s$.

Example 3. The *slicing wrt outputs* algorithm, applied for the specification and the test purpose from Figure 3, produces the specification shown in Figure 4. The transitions labeled $y := 1$ and $y := y * i$ are relabeled with τ and the output $co!pa(y)$ become $co!pa(\bot)$ because $\neg Use(co!pa)$.

Intuitively, the slicing wrt relevant outputs preserves the model of the specification up to concrete values carried by signals not observed in the test purpose. We define the renaming of the specification model $\widehat{SP}$ with respect to the set of output actions Σ_o in the following way: each visible output action $c!s(v)$ which is not specified by the test purpose i.e., $c!s(*) \notin \Sigma_o$, is renamed into $c!s(\bot)$. The other actions are left unchanged. In this way, we left out the exact parameter values for outputs, other than ones occurring in the test purpose. We note the renamed model with $\widehat{SP} \downarrow \Sigma_o$. The following proposition holds.

Proposition 2 (slicing wrt outputs correctness). *Let $SP = (S, C, P)$ be a specification and $TP = (Q_{tp}, T_{tp}, q_{tp}^0, Q_{tp}^{acc})$. The model of SP renamed with respect to the observable outputs Σ_o and respectively the model of $SP \setminus_o \Sigma_o$ are strongly bisimilar, that is, $\widehat{SP} \downarrow \Sigma_o \sim \widehat{SP \setminus_o \Sigma_o}$.*

A final remark concerns a more general utility of relevant variables. In fact, we tried here to exploit them at a purely syntactic level e.g., by eliminating

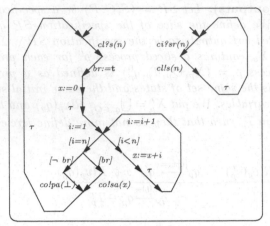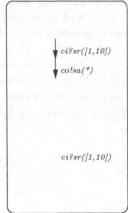

Fig. 4. Example slicing wrt outputs

the irrelevant ones and their dependencies in the specification. However, it is possible to take them into account in a deeper manner. For instance, using a technique similar to [4], one can reinitialize them with a default value as soon as they become irrelevant, thereby achieving a bisimilar reduced model.

3.3   Constraint Propagation

This section provides an approach to simplify the specification, using the constraints imposed on the feeds and the inputs of the test purpose. First, these constraints will be attached to possible matching inputs. Then, by using some intra/interprocesses data flow analysis algorithms, the constraints are propagated in the specification. Thus, for each control state, a conservative approximation of the set of possible values for each variable is computed. Finally, this information is used to evaluate the transitions guards and to eliminate those ones never firable.

In the following we will sketch the *constraint propagation* problem and how to solve it. It is a data flow analysis problem whose basic components are :

1. the flow graph is composed of the states and the transitions of each process and some auxiliary constructions in order to simulate the internal queues,
2. the complete powerset lattice of D, the constraints being some of its elements,
3. the class of *transfer* functions $Transfer_{t_p}$, for each transition t_p.
4. the confluence functions $\bigsqcup$, one for each state.

Let us observe that by choosing the constraints to be the elements of 2^D we have ensured the possibility of testing the emptiness of a constraint and also the possibility of having a partial order among them.

In order to define the transfer functions for transitions, one has to ensure that the actions of transitions (assignments and arithmetic operations) can be realized with constraints (that is, with set of values of D instead of only one value of D). This requirement is fulfilled by defining the operations with set of values similarly as in the *interval arithmetic* [19].

Having seen what are the basic requirements and an approach to fulfill them, the definition of constraint propagation problem follows below.

Definition 9 (constraint propagation). *Let $SP = (S, C, P)$ be the specification and Σ_f the set of feeds. Constraints are represented, for each process, as a function $Val : Q_p \rightarrow 2^D$. With the notations presented before, the constraint propagation problem is defined as finding the least fix point solution of the following equation system:*

$$Val(q'_p) = \bigsqcup\nolimits_{t_p : q_p \xrightarrow{\alpha} q'_p} Transfer_{t_p}(Val(q_p))$$

In order to solve this problem we have considered the cases where constraints are expressed by means of constants and by integer intervals. This is due to the fact that in TTCN [12] the constraints have this kind of simple forms. The formal framework defined above is applicable in these cases, using the Galois connection, a classical abstract interpretation technique [8].

The algorithm used for solving the constraint propagation problem in the case of the lattice of constants is the classical iterative algorithm from [16] with an interprocesses variant such as [9]. In the case of the integer intervals lattice, due to the fact that it has infinite height, we use for each process a widening technique as in [3].

The results of the constraint propagation problem are used in simplifying the specification by means of slicing. However, they also allow, for the outgoing output transitions of a control state, to have a conservative approximation of the parameters of the signals, thereby enabling generation of symbolic test cases.

Definition 10 (slicing wrt constraints). *Let $SP = (S, C, P)$ be a specification and Σ_f a set of feeds. We define the slice of the specification SP given the constraints computed wrt feeds to be the specification $SP \setminus_c \Sigma_f = (S, C, P \setminus_c \Sigma_f)$, where $P \setminus_c \Sigma_f$ contains a sliced process p' for each process $p \in P$. The slice for a process $p = (X_p, Q_p, T_p, q_p^0)$ is defined as a process $p' = (X_p, Q'_p, T'_p, q_p^0)$, which operates on the same set of variables X_p. The sets of states $Q'_p \subseteq Q_p$ and transitions $T'_p \subseteq T_p$ are the smallest ones which satisfy the following rules:*

$$\frac{-}{q_p^0 \in Q'_p} \qquad \frac{q_p \in Q'_p \; t_p = q_p \xrightarrow{\alpha} q'_p \; Transfer_{t_p}(Val_p(q_p)) \neq \emptyset}{q'_p \in Q'_p \; t_p = q_p \xrightarrow{\alpha} q'_p \in T'_p}$$

Example 4. The *slicing wrt constraints* algorithm, applied for the specification and the test purpose from Figure 4, produces the specification shown in Figure 5. The value t for br is propagated to the source state of the transition with the guard $[\neg br]$ and thus determining that this transition and the following $co!pa(\perp)$ will be never fired. These transitions are detached from the specification. The constraint propagation problem, in this case, given the feed $ci?sr([1, 10])$, provides for the parameter x in the transition $co!sa(x)$ the interval $[1, 100]$.

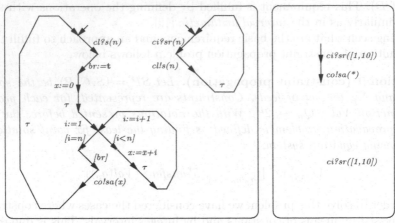

Fig. 5. Example slicing wrt constraints

We have the following preservation result.

Proposition 3 (slicing wrt constraints correctness). *Let $SP = (S, C, P)$ be a specification, $TP = (Q_{tp}, T_{tp}, q_{tp}^0, Q_{tp}^{acc})$ and Σ_f a set of feeds which cover TP. The synchronous product between the models of SP and respectively $SP \setminus_c \Sigma_f$ with the test purpose given the feeds Σ_f are strongly bisimilar, that is* $\prod(\widehat{SP}, TP, \Sigma_f) \sim \prod(\widehat{SP \setminus_c \Sigma_f}, TP, \Sigma_f)$

4   Experimentation

These techniques were implemented and currently we are experimenting with them on some case studies. We use the IF [5] framework, which is an intermediate program representation for protocols, based on *asynchronously communicating timed automata*. IF was designed right from the beginning to support the application of static analysis techniques used in compiler optimization [1,17].

The techniques presented before were applied to improve test case generation for the SSCOP protocol [6], a layer from the ATM protocols stack. Previous work was already done on it in the context of the FORMA research action [6] and despite its success, it shows also the limitations of the existing test generation technology. We were interested to see what are the concrete benefits of our add-ons.

We started with an SDL version of the protocol provided by CNET France Telecom. It is about 2000 lines of code which describes the whole protocol as a single SDL process. It was translated into an IF extended automaton, with 1075 states, 1291 transitions and 134 variables. We considered 10 test purposes conceived for different phases of the protocol (connection, data transmission). The results obtained using previous analysis are summarized below:

slicing wrt feeds: By carefully choosing the appropriate set of feeds for each test purpose, we obtained reductions up to 80% of the specification. That is, we started usually with the smallest set of feeds covering the test purpose inputs. This choice is often too restrictive i.e., test cases cannot be constructed from the model of sliced specification. Thus, we iteratively added other inputs to the feeds until the model became sufficiently large to cover the test purpose behavior. In this way, we are able to work on some minimal version of the specification, still allowing the generation of test cases.

slicing wrt outputs: This analysis gives very good results too. When applied on the sliced specification wrt to feeds, it reduces the number of variables up to 40%. More generally, for the SSCOP protocol we obtained, in average, that, from total number of variables, 30% are relevant with respect to outputs, while the maximum reaches 60%. Also, when used at the model generation time, the relevant variables still allow important reductions on the number of model states and transitions.

constraint propagation: The constraint propagation is still under development. At this time, we experimented only the constant propagation algorithm. The results obtained are good, mainly when the test purpose and the feeds contains punctual constraints i.e., the values provided in test purpose inputs are fixed at some constants. We work currently to adapt the interval propagation algorithm.

These results are very encouraging. However, given the particular nature of the SSCOP protocol, we need further experimentations to clearly set up our techniques. We will consider experimentations for interprocesses slicing and the interaction between the three slicing techniques.

5   Conclusion and Future Work

In this paper, we show that automatic test generation can take advantages of static analysis. Our test generation method, derived from the so-called on the fly model checking, consists in traversing a product defined between the specification and the test purpose. Before test generation, simplifications may be made on the specification, by collecting informations on the test purposes.

Our general approach to define static analysis is based on the following considerations and remarks. The specification is a set of extended automata, asynchronously communicating via a set of queues. The test purpose is also an extended automaton with constraints. In the context of test generation, we distinguish between inputs and outputs. The static analysis we define transform specifications into others, smaller ones, without loss of information with respect to test purpose. This approach is compatible with the standard definition of conformance testing.

In this work, we proposed three kinds of slicing, based on different analysis. The first one consists in restricting each automaton, starting from the set of feeds. It includes the propagation through the dependence relation between the input of a process and the outputs of the others process. The second analysis computes the set of variables, necessary to determine values occurring into the outputs, and safely discards the others. The last analysis is the constraint propagation.

We have shown that the combination of these three interprocesses analyses may reduce the specification. We have implemented these analysis in the context of IF tools and we obtain very good results on the SSCOP protocol.

Our results can be further extended in several directions. Firstly, we aim at experimenting more systematically the static analysis in the context of test case generation for industrial protocols. The results on SSCOP were very encouraging but other experimentations are further needed to conclude the practical use of our techniques.

At short term too, we plan to extend these analysis techniques to work on timed specifications. In fact, the generated test cases usually uses timers, which are set and test to more or less arbitrarily values in order to observe deadlocks or livelocks in the implementation. However, a more fine analysis can be done on timed specifications to obtain relevant values to be used in this context.

A more speculative direction concerns the generation of symbolic tests. In this respect, we are currently thinking about the appropriate extension for the test purposes concept. For instance, the explicit use of variables in addition to constraints can make them much more expressive. Furthermore, it may be interesting to reconsider the definition of the synchronous product i.e., to be done at a higher level in such a way that it will allow the derivation of symbolic test cases.

References

1. A. Aho, R. Sethi, and J.D. Ullman. *Compilers: Principles, Techniques and Tools.* Addison-Wesley, 1986. 247
2. A. Belinfante, J. Feenstra, R.G. de Vries, J. Tretmans, N. Goga, L. Feijs, S. Mauw, and L. Heerink. Formal Test Automation : a Simple Experiment. In G. Csopaki, S. Dibuz, and K. Tarnay, editors, 12th *International Workshop on Testing of Communicating Systems.* Kluwer Academic Publishers, 1999. 235
3. F. Bourdoncle. Efficient Chaotic Iteration Strategies with Widenings. In *International Conference on Formal Methods in Programming and their Applications*, volume 735 of *LNCS*. Springer-Verlag, 1993. 246
4. M. Bozga, J.-C. Fernandez, and L. Ghirvu. State Space Reduction based on Live Variables Analysis. In *SAS*, volume 1694 of *LNCS*, Venezia, IT, 1999. 242, 245
5. M. Bozga, J.-C. Fernandez, L. Ghirvu, S. Graf, J.-P. Krimm, L. Mounier, and J. Sifakis. IF : An Intermediate Representation for SDL and its Applications. In *SDL Forum Proceedings*, Montreal, CA, June 1999. 247
6. M. Bozga, J.-C. Fernandez, L. Ghirvu, C. Jard, T. Jéron, A. Kerbrat, P. Morel, and L. Mounier. Verification and Test Generation for the SSCOP Protocol. *Science of Computer Programming*, 1999. 247
7. E. Brinksma, R. Alderden, R. Langerak, J. Van de Lagemaat, and J. Tretmans. A Formal Approach to Conformance Testing. In J. De Meer, L. Mackert, and W. Effelsberg, editors, 2nd *International Workshop on Protocol Test Systems*. North Holland, 1990. 235
8. P. Cousot and R. Cousot. Comparing the Galois Connection and Widening/Narrowing Approaches to Abstract Interpretation. Technical report, LIX, Ecole Polytechnique, 91128 Palaiseau Cedex FR, May 1990. 246

9. M. Dwyer. Data Flow Analysis Frameworks for Concurrent Programs. Technical Report UM-CS-1995-062, University of Massachusetts at Amherst, US, 1995. 246

10. J.-C. Fernandez, C. Jard, T. Jéron, and C. Viho. Using on-the-fly verification techniques for the generation of test suites. In *Proceedings of the 8th International Conference on Computer Aided Verification*, number 1102 in LNCS. Springer-Verlag, 1996. 237

11. J.-C. Fernandez, C. Jard, T. Jéron, and C. Viho. An Experiment in Automatic Generation of Test Suites for Protocols with Verification Technology. *Science of Computer Programming*, 29, 1997. 235

12. International Organization for Standardization. OSI-Open Systems Interconnection, Information Technology - Open Systems Interconnection Conformance Testing Methodology and Framework, 1992. Standard ISO/IEC 9646-1/2/3. 235, 236, 239, 246

13. R. Gupta, M.J. Harrold, and M.L. Soffa. Program Slicing-Based Regression Testing Techniques. *Journal of Software Testing, Verification and Reliability,*, June 1996. 236

14. J. Hatcliff, J. Corbett, M. Dwyer, S. Sokolowski, and H. Zheng. A Formal Study of Slicing for Multi-Threaded Programs with JVM Concurrency Primitives. In *SAS*, volume 1694 of *LNCS*, Venezia, IT, 1999. Springer-Verlag. 236

15. ITU-T SG 10/Q.8. ISO/IEC JTC1/SC21 WG7. Information Retrieval, Transfer and Management for OSI; Framework: Formal Methods in Conformance Testing. Technical report, International Organization for Standardization - ISO, 1996. 235

16. G. Kildall. A Unified Approach to Global Program Optimization. In *ACM Symposium on Principles of Programming Languages*, 1973. 246

17. S. Muchnick. *Advanced Compiler Design Implementation*. Morgan Kaufmann Publishers, 1997. 241, 247

18. M. Phalippou. Test Sequence using Estelle or SDL Structure Information. In *FORTE*, Berne, CH, October 1994. 235, 236

19. H. Ratschek and J. Rokne. *New Computer Methods for Global Optimization*. Ellis Horwood, John Wiley, 1988. 246

20. D. Rayner. OSI Conformance Testing. *Computer Networks and ISDN Systems*, 14, 1987. 236

21. M. Schmitt, B. Koch, J. Grabowski, and D. Hogrefe. Autolink - A Tool for Automatic and Semi-automatic Test Generation from SDL Specifications. Technical Report A-98-05, Medical Univ. of Lübeck, DE, 1998. 235

22. J. Tretmans. A Formal Approach to Conformance Testing. In *6th International Workshop on Protocols Test Systems*, number C-19 in IFIP Transactions, pages 257–276, 1994. 235, 236

23. M. Weiser. Program Slicing. *IEEE Transactions on Software Engineering*, SE-10(4), July 1984. 236

Efficient Diagnostic Generation
for Boolean Equation Systems

Radu Mateescu

INRIA Rhône-Alpes / VASY
655, avenue de l'Europe, F-38330 Montbonnot Saint Martin, France
Radu.Mateescu@inria.fr

Abstract. Boolean Equation Systems (BESs) provide a useful framework for the verification of concurrent finite-state systems. In practice, it is desirable that a BES resolution also yields diagnostic information explaining, preferably in a concise way, the truth value computed for a given variable of the BES. Using a representation of BESs as extended boolean graphs (EBGs), we propose a characterization of full diagnostics (i.e., both examples and counterexamples) as a particular class of subgraphs of the EBG associated to a BES. We provide algorithms that compute examples and counterexamples in linear time and can be straightforwardly used to extend known (global or local) BES resolution algorithms with diagnostic generation facilities.

1 Introduction

It is well-known that several equivalence/preorder checking and temporal logic model-checking problems occurring in the verification of concurrent finite-state systems can be reduced to the resolution of Boolean Equation Systems (BESs). Various algorithms have been proposed for solving this problem, either *globally*, i.e., by computing the values of all variables in a BES [3,9,28,1,29,2,20,19], or *locally*, i.e., by computing the value of a single variable [17,1,29,30,20,18,19]. However, practical applications of BES resolution often need more detailed feedback than a simple yes/no answer. For instance, when solving a BES encoding the bisimilarity check between two transition systems, it is desirable to have, in case of a negative result, a *diagnostic* (e.g., a transition sequence) explaining why the two systems are not bisimilar.

In general, both positive diagnostics (examples) and negative diagnostics (counterexamples) are needed in order to be capable of fully explaining the truth value of a boolean variable. This is the case for instance when verifying CTL [5] formulas over a transition system: a positive answer obtained for an $E[T \cup \varphi]$ formula should be explained by an example (e.g., a transition sequence leading to a φ-state), whereas a negative answer obtained for an $A[T \cup \varphi]$ formula should be explained by a counterexample (e.g., a transition sequence leading to a deadlock or to a circuit without reaching a φ-state).

The problem of generating diagnostics for finite-state verification has been studied using various approaches. Explicit state enumeration techniques have

S. Graf and M. Schwartzbach (Eds.): TACAS/ETAPS 2000, LNCS 1785, pp. 251–265, 2000.

been applied to compute diagnostics for bisimulation/preorder checking [8,15,13] and CTL model-checking [5,23], in tools like ALDÉBARAN [4] and EMC [5], respectively. Symbolic techniques based on (ordered) binary decision diagrams have been used to generate examples (witnesses) and counterexamples for CTL formulas [7,6], in tools like SMV [21]. Recently, game-based techniques [25] have been applied to verify modal μ-calculus [16] formulas and to interactively generate diagnostics, in tools like the Edinburgh Concurrency Workbench [24].

In this paper we address the problem of characterizing and computing full diagnostics (examples and counterexamples) for BESs. We focus on single fixed point BESs, which allow to encode the alternation-free fragment of the modal μ-calculus [9], and attempt to devise efficient algorithms handling this case. The solutions that we propose can be easily instantiated in order to obtain diagnostic generation facilities for particular verification problems reducible to BES resolution, such as bisimulation/preorder checking and model-checking of branching-time temporal logics like CTL.

We use a representation of BESs as extended boolean graphs (EBGs), which allow to define an appropriate subgraph relation between EBGs. We start by characterizing the solution of a BES by means of two particular temporal logic formulas EX and CX interpreted on the corresponding EBG. This allows, on one hand, to reduce the problem of solving a BES to the problem of verifying these formulas over its EBG and, on the other hand, to characterize minimal diagnostics (w.r.t. the subgraph relation) as particular models of EX or CX. We also propose two efficient (linear-time) algorithms for computing minimal examples and counterexamples and we indicate how they can be used in conjunction with existing (global or local) BES resolution algorithms. Our characterizations of minimal examples and counterexamples turned out to be very similar to the winning strategies for player I and player II of a model-checking game [24]. However, as far as we know, there is no equivalent linear-time complexity result about the game-based algorithms applied to the alternation-free μ-calculus.

The paper is organized as follows. Section 2 defines BESs and their associated EBGs, and gives a characterization of the BES solution using temporal formulas. Section 3 defines diagnostics in terms of subgraphs of an EBG and provides a characterization of minimal diagnostics. Section 4 presents algorithms for computing minimal examples and counterexamples. Finally, Section 5 shows some practical applications of these results and indicates directions for future work.

2   BESs and Extended Boolean Graphs

A *boolean equation system* (BES) M is a set of fixed point equations whose left-hand-sides are boolean variables and whose right-hand-sides are pure disjunctive or conjunctive formulas (see Figure 1). Empty disjunctions and conjunctions are equivalent to F and T, respectively. Variables $\{x_1, ..., x_n\}$ are *bound* and variables in $(\bigcup_{1 \le i \le n} X_i) \setminus \{x_1, ..., x_n\}$ are *free* in M. A BES is *closed* if it has no free variables. In the sequel, we consider only minimal fixed point BESs ($\sigma = \mu$), the formalization for maximal fixed point BESs being completely dual.

Syntax of Boolean Equation Systems (BESs):

$$M = \{x_i \overset{\sigma}{=} op_i X_i\}_{1 \le i \le n}$$

where $\sigma \in \{\mu, \nu\}$, $x_i \in \mathcal{X}$, $op_i \in \{\vee, \wedge\}$, $X_i \subseteq \mathcal{X}$ for all $1 \le i \le n$

Semantics w.r.t. Bool $= \{F, T\}$ and a context $\delta : \mathcal{X} \to$ Bool:

$$[\![op\{x_1, ..., x_k\}]\!]\,\delta = \delta(x_1) \; op \; ... \; op \; \delta(x_k)$$

$$[\![M]\!]\,\delta = \sigma\Psi_\delta$$

where $\Psi_\delta : \text{Bool}^n \to \text{Bool}^n$, $\Psi_\delta(b_1, ..., b_n) = ([\![op_i X_i]\!]\,\delta[b_1/x_1, ..., b_n/x_n])_{1 \le i \le n}$

Fig. 1. Syntax and semantics of Boolean Equation Systems

An *extended boolean graph* (EBG) is a tuple $G = (V, E, L, F)$, where: V is the set of vertices; $E \subseteq V \times V$ is the set of edges; $L : V \to \{\vee, \wedge\}$ is the vertex labeling; and $F \subseteq V$ is the *frontier* of G. The notion of frontier will be useful later for defining a suitable subgraph relation between EBGs (see Section 3). The sets of successors and predecessors of a vertex $x \in V$ are noted $E(x)$ and $E^{-1}(x)$, respectively. The set of vertices reachable from x via E is noted $E^*(x)$. The restriction of E to a subset $U \subseteq V$ is defined as $E|_U = \{(x, y) \in E \mid x \in U\}$. Every EBG G induces a Kripke structure $\mathbf{G} = (V, E, L)$. A closed BES can be represented by an EBG, where V denotes the set of boolean variables, E denotes the dependencies between variables, and L labels the vertices as disjunctive or conjunctive according to the operator in the corresponding equation of the BES.

We can characterize the solution of a closed BES using temporal logic formulas interpreted over the Kripke structure induced by the corresponding EBG. The logic we use (see Figure 2) is a variant of the alternation-free μ-calculus [10].

Syntax of temporal formulas:

$$\varphi ::= P_\vee \mid P_\wedge \mid \varphi_1 \vee \varphi_2 \mid \varphi_1 \wedge \varphi_2 \mid \langle - \rangle\,\varphi \mid [-]\,\varphi \mid Y \mid \mu Y.\varphi \mid \nu Y.\varphi$$

where $Y \in \mathcal{Y}$

Semantics w.r.t. a Kripke structure $\mathbf{G} = (V, E, L)$ and a context $\rho : \mathcal{Y} \to 2^V$:

$$[\![P_\vee]\!]_{\mathbf{G}}\rho = \{x \in V \mid L(x) = \vee\}$$
$$[\![P_\wedge]\!]_{\mathbf{G}}\rho = \{x \in V \mid L(x) = \wedge\}$$
$$[\![\varphi_1 \vee \varphi_2]\!]_{\mathbf{G}}\rho = [\![\varphi_1]\!]_{\mathbf{G}}\rho \cup [\![\varphi_2]\!]_{\mathbf{G}}\rho$$
$$[\![\varphi_1 \wedge \varphi_2]\!]_{\mathbf{G}}\rho = [\![\varphi_1]\!]_{\mathbf{G}}\rho \cap [\![\varphi_2]\!]_{\mathbf{G}}\rho$$
$$[\![\langle - \rangle\,\varphi]\!]_{\mathbf{G}}\rho = \{x \in V \mid E(x) \cap [\![\varphi]\!]_{\mathbf{G}}\rho \ne \emptyset\}$$
$$[\![[-]\,\varphi]\!]_{\mathbf{G}}\rho = \{x \in V \mid E(x) \subseteq [\![\varphi]\!]_{\mathbf{G}}\rho\}$$
$$[\![Y]\!]_{\mathbf{G}}\rho = \rho(Y)$$
$$[\![\mu Y.\varphi]\!]_{\mathbf{G}}\rho = \bigcap\{U \subseteq V \mid \Phi_{\mathbf{G}\rho}(U) \subseteq U\}$$
$$[\![\nu Y.\varphi]\!]_{\mathbf{G}}\rho = \bigcup\{U \subseteq V \mid U \subseteq \Phi_{\mathbf{G}\rho}(U)\}$$

where $\Phi_{\mathbf{G}\rho} : 2^V \to 2^V$, $\Phi_{\mathbf{G}\rho}(U) = [\![\varphi]\!]_{\mathbf{G}}\rho[U/Y]$

Fig. 2. Syntax and semantics of the logic for diagnostic characterization

Given a Kripke structure $\mathbf{G} = (V, E, L)$, the two atomic propositions $P_\vee$ and $P_\wedge$ denote the disjunctive and conjunctive vertices of V, respectively. The boolean operators $\vee$ and $\wedge$ have their usual semantics. The possibility and necessity modal formulas $\langle - \rangle\, \varphi$ and $[-]\, \varphi$ denote the vertices for which some (all) successors satisfy φ. The fixed point formulas $\mu Y.\varphi$ and $\nu Y.\varphi$ denote the minimal and maximal solutions (over 2^V) of the equation $Y = \varphi$, respectively. Formulas φ are assumed to be *alternation-free* (without mutual recursion between minimal and maximal fixed points). A vertex $x \in V$ satisfies a formula φ in $\mathbf{G}$, noted $x \models_{\mathbf{G}} \varphi$, iff $x \in \llbracket \varphi \rrbracket_{\mathbf{G}}$. $\mathbf{G}$ is a φ-*model* iff $V = \llbracket \varphi \rrbracket_{\mathbf{G}}$.

The two particular formulas defined below will be useful in the sequel.

Definition 1 (example and counterexample formulas).
The formulas Ex *and* Cx *defined as follows:*

$$\mathrm{Ex} = \mu Y.(P_\vee \wedge \langle - \rangle\, Y) \vee (P_\wedge \wedge [-]\, Y)$$
$$\mathrm{Cx} = \nu Y.(P_\vee \wedge [-]\, Y) \vee (P_\wedge \wedge \langle - \rangle\, Y)$$

are called example formula *and* counterexample formula, *respectively.*

Since Ex and Cx are complementary (Ex $\vee$ Cx $=$ T and Ex $\wedge$ Cx $=$ F), their interpretations on a Kripke structure $\mathbf{G} = (V, E, L)$ associated to a closed Bes induce a partition of V. The following theorem states that this partition corresponds exactly to the true and false variables in the Bes solution.

Theorem 1 (characterization of BES solution).
Let $M = \{x_i \overset{\mu}{=} op_i X_i\}_{1 < i \leq n}$ *be a closed* Bes *and let* $\mathbf{G} = (V, E, L)$ *be its associated Kripke structure. Then:*

$$\llbracket M \rrbracket_i = \mathsf{T} \iff x_i \models_{\mathbf{G}} \mathrm{Ex}$$

for all $1 \leq i \leq n$.

Theorem 1 can be easily extended to alternation-free BESs, whose solution can be characterized using an alternation-free μ-calculus formula containing an Ex-subformula for each single fixed point subsystem[1] of the BES. The equivalence between alternation-free BESs and alternation-free μ-calculus formulas has been extensively studied in [20]. Together with the classical results of reducing μ-calculus model-checking to BES resolution [9,1], Theorem 1 provides another proof of this equivalence.

In the following, we will develop the formalization of diagnostics by reasoning exclusively in terms of EBGs associated to BESs and the interpretations of Ex and Cx formulas on the corresponding Kripke structures.

3   Examples and Counterexamples

Consider a Bes M and a boolean variable x that is bound in M. What would be a *diagnostic* for x? From the BES point of view, a diagnostic for x could be a

---

[1] For ν-subsystems, the formula Ex $= \nu Y.(P_\vee \wedge \langle - \rangle\, Y) \vee (P_\wedge \wedge [-]\, Y)$ must be used.

subsystem M' of M containing x as a bound variable and having the property that by solving M' one obtains for x the same truth value as by solving M. In other words, the value computed for x in M' should not depend upon the context of M' imposed by M (i.e., upon the values of variables that are free in M' and bound in M); that is, it should not depend upon *any* context of M'.

Figure 3 shows a BES and its associated EBG, where black vertices denote variables that are T and white vertices denote variables that are F in the BES solution. According to the informal definition above, a "diagnostic" showing why x_0 is T (an "example" for x_0) would be, for instance, the subsystem defining the variables $\{x_0, x_1, x_2, x_3, x_4\}$, whose vertices are surrounded by a dotted box in the EBG. Similarly, a "diagnostic" showing why x_5 is F (a "counterexample" for x_5) would be the other subsystem $\{x_5, x_6, x_7, x_8, x_9\}$ outlined in the figure. It is easy to see that these two subsystems can be solved individually and the truth values obtained in this way for x_0 and x_5 are the same as those obtained by solving the whole system.

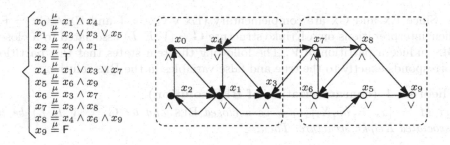

$$\begin{cases} x_0 \overset{\mu}{=} x_1 \wedge x_4 \\ x_1 \overset{\mu}{=} x_2 \vee x_3 \vee x_5 \\ x_2 \overset{\mu}{=} x_0 \wedge x_1 \\ x_3 \overset{\mu}{=} \mathsf{T} \\ x_4 \overset{\mu}{=} x_1 \vee x_3 \vee x_7 \\ x_5 \overset{\mu}{=} x_6 \wedge x_9 \\ x_6 \overset{\mu}{=} x_3 \wedge x_7 \\ x_7 \overset{\mu}{=} x_3 \wedge x_8 \\ x_8 \overset{\mu}{=} x_4 \wedge x_6 \wedge x_9 \\ x_9 \overset{\mu}{=} \mathsf{F} \end{cases}$$

Fig. 3. A closed BES and its associated EBG

In general, for a given variable of a BES there can be several subsystems having the property above (an obvious one being the BES itself). For instance, the reader may check that for the BES on Figure 3, the subsystems $\{x_0, x_1, x_2, x_3, x_4, x_6, x_7, x_8\}$ and $\{x_3, x_4, x_5, x_6, x_7, x_8, x_9\}$ can also be considered as "diagnostics" for the variables x_0 and x_5, respectively.

From the EBG point of view (and using Theorem 1), a diagnostic for a vertex x of an EBG G_2 would be a subgraph G_1 of G_2 containing x and having the property that $x \models_{\mathbf{G_1}} \mathrm{Ex}$ iff $x \models_{\mathbf{G_2}} \mathrm{Ex}$. A suitable subgraph relation between EBGs can be defined using the notion of frontier. Intuitively, the frontier of a subgraph G_1 contains all vertices starting at which new edges can be added when G_1 is embedded in another graph G_2 (note that G_2 may have the same vertices as G_1, but more edges). To obtain a correct subgraph relation, the notion of frontier must be *intrinsic* to an EBG: therefore, when embedding G_1 in G_2, the frontier of G_2 must not contain vertices of G_1 which are not already in the frontier of G_1. The frontier of an EBG that is not meant to be embedded in another one (e.g., an EBG associated to a closed BES) is empty.

Definition 2 (subgraph of an EBG).
Let $G_1 = (V_1, E_1, L_1, F_1)$ and $G_2 = (V_2, E_2, L_2, F_2)$ be two EBGs. G_1 is a subgraph of G_2, written $G_1 \preceq G_2$, iff the following conditions hold:

- $V_1 \subseteq V_2$ and $F_2 \cap V_1 \subseteq F_1$;
- $E_1 \subseteq E_2$ and $(E_2 \setminus E_1)|_{V_1} = (E_2 \setminus E_1)|_{F_1}$;
- $L_1 = L_2|_{V_1}$.

It is easy to check that $\preceq$ is a partial order relation on EBGs. For the EBG on Figure 3, the subgraphs enclosed in the left and right dotted boxes have the frontiers $\{x_1, x_4\}$ and $\{x_6, x_7, x_8\}$, respectively.

The two definitions below precise the notion of diagnostics in terms of EBGs.

Definition 3 (solution-closed EBG).
An EBG $G_1 = (V_1, E_1, L_1, F_1)$ is solution-closed iff, for any EBG $G_2 = (V_2, E_2, L_2, F_2)$ such that $G_1 \preceq G_2$:

$$[\![Ex]\!]_{\mathbf{G_1}} = [\![Ex]\!]_{\mathbf{G_2}} \cap V_1$$

or, equivalently:

$$[\![Cx]\!]_{\mathbf{G_1}} = [\![Cx]\!]_{\mathbf{G_2}} \cap V_1$$

where $\mathbf{G_1}$ and $\mathbf{G_2}$ are the Kripke structures associated to G_1 and G_2.

Definition 4 (examples and counterexamples).
Let $G = (V, E, L, F)$ be an EBG, $\mathbf{G}$ its associated Kripke structure, and $x \in V$. A diagnostic for x is a solution-closed subgraph of G containing x. A diagnostic for x is called example if $x \models_{\mathbf{G}} Ex$ and counterexample if $x \models_{\mathbf{G}} Cx$.

The following theorem provides a characterization of solution-closed EBGs that will be useful in the sequel. Intuitively, an EBG G is solution-closed if the satisfaction of Ex (or Cx) on its frontier (which contains the only vertices of G that may directly depend on some external context when G is embedded in another EBG) can be completely decided using only the information in G.

Theorem 2 (characterization of solution-closed EBGs).
Let $G = (V, E, L, F)$ be an EBG. G is solution-closed iff:

$$F \subseteq [\![(P_\vee \wedge Ex) \vee (P_\wedge \wedge Cx)]\!]_{\mathbf{G}}$$

where $\mathbf{G}$ is the Kripke structure associated to G.

Using Theorem 2, we can easily see that the left and right subgraphs of the EBG outlined on Figure 3 are solution-closed (i.e., they are diagnostics for x_0 and x_5). The same holds for the subgraphs corresponding to the other two subsystems $\{x_0, x_1, x_2, x_3, x_4, x_6, x_7, x_8\}$ and $\{x_3, x_4, x_5, x_6, x_7, x_8, x_9\}$ having the frontiers $\{x_1, x_8\}$ and $\{x_4\}$. However, in practice it is desirable to explain the value of a variable in a concise manner, and therefore diagnostics should be as small as possible. The following theorem states that minimal diagnostics (w.r.t. $\preceq$) can be obtained as particular Ex-models or Cx-models.

Theorem 3 (characterization of minimal diagnostics).
Let $G = (V, E, L, F)$ be an example for $x \in V$ and $\mathbf{G}$ its associated Kripke structure. G is minimal (w.r.t. $\preceq$) iff the following conditions hold:

a) $\mathbf{G}$ is an Ex-model;
b) $\forall y \in V.L(y) = \vee \Rightarrow |E(y)| = 1$;
c) $V = E^*(x)$;
d) $F = \{y \in V \mid L(y) = \vee\}$.

The same holds for minimal counterexamples (replacing Ex by Cx and $\vee$ by $\wedge$).

The characterization provided by Theorem 3 is sufficiently concrete to allow the design of efficient algorithms for generating minimal diagnostics.

4 Diagnostic Generation Algorithms

We give in this section algorithms for efficiently computing minimal examples and counterexamples for a given variable of an EBG G by exploring the Kripke structure $\mathbf{G}$ induced by G. These algorithms exploit the information in $[\![\text{Ex}]\!]_{\mathbf{G}}$ and $[\![\text{Cx}]\!]_{\mathbf{G}}$ and therefore they must rely upon a resolution algorithm that first computes the semantics of Ex (or Cx) on $\mathbf{G}$. We start by giving a global resolution algorithm and then we present our diagnostic generation algorithms.

4.1 Global Resolution Revisited

The global resolution algorithm SOLVE that we consider here (see Figure 4) is a slightly extended version of the global graph-based algorithm given in [1]. The pre- and post-conditions and the invariants of the while-loop are enclosed in rectangular boxes on Figure 4. The SOLVE procedure takes as input a Kripke structure $\mathbf{G} = (V, E, L)$ induced by an EBG G and computes two informations for the vertices $x \in V$: a natural value $c(x)$ such that $c(x) = 0$ iff $x \in [\![\text{Ex}]\!]_{\mathbf{G}}$; and (only for $\vee$-vertices $x \in [\![\text{Ex}]\!]_{\mathbf{G}}$) a successor $s(x) \in E(x)$ such that there is no path from $s(x)$ to x passing only through vertices in $[\![\text{Ex}]\!]_{\mathbf{G}}$.

It is a straightforward exercise to check the validity of the $\mathbf{I_1}$ and $\mathbf{I_2}$ invariants ($\Phi_{\mathbf{G}}^{\text{Ex}}$ is the functional associated to Ex), which ensure that after termination of SOLVE the vertices in $[\![\text{Ex}]\!]_{\mathbf{G}}$ will have $c(x) = 0$. Here we expressed $\mathbf{I_1}$ and $\mathbf{I_2}$ in terms of Ex (we could have done this equivalently in terms of Cx). In the light of Theorem 1, we see that SOLVE is in fact a model-checking algorithm for Ex. This holds also for other global BES resolution algorithms [3,9,28,30].

Invariant $\mathbf{I_3}$ ensures that after termination of SOLVE, all the $\vee$-vertices $x \in [\![\text{Ex}]\!]_{\mathbf{G}}$ will have a successor $s(x) \in [\![\text{Ex}]\!]_{\mathbf{G}}$ such that the satisfaction of Ex by $s(x)$ does not depend upon x. As we will see in the next section, the computation of s is necessary to obtain an efficient algorithm for generating minimal examples.

Figure 5 shows the result of executing SOLVE on the EBG previously considered on Figure 3. Vertices x for which $c(x) = 0$ are black and the others are white. Edges $(x, s(x))$ are drawn as thick arrows.

$\boxed{G = (V, E, L)}$

procedure SOLVE (V, E, L) **is**
  forall $x \in V$ **do**
    $c(x) :=$ **if** $L(x) = \wedge$ **then** $|E(x)|$ **else** 1 **endif**
  end;
  $A := \{x \in V \mid c(x) = 0\}$;
  while $A \neq \emptyset$ **do** $\boxed{I_1 \wedge I_2 \wedge I_3}$
    let $y \in A$;
    $A := A \setminus \{y\}$;
    forall $z \in E^{-1}(y)$ **do**
      if $c(z) > 0$ **then**
        $c(z) := c(z) - 1$;
        if $c(z) = 0$ **then**
          $A := A \cup \{z\}$;
          if $L(z) = \vee$ **then**
            $s(z) := y$
          endif
        endif
      endif
    end
  end
end

$\{x \in V \mid c(x) = 0\} = [\![\text{Ex}]\!]_G \wedge$
$\{(x, y) \in E \mid x, y \in [\![\text{Ex}]\!]_G \wedge (L(x) = \vee \Rightarrow y = s(x))\}$ is acyclic

$I_1 : \Phi_G^{\text{Ex}}(\{x \in V \mid c(x) = 0\} \setminus A) = \{x \in V \mid c(x) = 0\}$
$I_2 : \{x \in V \mid c(x) = 0\} \subseteq \mu\Phi_G^{\text{Ex}} = [\![\text{Ex}]\!]_G$
$I_3 : \{(x, y) \in E \mid c(x) = c(y) = 0 \wedge (L(x) = \vee \Rightarrow y = s(x))\}$ is acyclic

Fig. 4. Extended global resolution algorithm

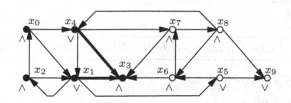

Fig. 5. Computation of c and s by SOLVE

One can easily adapt other global BES resolution algorithms like those in [3,9,28,30] in order to perform the computation of s. Moreover, we claim that local algorithms like those in [1,29,19] can be adapted as well, since they function by exploring forwards the boolean graph and by propagating backwards the vertices found to be true (which is done in a way similar to the SOLVE algorithm above). In fact, it can be shown that these local algorithms actually compute solution-closed subgraphs containing the boolean variable of interest.

4.2 Generation of Minimal Examples

The algorithm ExSEARCH that we propose for computing minimal examples (see Figure 6) takes as input a Kripke structure $\mathbf{G} = (V, E, L)$ induced by an EBG G, a vertex $x \in [\![\mathrm{Ex}]\!]_{\mathbf{G}}$, and for every $\vee$-vertex $y \in [\![\mathrm{Ex}]\!]_{\mathbf{G}}$ a successor $s(y)$ as computed by the SOLVE algorithm given in Section 4.1.

$\mathbf{G} = (V, E, L) \wedge x \in [\![\mathrm{Ex}]\!]_{\mathbf{G}} \wedge$
$R = \{(y, z) \in E \mid y, z \in [\![\mathrm{Ex}]\!]_{\mathbf{G}} \wedge (L(y) = \vee \Rightarrow z = s(y))\}$ is acyclic

procedure ExSEARCH $(x, (V, E, L), s)$ **is**
   $V_0 := \{x\}$; $E_0 := \emptyset$; $A := \{x\}$;
   while $A \neq \emptyset$ **do** $\boxed{\mathbf{J_1 \wedge J_2 \wedge J_3}}$
     let $y \in A$;
     $A := A \setminus \{y\}$;
     if $L(y) = \vee$ **then**
       $E_0 := E_0 \cup \{(y, s(y))\}$;
       if $s(y) \notin V_0$ **then**
         $V_0 := V_0 \cup \{s(y)\}$; $A := A \cup \{s(y)\}$
       endif
     else
       forall $z \in E(y)$ **do**
         $E_0 := E_0 \cup \{(y, z)\}$;
         if $z \notin V_0$ **then**
           $V_0 := V_0 \cup \{z\}$; $A := A \cup \{z\}$
         endif
       end
     endif
   end
end

$G_0 = (V_0, E_0, L|_{V_0}, \{y \in V_0 \mid L(y) = \vee\})$ is a minimal example for x

$\mathbf{J_1} : \exists k \geq 0.(V_0 \subseteq \bigcup_{i=0}^{k} \Phi^{\mathrm{Ex}\ i}_{(V_0, E_0, L|_{V_0})}(A))$
$\mathbf{J_2} : E_0 = R|_{V_0}$
$\mathbf{J_3} : V_0 = E_0^*(x)$

Fig. 6. Minimal example generation algorithm

ExSEARCH iteratively accumulates in V_0 all the vertices in $[\![Ex]\!]_G$ that are reachable from x by traversing only edges $(y, s(y))$ if $L(y) = \vee$ and edges $(y, z) \in E$ if $L(y) = \wedge$. All traversed edges are accumulated in E_0.

Invariant $\mathbf{J_1}$ (ensured by the properties of s) implies that after termination of ExSEARCH, $\mathbf{G_0} = (V_0, E_0, L|_{V_0})$ is an Ex-model. Indeed, at the end of the while-loop $A = \emptyset$ and thus $V_0 \subseteq \bigcup_{i \geq 0} \Phi_{\mathbf{G_0}}^{Ex}{}^i(\emptyset) = \mu\Phi_{\mathbf{G_0}}^{Ex} = [\![Ex]\!]_{\mathbf{G_0}} \subseteq V_0$. Invariant $\mathbf{J_2}$ implies that all $\vee$-vertices $y \in V_0$ have only one successor (namely $s(y)$), and invariant $\mathbf{J_3}$ implies that all vertices in V_0 are reachable from x via E_0. $\mathbf{G_0}$ being an Ex-model, Theorem 2 ensures that $\mathbf{G_0}$ is solution-closed, i.e., it is an example for x. Moreover, $\mathbf{G_0}$ meets the conditions of Theorem 3 and thus it is minimal.

Figure 7 shows a minimal example $\mathbf{G_0}$ computed by ExSEARCH for the variable x_0 in the EBG considered earlier on Figure 5. The edges in E_0 are drawn as thick arrows and the vertices on the frontier of $\mathbf{G_0}$ are surrounded by dashed circles. The $\vee$-vertices x_1 and x_4 have in E_0 a unique successor $s(x_1) = s(x_4) = x_3$ that was previously computed by SOLVE.

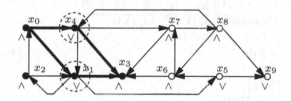

Fig. 7. A minimal example for x_0 computed by ExSEARCH

Note that the use of the information in s is crucial for ensuring the correctness of ExSEARCH: if we chose for x_1 the successor x_2 instead of x_3, the algorithm would compute the subgraph $\mathbf{G_0}$ outlined on Figure 8, which is *not* an example for x_0 because $x_0 \not\models_{\mathbf{G_0}} Cx$. A correct version of ExSEARCH that does not use s would require a backtracking graph search algorithm in order to determine the "good" successor for each $\vee$-vertex of the example. It is not obvious how to obtain a linear-time algorithm for computing minimal examples in this way.

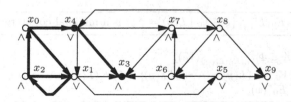

Fig. 8. An erroneous example for x_0 computed in absence of s

EXSEARCH has a complexity $O(|V_0| + |E_0|)$, since all vertices (edges) in the constructed example G_0 are visited (traversed) only once. Since this is the lowest possible complexity for an algorithm that must entirely explore G_0, it appears that (modulo the linear-time precomputation of s) EXSEARCH is an optimal algorithm for finding minimal examples. In practice, EXSEARCH runs very quickly when computing examples whose sizes are significantly smaller than $[\![\mathrm{Ex}]\!]_{\mathbf{G}}$ (this happens for CTL formulas like $\mathsf{E}\,[\mathsf{T}\,\mathsf{U}\,\varphi]$).

4.3   Generation of Minimal Counterexamples

The algorithm CXSEARCH that we propose for computing minimal counterexamples (see Figure 9) takes as input a Kripke structure $\mathbf{G} = (V, E, L)$ induced by an EBG G, a vertex $x \in [\![\mathrm{Cx}]\!]_{\mathbf{G}}$, and for every vertex $y \in V$ a counter $c(y)$ as computed by the SOLVE algorithm given in Section 4.1.

$\mathbf{G} = (V, E, L) \wedge x \in [\![\mathrm{Cx}]\!]_{\mathbf{G}} = \{y \in V \mid c(y) > 0\}$

procedure CXSEARCH $(x, (V, E, L), c)$ **is**
   $V_0 := \{x\};\ E_0 := \emptyset;\ A := \{x\};$
   while $A \neq \emptyset$ **do** $\boxed{\mathbf{K_1} \wedge \mathbf{K_2} \wedge \mathbf{K_3}}$
     let $y \in A$;
     $A := A \setminus \{y\}$;
     if $L(y) = \wedge$ **then**
       let $z \in E(y)$ such that $c(z) > 0$;
       $E_0 := E_0 \cup \{(y, z)\}$;
       if $z \notin V_0$ **then**
         $V_0 := V_0 \cup \{z\};\ A := A \cup \{z\}$
       endif
     else
       forall $z \in E(y)$ **do**
       $E_0 := E_0 \cup \{(y, z)\}$;
       if $z \notin V_0$ **then**
         $V_0 := V_0 \cup \{z\};\ A := A \cup \{z\}$
       endif
       end
     endif
   end
end

$G_0 = (V_0, E_0, L|_{V_0}, \{y \in V_0 \mid L(y) = \wedge\})$ is a minimal counterexample for x

$\mathbf{K_1} : V_0 \setminus A \subseteq \Phi^{\mathrm{Cx}}_{(V_0, E_0, L|_{V_0})}(V_0)$
$\mathbf{K_2} : \forall y \in V_0 \setminus A.(L(y) = \wedge \Rightarrow |E_0(y)| = 1) \wedge (L(y) = \vee \Rightarrow |E_0(y)| = |E(y)|)$
$\mathbf{K_3} : V_0 = E_0^*(x)$

Fig. 9. Minimal counterexample generation algorithm

CxSearch iteratively accumulates in V_0 all the vertices in $[\![Cx]\!]_G$ that are reachable from x by traversing either a single edge $(y, z) \in E$ if $L(y) = \wedge$, or all edges $(y, z) \in E$ if $L(y) = \vee$. All traversed edges are accumulated in E_0.

Invariant $\mathbf{K_1}$ ($\varPhi_G^{Cx}$ is the functional associated to Cx) ensures that after termination of CxSearch, $\mathbf{G_0} = (V_0, E_0, L|_{V_0})$ is a Cx-model. Indeed, at the end of the while-loop $A = \emptyset$ and thus $V_0 \subseteq \varPhi_{G_0}^{Cx}(V_0)$. By Tarski's theorem [27], this implies $V_0 \subseteq \nu\varPhi_{G_0}^{Cx} = [\![Cx]\!]_{G_0} \subseteq V_0$. Invariant $\mathbf{K_2}$ implies that after the while-loop $\wedge$-vertices of V_0 have only one successor in V_0 and $\vee$-vertices have all their successors in V_0. Invariant $\mathbf{K_3}$ implies that all vertices in V_0 are reachable from x via E_0. Since $\mathbf{G_0}$ is a Cx-model, Theorem 2 ensures that G_0 is solution-closed, i.e., it is a counterexample for x. Moreover, G_0 meets the conditions of Theorem 3 and thus it is minimal.

Figure 10 shows a minimal counterexample G_0 computed by CxSearch for the variable x_5 in the EBG considered earlier on Figure 5.

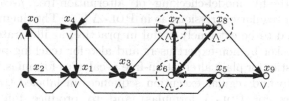

Fig. 10. A minimal counterexample for x_5 computed by CxSearch

CxSearch has a complexity $O(|V_0| + |E_0|)$, since all vertices (edges) in the constructed counterexample G_0 are visited (traversed) only once. Since this is the lowest possible complexity for an algorithm that must entirely explore G_0, CxSearch appears to be an optimal algorithm for finding minimal counterexamples. In practice, CxSearch runs very quickly when computing counterexamples whose sizes are significantly smaller than $[\![Cx]\!]_G$ (this happens for CTL formulas like $A[T \cup \varphi]$).

5   Conclusion and Future Work

By representing a boolean equation system M as an extended boolean graph G, we characterized the solution of M by means of two particular alternation-free μ-calculus formulas Ex and Cx interpreted on the Kripke structure $\mathbf{G}$ induced by G. This allowed to identify full diagnostics (examples and counterexamples) explaining the truth value of a boolean variable x of M as being particular subgraphs of G containing x. Moreover, minimal examples and counterexamples (w.r.t. a subgraph relation that we defined) are obtained as particular models of Ex and Cx, respectively.

The temporal logic-based formalization that we proposed provides a uniform framework for analyzing graph-based BES resolution algorithms such as those in [3,9,28,1,19]. For instance, in Section 4.1 we used our formalization to prove the correctness of a global resolution algorithm from [1], which can be seen in fact as an algorithm for checking the EX formula on a boolean graph.

We presented two linear-time algorithms EXSEARCH and CXSEARCH that compute minimal examples and counterexamples for a given variable of a BES. We also indicated how these algorithms can be used to extend existing (global or local) BES resolution algorithms with diagnostic generation facilities.

These two algorithms have been included in the model-checker EVALUATOR version 3.0 that we developed as part of the CADP (CÆSAR/ALDÉBARAN) protocol engineering toolset [11] using the generic OPEN/CÆSAR environment for on-the-fly verification [14]. EVALUATOR 3.0 performs on-the-fly model-checking of alternation-free μ-calculus formulas extended with regular expressions as in PDL-Δ [26]. The diagnostic generation facilities proved to be extremely useful in practice, as illustrated by the use of the model-checker by non-expert users and also for teaching purposes. Besides giving diagnostics for plain alternation-free μ-calculus formulas, EVALUATOR 3.0 can be used to find regular execution sequences in labeled transition systems (as diagnostics for PDL-Δ formulas) and to produce full diagnostics for CTL [5] and ACTL [22] formulas (by encoding the operators of these logics as macro-definitions in the input language of the tool).

The EXSEARCH and CXSEARCH algorithms compute diagnostics that are minimal w.r.t. the EBG subgraph relation that we proposed. The diagnostics obtained contain no redundant information, since every $\vee$-vertex in a minimal example and every $\wedge$-vertex in a minimal counterexample has only one successor. This is reasonably good in practice, as confirmed by the experiments performed using EVALUATOR 3.0. However, there are other additional criteria that may be considered for further reducing the diagnostic size (e.g., minimizing the number of vertices, number of edges, depth, diameter, etc.). Some of these optimizations can be done efficiently in particular cases, e.g., generating minimal length transition sequences as diagnostics for PDL-Δ diamond modalities or CTL formulas $E[T \cup \varphi]$ (which both translate into BESs containing only $\vee$ operators in the non-trivial right-hand sides). An interesting issue would be to investigate the general extension of EXSEARCH and CXSEARCH with such optimization features.

We also plan to apply our diagnostic generation techniques in the context of bisimulation checking [9,2] and of test generation [12]. Another potentially fruitful direction of research is to extend our formalization to BESs of higher alternation depth [29,2,20,18]. The characterizations of the solution and diagnostics for these BESs would certainly require formulas of the full modal μ-calculus.

Acknowledgements

We are grateful to the anonymous referees for their valuable comments and suggestions. We also thank Mihaela Sighireanu for largely contributing to the design and implementation of the EVALUATOR version 3.0 model-checker.

References

1. H. R. Andersen. Model Checking and Boolean Graphs. *TCS*, 126(1):3–30, 1994. 251, 254, 257, 259, 263
2. H. R. Andersen and B. Vergauwen. Efficient Checking of Behavioural Relations and Modal Assertions using Fixed-Point Inversion. In P. Wolper, editor, *Proceedings of CAV'95 (Liege, Belgium)*, vol. 939 of LNCS, pp. 142–154. Springer Verlag, July 1995. 251, 263
3. A. Arnold and P. Crubillé. A Linear Algorithm to Solve Fixed-point Equations on Transition Systems. *Information Processing Letters*, 29:57–66, 1988. 251, 257, 259, 263
4. M. Bozga, J-C. Fernandez, A. Kerbrat, and L. Mounier. Protocol Verification with the ALDEBARAN toolset. *Springer International Journal on Software Tools for Technology Transfer (STTT)*, 1(1-2):166–183, 1997. 252
5. E. M. Clarke, E. A. Emerson, and A. P. Sistla. Automatic Verification of Finite-State Concurrent Systems using Temporal Logic Specifications. *ACM Transactions on Programming Languages and Systems*, 8(2):244–263, April 1986. 251, 252, 263
6. E. M. Clarke, O. Grumberg, K. L. McMillan, and X. Zhao. Efficient Generation of Counterexamples and Witnesses in Symbolic Model Checking. In *Proceedings of DAC'95 (San Francisco, CA, USA)*, pp. 427–432. ACM, June 1995. 252
7 E. M. Clarke, O. Grumberg, and D. Long. Verification Tools for Finite-State Concurrent Systems. In J. W. de Bakker, W-P. de Roever, and G. Rozenberg, editors, *Proceedings of the REX School/Symposium (Noordwijkerhout, The Netherlands)*, vol. 803 of LNCS, pp. 124–175. Springer Verlag, June 1993. 252
8. R. Cleaveland. On Automatically Explaining Bisimulation Inequivalence. In E. M. Clarke and R. P. Kurshan, editors, *Proceedings of CAV'90 (New Brunswick, NJ, USA)*, vol. 531 of LNCS, pp. 364–372. Springer Verlag, June 1990. 252
9. R. Cleaveland and B. Steffen. A Linear-Time Model-Checking Algorithm for the Alternation-Free Modal Mu-Calculus. In K. G. Larsen and A. Skou, editors, *Proceedings of CAV'91 (Aalborg, Denmark)*, vol. 575 of LNCS, pp. 48–58. Springer Verlag, July 1991. 251, 252, 254, 257, 259, 263
10. E. A. Emerson and C-L. Lei. Efficient Model Checking in Fragments of the Propositional Mu-Calculus. In *Proceedings of the 1st LICS*, pp. 267–278, 1986. 253
11. J-C. Fernandez, H. Garavel, A. Kerbrat, R. Mateescu, L. Mounier, and M .Sighireanu. CADP (CÆSAR/ALDEBARAN Development Package): A Protocol Validation and Verification Toolbox. In R. Alur and T. A. Henzinger, editors, *Proceedings of CAV'96 (New Brunswick, NJ, USA)*, vol. 1102 of LNCS, pp. 437–440. Springer Verlag, August 1996. 263
12. J-C. Fernandez, C. Jard, T. Jéron, L. Nedelka, and C. Viho. Using On-the-Fly Verification Techniques for the Generation of Test Suites. In R. Alur and T. A. Henzinger, editors, *Proceedings of CAV'96 (New Brunswick, NJ, USA)*, vol. 1102 of LNCS, pp. 348–359. Springer Verlag, August 1996. 263

13. J-C. Fernandez and L. Mounier. "On the Fly" Verification of Behavioural Equivalences and Preorders. In K. G. Larsen and A. Skou, editors, *Proceedings of CAV'91 (Aalborg, Denmark)*, vol. 575 of LNCS. Springer Verlag, July 1991. 252

14. H. Garavel. OPEN/CÆSAR: An Open Software Architecture for Verification, Simulation, and Testing. In B. Steffen, editor, *Proceedings of TACAS'98 (Lisbon, Portugal)*, vol. 1384 of LNCS, pp. 68–84. Springer Verlag, March 1998. 263

15. H. Korver. Computing Distinguishing Formulas for Branching Bisimulation. In K. G. Larsen and A. Skou, editors, *Proceedings of CAV'91 (Aalborg, Denmark)*, vol. 575 of LNCS, pp. 13–23. Springer Verlag, July 1991. 252

16. D. Kozen. Results on the Propositional μ-calculus. *TCS*, 27:333–354, 1983. 252

17. K. G. Larsen. Efficient Local Correctness Checking. In G. v. Bochmann and D. K. Probst, editors, *Proceedings of CAV'92 (Montréal, Canada)*, vol. 663 of LNCS, pp. 30–43. Springer Verlag, June-July 1992. 251

18. X. Liu, C. R. Ramakrishnan, and S. A. Smolka. Fully Local and Efficient Evaluation of Alternating Fixed Points. In B. Steffen, editor, *Proceedings of TACAS'98 (Lisbon, Portugal)*, vol. 1384 of LNCS. Springer Verlag, March 1998. 251, 263

19. X. Liu and S. A. Smolka. Simple Linear-Time Algorithms for Minimal Fixed Points. In K. G. Larsen, S. Skyum, and G. Winskel, editors, *Proceedings of ICALP'98 (Aalborg, Denmark)*, vol. 1443 of LNCS. Springer Verlag, July 1998. 251, 259, 263

20. A. Mader. *Verification of Modal Properties Using Boolean Equation Systems*. VERSAL 8, Bertz Verlag, Berlin, 1997. 251, 254, 263

21. K. L. McMillan. *Symbolic Model Checking*. Kluwer Academic Publishers, 1993. 252

22. R. De Nicola and F. W. Vaandrager. *Action versus State based Logics for Transition Systems*. In *Proceedings Ecole de Printemps on Semantics of Concurrency*, vol. 469 of LNCS, pp. 407–419. Springer Verlag, 1990. 263

23. A. Rasse. Error Diagnosis in Finite Communicating Systems. In K. G. Larsen and A. Skou, editors, *Proceedings of CAV'91 (Aalborg, Denmark)*, vol. 575 of LNCS, pp. 114–124. Springer Verlag, July 1991. 252

24. P. Stevens and C. Stirling. Practical Model-Checking using Games. In B. Steffen, editor, *Proceedings of TACAS'98 (Lisbon, Portugal)*, vol. 1384 of LNCS, pp. 85–101. Springer Verlag, March 1998. 252

25. C. Stirling. Bisimulation, model checking and other games. In Notes for Mathfit instructional meeting on games and computation, Edinburgh, June 1997. 252

26. R. Streett. Propositional Dynamic Logic of Looping and Converse. *Information and Control*, (54):121–141, 1982. 263

27. A. Tarski. A Lattice-Theoretical Fixpoint Theorem and its Applications. *Pacific Journal of Mathematics*, (5):285–309, 1955. 262

28. B. Vergauwen and J. Lewi. A Linear Algorithm for Solving Fixed-point Equations on Transition Systems. In *Proceedings of CAAP'92 (Rennes, France)*, vol. 581 of LNCS, pp. 322–341. Springer Verlag, February 1992. 251, 257, 259, 263

29. B. Vergauwen and J. Lewi. Efficient Local Correctness Checking for Single and Alternating Boolean Equation Systems. In S. Abiteboul and E. Shamir, editors, *Proceedings of ICALP'94 (Vienna)*, vol. 820 of LNCS, pp. 304–315. Springer Verlag, July 1994. 251, 259, 263

30. B. Vergauwen, J. Wauman, and J. Lewi. Efficient FixPoint Computation. In *Proceedings of SAS'94 (Namur, Belgium)*, vol. 864 of LNCS, pp. 314–328. Springer Verlag, September 1994. 251, 257, 259

Compositional State Space Generation with Partial Order Reductions for Asynchronous Communicating Systems

Jean-Pierre Krimm and Laurent Mounier

VERIMAG – Joint Laboratory of CNRS, UJF and INPG
Centre Equation, 2, avenue de Vignate F-38610 Gières
{Jean-Pierre.Krimm,Laurent.Mounier}@imag.fr

Abstract. Compositional generation is an incremental technique for generating a reduced labelled transition system representing the behaviour of a set of communicating processes. In particular, since intermediate reductions can be performed after each generation step, the size of the LTS can be kept small and state-explosion can be avoided in many cases. This paper deals with compositional generation in presence of asynchronous communications via shared buffers. More precisely, we show how partial-order reduction techniques can be used in this context to define equivalence relations: that preserve useful properties, are congruence w.r.t asynchronous composition, and rely on a (syntactic) notion of preorder on execution sequences characterizing their "executability" in any buffer environment. Two such equivalences are proposed, together with dedicated asynchronous composition operators able to directly produce reduced LTS.

1 Introduction

This work takes place in the context of *formal verification* of distributed programs, those purpose is to evaluate a set of expected requirements on a formal program description. To automate this activity, one of the promising technique is the well-known *model-checking* approach, which consists of performing the verification on an explicit model of the system behaviour (e.g., a labelled transition system, or LTS). However, the main drawback of model-checking is the model explosion occurring when dealing with complex systems. This still limits its large scale utilisation in the industry.

Several interesting solutions have already been investigated to overcome this problem, for instance by avoiding an explicit storage of the whole model ("on-the-fly" techniques), or by processing it using efficient representations ("symbolic" techniques), or by generating a model simpler than the initial one ("abstraction" techniques). A particular instance of this latter solution consists of performing the verification not on the LTS S obtained from the original program description, but rather on its S/R quotient where R is an equivalence relation preserving the properties under verification. The main difficulty is then to get this quotient without generating first the initial LTS.

S. Graf and M. Schwartzbach (Eds.): TACAS/ETAPS 2000, LNCS 1785, pp. 266–282, 2000.

When the program under consideration is described by a *composition expression* between communicating LTS, and provided that R is a congruence with respect to the operators of this expression, the quotient S/R can easily be generated with a so-called *compositional approach*: it consists of (repeatedly) generating the LTS S' associated with a given sub-expression, and replacing this sub-expression in the initial one by the quotient S'/R. This approach has been widely studied [GS90,CK93,Val96,KM97], and has already been applied in some succesfull case studies. However, most of this works was done in the context of *synchronous* communicating systems (described for instance using process algebras like LOTOS [ISO87] or CSP [Hoa85]).

In this paper we propose a way to efficiently extend this compositional generation strategy to *asynchronous* systems communicating by message exchange through shared buffers. In fact, this communication scheme is very suitable for describing distributed systems or communication protocols, and it is the underlying model of popular specification formalisms such as the international standard SDL [IT92], or the PROMELA language [Hol91].

One of the main difficulties encountered during a compositional generation is to correctly handle the effect of the environment (i.e., the rest of the system) in order to restrict the generation of a given subset of components (otherwise the model obtained for this subset may be larger than the one corresponding to the whole system). This problem was addressed in [GS90,CK93,KM97] by expressing the constraints provided from the environment in terms of *process interfaces*, allowing to "cut off" some parts of a component behaviour. Unfortunately, this solution is not applicable in case of asynchronous communications, since the effects of the external buffers cannot precisely be statically approximated. Thus, many useless interleavings are computed when generating a subsystem independently of its buffer environment.

To avoid these interleavings, the solution we propose relies on the (well-known) *partial order* approach which consists of identifying *independent* execution sequences that can be safely sequentialized (instead of being fully interleaved). Such techniques have already been rather intensively been studied, and their efficiency has been established in practice, in particular for asynchronous communicating systems [Val90,GW91,Pel96,KLM+98]. However, to our knowledge, their application in this framework is original by its combination of two aspects:

— First, partial order reductions are usually performed on the whole system, considering the explicit behaviour of each of its components. *A contrario*, the approach we describe here can be applied on a partial sub-system, and it allows generation of a reduced LTS (with less interleavings) that can be re-used during further compositions.

— Second, the reductions we consider are not only based on a symmetrical *independence* relation of actions (leading to an equivalence relation between independent execution sequences), but also on an asymmetrical notion of *precedence* relation of actions, leading to a preorder between execution sequences. According to this preorder, smallest sequences are always "*more executable*" than larger ones in any buffer environment.

This notion of non commutative independence relation between actions was first introduced by [Lip75] to study the correctness of concurrents processes synchronized by means of semaphores. It was also used in [AJKP98] within a symbolic verification framework.

The paper is organized as follows:

First, we give in section 2 the program syntax we consider (a set of asynchronous communicating processes), and we briefly explain how the LTS denoting a program semantics can be compositionally generated in this framework. Then, we introduce in section 3 a (syntactic) notion of preorder between execution sequences, and we show how it characterizes the executability of an execution sequence in any buffer environment. Using this preorder, we consider in section 4 a first equivalence relation $\approx_\delta$, deadlock preserving, and which is a congruence w.r.t asynchronous composition. We then propose a new asynchronous composition operator, allowing to directly compute a reduced LTS w.r.t $\approx_\delta$ and thus avoiding many useless interleavings. Finally, in section 5 we extend these results to a stronger equivalence relation $\approx_o$, able to preserve the language w.r.t a set of observable actions.

2   Asynchronous Communicating Systems

In this section we give the abstract syntax and semantics used to represent asynchronous communicating systems by means of a parallel composition of labelled transition systems. Then we indicate how the global state space of such systems can be obtained in a compositional way.

2.1   Program Syntax and Semantics

A Labelled Transition System (LTS, for short) is a tuple $S = (Q, A, T, q_0)$ where Q is a finite set of (reachable) states, A a finite set of actions (or labels), $T \subseteq Q \times A \times Q$ a transition relation, and $q_0 \in Q$ the initial state of S. As usual, we shall note $p \xrightarrow{a}_T q$ instead of $(p, a, q) \in T$.

Let $\mathcal{M}$ be a set of *message* names, and Buf a set of *unbounded buffers* over $\mathcal{M}$. A buffer $B \in Buf$ is an abstract type with the following signature, and those concrete implementation depends on the exact nature of the buffer (e.g., bags, stacks, fifo queues, ...):

- $\perp$ is an empty buffer;
- **first**: $\mathcal{M} \times B \to$ **bool**.
  first(m, B) is true iff message m can be consumed in buffer B.
- **remove**: $\mathcal{M} \times B \to B$.
  When **first**(m, B) holds **remove**(m, B) returns the new buffer obtained from B by eliminating message m, otherwise B is returned unchanged.
- **append**: $\mathcal{M} \times B \to B$.
  append(m, B) adds the message m to buffer B.

Finally, a *program* is a couple $\mathcal{P} = (\mathcal{S}_n, \mathcal{B}_p)$ where $\mathcal{S}_n = \{S_1, S_2, \ldots S_n\}$ is a finite set of *elementary processes* represented by LTS $S_i = (Q_i, A_i, T_i, q_{0i})$, and $\mathcal{B}_p = \{B_1, B_2, \ldots B_p\}$ is a finite set of buffers over $\mathcal{M}$. Moreover, for each S_j in $\mathcal{S}_n$, action sets $A_j \subseteq \mathcal{A} = \mathcal{A}^+ \cup \mathcal{A}^- \cup \{\tau\}$ where:

$$\mathcal{A}^+ = \{+(i, m) \mid i \in [1, p] \wedge m \in \mathcal{M}\} \quad ; \quad \mathcal{A}^- = \{-(i, m) \mid i \in [1, p] \wedge m \in \mathcal{M}\}$$

Informally, for an LTS S_j, action $+a = +(i, m)$ denotes the output of message m to the buffer B_i, action $-a = -(i, m)$ denotes the input of message m from buffer B_i and τ denotes any internal (non communication) action.

Definition 1 (Program semantics). *The semantics of a program $\mathcal{P} = (\mathcal{S}_n, \mathcal{B}_p)$ is defined as the LTS $\mathbf{sem}(\mathcal{P}) = (Q, \mathcal{A}, T, q_0)$ where:*

$-\ Q \subseteq Q_1 \times Q_2 \times \cdots \times Q_n \times B_1 \times B_2 \times \cdots \times B_p$
$-\ q_0 = (q_{0_1}, q_{0_2}, \ldots, q_{0_n}, \bot, \ldots \bot)$
$-\ Q$ *and* T *are the smallest sets obtained when applying the following rules:*

$$q_0 \in Q \qquad \qquad [R0]$$

$$\frac{p = (p_1, \ldots, p_j, \ldots p_n, B_1, \ldots, B_i, \ldots B_p) \in Q, \ p_j \xrightarrow{-(i,m)}_{T_j} q_j, \ \mathbf{first}(m, B_i)}{q = (p_1, \ldots, q_j, \ldots p_n, B_1, \ldots, \mathbf{remove}(m, B_i), \ldots B_p) \in Q, \ p \xrightarrow{-(i,m)}_T q} \quad [R1]$$

$$\frac{p = (p_1, \ldots, p_j, \ldots p_n, B_1, \ldots, B_i, \ldots B_p) \in Q, \ p_j \xrightarrow{+(i,m)}_{T_j} q_j}{q = (p_1, \ldots, q_j, \ldots p_n, B_1, \ldots, \mathbf{append}(m, B_i), \ldots B_p) \in Q, \ p \xrightarrow{+(i,m)}_T q} \quad [R2]$$

$$\frac{p = (p_1, \ldots, p_j, \ldots p_n, B_1, \ldots, B_i, \ldots B_p) \in Q, \ p_j \xrightarrow{\tau}_{T_j} q_j}{q = (p_1, \ldots, q_j, \ldots p_n, B_1, \ldots, B_i, \ldots B_p) \in Q, \ p \xrightarrow{\tau}_T q} \quad [R3]$$

2.2   Compositional State Space Generation

The generation of $\mathbf{sem}(\mathcal{P})$ using definition 1, needs to consider *simultaneously* the whole sets of buffers and elementary processes. However, this resulting LTS can also be built in a more compositional way by taking into account each program component (i.e., buffer or elementary process) incrementally. To this purpose we first introduce two auxiliary operators, the *asynchronous product* between LTS and the execution of an LTS within a given *buffer environment*.

The asynchronous product ($\|$) between two LTS $S_i = (Q_i, A_i, T_i, q_{0i})$ is defined in the usual manner: $S_1 \| S_2$ is the LTS $S = (Q, A, T, q_0)$ where $Q = Q_1 \times Q_2$, $T = \{((p_1, p_2), a, (q_1, q_2)) \mid (p_1 \xrightarrow{a}_{T_1} q_1 \wedge p_2 = q_2) \vee (p_2 \xrightarrow{a}_{T_2} q_2 \wedge p_1 = q_1)\}$, $A = A_1 \cup A_2$, $q_0 = (q_{01}, q_{02})$.

Definition 2 (Execution of an LTS within a buffer environment). *For an LTS $S = (Q, A, T, q_0)$ and a buffer environment $\mathcal{B}_p$, we note $S[\mathcal{B}_p]$ the LTS (Q_s, A, T_s, q_{s_0}) obtained by executing S within $\mathcal{B}_p$, and defined as follows:*

- $Q_s \subseteq Q \times B_1 \times B_2 \times \cdots \times B_p$
- $q_{s_0} = (q_0, \perp, \ldots, \perp)$
- Q_s and T_s are the smallest sets obtained when applying the following rules:

$$q_{s_0} \in Q_s \qquad \qquad [R0]$$

$$\frac{p_s = (p, B_1, \ldots, B_i, \ldots B_p) \in Q_s, \ p \xrightarrow{-(i,m)}_T q, \ \mathbf{first}(m, B_i)}{q_s = (q, B_1, \ldots, \mathbf{remove}(m, B_i), \ldots B_p) \in Q_s, \ p_s \xrightarrow{-(i,m)}_{T_s} q_s} \qquad [R1]$$

$$\frac{p_s = (p, B_1, \ldots, B_i, \ldots B_p) \in Q_s, \ p \xrightarrow{+(i,m)}_T q}{q_s = (q, B_1, \ldots, \mathbf{append}(m, B_i), \ldots B_p) \in Q_s, \ p_s \xrightarrow{+(i,m)}_{T_s} q_s} \qquad [R2]$$

$$\frac{p_s = (p, B_1, \ldots, B_i, \ldots B_p) \in Q_s, \ p \xrightarrow{\tau}_T q}{q_s = (q, B_1, \ldots, B_i, \ldots B_p) \in Q_s, \ p_s \xrightarrow{\tau}_{T_s} q_s} \qquad [R3]$$

It is easy to show that the global LTS $\mathbf{sem}(\mathcal{P})$ can be obtained by considering first the asynchronous product of its elementary processes, then executing it w.r.t its buffer environment:

Proposition 1. *For a program* $\mathcal{P} = (\mathcal{S}_n, \mathcal{B}_p)$, $\mathbf{sem}(\mathcal{P}) = (S_1 \| S_2 \| \ldots \| S_n)[\mathcal{B}_p]$.

Furthermore, this approach can be made even more flexible by partially distributing buffers $\mathcal{B}_p$ w.r.t a subset of elementary processes. More formally:

Proposition 2. *Let* S_1 *and* S_2 *be two* LTS *and* $\mathcal{B}_p$ *a buffer environment.*

Consider a split of $\mathcal{B}_p$ *into three sets* $\mathcal{B}_{p1}$, $\mathcal{B}_{p2}$ *and* $\mathcal{B}_{p3}$ *such that: buffers of* $\mathcal{B}_{p1}$ *are not accessed by* S_2, *buffers of* $\mathcal{B}_{p2}$ *are not accessed by* S_1, *and buffers of* $\mathcal{B}_{p3}$ *are accessed by both* S_1 *and* S_2. *(such a split always exists since* $\mathcal{B}_{p1}$ *and* $\mathcal{B}_{p2}$ *can be empty).*

Then, the following holds: $(S_1 \| S_2)[\mathcal{B}_p] = (S_1[\mathcal{B}_{p1}] \| S_2[\mathcal{B}_{p2}])[\mathcal{B}_{p3}]$

Finally, depending on the program properties under consideration, intermediate LTS reductions can now be introduced between successive generation steps. Furthermore, since internal communications within a sub-system can be abstracted away *before* its composition with the other program components, powerful reduction operations are possible when only the external program behaviour is relevant. In particular most of the usual bisimulation based weak equivalence relations (such as observational equivalence [Mil89], branching bisimulation [vGW89] or safety equivalence [BFG+91]) happen to be congruences w.r.t. operators $\|$ and [...] and can be used in this framework.

However, due to asynchronous nature of communications, this (straightforward) compositional approach may still suffer from state explosion problems. In fact, when generating a subsystem, each **append** or **remove** operations concerning external buffers is considered as fully asynchronous. This leads to many possible interleavings, and, therefore, the size of the resulting intermediate LTS may become very large.

We propose in this paper a solution to decrease the number of these useless interleavings by taking advantage of some (well-known) considerations about the concurrent execution of *independent* actions.

3 Equivalence and Preorder on Execution Sequences

First, we give some notations related to the execution sequences of an LTS. Then we introduce some equivalence and preorder relations between execution sequences.

Definition 3 (Execution sequences of an LTS).
Let $S = (Q, A, T, q_0)$ be an LTS, and p a given set of Q:

- $Act(p)$ is the set of actions the state p can perform, and $Pre(p)$ the set of actions that may reach it:

$$Act(p) = \{a \in \mathcal{A} \mid \exists q . p \xrightarrow{a}_T q\} \quad ; \quad Pre(p) = \{a \in \mathcal{A} \mid \exists q . q \xrightarrow{a}_T p\}$$
$$Act^-(p) = Act(p) \cap \mathcal{A}^- \quad ; \quad Act^+(p) = Act(p) \cap \mathcal{A}^+$$

- An (execution) sequence σ from p is an element $\sigma = a_1.a_2.\cdots a_n$ of A^* such that: $\sigma = p \xrightarrow{a_1}_T p_1 \xrightarrow{a_2}_T \cdots \xrightarrow{a_n}_T p_n$ We shall also use the notation $p \xrightarrow{\sigma}_T p_{n+1}$, or simply $p \xrightarrow{\sigma}_T$.

3.1 Equivalence between Execution Sequences

The equivalence relation between execution sequences we consider is based on an *independency* relation I on actions. Roughly speaking, two actions a_1 and a_2 will be considered as independent $((a_1, a_2) \in I)$ if, whenever they are both enabled in a given state p, their execution order has no influence on the subsequent execution sequences p will be able to perform.

Definition 4 (Independance of actions).
A relation $I \subseteq \mathcal{A} \times \mathcal{A}$ is an independency *relation for an* LTS $S = (Q, A, T, q_0)$ *if, for all $p \in Q$, and for all $(a_1, a_2) \in I$ then:*

$$a_1, a_2 \subseteq Act(p) \Rightarrow \begin{cases} \forall q_1, q_2 \in Q . p \xrightarrow{a_1}_T q_1 \wedge p \xrightarrow{a_2}_T q_2 \\ \qquad\qquad\qquad \Rightarrow (a_2 \in Act(q_1) \wedge a_1 \in Act(q_2)) \\ \wedge \\ \forall q \in Q . p \xrightarrow{a_1.a_2}_T q \Leftrightarrow p \xrightarrow{a_2.a_1}_T q \end{cases}$$

We give below some examples of independency relations defined on communication actions performed by *distinct* processes, depending on the kind of buffers that are considered.

Example 1. When buffers are defined as *bags*, the order of two **append** operations does not matter. Therefore, two **append** (resp. **remove**) operations are always independent each others. Moreover, an **append** and a **remove** operation will be independent if they occur in two different bags. Therefore, I_{bag} is defined as follows: $I_{bag} = \mathcal{A}^+ \times \mathcal{A}^+ \cup \mathcal{A}^- \times \mathcal{A}^- \cup \{(\pm(i_1, m_1), \mp(i_2, m_2)) \mid i_1 \neq i_2\}$ When buffers are defined as fifo queues, the order of two **append** or **remove** operations does not matter only if they occur in different queues. The corresponding independency relation is then:

$$I_{fifo} = \{(\pm(i_1, m_1), \pm(i_2, m_2)) \mid i_1 \neq i_2\} \cup \{(\pm(i_1, m_1), \mp(i_2, m_2)) \mid i_1 \neq i_2\}$$

Note that internal transitions (τ) performed by distinct processes are always independent. $\square$.

Independency relations allow to define equivalence relations on execution sequences: two sequences u and v will be considered as equivalent iff u can be obtained from v by repeatedly permuting two of its *adjacent* independent actions.

Definition 5 (Equivalence between execution sequences).
Let I be an independency relation. For two sequences $u, v \in \mathcal{A}^*$, write $u \sim^1_I v$ if there exist sequences w_1, w_2 and actions a, b such that $(a, b) \in I$, $u = w_1 a b w_2$ and $v = w_1 b a w_2$. Let $\sim_I$ be the reflexive and transitive closure of the relation $\sim^1_I$. We say that u is I-equivalent with v if $u \sim_I v$.

Intuitively, if two equivalent sequences σ_1 and σ_2 are enabled on a state p, then, any buffer environment allowing the execution of σ_1 also allows the execution of σ_2 (and conversely). Furthermore, buffer contents are updated similarly during execution of σ_1 or σ_2. More formally:

Proposition 3. *Let $S = (Q, A, T, q_0)$ be an LTS, I an independence relation, p a state of Q, and σ_1 and σ_2 two execution sequences of S such that $\exists\ q_1, q_2 \in Q$, $p \xrightarrow{\sigma_1}_T q_1$, $p \xrightarrow{\sigma_2}_T q_2$ and $\sigma_1 \sim_I \sigma_2$.*
For a given buffer environment $\mathcal{B}_p$, let $S' = S[\mathcal{B}_p]$ where $S' = (Q', A, T', q_0')$. Then, for any state $(p, b_1, b_2, \ldots, b_p)$ of Q', the following holds:

$$(p, b_1, b_2, \ldots, b_p) \xrightarrow{\sigma_1}_{T'} (q_1, b_1', b_2', \ldots, b_p') \Leftrightarrow (p, b_1, b_2, \ldots, b_p) \xrightarrow{\sigma_2}_{T'} (q_2, b_1', b_2', \ldots, b_p')$$

3.2   Preorder between Execution Sequences

As stated above, the equivalence relation between execution sequences *exactly* preserves the executability within any buffer environment. We introduce here a weaker relation, able to characterize the fact that a given sequence σ_1 is *more executable* than another sequence σ_2 (that is, whenever σ_2 is executable, then σ_1 is). This preorder relation between execution sequence relies itself on a *precedency* relation P between actions:

Definition 6 (Precedence of actions).
A relation $P \subseteq \mathcal{A} \times \mathcal{A}$ is a precedency relation for an LTS $S = (Q, A, T, q_0)$ if, for all $p \in Q$, and for all $(a_1, a_2) \in P$ then:

$$a_1, a_2 \subseteq Act(p) \Rightarrow \begin{cases} \forall q_2 \in Q \,.\, p \xrightarrow{a_2}_T q_2 \Rightarrow a_1 \in Act(q_2) \\ \wedge \\ \forall q \in Q \,.\, p \xrightarrow{a_2.a_1}_T q \Rightarrow p \xrightarrow{a_1.a_2}_T q \end{cases}$$

Example 2. When communications buffers are defined as *unbounded* bags, an **append** action performed by a process cannot prevent any **append** or **remove** action performed by another process. The precedency relation on communication actions between distinct processes is then: $P_{bag} = I_{bag} \cup \mathcal{A}^+ \times \mathcal{A}^-$
□.

This preorder on $\mathcal{A}$ is then extended to $\mathcal{A}^*$: a sequence σ_1 is smaller than a sequence σ_2 iff σ_1 can be obtained from σ_2 by repeatedly permuting any pair of its adjacent action belonging to the precedence relation.

Definition 7 (Preorder between execution sequences).
For two sequences $u, v \in \mathcal{A}^*$, write $u \lesssim_P^1 v$ if there exist sequences w_1, w_2 and actions a, b such that $(a, b) \in P$, $u = w_1 ab w_2$ and $v = w_1 ba w_2$. Let $\lesssim_P$ be the reflexive and transitive closure of $\lesssim_P^1$. We say that u is smaller than v (or more executable) if $u \lesssim_P v$.

Proposition 3 can now be rephrased as follows:

Proposition 4. *Let $S = (Q, A, T, q_0)$ be an LTS, P a precedence relation, p a state of Q, and σ_1 and σ_2 two execution sequences of S such that $\exists\ q_1, q_2 \in Q$, $p \xrightarrow{\sigma_1}_T q_1$ and $p \xrightarrow{\sigma_2}_T q_2$ and $\sigma_1 \lesssim_P \sigma_2$. For a given buffer environment $\mathcal{B}_p$, let $S' = S[\mathcal{B}_p]$ where $S' = (Q', A, T', q'_0)$. Then, for any state $(p, b_1, b_2, \dots, b_p)$ of Q', the following holds:*

$$(p, b_1, b_2, \dots, b_p) \xrightarrow{\sigma_2}_{T'} (q_1, b'_1, b'_2, \dots, b'_p) \;\Rightarrow\; (p, b_1, b_2, \dots, b_p) \xrightarrow{\sigma_1}_{T'} (q_2, b'_1, b'_2, \dots, b'_p)$$

In the following sections we show how this preorder on execution sequences allows to define equivalence relations between LTS that are able to preserve various kinds of reachability properties. Moreover, since this preorder characterizes the executability of execution sequences, it turns out that these equivalence relations are congruence w.r.t. the [..] operator and therefore can be used during a compositional state space generation.

Note 1. We will consider in the sequel that buffers are *unbounded bags*. Thus, we shall note $\lesssim$ instead of $\lesssim_{P_{bag}}$. The extension of this work to *fifo* queues will be briefly discussed in the conclusion.

4 Deadlock Preservation

We consider here a first property based on a simple reachability analysis, the *deadlock freedom* of a given program $\mathcal{P}$. More precisely, this property can be verified by compositionally generating a reduced LTS S', equivalent to **sem**($\mathcal{P}$) w.r.t. its deadlock states. To this purpose, we introduce an equivalence relation $\approx_\delta$ preserving the reachability of any ("equivalent") potential deadlock states. Then, we show that $\approx_\delta$ is a congruence w.r.t. operators $\|$ and $[...]$. Finally, we propose a new asynchronous composition operator for the direct generation of a reduced LTS w.r.t to $\approx_\delta$.

4.1   A Deadlock Preserving Equivalence between LTS

In our framework the only "blocking" actions performed by a program component are the **remove** operations. Consequently, potential deadlock states are the
state not able to perform any **append** (or internal) operation. This set of states
can be even reduced by considering that a subsequence of adjacent potential
deadlock states of a same execution sequence can be collapsed into a single one
(the first state of this subsequence). Furthermore, two potential deadlock states
will be considered as equivalent iff a same buffer environment is able to "unlock"
them (i.e., they can perform the same sets of consecutive **remove** operations).

More formally, these potential deadlock states are defined as the *stable states*
of an LTS:

Definition 8 (Stable state).
Let $S = (Q, A, T, q_0)$ be an LTS. For each state q of Q:

$$stable(q) \equiv (q = q_0) \vee (Act(q) \subseteq \mathcal{A}^- \wedge Pre(q) \cap \mathcal{A}^+ \neq \emptyset) \vee (Act(q) = \emptyset)$$

We note stable(S) *the set of stable states of S. The equivalence $\sim_\delta$ between stable
states q_1 and q_2 is then the following:*

$$q_1 \sim_\delta q_2 \equiv \begin{cases} \forall \sigma_1 \in \mathcal{A}^{-^*} . \ q_1 \xrightarrow{\sigma_1}_T \Rightarrow \exists \sigma_2 . \ q_2 \xrightarrow{\sigma_2}_T \wedge \sigma_2 \sim \sigma_1 \\ \wedge \\ \forall \sigma_2 \in \mathcal{A}^{-^*} . \ q_2 \xrightarrow{\sigma_2}_T \Rightarrow \exists \sigma_1 . \ q_1 \xrightarrow{\sigma_1}_T \wedge \sigma_1 \sim \sigma_2 \end{cases}$$

The purpose of equivalence $\approx_\delta$ is to preserve reachability of $\sim_\delta$-equivalent
stable states in any buffer environment. Thus, a sufficient definition would be to
consider two LTS S_1 and S_2 as equivalent if, for any stable state of S_1 reachable
by an execution sequence σ_1, it corresponds an equivalent stable state of S_2,
reachable by an execution sequence σ_2, such that $\sigma_2 \lesssim \sigma_1$ (and reciprocally
for any stable state of S_2). However, we will use here a stronger definition,
which better corresponds to the behaviour of the composition operator we will
introduce later (see section 4.2).

Definition 9 (Equivalence between LTS).
*Let $S_i = (Q_i, A_i, T_i, q_{0_i})_{i=1,2}$ be two LTS. $\approx_\delta \subseteq Q_1 \times Q_2$ is the largest symmet-
rical relation verifying:*

$$p_1 \approx_\delta p_2 \Leftrightarrow \forall q_1 \in stable(S_1) . \ p_1 \xrightarrow{\sigma_1}_{T_1} q_1 \Rightarrow \exists q_2 \in stable(S_2) .$$
$$p_2 \xrightarrow{\sigma_2}_{T_2} q_2 \wedge q_1 \sim_\delta q_2 \wedge \sigma_2 \lesssim \sigma_1 \wedge q_1 \approx_\delta q_2$$

We extend $\approx_\delta$ to LTS saying that $S_1 \approx_\delta S_2$ iff $q_{0_1} \approx_\delta q_{0_2}$.

Relation $\approx_\delta$ preserves deadlocks in any buffer environment:

Proposition 5. *Let $S_i = (Q_i, A_i, T_i, q_{0_i})_{i=1,2}$ be two LTS and $\mathcal{B}_p$ a buffer environment. For a given LTS S let* **sink**(S) *denote the set of state of S without any
successors by its transition relation. Then:*

$$S_1 \approx_\delta S_2 \ \Rightarrow \ (\textbf{sink}(S_1[\mathcal{B}_p]) = \emptyset \ \Leftrightarrow \ \textbf{sink}(S_2[\mathcal{B}_p]) = \emptyset)$$

Example 3.

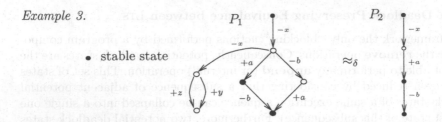

- stable state

To each execution sequence of P_1 leading to a stable state there exists a *smaller* execution sequence of P_2, leading to an equivalent stable state (and reciprocally). In particular, sequence $-x. - x.(+y. + z)^*$ of P_1 which not lead to any stable state is not preserved by $\approx_\delta$ (since it will never lead to a deadlock even after further compositions). □.

Finally, proposition 6 states that relation $\approx_\delta$ is a congruence w.r.t operators $\|$ (asynchronous composition) and [...] (execution within a given buffer environment). The proof of this proposition will rely on the following lemma:

Lemma 1. *For two execution sequences σ_1 and σ_2 of $\mathcal{A}^*$, we note $\sigma_1 \| \sigma_2$ the set of sequences obtained by "asynchronous composition" of σ_1 and σ_2. $\sigma_1 \| \sigma_2$ contains any sequence of $\mathcal{A}^*$ resulting of an interleaving of σ_1 and σ_2. Then, the following holds:*

$$\forall \sigma \in \mathcal{A}^* . \sigma_1 \lesssim \sigma_2 \Rightarrow \forall \sigma'_2 \in (\sigma_2 \| \sigma) . \exists \sigma'_1 \in (\sigma_1 \| \sigma) \text{ such that } \sigma'_1 \lesssim \sigma'_2$$

Proposition 6 (Congruence of $\approx_\delta$). *Let S_1, S_2 and S be three LTS, and $\mathcal{B}_p$ a buffer environment. If $S_1 \approx_\delta S_2$ then the following holds:*

$$S_1[\mathcal{B}_p] \approx_\delta S_2[\mathcal{B}_p] \tag{1}$$

$$S_1 \| S \approx_\delta S_2 \| S \tag{2}$$

4.2   A Deadlock Preserving Composition Operator

The deadlock preserving composition operator $S_1 \otimes_\delta S_2$ is based on the standard operator $\|$ of asynchronous composition between processes. Intuitively, the resulting LTS could be defined by "cutting off" any non minimal sequences of $S_1 \| S_2$ leading to a stable state (according to the pre-order $\lesssim$, definition 7).

In practice, this LTS will be obtained by considering as atomic some particular subsequences of S_1 and S_2, thus avoiding their full interleaving. Moreover, this generation can be performed "on-the-fly" without generating $S_1 \| S_2$. More precisely, atomic subsequences that we consider are delimited not only by stable states, but also using a particular set of states. These distinguished states are called "interleaving" in the sequel and are defined as follows:

Definition 10 (Interleaving states).
Let $P = (Q, A, T, q_0)$ an LTS. We note $int(P)$ the set of interleaving states of P:
$int(P) = stable(P) \cup \{q \in Q \mid Act^-(p) \neq \emptyset \wedge Act^+(p) \neq \emptyset \wedge Pre(p) \cap \mathcal{A}^+ \neq \emptyset\}$

Formally, *atomic subsequences* are defined as follows:

$$atom(\sigma) \equiv \sigma = p_1 \xrightarrow{-a_1} p_1' \xrightarrow{-a_i^*} p_1'' \xrightarrow{+b_i^*} q_1$$

where p_1 is an interleaving state, q_1 a stable state, and each p_i'' such that $Act^-(p_i'') \neq \emptyset$ is an interleaving state.

The deadlock preserving composition operator between processes can now be defined as follows:

Definition 11 (Deadlock preserving composition operator between LTS).

Let $P = P_1 \otimes_\delta P_2$ with $P = (Q, A, T, q_0)$ and $P_i = (Q_i, A_i, T_i, q_{0_i})_{i=1,2}$ s.t.:

- $q_0 = (q_{0_1}, q_{0_2})$;
- $A \subseteq A_1 \cup A_2$;
- Q is the smallest set reachable from q_0 using T.
- The set of transitions T is computed using the four following rules. For each of them we note $\mathcal{H}$ the statement:

$$\mathcal{H} = p_1 \xrightarrow{\sigma_1}_{T_1} q_1 \wedge p_2 \xrightarrow{\sigma_2}_{T_2} q_2 \wedge p_1 \in int(P_1) \wedge p_2 \in int(P_2)$$
$$\wedge\, atom(\sigma_1) \wedge atom(\sigma_2) \wedge stable(q_1) \wedge stable(q_2)$$

$$\frac{\mathcal{H},\ \sigma_1 \notin A^{-^*},\ \sigma_2 \notin A^{-^*}}{(p_1,p_2) \xrightarrow{\sigma_1}_T (q_1,p_2) \xrightarrow{\sigma_2}_T (q_1,q_2),\ (p_1,p_2) \xrightarrow{\sigma_2}_T (p_1,q_2) \xrightarrow{\sigma_1}_T (q_1,q_2)} \quad [R1]$$

$$\frac{\mathcal{H},\ \sigma_1 \in A^{-^*},\ \sigma_2 \notin A^{-^*}}{(p_1,p_2) \xrightarrow{\sigma_2}_T (p_1,q_2) \xrightarrow{\sigma_1}_T (q_1,q_2)} \quad [R2]$$

$$\frac{\mathcal{H},\ \sigma_1 \notin A^{-^*},\ \sigma_2 \in A^{-^*}}{(p_1,p_2) \xrightarrow{\sigma_1}_T (q_1,p_2) \xrightarrow{\sigma_2}_T (q_1,q_2)} \quad [R3]$$

$$\frac{\mathcal{H},\ \sigma_1 \in A^{-^*},\ \sigma_2 \in A^{-^*}}{(p_1,p_2) \xrightarrow{\sigma_1}_T (q_1,p_2) \xrightarrow{\sigma_2}_T (q_1,q_2)\ or\ (p_1,p_2) \xrightarrow{\sigma_2}_T (p_1,q_2) \xrightarrow{\sigma_1}_T (q_1,q_2)} \quad [R4]$$

Example 4. Let P_1 and P_2 be the two LTS represented below. LTS P is the product $P_1 \otimes_\delta P_2$. Dotted arrows indicate non minimal subsequences of $P_1 \parallel P_2$ that have been "cut off".

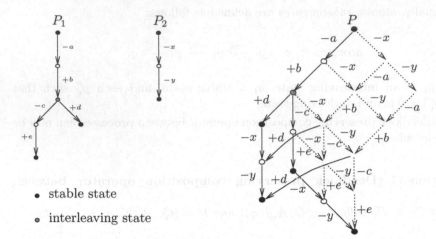

- stable state
- interleaving state

□.

Note 2.
For applying this method, all actions of σ_1 must be independent with actions of σ_2, which is the case when buffers are bags.

It remains to prove that this new operator of composition between processes preserves $\approx_\delta$ w.r.t. the standard asynchronous composition. This is expressed in the following proposition:

Proposition 7. *Let P_1 and P_2 be two* LTS. *Then we have $P_1 \parallel P_2 \approx_\delta P_1 \otimes_\delta P_2$.*

5   Observable Language Preservation

We consider now another kind of reachability property, the (finite) observable language generated by a given program $\mathcal{P}$. Here again, our objective is to compositionally generate a reduced LTS S', able to produce the same set of observable execution sequences as $\mathbf{sem}(\mathcal{P})$. Therefore, we introduce a relation $\approx_o$ preserving the language equivalence over a distinguished set $\mathcal{O} \subseteq \mathcal{A}$ of observable actions. Then, we show that $\approx_o$ is a congruence w.r.t. operators $\parallel$ and [...], and we propose another asynchronous composition operator preserving $\approx_o$.

5.1   A Language Preserving Equivalence

For a given LTS S, we denote by $L_\mathcal{O}(S)$ the set of (finite) execution sequences S can perform up to a set of observable actions $\mathcal{O}$. Thus, *observable* states of S are the states able to perform any observable actions, and two (observable) states will be considered as equivalent iff they can perform the same observable actions.

Definition 12 (Observable language, observable states).
Let $S = (Q, A, T, q_0)$ be an LTS. *The observable language over $\mathcal{O}$ of S is the following set:*

$$L_{\mathcal{O}}(S) = \{\sigma_o \in \mathcal{O}^* \mid \sigma_o = o_1.o_2.\cdots.o_n \ \wedge$$
$$\exists \sigma = x_0^*.o_1.x_1^*.o_2.\cdots.x_{n-1}^*.o_n.x_n^* \cdot q_0 \xrightarrow{\sigma}_T \ \wedge \ x_i \notin \mathcal{O}\}$$

For each state q of Q: $obs(q) \equiv Act(q) \cap \mathcal{O} \neq \emptyset$. We note $obs(S)$ the set of stable states of S and $\sim_o$ the equivalence relation between two states q_1 and q_2 defined as follows: $q_1 \sim_o q_2 \equiv (Act(q_1) \cap \mathcal{O} = Act(q_2) \cap \mathcal{O})$

Clearly, to preserve the observable language of an LTS it is sufficient to preserve the reachability of each of its observable states (in any buffer environment) by execution sequences identical w.r.t. observable actions. Consequently, by replacing "stable" by "observable" (and $\sim_\delta$ by $\sim_o$) in definition 9, one could easily obtain a suitable equivalence relation.

Unfortunately this straightforward definition of $\approx_o$ is not satisfying, at least for two reasons:

1. Since it completely ignores the effect of execution sequences not containing any observable state, the resulting equivalence is not a congruence w.r.t. the $\parallel$ operator [1]. Therefore, such execution sequences also have to be explicitly taken into account, this can be done in practice by preserving not only observable states but also the "interleaving" states introduced in section 4.2.

2. A "composed" state $(p_1, p_2, \ldots p_n)$ becomes observable as soon as one of its component p_i is able to perform an observable action. Thus, asynchronous composition produces many "stuttering equivalent" observable states, not identified by this definition (since they are reachable by execution sequences not comparable w.r.t. $\lesssim$). Relation $\lesssim$ should be weakened into a new relation $\lesssim^{\#}$ in order to not distinguish these "stuttering equivalent" observable states.

Relation $\lesssim^{\#}$ relies on the following observation: since an **append** operation performed by a given component can never be prevented by its environment (and resp. a **remove** operation may always be prevented), execution sequence $+a.\omega$ can be considered as "more executable" than ω (resp. sequence $\omega.a-$ is "less executable" than ω). This suggests to extend the precedency relation P to the relation $P^{\#}$ such that: $P^{\#} = P \cup \{\mathcal{A}^+ \times \{\epsilon\}\} \cup \{\{\epsilon\} \times \mathcal{A}^-\}$

Relation $\lesssim^{\#}$ is then the extension of $P^{\#}$ to execution sequences (applying definition 7, where $\lesssim^{\#} = \lesssim_{P^{\#}}$). It is easy to see that proposition 4 still holds for $\lesssim^{\#}$, that is, according to this new preorder, smallest execution sequences are always more executable than largest ones in any buffer environment.

The definition of the language preserving equivalence $\approx_o$ is now the following:

---

[1] this problem did not occur with $\approx_\delta$ because execution sequences without stable state cannot lead to a deadlock even after composition with other components.

Definition 13 (Equivalence between LTS).
Let $S_i = (Q_i, A_i, T_i, q_{0_i})_{i=1,2}$ be two LTS. $\approx_o \subseteq Q_1 \times Q_2$ is the largest symmetrical relation verifying:

$$p_1 \approx_o p_2 \Leftrightarrow \forall q_1 \in (obs(S_1) \cup int(S_1)) \cdot p_1 \xrightarrow{\sigma_1}_{T_1} q_1 \Rightarrow \exists q_2 \in (obs(S_2) \cup int(S_2)) \cdot$$
$$p_2 \xrightarrow{\sigma_2}_{T_2} q_2 \wedge q_1 \sim_\emptyset q_2 \wedge \sigma_2 \lesssim^\# \sigma_1 \wedge q_1 \approx_o q_2 \wedge$$
$$\forall \omega_1 \in A^* \cdot q_1 \xrightarrow{\omega_1}_{T_1} \Rightarrow \exists \omega_2 \in A^* \cdot q_2 \xrightarrow{\omega_2}_{T_2} \wedge \omega_2 \lesssim^\# \omega_1$$

We say that $S_1 \approx_o S_2$ iff $q_{0_1} \approx_o q_{0_2}$.

Relation $\approx_o$ preserves observable language over $\mathcal{O}$

Proposition 8. Let S_1 and S_2 be two LTS and $\mathcal{B}_p$ a buffer environment.

$$S_1 \approx_o S_2 \Rightarrow L_{\mathcal{O}}(S_1[\mathcal{B}_p]) = L_{\mathcal{O}}(S_2[\mathcal{B}_p])$$

Finally, we show that relation $\approx_o$ is a congruence w.r.t operators $\|$ (asynchronous composition) and [...] (execution within a given buffer environment). Here again, the proof of this proposition will rely on lemma 1, which also applies to preorder $\lesssim^\#$.

Proposition 9. Let S_1, S_2 and $S = (Q, A, T, q_0)$ be three LTS, and $\mathcal{B}_p$ a buffer environment. If $S_1 \approx_o S_2$ then the following holds:

$$S_1 \| S \approx_o S_2 \| S \tag{3}$$
$$S_1[\mathcal{B}_p] \approx_o S_2[\mathcal{B}_p] \tag{4}$$

5.2 A Language Preserving Composition Operator

We briefly explain here how the composition operator $\otimes_\delta$ defined in section 4.2 can be modified into a $\otimes_o$ operator preserving $\approx_o$ -equivalence. The underlying idea is now to consider as *atomic* parts of execution sequences delimited either by "interleaving" states or observable states. However, the set of interleaving states considered in definition 10 have to be augmented in order to deal with "terminal" subsequences which do no contain any interleaving state (such sequences are necessarily ended by a loop of A^+-actions). A practical way is to add to the interleaving set of states any element of this A^+-loop (these states are computed during the construction of $S_1 \otimes_o S_2$).

Such sequences are then of the form: $atom(\sigma) \equiv \sigma = p_1 \xrightarrow{-a_i^*} p_1' \xrightarrow{+b_i^*} q_1$

Moreover, as in section 4.2, a complete interleaving between a pair of atomic sequences σ_1 and σ_2 is required only when both σ_1 and σ_2 contain a combination of **append** and **remove** actions (otherwise it is enough to consider only the smallest element of the ordered set $\{\sigma_1.\sigma_2, \sigma_2.\sigma_1\}$).

Formally, operator $\otimes_o$ is obtained by modifying definition of $\otimes_\delta$ (definition 11) as follows:

Definition 14 (Language preserving composition operator).
Let $P = P_1 \otimes_o P_2$ with $P = (Q, A, T, q_0)$ and $P_i = (Q_i, A_i, T_i, q_{0_i})_{i=1,2}$ s.t.:

- $q_0 = (q_{0_1}, q_{0_2})$;
- $A \subseteq A_1 \cup A_2$;
- Q is the smallest set reachable from q_0 using T.
- The set of transitions T is computed using the following four rules. For each of them, we note $\mathcal{H}$ the following statement:

$$\mathcal{H} = p_1 \xrightarrow{\sigma_1}_{T_1} q_1 \wedge p_2 \xrightarrow{\sigma_2}_{T_2} q_2 \wedge p_1 \in int(P_1) \cup obs(P_1) \wedge p_2 \in int(P_2) \cup obs(P_2)$$
$$\wedge\; atom(\sigma_1) \wedge atom(\sigma_2) \wedge (int(q_1) \vee obs(q_1)) \wedge (int(q_2) \vee obs(q_2))$$

$$\frac{\mathcal{H},\; \sigma_1 \notin A^{-*},\; \sigma_2 \notin A^{-*}\; \sigma_1 \notin A^{+*},\; \sigma_2 \notin A^{+*}}{(p_1, p_2) \xrightarrow{\sigma_1}_T (q_1, p_2) \xrightarrow{\sigma_2}_T (q_1, q_2),\; (p_1, p_2) \xrightarrow{\sigma_2}_T (p_1, q_2) \xrightarrow{\sigma_1}_T (q_1, q_2)} \quad [R1]$$

$$\frac{\mathcal{H},\; \sigma_1 \in A^{-*},\; \sigma_2 \notin A^{-*}}{(p_1, p_2) \xrightarrow{\sigma_2}_T (p_1, q_2) \xrightarrow{\sigma_1}_T (q_1, q_2)} \quad [R2]$$

$$\frac{\mathcal{H},\; \sigma_1 \notin A^{-*},\; \sigma_2 \in A^{-*}}{(p_1, p_2) \xrightarrow{\sigma_1}_T (q_1, p_2) \xrightarrow{\sigma_2}_T (q_1, q_2)} \quad [R3]$$

$$\frac{\mathcal{H},\; (\sigma_1 \in A^{-*} \wedge \sigma_2 \in A^{-*}) \vee (\sigma_1 \in A^{+*} \wedge \sigma_2 \in A^{+*})}{(p_1, p_2) \xrightarrow{\sigma_1}_T (q_1, p_2) \xrightarrow{\sigma_2}_T (q_1, q_2) \text{ or } (p_1, p_2) \xrightarrow{\sigma_2}_T (p_1, q_2) \xrightarrow{\sigma_1}_T (q_1, q_2)} \quad [R4]$$

Using similar arguments than in section 4.2 it is possible to show that this operator preserves $\approx_o$ w.r.t. the standard asynchronous composition:

Proposition 10. Let P_1 and P_2 be two LTS. Then we have $P_1 \parallel P_2 \approx_o P_1 \otimes_o P_2$

6 Conclusion and Future Works

We have proposed a state space generation method for asynchronous communicating processes which combines the benefits of both *compositionality* (generation and reduction steps are performed incrementally), and *partial-order reduction* techniques (only some representative elements of the set of execution sequences are considered).

More precisely, our approach was based on a syntactic notion of *precedence* of communication actions, leading to a preorder between execution sequences able to characterize their "executability" in any external buffer environments (smallest sequences are the most executable). Using this preorder, we proposed two equivalence relations between LTS, based on a similar notion of reachability of a distinguished set of states through most executable execution sequences. These two equivalence relations respectively preserve deadlock states and the system language up to a given set of observable actions. Moreover, they are congruences w.r.t. asynchronous composition. Finally, we have also defined two asynchronous composition operators, able to directly generate reduced LTS w.r.t. each of these relations. These operators differ on the standard one by considering as *atomic* particular subsequences of each process, thus saving many useless interleavings.

A first prototype implementation has been experimented within the IF environment developed at VERIMAG for the verification of asynchronous communicating systems [BFG+99]. The results obtained on a "benchmark" example (a leader election algorithm) largely confirm the interest of this compositional approach (about 5 000 generated states instead of 20 000 using a simultaneous composition, when verifying observable language preservation). It now remains to extend this experience to others case-studies, in particular to see how our approach compares with more "classical" partial-order reduction techniques (for instance the one implemented in SPIN [Hol91]).

One of the practical motivation behind this work is to apply compositional generation techniques to the verification of industrial size SDL specifications. To this purpose, the results proposed here will have to be (fully) extended to the case of asynchronous communications via *fifo queues* (instead of their abstraction in terms of *bags*). In this case, the "purely syntactic" definition of *precedence* relation between actions we considered here may be to strict, and it would be interesting to see how it can be enlarged using more sophisticated *static analysis* techniques (for instance depending on the communication topology between processes). To this purpose, a suitable framework could be provided by the notion of *conditional independence* proposed in [KP92].

Acknowledgements

Parts of this work were largely improved during fruitful discussions with M. Bozga, S. Graf and J. Sifakis. Thanks are also due to the anonymous referees for their helpful comments and suggestions.

References

AJKP98. P. Abdulla, B. Jonsson, M. Kindhal, and D. Peled. A General Approach to Partial Order Reductions in Symbolic Verification. In *Proceedings of CAV'98, Vancouver, Canada*, volume 1427 of *LNCS*, June 1998. 268

BFG+91. Ahmed Bouajjani, Jean-Claude Fernandez, Susanne Graf, Carlos Rodríguez, and Joseph Sifakis. Safety for Branching Time Semantics. In *Proceedings of 18th ICALP*. Springer Verlag, July 1991. 270

BFG+99. M. Bozga, J.-C. Fernandez, L. Ghirvu, S. Graf, J.P. Krimm, and L. Mounier. IF: An Intermediate Representation and Validation Environment for Timed Asynchronous Systems. In *Proceedings of FM'99, Toulouse, France*, LNCS 1708, 1999. 281

CK93. S.C. Cheung and J. Kramer. Enhancing Compositional Reachability Analysis with Context Constraints. In *Proceedings of the 1st ACM International Symposium on the Foundations of Software Engineering*, pages 115–125, Los Angeles, California, December 1993. 267

GS90.   S. Graf and B. Steffen. Compositional Minimization of Finite State Processes. In *Workshop on Computer-Aided Verification*, Rutgers, USA, June 1990. DIMACS, R.P. Kurshan and E.M. Clarke. 267

GW91.   P. Godefroid and P. Wolper. Using Partial Orders for the Efficient Verification of Deadlock Freedom and Safety Properties. In K. G. Larsen, editor, *Proceedings of CAV'91 (Aalborg, Denmark)*, July 1991. 267

Hoa85.   C. A. R. Hoare. *Communicating Sequential Processes*. Prentice-Hall, 1985. 267

Hol91.   Gerard J. Holzmann. *Design and Validation of Computer Protocols*. Software Series. Prentice Hall, 1991. 267, 281

ISO87.   ISO/IEC. LOTOS — A Formal Description Technique Based on the Temporal Ordering of Observational Behaviour. Information Processing Systems — OSI , Genève, July 1987. 267

IT92.   ITU-T. Specification and Description Language (SDL). ITU-T Recommendation Z.100, International Telecommunication Union, Genève, 1992. 267

KLM⁺98.   R. Kurshan, V. Levin, M. Minea, D. Peled, and H. Yenigün. Static Partial Order Reduction. In *Proceedings of TACAS'98, Lisbon, Portugal*, volume 1384 of *LNCS*, 1998. 267

KM97.   Jean-Pierre Krimm and Laurent Mounier. Compositional State Space Generation from Lotos Programs. In Ed Brinksma, editor, *Proceedings of TACAS'97*, Enschede, The Netherlands, April 1997. Springer Verlag. 267

KP92.   S. Katz and D. Peled. Defining conditional independence usin collapses. *Theoretical Computer Science*, 101(1):337–359, 1992. 281

Lip75.   Lipton. Reduction, a method of proving properties of parallel programs. *Communications of the ACM*, 18(12):717–721, dec 1975. 268

Mil89.   Robin Milner. *Communication and Concurrency*. Prentice-Hall, 1989. 270

Pel96.   Doron Peled. Combining partial-order reductions with on-the-fly model-checking. *Formal Methods in System Design*, 8:39–64, 1996. 267

Val90.   A. Valmari. A Stubborn Attack on State Explosion. In *Workshop on Computer Aided Verification*, Rutgers, USA, June 1990. DIMACS, R.P. Kurshan and E.M. Clarke. 267

Val96.   Antti Valmari. Compositionality in State Space Verification. In *Application and Theory of Petri Nets*, volume 1091 of *LNCS*, pages 29–56, Springer Verlag, June 1996. 267

vGW89.   R. J. van Glabbeek and W. P. Weijland. Branching-Time and Abstraction in Bisimulation Semantics (extended abstract). CS R8911, Centrum voor Wiskunde en Informatica, Amsterdam, 1989. 270

Checking for CFFD-Preorder with Tester Processes

Juhana Helovuo and Antti Valmari

Tampere University of Technology, Software Systems Laboratory
PO Box 553, FIN-33101 Tampere, FINLAND
{juhe,ava}@cs.tut.fi

Abstract. This paper describes an on-the-fly technique for computing the CFFD-preorder relation on two labelled transition systems (LTSs). CFFD is a process-algebraic semantic model for comparing processes. It is a modification of the CSP model. LTSs are used as a representation of processes. The presented technique is based on transforming the specification process into a special *tester process*. The tester is then composed in parallel with the processes of the implementation. Violations against the specification are detected as illegal states, deadlocks and livelocks during the computation of the composition. Tester processes are an extension of Brinksma's canonical testers. Using a tester process can be a substantially faster method of computing CFFD-preorder than the previously used method of comparing acceptance graphs.

1 Introduction and Motivation

This work is based on process-algebraic theories such as Calculus of Communicating Systems (CCS) [11], Communicating Sequential Processes (CSP) [5] [14], and Chaos-Free Failures-Divergences (CFFD) [18,19]. These theories define ways to compare processes. Each of them defines its own notion of equivalence, that is, defines when the behaviours of two processes are considered equivalent.

The semantic model used in this paper is CFFD, which is a further development of CSP. Unlike CSP, the CFFD theory can distinguish between different behaviours after a possible livelock. CSP considers all livelock situations as "chaos" and therefore equivalent, no matter what can happen after the potential livelock. CFFD avoids this problem, hence the name "Chaos-Free Failures-Divergences".

In this paper it is assumed that the processes are formally modelled as *labelled transition systems* (LTS), or parallel compositions thereof. LTSs resemble nondeterministic automata. The key difference is that an LTS has no accepting states, and, in addition to the normal alphabet, there is a special *invisible* action τ. τ resembles the ε of automata theory, but is usually given more significance.

Many process-algebraic theories contain a *preorder* relation that can be considered as an implementation relation: a system *Sys* is a legal implementation of a specification *Spec*, if and only if $Sys \leq Spec$. A detailed analysis of many of them is in [9]. The CFFD-preorder "$\leq_{\mathrm{CFFD}}$" is particularly interesting, because

S. Graf and M. Schwartzbach (Eds.): TACAS/ETAPS 2000, LNCS 1785, pp. 283–298, 2000.
© Springer-Verlag Berlin Heidelberg 2000

- it has nice compositional properties, so it is suitable for compositional verification;
- it handles livelocks in a satisfactory way; and
- it has an interesting connection to ordinary state-based linear-time temporal logic (LTL) [10].

Namely, if $Sys \leq_{\text{CFFD}} Spec$ holds and $Spec$ satisfies an LTL formula, then also Sys satisfies it, provided that the values of the atomic propositions of the formula are fully determined by the non-τ actions executed so far, and the formula does not contain the "next state" operator [7]. (Notice that Sys may satisfy also formulas that $Spec$ does not satisfy.) This is an important property, because LTL is one of the most important formalisms used for specifying systems, "next state" is usually considered irrelevant in concurrency contexts, and the τ-actions can be chosen according to the atomic propositions of the formula. Furthermore, all major process-algebraic preorders lack this property because of the way they handle livelocks. There are less well known preorders that have the property and some that also preserve deadlocks, but CFFD-preorder can be shown to be the coarsest compositional one among them [7].

CFFD-preorder guarantees that Sys has only "legal" execution traces (those specified by $Spec$), Sys has only legal refusal sets (a generalization of deadlocks), and Sys can livelock only when specified by $Spec$. It implies *testing preorder*, or *failure preorder* [1].

Checking of $Sys \leq_{\text{CFFD}} Spec$ is PSPACE-complete in the size of $Spec$. On the other hand, it can be done in low-order polynomial time in the size of Sys. We will develop an algorithm that is exponential in the size of $Spec$ and fast in the size of Sys. It is based on converting $Spec$ into a special *tester process*, putting it in parallel with Sys, and checking for certain conditions when computing the parallel composition of Sys and $tester(Spec)$. In addition to being cheap in terms of the size of Sys, the algorithm has the advantage that it can detect errors *on-the-fly*, that is, during the construction of an LTS for Sys. This is obtained by presenting Sys as a parallel composition of several processes $P_1, P_2, \ldots, P_n$, and computing $P_1 \parallel P_2 \parallel \cdots \parallel P_n \parallel tester(Spec)$ and simultaneously checking for the error detection conditions. As was discussed in detail in [16] Section 4.2, on-the-fly verification may save a lot of effort when analysing erroneous systems, compared to fully computing the LTSs of $Spec$ and Sys before comparing them.

Many of the fundamental ideas presented in this paper are not new. They can be found from the literature on reduction algorithms in classic automata theory, the theory of canonical testers [2], and the CSP model checking in the FDR tool [13,14]. However, as far as we know, this is the first time that the theory of tester processes is put together and presented in an organized manner. Furthermore, nontrivial new ideas were needed for adding the handling of divergences in an appropriate way, and, as we pointed out above, divergences are necessary for checking the absence of illegal livelocks.

Other algorithms for checking a preorder that resembles CFFD have been proposed in [3,13]. The [3] approach is exponential also in the size of Sys. The [13] approach is rather similar to ours and has more or less the same complexity. The main difference, in addition to the important fact that our approach handles also livelocks, is that some things that the [13] approach postpones to the computation of the parallel composition are done already during the tester construction in our method. Therefore, our method states less requirements to the parallel composition tool. (Please be not confused by the fact that the handling of livelocks causes a rather strict requirement in our method — this should not be taken into account when comparing to [13], because the latter treats livelocks as "chaos".)

The algorithm described in Section 4 has been implemented as an addition to the "Advanced Reachability Analysis" verification tool set, which has been developed by VTT Electronics and the Verification Algorithm Research Group at Tampere University of Technology [17].

Section 2 recalls the basic definitions. In Section 3 the notion of acceptance graphs is introduced. Our new method is described in Section 4.

2   Background

2.1   CFFD Semantics

The CFFD semantics is a semantic model for labelled transition systems (LTS). It is a modification of the CSP model [5] [14]. The CFFD model differs from the CSP model in the handling of (possible) divergences. The CFFD model records the behavior of the system after divergences whereas the CSP model disregards any behavior after the first divergence. The CFFD model is described in detail in [18] and [19]. Here are some definitions of the concepts used in this paper.

Definition 1 (Labelled transition system) *LTS P is the 4-tuple $P = (S, \Sigma, \Delta, \hat{s})$, where S is the set of* states, *Σ is the finite set of* visible action symbols. *There is also the* invisible action $\tau \notin \Sigma$. $\Delta \subseteq S \times (\Sigma \cup \{\tau\}) \times S$ *is the set of* transitions *and $\hat{s} \in S$ is the* initial state.

In addition to the alphabet symbols in Σ there is the invisible action τ. It denotes some execution step which is internal to the system and its execution cannot be directly observed in the execution behavior of the LTS.

Definition 2 (Arrow notation) *The following are more convenient notations for executions of an LTS.*

- $s -a\rightarrow s'$ *iff* $(s, a, s') \in \Delta$
- $s -a_1a_2 \ldots a_n\rightarrow s'$ *iff*
  $\exists s_0, s_1, \ldots, s_n : s = s_0 \wedge s_0 -a_1\rightarrow s_1 -a_2\rightarrow \cdots -a_n\rightarrow s_n \wedge s' = s_n.$
- *If* $\sigma = a_1a_2 \ldots a_n$ *then* $s -a_1a_2 \ldots a_n\rightarrow s'$ *can be written* $s -\sigma\rightarrow s'$.
- $s -\sigma\rightarrow$ *iff* $\exists s' : s -\sigma\rightarrow s'$
- $s =a_1a_2 \ldots a_n\Rightarrow s'$ *iff* $s -\tau^*a_1\tau^*a_2\tau^* \ldots \tau^*a_n\tau^*\rightarrow s'$, *where each τ^* denotes any sequence of zero or more τ-actions, and none of a_i is τ.*
- $s =\sigma\Rightarrow$ *iff* $\exists s' : s =\sigma\Rightarrow s'$

Parallel composition is an operator which combines many LTSs into one. We use a parallel composition operator that synchronizes all visible actions which occur in the alphabets of more than one component LTS.

Definition 3 (Parallel composition) *Let* $L_1 = (S_1, \Sigma_1, \Delta_1, \hat{s}_1), \ldots, L_n = (S_n, \Sigma_n, \Delta_n, \hat{s}_n)$. *Their parallel composition* $L_1 \| \cdots \| L_n = (S, \Sigma, \Delta, \hat{s})$, *where*

- $S = S_1 \times S_2 \times \cdots \times S_n$
- $\Sigma = \Sigma_1 \cup \Sigma_2 \cup \cdots \cup \Sigma_n$
- $(s, a, s') \in \Delta$, *where*
  $s = (s_1, \ldots, s_n) \in S \wedge s' = (s'_1, \ldots, s'_n) \in S,$

$$\text{iff either} \begin{cases} a = \tau \wedge \exists i \in \{1, \ldots, n\} : \begin{cases} (s_i, \tau, s'_i) \in \Delta_i \text{ and} \\ \forall j : (j \neq i \Rightarrow s'_j = s_j) \text{ or} \end{cases} \\ a \in \Sigma \wedge \forall i \in \{1, \ldots, n\} : \begin{cases} a \in \Sigma_i \Rightarrow (s_i, a, s'_i) \in \Delta_i \text{ and} \\ a \notin \Sigma_i \Rightarrow s'_i = s_i \end{cases} \end{cases}$$

- $\hat{s} = (\hat{s}_1, \hat{s}_2, \ldots, \hat{s}_n)$

The LTSs generated by this definition of composition contain *unreachable* states. In practice, these states can be ignored, since they don't affect the behavior of the LTS. In other words, only states s which satisfy $\exists \sigma : \hat{s} - \sigma \rightarrow s$ are important.

Definition 4 (Traces) *The set of* traces *of an LTS* $P = (S, \Sigma, \Delta, \hat{s})$ *is* $tr(P) = \{ \sigma \in \Sigma^* \mid \hat{s} = \sigma \Rightarrow \}$

Definition 5 (Stable failures) *The set of* stable failures *of an LTS* P *is the set of pairs* $sfail(P) = \{ (\sigma, R) \in \Sigma^* \times 2^\Sigma \mid \exists s : \hat{s} = \sigma \Rightarrow s \wedge \forall a \in R \cup \{\tau\} : \neg(s - a \rightarrow) \}$. *The set* R *is called a* refusal set.

The number of refusal sets for a given σ is often very large. All subsets of a refusal set are also refusal sets, that is $(\sigma, R) \in sfail(P) \wedge R' \subseteq R \Rightarrow (\sigma, R') \in sfail(P)$. Therefore, the stable failures with *maximal* refusal sets with respect to $\subseteq$ completely determine the set of stable failures.

Sometimes it is more convenient to use *acceptance sets* instead of refusal sets. Acceptance sets are the complements of refusal sets. Complements of the maximal refusal sets are the *minimal acceptance sets*.

Definition 6 (Deadlock traces) *The set of* deadlock traces *of an LTS* P *is the set* $dltr(P) = \{ \sigma \in tr(P) \mid \exists s : (\hat{s} = \sigma \Rightarrow s \wedge \forall a \in \Sigma \cup \{\tau\} : \neg(s - a \rightarrow)) \}$

Thus

Theorem 1 $dltr(P) = \{ \sigma \mid (\sigma, \Sigma) \in sfail(P) \}$.

Definition 7 (Divergence traces) *The set of* divergence traces *of an LTS* P *is the set* $divtr(P) = \{ \sigma \mid \exists s : \hat{s} = \sigma \Rightarrow s \wedge s - \tau^\omega \rightarrow \}$

Here τ^ω denotes an infinite sequence of invisible events. Similarly, Σ^ω denotes all infinite sequences of visible actions.

Traces can be derived from stable failures and divergence traces [15]:

Theorem 2 $tr(P) = divtr(P) \cup \{\, \sigma \mid (\sigma, \emptyset) \in sfail(P) \,\}.$

Definition 8 (Infinite traces) *If P is an LTS, then*
$inftr(P) = \{\, \sigma \in \Sigma^\omega \mid \hat{s} =\sigma\!\Rightarrow \,\}$

Definition 9 (Stability) *State s is stable iff there are no invisible transitions from it: $stable(s) \Leftrightarrow \neg(s -\tau\!\rightarrow)$. An LTS P is stable iff its initial state is stable.*

Definition 10 (CFFD-equivalence) *LTSs P and Q are CFFD-equivalent, written $P \equiv_{CFFD} Q$, iff $\Sigma(P) = \Sigma(Q) \wedge stable(P) = stable(Q) \wedge sfail(P) = sfail(Q) \wedge divtr(P) = divtr(Q) \wedge inftr(P) = inftr(Q)$*

There are five components $(\Sigma, stable(), sfail(), divtr()$ and $inftr())$ in the CFFD-equivalence. In the case of finite state systems the $inftr()$-component follows from the other components:

Theorem 3 *If P is a finite state LTS, then $inftr(P) = \{\, \omega \in \Sigma^\omega \mid \forall \sigma < \omega : \sigma \in tr(P) \,\}.$*

The proof can be found in [19].

The following formulae are intended to illustrate the relation between CFFD and CSP [12,15]. Let $\rho \le \sigma$ denote that ρ is a prefix of σ. Let P be an LTS. Then its *CSP-divergences* and *CSP-failures* are

Definition 11 (CSP-divergences and CSP-failures) $CSPdiv(P) = \{\, \sigma \in \Sigma^* \mid \exists \rho \in divtr(P) : \rho \le \sigma \,\}$ *and* $CSPfail(P) = sfail(P) \cup (CSPdiv(P) \times 2^\Sigma).$

2.2 CFFD-Preorder

The CFFD-preorder is a relation which is used to compare two LTSs. One of the LTSs represents the *specification* (S) and the other represents the *implementation* (I). The relation is written $I \le_{CFFD} S$.

Definition 12 (CFFD-preorder) *If P and Q are LTSs, then $P \le_{CFFD} Q$ iff*
1. $\Sigma(P) = \Sigma(Q)$,
2. $stable(P) \vee \neg stable(Q)$, *(or, equivalently, $stable(Q) \Rightarrow stable(P)$)*
3. $sfail(P) \subseteq sfail(Q)$,
4. $divtr(P) \subseteq divtr(Q)$ *and*
5. $inftr(P) \subseteq inftr(Q)$

This relation is both reflexive and transitive, so it is a preorder. The equivalence induced by this preorder is the CFFD-equivalence. That is, $P \le_{CFFD} Q \wedge Q \le_{CFFD} P \iff P \equiv_{CFFD} Q$.

If the LTSs are both finite, then the fifth property follows from the 3rd and 4th.

Property 1 tells that the implementation and specification should be interested in the same set of actions. Property 2 tells that if the specification is stable, then the implementation must be also stable. In general, the specification may contain more nondeterminism than the implementation but not the other way around. Property 3 states that the implementation is allowed to refuse some set $R \subseteq \Sigma$ of actions after executing a trace $\sigma \in \Sigma^*$ only if the specification can execute σ and then refuse R.

The implementation does not have to refuse everything that the specification may refuse. When considering the acceptance sets instead of refusal sets, the situation is complementary: After executing σ the implementation should always be able to accept some superset of one of the specification's acceptance sets. Note that this property only speaks of the stable states.

Property 4 means that the implementation is allowed to diverge (livelock) after executing some trace only if also the specification can diverge after that trace. The implementation may also choose not to livelock even if the specification allows it to do so, but then the implementation refuses at least $\emptyset$ after the trace, which may violate property 3.

Property 5 is important only in the case of infinite state systems as Theorem 3 states. In [19] this issue is presented in more detail.

Definition 12 (properties 3 and 4) with theorems 1 and 2 implies two additional properties:

Theorem 4 *If* $P \leq_{CFFD} Q$ *then 6.* $tr(P) \subseteq tr(Q)$ *and 7.* $dltr(P) \subseteq dltr(Q)$

2.3   The Complexity of Checking CFFD-Preorder

The checking of equivalence according to a semantics that is based on failures is typically PSPACE-complete [8]. This applies also to CFFD-semantics. Because $P \equiv_{CFFD} Q \leftrightarrow P \leq_{CFFD} Q \wedge Q \leq_{CFFD} P$, the problem of checking $P \leq_{CFFD} Q$ must be PSPACE-hard in the size of at least one of P and Q. The next theorem states that it is hard in the size of Q. On the other hand, as will be described in Section 4.1, it can be done in low-order polynomial time in the size of P.

Theorem 5 *Checking that* $P \leq_{CFFD} Q$ *is PSPACE-complete in the size of* Q.

Proof. If $P \leq_{CFFD} Q$ does not hold, then at least one of properties 1 to 4 of Definition 12 does not hold. The first two are trivial to check. If the property 3 or 4 does not hold, P and Q have a trace σ such that either there is an action a such that $\sigma a \in tr(P)$ but $\sigma a \notin tr(Q)$; or there is $A \subseteq \Sigma$ such that $(\sigma, A) \in sfail(P)$ but $(\sigma, A) \notin sfail(Q)$; or $\sigma \in divtr(P)$ but $\sigma \notin divtr(Q)$. A nondeterministic algorithm can guess the kind of error and then one by one guess the steps of an execution of P that yields σ as the trace, and leads P to a state with an illegal next action a, refusal set A, or divergence. The algorithm simultaneously keeps track of all the states that Q may be in after executing the same trace as P has so far executed.

At some point the algorithm guesses that the execution has been completed. Then it verifies that P can continue with a or refuse A or diverge from its current state, but Q cannot from any of the states in its current set of states. Thanks to the interleaving of the steps of P and Q, neither the (possibly exponentially long) execution nor its trace σ needs to be stored. Keeping track of the set of states of Q requires two or three bits per each state of Q. So polynomial space suffices. Thus $P \nleq_{\text{CFFD}} Q$ can be checked in nondeterministic polynomial space, and NPSPACE is know to be the same as PSPACE.

It remains to be proven that checking $P \leq_{\text{CFFD}} Q$ is PSPACE-hard. The checking whether a nondeterministic finite automaton $N = (S, \Sigma, \Delta, \hat{s}, F)$ accepts all traces (known as "words" in automata theory) in its alphabet is a well-known PSPACE-complete problem. ($F \subseteq S$ is the set of *acceptance states*; the other components are like in an LTS; and the automaton accepts a trace if and only if it has an execution that produces that trace and ends in an acceptance state.) This problem can be reduced to the checking of $P \leq_{\text{CFFD}} Q$ in polynomial time as follows.

First, N is converted to the LTS $L_1 = (S_1, \Sigma_1, \Delta_1, \hat{s})$, where $S_1 = S \cup \{s_\#\}$, $\Sigma_1 = \Sigma \cup \{a_\#\}$, $\Delta_1 = \Delta \cup \{(s, a_\#, s_\#) \mid s \in F\} \cup \{(s_\#, a, s_\#) \mid a \in \Sigma_1\}$, and $s_\#$ and $a_\#$ are new (i.e., $s_\# \notin S$ and $a_\# \notin \Sigma$). That is, a new state is added such that it can be reached from each original acceptance state by $a_\#$, and from itself by just any visible action. If N rejects some trace σ, then $\sigma a_\# \notin tr(L_1)$. Otherwise, L_1 can execute any $\sigma \in \Sigma^*$ in such a way that it can then continue with $a_\#$ and any element of Σ_1^*. Thus N accepts all traces if and only if $tr(L_1) = \Sigma_1^*$.

Next S_1, Δ_1 and $\hat{s}$ are replaced with $S_2 = \{[[s]] \mid s \in S_1\}$ and $\Delta_2 = \{([[s]], a, [[s']]) \mid (s, a, s') \in \Delta_1\}$ and $\hat{s}_2 = [[\hat{s}]]$, where $[[s]] = \{s' \in S_1 \mid s = \varepsilon \Rightarrow s' \wedge s' = \varepsilon \Rightarrow s\}$, yielding $L_2 = (S_2, \Sigma_1, \Delta_2, \hat{s}_2)$. In other words, each strongly connected component is collapsed into an individual state, where only τ-transitions are taken into account when checking strong connectivity. Very efficient algorithms are known for this, and $tr(L_1)$ is not changed, that is, $tr(L_2) = tr(L_1)$.

Finally a new initial state and τ-transition are added, a new deadlock state is added and made reachable from any old state by one τ-transition, and all "self-loop" τ-transitions are removed. More formally: $S_3 = S_2 \cup \{s_I, s_D\}$, $\Delta_3 = \Delta_2 \cup \{(s_I, \tau, \hat{s}_2)\} \cup \{(s, \tau, s_D) \mid s \in S_2\} - \{(s, \tau, s) \mid s \in S_3\}$, and $\hat{s}_3 = s_I$, where $s_I \notin S_2$ and $s_D \notin S_2$. This conversion leaves $tr(L_2)$ intact, and ensures that $stable(L_3) = \text{false}$, $sfail(L_3) = tr(L_3) \times 2^{\Sigma_1}$, and $divtr(L_3) = \emptyset$.

Consider the LTS $L' = (\{s_1, s_2\}, \Sigma_1, \Delta', s_1)$, where $\Delta' = \{(s_1, \tau, s_2)\} \cup \{(s_1, a, s_1) \mid a \in \Sigma_1\}$. We have $stable(L') = \text{false}$, $sfail(L') = \Sigma_1^* \times 2^{\Sigma_1}$, and $divtr(L') = \emptyset$. Therefore, $L' \leq_{\text{CFFD}} L_3$ holds if and only if $\Sigma_1^* \subseteq tr(L_3)$. On the other hand, $tr(L_3) \subseteq \Sigma_1^*$ by definition, and $tr(L_3) = tr(L_1)$ by construction. So $L' \leq_{\text{CFFD}} L_3$ holds if and only if $tr(L_1) = \Sigma_1^*$, which, in turn, was shown equivalent to N accepting all traces in its alphabet. $\square$

3   Acceptance Graphs

In order to check whether the relation $P \leq_{\mathrm{CFFD}} Q$ holds, we have to check if the properties 1-5 of Definition 12 hold for them. If we assume that Q does not have an infinite number of states, then property 5 need not be checked.

Properties 1 and 2 are simple. Equivalence of alphabets is just a set comparison. The values of $stable(P)$ and $stable(Q)$ can be obtained by inspecting the output transitions of the initial states of P and Q, and from then on the check of property 2 consists of simple Boolean arithmetic.

To check for properties 3 and 4 we rely on the idea of *acceptance graphs*, which are a modification of acceptance trees of [4]. They are deterministic LTSs with some additional information.

Definition 13 (Acceptance Graph) *An* acceptance graph *(AG) is the 7-tuple* $(S, \Sigma, \delta, \hat{s}, accsets, divok, stable)$, *where*

- S *is the set of states.*
- Σ *is the alphabet.*
- δ *is a set of transitions, unlike in LTSs, it is a partial function* $S \times \Sigma \rightarrow S$.
- $\hat{s} \in S$ *is the* initial state.
- $accsets(s)$ *is an attribute of each state in* S. *Its value is a set of subsets of* Σ *such that no set is a subset of another. That is, if* $accsets(s) = \{A_1, A_2, \ldots, A_k\}$, *then* $A_i \not\subseteq A_j$ *whenever* $i \neq j$.
- $divok(s)$ *is a Boolean attribute of each state in* S.
- $stable$ *is a Boolean attribute of the entire AG.*

Because an acceptance graph is deterministic, it can be exponentially bigger than a CFFD-equivalent LTS. Acceptance graphs may thus be expensive to use.

Acceptance graphs and their construction are described in more detail in [18]. Now we will only briefly review the structure of an AG.

An acceptance graph can represent the same information as the CFFD-model of finite LTSs, namely the alphabet, stability, stable failures, and divergence traces. The main difference is that an AG contains no invisible transitions and it is deterministic.

Since the AG is deterministic, each trace σ leads to a unique state s. If $\sigma \in divtr(P)$ in the LTS representation, then the corresponding state in the AG has its $divok =$ true. The stable failures are stored as minimal acceptance sets in each state. If there are stable failures $(\sigma, R_1), (\sigma, R_2), \ldots$ associated with trace σ, then we take the maximal ones among the refusal sets $R_1, R_2, \ldots$, compute their complements in order to save space and store these complements (minimal acceptance sets) as an attribute to the AG state s reachable with trace σ. The initial stability information is stored as a separate attribute of the entire AG.

4   Checking CFFD-Preorder with Tester Processes

4.1   Use of the Tester

A *tester process* is an augmented LTS which can be used to check CFFD-preorder $P \leq_{\mathrm{CFFD}} Q$ without determinising P. Like in the previous checking method, the parts 1 and 2 of Definition 12 are checked separately. The parts 3 and 4 are checked by computing the parallel composition of the tester and the original LTS P. Any violations of the conditions 3 and 4 for CFFD-preorder can be seen as a result of this construction.

The tester is "almost" deterministic. Given any trace σ, either the tester cannot execute it at all, or the tester is in a unique state immediately after executing σ. From this state there may be zero or more τ-transitions, but their end states are stable.

In addition to the components of a normal LTS, the tester will have up to three checks in each of its states. These may be considered as Boolean values attached to the states. Each state can be marked as a *rejection state*, *deadlock rejection state* or *livelock rejection state*, or any combination of these. The values of these flags on the state s are given by the functions reject(s), DL-reject(s) and LL-reject(s). They should be observed when constructing the parallel composition of the tester and the implementation under test.

If the parallel composition ever reaches a state where the tester is in a rejection state, it is considered an error of the implementation. Similarly, if the parallel composition deadlocks when the tester is in a deadlock rejection state, or livelocks when the tester is in a livelock rejection state, then these are considered illegal behavior of the implementation.

Violations against rejection and deadlock rejection states are easy to detect on-the-fly, that is, during the construction of the parallel composition. An efficient algorithm for on-the-fly detection of also violations against livelock rejection states was described in [20]. The algorithm is based on constructing the parallel composition in a certain order, and monitoring for loops consisting solely of τ-transitions. Also the "non-progress cycle" detection algorithm of [6] can be used for the task, but [16] argues that it is usually less efficient.

4.2   Construction of the Tester

We shall present an algorithm that converts the acceptance graph of Q into a tester process $tester(Q)$. It needs the notion of the *minimal mirror collection* [2] of a collection of sets.

Definition 14 (Set mirroring) *Let* $\mathbb{A} = \{A_1, A_2, \dots, A_n\}$, *where* $A_i \subseteq \Sigma$ *when* $i = 1, \dots, n$ *be a collection of subsets of* Σ. *Define* intersect($\mathbb{A}$) $= \{ B \subseteq \Sigma \mid \forall j \in \{1, \dots, n\} : A_j \cap B \neq \emptyset \}$. *The* minimal mirror collection *of* $\mathbb{A}$ *is the set of the minimal members of* intersect($\mathbb{A}$):
$Mirror(\mathbb{A}) = \{ M \in intersect(\mathbb{A}) \mid \neg \exists M' : M' \subset M \wedge M' \in intersect(\mathbb{A}) \}$.

Notice that this definition implies $Mirror(\{a_1, a_2, \dots, a_n\}) = \{\{a_1\}, \{a_2\}, \dots, \{a_n\}\}$, $Mirror(\emptyset) = \{\emptyset\}$ and $Mirror(\{\emptyset\}) = \emptyset$. The name suggests that the mirror image of a mirror image of a collection should be the original collection. This is not true in general, but holds if no set in the original collection is a subset of another.

Algorithm 1 *Tester LTS Construction*

Input: An acceptance graph $AG(Q) = (S_Q, \Sigma_Q, \Delta_Q, \hat{s}_Q, accsets_Q, divok_Q, stable_Q)$
of LTS Q.
Create a new state s_{fail}. ; $S'_Q := S_Q \cup \{s_{\text{fail}}\}$
reject(s_{fail}) := true ; LL-reject(s_{fail}) := true ; DL-reject(s_{fail}) := true
For each state $s \in S_Q$ such that $s \neq s_{\text{fail}}$:
    reject(s) := false ; LL-reject(s) := $\neg divok(s)$
    DL-reject(s) := ($accsets_Q(s) \neq \{\emptyset\}$)
    For each $a \in \Sigma_Q$ such that $\neg(s -a \rightarrow)$:
        Create a new transition $s -a \rightarrow s_{\text{fail}}$.
    end
    $M := Mirror(accsets(s))$
    For each $A \in M$:
        Create a new state s_A. ; $S'_Q := S'_Q \cup \{s_A\}$
        Create a new transition $s -\tau \rightarrow s_A$.
        reject(s_A) := false ; DL-reject(s_A) := DL-reject(s)
        LL-reject(s_A) := LL-reject(s)
        For each $a \in A$ and $s' \in S_Q$ such that $s -a \rightarrow s'$:
            Create a new transition $s_A -a \rightarrow s'$.
            Mark the transition $s -a \rightarrow s'$ for removal.
        end
    end
    Remove marked transitions.
end
Output: $tester(Q) = (S'_Q, \Sigma_Q, \Delta_Q, \hat{s}_Q, \text{reject}, \text{DL-reject}, \text{LL-reject})$

end

Theorem 6
1. *If $A_1 \subseteq A$, then $Mirror(\{A_1, A_2, \ldots, A_k, A\}) = Mirror(\{A_1, A_2, \ldots, A_k\})$.*
2. *If no member of $\mathbb{A}$ is a subset of another, then $Mirror(Mirror(\mathbb{A})) = \mathbb{A}$.*

The proof is skipped because of lack of space.
We are now ready to present the tester construction algorithm. It is the enclosed Algorithm 1. It works by adding new states and transitions to $AG(Q)$, deleting some old transitions, and setting the reject- etc. flags of all states. These operations are guided by the *accsets*- and *divok*-attributes of $AG(Q)$.

In theory, the reject flag is not necessary. The only state where it is on, namely s_{fail}, has no output transitions. Furthermore, the tester has the same visible actions as the specification Q and the implementation P. Therefore, if $P \parallel tester(Q)$ reaches a state where $tester(Q)$ is in s_{fail}, then it can continue only with invisible actions. If it can do an infinite number of them, then it livelocks, otherwise it eventually deadlocks. Thus the reaching of s_{fail} would be detected as a violation against LL-reject(s_{fail}) or DL-reject(s_{fail}). However, the reject flag is extremely easy to implement, and it makes it possible to catch the error sooner. Early catching of errors is a virtue of on-the-fly verification.

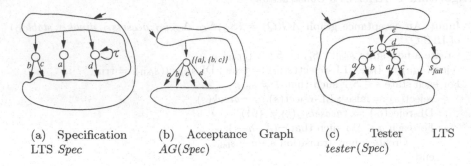

(a) Specification   (b) Acceptance Graph   (c)   Tester   LTS
LTS *Spec*   *AG(Spec)*   *tester(Spec)*

Fig. 1. Stages of the tester construction

Also the DL-reject-flags are unnecessary in theory, but helpful in practice. They could be avoided by adding the transition $s -\tau\to s$ to every original state s of $AG(Q)$ when starting to process s in the algorithm, and treating every state as a DL-reject-state. Then the parallel composition cannot deadlock in s because the tester can livelock there; it can deadlock only when the tester is in some state s_A that the algorithm added to cater for a set A in $Mirror(accsets(s))$. If the specification allows deadlocking, then $accsets(s) = \{\emptyset\}$ and $Mirror(accsets(s)) = \emptyset$, so there will be no s_A. However, letting the tester livelock would complicate the use of the LL-reject-flags, as one would then have to distinguish those livelocks that are not due to the tester. It would also cause a small increase in the size of the parallel composition LTS.

The construction of the tester may be sped up by minimizing $AG(Q)$ [18] before tester construction.

4.3 An Example Tester

The LTS *Spec* in Figure 1 contains three explicitly shown states, which represent possible states after some trace σ. All three are reachable with the same trace from the initial state somewhere in the "cloud". The alphabet of this specification is $\Sigma = \{a, b, c, d, e\}$.

In the acceptance graph fragment all three states are combined into one, since they are reachable by the same trace and different stable failures are represented by different acceptance sets in this state. Notice that the state with divergence is unstable and therefore does not generate an acceptance set of its own. However, the divergence state causes the *divok*-flag of the AG state to be set. The mirror image of these acceptance sets is $Mirror(\{\{a\}, \{b, c\}\}) = \{\{a, b\}, \{a, c\}\}$.

The tester generated from the acceptance graph shows a new "child" state and a τ-transition to it for each mirrored acceptance set. The visible transitions from the original state have been moved and possibly duplicated to begin from the child states. The transition labelled d is not a member of any acceptance set, so it has been left intact. The trace σe is illegal, so that trace leads the tester immediately to the failure state s_{fail}.

4.4 How Does the Tester Work

Consider the parallel composition of a tester with another LTS. From it one should be able to tell if any of the properties of the CFFD-preorder are violated. In fact, $sfail(P) \subseteq sfail(Q)$ and $divtr(P) \subseteq divtr(Q)$ are the only interesting properties, since the alphabet and stability are easy to check without testers, and infinite traces are relevant only if Q has infinitely many states.

Traces First of all, the parallel composition can verify $tr(P) \subseteq tr(Q)$. Due to its construction, $AG(Q)$ has the same set of traces as Q. If P has a finite trace σ_{fail} that Q cannot execute, then it has a (possibly empty) longest prefix $\sigma'_{\mathsf{fail}} \le \sigma_{\mathsf{fail}}$ which is a trace of both processes. After executing σ'_{fail}, $AG(Q)$ will be in a state where it cannot continue with the next visible action in σ_{fail}. An attempt to execute this action will lead $tester(Q)$ immediately to s_{fail}. On the other hand, because $AG(Q)$ is deterministic and $tester(Q)$ inherits its structure from $AG(Q)$, s_{fail} can be reached only by an illegal trace. Therefore, $tr(P) \not\subseteq tr(Q)$ if and only if the parallel composition will contain a transition to s_{fail}.

Divergence Traces Since $AG(Q)$ is deterministic, each of its traces uniquely determines a state, where execution ends up after that trace. The LTS Q can diverge after some trace σ iff $AG(Q)$ has its *divok*-flag set in the state s determined by σ. The tester constructed using the above algorithm has all the states of $AG(Q)$ and some more. In the tester, the trace σ leads to state s or one of its "child states" s_A added during the algorithm. In all these states the flag LL-reject has the opposite value from $divok(s)$ in $AG(Q)$.

This means that if the testee process P in the composition has a divergence after σ, and if σ is not rejected as an illegal trace, then the parallel composition will livelock after σ. If σ is in $divtr(Q)$ (legal divergence), then the LL-reject-flags in the states immediately after σ are off, so no error is declared. In the opposite case, the tester component is in a livelock rejection state, so an illegal livelock will be detected during the computation of the parallel composition.

Stable Failures We still have the check $sfail(P) \subseteq sfail(Q)$. If $(\sigma, R) \in sfail(P)$ but $\sigma \notin tr(Q)$, then σ is an illegal trace and will be detected as such. Therefore, let us from now on assume that $\sigma \in tr(Q)$ but $(\sigma, R) \notin sfail(Q)$.

Let s_P be a stable state of P that can be reached with σ and refuses all actions in R. Let $R_1, \ldots, R_n$ be the maximal refusal sets of Q after σ. Because the refusal of R is illegal, for each i, R contains an action a_i that is not present in R_i. Thus $a_i \in \Sigma - R_i$, and we can reason that each minimal acceptance set of $AG(Q)$ after σ contains an action a_i that is also in R. The mirror image of the collection of the minimal acceptance sets contains a subset A of the set of those actions, so that $A \subseteq \{a_1, \ldots, a_n\}$. The tester has a state s_A that is reachable with σ and offers precisely the actions in A as the next actions. Because s_P

refuses all of $a_1, \ldots, a_n$ and both s_P and s_A are stable, the parallel composition is in a deadlock. Because refusing of R is illegal, we see that Σ is not a refusal set of Q after σ, so the collection of minimal acceptance sets is not $\{\emptyset\}$, its mirror image is not $\emptyset$, and DL-reject(s_A) = true. Thus the deadlock is illegal, and the error is detected. We have now shown that all illegal stable failures are detected.

It remains to be proven that if the parallel composition deadlocks while the tester is in a deadlock rejection state, then P has an illegal stable failure. The deadlock state is of the form (s_P, s_Q), and is reached by some common trace σ of P and Q. The state s_Q is either s_{fail}, or one of the s_A-states added by the tester construction algorithm, or one of the original states of $AG(Q)$. If it is s_{fail}, then already σ is illegal. An original state can be a component of a deadlock state only if it has no τ-transitions to the s_A-states. This is possible only if $Mirror(accsets(s_Q)) = \emptyset$, in which case $accsets(s_Q) = \{\emptyset\}$, so DL-reject($s_Q$) = false, and no error is reported. Therefore, assume from now on that s_Q is one of the s_A-states. It corresponds to some set A in $Mirror(accsets(s_Q))$. By construction, A contains at least one action from each minimal acceptance set of Q after σ. Thus for each refusal set R_i, $1 \leq i \leq n$, of Q after σ there is $a_i \in A$ such that $a_i \notin R_i$. However, because (s_P, s_Q) is a deadlock, s_P refuses all of a_i. Thus s_P refuses $\{a_1, \ldots, a_n\}$ that is not a refusal set of s_Q.

4.5   Implementation Considerations

The tester construction algorithm is otherwise quite straightforward to implement, but it contains operations on sets of subsets of Σ. Choosing appropriate data structures is important for fast set operations. The most effective set representation in a typical computer depends on the size of Σ. For a small Σ a bit vector representation is most efficient.

Excluding the handling of the acceptance sets (the "for each $A \in M$" loop and the preceding line, which does set mirroring), the complexity of the algorithm is of the order $|\Sigma||S|$. The cost of processing the acceptance sets, and the number of the states and transitions in the constructed tester, depend greatly on the results of the acceptance set mirroring. If the average number of sets in the mirror images is high, then the resulting tester will be large.

Suppose $\Sigma = \{a_1, a_2, \ldots, a_{2n}\}$, where $a_i \neq a_j$ whenever $i \neq j$. Then some state may have the acceptance sets $\mathbb{A} = \{\{a_1, a_2\}, \{a_3, a_4\}, \ldots, \{a_{2n-1}, a_{2n}\}\}$. Because all the elements in these n sets are different, the mirror image will be $\{a_1, a_2\} \times \{a_3, a_4\} \times \cdots \times \{a_{2n-1}, a_{2n}\}$. The number of these sets is 2^n or $2^{(\frac{|\Sigma|}{2})}$. Therefore, any algorithm for computing the mirror image has a worst-case exponential run time with respect to the size of Σ.

A brute-force method for computing $Mirror(\{A_1, A_2, \ldots, A_n\})$ is to first compute the Cartesian product $A_1 \times A_2 \times \cdots \times A_n$. The result is formally a set of vectors, but these vectors can be converted into sets by dropping the duplicate elements and disregarding the order of elements. Then we only have to find the minimal ones among these sets. This can be done simply by comparing each set to all the others and removing the set if any of its proper subsets is found.

The computation of a long chain of Cartesian products can be done one product at a time. In this case the computation can be optimized by checking for minimality already at this stage, and discarding sets which have subsets in the already-computed result.

4.6 Measurements

The tester construction algorithm has been implemented as an extension to the "Advanced Reachability Analysis" verification tool set [17]. The following measurements are intended to give only a rough estimate of the time consumed by the tester construction algorithm starting from the acceptance graph. The time indicated includes inputting the acceptance graph from a file, constructing the tester and outputting the result into a file. The measurements were made on a Sun SPARCStation 5 with a 70MHz sparc CPU. The time program provided with the operating system (Solaris 2.5) was used to measure program run times. The first test case is a simple artificial example LTS, the second case is a model of the alternating bit protocol with buffers and the third test case is an incorrect version of the same protocol.

Test case		Simple	ABP	BABP
Size of Σ		5	5	13
Specification AG	Size of S	5	150	1500
	Size of Δ	7	270	3600
Tester LTS	Size of S	10	310	4100
	Size of Δ	30	750	21000
CPU time used		0.2s	1.7s	31s
Real time used		0.4s	1.9s	32s

5 Conclusions

We have developed an on-the-fly CFFD-preorder verification method which is based on tester processes. Tester processes are ordinary LTSs extended with three kinds of error detection states: reject, reject if deadlock, and reject if livelock. The implementation process is represented as an LTS or a parallel composition of several LTSs. The specification LTS is converted into a tester by determinising, mirroring of the refusal information, adding new states and τ-transitions, and declaring certain states as error detection states. Implementation errors according to $\leq_{CFFD}$ can be detected on-the-fly with an ordinary LTS parallel composition algorithm augmented with three relatively easy checks based on the local state of the tester. The check for livelocks uses an algorithm that has been published earlier, [6] or [20].

The use of testers requires computationally expensive things to be done only to the specification LTS. A software tool for computing these tester processes from specification LTSs has been implemented.

Acknowledgments

This research was funded by the National Technology Agency of Finland (Tekes) in conjunction with the RATE-project, which studies automated testing of reactive systems; and by the Academy of Finland, project "Software Verification with CFFD-Semantics".

References

1. E. Brinksma, G. Scollo, and C. Steenbergen. LOTOS specifications, their implementations and their tests. *Protocol Specification, Testing and Verification VI, IFIP 1987*, pages 349–360, 1987. 284
2. Ed Brinksma. A theory for the derivation of tests. In *Protocol Specification, Testing and Verification VIII*, pages 63–74. North-Holland, 1989. 284, 291
3. Rance Cleaveland and Matthew Hennessy. Testing equivalence as a bisimulation equivalence. *Formal Aspects of Computing*, 5(1):1–20, 1993. 284
4. M. Hennessy. Acceptance trees. *Journal of the ACM 32(4)*, pages 896–928, 1985. 290
5. C.A.R. Hoare. *Communicating Sequential Processes*. Prentice-Hall, 1985. 283, 285
6. Gerard J. Holzmann. *Design and Validation of Computer Protocols*. Prentice Hall, 1990. 291, 296
7. Roope Kaivola and Antti Valmari. The weakest compositional semantic equivalence preserving nexttime-less linear temporal logic. In *CONCUR '92: Third International Conference on Concurrency Theory*, volume 630 of *Lecture Notes in Computer Science*, pages 207–221. Springer-Verlag. 284
8. Paris C. Kanellakis and Scott A. Smolka. CCS expressions, finite state processes, and three problems of equivalence. *Information and Computation*, 86(1):43–68, May 1990. 288
9. Guy Leduc. *On the Role of Implementation Relations in the Design of Distrubuted Systems using LOTOS*. PhD thesis, Université de Liège, July 1990. 283
10. Z. Manna and A. Pnueli. *The Temporal Logic of Reactive and Concurrent Systems-Specification*. Springer-Verlag, 1992. 284
11. R. Milner. *Communication and Concurrency*. Prentice-Hall, 1989. 283
12. Ernst-Rüdiger Olderog. TCSP: Theory of communicating sequential processes. In *Petri Nets: Applications an Relationships to Other Models of Concurrency*, volume 255 of *Lecture Notes in Computer Science*, pages 441–465. Springer-Verlag, July 1986. 287
13. A. W. Roscoe. Model-checking CSP. In *A Classical Mind: Essays in Honour of C. A. R. Hoare*, pages 353–378. Prentice-Hall, 1994. 284, 285
14. A. W. Roscoe. *The Theory and Practice of Concurrency*. Prentice-Hall, 1998. 283, 284, 285
15. A. Valmari. Compositionality in state space verification methods. In *Application and Theory of Petri Nets 1996, 17th International Conference*, volume 1091, pages 29–56, 1996. 287
16. A. Valmari. The state explosion problem. In *Lectures on Petri Nets I: Basic Models*, volume 1491, pages 429–528, 1998. 284, 291

17. Antti Valmari, Jukka Kemppainen, Matthew Clegg, and Mikko Levanto. Putting advanced reachability analysis techniques together: the "ARA" tool. In *FME'93: Industrial-Strength Formal Methods*, pages 597–616. Formal Methods Europe, Springer-Verlag, April 1993. Lecture Notes in Computer Science 670. 285, 296
18. Antti Valmari and Martti Tienari. An improved failures equivalence for finite-state systems with a reduction algorithm. In *Proceedings of the IFIP WG 6.1 Eleventh International Symposium on Protocol Specification, Testing and Verification, Stockholm, Sweden*, pages 3–18. North-Holland, 1991. 283, 285, 290, 293
19. Antti Valmari and Martti Tienari. Compositional failure-based semantic models for Basic LOTOS. *Formal Aspects of Computing*, 7:440–468, 1995. 283, 285, 287, 288
20. Valmari, A. On-the-fly verification with stubborn sets. In *Proc. of the 1993 Workshop on Computer-Aided Verification*, 1993. 291, 296

Fair Bisimulation[*]

Thomas A. Henzinger[1] and Sriram K. Rajamani[2]

[1] University of California at Berkeley
tah@eecs.berkeley.edu
[2] Microsoft Research
sriram@microsoft.com

Abstract. Bisimulations enjoy numerous applications in the analysis of labeled transition systems. Many of these applications are based on two central observations: first, bisimilar systems satisfy the same branching-time properties; second, bisimilarity can be checked efficiently for finite-state systems. The local character of bisimulation, however, makes it difficult to address liveness concerns. Indeed, the definitions of fair bisimulation that have been proposed in the literature sacrifice locality, and with it, also efficient checkability. We put forward a new definition of fair bisimulation which does not suffer from this drawback.

The bisimilarity of two systems can be viewed in terms of a game played between a protagonist and an adversary. In each step of the infinite bisimulation game, the adversary chooses one system, makes a move, and the protagonist matches it with a move of the other system. Consistent with this game-based view, we call two fair transition systems bisimilar if in the bisimulation game, the infinite path produced in the first system is fair iff the infinite path produced in the second system is fair.

We show that this notion of fair bisimulation enjoys the following properties. First, fairly bisimilar systems satisfy the same formulas of the logics Fair-AFMC (the fair alternation-free μ-calculus) and Fair-CTL*. Therefore, fair bisimulations can serve as property-preserving abstractions for these logics and weaker ones, such as Fair-CTL and LTL. Indeed, Fair-AFMC provides an exact logical characterization of fair bisimilarity. Second, it can be checked in time polynomial in the number of states if two systems are fairly bisimilar. This is in stark contrast to all trace-based equivalences, which are traditionally used for addressing liveness but require exponential time for checking.

1 Introduction

In system analysis, a key question is when two systems should be considered equivalent. One way of answering this question is to consider a class of queries and to identify those systems which cannot be distinguished by any query from the considered class. Queries typically have the form "does a system satisfy

[*] This research was supported in part by the DARPA (NASA) grant NAG2-1214, the SRC contract 99-TJ-683.003, the MARCO grant 98-DT-660, the DARPA (MARCO) grant MDA972-99-1-0001, and the NSF CAREER award CCR-9501708.

S. Graf and M. Schwartzbach (Eds.): TACAS/ETAPS 2000, LNCS 1785, pp. 299–314, 2000.
© Springer-Verlag Berlin Heidelberg 2000

a requirement specified in a given logic?" If one considers finite behaviors of systems, then a useful model is the labeled transition graph, whose states or transitions are labeled with observations, and the finest reasonable equivalence on labeled transition graphs is bisimilarity [Par80,Mil89]. On one hand, no μ-calculus query, no matter how complex, can distinguish bisimilar systems. On the other hand, bisimilarity is not too fine for constructing an abstract quotient system if branching-time properties are of interest. This is because simple Hennessy-Milner queries, which correspond to the quantifier-free subset of the μ-calculus, can distinguish systems that are not bisimilar.

If one wishes to consider infinite limit behaviors also, then the labeled transition graph needs to be equipped with fairness constraints. The most common fairness constraints have either Büchi form (requiring that a transition cannot be enabled forever without being taken) or Streett form (requiring that a transition cannot be enabled infinitely often without being taken). If we can observe whether a transition is enabled or taken —that is, if the query logic can refer to these events— then bisimilarity still captures the equivalence induced by branching-time queries. However, if, as is often the case in system design, the private (i.e., unobservable) part of the system state contributes both to whether a transition is enabled and to the result of the transition, then bisimilarity is too coarse for branching-time queries. For example, if we ask whether a system has an infinite fair behavior along which some observation repeats infinitely often, then the answer may be Yes and No, respectively, for two bisimilar systems, because infinite behaviors may be identical in their observations yet different in their fairness. (One should note that one solution, albeit a nonoptimal one, is simply to define bisimilarity with respect to an extended set of observations whose new elements make fairness observable. This solution is nonoptimal as the resulting "extended-bisimilarity" relation is generally too fine: there can be systems that are not extended bisimilar, yet cannot be distinguished by queries that refer to the newly introduced observations in a restricted way, namely, only for checking if an infinite behavior is fair. An example of this is given in Section 5).

It is therefore not surprising that generalized notions of bisimilarity have been proposed which take into account fairness constraints. These notions generally have in common that they start from a query logic, such as Fair-CTL [ASB⁺94] or Fair-CTL* [GL94] (where all path quantifiers range over fair behaviors only), and define the equivalence induced by that logic: two systems are equivalent iff no query can distinguish them. Unfortunately, the resulting equivalences are unsuitable for use in automatic finite-state tools, because checking equivalence between two systems is either not known to be polynomial (for Fair-CTL based bisimilarity) or known to be PSPACE-hard (for Fair-CTL* based bisimilarity) in the combined number of states [KV96]. This is in stark contrast to the unfair case, where bisimilarity for finite-state systems can be checked efficiently [PT87,KS90,CPS93].

Borrowing ideas from earlier work on fair simulations [HKR97], we show that a fair refinement of bisimilarity can be defined which (1) corresponds to a natural query logic and (2) can be checked efficiently. Our starting point is the game-

based view of bisimilarity. The bisimilarity of two systems can be viewed in terms
of a two-player game between a protagonist and an adversary. In each step of the
game, the adversary chooses one of the systems together with a transition, and
the protagonist must match the resulting observation by a transition of the other
system. The game proceeds either until the protagonist cannot match, in which
case the adversary wins, or for an infinite number of steps, in which case the
protagonist wins. If the adversary has a winning strategy, then the two systems
are not bisimilar; if the protagonist has a winning strategy, then the systems
are bisimilar. In the presence of fairness constraints, we generalize this game
as follows. If the bisimulation game is played for a finite number of steps, then
the adversary wins as before. However, if the bisimulation game is played for an
infinite number of steps, then the winner is determined differently. If the infinite
paths traversed in the two systems are either both fair or both unfair, then the
protagonist wins; otherwise the adversary wins. In other words, the objective of
the protagonist is not only to match observations but also to match both the
satisfaction and the violation of fairness constraints.

In Section 2, we define our notion of fair bisimilarity formally and show that
it is finer than the previously proposed notions; that is, it distinguishes states
that cannot be distinguished by Fair-CTL*. The main benefit of our definition
is its efficient implementability in finite-state tools: it can be checked in time
polynomial in the combined number of states if two systems are fairly bisimilar
according to our definition. A tree-automata based algorithm is given in Section 3
together with its complexity analysis. In Section 4, we prove that two systems
with Büchi or Streett constraints are fairly bisimilar, in our sense, iff they satisfy the same formulas of Fair-AFMC (the fair alternation-free μ-calculus). It
follows that Fair-AFMC provides an exact logical characterization and a query
language for our fair bisimilarity. Finally, in Section 5, we discuss several issues
in constructing system abstractions using fair-bisimilarity quotients.

Related work. In process algebra, several preorders and equivalences on labeled transition systems have been defined to account for fairness and have been
studied from axiomatic and denotational angles [BW90,HK96]. That line of research usually considers fairness in the context of divergence (infinitely many
silent τ actions). By contrast, our model has no silent actions, and our notions
of Büchi and Streett fairness are inspired from ω automata. Also, our focus is
on efficient algorithms. In contrast, all fair preorders based on failures [BKO87]
and testing [Hen87,VEB95,NC95] are closely related to fair trace containment,
and the problems of checking them are hard for PSPACE.

2   Defining Fair Bisimilarity, Game-Theoretically

A (*Kripke*) *structure* is a 5-tuple $K = \langle \Sigma, W, \hat{w}, R, L \rangle$ with the following components:

- A finite alphabet Σ of observations. Usually, we have a finite set P of propositions and $\Sigma = 2^P$.

- A finite set W of states.
- An initial state $\hat{w} \in W$.
- A transition relation $R \subseteq W \times W$.
- A labeling function $L : W \to \Sigma$ that maps each state to an observation.

The structure K is *deterministic* if whenever $R(w, w_1)$ and $R(w, w_2)$ for $w_1 \neq w_2$, then $L(w_1) \neq L(w_2)$. For a state $w \in W$, a *w-run* of K is a finite or infinite sequence $\overline{w} = w_0 \cdot w_1 \cdot w_2 \cdots$ of states $w_i \in W$ such that $w_0 = w$ and $R(w_i, w_{i+1})$ for all $i \geq 0$. If $\overline{w} = w_0 \cdot w_1 \cdot w_2 \cdots w_n$ then $|\overline{w}|$ is n. If $\overline{w}$ is infinite, then $|\overline{w}|$ is ω. We write $\inf(\overline{w})$ for the set of states that occur infinitely often in $\overline{w}$. A *run* of K is a $\hat{w}$-run, for the initial state $\hat{w}$. Let σ be the a finite or infinite sequence.

A *fairness constraint* for K is a function that maps every infinite run of K to the binary set $\{fair, unfair\}$. We consider two kinds of fairness constraints:

- A *Büchi* constraint F is specified by a set $F_B \subseteq W$ of states. Then, for an infinite run $\overline{w}$ of K, we have $F(\overline{w}) = fair$ iff $\inf(\overline{w}) \cap F_B \neq \emptyset$. Büchi constraints can be used for specifying the weak fairness of transitions (e.g., a transition is infinitely often either taken or disabled).
- A *Streett* constraint F is specified by a set $F_S \subseteq 2^W \times 2^W$ of pairs of state sets. Then, for an infinite run $\overline{w}$ of K, we have $F(\overline{w}) = fair$ iff for every pair $\langle l, r \rangle \in F_S$, if $\inf(\overline{w}) \cap l \neq \emptyset$ then $\inf(\overline{w}) \cap r \neq \emptyset$. Streett constraints can be used for specifying the strong fairness of transitions (e.g., if a transition is infinitely often enabled, then it is infinitely often taken).

A *fair structure* $\mathcal{K} = \langle K, F \rangle$ consists of a structure K and a fairness constraint F for K. The fair structure $\mathcal{K}$ is a Büchi structure if F is a Büchi constraint, and $\mathcal{K}$ is a Streett structure if F is a Streett constraint. In particular, every Büchi structure is also a Streett structure. For a state $w \in W$, a *fair w-run* of $\mathcal{K}$ is either a finite w-run of K or an infinite w-run $\overline{w}$ of K such that $F(\overline{w}) = fair$. A fair run of $\mathcal{K}$ is a fair $\hat{w}$-run, for the initial state $\hat{w}$.

In the following, we consider two structures $K_1 = \langle \Sigma, W_1, \hat{w}_1, R_1, L_1 \rangle$ and $K_2 = \langle \Sigma, W_2, \hat{w}_2, R_2, L_2 \rangle$ over the same alphabet, and two fair structures $\mathcal{K}_1 = \langle K_1, F_1 \rangle$ and $\mathcal{K}_2 = \langle K_2, F_2 \rangle$.

Bisimulation

A binary relation $S \subseteq W_1 \times W_2$ is a *bisimulation* between K_1 and K_2 if the following three conditions hold [Par80,Mil89]:

1. If $S(w_1, w_2)$, then $L_1(w_1) = L_2(w_2)$.
2. If $S(w_1, w_2)$ and $R_1(w_1, w_1')$, then there is a state $w_2' \in W_2$ such that $R_2(w_2, w_2')$ and $S(w_1', w_2')$.
3. If $S(w_1, w_2)$ and $R_2(w_2, w_2')$, then there is a state $w_1' \in W_1$ such that $R_1(w_1, w_1')$ and $S(w_1', w_2')$.

The structures K_1 and K_2 are *bisimilar* if there is a bisimulation S between K_1 and K_2 such that $S(\hat{w}_1, \hat{w}_2)$. The problem of checking if K_1 and K_2 are bisimilar can be solved in time $O((|R_1| + |R_2|) \cdot \log(|W_1| + |W_2|))$ [PT87]. The following alternative definitions of bisimilarity are equivalent to the definition above.

The game-theoretic view. Consider a two-player game whose positions are pairs $\langle w_1, w_2 \rangle \in W_1 \times W_2$ of states. The initial position is $\langle \hat{w}_1, \hat{w}_2 \rangle$. The game is played between an adversary and a protagonist and it proceeds in a sequence of rounds. In each round, if $\langle w_1, w_2 \rangle$ is the current position, the adversary chooses a structure and makes a move that respects its transition relation. Then, the protagonist makes a matching move in the other structure. If the adversary chooses to move in K_1, and updates the first component w_1 to an R_1-successor w_1', then the protagonist must update the second component w_2 to some R_2-successor w_2' such that $L_1(w_1') = L_2(w_2')$. If no such w_2' exists, then the protagonist loses. Similarly, if the adversary chooses to move in K_2, and updates the second component w_2 to an R_2-successor w_2', then the protagonist must update the first component w_1 to some R_1-successor w_1' such that $L_1(w_1') = L_2(w_2')$. If no such w_1' exists, then the protagonist loses. If the game proceeds ad infinitum, for ω rounds, then the adversary loses. It is easy to see that K_1 and K_2 are bisimilar iff the protagonist has a winning strategy.

The temporal-logic view. Bisimilarity provides a fully abstract semantics for the branching-time logics CTL, CTL*, AFMC (the alternation-free fragment of the μ-calculus), and MC (the μ-calculus) [BCG88]. Formally, two structures K_1 and K_2 are bisimilar iff for every formula ψ of CTL (or CTL* or AFMC or MC), K_1 satisfies ψ iff K_2 satisfies ψ.

Previous Definitions of Fair Bisimulation

In the literature, we find two extensions of bisimilarity that account for fairness constraints. The two extensions are motivated by the branching-time logics Fair-CTL and Fair-CTL*, which are interpreted over fair structures with the path quantifiers being restricted to the infinite runs that are fair [CES86].

CTL-bisimulation [ASB+94]. A binary relation $S \subseteq W_1 \times W_2$ is a CTL-*bisimulation* between $\mathcal{K}_1$ and $\mathcal{K}_2$ if the following three conditions hold:

1. S is a bisimulation between K_1 and K_2.
2. If $S(w_1, w_2)$, then for every periodic fair w_1-run $\overline{w} = u_0 \cdot u_1 \cdot u_2 \cdots u_n \cdot (u_{n+1} \cdot u_{n+2} \cdots u_{n+k})^\omega$ of $\mathcal{K}_1$, there is a fair w_2-run $\overline{w}' = u_0' \cdot u_1' \cdot u_2' \cdots$ of $\mathcal{K}_2$ such that for $1 \leq i \leq n$ we have $S(u_i, u_i')$, and for $i > n$ there exists $u \in \inf(\overline{w})$ such that $S(u, u_i')$.
3. If $S(w_1, w_2)$, then for every periodic fair w_2-run $\overline{w}' = u_0' \cdot u_1' \cdot u_2' \cdots u_n' \cdot (u_{n+1}' \cdot u_{n+2}' \cdots u_{n+k}')^\omega$ of $\mathcal{K}_2$, there is a fair w_1-run $\overline{w} = u_0 \cdot u_1 \cdot u_2 \cdots$ of $\mathcal{K}_1$ such that for $1 \leq i \leq n$ we have $S(u_i, u_i')$, and for $i > n$ there exists $u' \in \inf(\overline{w}')$ such that $S(u_i, u')$.

The fair structures $\mathcal{K}_1$ and $\mathcal{K}_2$ are CTL-*bisimilar* if there is a CTL-bisimulation S between $\mathcal{K}_1$ and $\mathcal{K}_2$ such that $S(\hat{w}_1, \hat{w}_2)$. For Büchi or Streett constraints F_1 and F_2, the problem of checking if there is a CTL-bisimulation between $\mathcal{K}_1$ and

K_2 is known to be in PSPACE. No matching lower bound is known, but the best known algorithm has a time complexity exponential in the number of states. Two fair structures $\mathcal{K}_1$ and $\mathcal{K}_2$ are CTL-bisimilar iff for every formula ψ of Fair-CTL, $\mathcal{K}_1$ satisfies ψ iff $\mathcal{K}_2$ satisfies ψ [ASB+94].

CTL*-bisimulation [ASB+94,GL94]. A binary relation $S \subseteq W_1 \times W_2$ is a CTL*-*bisimulation* between $\mathcal{K}_1$ and $\mathcal{K}_2$ if the following three conditions hold:

1. If $S(w_1, w_2)$, then $L_1(w_1) = L_2(w_2)$.
2. If $S(w_1, w_2)$, then for every fair w_1-run $\overline{w} = u_0 \cdot u_1 \cdot u_2 \cdots$ of $\mathcal{K}_1$, there is a fair w_2-run $\overline{w}' = u_0' \cdot u_1' \cdot u_2' \cdots$ of $\mathcal{K}_2$ such that $\overline{w}'$ *S-matches* $\overline{w}$; that is, $|\overline{w}'| = |\overline{w}|$ and $S(u_i, u_i')$ for all $0 \le i \le |\overline{w}|$.
3. If $S(w_1, w_2)$, then for every fair w_2-run $\overline{w}' = u_0' \cdot u_1' \cdot u_2' \cdots$ of $\mathcal{K}_2$, there is a fair w_1-run $\overline{w} = u_0 \cdot u_1 \cdot u_2 \cdots$ of $\mathcal{K}_1$ such that $\overline{w}'$ *S-matches* $\overline{w}$.

Every CTL*-bisimulation between $\mathcal{K}_1$ and $\mathcal{K}_2$ is a bisimulation between K_1 and K_2. The fair structures $\mathcal{K}_1$ and $\mathcal{K}_2$ are CTL*-*bisimilar* if there is a CTL*-bisimulation S between $\mathcal{K}_1$ and $\mathcal{K}_2$ such that $S(\hat{w}_1, \hat{w}_2)$. For Büchi or Streett constraints F_1 and F_2, the problem of checking if there is a CTL*-bisimulation between $\mathcal{K}_1$ and $\mathcal{K}_2$ is complete for PSPACE. In particular, the problem is PSPACE-hard in the combined number $|W_1| + |W_2|$ of states [KV96]. Two fair structures $\mathcal{K}_1$ and $\mathcal{K}_2$ are CTL*-bisimilar iff for every formula ψ of Fair-CTL*, $\mathcal{K}_1$ satisfies ψ iff $\mathcal{K}_2$ satisfies ψ [ASB+94,GL94].

CTL*-bisimilarity is strictly stronger than CTL-bisimilarity [ASB+94]. Formally, for all fair structures $\mathcal{K}_1$ and $\mathcal{K}_2$, if $\mathcal{K}_1$ and $\mathcal{K}_2$ are CTL*-bisimilar, then $\mathcal{K}_1$ and $\mathcal{K}_2$ are CTL-bisimilar. Moreover, there are two Büchi structures $\mathcal{K}_1$ and $\mathcal{K}_2$ such that $\mathcal{K}_1$ and $\mathcal{K}_2$ are CTL-bisimilar, but $\mathcal{K}_1$ and $\mathcal{K}_2$ are not CTL*-bisimilar. This is in contrast to the unfair case, where CTL and CTL* have the same distinguishing power on Kripke structures.

Our Definition of Fair Bisimulation

Let $\mathcal{K}_1$ and $\mathcal{K}_2$ be fair structures. Recall the bisimulation game played between the adversary and the protagonist. A *strategy* τ is a pair of functions, $\tau = \langle \tau_1, \tau_2 \rangle$, where τ_1 is a partial function from $(W_1 \times W_2)^* \times W_1$ to W_2, and τ_2 is a partial function from $(W_1 \times W_2)^* \times W_2$ to W_1. The strategy is used by the protagonist to play a game against the adversary. The game proceeds as follows. The game starts at some position in $W_1 \times W_2$. If the game so far has produced the sequence $\pi \in (W_1 \times W_2)^*$ of positions, and $\langle u, u' \rangle$ is the last position in π, the adversary has two sets of choices. It can move either in K_1 or in K_2. If the adversary moves to w in K_1, such that $R_1(u, w)$, then the first component τ_1 of the strategy instructs the protagonist to move to $w' = \tau_1(\pi, w)$, where $R_2(u', w')$, thus resulting in the new position $\langle w, w' \rangle$. If the adversary moves to w' in K_2, such that $R_2(u', w')$ then the second component τ_2 of the strategy instructs the protagonist to move to $w = \tau_2(\pi, w')$, where $R_1(u, w)$, thus resulting in the new position $\langle w, w' \rangle$. A finite or infinite sequence $\overline{w}$ is an *outcome* of the strategy τ if $\overline{w}$ results from letting the adversary make an arbitrary move at each step, and making the protagonist respond using τ in each step. Formally, $\overline{w} = \langle w_0, w_0' \rangle \cdot \langle w_1, w_1' \rangle \cdots \in (W_1 \times W_2)^* \cup (W_1 \times W_2)^\omega$ is an *outcome* of the strategy τ if for all $0 \leq i < |\overline{w}|$, either (1) $w_{i+1}' = \tau_1(\langle w_0, w_0' \rangle \cdots \langle w_i, w_i' \rangle \cdot w_{i+1})$, or (2) $w_{i+1} = \tau_2(\langle w_0, w_0' \rangle \cdots \langle w_i, w_i' \rangle \cdot w_{i+1}')$.

A binary relation $S \subseteq W_1 \times W_2$ is a *fair bisimulation* between $\mathcal{K}_1$ and $\mathcal{K}_2$ if the following two conditions hold:

1. If $S(w, w')$, then $L_1(w) = L_2(w')$.
2. There exists a strategy τ such that, if $S(u, u')$, then every outcome $\overline{w} = \langle w_0, w_0' \rangle \cdot \langle w_1, w_1' \rangle \cdots$ of τ with $w_0 = u$ and $w_0' = u'$ has the following two properties: (1) for all $0 \leq i \leq |\overline{w}|$, we have $S(w_i, w_i')$, and (2) the projection $w_0 \cdot w_1 \cdots$ of $\overline{w}$ to W_1 is a fair w_0-run of $\mathcal{K}_1$ iff the projection $w_0' \cdot w_1' \cdots$ of $\overline{w}$ to W_2 is a fair w_0'-run of $\mathcal{K}_2$.

Every fair bisimulation between $\mathcal{K}_1$ and $\mathcal{K}_2$ is a bisimulation between K_1 and K_2. The fair structures $\mathcal{K}_1$ and $\mathcal{K}_2$ are *fairly bisimilar* if there is a fair bisimulation S between $\mathcal{K}_1$ and $\mathcal{K}_2$ such that $S(\hat{w}_1, \hat{w}_2)$. In Section 3 we give an efficient (polynomial in the combined number of states) algorithm to check if two fair structures are fairly bisimilar. For two fair structures $\mathcal{K}_1$ and $\mathcal{K}_2$, we show in Section 4 that $\mathcal{K}_1$ and $\mathcal{K}_2$ are fairly bisimilar iff for every formula ψ of Fair-AFMC, $\mathcal{K}_1$ satisfies ψ iff $\mathcal{K}_2$ satisfies ψ. The following propositions state that fair bisimilarity is stronger than CTL*-bisimilarity.

Proposition 1. *For all fair structures $\mathcal{K}_1$ and $\mathcal{K}_2$, if $\mathcal{K}_1$ and $\mathcal{K}_2$ are fairly bisimilar, then $\mathcal{K}_1$ and $\mathcal{K}_2$ are CTL*-bisimilar.*

Proposition 2. *There are two Büchi structures $\mathcal{K}_1$ and $\mathcal{K}_2$ such that $\mathcal{K}_1$ and $\mathcal{K}_2$ are CTL*-bisimilar, but $\mathcal{K}_1$ and $\mathcal{K}_2$ are not fairly bisimilar.*

Proof. Consider the Büchi structures $\mathcal{K}_1$ and $\mathcal{K}_2$ shown in Figure 1 (the Büchi states are marked). Consider the relation $S \subseteq W_1 \times W_2$, where $S = \{(w, w') \mid w \in W_1, w' \in W_2, \text{ and } L_1(w) = L_2(w')\}$. It can be checked that S is a CTL*-bisimulation between $\mathcal{K}_1$ and $\mathcal{K}_2$. Consider the bisimulation game starting at position $\langle s_1, t_1 \rangle$. The adversary first chooses to move in $\mathcal{K}_2$ and moves to t_2''. The protagonist can respond by moving to either s_2 or s_2'. If the protagonist moves to s_2, then the adversary switches to $\mathcal{K}_1$ and moves to s_3, forcing the protagonist to move in $\mathcal{K}_2$ to t_3''. If the protagonist moves to s_2', then the adversary switches to $\mathcal{K}_1$ and moves to s_4', forcing the protagonist to move in $\mathcal{K}_2$ to t_4''. In both cases, the game goes back to the initial state $\langle s_1, t_1 \rangle$ in the next round. By repeating this sequence ad infinitum, the adversary ensures that the run produced in $\mathcal{K}_1$ is fair, while the run produced in $\mathcal{K}_2$ is not. Thus $\mathcal{K}_1$ and $\mathcal{K}_2$ are not fairly bisimilar. $\square$

Our game-theoretic definition of fair bisimulation is inspired by the notion of fair simulation from [HKR97]. It should be noted that, as in the unfair case, fair bisimulation is stronger than mutual fair simulation. Consider again the two structures in Figure 1. Then $\mathcal{K}_1$ fairly simulates $\mathcal{K}_2$ and $\mathcal{K}_2$ fairly simulates $\mathcal{K}_1$, despite the fact that $\mathcal{K}_1$ and $\mathcal{K}_2$ are not fairly bisimilar. It should also be noted that, in the example of Figure 1, the adversary needs to switch between $\mathcal{K}_1$ and $\mathcal{K}_2$ infinitely often to win the fair-bisimulation game.

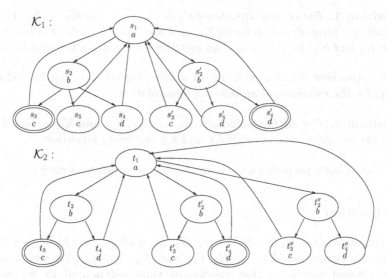

Fig. 1. Fair bisimilarity is stronger than CTL*-bisimilarity

3   Checking Fair Bisimilarity, Efficiently

We present an algorithm for checking if two fair structures are fairly bisimilar. The time complexity of our algorithm is polynomial in the combined number of states. The algorithm exploits properties of a weak version of fair bisimulation, where the game is required to start at the initial states.

Init-fair Bisimulation

A binary relation $S \subseteq W_1 \times W_2$ is an *init-fair bisimulation* between $\mathcal{K}_1$ and $\mathcal{K}_2$ if the following three conditions hold:

1. $S(\hat{w}_1, \hat{w}_2)$.
2. If $S(s, t)$, then $L_1(s) = L_2(t)$.
3. There exists a strategy τ such that every outcome $\overline{w} = \langle w_0, w_0' \rangle \cdot \langle w_1, w_1' \rangle \cdots$ of τ with $w_0 = \hat{w}_1$ and $w_0' = \hat{w}_2$ has the following two properties: (1) for all $0 \leq i \leq |\overline{w}|$, we have $S(w_i, w_i')$, and (2) the projection $w_0 \cdot w_1 \cdots$ of $\overline{w}$ to W_1 is a fair run of $\mathcal{K}_1$ iff the projection $w_0' \cdot w_1' \cdots$ of $\overline{w}$ to W_2 is a fair run of $\mathcal{K}_2$.

The fair structures $\mathcal{K}_1$ and $\mathcal{K}_2$ are *init-fairly bisimilar* if there is an init-fair bisimulation S between $\mathcal{K}_1$ and $\mathcal{K}_2$. Every fair bisimulation S between $\mathcal{K}_1$ and $\mathcal{K}_2$ with $S(\hat{w}_1, \hat{w}_2)$ is also an init-fair bisimulation between $\mathcal{K}_1$ and $\mathcal{K}_2$, but not every init-fair bisimulation is necessarily a fair bisimulation. Init-fair bisimulations are useful to us because of the following monotonicity property.

Proposition 3. *For all fair structures $\mathcal{K}_1 = \langle K_1, F_1 \rangle$ and $\mathcal{K}_2 = \langle K_2, F_2 \rangle$, if S is an init-fair bisimulation between $\mathcal{K}_1$ and $\mathcal{K}_2$, and $S' \supseteq S$ is a bisimulation between K_1 and K_2, then S' is also an init-fair bisimulation between $\mathcal{K}_1$ and $\mathcal{K}_2$.*

Moreover, checking for the existence of a fair bisimulation can be reduced to checking for the existence of an init-fair bisimulation.

Proposition 4. *For all fair structures $\mathcal{K}_1 = \langle K_1, F_1 \rangle$ and $\mathcal{K}_2 = \langle K_2, F_2 \rangle$, $\mathcal{K}_1$ and $\mathcal{K}_2$ are init-fairly bisimilar iff $\mathcal{K}_1$ and $\mathcal{K}_2$ are fairly bisimilar.*

The proofs of both propositions are similar to the simulation case [HKR97].

The Algorithm

Given two structures $K_1 = \langle \Sigma, W_1, \hat{w}_1, R_1, L_1 \rangle$ and $K_2 = \langle \Sigma, W_2, \hat{w}_2, R_2, L_2 \rangle$, and two fair structures $\mathcal{K}_1 = \langle K_1, F_1 \rangle$ and $\mathcal{K}_2 = \langle K_2, F_2 \rangle$, we present an automata-based algorithm that checks, in time polynomial in K_1 and K_2, whether there is a fair bisimulation between $\mathcal{K}_1$ and $\mathcal{K}_2$.

A *coarsest bisimulation* between K_1 and K_2 is a binary relation $\hat{S} \subseteq W_1 \times W_2$ such that (1) $\hat{S}$ is a bisimulation between K_1 and K_2, and (2) for every bisimulation S between K_1 and K_2, we have $S \subseteq \hat{S}$. The following proposition, which follows from Propositions 3 and 4, reduces the problem of checking if there is a fair bisimulation between $\mathcal{K}_1$ and $\mathcal{K}_2$ to checking if the (unique) coarsest bisimulation between K_1 and K_2 is an init-fair bisimulation between $\mathcal{K}_1$ and $\mathcal{K}_2$.

Proposition 5. *For all fair structures $\mathcal{K}_1 = \langle K_1, F_1 \rangle$ and $\mathcal{K}_2 = \langle K_2, F_2 \rangle$, if $\hat{S}$ is the coarsest bisimulation between K_1 and K_2, then $\mathcal{K}_1$ and $\mathcal{K}_2$ are fairly bisimilar iff $\hat{S}$ is an init-fair bisimulation between $\mathcal{K}_1$ and $\mathcal{K}_2$.*

The coarsest bisimulation between K_1 and K_2 can be constructed in time $O((|R_1| + |R_2|) \cdot \log(|W_1| + |W_2|))$ using the Paige-Tarjan algorithm [PT87]. Hence, we are left to find an algorithm that efficiently checks, given a relation $S \subseteq W_1 \times W_2$, if S is an init-fair bisimulation between $\mathcal{K}_1$ and $\mathcal{K}_2$. For this purpose, consider the structure $K_S = \langle \Sigma_S, W, \hat{w}, R, L \rangle$ with the following components:

- $\Sigma_S = W_1 \cup W_2$. Thus, each state of K_S is labeled by a state of K_1 or K_2.
- $W = (S \times \{\mathbf{a}\}) \cup (W_1 \times W_2 \times \{1, 2\} \times \{\mathbf{p}\})$. Thus, there are two types of states: adversary-states, in which the W_1-component is related by S to the W_2-component, and protagonist-states, which are not restricted. We regard the states of K_S as positions in a game, with the adversary moving in adversary-states and the protagonist moving in protagonist-states. Since the adversary can choose to move either in $\mathcal{K}_1$ or in $\mathcal{K}_2$, we record this choice in the protagonist states. If the third component of a protagonist state is 1 (2), then the protagonist needs to make a move in $\mathcal{K}_2$ ($\mathcal{K}_1$).
- $\hat{w} = \langle \hat{w}_1, \hat{w}_2, \mathbf{a} \rangle$. This is the initial game position.

- $R = \{(\langle w_1, w_2, \mathbf{a}\rangle, \langle w_1', w_2, 1, \mathbf{p}\rangle) \mid R_1(w_1, w_1')\} \cup \{(\langle w_1, w_2, \mathbf{a}\rangle, \langle w_1, w_2', 2, \mathbf{p}\rangle) \mid R_2(w_2, w_2')\} \cup \{(\langle w_1, w_2, 2, \mathbf{p}\rangle, \langle w_1', w_2, \mathbf{a}\rangle) \mid R_1(w_1, w_1')\} \cup \{(\langle w_1, w_2, 1, \mathbf{p}\rangle, \langle w_1, w_2', \mathbf{a}\rangle) \mid R_2(w_2, w_2')\}$. Thus, the adversary and the protagonist alternate moves. The adversary moves along transitions that correspond to transitions of either K_1 or K_2. If the adversary makes a move along a transition of K_1 (K_2), the protagonist must reply with a move along a transition of K_2 (K_1). Since adversary-states consist only of pairs in S, the protagonist must reply to each move of the adversary with a move to a state $\langle w_1, w_2, \mathbf{a}\rangle$ for which $S(w_1, w_2)$.
- We label an adversary-state by its W_1-component and we label a protagonist-state by its W_2-component: $L(\langle w_1, w_2, \mathbf{a}\rangle) = \{w_1\}$, and $L(\langle w_1, w_2, \cdot, \mathbf{p}\rangle) = \{w_2\}$.

We say that a run $\overline{w}$ of K_S satisfies a fairness constraint F if $F(L(\overline{w})) = \textit{fair}$. The protagonist wins the game on K_S if (1) whenever the game position is a protagonist-state, the protagonist can proceed with a move, and (2) whenever the game produces an infinite run of K_S, the run satisfies F_1 iff it satisfies F_2. Then, the protagonist has a winning strategy in this game iff S is an init-fair bisimulation between K_1 and K_2.

The problem of checking the existence of a winning strategy (and the synthesis of such a strategy) can be reduced to the nonemptiness problem for tree automata. We construct two tree automata:

1. The tree automaton $\mathcal{A}_S$ accepts all infinite $(W_1 \cup W_2)$-labeled trees that can be obtained by unrolling K_S and pruning it such that every adversary-state retains all its successors, and every protagonist-state retains exactly one of its successors. The intuition is that each tree accepted by $\mathcal{A}_S$ corresponds to a strategy of the protagonist. The automaton $\mathcal{A}_S$ has $O(|W_1| \cdot |W_2|)$ states, and it has a vacuous acceptance condition.
2. The tree automaton $\mathcal{A}_F$ accepts all $(W_1 \cup W_2)$-labeled trees in which all paths have the following property: F_1 is satisfied iff F_2 is satisfied. When K_1 and K_2 are Büchi structures, the automaton $\mathcal{A}_F$ can be defined as a Streett automaton with two states and two pairs in the Streett constraint. When K_1 and K_2 are Streett structures, the automaton $\mathcal{A}_F$ can be defined as a Streett automaton with $3^{(|F_1|+|F_2|)} \cdot |F_1| \cdot |F_2|$ states, and $3 \cdot (|F_1| + |F_2|)$ pairs in the Streett constraint.

The protagonist has a winning strategy iff the intersection of the Streett automata $\mathcal{A}_S$ and $\mathcal{A}_F$ is nonempty. To check this, we define and check the nonemptiness of the product automaton $\mathcal{A}_S \times \mathcal{A}_F$. Since $\mathcal{A}_S$ has a vacuous acceptance condition, the product automaton is a Streett automaton with the same number of pairs as $\mathcal{A}_F$. Finally, since checking the nonemptiness of a Streett tree automaton with n states and f pairs requires time $O(n^{(2f+1)} \cdot f!)$ [KV98], the theorem below follows.

Theorem 1. *Given two fair structures K_1 and K_2 with state sets W_1 and W_2, transition relations R_1 and R_2, and fairness constraints F_1 and F_2, we can check whether K_1 and K_2 are fairly bisimilar in time:*

- $O((|W_1| \cdot |W_2|)^5)$, *for Büchi structures.*
- $O(n^{(2f+1)} \cdot 3^{(2f^2+f)/3} \cdot f!)$, *where* $n = |W_1| \cdot |W_2| \cdot |F_1| \cdot |F_2|$ *and* $f = 3 \cdot (|F_1| + |F_2|)$, *for Streett structures.*

4   Characterizing Fair Bisimilarity, Logically

We show that fair bisimilarity characterizes precisely the distinguishing power of the fair alternation-free μ-calculus (Fair-AFMC). A formula of the μ-calculus (MC) is one of the following:

- **true, false**, p, or $\neg p$, for a proposition $p \in P$.
- y, for a propositional variable $y \in V$.
- $\varphi_1 \vee \varphi_2$ or $\varphi_1 \wedge \varphi_2$, where φ_1 and φ_2 are MC formulas.
- $\exists \bigcirc \varphi$ or $\forall \bigcirc \varphi$, where φ is a MC formula.
- $\mu y.f(y)$ or $\nu y.f(y)$, where $f(y)$ is a MC formula. All free occurrences of the variable y in $\mu y.f(y)$ and $\nu y.f(y)$ are bound by the initial fixpoint quantifier.

A MC formula is *alternation-free* if for all variables $y \in V$, there are respectively no occurrences of ν (μ) in any syntactic path from a binding occurrence μy (νy) to a corresponding bound occurrence of y. For example, the formula $\mu x.(p \vee \mu y.(x \vee \exists \bigcirc y))$ is alternation-free; the formula $\mu x.(p \vee \nu y.(x \wedge \exists \bigcirc y))$ is not. The AFMC formulas are the MC formulas that are alternation-free.

The semantics of AFMC is defined for formulas without free occurrences of variables. We interpret the closed AFMC formulas over fair structures, thus obtaining the logic Fair-AFMC. Unlike in Fair-CTL and Fair-CTL*, where the path quantifiers are restricted to fair runs, the μ-calculus does not explicitly refer to paths, and the definition of the satisfaction relation for Fair-AFMC is more involved. An AFMC formula can be thought of being evaluated by "unrolling" the fixpoint quantifiers; for example, $\nu y.f(y)$ is unrolled to $f(\nu y.f(y))$. Least-fixpoint (μ) quantifiers are unrolled a finite number of times, but greatest-fixpoint (ν) quantifiers are unrolled ad infinitum. In Fair-AFMC, we need to ensure that all ν-unrollings are fair. This is done formally using the notion of sat-trees.

The *closure* $cl(\psi)$ of a Fair-AFMC formula ψ is the least set of formulas that satisfies the following conditions:

- **true** $\in cl(\psi)$ and **false** $\in cl(\psi)$.
- $\psi \in cl(\psi)$.
- If $\varphi_1 \wedge \varphi_2$ or $\varphi_1 \vee \varphi_2$ is in $cl(\psi)$, then $\varphi_1 \in cl(\psi)$ and $\varphi_2 \in cl(\psi)$.
- If $\exists \bigcirc \varphi$ or $\forall \bigcirc \varphi$ is in $cl(\psi)$, then $\varphi \in cl(\psi)$.
- If $\mu y.f(y) \in cl(\psi)$, then $f(\mu y.f(y)) \in cl(\psi)$.
- If $\nu y.f(y) \in cl(\psi)$, then $f(\nu y.f(y)) \in cl(\psi)$.

Each Fair-AFMC formula ψ specifies a set of "obligations" — a subset of formulas in $cl(\psi)$ — that need to be satisfied. The witness to the satisfaction of a formula is a tree called a sat-tree.

We first define labeled trees formally. A (finite or infinite) *tree* is a set $t \subseteq \mathbb{N}^*$ such that if $xn \in t$, for $x \in \mathbb{N}^*$ and $n \in \mathbb{N}$, then $x \in t$ and $xm \in t$ for all $0 \le m < n$. The elements of t represent nodes: the empty word ϵ is the root of t, and for each node x, the nodes of the form xn, for $n \in \mathbb{N}$, are the children of x. The number of children of the node x is denoted by $deg(x)$. A *path* ρ of t is a finite or infinite set $\rho \subseteq t$ of nodes that satisfies the following three conditions: (1) $\epsilon \in \rho$, (2) for each node $x \in \rho$, there exists at most one $n \in \mathbb{N}$ with $xn \in \rho$, and (3) if $xn \in \rho$, then $x \in \rho$. Given a set A, an *A-labeled tree* is a pair $\langle t, \lambda \rangle$, where t is a tree and $\lambda : t \to A$ is a labeling function that maps each node of t to an element in A. Then, every path $\rho = \{\epsilon, n_0, n_0 n_1, n_0 n_1 n_2, \ldots\}$ of t generates a sequence $\lambda(\rho) = \lambda(\epsilon) \cdot \lambda(n_0) \cdot \lambda(n_0 n_1) \cdots$ of elements in A.

Given a fair structure $\mathcal{K} = \langle K, F \rangle$ with $K = \langle \Sigma, W, w, R, L \rangle$, and a Fair-AFMC formula ψ, a *sat-tree* $\langle t, \lambda \rangle$ of $\mathcal{K}$ for ψ is a $(W \times cl(\psi))$-labeled tree $\langle t, \lambda \rangle$ that satisfies the following conditions:

- $\lambda(\epsilon) = \langle \hat{w}, \psi \rangle$. Thus, the root of the tree, which corresponds to the initial obligation, is labeled by the initial state of K and ψ itself.
- If $\lambda(x) = \langle w, \mathbf{false} \rangle$ or $\lambda(x) = \langle w, \mathbf{true} \rangle$, then $deg(x) = 0$.
- If $\lambda(x) = \langle w, p \rangle$, where $p \in P$, then $deg(x) = 1$. If $p \in L(w)$, then $\lambda(x0) = \langle w, \mathbf{true} \rangle$; otherwise $\lambda(x0) = \langle w, \mathbf{false} \rangle$.
- If $\lambda(x) = \langle w, \neg p \rangle$, where $p \in P$, then $deg(x) = 1$. If $p \in L(w)$, then $\lambda(x0) = \langle w, \mathbf{false} \rangle$; otherwise $\lambda(x0) = \langle w, \mathbf{true} \rangle$.
- If $\lambda(x) = \langle w, \varphi_1 \vee \varphi_2 \rangle$, then $deg(x) = 1$ and $\lambda(x0) \in \{\langle w, \varphi_1 \rangle, \langle w, \varphi_2 \rangle\}$.
- If $\lambda(x) = \langle w, \varphi_1 \wedge \varphi_2 \rangle$, then $deg(x) = 2$, $\lambda(x0) = \langle w, \varphi_1 \rangle$, and $\lambda(x1) = \langle w, \varphi_2 \rangle$.
- If $\lambda(x) = \langle w, \exists \bigcirc \varphi \rangle$, then $deg(x) = 1$ and $\lambda(x0) \in \{\langle w', \varphi \rangle \mid R(w, w')\}$.
- If $\lambda(x) = \langle w, \forall \bigcirc \varphi \rangle$, and $\{w_0, w_1, \ldots, w_n\}$ are the successors of w in K, in some arbitrary (but fixed) order, then $deg(x) = n+1$, and for $0 \le i \le n$, we have $\lambda(xi) = \langle w_i, \varphi \rangle$.
- If $\lambda(x) = \langle w, \nu y. f(y) \rangle$, then $deg(x) = 1$ and $\lambda(x0) = \langle w, f(\nu y. f(y)) \rangle$.
- If $\lambda(x) = \langle w, \mu y. f(y) \rangle$, then $deg(x) = 1$ and $\lambda(x0) = \langle w, f(\mu y. f(y)) \rangle$.

Consider a sat-tree $\langle t, \lambda \rangle$ of $\mathcal{K}$ for ψ. If $\langle t, \lambda \rangle$ contains no node labeled $\langle w, \mathbf{false} \rangle$, then it provides a witness to the satisfaction of all local obligations induced by ψ. In addition, we have to make sure that least-fixpoint obligations are not propagated forever, and that greatest-fixpoint obligations are satisfied along fair runs of $\mathcal{K}$. Formally, the sat-tree $\langle t, \lambda \rangle$ of $\mathcal{K}$ for ψ is *convincing* if the following three conditions hold:

1. The sat-tree $\langle t, \lambda \rangle$ contains no node labeled $\langle w, \mathbf{false} \rangle$. Thus, all local obligations induced by ψ are satisfied.
2. For all infinite paths ρ of $\langle t, \lambda \rangle$, the projection of $\lambda(\rho)$ on the $cl(\psi)$-component contains only finitely many occurrences of formulas of the form $\mu y. f(y)$. Thus, no least-fixpoint obligation is propagated forever.
3. For all infinite paths ρ of $\langle t, \lambda \rangle$, the projection of $\lambda(\rho)$ on the W-component satisfies the fairness constraint F of $\mathcal{K}$.

The fair structure $\mathcal{K}$ *satisfies* the Fair-AFMC formula ψ if there is a convincing sat-tree $\langle t, \lambda \rangle$ of $\mathcal{K}$ for ψ.

If $\mathcal{K}_1$ and $\mathcal{K}_2$ are not fairly bisimilar, we can construct a Fair-AFMC formula ψ such that $\mathcal{K}_1$ satisfies ψ and $\mathcal{K}_2$ does not satisfy ψ. Consider the structures from Figure 1. The formula $\nu z.\forall \bigcirc \ (\exists \bigcirc \ (c \wedge \exists \bigcirc \ z) \vee \exists \bigcirc \ (d \wedge \exists \bigcirc \ z))$ is satisfied in $\mathcal{K}_1$ and not satisfied in $\mathcal{K}_2$. Conversely, if $\mathcal{K}_1$ and $\mathcal{K}_2$ are bisimilar, and $\mathcal{K}_1$ satisifes a Fair-AFMC formula ψ, we can use the convincing sat-tree of $\mathcal{K}_1$ for ψ and the winning strategy of the bisimulation game, to construct a convincing sat-tree of $\mathcal{K}_2$ for ψ.

Theorem 2. *For all fair structures $\mathcal{K}_1$ and $\mathcal{K}_2$, the following two statements are equivalent:*

1. *$\mathcal{K}_1$ and $\mathcal{K}_2$ are fairly bisimilar.*
2. *For every formula ψ of Fair-AFMC, $\mathcal{K}_1$ satisfies ψ iff $\mathcal{K}_2$ satisfies ψ.*

It is an open problem if the full μ-calculus over fair structures (Fair-MC) can be defined in a meaningful way, and to characterize its distinguishing power. In particular, condition 2 in the definition of convincing sat-trees for Fair-AFMC is no longer appropriate in the presence of alternating fixpoint quantifiers.

5   Discussion

An important topic that we have not addressed in this paper is the construction of fair abstractions. Here, we discuss some issues and difficulties in doing this. Let $K = \langle \Sigma, W, \hat{w}, R, L \rangle$ be a structure. Let $E \subseteq W \times W$ be an equivalence relation that is *observation-preserving*, i.e., if $E(s, t)$, then $L(s) = L(t)$. We define the *quotient* of K with respect to E, denoted $K/_E = \langle \Sigma, W', \hat{w}', R', L' \rangle$, as follows:

- The state set is $W' = W/_E$, the set of equivalence classes of W with respect to E. We denote the equivalence class of state $w \in W$ by $[w]_E$.
- The initial state is $\hat{w}' = [\hat{w}]_E$.
- The transition relation is $R' = \{([w]_E, [w']_E) \mid R(w, w')\}$.
- The labeling function L' is given by $L'([w]_E) = L(w)$. Note that L' is well-defined, because E is observation-preserving.

If S is the coarsest bisimulation between K and K, then $K/_S$ is called the *bisimilarity quotient* of K. It is not difficult to check that K and $K/_S$ are bisimilar, and that $K/_S$ is the smallest structure that is bisimilar to K. Since the construction of $K/_S$ is efficient, it may be a useful preprocessing step for model checking CTL, CTL*, and the μ-calculus.

Let $\mathcal{K} = \langle K, F \rangle$ be a fair structure. We are interested in finding a fair structure $\mathcal{K}'$ which (1) is fairly bisimilar to $\mathcal{K}$, and (2) has fewer states than $\mathcal{K}$. Such a $\mathcal{K}'$ is an abstraction of $\mathcal{K}$ which preserves all Fair-AFMC properties, and by Proposition 1, also all Fair-CTL* properties. If the construction of $\mathcal{K}'$ is efficient, then it may be a useful preprocessing step for Fair-AFMC and Fair-CTL* model

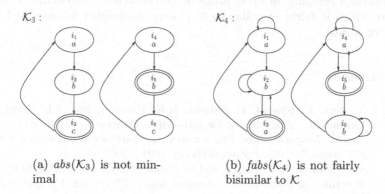

(a) $abs(\mathcal{K}_3)$ is not minimal

(b) $fabs(\mathcal{K}_4)$ is not fairly
bisimilar to $\mathcal{K}$

Fig. 2. Constructing minimal fairly bisimilar abstractions

checking. We present two attempts at defining $\mathcal{K}'$ and point out why neither attempt is satisfactory.

The first attempt makes the fair states observable before constructing a minimal quotient. This attempt produces a fairly bisimilar abstraction, but not necessarily a minimal one. Define the binary relation $H \subseteq W \times W$ such that $H(w, w')$ iff (1) $L(w) = L(w')$, and (2) the fairness constraint F treats w and w' identically (i.e, if F is a Büchi constraint, then $w \in F$ iff $w' \in F$; if F is a Streett constraint, then for every Streett pair $\langle l, r \rangle$, we have $w \in l$ iff $w' \in l$, and $w \in r$ iff $w' \in r$). Clearly, H is an equivalence relation. Let $\hat{H} \subseteq W \times W$ be the coarsest bisimulation between $\mathcal{K}$ and $\mathcal{K}$ that refines H. Let $abs(K) = \langle K/_{\hat{H}}, F' \rangle$, where F' is obtained by lifting the fairness constraint F to $K/_{\hat{H}}$. Formally, given a set $A \subseteq W$ of states, define $\alpha(A) = \{[w]_{\hat{H}} \mid [w]_{\hat{H}} \cap A \neq \emptyset\}$. If F is a Büchi constraint, let $F' = \alpha(F)$; if F is a Streett constraint, let $F' = \{\langle \alpha(l), \alpha(r) \rangle \mid \langle l, r \rangle \in F\}$. It can be checked that $\mathcal{K}$ and $abs(K)$ are fairly bisimilar. However, $abs(K)$ is, in general, not the minimal fair structure which is fairly bisimilar to $\mathcal{K}$. For example, consider the Büchi structure $\mathcal{K}_3$ of Figure 2(a). In this example, $abs(K_3)$ is isomorphic to $\mathcal{K}_3$. But we can merge the states i_1 and i_4 to produce a fairly bisimilar abstraction which has only 5 states, and thus is smaller.

The second attempt constructs a minimal fair quotient, which is then equipped with a fairness constraint. However, there are cases where the straightforward way of equipping the fair quotient with a fairness constraint does not result in a fairly bisimilar system. Let $S \subseteq W \times W$ be the coarsest fair bisimulation between $\mathcal{K}$ and $\mathcal{K}$. Define the relation $J \subseteq W \times W$ such that $J(w, w')$ iff (1) $S(w, w')$, and (2) the fairness constraint F treats w and w' identically. Clearly, J is an equivalence relation. Let $fabs(\mathcal{K}) = \langle K/_J, F' \rangle$, where F' is obtained by lifting the fairness constraint F to $K/_J$. Returning to the structure $\mathcal{K}_3$ of Figure 2(a), we find that $fabs(\mathcal{K}_3)$ indeed merges i_1 and i_4 and produces a fairly bisimilar abstraction with 5 states. However, for the Büchi structure $\mathcal{K}_4$ of Figure 2(b), $fabs(\mathcal{K}_4)$ and $\mathcal{K}_4$ are not fairly bisimilar.

It therefore remains an open problem to construct, in general, a minimal structure which is fairly bisimilar to $\mathcal{K}$ (where minimality is measured in the number of states).

References

ASB⁺94.   A. Aziz, V. Singhal, F. Balarin, R.K. Brayton, and A.L. Sangiovanni-Vincentelli. Equivalences for fair kripke structures. In *ICALP 94: Automata, Languages, and Programming*, Lecture Notes in Computer Science 820, pages 364–375. Springer-Verlag, 1994. 300, 303, 304

BCG88.   M.C. Browne, E.M. Clarke, and O. Grumberg. Characterizing finite Kripke structures in propositional temporal logic. *Theoretical Computer Science*, 59:115–131, 1988. 303

BKO87.   J.A. Bergstra, J.W. Klop, and E.R. Olderog. Failures without chaos: a new process semantics for fair abstraction. In *Formal Description Techniques III*, pages 77–103. Elsevier, 1987. 301

BW90.   J.C.M. Baeten and W.P. Weijland. *Process Algebra*. Cambridge University Press, 1990. 301

CES86.   E.M. Clarke, E.A. Emerson, and A.P. Sistla. Automatic verification of finite-state concurrent systems using temporal-logic specifications. *ACM Transactions on Programming Languages and Systems*, 8(2):244–263, 1986. 303

CPS93.   R.J. Cleaveland, J. Parrow, and B. Steffen. The Concurrency Workbench: a semantics-based tool for the verification of finite-state systems. *ACM Transactions on Programming Languages and Systems*, 15(1):36–72, 1993. 300

VEB95.   W. Vogler, E. Brinksma, and A. Rensink. Fair testing. In *CONCUR 95: Theories of Concurrency*, Lecture Notes in Computer Science 962, pages 313–327. Springer-Verlag, July 1995. 301

GL94.   O. Grumberg and D.E. Long. Model checking and modular verification. *ACM Transactions on Programming Languages and Systems*, 16(3):843–871, 1994. 300, 304

Hen87.   M.C.B. Hennessy. An algebraic theory of fair asynchronous communicating processes. *Theretical Computer Science*, 49:121–143, 1987. 301

HK96.   M. Huth and M. Kwiatkowska. The semantics for fair recursion with divergence. Technical Report CSR-96-4, University of Birmingham, 1996. 301

HKR97.   T.A. Henzinger, O. Kupferman, and S. K. Rajamani. Fair simulation. In *CONCUR 97: Theories of Concurrency*, Lecture Notes in Computer Science 1243, pages 273–287. Springer-Verlag, July 1997. 300, 305, 307

KS90.   P.C. Kanellakis and S.A. Smolka. CCS expressions, finite-state processes, and three problems of equivalence. *Information and Computation*, 86:43–68, 1990. 300

KV96.   O. Kupferman and M.Y. Vardi. Verification of fair transition systems. In *CAV 96: Computer Aided Verification*, Lecture Notes in Computer Science 1102, pages 372–381. Springer-Verlag, 1996. 300, 304

KV98.   O. Kupferman and M.Y. Vardi. Weak alternating automata and tree automata emptiness. In *Proceedings of the 30th ACM Symposium on Theory of Computing*, pages 224–233. ACM Press, 1998. 308

314   Thomas A. Henzinger and Sriram K. Rajamani

Mil89.   R. Milner. *Communication and Concurrency*. Prentice-Hall, 1989. 300, 302

NC95.   V. Natarajan and R. Cleaveland. Divergence and fair testing. In *ICALP 95: Automata, Languages, and Programming*, Lecture Notes in Computer Science 944, pages 648–659. Springer-Verlag, 1995. 301

Par80.   D.M.R. Park. *Concurrency and Automata on Infinite Sequences*. Lecture Notes in Computer Science 104. Springer-Verlag, 1980. 300, 302

PT87.   R. Paige and R.E. Tarjan. Three partition-refinement algorithms. *SIAM Journal of Computing*, 16(6):973–989, 1987. 300, 303, 307

Integrating Low Level Symmetries into Reachability Analysis

Karsten Schmidt

Institut für Informatik, Humboldt–Universität zu Berlin
10099 Berlin, Germany
kschmidt@informatik.hu-berlin.de

Abstract. We present three methods for the integration of symmetries into reachability analysis. Two of them lead to maximal reduction but their runtime depends on the symmetry structure. The third one works always fast but does not always yield maximal reduction.

Keywords: symmetries, automorphisms, reachability analysis

1 Introduction

Symmetric structure yields symmetric behavior. Thus, symmetries can be employed to reduce the size of reachability graphs for analyzing particular properties [HJJJ84,Sta91,ID96] or for model checking [ES96,CEFJ96]. Instead of storing all states, only (representatives of) equivalence classes of states are stored. There are two major problems that need to be solved in the context of symmetries. Before starting reachability graph generation, we need to investigate the symmetries of the system. During graph generation, we need to decide repeatedly whether for a (recently generated) state an equivalent one has been explored earlier.

In the context of *high level Petri nets* or structured programming languages, we can use operations and relations on the data domains or replicated components to describe the symmetries symbolically [HJJJ84,Jen92]. Then the user can provide the description of the symmetries together with the system using terms (such as data operations) of the structured language. For instance, having the integer numbers as data type, one can map a state where a certain variable has value i to a state where that variable has value $i + 1$. For some classes of high level nets or other system descriptions, a symbolic description of a set of symmetries can be deduced automatically [CDFH90,Jun98,ID96], though this approach seems to be rather sensitive to the syntax used for system descriptions. Furthermore it is sometimes necessary to model the system very carefully to make the symmetries visible to the deduction tool [Chi98,CFG94]. For the decision of equivalence between states, one uses the symmetries to transform the current state into an equivalent one which is minimal with respect to some, say lexicographical, order. The transformed state is called *canonical representative*, is unique, and is used to represent its equivalence class. Currently, this approach is

S. Graf and M. Schwartzbach (Eds.): TACAS/ETAPS 2000, LNCS 1785, pp. 315–330, 2000.

more or less restricted to symmetry groups that can be composed of full permutation groups and rotation groups over the involved data domains. As an efficient alternative, non–unique representatives have been proposed in [CEFJ96,ID96] which potentially lead to a larger graph and some problems for reachability tests on the reduced graph.

Using low level symmetries [Sta91][1] arbitrary symmetry groups can be handled in a uniform manner as graph automorphisms of the Petri net graph representation. There is no straightforward symbolic description of low level symmetries. Thus, calculation is the only way to get the information about symmetries. However, the algorithm proposed in [Sch97] and implemented in INA [RS97] is able to calculate polynomially large generating sets of (in worst case exponentially large) maximal symmetry groups in reasonable space and time. For instance, the symmetry group calculation for a net with 10000 vertices requires usually less than 5 minutes. For nets of that size, reachability analysis is faced with a lot of other challenges than symmetry calculation.

This paper surveys three solutions of the problem of using low level symmetries in reduced graph generation and reports experimental results.

With the present low level symmetry technology, we fill the following gaps left by the symbolic high level calculus:

- We can deal with systems where a structured representation is not available (for instance, translations from other formalisms into low level nets);
- We offer a fully automated approach to high level (structured) systems with small or medium size data domains (prototypes of larger systems) independently of the net inscription syntax;
- We can handle small or medium size systems having non–standard symmetry groups

2   Petri Nets

For the purpose of simplicity (in particular due to the immediate correspondence between net symmetries and graph automorphisms) , we present the approach for place/transition nets. However, it should not be difficult to transfer the results to other formalisms, whether Petri net based or not.

Definition 1 (Petri net). *A tuple* $N = [P, T, F, W, m_0]$ *is a Petri net iff* P *and* T *are finite, nonempty, and disjoint sets (of places and transitions),* $F \subseteq (P \times T) \cup (T \times P)$ *(the set of arcs),* $W : (P \times T) \cup (T \times P) \longrightarrow \mathbb{N}$ *such that* $W([x, y]) > 0$ *iff* $[x, y] \in F$ *(the arc multiplicities), and* m_0 *is a state, i.e. a mapping* $m_0 : P \longrightarrow \mathbb{N}$.

---

[1] throughout the paper, we use the term *low level* for the symmetry approach to place/transition nets, i.e. Petri nets with unstructured, uniform tokens. In contrast, high level symmetries rely on the ability to use data specific terms for symbolic description of symmetries.

Throughout the paper, we assume that places and transitions are totally ordered.

For a place or transition x, $\bullet x = \{y \mid [y, x] \in F\}$ denotes the *pre–set* of x, and $x^\bullet = \{y \mid [x, y] \in F\}$ denotes its *post–set*.

Definition 2 (Transition relation). *We say that t can fire at a state m yielding state m' (written: $m@ > t >> m'$) iff for all $p \in P$, $m(p) \geq W([p, t])$ and $m'(p) = m(p) - W([p, t]) + W([t, p])$.*

If, for a given state m and transition t there exists a state m' such that $m@ > t >> m'$, then we say that t is enabled at m. We extend the transition relation to sequences of transitions. Define $m@ > e >> m$ for an arbitrary m and the empty sequence e, and $m@ > wt >> m'$ (w being a transition sequence and t a transition) iff there is an m^* such that $m@ > w >> m^*$ and $m^*@ > t >> m'$. If there is a transition sequence w such that $m@ > w >> m'$, we write $m@ > * >> m'$.

Definition 3 (Reachability graph). *A directed labeled graph is the reachability graph of a Petri net $N = [P, T, F, W, m_0]$ iff its set of vertices is the set of all reachable states, i.e. $\{m \mid m_0@ > * >> m\}$, and $[m, m']$ is an edge labeled with t iff $m@ > t >> m'$.*

3   Graph Automorphisms

Consider a directed graph $[V, E]$ (with a finite set V of vertices and a set $E \subseteq V \times V$ of edges) together with a mapping $\phi : V \cup E \longrightarrow C$ that assigns a *color* of a set C to every graph element.

Definition 4 (Graph automorphism). *A graph automorphism is a bijection $\sigma : V \to V$ of the vertices of a directed colored graph that respects adjacency and coloring, i.e.*

- *$e = [x, y] \in E$ iff $\sigma(e) = [\sigma(x), \sigma(y)] \in E$;*
- *$\phi(\sigma(z)) = \phi(z)$ for $z \in V \cup E$.*

The set of all automorphisms of a graph forms a group under composition and inversion. The identity is always an automorphism and serves as neutral element of the group. For the remainder of this section, consider an arbitrary graph and its automorphism group. There can be exponentially many automorphisms. However, there is always a generating set of at most $\frac{|V| \cdot (|V| - 1)}{2}$ elements for the whole automorphism group. In the sequel we consider a rather well formed generating set that enjoys a regular structure though it is not necessarily of minimal size. The algorithm proposed in [Sch97] returns a generating set as described below. Assume a total ordering of V, i.e. $V = \{v_1, \ldots, v_n\}$. A well formed generating set G for all graph automorphisms consists of $|V|$ families $G_1, \ldots, G_{|V|}$. If, for $i \in \{1, \ldots, |V|\}$ and $j \in \{i, \ldots, |V|\}$, there exist automorphisms σ such that $\sigma(v_1) = v_1, \ldots, \sigma(v_{i-1}) = v_{i-1}$ and $\sigma(v_i) = v_j$ then family G_i contains exactly one of them. In other words, the elements of family G_i are equal to the identity on all vertices smaller than v_i and cover all possible images of v_i.

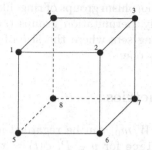

Fig. 1. 3 dimensional grid

Example 1. Consider the graph depicted in Fig. 1. Every drawn line between two vertices x and y corresponds to a pair $[x, y]$ and $[y, x]$ of edges. Table 1 lists a generating set for the 48 graph automorphisms that fits to the rules above. The generating set is not minimal. For instance, $\sigma_2 = \sigma_1 \circ \sigma_1$.

Table 1. Generating set of the grid automorphisms

Argument	Images												
	Family 1								Family 2			Family 3	
1	**1**	**2**	**3**	**4**	**5**	**6**	**7**	**8**	1	1	1	1	1
2	2	3	4	1	1	5	8	7	**2**	4	5	2	2
3	3	4	1	2	4	8	5	6	3	8	6	**3**	**6**
4	4	1	2	3	8	7	6	5	4	5	2	4	5
5	5	6	7	8	6	2	3	4	5	2	4	5	4
6	6	7	8	5	2	1	4	3	6	3	8	6	3
7	7	8	5	6	3	4	1	2	7	7	7	7	7
8	8	5	6	7	7	3	2	1	8	6	3	8	8
	id	σ_1	σ_2	σ_3	σ_4	σ_5	σ_6	σ_7	id	σ_8	σ_9	id	σ_{10}

Proposition 1 (Generating set). *Every set of automorphisms that fits to the rules described above is a generating set for all automorphisms. In particular, every automorphism can be represented as the composition $\sigma_1 \circ \cdots \circ \sigma_{|V|}$ where σ_i belongs to family G_i of the generating set.*

Proposition 2 (Non–repetition). *If for all i, σ_i and τ_i are members of family G_i of a generating set as described above, then $\sigma_1 \circ \cdots \circ \sigma_n = \tau_1 \circ \cdots \circ \tau_n$ implies $\sigma_1 = \tau_1, \ldots, \sigma_n = \tau_n$.*

These two propositions state that every automorphism can be generated in exactly one way as the composition of one member per family of the generating set. As a corollary, the product of the sizes of the families yields the size of the automorphism group. For instance, our grid has $8 \cdot 3 \cdot 2 = 48$ automorphisms.

Rotation groups (automorphism groups of ring–like graphs) have a generating set consisting of one family, permutation groups (symmetry groups of clique–like graphs) have generating sets where the size of subsequent families of the generating set decreases by one.

4 Petri Net Symmetries

A Petri net $N = [P, T, F, W, m_0]$ can be regarded as colored graph with $V = P \cup T$, $E = F$, $\phi(p) = \texttt{place}$ for $p \in P$, $\phi(t) = \texttt{transition}$ for $t \in T$, and $\phi(f) = W(f)$ for $f \in F$.

Definition 5 (Symmetry). *A Petri net symmetry is an automorphism of the underlying colored graph.*

We denote the symmetry group of a Petri net by Σ. A symmetry group Σ induces equivalence relations on the Petri net vertices as well as on the states.

Definition 6 (Equivalence of vertices/states). *Two vertices x and y in $P \cup T$ are equivalent with respect to Σ ($x \sim_\Sigma y$) iff there is a $\sigma \in \Sigma$ such that $\sigma(x) = y$. For a state m, let $\sigma(m)$ be the state satisfying, for all $x \in P \cup T$, $\sigma(m)(\sigma(x)) = m(x)$. A state m_1 is equivalent to a state m_2 with respect to Σ ($m_1 \sim_\Sigma m_2$) iff there is a $\sigma \in \Sigma$ such that $\sigma(m_1) = m_2$.*

$\sim_\Sigma$ is an equivalence relation. We denote the $\sim_\Sigma$ equivalence class containing some state m by $[m]_\Sigma$.

5 The Integration Problem

During generation of the reduced reachability graph, we want to merge equivalent states. As soon as a new state m is generated, we compare it against the set of already existing states M. If, among those states, there is one equivalent to m, we do not store m. Instead, we redirect all arcs to m to the equivalent state. Thus, the problem we are confronted with (and which we call the integration problem) is:

> *Given a symmetry group Σ, a set M of states, and a state m, decide whether there exist an $m' \in M$ and a $\sigma \in \Sigma$ such that $\sigma(m) = m'$; in the case that such an m' exists, return m'.*

Here, Σ is given by a well formed generating set. M is the set of already calculated states and is usually organized as a search structure (tree, hash table or whatsoever).

We study three approaches to the integration problem. The first two procedures implement one of the existential quantifiers appearing in the integration problem as a loop. The third method implements the canonical representative method to low level Petri nets.

6 Iterating the Symmetries

The integration problem quantifies a symmetry existentially. If we implement this quantification as a loop on all symmetries, we obtain the following brute force solution:

FOR ALL $\sigma \in \Sigma$ **DO**
    IF $\sigma^{-1}(m) \in M$ **THEN**
        RETURN yes;
    END;
END;
RETURN no;

The test $\sigma^{-1}(m) \in R$ is a standard operation on sets of states and can be efficiently implemented. So the costs of the procedure depend on the number of iterations of the outer loop which is, in the worst case (the case where m is not in M), equal to the size of the symmetry group. Due to the up to exponential size of symmetry groups, this approach does not work well. However, using decision trees for storing the states in M enables a nice reduction concerning the number of loops.

A decision tree treats states as strings and merges common prefixes. Fig. 2 depicts a decision tree storing the set $\{(1,0,0),(1,0,1),(1,2,2),(1,3,1)\}$.

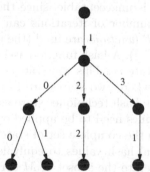

If we find $\sigma^{-1}(m)$ in the decision tree, we exit the loop. Otherwise, there is some prefix of $\sigma^{-1}(m)$ that is not contained in the tree and the length i of this prefix is available through the search process. This means that any other state with the same prefix is not contained in M as well. However, the σ^{-1}–image of m on the first i places is determined by the generators of the first i families of the generating set. That is, every symmetry that is composed of the same elements of the first i families as σ, but different elements of the last $|P| - i$ families of the generating set,

Fig. 2. Decision tree

yields the same i–prefix as $\sigma^{-1}(m)$ and is consequently not contained in M. Using this observation, we can skip all such combinations of generators and continue with one where at least one of the first i ones is different. This method reduces significantly the number of iterations of the outer loop in the above code fragment.

Having implemented this iteration, we found out that the loop reduction was powerful enough to make reduced graph generation faster than complete iteration even if complete iteration runs on an explicitly stored list of *all* symmetries (i.e. re–initialization of the loop is just a jump to the next list element instead of composing a symmetry from generators). The current version of INA uses the generating set and the described loop reduction. Older versions of INA maintain an explicit list of all symmetries. The algorithm works quite well if the symmetry group is sparse. Unfortunately, larger symmetry groups require still too many iterations of the symmetry loop and graph generation tends to fail. Therefore, we need other integration technologies.

7   Iterating the States

In this section, we develop another solution of the integration problem where the outer loop iterates on states. The principal solution is:

FOR ALL $m' \in M$ **DO**
   IF $\exists \sigma : \sigma(m) = m'$ **THEN**
      RETURN yes;
   END;
END;
RETURN no;

For the test $\exists \sigma : \sigma(m) = m'$ we do not need to iterate the symmetries. The algorithm in [Sch97], otherwise used to compute the generating set, can as well be customized such that it computes a symmetry mapping m to m' (or recognize that such a symmetry does not exist).

Of course, iterating all states in the outer loop is unacceptable, since there are usually too many of them. Fortunately, the number of iterations can be reduced significantly when *symmetry respecting hash functions* are used (the use of hash functions has already been studied in [HJJJ84]). A hash function assigns an index $h(m)$ from a finite index set I to every state m. This way, the set of states M can be partitioned into $card(I)$ classes where two states are in the same class iff they have the same hash value. Simple hash techniques store each hash class separately such that other search techniques need to be applied only to the (hopefully small) hash classes rather than to the complete set of states.

Symmetry respecting hash functions assign equal hash values to equivalent states. Using such a function h, it is sufficient to iterate the subset of M corresponding to $h(m)$ rather than the whole M.

As a simple way to get a symmetry respecting hash function, one can use a weighted sum of component values. For this purpose, one assigns a number c_p to each place p and sets $h(m) = \sum_{p \in P} c_p \cdot m(p) \quad mod \quad k$ where k is the size of the hash table. In order to make this function symmetry respecting, one guarantees $c_p = c_{p'}$ for all equivalent places. The equivalence relation for places can be efficiently deduced from the generating set without iterating all symmetries. In fact, it is sufficient to start with a family of singleton sets $\{\{p\} \mid p \in P\}$ and then to build repeatedly the union of the set containing p with the set containing $\sigma(p)$ (for all $p \in P$ and all σ *of the generating set*). This task can be efficiently done by TARJAN's union/find algorithm [Tar75] and produces directly the equivalence classes. The implementation used for computing the examples at the end of the paper uses weighted component sums as hash function where the c_p are otherwise randomly chosen. Random choice appears to spread hash values well enough.

The proposed method depends on the number of states in M that share the same hash value. Besides the general uncertainties of hash functions, there are general problems with symmetry respecting hash functions for sparse symmetry groups. Consider Fig. 3 and assume that (maybe by some additional hidden net structure) the rotations along the ring are the only symmetries.

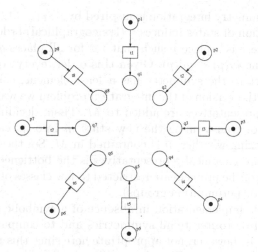

Fig. 3. Difficult situation for symmetry respecting hash functions

In this net, for every pair of outer places there is a symmetry mapping one to another. The same holds for inner places. However, there is no symmetry mapping an outer place to an inner place. Therefore, a hash function following our proposal assigns some weight c_o to all outer places and some weight c_i to all inner places. Consequently, the best symmetry respecting hash function would produce at most 9 different used hash values for the 36 states of the symmetrically reduced reachability graph of this net (the hash value depends only on *how many* inner places are marked, but equivalence depends on the distances between two marked inner places). In a ring of the same kind but length 20, the 52488 states of the reduced graph would share only 21 different values of any symmetry respecting hash function (in general, at least $\frac{2^n}{n}$ states share at most $n + 1$ hash values).

A situation as described above is typical for all rotation–like symmetry groups. Fortunately, this effect is due to the low number of symmetries (where the integration method of the previous section behaves well). If we use all permutations between the p_i (and corresponding mappings on the t_i and q_i) as symmetry group of the system depicted in Fig. 3, the problem does not appear since those states that share the same hash value become equivalent. Thus, the reduced reachability graph contains only one of them. Assigning, for example, weight 1 to the p_i and weight 2 to the q_i, we get 9 different hash values for the 9 states of the reduced reachability graph (in general, n values for n states). Thus, iterating the states of a hash class is a method for integrating symmetries that displays its best behavior with large symmetry groups. This complements the behavior of the method discussed in the previous section.

8   Canonical Representatives

This version of symmetry integration is inspired by [HJJJ84,ID96,CEFJ96]. The vector representation of states induces a (lexicographical) order between states: Let $m < m'$ iff there is a place p such that for for all places q $(q < p)$, one has $m(q) = m'(q)$ while $m(p) < m'(p)$. Given this order, every equivalence class of states with respect to the symmetry has a least element, called the *canonical representative*. In the version of the integration problem we want to discuss now, only canonical representatives are added to M. Then, deciding the integration problem consists of transforming the new state m into its canonical representative $\overline{m}$ and checking whether $\overline{m}$ is contained in M. So, the transformation of arbitrary states into canonical representatives is the bottleneck of this method. Efficient solutions of the problem are restricted to few classes of symmetry groups (such as rotation or permutation groups).

The brute force implementation in absence of a symbolic description of the symmetries would be to iterate all symmetries and to compare their images of the given m. This is, however, not appropriate here since this method would not work at all for larger groups. Therefore, we try once more to benefit from the structure of the generating set introduced in Sect. 3, in particular from the fact that elements of larger families do not change values on the first places. Thus, we could try the following procedure to transform states (σ_{ij} is the j-th member of family G_i of the generating set, $\#_i$ is the size of family G_i):

```
PROCEDURE transform(m:state): state:
VAR globalmin,localmin: state;
    i,j:Nat;
BEGIN
    globalmin := m;
    FOR i := 1 TO n DO  (* for all families *)
        localmin := globalmin;
        FOR j := 1 TO n DO
            IF σij(globalmin) < localmin THEN
                localmin := σij(globalmin);
            END
        END
        globalmin := localmin;
    END
    RETURN globalmin;
END.
```

This procedure has the advantage that it works in polynomial time in the size of the net. It has, however, one big disadvantage: it does not always produce canonical representatives! For an example, consider the grid example of Sect. 3. Assume for the purpose of simplicity that all vertices of the grid are places and transform the state $m = (1, 2, 2, 3, 3, 2, 1, 3)$. In the first family, only the identity and σ_6 produce 1 on the first place. $\sigma_6(m) = (1, 3, 3, 2, 2, 3, 1, 2)$. Thus, the minimal state produced by the first family is the state itself. In the second family, both σ_8 and σ_9 would produce 3 on the third place, thus m itself remains the minimal state. In the third family, σ_{10} does not change the state. Therefore the transform procedure would return m itself. However, applying σ_9 to $\sigma_6(m)$ leads to $(1, 2, 2, 2, 3, 3, 1, 3)$ which is smaller than m. Thus, the procedure does not always return canonical representatives. The way to the global minimum does not always lead via the minima at the intermediate steps of the algorithm.

The problem is limited to symmetry groups other than rotation and permutation groups. For rotation groups, we have a generating set consisting of a single family containing all symmetries. Thus, no symmetry is forgotten. For full permutation groups, the transform procedure performs a real sorting on the state. Thus, the global minimum is returned.

There are two ways out of the problem of non–minimality. The first one would be to replace the above transform procedure by one returning the actual canonical representative. However, the complexity of this problem is closely related to deciding graph isomorphism [CEFJ96,ES96] and therefore it is unlikely that there is a polynomial solution at all. Therefore we tried the other way which is to study which problems arise from non–unique representatives. The first observation is that a reduced graph using non–unique representatives can contain more than one element of some equivalence classes. Thus, the reduced graph is larger than a perfectly reduced one (i.e. one that contains exactly one representative per reachable class). On the other hand, most global properties do not depend on perfect reduction. In particular, the proof rules described in [Jen95] for boundedness, liveness, reversibility and other properties as well as model checking using formula respecting symmetries [ES96] are still valid. On the other hand, checking reachability of a given state m^* against a reduced reachability graph might be dangerous. It can happen that the transformed image of m^* is different from all representatives of its equivalence class in the reduced state space. Thus, not finding the image of m^* in M does not yet mean that the equivalence class of m^* is not represented in M. The problem can be circumvented in the following way: use the canonical representative method for generating the graph, but use one of the other methods to check reachability. This compromise should work well as long as only some states are to be tested for reachability.

9   Experiments

We have implemented all three methods in a new reachability oriented Petri net tool called LoLA (Low Level Analyzer). So reduced and full graph generation share the same code for all tasks not depending on the integration method.

ItSymm corresponds to the iteration of symmetries (Sect. 6), *ItState* to the iteration of states (Sect.7), and *CanRep* to the canonical representative method of Sect. 8. Times have been taken on a LINUX PC with 64MB RAM and a 400MHz Pentium processor. The times are written as <minutes>:<seconds>. We used a hash table of size 65536.

The first three tables show the behavior of symmetric reduction for different kinds of symmetry groups. We demonstrate the reduction in space, compared with full graph generation and give an impression concerning the running time. Furthermore we provide experimental evidence for the run time predictions we derived in the theoretical sections. There, we expected ItSymm to be fast on sparse groups but slow on large groups, we expected ItStates to be slow on sparse, but acceptable on large groups, and we expected CanRep to be fast anyway but to produce larger graphs. For these goals, small examples should be sufficient.

The first table concerns a deadlocking version of the *n* dining philosophers example. This is an example of a ring–like agents network.

Table 2. Results for the dining philosophers

	number of phil.		
	5	10	13
Places	25	50	65
Transitions	20	40	52
States in full graph	242	59048	$3^{13}-1$
Edges in full graph	805	393650	?
Hash entries in full graph	242	38048	?
Time for full graph	0:00.085	0:05.9	?
Symmetries	5	10	13
States in red. graph	50	5933	122642
Edges in red. graph	165	39550	1062893
nonempty hash classes in red. graph	20	65	104
time for ItSymm	0:00.077	0:02	1:38
time for ItState	0:00.22	11:31	?
time for CanRep	0:00.077	0:01.1	0:33.5

The symmetry group is a rotation–like group. Thus, we would store all symmetries explicitly as our generating set. They are organized in a single family. Therefore, the canonical representative method *must* yield full reduction. The times of iteration of states and canonical representatives are acceptable. The long time for the iteration of states is due to the hashing problem discussed in Sect. 7 and makes the method unacceptable for this kind of net. Though the times for the reduced graphs include the calculation of the symmetries, they are smaller than the corresponding full graph generation. Note that the number of instances of the integration problem to be solved corresponds to the number of edges of the reduced graph.

The second example is a data access scheme where r readers can access some data concurrently while w writers access it in mutual exclusion (and excluded from the readers). The readers are not distinguishable from each other and the writers are not distinguishable from each other. Thus, the symmetry group is close to full permutation.

Table 3. Results for the data access scheme

	readers / writers			
	5/5	13/13	20/20	40/40
Places	31	79	121	241
Transitions	25	65	100	200
States in full graph	217	114857	$21 \cdot (2^{20} + 20)$	$41 \cdot (2^{40} + 40)$
Edges in full graph	770	905554	?	?
Hash entries in full graph	217	54952	?	?
Time for full graph	0:00.1	2:54	?	?
Generators of Symm.	20	156	380	1560
Families of gen. set	8	24	38	78
Symmetries	14400	$13! \cdot 13!$	$20! \cdot 20!$	$40! \cdot 40!$
States in red. graph	14	30	44	84
Edges in red. graph	82	470	1072	4142
nonempty hash classes in red. graph	14	30	44	84
time for ItSymm	0:00.64	> 60:00	?	?
time for ItState	0:00.2	0:05.8	0:33	9:44
time for CanRep	0:00.084	0:00.4	0:01.7	0:34
States generated by CanRep	17	41	62	122
Edges generated by CanRep	85	481	1090	4180

For this system, iteration of symmetries fails due to the huge number of symmetries even in cases where the full graph can be generated without problems. Iteration of states works for this system though it cannot reach the speed of iterating the symmetries for a rotation symmetry group. However, compared to the time needed for the complete graph we can be satisfied with the result. Observe that the number of used hash entries shows that every instance of the integration problem involves at most one attempt to calculate a symmetry. The fastest method is once more the canonical representative approach. However, the example shows that it produces slightly larger graphs. This is due to the interlacing of two permutation groups. This problem could be avoided by rearranging the order of places which would require knowing the symmetries in advance; but that is not the intended application area of the low level Petri net method. However, the advantage with respect to time could justify a few more states. Again, one of the perfectly reducing methods and the canonical representative method were able to outperform the full graph generation.

The third example is designed to study the behavior of our procedures on grid–like networks. For this purpose we arranged several identical agents in a grid network. The agents have two states. The second state can only be entered in mutual exclusion to the direct neighbors, controlled by a set of semaphores. We vary the number of dimensions of the grid and the number of agents per row (our running example would have dimension 3 and two agents per row).

Table 4. Results for the grid network

| | dimensions / agents per row | | | |
	2/5	3/3	4/2	5/2
Places	75	81	48	96
Transitions	50	54	32	64
States of full graph	55447	70633	734	?
Edges of full graph	688478	897594	5664	?
Time for full graph	0: 10	0:15	0:00.18	?
Generators	4	10	21	41
Nontrivial families	2	3	4	5
Symmetries	8	48	384	3840
States of red. graph	7615	2352	21	332
Edges of red. graph	94850	29912	172	4937
nonempty hash entries of red. graph	192	106	9	17
Time for ItSymm	0:03.8	0:03.7	0:00.18	0:26.6
Time for ItState	12:29	4:38	0:00.72	1:20
Time for CanRep	0:04.7	0:04.9	0:00.15	0:27
States gen. by CanRep	15138	10832	29	3032
Edges gen. by CanRep	188706	137345	234	44650

For this example, the a lot of symmetries can be skipped during the iteration of symmetries in ItSymm, so ItSymm is even able to outperform the canonical representative method (which has, in addition, the disadvantage of generating more states). The grid symmetries can be considered as a sparse symmetry group, which explains the bad behavior of ItState. The reason for the slow ItState can be found in the small number of used hash classes compared with the large number of states.

The grid example demonstrates the benefits of using low level net symmetries on non–standard symmetry groups. In the 3–dimensional case we have 48 symmetries. The size of the reduced graph is approximately 30 times smaller than the full one. Since every equivalence class of reachable states should appear in the reduced graph, and the size of an equivalence class is bounded by the number of symmetries, a reduced graph can never be smaller than the size of the full graph divided by the number of symmetries. As outlined in [CFG94,CDFH90], the symbolic symmetry approach based on rotation and permutation groups considers only a rotation (sub-)group of grid structures that consists only of four symmetries. Thus, instead of a reduction factor 30, a reduction factor smaller than 4 is achieved.

The symmetry approach has been criticized for its lack of practical feasibility. Extrapolation of the previous tables to larger examples supports this criticism. In particular, sparse symmetry groups do not yield sufficient reduction to keep pace with the growth of the reachability graph. However, things look different if we take into consideration that symmetries can be applied jointly with several other reduction techniques, for instance the stubborn set method [Val88]. Benefits of combined application have been reported earlier [Val91,DBDS93,EJP97]. We report results for our particular symmetry approach. Applying symmetries alone leads to memory overflow on all reported instances, not to mention full graphs.

Table 5. Stubborn sets versus stubborn sets with symmetries (for the dining philosophers)

	number of phil.			
	100	200	300	900
Places	500	1000	1500	4500
Transitions	400	800	1200	3200
States in full graph	$3^{100} - 1$	$3^{200} - 1$	$3^{300} - 1$	$3^{900} - 1$
Symmetries	100	200	300	900
States in symm./stubb. red. graph	299	599	899	2699
Edges in symm./stubb. red. graph	496	996	1496	4496
time for ItSymm+ stubborn	0:02	0:10	0:26	7: 00
States in stubb. red. graph	29702	119402	overflow	-
Edges in stubb. red. graph	39700	159400	-	-
Time for stubb. red. graph	0:05	1:08	-	-

In the grid example, stubborn sets do not reduce the number of states. Concerning the data access scheme (40 readers/40 writers), stubborn sets produce 121 states while combined application of stubborn sets and symmetries leads to 4 states, independently of the number of readers and writers.

10   Conclusion

We have presented three solutions of the integration problem (deciding whether for the current state there is a symmetrical one in the set of already computed states). All methods have their advantages and disadvantages. The advantage of the iteration of symmetries and iteration of states is that they yield a completely reduced graph. Unfortunately they work well only on sparse (iteration of symmetries) or large (iteration of states) symmetry groups. The canonical representative method is the fastest method that works for all kind of symmetries, but it often produces more than one representative for some equivalence classes of states. The canonical representative method cannot be used for testing the reachability of states. This problem can be repaired by using one of the other method for testing the reachability on a graph produced by the canonical representative method.

With the set of methods presented in this paper, low level symmetries are no longer a restricting factor for reduced reachability graph generation. In most cases, the remaining size of the reduced graph limited the analysis. This in turn is due to the limitation of the symmetry approach *as it* and not due to its *low level* version (low level symmetries do not produce larger graphs than high level (symbolic) symmetries).

In connection with other reduction techniques (such as stubborn sets), much larger systems can be analyzed than using either method in isolation. The easy use of maximal symmetry groups other than rotation and permutation groups is another argument in favor of the low level symmetry approach.

References

CDFH90. G. Chiola, C. Dutheillet, G. Franceschinis, and S. Haddad. On well–formed colored nets and their symbolic reachability graph. *Proc. of the 11th Int. Conf. on Application and Theory of Petri Nets*, pages 387–410, 1990. 315, 328

CEFJ96. E.M. Clarke, R. Enders, T. Filkorn, and S. Jha. Exploiting symmetry in temporal logic model checking. *Formal Methods in System Design 9*, pages 77–104, 1996. 315, 316, 323, 324

CFG94. G. Chiola, G. Franceschinis, and R. Gaeta. Modelling symmetric computer architectures by swn's. *Proc. 15th Int. Conf. on Application and Theory of Petri Nets, LNCS 815*, pages 139–158, 1994. 315, 328

Chi98. G. Chiola. Manual and automatic exploitation of symmetries in spn models. *Proc. 19th International Conference on Application and Theory of Petri nets, LNCS 1420*, pages 28–43, 1998. 315

DBDS93. S. Duri, U. Buy, R. Devarapalli, and S. Shatz. Using state space methods for deadlock analysis in ada tasking. *ACM Proc. Int. Symp. on Software Testing and Analysis*, pages 51–60, 1993. 328

EJP97. E.A. Emerson, S. Jha, and D. Peled. Combining partial order and symmetry reductions. *Proc. TACAS '97, LNCS 1217*, pages 19–34, 1997. 328

ES96. E.A. Emerson and A.P. Sistla. Symmetry and model checking. *Formal Methods in System Design 9*, pages 105–131, 1996. 315, 324

HJJJ84. Huber, A. Jensen, Jepsen, and K. Jensen. Towards reachability trees for high–level petri nets. In *Advances in Petri Nets 1984, Lecture Notes on Computer Science 188*, pages 215–233, 1984. 315, 321, 323

ID96. C.N. Ip and D.L. Dill. Better verification through symmetry. *Formal Methods in System Design 9*, pages 41–75, 1996. 315, 316, 323

Jen92. K. Jensen. *Coloured Petri Nets*, volume 1 of *EATCS Monographs on Theoretical Computer Science*. Springer, 1992. 315

Jen95.   K. Jensen. *Coloured Petri Nets Vol. 2: Analysis Methods*. Springer, 1995.
          324

Jun98.   T. Junttila. Towards well-formed algebraic system nets. *Workshop CSP'98
          Berlin, Technical Report 110, Humboldt–University Berlin*, pages 116–127,
          1998. 315

RS97.   S. Roch and P. Starke. *INA – Integrierter Netz–Analysator Version 1.7.
          Handbuch.* Humboldt–University Berlin, Institute of Computer Science,
          1997. 316

Sch97.   K. Schmidt. How to calculate symmetries of petri nets. To appear in Acta
          Informatica. 316, 317, 321

Sta91.   P. Starke. Reachability analysis of petri nets using symmetries. *J. Syst.
          Anal. Model. Simul.*, 8:294–303, 1991. 315, 316

Tar75.   R.E. Tarjan. Efficiency ofa good but not linear set union algorithm. *Journal
          of the ACM 22(2)*, pages 215–225, 1975. 321

Val88.   A. Valmari. Error detection by reduced reachability graph generation. *Proc.
          of the 9th European Workshop on Application and Theory of Petri Nets,
          Venice*, 1988. 328

Val91.   A. Valmari. Stubborn sets for coloured petri nets. In *The Proceedings of
          the 12th International Conference on Application and Theory of Petri Nets*,
          pages 102–121, 1991. 328

Model Checking Support for the ASM High-Level Language

Giuseppe Del Castillo[1]* and Kirsten Winter[2]

[1] Heinz Nixdorf Institut, Universität-GH Paderborn
Fürstenallee 11, D-33102 Paderborn, Germany
giusp@uni-paderborn.de
[2] GMD FIRST
Kekuléstr.7, D-12489 Berlin, Germany
kirsten@first.gmd.de

Abstract Gurevich's Abstract State Machines (ASM) constitute a high-level specification language for a wide range of applications. The existing tool support for ASM–currently including type-checking, simulation and debugging–should be extended to support computer-aided verification, in particular by model checking. In this paper we introduce an interface from our existing tool environment to the model checker SMV, based on a transformation which maps a large subset of ASM into the SMV language. Through a case study we show how the proposed approach can ease the validation process.

1 Introduction

Gurevich's Abstract State Machines (ASM) [7] constitute a simple but powerful method for specifying and modeling software and hardware systems. Existing case studies include specifications of distributed protocols, architectures, embedded systems, programming languages, etc. (see [1] and [8]).

The advantage of ASMs is in the simple language and its intuitive understanding. The method is based on general mathematics which allows to naturally model systems on a suitable level of abstraction. Traditionally, the verification task is done by means of hand-written mathematical proofs. Tool support for the verification process is obviously needed for a broader acceptance.

Our contribution to this task is the development of an interface between the *ASM Workbench* [2] and the SMV model checker [11]. The ASM Workbench is a tool environment, based on a typed version of ASM, which includes a type checker and a simulator for ASMs. SMV has been chosen as a typical representative of a class of model checkers based on transition systems and could be easily replaced by any other similar model checker, e.g., SVE [5] or VIS [6].

On the other hand our transformation tool supplies SMV with a higher level modeling language, namely ASMs. This facilitates the specification task by allowing the use of more complex data types and of *n-ary dynamic functions* for

---

* Partially supported by the DFG Schwerpunktprogramm "Softwarespezifikation".

S. Graf and M. Schwartzbach (Eds.): TACAS/ETAPS 2000, LNCS 1785, pp. 331–346, 2000.

parameterization (a peculiar feature of the ASM language, which generalizes the classical notion of state variables).

Since model checking is only applicable to finite-state systems, we have to put restrictions on the ASM model to be checked in order to make it finite: all function ranges have to be restricted to a fixed finite set of values. To cope with a broader subset of the ASM language, we extend the basic work of [14], which introduced a simple transformation schema, to support the transformation of *n-ary dynamic functions* for $n > 0$. To ease the transition from infinite or large models to finite and feasible ones, we introduce a language feature for adjusting the function ranges in the declaration part of the system specification. Thus, such changes can be done locally and are not spread over the whole model.

From a methodical point of view, model checking can *support the early design phase*: checking properties of the system behavior may yield counterexamples which help to "debug" the system specification. The simulator provided by the ASM Workbench can be fed with the counterexamples in order to illustrate the erroneous behavior. After locating and correcting the error that causes the counterexample, the transformation and model checking should be repeated. This debugging process gives a deeper insight into the model at hand. Errors become visible that can be easily over seen when carrying out mathematical proofs which are not mechanically checked, borderline cases become visible that are mostly not found when simulating isolated test cases.

We are not claiming that model checking can replace, in general, mathematical proofs (developed with or without the help of theorem provers), as the range of applicability of model checking techniques is restricted to the verification of finite instances of the problem at hand and is in most cases insufficient to prove correctness of a system or protocol in general. However, we argue that using tool support in the way we suggest helps to find errors with small additional effort.

This paper is structured as follows: after introducing the main features of ASM (Sect. 2), we show how the transformation from ASM into the SMV language is performed (Sect. 3). Sect. 4 presents results from applying our approach to a case study, an ASM specification of the FLASH cache coherence protocol. Sect. 5 outlines related work. We conclude in Sect. 6 with an outlook to further possible improvements of our tool.

2 Basic Notions of Abstract State Machines

In this section we introduce some basic notions of ASM (see [7] for the complete definition). We first describe the underlying computational model and then the syntax and semantics of the subset of the ASM language needed in this paper.

2.1 Computational Model

Computations Abstract State Machines define a state-based computational model, where computations (*runs*) are finite or infinite sequences of states $\{S_i\}$, obtained from a given *initial state* S_0 by repeatedly executing *transitions* δ_i:

$$S_0 \xrightarrow{\delta_1} S_1 \xrightarrow{\delta_2} S_2 \ldots \xrightarrow{\delta_n} S_n \ldots$$

States The *states* are algebras over a given *signature* Σ (or Σ-*algebras* for short). A signature Σ consists of a set of *basic types* and a set of *function names*, each function name f coming with a fixed arity n and type $T_1 \ldots T_n \to T$, where the T_i and T are basic types (written $f : T_1 \ldots T_n \to T$, or simply $f : T$ if $n = 0$). for each function name $f : T_1 \ldots T_n \to T$ in Σ (the *interpretation* of the function name f in S). Function names in Σ can be declared as:

- *static*: static function names have the same (fixed) interpretation in each computation state;
- *dynamic*: the interpretation of dynamic function names can be altered by transitions fired in a computation step (see below);
- *external*: the interpretation of external function names is determined by the environment (thus, external functions may change during the computation as a result of environmental influences, but are not controlled by the system).

Any signature Σ must contain at least a basic type $BOOL$, static nullary function names (constants) $true : BOOL$, $false : BOOL$, the usual boolean operations ($\wedge$, $\vee$, etc.), and the equality symbol $=$. We also assume that there is a (polymorphic) type $SET(T)$ of finite sets with the usual set operations. When no ambiguity arises we omit explicit mention of the state S (e.g., we write T instead of T^S for the carrier sets, and $\mathbf{f}$ instead of $\mathbf{f}_S$ for static functions, as they never change during a run).

Locations If $f : T_1 \ldots T_n \to T$ is a dynamic or external function name, we call a pair $l = (f, \overline{x})$ with $\overline{x} \in T_1 \times \ldots \times T_n$ a *location* (then, the *type* of l is T and the *value* of l in a state S is given by $\mathbf{f}_S(\overline{x})$). Note that, within a run, two states S_i and S_j are equal iff the values of all locations in S_i and S_j are equal (i.e., they coincide iff they coincide on all locations).

Transitions Transitions transform a state S into its successor state S' by changing the interpretation of some dynamic function names on a finite number of points (i.e., by updating the values of a finite number of *locations*).

  More precisely, the transition transforming S into S' results from firing a finite *update set* Δ at S, where *updates* are of the form $((f, \overline{x}), y)$, with $(f, \overline{x})$ being the location to be updated and y the value. In the state S' resulting from firing Δ at S the carrier sets are unchanged and, for each function name f:

$$\mathbf{f}_{S'}(\overline{x}) = \begin{cases} y & \text{if } ((f, \overline{x}), y) \in \Delta \\ \mathbf{f}_S(\overline{x}) & \text{otherwise.} \end{cases}$$

Note that the above definition is only applicable if Δ does not contain *conflicting updates*, i.e., any updates $((f, \overline{x}), y)$ and $((f, \overline{x}), y')$ with $y \neq y'$.

  The update set Δ–which depends on the state S–is determined by evaluating in S a distinguished closed *transition rule* P, called the *program*. The program consists usually of a set (block) of rules, describing system behavior under different–usually mutually exclusive–conditions.[1]

---

[1] See, for instance, the example in Sect. 4, containing a rule for each message type.

2.2 The ASM Language

Terms Terms are defined as in first-order logic: *(i)* if $f : T_1 \ldots T_n \to T$ is a function name in Σ, and t_i are terms of type T_i (for $i = 1, \ldots, n$), then $f(t_1, \ldots, t_n)$ is a term of type T (written $t : T$) (if $n = 0$ the parentheses are omitted, i.e. we write f instead of $f()$); *(ii)* a variable v (of a given type T) is a term. The meaning of a term $t : T$ in a state S and environment ρ is a value $S_\rho(t) \in T$ defined by:[2]

$$S_\rho(t) = \begin{cases} \mathbf{f}_S(S_\rho(t_1), \ldots, S_\rho(t_n)) & \text{if } t \equiv f(t_1, \ldots, t_n) \\ \rho(v) & \text{if } t \equiv v. \end{cases}$$

As opposed to first-order logic, there is no notion of formula: boolean terms are used instead. Finite quantifications of the form "$(Q \ v \ \text{in} \ A : G)$", where Q is $\forall$ or $\exists$, $v : T$, $A : SET(T)$, and $G : BOOL$, are also valid boolean terms.[3]

Transition rules While terms denote values, transition rules (*rules* for short) denote *update sets*, and are used to define the dynamic behavior of an ASM: the meaning of a rule R in a state S and environment ρ is an update set $\Delta_{S,\rho}(R)$.

ASM runs starting in a given initial state S_0 are determined by the program P: each state S_{i+1} ($i \geq 0$) is obtained by firing the update set $\Delta_{S_i}(P)$ at S_i:

$$S_0 \xrightarrow{\Delta_{S_0}(P)} S_1 \xrightarrow{\Delta_{S_1}(P)} S_2 \ldots \xrightarrow{\Delta_{S_{n-1}}(P)} S_n \ldots$$

Basic transition rules are the *skip*, *update*, *block*, and *conditional* rules. Additional rules are the *do-forall* (a generalized block rule) and *choose* rules (for non-deterministic choice).[4]

$$R ::= \ \mathbf{skip} \ | \ f(t_1, \ldots, t_n) := t \ | \ R_1 \ldots R_n \ | \ \mathbf{if} \ G \ \mathbf{then} \ R_T \ \mathbf{else} \ R_F$$
$$| \ \mathbf{do \ forall} \ v \ \mathbf{in} \ A \ \mathbf{with} \ G \ \ R' \ | \ \mathbf{choose} \ v \ \mathbf{in} \ A \ \mathbf{with} \ G \ \ R'$$

The form "$\mathbf{if} \ G \ \mathbf{then} \ R$" is a shortcut for "$\mathbf{if} \ G \ \mathbf{then} \ R \ \mathbf{else \ skip}$". Omitting "$\mathbf{with} \ G$" in *do-forall* and *choose* rules corresponds to specifying "$\mathbf{with \ true}$". The semantics of transition rules is as follows:

$$\Delta_{S,\rho}(\mathbf{skip}) = \{ \}$$
$$\Delta_{S,\rho}(f(t_1, \ldots, t_n) := t) = \{ ((f, (S_\rho(t_1), \ldots, S_\rho(t_n))), S_\rho(t)) \}$$
$$\Delta_{S,\rho}(R_1 \ldots R_n) = \bigcup_{i=1}^{n} \Delta_{S,\rho}(R_i)$$
$$\Delta_{S,\rho}(\mathbf{if} \ G \ \mathbf{then} \ R_T \ \mathbf{else} \ R_F) = \begin{cases} \Delta_{S,\rho}(R_T) \ \text{if} \ S_\rho(G) = \mathbf{true} \\ \Delta_{S,\rho}(R_F) \ \text{otherwise} \end{cases}$$

---

[2] Environments–denoted by the letter ρ–are finite maps containing bindings which associate (free) variables to their corresponding values. We adopt the following notation: $\rho[v \mapsto x]$ is the environment obtained by modifying ρ to bind v to x, while $\rho \backslash v$ is the environment with the binding of variable v removed from ρ. For closed terms and rules, we omit explicit mention of ρ (e.g., if t is a closed term, $S(t) = S_\emptyset(t)$).

[3] Also in the rest of this paper we use A for set-typed terms and G for boolean terms.

[4] The ASM Workbench support more rules, such as *let* and *case* rules with pattern matching: however, for reasons of space, we have to skip them here.

$$\Delta_{S,\rho}(\texttt{do forall } v \texttt{ in } A \texttt{ with } G\ R') \ = \ \bigcup_{x \in X} \Delta_{S,\rho[v \to x]}(R')$$
$$\text{where } X = \{x \mid x \in S_\rho(A) \wedge S_{\rho[v \to x]}(G) = \textbf{true}\}.$$

Note that executing a block (or a do-forall) rule corresponds to *simultaneous* execution of its subrules[5] and may lead to conflicts.

Choose rules are not directly supported by our transformation tool, but can always be replaced by external functions for arbitrary choice of a value (by a transformation similar to skolemization). For example, let A_i be terms of type $SET(T_i)$, $i = 1, 2, 3$, and $f_x : T_1$, $f_z : T_2 \to T_3$ external functions with $f_x \in A_1$ and $f_z(y) \in A_3$ for each $y \in A_2$. Then the following two rules are equivalent:

> choose x in A_1
> > do forall y in A_2
> > > choose z in A_3
> > > > $a(x, y, z) := x + y + z$

$\cong$

> do forall y in A_2
> > $a(f_x, y, f_z(y)) := f_x + y + f_z(y)$

Multi-Agent ASM Concurrent systems can be modelled in ASM by the notion of multi-agent ASM (called *distributed ASM* in [7]). The basic idea is that the system consists of more *agents*, identified with the elements of a finite set $AGENT$ (which are actually sort of "agent identifiers"). Each agent $a \in AGENT$ executes its own program $prog(a)$ and can identify itself by means of a special nullary function $self : AGENT$, which is interpreted by each agent a as a.

As a semantics for multi-agent ASM we consider here a simple interleaving model, which allows us to model concurrent systems in the basic ASM formalism as described above. In particular, we consider $self$ as an external function, whose interpretation $self_{S_i}$ determines the agent which fires at state S_i. We assume that there is one program P, shared by all agents, possibly performing different actions for different agents, e.g.:

> if $self = a_1$ then $prog(a_1)$
> ...
> if $self = a_n$ then $prog(a_n)$

where $\{a_1, \ldots, a_n\}$ are the agents and $prog(a_i)$ is the rule to be executed by agent a_i, i.e., the "program" of a_i. (The FLASH model presented in Sect. 4 is an example of this style of modelling, except that all agents execute exactly the same program, but on different data.)

The ASM-SL Notation The ASM language, including all constructs above, is supported by the "ASM Workbench" tool environment [2], which provides syntax- and type-checking of ASM specifications as well as their simulation and debugging. The source language for the ASM Workbench, called ASM-SL, includes some additional features which are necessary for practical modelling tasks: constructs for defining types, functions, and named transition rules ("macros"), as well as a set of predefined data types (booleans, integers, tuples, lists, finite sets, etc.): as the ASM-SL notation is quite close to usual mathematical notation, no further explanation of ASM-SL will be needed.

---

[5] For example, a block rule a := b, b := a exchanges a and b.

3   Translating Abstract State Machines into SMV

In this section, after a brief comparison of the ASM and SMV specification languages, we describe the transformation from ASM to SMV in two stages. First we recall the translation scheme introduced in [14], defined for a subset of ASM called ASM_0 in this paper (Sect. 3.1). Then we define a transformation technique to reduce any ASM specification to ASM_0, such that the first translation scheme can then be applied (Sect. 3.2).

ASM versus SMV   While the computational model underlying both SMV and ASM is essentially the well-known model of *transition systems*, there are some significant differences: **(1.)** Abstract State Machines define, in general, systems with a possibly infinite number of states (as both the number of locations and the location ranges may be infinite); **(2.)** the way of specifying transitions in ASM and SMV is different: in SMV transitions are specified by **next**-expressions, which completely define the value which a state variable assumes in the next state, while updates of dynamic functions in ASM may be scattered troughout the program; **(3.)** the ASM notions of *dynamic function* and *external function* generalize the notion of *state variable* typical of basic transition systems (state variables correspond to nullary dynamic/external functions of ASM).

The first issue is solved by introducing *finiteness constraints*, the second and third are addressed by the transformations of Sect. 3.1 and 3.2, respectively.

Finiteness constraints   In order to ensure that the ASM programs to be translated into SMV define finite-state systems, the user has to specify, for each dynamic or external function $f : T_1 \ldots T_n \to T$, a finiteness constraint of the form $f(x_1, \ldots, x_n) \in t[x_1, \ldots, x_n]$, where $t : SET(T)$ is a term denoting a finite set, possibly depending on the arguments of f (see Fig. 1 for an example). For external functions, finiteness constraints correspond to environment assumptions, expressed in the resulting SMV model by the range of the generated state variables; for dynamic functions, it must be checked that the constraints are not violated by the rules, resulting in the SMV code in appropriate proof obligations, which we call *range conditions*.[6]

3.1   The Basic Translation Scheme

The translation scheme introduced in [14] can be applied to transform into SMV a subset ASM_0 of ASM, where: *(i)* only **nullary** dynamic and external functions are allowed; *(ii)* the only available data types are integers, booleans and enumerated types; *(iii)* the only defined static functions are those corresponding to predefined operations in SMV (boolean operations, +, -, etc.).

As the semantic models for ASM_0 are essentially basic transition systems, the translation of ASM into SMV is very close:

---

[6] Note, however, that the range conditions can often be discarded by a simple static analysis of the rules, which prevents their expensive proof by model-checking.

- non-static functions (i.e., dynamic and external functions) are identified with locations and thus mapped one-to-one to SMV state variables;
- values of the ASM data types are mapped one-to-one to SMV constants;
- applications of static functions are translated to applications of the corresponding built-in operators of SMV.

What remains to be done is to restructure the ASM program into a form where updates of the same location, together with their guards, are collected together. This is done in two steps. First, we transform an ASM program P into an equivalent ASM program P' consisting only of a block of guarded updates (i.e., rules of the form if G then $f(\bar{t}) := t$) by means of a "flattening" transformation:

$[\![\text{skip}]\!] = \text{(empty block)}$
$[\![f(\bar{t}) := t]\!] = \text{if } true \text{ then } f(\bar{t}) := t$
$[\![R_1 \ldots R_n]\!] = [\![R_1]\!] \ldots [\![R_n]\!]$

$$[\![R_T]\!] = \begin{cases} \text{if } G_T^1 \text{ then } R_T^1 \\ \ldots \\ \text{if } G_T^n \text{ then } R_T^n \end{cases} \Rightarrow [\![\text{if } G \text{ then } R_T \text{ else } R_F]\!] = \begin{cases} \text{if } G \wedge G_T^1 \text{ then } R_T^1 \\ \ldots \\ \text{if } G \wedge G_T^n \text{ then } R_T^n \\ \text{if } \neg G \wedge G_F^1 \text{ then } R_F^1 \\ \ldots \\ \text{if } \neg G \wedge G_F^m \text{ then } R_F^m \end{cases}$$
$$[\![R_F]\!] = \begin{cases} \text{if } G_F^1 \text{ then } R_F^1 \\ \ldots \\ \text{if } G_F^m \text{ then } R_F^m \end{cases}$$

Second, we collect all guarded updates of the same location, thus obtaining, for each location loc occurring on the left-hand side of an update in P', a pair $(loc, \{(G_1, t_1), \ldots, (G_n, t_n)\})$ which maps loc to a set of pairs (guard, right-hand side). Such a pair is translated into the following SMV assignment:[7]

```
ASSIGN next(C[[loc]]) :=
    case C[[G_1]] : C[[t_1]] ;  ...  C[[G_n]] : C[[t_n]] ;  1 : C[[loc]] esac;
```

where $C[\![.]\!]$ denotes here the ASM $\rightarrow$ SMV compiling function for terms, which is straightforward for ASM$_0$. For each location l of a dynamic function f, in addition to the next assignment above, the transformation also generates the location's initialization (an init assignment in SMV) as well as two proof obligations, a *range condition* (see discussion of finiteness constraints above) and a *no-conflict condition*, which ensures that no conflicts arise on this location. In fact, due to the semantics of case in SMV, the translation scheme is correct only if for all i, j with $i \neq j$, $S \models \neg(G_i \wedge G_j) \vee (t_i = t_j)$ in any reachable state S: if, in some state S, this condition is not satisfied, the ASM transition produces a conflict (i.e., an error), while the corresponding SMV transition simply picks one of the updates (the first one in the case whose guard is satisfied).[8]

3.2 The Extended Translation Scheme

In this section we show how to reduce an arbitrary (finite-state) ASM to ASM$_0$. This transformation allows to deal with the complete ASM language as in [7],

---

[7] Note that we have to specify the default case explicitly (if none of the guards is true) which is given implicitly in ASM rules (see ASM semantics above).

[8] Like range conditions, no-conflict conditions can be often discarded statically.

with the exception of **import** rules (rules which allow the dynamic creation of elements at run-time) and **choose** rules. (However, one can deal with **choose** as explained in Sect. 2.2.) Arbitrary data types and operations (in particular, lists, finite sets, finite maps and user-definable freely generated types, as provided by ASM-SL) can be used without any restriction. Finite quantifications are also supported.

The main problem here, as opposed to ASM_0, is that in general we do not know which location is updated by an update rule $f(t_1, \ldots, t_n) := t$ (if $n > 0$): the updated location may differ from state to state if some t_i contains non-static function names. However, if all terms t_i contain only static function names, they can be evaluated statically to values x_i, and the term $f(t_1, \ldots, t_n)$ to the location $l = (f, \overline{x})$. Thus, the basic idea of the transformation is to iteratively unfold and simplify rules until all terms can be reduced to values or locations.

To formally define the transformation, we extend the syntactic category of terms to "partially evaluated terms" (simply called "terms" in the sequel) by adding values and locations:

$$t ::= f(t_1, \ldots, t_n) \mid v \mid (Q\ v \text{ in } A : G) \mid x \mid l$$

(We adopt the convention that x stands for a value and l for a location).

Terms can be simplified by means of the transformation $[\![.]\!]_\rho$ defined in Table 1, which is then extended to rules in a canonical way. Note that, whenever ρ contains bindings for all free variables occurring in t: *(i)* if t is a static term, then $[\![t]\!]_\rho$ is a value x (coinciding with $S_\rho(t)$ in every state S); *(ii)* if $t = f(t_1, \ldots, t_n)$ is a term where f is a dynamic or external function name and all the subterms t_i are static (we call such a term a *locational* term), then $[\![t]\!]_\rho$ is a location l.[9]

The rule-unfolding transformation $\mathcal{E}$, which operates on closed rules such as the program P, is formally defined in Table 2. It works as follows:

- if the rule R consists of a block of update rules of the form *location := value*, it terminates and yields R as result (there is nothing left to unfold);
- otherwise, it looks for the first location l occurring in R (but not as left-hand side of some update rule) and unfolds R according to the possible values[10] of l. In turn, the unfolding has to be applied to the subrules $[\![R[l/x_i]]\!]$ obtained by substituting the values x_i for l in R and simplifying.

Applying $\mathcal{E}$ to the (simplified) ASM program $[\![P]\!]_\emptyset$ yields a program $P' = \mathcal{E}([\![P]\!]_\emptyset)$ which is essentially an ASM_0 program (formally, the locations have still to be replaced by nullary dynamic or external function names and the values by nullary static function names, i.e. by constants).[11]

---

[9] A simple consequence of this fact is that every closed static term simplifies to a value and every closed locational term to a location.

[10] The finite range of location $l = (f, \overline{x})$ is derived from the finiteness constraint for f.

[11] The unfolding transformation often results in very large decision trees (**case**-structures in SMV): however, this does not have a negative influence on the efficiency of verification with SMV, as the verification costs depend on the size of the BDDs representing the transition relation and not on the size of the SMV source code (and BDDs, for a given variable ordering, are a canonical representation).

Table 1. Term and Rule Simplification

Term Simplification

$$[\![x]\!]_\rho = x \qquad\qquad [\![l]\!]_\rho = l$$

$$[\![v]\!]_\rho = \begin{cases} x = \rho(v) & \text{if } v \in \text{dom}(\rho) \\ v & \text{otherwise} \end{cases}$$

$$[\![t_i]\!]_\rho = x_i \text{ for each } i \in \{1, \dots, n\} \Rightarrow$$

$$[\![f(t_1, \dots, t_n)]\!]_\rho = \begin{cases} x = \mathsf{f}(x_1, \dots, x_n) & \text{if } f \text{ static function name} \\ l = (f, (x_1, \dots, x_n)) & \text{if } f \text{ dynamic/external function name} \end{cases}$$

$$[\![t_i]\!]_\rho = l \text{ or } [\![t_i]\!]_\rho = f'(\bar{t'}) \text{ for some } i \in \{1, \dots, n\} \Rightarrow$$
$$[\![f(t_1, \dots, t_n)]\!]_\rho = f([\![t_1]\!]_\rho, \dots, [\![t_n]\!]_\rho)$$

$$[\![(Q \ v \ \text{in} \ A : G)]\!]_\rho = \begin{cases} [\![G]\!]_{\rho[v \mapsto x_1]} \ op \ \cdots \ op \ [\![G]\!]_{\rho[v \mapsto x_n]} \\ \qquad \text{if } [\![A]\!]_\rho = x = \{x_1, \dots, x_n\} \quad \text{(i.e., if } [\![A]\!]_\rho \text{ is a value)} \\ (Q \ v \ \text{in} \ [\![A]\!]_\rho : [\![G]\!]_{(\rho \backslash v)}) \\ \qquad \text{otherwise.} \end{cases}$$

(where $op \equiv \wedge$ if $Q \equiv \texttt{forall}$, $op \equiv \vee$ if $Q \equiv \texttt{exists}$).

Rule Simplification

$$[\![\texttt{skip}]\!]_\rho = \texttt{skip}$$
$$[\![t_L := t_R]\!]_\rho = [\![t_L]\!]_\rho := [\![t_R]\!]_\rho$$
$$[\![R_1 \ \dots \ R_n]\!]_\rho = [\![R_1]\!]_\rho \ \dots \ [\![R_n]\!]_\rho$$

$$[\![\texttt{if } G \texttt{ then } R_T \texttt{ else } R_F]\!]_\rho = \begin{cases} [\![R_T]\!]_\rho & \text{if } [\![G]\!]_\rho = \textbf{true} \\ [\![R_F]\!]_\rho & \text{if } [\![G]\!]_\rho = \textbf{false} \\ \texttt{if } [\![G]\!]_\rho \texttt{ then } [\![R_T]\!]_\rho \texttt{ else } [\![R_F]\!]_\rho & \text{otherwise.} \end{cases}$$

$$[\![\texttt{do forall } v \texttt{ in } A \texttt{ with } G \ R']\!]_\rho =$$
$$= \begin{cases} [\![\texttt{if } G \texttt{ then } R']\!]_{\rho[v \mapsto x_1]} \ \cdots \ [\![\texttt{if } G \texttt{ then } R']\!]_{\rho[v \mapsto x_n]} \\ \qquad \text{if } [\![A]\!]_\rho = x = \{x_1, \dots, x_n\} \quad \text{(i.e., if } [\![A]\!]_\rho \text{ is a value)} \\ \texttt{do forall } v \texttt{ in } [\![A]\!]_\rho \texttt{ with } [\![G]\!]_{(\rho \backslash v)} \ [\![R']\!]_{(\rho \backslash v)} \\ \qquad \text{otherwise.} \end{cases}$$

Table 2. Rule Unfolding

Rule Unfolding

If R has the form $l_1 := x_1 \ \dots \ l_n := x_n$, then $\mathcal{E}(R) = R$.
Otherwise:
$$\mathcal{E}(R) = \texttt{if } l = x_1 \texttt{ then } \mathcal{E}([\![R[l/x_1]]\!]_\emptyset)$$
$$\qquad\qquad \texttt{else if } l = x_2 \texttt{ then } \mathcal{E}([\![R[l/x_1]]\!]_\emptyset)$$
$$\cdots$$
$$\qquad\qquad \texttt{else if } l = x_n \texttt{ then } \mathcal{E}([\![R[l/x_n]]\!]_\emptyset)$$
where l is the first location occurring in R (but not as lhs of an update rule)
and $\{x_1, \dots, x_n\}$ is the range of location l.

Fig. 1 illustrates graphically the transformation technique (for simplicity, we consider a rule without variables, such that we can omit mentioning environments). The root of the tree–enclosed in the dashed box–is the (simplified) ASM program $[\![P]\!]$ to be transformed. The successors of each node in the tree are obtained as result of an unfolding step (under the given finiteness constraints): for instance, the successors of the root node are the rules $[\![P]\!][a/1]\!]$, $[\![P]\!][a/2]\!]$, and $[\![P]\!][a/3]\!]$, respectively. Locations are emphasized by enclosing them in boxes: note that, at the leaves, locations occur only as left-hand side of updates, thus they cause no further unfolding. The dashed box on the right contains the ASM_0 program produced by the transformation: note that the locations actually affected by the ASM program–which are revealed by the unfolding–are mapped to nullary functions ("state variables"), whose ranges are derived from the finiteness constraints (see box at the top right corner).

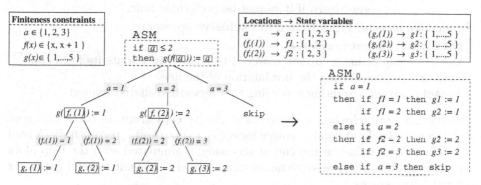

Fig. 1. Rule Transformation Example

4 Case Study: The FLASH Cache Coherence Protocol

As an example for our model checking approach we chose a formalization of the FLASH protocol [9] with ASM. Our model is based on the work of Durand [4]. In Sect. 4.1, after a short introduction to FLASH, we describe an ASM model derived from [4] and motivate our refinements. Then we sketch the debugging process supported by the transformation and checking with SMV (in Sect. 4.2).

4.1 FLASH Cache Coherence Protocol

The Stanford FLASH multiprocessor integrates support for cache coherent shared memory for a large number of interconnected processing nodes. Each line-sized block of the distributed memory is associated with a *home* node containing the part of the physical memory where that line resides. Every read or write miss concerning a remote memory line triggers a line request to its *home* node that in turn initiates the corresponding part of the protocol. The request may ask for *shared* or *exclusive* access depending on whether reading or writing access is wanted.

The ASM description of the protocol is based on agents. A set of transition rules describes the behavior of a single agent. The behavior is determined by the currently processed message type – a notion that yields the clear model structure that is sketched in Fig. 2.

Message Structure. A message is modeled as a quintuple consisting of the type of the message, the addressed agent, sender agent, agent initiating the request and requested line[12]. Message types related to **shared** access are:

get: requesting a line from its *home*
put: granting a line to the requester (*source* of the request)
fwdget: forwarding the request to an exclusive owner of the line
swb: requesting a write-back of an owned line that is to be shared
nack, nackc: negatively acknowledging the request or forwarded request respectively, if it cannot be performed now.

In analogy, message types related to **exclusive** access are:

getx, putx, fwdgetx, and also
inv: requesting a current *sharer* of the line to invalidate its local copy
invAck: acknowledging the invalidation of the line
fwdAck: owner's granting according to a forwarded shared request.

Additionally, for releasing a shared or exclusive copy from its cache an agent sends a write_back (wb) and a replace message (rpl) to *home*, respectively. A read or write miss of a line, or the end of accessing, is simulated with the help of an oracle function which non-deterministically triggers an agent to send get/getx or rpl/wb messages.

State Functions. Besides the message type, the agent's behavior depends on several local state variables: *curPhase(line)* (phase of the current request), *State(line)* (state of the local line copy in use), and *pending(line)* (flag for currently processed request). *Owner(line)* and the set of *Sharers* of a line are also taken into account.

Adjustable Parameters. The transition rules are parameterized by *self*, the agent that is currently active (this is implicit in Fig. 2), and the requested line. The domains of these parameters, *Agents* and *Lines*, and their extent are easily adjustable in the declaration part of the specification.

Necessary Refinements. Sending a message is given as a macro definition. In the abstract model of [4] *SendMsg* adds a message to a (possibly infinite) set of messages in transit. The strategy for receiving a message from this set is not specified. For the proof it is just assumed that the messages are received in the right order. In order to keep the model finite and to formalize the assumption on the model behavior we have to refine the model. We replace the set of messages in transit by a finite queue for each agent, and we extend the overall behavior by means of a sub-step for synchronization. In the synchronization step the messages are passed through to the addressed agent in the proper order.

---

[12] In our adaptation of the model the parts related to data are discarded.

if $MessType =$ get

   then if $pending(l)$ **then** $SendMsg(\textbf{nack}, source, self, source, l)$
                       else if $Owner(l) \neq undef$
                                then $SendMsg(\textbf{fwdget}, Owner(l), self, source, l)$
                                    $pending(l) := true$
                              else $SendMsg(\textbf{put}, source, self, source, l)$
                                  $Sharer(l, \textbf{source}) := true$

if $MessType =$ fwdget   **if** $MessType =$ put   **if** $MessType =$ swb
  then ...   **then** ...   **then** ...

if $MessType =$ nack   **if** $MessType =$ nackc
  then $curPhase(l) := ready$ **then** $pending(l) := false$

if $MessType =$ getx

  then if $pending(l)$
             then $SendMsg(\textbf{nack}, source, self, source, l)$
             else if $Owner(l) \neq undef$
                     then $SendMsg(\textbf{fwdgetx}, Owner(l), self, source, l)$
                           $pending(l) := true$
                     else if $\exists u : Sharer(l, u)$
                           then $\forall u : Sharer(l, u) SendMsg(\textbf{inv}, u, self, source, l)$
                                $pending(l) := true$
                           else $SendMsg(\textbf{putx}, source, self, source, l)$
                                 $Owner(l) := source$

if $MessType =$ fwdgetx   **if** $MessType =$ fwdAck
  then ...   **then** ...

if $MessType =$ inv

  then $SendMsg(\textbf{invAck}, home, self, source, l)$
             if $State(l) = shared$
                   then $State(l) := invalid$
                   else if $curPhase(l) = wait$
                         then $curPhase(l) := invalidPhase$

if $MessType =$ invAck

  then $Sharer(l, MessSender) := false$
             if $\forall a : Agents \mid a \neq MessSender \wedge Sharer(l, a) = false$
             then $SendMsg(\textbf{putx}, source, self, source, l)$
                     $pending(l) := false$

if $MessType =$ putx   **if** $MessType =$ rpl   **if** $MessType =$ wb
  then ...   **then** ...   **then** ...

Fig. 2. Agent behavior modeled by ASM transition rules

In an ASM model, introducing a sub-step is structure preserving: in addition to the ASM for message computation (explained above) we specify an ASM for the message passing through. An overall ASM invokes both "sub-ASMs" in turn. Taking this, we benefit from the clear and understandable structure of the abstract model. The entire refined ASM-model is available on the web at `http://www.first.gmd.de/~kirsten/publications/flash_param.asm`.

4.2   Model Checking the Transformed System Specification

We take model checking of the transformed ASM model as an evolutionary process of debugging: we edit the ASM model, transform it automatically into an SMV model, run SMV to check the properties under investigation, investigate the resulting counterexample (if any) within the ASM model, and debug the ASM model. Since there are no restrictions on the behavior of the environment (producing requests on a line), we do not suffer from "wrong" counterexamples that are not suitable for debugging the ordinary system behavior. (We call counterexamples wrong, if they are caused by non-reasonable environment behavior that should be excluded. They obstruct the debugging process, since only one counterexample will be produced.)

As the debugging process is more efficient if the model checking terminates in a reasonable span of time, we keep our model as small as possible. We find that, even when the model is restricted to few agents and lines, we detect errors in the abstract model as well as in our refinement. In the following we describe two of them as examples. We check the model for **safety** and **liveness**, i.e.:

– No two agents have exclusive access on the same line simultaneously.
– Each request will eventually be acknowledged.
– Whenever an agent gets shared access, home will note it as a sharer.

We formalize these requirements in CTL, e.g.[13]:

$\bigwedge_{i \neq j}$[AG (!(State(a(i),l)=exclusive & State(a(j),l)=exclusive))]

$\bigwedge_{i}$[AG (curPhase(a(i),l) = wait -> AF (curPhase(a(i),l) = ready))]

$\bigwedge_{i}$[AG (State(a(j),l)=shared -> AX (Sharer(l,a(i)) = true))]

Our first counterexample shows simultaneous exclusive access (for reasons of space we have to omit the listing here). The error that caused the counterexample can also be found in the abstract ASM model of [4]:

> Whenever a `putx`-message is sent to grant exclusive access the addressed requester has to be noted as owner of the line. This is specified in the `getx`-rule but it is missing in the `invAck`-rule that might also cause a `putx`-message to be send (see also Fig. 2). The protocol is unsafe since simultaneous exclusive access may occur, and written data may be lost.

---

[13] Though the third specification is rather weak, it yields helpful counterexamples.

The following counterexamples are dedicated to the problem of racing (i.e., conflicts) on the finite message queue. Although our data space is limited to a very short queue, we can derive more general remarks, e.g.:

Each sharer of a requested line has to process the rule for invalidation (inv-rule). It sends an invAck-message to *home* for acknowledging the invalidation. When receiving an invAck-message, *home* deletes the sender from the list of sharers. If *home* is sharer too,[14] a deadlock may occur if the number of sharers is greater or equal than the length of the message queue: *home* may fail to complete with the inv-rule when the queue is full and sending a message is not possible (since every other sharer may have sent before); *home* stays busy and can not process the incoming invAck-rule to clear the queue. In general, we found out that the message queue must be larger or equal than the number of agents since in the worst case each agent is a sharer and will send simultaneously an invAck-message to the home node.

The examples show that helpful borderline cases can be detected more easily by a model checker than by pure simulation. The computational effort for the automated transformation of our models ranges from three to five seconds. The size of the resulting SMV models is given below.[15] The variable ordering is determined by the automatic reordering facility that is given by the SMV.

resources used:	2 agents, 1 line	3 agents, 1 line	2 agents, 2 lines
user time/system time:	4.69 s/0.13 s	5687.52 s/0.6 s	17263.2 s/0.86 s
BDD nodes allocated:	70587	1612740	2975127
Bytes allocated:	4849664	37748736	54657024
BDD nodes repr. transition relation:	19261 + 78	288986 + 82	78365 + 96

Although checking our model of the FLASH protocol is only feasible for a small number of agents and lines, the results show that the counterexamples yield extremely helpful scenarios for locating errors.

5   Related Work

Extending tool environments for high-level specification languages with an interface to a model checker is an upcoming topic. One can find approaches that are quite similar to ours but work on a different language: [3] suggests a transformation from Statecharts into SMV, in [10] Controller Specification (CSL) models are transformed and model checked by SVE, [12] equips the multi-language environment SYNCHRONIE with an interface to the VIS model checker, etc.

Closer to our approach from the language point of view, [13] also investigates automatic verification of ASM. Spielmann represents an ASM model independently of its possible input by means of a logic for computation graphs (called

---

[14] This is possible if we allow intra-node communication.

[15] The experiments were carried out on an UltraSPARC-II station with 296MHz and 2048 Mb memory, the operating system is Solaris 2.6.

CGL*). The resulting formula is combined with a CTL*-like formula which specifies properties and checked by means of deciding its finite validity. This approach addresses the problem of checking systems with infinitely many inputs, but it is only applicable to ASM with only 0-ary dynamic functions (i.e. ASM_0 programs) and relational input, which is the second result of [13].

6 Conclusions

We presented an interface from the ASM Workbench to SMV, based on a transformation from ASM to the SMV language extending the one defined in [14] by the treatment of dynamic functions of arity $n > 0$. This is essential, as most ASM specifications benefit from the abundant use of parametric dynamic functions.

The practicability of our approach is demonstrated by a non-trivial case study: the ASM model of the FLASH protocol. By example we show that errors can be found in the ASM model that will hardly be detected by pure mathematical proofs, and deduce more general constraints for the model at hand from the counterexamples.

We support the exploitation of the model checking facility by means of introducing *finiteness constraints* into the ASM specification language for easy control of the function ranges in order to restrict the state space of the model. Additionally, the developer benefits from the automatically generated proof obligations to be checked by SMV: the *no-conflict* conditions and the *range* conditions.

Some improvements of our tool, which are still to be implemented in order to make the transition between ASM and SMV smoother and thus ease the validation process, include the automatic translation of the counterexamples into a form which can be immediately read and simulated by the Workbench and the embedding of CTL operators into the ASM-SL language.

References

1. E. Börger. *Specification and Validation Methods.* Oxford University Press, 1995. 331
2. G. Del Castillo. Towards comprehensive tool support for Abstract State Machines: The ASM Workbench tool environment and architecture. In D. Hutter et al., eds., *Applied Formal Methods – FM-Trends 98*, LNCS 1641, pp. 311–325. Springer, 1999. 331, 335
3. N. Day. A model checker for Statecharts (linking case tools with formal methods). TR 93-35, CS Dept., Univ. of British Columbia, Vancouver, B.C., Canada, 1993. 344
4. A. Durand. Modeling cache coherence protocol - a case study with FLASH. In U. Glässer and P. Schmitt, editors, *Procs. of the 5th International ASM Workshop*, pages 111–126, Magdeburg University, 1998. 340, 341, 343
5. T. Filkorn et. al. *SVE Users' Guide.* Siemens AG, München, 1996. 331
6. The VIS Group. Vis: A system for verification and synthesis. In T. Henzinger and R. Alur, editors, *8th Int. Conf. on Computer Aided Verification, CAV'96*, number 1102 in LNCS, pages 428–432, July 1996. 331

7. Y. Gurevich. Evolving Algebras 1993: Lipari Guide. In E. Börger, editor, *Specification and Validation Methods*. Oxford University Press, 1995.   331, 332, 335, 337

8. J.K. Huggins. Abstract State Machines home page. EECS Department, University of Michigan. http://www.eecs.umich.edu/gasm/.   331

9. J. Kuskin et al. The Stanford FLASH multiprocessor. In *21th Int. Symp. on Computer Architecture*. Chicago, IL, 1994.   340

10. P. Liggesmeyer and M. Rothfelder. Towards automated proof of fail-safe behavior. In W. Ehrenberger, editor, *Computer Safety, Reliablity and Security, SAFECOMP'98*, LNCS 1516, pages 169–184, 1998.   344

11. K. McMillan. *Symbolic Model Checking*. Kluwer Academic Publishers, 1993.   331

12. A. Merceron, M. Müllerburg, and G.M. Pinna. Verifying a time-triggered protocol in a multi-language environment. In W. Ehrenberger, editor, *Computer Safety, Reliablity and Security, SAFECOMP'98*, LNCS 1516, pages 185–195, 1998.   344

13. M. Spielmann. Automatic verification of Abstract State Machines. In N. Halbwachs and D. Peled, editors, *Computer Aided Verification, CAV '99*, number 1633 in LNCS, pages 431–442, Trento, Italy, 1999.   344, 345

14. K. Winter. Model checking for abstract state machines. *J.UCS Journal for Universal Computer Science (special issue)*, 3(5):689–702, 1997.   332, 336, 345

A Markov Chain Model Checker

Holger Hermanns[1], Joost-Pieter Katoen[1],
Joachim Meyer-Kayser[2*], and Markus Siegle[2]

[1] Formal Methods and Tools Group, University of Twente
P.O. Box 217, 7500 AE Enschede, The Netherlands
[2] Lehrstuhl für Informatik 7, University of Erlangen-Nürnberg
Martensstraße 3, 91058 Erlangen, Germany

Abstract. Markov chains are widely used in the context of performance and reliability evaluation of systems of various nature. Model checking of such chains with respect to a given (branching) temporal logic formula has been proposed for both the discrete [17,6] and the continuous time setting [4,8]. In this paper, we describe a prototype model checker for discrete and continuous-time Markov chains, the *Erlangen–Twente Markov Chain Checker* ($E \vdash MC^2$), where properties are expressed in appropriate extensions of CTL. We illustrate the general benefits of this approach and discuss the structure of the tool. Furthermore we report on first successful applications of the tool to non-trivial examples, highlighting lessons learned during development and application of $E \vdash MC^2$.

1 Introduction

Markov chains are widely used as simple yet adequate models in diverse areas, ranging from mathematics and computer science to other disciplines such as operations research, industrial engineering, biology and demographics. Markov chains can be used to estimate performance characteristics of various nature, for instance to quantify throughput of manufacturing systems, locate bottlenecks in communication systems, or to estimate reliability in aerospace systems.

Model checking is a very successful technique to establish the *correctness* of systems from similar application domains, usually described in terms of a non-deterministic finite-state model. If non-determinism is replaced by randomized, i.e. probabilistic decisions, the resulting model boils down to a finite-state discrete-time Markov chain (DTMC). For these models, qualitative and quantitative model checking algorithms have been investigated extensively, see e.g. [3,5,6,10,13,17,29]. In a qualitative setting it is checked whether a property holds with probability 0 or 1; in a quantitative setting it is verified whether the probability for a certain property meets a given lower- or upper-bound.

Markov chains are *memoryless*. In the discrete-time setting this is reflected by the fact that probabilistic decisions do not depend on the outcome of decisions taken earlier, only the state currently occupied is decisive to completely

---

* supported by the German Research Council DFG under HE 1408/6-1.

S. Graf and M. Schwartzbach (Eds.): TACAS/ETAPS 2000, LNCS 1785, pp. 347–362, 2000.

determine the probability of next transitions. For continuous-time Markov chains (CTMCs), where time ranges over (positive) reals (instead of discrete subsets thereof) the memoryless property further implies that probabilities of taking next transitions do not depend on the amount of time spent in the current state. The vast majority of applications of Markov chain modelling involves CTMCs, as opposed to DTMCs.[1] In particular, CTMCs are the underlying semantic model of major high-level performance modelling formalisms such as stochastic Petri nets [1], stochastic automata networks [26], stochastic process algebras [24,21], Markovian queueing networks [12], and various extensions thereof.

Model checking of CTMCs has been discussed in [8], introducing a (branching) temporal logic called *continuous-time stochastic logic* (**CSL**) to express properties over CTMCs. This logic is an extension of the (equally named) logic by Aziz et al. [4] with an operator to reason about steady-state probabilities: e.g. the formula $\mathcal{S}_{\geq p}(\Phi)$ asserts that the steady-state probability for being in a Φ-state is at least p, for $p \in [0,1]$. Apart from the usual quantifiers like next and until, a time-bounded until $\mathcal{U}^{\leq t}$, for t a non-negative real, is incorporated, for which standard derivatives, such as a time-bounded eventually $\Diamond^{\leq t}$, can be defined. The usual path quantifiers $\forall$ and $\exists$ are replaced by the probabilistic operator $\mathcal{P}_{\bowtie p}(.)$ for comparison operator $\bowtie$ and $p \in [0,1]$. For instance, $\mathcal{P}_{<10^{-9}}(\Diamond^{\leq 4} error)$ asserts that the probability for a system error within 4 time-units is less than 10^{-9}. Such properties are out of the scope of what can be computed with standard Markov chain analysis algorithms, yet they are highly interesting to study.

In this paper we describe the *Erlangen–Twente Markov Chain Checker* ($E \vdash MC^2$), to our knowledge the first implementation of a model checker for CTMCs It uses numerical methods to model check **CSL**-formulas, based on [8]. Apart from standard graph algorithms, model checking **CSL** involves matrix-vector multiplications (for next-formulas), solutions of linear systems of equations (for until- and steady-state formulas), and solutions of systems of Volterra integral equations (for time-bounded until). Linear systems of equations are iteratively solved by standard numerical methods [27]. Systems of integral equations are iteratively solved by piecewise integration after discretization. As a side result, $E \vdash MC^2$ is also capable to model check DTMCs against properties expressed in **PCTL** [17]. This is not surprising, taking into account that the algorithms needed for **CSL** are a superset of what is needed to check **PCTL**. The tool has been implemented in JAVA (version 1.2), and uses sparse matrix representations. The paper illustrates how $E \vdash MC^2$ can be linked (among others) to (generalized) stochastic Petri nets (GSPN) and to Markovian queueing networks by reporting on the model checking of a GSPN-model of a cyclic server system and of a tandem queueing network.

Other model checkers for probabilistic systems are the DTMC-model checkers PROBVERUS [18] and TPWB (the Timing and Probability Work-Bench) [15],

---

[1] DTMCs are mostly applied in strictly synchronous scenarios, while CTMCs have shown to fit well to (interleaving) asynchronous scenarios.

and the recent symbolic model checker for (discrete-time) Markov decision processes [2].

The paper is organized as follows. Section 2 briefly introduces CTMCs and **CSL**. Section 3 discusses the tool architecture together with the model checking algorithm and some implementation details. Section 4 reports on practical experiences with two case studies and Section 5 concludes the paper.

2   Continuous-Time Markov Chains and CSL

This section reviews continuous-time Markov chains [27] and **CSL** [8].

Continuous-time Markov chains. Let AP be a fixed, finite set of atomic propositions. A (labelled) *continuous-time Markov chain* (CTMC for short) is a tuple $\mathcal{M} = (S, \mathbf{R}, L)$ where S is a finite set of *states*, $\mathbf{R} : S \times S \to \mathbb{R}_{\geqslant 0}$ the *rate matrix*, and $L : S \to 2^{AP}$ the *labelling* function which assigns to each state $s \in S$ the set $L(s)$ of atomic propositions $a \in AP$ that are valid in s.

Intuitively, $\mathbf{R}(s, s')$ specifies that the probability of moving from state s to s' within t time-units (for positive t) is $1 - e^{-\mathbf{R}(s,s') \cdot t}$, an exponential distribution with rate $\mathbf{R}(s, s')$. If $\mathbf{R}(s, s') > 0$ for more than one state s', a competition between the transitions exists, known as the *race condition*. Let $\mathbf{E}(s) = \sum_{s' \in S} \mathbf{R}(s, s')$, the total rate at which any transition emanating from state s is taken. This rate is the reciprocal of the mean sojourn time in s. More precisely, $\mathbf{E}(s)$ specifies that the probability of leaving s within t time-units (for positive t) is $1 - e^{-\mathbf{E}(s) \cdot t}$, due to the fact that the minimum of exponential distributions (competing in a race) is again exponentially distributed, and characterized by the sum of their rates. Consequently, the probability of moving from state s to s' by a single transition, denoted $\mathbf{P}(s, s')$, is determined by the probability that the delay of going from s to s' finishes before the delays of other outgoing edges from s; formally, $\mathbf{P}(s, s') = \mathbf{R}(s, s')/\mathbf{E}(s)$ (except if s is an absorbing state, i.e. if $\mathbf{E}(s) = 0$; in this case we define $\mathbf{P}(s, s') = 0$). Remark that the matrix $\mathbf{P}$ describes an embedded DTMC.

A *path* σ is a finite or infinite sequence $s_0, t_0, s_1, t_1, s_2, t_2, \ldots$ with for $i \in \mathbb{N}$, $s_i \in S$ and $t_i \in \mathbb{R}_{>0}$ such that $\mathbf{R}(s_i, s_{i+1}) > 0$, if σ is infinite. For infinite path σ, $t \in \mathbb{R}_{\geqslant 0}$ and i the smallest index with $t \leqslant \sum_{j=0}^{i} t_j$ let $\sigma@t = s_i$, the state of σ at time t. If σ is finite and ends in s_l, we require that s_l is absorbing, and $\mathbf{R}(s_i, s_{i+1}) > 0$ for all $i < l$. For finite σ, $\sigma@t = s_l$ for $t > \sum_{j=0}^{l-1} t_j$, for other t it is defined as above. Let $Path(s)$ be the set of paths starting in s.

Continuous stochastic logic. **CSL** is a branching-time, CTL-like temporal logic where the state-formulas are interpreted over states of a CTMC.

Definition 1. *For $a \in AP$, $p \in [0, 1]$ and $\bowtie \; \in \{\leqslant, <, \geqslant, >\}$, the state-formulas of* **CSL** *are defined by the grammar*

$$\Phi ::= a \;\Big|\; \Phi \wedge \Phi \;\Big|\; \neg \Phi \;\Big|\; \mathcal{P}_{\bowtie p}(X\Phi) \;\Big|\; \mathcal{P}_{\bowtie p}(\Phi \mathcal{U} \Phi) \;\Big|\; \mathcal{P}_{\bowtie p}(\Phi \mathcal{U}^{\leqslant t} \Phi) \;\Big|\; \mathcal{S}_{\bowtie p}(\Phi)$$

The other boolean connectives are derived in the usual way. The probabilistic operator $\mathcal{P}_{\bowtie p}(.)$ replaces the usual CTL path quantifiers $\exists$ and $\forall$ that can be re-invented – up to fairness [9] – as the extremal probabilities $\mathcal{P}_{>0}(.)$ and $\mathcal{P}_{\geq 1}(.)$. Formula $\mathcal{P}_{\bowtie p}(X\Phi)$ ($\mathcal{P}_{\bowtie p}(\Phi_1 \mathcal{U} \Phi_2)$, respectively) asserts that the probability measure of the paths satisfying $X\Phi$ ($\Phi_1 \mathcal{U} \Phi_2$) satisfies $\bowtie p$. The meaning of X ("next step") and $\mathcal{U}$ ("until") is standard. The temporal operator $\mathcal{U}^{\leq t}$ is the real-time variant of $\mathcal{U}$; $\Phi_1 \mathcal{U}^{\leq t} \Phi_2$ asserts that $\Phi_1 \mathcal{U} \Phi_2$ will be satisfied in the time interval $[0, t]$; i.e. there is some $x \in [0, t]$ such that Φ_1 continuously holds during the interval $[0, x[$ and Φ_2 becomes true at time instant x. The state formula $\mathcal{S}_{\bowtie p}(\Phi)$ asserts that the steady-state probability for a Φ-state satisfies $\bowtie p$. Temporal operators like $\Diamond$, $\Box$ and their real-time variants $\Diamond^{\leq t}$ or $\Box^{\leq t}$ can be derived, e.g. $\mathcal{P}_{\bowtie p}(\Diamond^{\leq t} \Phi) = \mathcal{P}_{\bowtie p}(true \, \mathcal{U}^{\leq t} \Phi)$ and $\mathcal{P}_{\geq p}(\Box \Phi) = \mathcal{P}_{\leq 1-p}(\Diamond \neg \Phi)$.

Semantics of CSL. Let $\mathcal{M} = (S, \mathbf{R}, L)$ with proposition labels in AP. The semantics for atomic propositions, negation, and conjunction is standard [11]. Let $Sat(\Phi) = \{ s \in S \mid s \models \Phi \}$. The steady-state operator is defined by:

$$s \models \mathcal{S}_{\bowtie p}(\Phi) \quad \text{iff} \quad \pi_{Sat(\Phi)}(s) \bowtie p$$

where $\pi_{S'}(s)$ denotes the steady-state probability for $S' \subseteq S$ when starting in s,

$$\pi_{S'}(s) = \lim_{t \to \infty} \Pr\{ \sigma \in Path(s) \mid \sigma@t \in S' \}.$$

This limit exists for finite S [27]. Obviously, $\pi_{S'}(s) = \sum_{s' \in S'} \pi_{s'}(s)$, where we write $\pi_{s'}(s)$ instead of $\pi_{\{s'\}}(s)$. We let $\pi_{\varnothing}(s) = 0$.

For path-formula φ of the form $X\Phi$, $\Phi_1 \mathcal{U} \Phi_2$, or $\Phi_1 \mathcal{U}^{\leq t} \Phi_2$ we have:

$$s \models \mathcal{P}_{\bowtie p}(\varphi) \quad \text{iff} \quad Prob(s, \varphi) \bowtie p, \quad \text{where} \quad Prob(s, \varphi) = \Pr\{ \sigma \in Path(s) \mid \sigma \models \varphi \}$$

i.e., $Prob(s, \varphi)$ denotes the probability measure of all paths $\sigma \in Path(s)$ satisfying φ. The fact that, for each state s, the set $\{ \sigma \in Path(s) \mid \sigma \models \varphi \}$ is measurable, follows by easy verification given the Borel space construction on paths through CTMCs in [8]. The semantics of next and until-formulas is standard [11] and is omitted here. For time-bounded until we have:

$$\sigma \models \Phi_1 \mathcal{U}^{\leq t} \Phi_2 \quad \text{iff} \quad \exists x \in [0, t]. \, (\sigma@x \models \Phi_2 \wedge \forall y \in [0, x[. \, \sigma@y \models \Phi_1).$$

3   The Model Checker E ⊢ MC^2

E ⊢ MC^2 is a prototype tool supporting the verification of **CSL**-properties over CTMCs. It is a *global* model checker, i.e. it checks the validity of a formula for all states in the model. E ⊢ MC^2 has been developed as a model checker that can easily be linked to a wide range of existing high-level modelling tools based on, for instance, stochastic process algebras, stochastic Petri nets, or queueing networks. A whole variety of such tools exists [20], most of them using dedicated formats to store the rate matrix $\mathbf{R}$ that is obtained from the high-level specification. The matrix $\mathbf{R}$, together with the proposition-labelling function L, constitutes the interface between the high-level formalism at hand and the model checker E ⊢ MC^2. Currently, E ⊢ MC^2 accepts CTMCs represented in the **tra**-format as generated by the stochastic process algebra tool TIPPTOOL [22], but the tool is designed in such a way that it enables a filter plug-in functionality to bridge to various other input formats. This is realized via JAVA's dynamic class loading capability.

3.1   The Model Checking Algorithm

Once the matrix $\mathbf{R}$ and the labelling L of a CTMC $\mathcal{M}$ have been initialised, the model checking algorithm implemented in $\mathsf{E} \vdash MC^2$ essentially proceeds in the same way as for model checking CTL [11]. For a given formula $\varPhi$ it recursively computes the sets of states $Sat(.)$ satisfying the sub-formulas of $\varPhi$, and constructs the set $Sat(\varPhi)$ from them. The verification of probabilistic and steady-state properties relies on the constructive characterizations for $Prob(s, \varphi)$ and $\pi_{S'}(s)$ as established in [8].

Steady-state properties. For calculating $\mathcal{S}_{\bowtie p}(\varPhi)$ the tool follows a two-phase approach: first, the bottom strongly connected components (BSCC) of $\mathcal{M}$ are determined by a standard graph algorithm [28]. Then, the steady-state probability distribution is calculated for each of the BSCC. Each step requires the solution of a *linear system of equations* in the size of the BSCC. More precisely, let G be the underlying directed graph of $\mathcal{M}$ where vertices represent states and where there is an edge from s to s' iff $\mathbf{R}(s, s') > 0$. Sub-graph B is a BSCC of G if it is a strongly connected component such that for any $s \in B$, $Reach(s) \subseteq B$. We have $\pi_{s'}(s) = 0$ iff s' does not occur in any BSCC reachable from s. Let B be a BSCC of G with $Reach(s) \cap B \neq \varnothing$, or equivalently, $B \subseteq Reach(s)$, and assume that a_B is an atomic proposition such that $a_B \in L(s)$ iff $s \in B$. Then $\Diamond a_B$ is a path-formula in **CSL** and $Prob(s, \Diamond a_B)$ is the probability of reaching B from s at some time t. For $s' \in B$, $\pi_{s'}(s)$ is given by $\pi_{s'}(s) = Prob(s, \Diamond a_B) \cdot \pi_B(s')$ where $\pi_B(s') = 1$ if $B = \{s'\}$, and otherwise π_B satisfies the linear system of equations[2]

$$\sum_{\substack{s \in B \\ s \neq s'}} \pi_B(s) \cdot \mathbf{R}(s, s') = \pi_B(s') \cdot \sum_{\substack{s \in B \\ s \neq s'}} \mathbf{R}(s', s) \quad \text{such that} \quad \sum_{s \in B} \pi_B(s) = 1. \quad (1)$$

Linear systems of equations can be solved either directly (e.g. Gaussian elimination or LU-decomposition) or by iterative methods such as the power method, Jacobi iteration, Gauß-Seidel iteration and successive over-relaxation [27]. Iterative methods compute approximations to the exact result up to a prespecified precision ε. Although (except for the power method) convergence of the iterative methods is not guaranteed, this problem only appears for pathological cases in practice. The major advantage of these methods is that the involved matrices do not change during the computation (i.e. fill-in is avoided), and hence the buildup of rounding errors is nonexistent [19,27]. In addition, direct methods are known

---

[2] In [8] the above linear system of equations is defined in a slightly different way, by characterizing the steady-state probabilities in terms of the embedded DTMC.

to be only practical for state spaces of up to a few hundred states, while itera-tive methods have successfully been applied for much larger systems (up to 10^7 states) [14]. For these reasons, $\mathsf{E} \vdash MC^2$ supports all of the above mentioned iterative methods to solve (1).

Probabilistic path-formulas. Calculating the probabilities $Prob(s, \varphi)$ pro-ceeds as in the discrete-time case [13,17,5], except for the time-bounded until that is particular to the continuous-time case. More precisely:

Next: $Prob(s, X\Phi)$ is obtained by multiplying the transition probability matrix $\mathbf{P}$ with the (boolean) vector $i_\Phi = (i_\Phi(s))_{s\in S}$ characterizing $Sat(\Phi)$, i.e. $i_\Phi(s) = 1$ if $s \models \Phi$, and 0 otherwise.

Until: $Prob(s, \Phi_1 \,\mathcal{U}\, \Phi_2)$ is obtained by solving a linear system of equations of the form $\mathbf{x} = \overline{\mathbf{P}} \cdot \mathbf{x} + i_{\Phi_2}$ where $\overline{\mathbf{P}}(s, s') = \mathbf{P}(s, s')$ if $s \models \Phi_1 \wedge \neg\Phi_2$ and 0 other-wise. $Prob(s, \Phi_1 \,\mathcal{U}\, \Phi_2)$ is the least solution of this set of equations. $\mathsf{E} \vdash MC^2$ computes the least solution by one of the standard methods mentioned above for the steady-state operator.

Time-bounded until: to compute the time-bounded until operator, we use the following characterization:

Theorem 1. [8] *The function* $S \times \mathbb{R}_{\geqslant 0} \to [0,1]$, $(s,t) \mapsto Prob(s, \Phi_1 \,\mathcal{U}^{\leqslant t}\, \Phi_2)$ *is the least fixed point of the higher-order operator* $\Omega : (S \times \mathbb{R}_{\geqslant 0} \to [0,1]) \to (S \times \mathbb{R}_{\geqslant 0} \to [0,1])$ *where[3]*

$$\Omega(F)(s,t) = \begin{cases} 1 & \text{if } s \models \Phi_2 \\ \sum_{s' \in S} \mathbf{R}(s, s') \cdot \int_0^t e^{-\mathbf{E}(s) \cdot x} \cdot F(s', t-x) \, dx & \text{if } s \models \Phi_1 \wedge \neg\Phi_2 \\ 0 & \text{otherwise.} \end{cases}$$

This result suggests the following iterative method to approximate $Prob(s, \Phi_1 \,\mathcal{U}^{\leqslant t}\, \Phi_2)$: let $F_0(s,t) = 0$ for all s, t and $F_{k+1} = \Omega(F_k)$. Then,

$$\lim_{k \to \infty} F_k(s,t) = Prob(s, \Phi_1 \,\mathcal{U}^{\leqslant t}\, \Phi_2).$$

Each step in the iteration amounts to solve an integral of the following form:

$$F_{k+1}(s,t) = \sum_{s' \in S} \mathbf{R}(s, s') \cdot \int_0^t e^{-\mathbf{E}(s) \cdot x} \cdot F_k(s', t-x) \, dx,$$

if $s \models \Phi_1 \wedge \neg\Phi_2$. In [8], we proposed to solve these integrals numerically based on quadrature formulas with, say, $N + 1$ equally spaced interpolation points $x_m = m \cdot \frac{t}{N}$ ($0 \leqslant m \leqslant N$) such as trapezoidal, Simpson, or Romberg integration schemes. For the trapezoidal method, for instance, this amounts to approximate

$$F_{k+1}(s, x_m) \approx \sum_{s' \in S} \mathbf{R}(s, s') \cdot \sum_{j=0}^{m} \alpha_j \cdot e^{-\mathbf{E}(s) \cdot x_j} \cdot F_k(s', x_m - x_j)$$

where for fixed m, $\alpha_0 = \alpha_m = \frac{t}{2N}$ and $\alpha_j = \frac{t}{N}$ for $0 < j < m$. However, practical experiments with $\mathsf{E} \vdash MC^2$ revealed that these schemes may result in inaccurate results by overestimating the impact of the 'leftmost' intervals. We therefore take a different route by using piecewise integration, and approximat-ing

---

[3] The underlying partial order on $S \times \mathbb{R}_{\geqslant 0} \to [0,1]$ is defined for F_1, $F_2 : S \times \mathbb{R}_{\geqslant 0} \to [0,1]$ by $F_1 \leqslant F_2$ iff $F_1(s,t) \leqslant F_2(s,t)$ for all s, t.

$$F_{k+1}(s, x_m) \approx \sum_{s' \in S} \mathbf{R}(s, s') \cdot \sum_{j=0}^{m} \int_{x_j - \beta_j}^{x_j + \beta_{j+1}} e^{-\mathbf{E}(s) \cdot x} \, dx \cdot F_k(s', x_m - x_j)$$

where $\beta_0 = \beta_{m+1} = 0$ and $\beta_j = \frac{1}{2N}$ for $0 < j \leqslant m$. Note that the resulting integrals are easily solved because they only involve exponential distributions. So, discretization is used merely to restrict the impact of possible state changes to the interpolation points $x_0, \ldots, x_N$. The influence of the number of interpolation points on the accuracy and the run-time of the algorithm is one of the interesting aspects discussed in Section 4.

As in [17] for until and time-bounded until some pre-processing is done (on the underlying graph G of CTMC $\mathcal{M}$) before the actual model checking is carried out. First we determine the set of states for which the (fair) CTL-formula $\exists(\Phi_1 \, \mathcal{U} \, \Phi_2)$ is valid, i.e. we compute $Sat(\exists(\Phi_1 \, \mathcal{U} \, \Phi_2))$. This is done in the usual iterative way [17]. For states not in this set the respective probabilistic until-formula will have probability 0. In a similar way, we compute the set of states for which the probability of these properties will be 1. This is done by computing the set of states $Sat(\forall(\Phi_1 \, \mathcal{U} \, \Phi_2))$ (up to fairness, cf. [9]) in the usual iterative way [17]. As a result, the actual computation, being it the solution of the linear system of equations in case of an unbounded until, or the solution of the system of Volterra integral equations in case of the time-bounded until, can be restricted to the remaining states. This not only reduces the number of states, but also speeds up the convergence of the iterative algorithms.

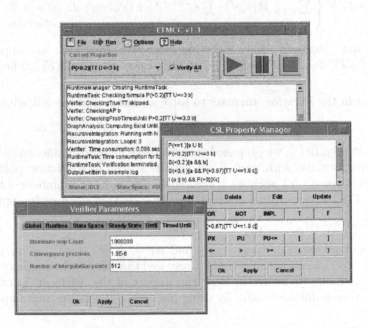

Fig. 1. User interface of $\mathsf{E} \vdash MC^2$

3.2 Tool Architecture

$E \vdash MC^2$ has been written entirely in JAVA (version 1.2), an object-oriented language known to provide platform independence and to enable fast and efficient program development. Furthermore, support for the development of graphical user interfaces as well as grammar parsers are at hand. For the sake of simplicity, flexibility and extensibility we abstained from low-level optimizations, such as minimization of object invocations. The design and implementation took approximately 8 man-months, with about 8000 lines of code for the kernel and 1500 lines of code for the GUI implementation, using the SWING library. The tool architecture consists of five components, see Fig. 2.

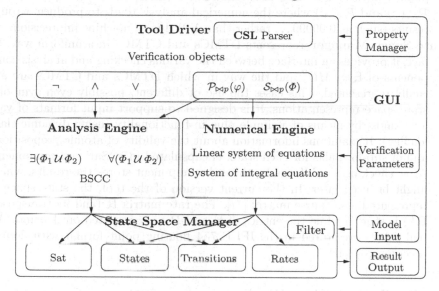

Fig. 2. The tool architecture

Graphical User Interface (cf. Fig. 1) enables the user to load a model $\mathcal{M}$, a labelling L, and the properties to be checked. It prints results on screen or writes them into file and allows the user to construct **CSL**-formulas by the 'CSL Property Manager'. Several verification parameters for the numerical analysis, such as solution method, precision ε and number of interpolation points N, can be set by the user.

Tool Driver controls the model checking procedure. It parses a **CSL**-formula and generates the corresponding parse tree. Subsequent evaluation of the parse tree results in calls to the respective verification objects that encapsulate the verification sub-algorithms. These objects, in turn, use the analysis and/or numerical engine. For instance, checking $\mathcal{P}_{\leqslant p}(\Phi_1 \, \mathcal{U} \, \Phi_2)$ involves a pre-processing step (as mentioned above) that isolates states satisfying $\exists(\Phi_1 \, \mathcal{U} \, \Phi_2)$ and $\forall(\Phi_1 \, \mathcal{U} \, \Phi_2)$. The results of this step are passed to the numerical engine that computes the corresponding (non-zero) probabilities.

Numerical Engine is the numerical analysis engine of $\mathsf{E} \vdash MC^2$. It computes the solution of linear systems of equations and of systems of Volterra integral equations in the way explained above on the basis of the parameters provided by the user via the GUI, such as the precision ε, the 'maximum loop count' (the maximal number of iterations before termination), or the number N of interpolation points used for the piecewise integration.

Analysis Engine is the engine that supports graph algorithms, for instance, to compute the BSCC in case of steady-state properties, and standard model checking algorithms for CTL-like until-formulas. The latter algorithms are not only used as a pre-processing phase of checking until-formulas (as explained above), but they also take care of instances of the special cases $\mathcal{P}_{\geqslant 1}(\varphi)$ and $\mathcal{P}_{>0}(\varphi)$ where the numerical analysis tends to produce 'wrong' results (such as $0.99999\ldots$ rather than 1.0) due to machine imprecision.

State Space Manager represents DTMCs and CTMCs in a uniform way. In fact, it provides an interface between the various checking and analysis components of $\mathsf{E} \vdash MC^2$ and the way in which DTMCs and CTMCs are actually represented. This eases the use of different, possibly even symbolic state space representations. It is designed to support input formats of various kinds, by means of a simple plug-in-functionality (using dynamic class loading). It maintains information about the validity of atomic propositions and of sub-formulas for each state, encapsulated in a 'Sat' sub-component. After checking a sub-formula, this sub-component stores the results, which might be used later. In the current version of the tool, the state space is represented as a sparse matrix [27]. The rate matrix $\mathbf{R}$ (and its transposed $\mathbf{R}^T$) is stored, while the entries of $\mathbf{E}$ and $\mathbf{P}$ are computed on demand. All real values are stored in the IEEE 754 floating point format with double precision (64 bit).

4   Application Case Studies

In this section we report on experiences with $\mathsf{E} \vdash MC^2$ in the context of model checking two Markov chain models that have been generated from high-level formalisms, namely queueing networks and generalized stochastic Petri nets. Based on these experiments we assess the sensitivity of the model checker with respect to various parameters. We ran the experiments on a 300 MHz SUN Ultra 5/10 workstation with 256 MB memory under the Solaris 2.6 operating system. In the case studies we solve linear systems of equations by means of the Gauß-Seidel method. All recorded execution times are wall clock times.

4.1   A Simple Tandem Queue

As a first, simple example we consider a queueing network (with blocking) taken from [23]. It consists of a $M/Cox_2/1$-queue sequentially composed with a $M/M/1$-queue, see Fig. 3. Due to space constraints, we have to refer to [12] for a thorough introduction to networks of queues. Both queueing stations have a capacity of c

Fig. 3. A simple tandem network with blocking [23]

jobs, $c > 0$. Jobs arrive at the first queueing station with rate λ. The server of the first station executes jobs in one or two phases; that is, with probability $1 - a_1$ a job is served with rate μ_1 only, and with probability a_1, the job has to pass an additional phase with rate μ_2. Once served, jobs leave the first station, and are queued in the second station where service takes place with rate κ. In case the second queueing station is fully occupied, i.e. its server is busy and its queue is full, the first station is said to be blocked. Note that in this situation, the second phase of the first server is blocked and the first server can only pass a job that just finished the first phase to the second phase (which happens with probability a_1), but the "bypass" of the second phase is also blocked. For the experiments we take the following values for the parameters of the queue: $\lambda = 4 \cdot c$, $\mu_1 = 2$, $\mu_2 = 2$, $\kappa = 4$, and $a_1 = 0.1$. We consider $c = 2$, which amounts to 15 states and 33 transitions, $c = 5$, i.e. 66 states and 189 transitions and $c = 20$, i.e. 861 states and 2851 transitions. The following atomic propositions are considered:

- *full* is valid iff the entire tandem network is entirely populated, i.e. iff both queueing stations contain c jobs,
- *fst* is valid iff no new arriving job (with rate λ) can be accepted anymore, because the first queue is entirely populated.
- *snd* is valid iff the first queueing station is blocked, because the second queue is entirely populated.

It should be noticed that *full* characterizes a single state, and hence, for large c identifies a rare event, i.e. a situation that appears with very low probability. The following steady-state properties are checked: $\mathcal{S}_{\bowtie p}(full)$, $\mathcal{S}_{\bowtie p}(fst)$, and $\mathcal{S}_{\bowtie p}(\mathcal{P}_{\bowtie q}(X\,snd))$, for arbitrary p and q. The latter property is valid if the steady-state probability to be in a state that can reach a state in which the first queueing station is blocked in a single step with probability $\bowtie q$ satisfies $\bowtie p$. We do not instantiate p and q, as the execution times and computed probabilities will be the same for all p and q (except for the extremal cases 0 and 1); only the comparison with the bounds might lead to a different outcome. Thus, $p, q \in\,]0, 1[$. For the steady-state properties we vary the precision ε of the computed probability, which is a parameter to the model checker. The results are listed in Table 1.

The third column indicates the number of iterations needed to reach the result with the desired precision. Recall that the model checker checks the validity of **CSL**-formulas for all states in the CTMC.

The following probabilistic path properties are checked: $\mathcal{P}_{\bowtie p}(\lozenge^{\leq t}\,full)$, $\mathcal{P}_{\bowtie p}(\lozenge^{\leq t}\,fst)$ and $\mathcal{P}_{\bowtie p}(snd\,\mathcal{U}^{\leq t}\,\neg snd)$. The latter property refers to the prob-

Table 1. Statistics for checking steady-state properties on the tandem queue

# states	ε	# iterations	$\mathcal{S}_{\bowtie p}(full)$ time (in sec)	$\mathcal{S}_{\bowtie p}(fst)$ time (in sec)	$\mathcal{S}_{\bowtie p}(\mathcal{P}_{\bowtie q}(X\,snd))$ time (in sec)
15	10^{-4}	62	0.012	0.012	0.013
	10^{-6}	107	0.016	0.017	0.016
$(c=2)$	10^{-8}	146	0.017	0.018	0.019
66	10^{-4}	77	0.028	0.028	0.065
	10^{-6}	121	0.041	0.042	0.076
$(c=5)$	10^{-8}	159	0.048	0.085	0.181
861	10^{-4}	74	0.569	0.498	1.567
	10^{-6}	118	0.644	0.643	1.935
$(c=20)$	10^{-8}	158	0.811	0.778	2.369

Table 2. Statistics for checking $\mathcal{P}_{\bowtie p}(\varPhi_1\,\mathcal{U}^{\leq t}\,\varPhi_2)$-formulas on the tandem queue

# states	t	# interpolation points	$\mathcal{P}_{\bowtie p}(\Diamond^{\leq t} full)$ # iter.	time (in sec)	$\mathcal{P}_{\bowtie p}(\Diamond^{\leq t} fst)$ # iter.	time (in sec)	$\mathcal{P}_{\bowtie p}(snd\,\mathcal{U}^{\leq t}\,\neg snd)$ # iter.	time (in sec)
15	2	64	18	2.497	11	1.045	4	0.144
		128	18	9.762	11	4.082	4	0.566
		256	18	22.19	11	16.30	4	2.248
		512	18	156.2	11	69.04	4	9.067
$(c=2)$		1000	18	602.3	11	248.6	4	34.27
15	10	64	45	6.506	12	1.140	4	0.145
		128	43	24.00	12	4.575	4	0.568
		256	43	52.85	12	17.94	4	2.309
		512	43	383.1	12	75.13	4	8.994
$(c=2)$		1000	43	1433	12	274.9	4	34.38
15	100	64	472	104.6	12	2.133	4	0.229
		128	344	284.9	12	7.682	4	0.817
		256	285	958.1	12	31.07	4	3.361
		512	260	3582	12	123.8	4	13.51
$(c=2)$		1000	252	13201	12	493.8	4	51.49
861	2	64	36	448.3	29	347.3	21	9.608
		128	36	1773	29	1336	21	38.90
		256	36	7028	29	5293	21	150.5
$(c=20)$		512	36	28189	29	21914	21	600.1

ability of leaving a situation in which the second queue is entirely populated. All path-properties are checked with precision $\varepsilon = 10^{-6}$. We vary the time-span t (over 2, 10 and 100), and the number of interpolation points for the piecewise integration from 64 up to 1000. The results for $c = 2$ are listed in the upper part of Table 2. Note the difference in computation time for the different properties. Whereas $\mathcal{P}_{\bowtie p}(snd\,\mathcal{U}^{\leq t}\,\neg snd)$ can be checked rather fast, calculating the probability for reaching a fst-state within a certain time bound, and — in particular — until reaching a $full$-state takes significantly more time. Since the CTMC is strongly connected, a $full$- or fst-state can (eventually) be reached from any other state, and hence for all states the probability for reaching these states within time t must be calculated. In addition, the probability of reaching the single $full$-state is low, especially for larger c, and quite a number of iterations are needed in that case to obtain results with the desired precision. Since there are several fst-states in the CTMC, this effect is less important for $\mathcal{P}_{\bowtie p}(\Diamond^{\leq t} fst)$. For the last property (last two columns), probabilities need only be computed for *snd*-states rather than for all states, and precision is reached rather quickly as the real probabilities are close to 1. These effects become more apparent when increasing the state space. This is reflected by the results in the lower part of Table 2 where we considered a CTMC of almost 1000 states.

4.2   A Cyclic Server Polling System

In this section, we consider a cyclic server polling system consisting of d stations and a server, modelled as a GSPN.[4] The example is taken from [25], where a

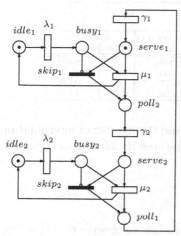

detailed explanation can be found. For $d = 2$, i.e. a two-station polling system, the GSPN model is depicted on the left. For a d-station polling system, the Petri net is extended in the obvious way. Place $idle_i$ represents the condition that station i is idle, and place $busy_i$ represents the condition that station i has generated a job. The server visits the stations in a cyclic fashion. After polling station i (place $poll_i$) the server serves station i (place $serve_i$), and then proceeds to poll the next station. The times for generating a message, for polling a station and for serving a job are all distributed exponentially with parameters λ_i, γ_i and μ_i, respectively. In case the server finds station i idle, the service time is zero which is modelled by the immediate transition $skip_i$ and the inhibitor arc from place $busy_i$ to transition $skip_i$. In this study we consider polling systems with $d = 3$, 5, 7 and 10 stations (like in [25]). The corresponding CTMCs have 36, 240, 1344 and 15360 states (84, 800, 5824 and 89600 transitions). The polling systems are assumed to be symmetric, i.e. all λ_i have the same numerical values, and the same is true for all $\gamma_i = 1$ and all $\mu_i = 200$. We set $\lambda_i = \mu_i/d$.

In the context of GSPNs, it is rather natural to identify the set of places that possess a token in a given marking — i.e. a state of our CTMC — with the set of atomic propositions valid in this state. Based on these atomic propositions, we check the following properties on the polling system: $\neg(poll_1 \land poll_2)$, stating that the server never polls both stations at the same time; $\mathcal{P}_{\bowtie p}(\neg serve_2 \, \mathcal{U} \, serve_1)$, i.e. with probability $\bowtie p$ station 1 will be served before station 2; $busy_1 \Rightarrow \mathcal{P}_{\geqslant 1}(\Diamond poll_1)$, so once station 1 has become busy, it will eventually be polled; $busy_1 \Rightarrow \mathcal{P}_{\bowtie p}(\Diamond^{\leqslant t} poll_1)$, once station 1 has become busy, with probability $\bowtie p$ it will be polled within t time units. (We let $t = 1.5$.) The following steady state

---

[4] We refer to [1] for details on the semantics of GSPNs. In particular, the existence of immediate transitions (i.e. the black transitions) leads to so-called vanishing markings in the reachability graph which, however, can be eliminated easily. Our model checker works on the resulting tangible reachability graph which is isomorphic to a CTMC.

formulas are considered: $S_{\bowtie p}(busy_1 \wedge \neg serve_1)$, which says that the probability of station 1 being waiting for the server is $\bowtie p$; and $S_{\bowtie p}(idle_1)$, stating that the probability of station 1 being idle is $\bowtie p$. Like before, $p \in]0,1[$. All path-

Table 3. Statistics for checking **CSL**-formulas on the polling system

d	# states	$\neg(poll_1 \wedge poll_2)$ time (in sec)	$P_{\bowtie p}(\neg serve_2 \, \mathcal{U} \, serve_1)$ time (in sec)	$busy_1 \Rightarrow P_{\geqslant 1}(\Diamond poll_1)$ time (in sec)
3	36	0.002	0.031	0.005
5	240	0.002	0.171	0.009
7	1344	0.005	1.220	0.011
10	15360	0.037	16.14	0.080

d	# states	$busy_1 \Rightarrow P_{\bowtie p}(\Diamond^{\leqslant 1.5} poll_1)$ # iter.	time (in sec)	$S_{\bowtie p}(busy_1 \wedge \neg serve_1)$ # iter.	time (in sec)	$S_{\bowtie p}(idle_1)$ # iter.	time (in sec)
3	36	8	2.308	39	0.044	39	0.038
5	240	12	30.92	61	0.103	61	0.102
7	1344	14	308.5	80	0.677	80	0.658
10	15360	18	7090	107	11.28	107	11.29

properties were checked with precision $\varepsilon = 10^{-6}$, and the number of interpolation points for numerical integration was set to 64. The steady-state properties were checked for $\varepsilon = 10^{-8}$.

4.3 Assessment of the Tool

Verification time. From the results of our case studies we observe that checking **CSL**-formulas consisting of just atomic propositions and logical connectives is very fast. Checking steady-state properties and unbounded until-formulas is also a matter of only a few seconds, even for the 15360 state case. Measurements have shown that the performance of our tool's steady-state solution algorithm is comparable to the one of TIPPtool [22] which is based on a sophisticated sparse matrix library implemented in C. The model checking algorithm for time-bounded until $P_{\bowtie p}(\Phi_1 \, \mathcal{U}^{\leqslant t} \, \Phi_2)$, which involves the approximate solution of a system of integral equations, becomes very time consuming for larger state spaces. Obviously, the execution times for checking time-bounded until strongly depend on the chosen number of interpolation points: each iteration in the piecewise integration in the worst case is of order $\mathcal{O}(N^2 \cdot K)$, where K is the number of transitions and N the number of interpolation points. In addition, the execution times depend on the arguments (i.e. Φ_1 and Φ_2) and the considered time-span (i.e. parameter t). For instance, checking $P_{\bowtie p}(\Diamond^{\leqslant t}\Phi_2)$ involves a computation for each state (that has a non-zero and non-trivial probability of reaching a Φ_2-state), while checking $P_{\bowtie p}(a\,\mathcal{U}^{\leqslant t} \, \Phi_2)$ only involves a computation for the a-labelled states (of this set). The case studies, and other experiments which we conducted showed that the main performance bottleneck of our tool is the algorithm for time-bounded until.

Accuracy of numerical results. In order to assess the numerical accuracy of the algorithm for time-bounded until, we used our tool to compute (amongst others) the cumulative distribution function of the Erlang k-distribution, that is, a convolution of k identical exponential distributions. For small k the results of the iterative algorithm are quite accurate, even for a small number of interpolation points N. The accuracy further improves as N is increased, as expected. For $k \geqslant 100$ and small N, the accuracy of the results is unacceptable, while for larger N the run-time becomes excessive.

Accuracy of verification result. Another issue — that is inherently present in all model checking approaches that rely on numerical recipes — is to avoid wrong outcomes of comparisons with a probability bound p in a sub-formula, that is then propagated upwards. Because round-off and truncation errors cannot be avoided (due to machine imprecision), this effect can happen if the computed value is very close to the bound p. For the extremal probability bounds (i.e. bounds > 0 and $\geqslant 1$), we have circumvented this problem by applying the standard model checking algorithms for $\forall$ and $\exists$ as in [17]. Furthermore we intend to use a three-valued logic such that the tool can avoid potentially wrong results, and answers 'don't know' in case some calculated (i.e. approximated) probability is within some tolerance to a probability bound p occurring in a (sub-)formula to be checked.

5   Conclusion

In this paper we have presented a model checker for (state labelled) discrete and continuous-time Markov chains. We reported on the structure of the tool, and on experiments using the model checker to verify CTMCs derived from high-level formalisms such as stochastic Petri nets and queueing networks. As far as we know, $\mathsf{E} \vdash MC^2$ is the first implementation of a bridge between such high-level specification formalisms for CTMCs and model checking.

$\mathsf{E} \vdash MC^2$ is a prototype, in particular for the moment it does not use symbolic, i.e. (MT)BDD-based, data structures. Although our own experience (and of others, cf. [16]) has shown that very compact encodings of Markov chains are possible with MTBDDs and similar data structures [23], and symbolic model checking algorithms for CTMCs do exist [8], we favor a separation of concerns: to our belief the issues of numerical stability, convergence, accuracy and efficiency are worth to be studied in isolation, without interference of the (sometimes unpredictable) effects of BDD-based computations. In addition, none of the high-level modelling tools for generating CTMCs uses BDD-based data structures, as far as we know.

Our decision to implement the model checker $\mathsf{E} \vdash MC^2$ in JAVA turned out to be a good choice. In particular it allowed us to develop an easy-to-use user interface along with the model checker engine. Also the numerical computations have a good performance in JAVA; e.g., the computation of steady-state properties is comparable to (optimised) existing C implementations. Our experiments with $\mathsf{E} \vdash MC^2$ have shown that the checking of time-bounded until-properties requires an efficiency improvement. We are currently considering alternative ways to model check this operator [7].

Acknowledgement

The authors thank Lennard Kerber (Erlangen) for his contribution to assessing the accuracy of the tool output and Christel Baier (Bonn) for her valuable contributions and discussions.

References

1. M. Ajmone Marsan, G. Conte, and G. Balbo. A class of generalised stochastic Petri nets for the performance evaluation of multiprocessor systems. *ACM Tr. on Comp. Sys.*, **2**(2): 93–122, 1984. 348, 358
2. L. de Alfaro, M.Z. Kwiatkowska, G. Norman, D. Parker and R. Segala. Symbolic model checking for probabilistic processes using MTBDDs and the Kronecker representation. In *TACAS*, LNCS (this volume), 2000. 349
3. A. Aziz, V. Singhal, F. Balarin, R. Brayton and A. Sangiovanni-Vincentelli. It usually works: the temporal logic of stochastic systems. In *CAV*, LNCS 939: 155–165, 1995. 347
4. A. Aziz, K. Sanwal, V. Singhal and R. Brayton. Verifying continuous time Markov chains. In *CAV*, LNCS 1102: 269–276, 1996. 347, 348
5. C. Baier. On algorithmic verification methods for probabilistic systems. Habilitation thesis, Univ. of Mannheim, 1999. 347, 352
6. C. Baier, E. Clarke, V. Hartonas-Garmhausen, M. Kwiatkowska, and M. Ryan. Symbolic model checking for probabilistic processes. In *ICALP*, LNCS 1256: 430–440, 1997. 347
7. C. Baier, B.R. Haverkort, H. Hermanns and J.-P. Katoen. Model checking continuous-time Markov chains by transient analysis. 2000 (submitted). 360
8. C. Baier, J.-P. Katoen and H. Hermanns. Approximate symbolic model checking of continuous-time Markov chains. In *CONCUR*, LNCS 1664: 146–162, 1999. 347, 348, 349, 350, 351, 352, 360
9. C. Baier and M. Kwiatkowska. On the verification of qualitative properties of probabilistic processes under fairness constraints. *Inf. Proc. Letters*, **66**(2): 71–79, 1998. 350, 353
10. I. Christoff and L. Christoff. Reasoning about safety and liveness properties for probabilistic systems. In *FSTTCS*, LNCS 652: 342-355, 1992. 347
11. E.M. Clarke, E.A. Emerson and A.P. Sistla. Automatic verification of finite-state concurrent systems using temporal logic specifications. *ACM Tr. on Progr. Lang. and Sys.*, **8**(2): 244-263, 1986. 350, 351
12. A.E. Conway and N.D. Georganas. *Queueing Networks – Exact Computational Algorithms*. MIT Press, 1989. 348, 355
13. C. Courcoubetis and M. Yannakakis. Verifying temporal properties of finite-state probabilistic programs. In *Proc. IEEE Symp. on Found. of Comp. Sci.*, pp. 338–345, 1988. 347, 352
14. D.D. Deavours and W.H. Sanders. An efficient disk-based tool for solving very large Markov models. In *Comp. Perf. Ev.*, LNCS 1245: 58–71, 1997. 352
15. L. Fredlund. The timing and probability workbench: a tool for analysing timed processes. Tech. Rep. No. 49, Uppsala Univ., 1994. 348
16. G. Hachtel, E. Macii, A. Padro and F. Somenzi. Markovian analysis of large finite-state machines. *IEEE Tr. on CAD of Integr. Circ. and Sys.*, **15**(12): 1479–1493, 1996. 360

17. H. Hansson and B. Jonsson. A logic for reasoning about time and reliability. *Form. Asp. of Comp.*, **6**(5): 512–535, 1994. 347, 348, 352, 353, 360

18. V. Hartonas-Garmhausen, S. Campos and E.M. Clarke. PROBVERUS: probabilistic symbolic model checking. In *ARTS*, LNCS 1601: 96–111, 1999. 348

19. B.R. Haverkort. *Performance of Computer Communication Systems: A Model-Based Approach.* John Wiley & Sons, 1998. 351

20. B.R. Haverkort and I.G. Niemegeers. Performability modelling tools and techniques. *Perf. Ev.*, **25**: 17–40, 1996. 350

21. H. Hermanns, U. Herzog and J.-P. Katoen. Process algebra for performance evaluation. *Th. Comp. Sci.*, 2000 (to appear). 348

22. H. Hermanns, U. Herzog, U. Klehmet, V. Mertsiotakis and M. Siegle. Compositional performance modelling with the TIPPTOOL. *Perf. Ev.*, **39**(1-4): 5–35, 2000. 351, 359

23. H. Hermanns, J. Meyer-Kayser and M. Siegle. Multi-terminal binary decision diagrams to represent and analyse continuous-time Markov chains. In *Proc. 3rd Int. Workshop on the Num. Sol. of Markov Chains*, pp. 188-207, 1999. 355, 356, 360

24. J. Hillston. *A Compositional Approach to Performance Modelling.* Cambridge University Press, 1996. 348

25. O.C. Ibe and K.S. Trivedi. Stochastic Petri net models of polling systems. *IEEE J. on Sel. Areas in Comms.*, **8**(9): 1649–1657, 1990. 358

26. B. Plateau and K. Atif, Stochastic automata networks for modeling parallel systems. *IEEE Tr. on Softw. Eng.*, **17**(10): 1093–1108, 1991. 348

27. W. Stewart. *Introduction to the Numerical Solution of Markov Chains.* Princeton Univ. Press, 1994. 348, 349, 350, 351, 355

28. R.E. Tarjan. Depth-first search and linear graph algorithms. *SIAM J. of Comp.*, **1**: 146–160, 1972. 351

29. M.Y. Vardi. Automatic verification of probabilistic concurrent finite state programs. In *Proc. IEEE Symp. on Found. of Comp. Sci.*, pp. 327–338, 1985. 347

Model Checking SDL with Spin[*]

Dragan Bošnački[1], Dennis Dams[2], Leszek Holenderski[1], and Natalia Sidorova[2]

[1] Dept. of Computing Sci., Eindhoven University of Technology
PO Box 513, 5600 MB Eindhoven, The Netherlands
{D.Bosnacki,L.Holenderski}@tue.nl
[2] Dept. of Electrical Eng., Eindhoven University of Technology
PO Box 513, 5600 MB Eindhoven, The Netherlands
{D.Dams,N.Sidorova}@tue.nl

Abstract. We present an attempt to use the model checker Spin as a
verification engine for SDL, with special emphasis put on the verification of timing properties of SDL models. We have extended Spin with a
front-end that allows to translate SDL to Promela (the input language
of Spin), and a back-end that allows to analyse timing properties. Compared with the previous attempts, our approach allows to verify not only
qualitative but also quantitative aspects of SDL timers, and our translation of SDL to Promela handles the SDL timers in a correct way. We
applied the toolset to the verification of a substantial part of a complex
industrial protocol. This allowed to expose several non-trivial errors in
the protocol's design.

1 Introduction

We present an approach to automating the formal verification of SDL, by model
checking SDL specifications with Spin. SDL [8] is a visual specification language,
especially well suited for communication protocols, and quite popular in industry.
Spin [5] is one of the most successful enumerative model checkers.

In order to connect the Spin verification engine to SDL, we had to extend
Spin in two ways. First, we had to implement a front-end which would allow to
automatically translate SDL to Promela (the input language of Spin). Second,
we had to extend Spin with the notion of discrete time, to be able to model SDL
timers. The extended version is called DT Spin and its input language is called
DT Promela (where DT stands for *discrete time*).

The translation of SDL to Promela is split into two steps. In the first step
we use the `sdl2if` tool, implemented in Verimag, Grenoble, which transforms
SDL programs to the intermediate format IF [3] that was designed for the representation of timed asynchronous systems. This first step flattens the hierarchic
structure of SDL blocks to bare processes which can then be directly transformed
to Promela processes, in the second step, by our tool `if2pml`.

---

[*] This research has been supported by the VIRES project (Verifying Industrial Reactive Systems, Esprit Long Term Research Project #23498).

S. Graf and M. Schwartzbach (Eds.): TACAS/ETAPS 2000, LNCS 1785, pp. 363–377, 2000.

We applied our method to the verification of a substantial part of MAS-CARA which is a complex telecommunication protocol developed by the WAND (Wireless ATM Network Demonstrator) consortium [13]. As a result, we exposed several non-trivial errors in the design of MASCARA.

In order to resolve the usual problems caused by the lack of the formal semantics of SDL, we decided to rely on the semantics of SDL as determined by the ObjectGEODE tool [11]. In particular, we assume that transitions are atomic and instantaneous, and timeout signals are not necessarily sent at the beginning of a time slice (in other words, the timer messages are treated like other messages, without any special priority). More details are given in Section 3.2.

We are aware of two other attempts to use Spin as a verification engine for SDL [6,10]. In our opinion, they were not fully successful. First, both ap-proaches tackle the qualitative aspects of SDL timers only, in the sense that they abstract out the concrete values of timers. Our approach allows to analyze the quantitative aspects of SDL timers as well. Second, the previous approaches are incorrect, as far as the timing issues are concerned. More precisely, instead of just introducing more behaviours, which is unavoidable when the concrete values of timers are abstracted out, they simultaneously remove some of the behaviours that are allowed by SDL, which may lead to unsound results (so called "false positives"). Some concrete examples are given in Section 3.3. The incorrectness of the previous attempts also shows that taking the timing issues of SDL into account, when using Spin to model check SDL, is not trivial.

We do not claim that our approach is correct, in the formal sense. Ideally, one should prove that the approach is sound (no "false positives" are possible) and complete (no "false negatives" are possible). In principle, such a correctness result cannot be established, due to the lack of formal semantics, both for SDL and Promela, which would be simple enough to carry such correctness proofs. However, we give some informal justification of the correctness of our approach.

We clearly separate the qualitative and quantitative aspects of SDL timers. This allows to analyze the SDL models that use timers, both in the abstract and concrete way. The two methods have their own benefits and drawbacks. In the abstract case, if DT Spin decides that some safety property holds then the property is true for all values of timers, and is thus time independent. This may be a desired feature of a model. On the other hand, proving the time independence may come at a price: "false negatives" are possible, in the case a property does depend on time. The analysis with the concrete values of timers does not lead to "false negatives", but the price may be a bigger state space that must be enumerated by DT Spin.

We put some effort in making DT Spin a "conservative" extension of Spin: DT Promela is designed in such a way that standard Spin can be used to model check DT Promela programs obtained from the SDL models with abstracted timers. This may be useful for those who prefer to use a proven technology, instead of our experimental DT Spin.

The paper is organized as follows. In Section 2, we give an overview of Spin and DT Spin. Section 3 is devoted to the translation of SDL to DT Promela. The verification method and its application to the MASCARA protocol is presented in Sections 4 and 5. Finally, we conclude with Section 6.

2   Spin and DT Spin

2.1   Spin and Promela

Spin [5] is a software tool that supports the analysis and verification of concurrent systems. The system descriptions are modelled in a high-level language, called Promela. Its syntax is derived from C, and extended with Dijkstra's guarded commands and communication primitives from Hoare's CSP.

In Promela, system components are specified as *processes* that can interact either by message passing, via *channels*, or memory sharing, via *global variables*. The message passing can either be buffered or unbuffered (as in Hoare's CSP). Concurrency is asynchronous (no assumptions are made on the relative speed of process executions) and modelled by interleaving (in every step only one *enabled* action is performed).

Given a Promela model as input, Spin generates a C program that performs a verification of the system by enumerating its state space, using a depth-first search algorithm. This way, both *safety* properties (such as absence of deadlock, unspecified message receptions, invalid end states, and assertions) and *liveness* properties (such as non-progress cycles and eventual reception of messages) can be checked. The most general way of expressing properties in Spin is via so-called *never claims*, which are best seen as monitoring processes that run in lock step with the rest of the system. The never claims are, in fact, Büchi Automata, and thus can express arbitrary omega-regular properties. Spin provides an automatic translator from formulae in linear-time temporal logic (LTL) to never claims, so it can be used as a full LTL model checker. In case the system violates a property, the trace of actions leading to an invalid state, or a cycle, is reported. The erroneous trace can be replayed, on the Promela source, by a guided simulation.

To cope with the problem of state space explosion, Spin employs several techniques, such as partial-order reduction, state-vector compression, and bit-state hashing.

2.2   DT Spin and DT Promela

DT Spin [2] is an extension of Spin with discrete time. In the time model used in DT Spin, time is divided into slices indexed by natural numbers that can be seen as readings of a fictitious global digital clock that ticks at the end of each slice. The events happening in the same slice are assigned the same clock value, so the elapsed time between events is measured in ticks. In our model, time passes only if no other action in the system is possible.

Since concurrency is modelled by interleaving, all the events happening in one run of a system are totally ordered and thus two events happening in the same slice are not considered necessarily simultaneous. Instead, they are considered to be ordered, and their ordering inside one slice is determined by the ordering of the run. The properties that depend only on the ordering of events are called *qualitative* while those depending on the elapsed time between events are called *quantitative*.

In order to capture timing features, standard Promela is extended to DT Promela. A new data type, called `timer`, is introduced. It is used to declare variables that represent discrete-time countdown timers. Three new statements that operate on timers are added: `set(`*tmr, val*`)` activates the timer *tmr*, by assigning the integer value *val* to *tmr*, `reset(`*tmr*`)` deactivates *tmr*, by setting it to −1, and `expire(`*tmr*`)` tests whether the value of *tmr* is 0. Initially, a timer has value −1.

In fact, the new statements are defined as Promela macros, in a special header file included at the beginning of every DT Promela model:

```
#define timer          short /* a short integer */
#define set(tmr,val)   tmr = val
#define reset(tmr)     tmr = -1
#define expire(tmr)    tmr == 0
```

The new statements allow to model a broad class of timing constraints, and other timed statements can easily be defined as Promela macros, by combining `set`, `reset` and `expire` with the control flow statements offered by Promela. There is yet another operation on timers: the `tick` statement decreases the value of all active timers by 1. It is used internally by DT Spin, at the end of every time slice, and is not available to the user.

DT Spin is fully compatible with Spin, and all features of Spin can be used to analyse discrete-time models. In particular, the partial order reduction algorithm of Spin [7,9] had to be adapted for timed systems [2]. Besides qualitative properties, a broad range of quantitative properties can be verified using boolean expressions on timer values, in the assertions and LTL formulae.

3   Translating SDL to DT Promela

The process of model checking an SDL specification is depicted in Figure 1. An SDL specification is pushed through the pipe of translators `sdl2if` and `if2pml`, to obtain a DT Promela program that serves as input to DT Spin or Spin. The result of a negative verification experiment (e.g., an erroneous trace) has to be checked manually against the SDL specification.

`sdl2if` translates SDL to the language IF (Intermediate Format, [3]) which is a specification language for timed concurrent systems consisting of a fixed number of communicating automata. IF was designed as an intermediate formalism for connecting several industrial formal description techniques, such as LOTOS and SDL, to a number of verification tools developed in the research community.

`sdl2if` is implemented with the help of the SDL/API Interface provided by the ObjectGEODE tool [11]. The current implementation of `sdl2if` is able to

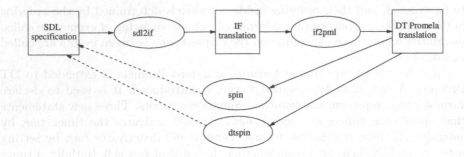

Fig. 1. The tools used in the verification.

translate a substantial subset of SDL. The only essential omissions are dynamically created processes and abstract data types.

In the overall SDL to DT Promela translation, sdl2if resolves the hierarchical aspects of SDL by "flattening" the hierarchy of blocks down to bare processes and resolving appropriately the sources, destinations and priorities of the signals exchanged between the processes. On the way, the SDL procedures are eliminated by inlining (when possible), and the syntactic sugar of SDL (enabling conditions, continuous signals, the special input *none*) is transformed to more primitive constructs. Moreover, some implicit constructs are made explicit (sender, offspring, parent, discarded signals). Details are given in [3].

On the other hand, if2pml performs the translation of the SDL core language, coping with issues that have more semantical flavor (like preserving the atomicity of the transitions or implementing the discard mechanism). Since IF is intended to be an intermediate language for a variety of high-level specification formalisms, it is quite expressive. As not all of its constructs are needed for representing SDL models, if2pml only translates the subset of IF that is relevant to SDL.

IF and sdl2if were developed at Verimag, Grenoble, while if2pml and DT Spin were developed at the Eindhoven University of Technology. All the tools were developed in the framework of the VIRES project [12].

In what follows we describe the translation from IF to DT Promela in more detail. The presentation is divided into three parts. In Section 3.1 we describe how the SDL processes (i.e., IF automata) are represented in Promela. In Section 3.2, the DT Promela representation of the SDL/IF timers is given. Finally, in Section 3.3, the abstraction from the concrete values of timers is described.

3.1   IF to Promela: Translating Automata

As in Promela, the IF models are sets of processes that communicate via buffers. This provides an almost one-to-one translation of these concepts. Also, the IF data types can directly be translated to their Promela counterparts (with some minor restrictions on the range types).

The way the SDL/IF automata are represented in Promela is fairly standard, and can be grasped by comparing the IF source given in Fig. 2 with its Promela translation in Fig. 3. A state is represented by a Promela label. All the outgoing transitions are translated to the branches of the choice statement associated with the label. The discard mechanism is implemented via self-looping to the same state, after reading a signal that has to be discarded in the state. The atomicity of SDL/IF transitions is preserved by putting the if statement inside the atomic statement.[1]

```
process proc: buffer buf;
    state
        state1 discard sig3, sig4 in buf
        state2
        ...
    transition
        from state1 input sig1 from buf do body1 to state2;
        from state1 input sig2 from buf do body2 to state3;
        ...
```

Fig. 2. A skeleton of an IF program.

```
proctype proc() {
    state1: atomic {
    if
    :: buf?sig1 -> translated_body1; goto state2;
    :: buf?sig2 -> translated_body2; goto state3;
    ...
    :: buf?sig3 -> goto state1; /* discard */
    :: buf?sig4 -> goto state1; /* discard */
    fi
    }
    state2: atomic{
    ...
    }
    ...
}
```

Fig. 3. Promela translation of the structure from Fig. 2

The implementation of if2pml is still in a prototype stage and some SDL features are not supported yet. The most notable omissions are the mechanism of saving a signal, the dynamic creation of processes, and the abstract data types. The implementation of the save mechanism in Promela is possible, but rather

---

[1] A special care is taken to correctly handle the stable and non-stable states in IF.

involved. It may lead to a substantial growth of the state space during model checking, and for this reason we have chosen to omit it. The dynamic process creation is a basic feature of Promela, so it can easily be implemented once sdl2if supports it. Finding a satisfactory solution for the abstract data types remains a future work for both sdl2if and if2pml.

3.2   IF to DT Promela: Translating Timers

The crucial issue about time in SDL is the detection of timer expirations (time-outs). In SDL, a timer expiration results in sending a timeout pseudo-signal to the input queue of the process the timer belongs to. The timeout signal is then handled as an ordinary signal: it is either consumed, by a transition that is guarded by the timeout signal, or discarded, in a state with no such transitions. In both cases, the corresponding timer is deactivated.

Our implementation of timers does not use such timeout signals. Instead, we associate with each SDL timer a DT Promela timer variable, and detect the expiration of the timer by testing whether the timer variable has value 0, and the timer is deactivated by setting the timer variable's value to -1.

More precisely, for each timer *tmr* declared in an SDL process, we add a new branch to all the choice statements associated with states (see figure 3). Assume a state, say state1, with an outgoing transition guarded by *tmr*. For such a state we add the branch

```
:: expire(tmr) -> reset(tmr); translated_body1; goto state2;
```

If state1 has no outgoing transitions guarded by *tmr*, we add the branch

```
:: expire(tmr) -> reset(tmr); goto state1; /* discard */
```

It turns out that under the time semantics given below (as determined by the ObjectGEODE tool [11]), these two approaches to timers are equivalent. However, the "variable" approach has an advantage over the "signal" approach, from the verification point of view, since it generates smaller state spaces. In the "signal" approach, an additional Promela process (or even several processes) would be needed, in order to generate the timeout signals in a right way. This, together with the overhead of exchanging timeout signals, increases the state space.

In what follows, we give an informal justification of the above mentioned equivalence.

The semantics of time in SDL. Transitions are instantaneous. Time can only progress if at least one timer is active and all SDL processes are waiting for further input signals (i.e., all input queues are empty, except for saved signals). Time progression amounts to performing a special transition that makes time increment until an active timer expires. In the sequel, we refer to the segments of time separated by the special transition as *time slices*. (Note that time progression is discretized.)

With each timer there is associated a pseudo-signal and an implicit transition, called a timeout transition. When a timer expires, in some time slice, its timeout transition becomes enabled and can be executed at any point of the time slice. The execution of this transition adds the associated pseudo-signal to the process queue. The timeout transitions of the timers that expire simultaneously can be executed in any order.

If the **set** or **reset** operation is performed on a timer after its timeout transition becomes enabled, the timeout transition is disabled. If the timer is set or reset after adding its associated pseudo-signal to the process queue, the pseudo-signal is removed from the queue.

Model equivalence. In order to justify the equivalence of the two models we need to show that any execution sequence in the signal model can be simulated by an execution sequence in the variable model, and vice versa. In what follows, we assume that SDL timers are never set to the special value *now* (i.e., our timer variables are never set to 0, explicitly), and we only concentrate on the simulation of the transitions which relate to timers, since the two models coincide on the untimed features. There are two issues which have to be considered: the **set** and **reset** operations on timers, and the expiration of timers.

The **set** and **reset** operations coincide in the two models, so this issue does not cause problems. As far as the expiration of timers is concerned, it should be obvious that the time slice in which a timer expires is recognized in the same way, in both models.

The only problematic issue is whether consuming/discarding the timeout signals, in the signal model, is properly simulated with our count-down timers, and vice versa. Our claim that, in fact, this is the case is based on the assumption that the following, more direct, translation of SDL/IF to Promela would be correct.

Assume ts_T denotes the timeout signal corresponding to timer T, in the signal model. In order to handle the consumption of ts_T like the consumption of an ordinary signal, by an SDL/IF transition guarded by ts_T, the following branch

```
:: buf?ts_T -> translated_body1; goto state2;
```

could be added to the Promela translation in figure 3.

Similarly, in order to handle the discarding of ts_T as an ordinary signal, the following branch

```
:: buf?ts_T -> goto state1; /* discard */
```

could be added to the choice statements that corresponds to the states with no outgoing transitions guarded by ts_T.

Observe that the

```
:: expire(tmr) -> reset(tmr); ...
```

branches, in our real Promela code, correspond directly to the above branches. More precisely, `expire(tmr) -> reset(tmr)` corresponds directly to `buf?ts_T`. Namely, `expire(tmr)` corresponds to the check whether ts_T is in the input queue, and `reset(tmr)` corresponds to the removal of ts_T from the queue.

3.3 Timer Abstraction

It turns out that standard Spin can also be used to model check a DT Promela model, for a property that does not depend on time. The advantage of using Spin instead of DT Spin is that Spin usually consumes less resources than DT Spin. In order to convert a DT Promela model into a Promela model, it suffices to change the special header file included at the beginning of every DT Promela model (see Section 2.2):

```
#define timer           bool
#define set(tmr,val)    tmr = true
#define reset(tmr)      tmr = false
#define expire(tmr)     tmr == true
```

The new definitions abstract out the concrete values of *active* timers, by consistently mapping them to `true`. The concrete value -1, which is used to mark an *inactive* timer, is consistently mapped to `false` (under the assumption that each timer is initialised to `false`). Obviously, such an abstraction is sound since no behaviours are lost. More precisely, any behaviour with concrete timers can be simulated with abstract timers, since the active timers are allowed to expire nondeterministically, at any time.

This is not the case in the related approaches [6,10], where some heuristic approximations of the timer behaviour are used rather than a proper abstraction. The approximations do not only add some behaviours, but also loose some of them, as shown in the following examples.

In [6] the authors try to minimize the number of timer expirations, in the abstract system, that do not correspond to expirations in the concrete system. They take advantage of the observation that, in practice, the transitions guarded by a timer expiration are supposed to resolve the kind of deadlocks when no other transitions except the ones triggered by timeout signals would be enabled. The timers are represented by processes that send the corresponding timeout signals when the special Promela statement `timeout` becomes enabled. The `timeout` statement becomes enabled when no other transition is enabled, in the system.

However, there are situations when a behaviour of the concrete system cannot be simulated by the approximate one. Let us consider two concurrent processes, say P_1 and P_2, specified by the following transition systems:

$$P_1 : \quad \bullet \xrightarrow{T_1/A} \bullet \xrightarrow{B/} \bullet$$

$$P_2 : \quad \bullet \xrightarrow{T_2/B} \bullet \xrightarrow{A/} \bullet$$

where T_1 and T_2 are timer signals, A and B are normal signals, and X/Y denotes "receive X and send Y to the other process".

If both T_1 and T_2 expire simultaneously then, in the concrete system, P_1 and P_2 may exchange signals A and B, and both reach their final states. However, in the abstract system, one of the processes will not be able to reach its final state. Initially, the first transitions of both processes are enabled. If P_1 performs its first transition (and thus sends A to P_2), the first transition of P_2 becomes disabled. P_2 must discard A, before its first transition becomes enabled again, and thus it will not be able to pass the $A/$ guard. Similarly, if P_2 performs its first transition, P_1 will not be able to pass the $B/$ guard.

In the approximation used in [10], one pseudo-process is used to handle all timer expirations. After each **set** operation this pseudo-process immediately sends the corresponding timeout signal to the input queue of the process that sets the timer. As a result, if an SDL process uses two timers, they can only expire in the order they are set, no matter what values they are set to. Obviously, the behaviour in which an SDL process sets the timers T_1 and T_2 (in that order) to such values that T_2 expires before T_1 cannot be simulated by the abstract system.

4   Verification Methodology

The aim of this section is to present the way the real verification process is performed. Industrial-size SDL models normally cannot be verified with existing model-checking tools as a whole, so the first natural task is to split a protocol in some relatively autonomous parts of a reasonable size and apply to them compositional verification. Fortunately, due to their block-structure, SDL-systems can be usually split in a natural way without much effort.

The obtained sub-models are not self-contained, i.e. the behaviour of their environment is not specified. Since Spin can only model-check closed systems we need to close our model first. We achieve this by adding an "environment" process specified in SDL at the same hierarchy level as the extracted model itself.

The simplest possible approach is to construct an environment producing all the "possible" behaviours but practice shows that this is not of much use in real life. Such an environment leads to adding to the model too many erroneous behaviours and thus one gets too many "false negatives" during model-checking. Local livelocks, cycles with non-progressing time, and non-existing deadlocks are the typical examples of those false-errors. Moreover, since many redundant behaviours are added, this may also lead to a state explosion. Another possibility is to construct an environment being able to send/receive a signal whenever the modelled system is ready to get/send it. Applying such an approach reduces the added behaviours but it still adds some unwanted behaviours caused by sending non-realistic signal sequences.

Both these approaches are not safe: in case of adding non-progressing time cycles, we loose some behaviour of the system. So they can be considered as a kind of heuristics only, that may be of some use at the first stage of system debugging.

A different approach is to provide an SDL-specification of the "right" environment, i.e. the one, which faithfully models the assumptions under which the component was designed, giving an abstraction of a real environment. Although it makes the soundness of verification results dependent on the quality of the environment model, it usually turns out to be a practical method.

The closed SDL-model can be automatically translated into DT Promela through the translators sdl2if and if2pml. Then one should choose between verification of the concrete model with DT Spin and verification of the model with abstracted time in the standard Spin. First, the built-in Spin features (finding deadlocks and livelocks, unreachable code) are used. After correcting discovered structural errors, functional properties defined by a designer or drawn from the informal specification of the system can be verified.

It would seem obvious to verify all non-timed properties with an abstracted-time model and all timed properties with a concrete model. However, sometimes it is more convenient to verify non-timed properties with a concrete model as well. If some functional property was proved with the abstracted-time model, it is proved for all possible values of timers. However if it was disproved, or a deadlock in the model was found, the next step is to check whether the erroneous trace given by Spin is a real error in the system or it is a false error caused by adding erroneous behaviour either with abstracting from time or with too abstract specification of the environment. It can happen that the property does not hold for the concrete model, however the erroneous trace given by Spin is one of the added behaviours. This behaviour cannot be reproduced for the SDL model with SDL-simulation tools and we cannot conclude whether the property holds or not.

One can not force Spin to give the trace from the non-added behaviours. DT Spin allows to reduce the set of added behaviours guaranteeing that timers are expiring in the correct order. In our verification experiments we had a number of cases when application of DT Spin, instead of Spin, gave a chance to get a real erroneous trace and disprove the property (see the next section).

5   Case Study: Verifying the MASCARA Protocol

We have applied our tools to the verification of an industrial-size communication protocol called MASCARA (Mobile Access Scheme based on Contention and Reservation for ATM), developed by the WAND (Wireless ATM Network Demonstrator) consortium [13]. The protocol is an extension of the ATM (Asynchronous Transfer Mode) networking protocol to wireless networks.

A wireless ATM network comprises of a fixed wire-based ATM network that links a number of geographically distributed access points, which transparently extend ATM services to mobile users, via radio links operating in the 5.2 GHz frequency band and achieving data rates of 23.5 MBits/s. The task of MASCARA is to mediate between the mobile users and the access points, to offer the mobile users the advantages of the standard wire-based ATM protocol: high reliability, capacity-on-demand, and service-independent transport. The transparent extension of ATM over radio links is a challenge, as standard ATM has not been designed to work in a wireless environment. The radio medium is characterised by a high bit error rate, the transmission mode is typically broadcast (or at least multicast) and the scarcity of available radio bandwidth calls for a time division duplex (i.e. half duplex) mode. All this leads to the necessity of extra functionality allowing to cope with these dissimilar environmental properties.

A crucial feature of MASCARA is the support of *mobility*. A mobile terminal (MT) can reliably communicate with an access point (AP) only within some area called the AP's *cell*. Whenever an MT moves outside the cell of its current AP it has to perform a so-called *handover* to an AP whose cell the MT has moved into. A handover must be managed transparently with respect to the ATM layer, maintaining the agreed quality of service for the current connections. So the protocol has to detect the need for a handover, select a candidate AP to switch to and redirect the traffic with minimal interruption.

The protocol is too large to be automatically verified as a whole so we have concentrated our efforts on the verification of a substantial part called MCL (MASCARA Control). The main purpose of MCL is to support the mobility issues. It contains 9 processes, each with up to 10 states (6 on average). Its main function is to monitor the current radio link quality, gather information about radio link qualities of its neighbouring APs (to make a quick handover, in the case of deterioration of the current link quality), and switch from one AP to another (during the handover procedure).

During the first phase of the verification, several deadlocks were found. Most of them were related to improper synchronisation between various request/confirm subprotocols (a component requests a service from another component and waits until the confirmation arrives that the request is either rejected or served). The second source of deadlocks was the potential race conditions between various components of MCL, due to the fully asynchronous communication in SDL (non-blocking sending of messages). The following example describes one of the race conditions we have found.

Most MASCARA components must be initialised before they are prepared to serve requests from other components. The components are grouped in various tree-like hierarchies, and the initialisation phase for a group is triggered by sending the INIT signal to the group's root. Each node that receives the INIT signal resends the signal to all its children. However, in such a cascade of INIT signals there is a possible race condition: Spin found a trace in MCL where an already initialised component tried to immediately request a service from a component that had not been initialised yet. Such a request was simply discarded and thus its confirmation was never sent back, leading to a deadlock in MCL.

After correcting these errors, we continued the verification, by exploiting another useful Spin feature—unreachable code diagnosis. The analysis of the unreachable code reported by Spin revealed that some code for serving one particular request is never reached and thus the request for that particular service was never confirmed. Further analysis showed that there was a local deadlock possible. (This local deadlock could not be discovered by Spin, in previous experiments, since Spin can only discover global deadlocks.)

Finally, we verified some functional properties that we derived from the informal specification. An example of such a property is given below.

One of the tasks of MCL is to periodically update a list that contains information about the quality of radio links with the neighbouring APs. This updating phase is called the *TI procedure*. In order to judge the quality of a radio link with a particular AP, MCL must connect to that particular AP, so the connection with the current AP is suspended during the whole TI procedure. Therefore, another procedure, checking the quality of the current connection and making the decision on the necessity of a handover, should not interfere with TI procedure.

This requirement was encoded as a simple observer for the following safety property: a handover request never comes in between the two messages that mark the beginning and the end of the TI procedure. The verification experiment with Spin, which was supposed to confirm this property, showed instead a trace violating it. Unfortunately, the erroneous trace could not be simulated by the SDL model of MCL (so we got a so-called "false negative"). However, when exactly the same experiment was repeated with DT Spin we got a different erroneous trace which could then be simulated by the SDL model. Thus, the property was indeed violated, DT Spin allowed us to find yet another error in MASCARA protocol.

The explanation of the different results obtained with Spin and DT Spin is obvious. The TI procedure is triggered by a timer, so the behaviour of the TI protocol could indeed depend on proper timing. In the model with abstracted time, as used in Spin, timers can expire at any time, so Spin can produce a wrongly timed trace that is not accepted by an SDL simulator (which allows only properly timed traces, of course). After finding a way to re-design the components, some other functional properties were proved.

When we planned the first series of verification experiments we expected to reach the limits of Spin and DT Spin quickly. We were proved wrong. In the experiment that consumed the most resources, Spin reported the following statistics:

```
State-vector 416 byte, depth reached 3450, errors: 0
    55959  states, stored
    23.727 memory usage for states (in MB)
    25.582 total memory usage (in MB)
    14.2   total time (in seconds)
```

which should be read in the following way:

State-vector 416 byte is the memory needed to represent one state.
55959 states, stored is the number of different states found in the model (all the states must be kept during the state space enumeration, so 23.727MB memory was needed for states).

`depth reached 3450` is the greatest depth reached during the depth-first search (since Spin must keep a state stack of at least this depth, about 1.7MB was needed in addition to the state memory).

It is quite likely that with our 2048MB memory we will be able to handle even more complex case studies.

6   Conclusions and Future Work

We have developed a tool, `if2pml`, that enables the translation from SDL to Promela. It can be used, together with the accompanying tool `sdl2if`, to model check SDL specifications with Spin.

Our approach preserves the timing aspects of SDL. This is in contrast to other translators that we know, which only approximate timing aspects. SDL timers, which expire by sending signals, are in our approach translated into the timer variables provided by DT Promela. We have argued the correctness of this translation.

The approach has been successfully used on an industrial case study. More information is available from `http://radon.ics.ele.tue.nl/~vires/public/results`.

As a future work, we consider to extend the tool by implementing the translation of dynamic process creation in SDL and the `save` construct. SDL supports various styles of specifying data types. It needs to be investigated how the specification of data aspects can be combined with the translation from SDL to Promela.

Acknowledgments

We gratefully acknowledge VERILOG for giving us free access to their *Object-GEODE* tool. We would also like to thank Marius Bozga, Lucian Ghirvu, Susanne Graf (Verimag, Grenoble) and Gerard Holzmann (Bell Labs) for fruitful discussions during the implementation of the `if2pml` tool.

References

1. R. Alur, D.L. Dill, *A Theory of Timed Automata*, Theoretical Computer Science, 126, pp.183-235, 1994.
2. D. Bošnački, D. Dams, *Integrating Real Time into Spin: A Prototype Implementation*, S. Budkowski, A. Cavalli, E. Najm, editors, Formal Description Techniques and Protocol Specification, Testing and Verification (FORTE/PSTV'98), Kluwer, 1998. 365, 366
3. M. Bozga, J-C. Fernandez, L. Ghirvu, S. Graf, J.P. Karimm, L. Mounier, J. Sifakis, *If: An Intermediate Representation for SDL and its Applications*, In Proc. of SDL-FORUM'99, Montreal, Canada, 1999. 363, 366, 367

4. I. Dravapoulos, N. Pronios, S. Denazis *et al.*, *The Magic WAND, Deliverable 3D2, Wireless ATM MAC*, September 1997.
5. G. J. Holzmann, *Design and Validation of Communication Protocols*, Prentice Hall, 1991. Also: http://netlib.bell-labs.com/netlib/spin/whatispin.html   363, 365
6. G.J. Holzmann, J. Patti, *Validating SDL Specification: an Experiment*, In E. Brinksma, G. Scollo, Ch.A. Vissers, editors, Protocol Specification, Testing and Verification, Enchede, The Netherlands, 6-9 June 1989, pp. 317-326, Amsterdam, 1990. North-Holland. 364, 371
7. G.J. Holzmann, D. Peled, *An Improvement of Formal Verification*, PSTV 1994 Conference, Bern, Switzerland, 1994. 366
8. A. Olsen *et al.*, *System Engineering Using SDL-92*, Elsevier Science, North-Holland, 1997. 363
9. D. Peled, *Combining Partial Order Reductions with On-the-Fly Model Checking*, Computer Aided Verification CAV 94, LCNS 818, pp. 377-390, 1994. 366
10. H. Tuominen, Embedding a Dialect of SDL in PROMELA, 6th Int. SPIN Workshop, LNCS 1680, pp. 245-260, 1999. 364, 371, 372
11. Verilog, *ObjectGEODE tutorial*, Version 1.2, Verilog SA, Toulouse, France, 1996. 364, 366, 369
12. VIRES, *Verifying Industrially Relevant Systems*, Esprit Long Term Research Project #23498, http://radon.ics.ele.tue.nl/~vires, 1996. 367
13. WAND consortium, *Magic WAND - Wireless ATM Network Demonstrator*, http://www.tik.ee.ethz.ch/~wand, 1996. 364, 373

Salsa: Combining Constraint Solvers with BDDs for Automatic Invariant Checking

Ramesh Bharadwaj[1] and Steve Sims[2]

[1] Center for High Assurance Computer Systems, Naval Research Laboratory
Washington, DC 20375-5320
ramesh@itd.nrl.navy.mil
[2] Reactive Systems, Inc.
sims@reactive-systems.com
www.reactive-systems.com

Abstract. *Salsa* is an invariant checker for specifications in SAL (the **SCR Abstract Language**). To establish a formula as an invariant without any user guidance, Salsa carries out an induction proof that utilizes tightly integrated decision procedures, currently a combination of BDD algorithms and a constraint solver for integer linear arithmetic, for discharging the verification conditions. The user interface of Salsa is designed to mimic the interfaces of model checkers; i.e., given a formula and a system description, Salsa either establishes the formula as an invariant of the system (but returns no proof) or provides a *counterexample*. In either case, the algorithm will terminate. Unlike model checkers, Salsa returns a state pair as a counterexample and not an execution sequence. Also, due to the incompleteness of induction, users must *validate* the counterexamples. The use of induction enables Salsa to combat the state explosion problem that plagues model checkers – it can handle specifications whose state spaces are too large for model checkers to analyze. Also, unlike general purpose theorem provers, Salsa concentrates on a single task and gains efficiency by employing a set of optimized heuristics.

1 Introduction

Model checking[17] has emerged as an effective technique for the *automated* analysis of descriptions of hardware and protocols. To analyze software system descriptions, however, a direct application of model checking to a problem (i.e., without a prior reduction of its state space size by the application of abstraction) rarely succeeds [9]. For such systems, theorem proving affords an interesting alternative. Conventional theorem proving systems, however, are often too general or too expensive to use in a practical setting because they require considerable user sophistication, human effort, and system resources. Additionally, the counterexample provided by a model checker when a check fails serves practitioners as a valuable debugging aid. However, in contrast, conventional theorem provers provide little or no diagnostic information (or worse, may not terminate) when a theorem is *not* true.

S. Graf and M. Schwartzbach (Eds.): TACAS/ETAPS 2000, LNCS 1785, pp. 378–395, 2000.
© Springer-Verlag Berlin Heidelberg 2000

Salsa is an invariant checker for system descriptions written in a language based on the tabular notation of SCR [24] called SAL (the **SCR A**bstract **L**anguage). Given a logical formula and a system description in SAL, Salsa uses induction to determine whether the formula is true in all states (or transitions) the system may reach. Unlike concurrent algorithms or protocol descriptions, on which model checkers are very effective, practical SAL models usually do not contain interleaving concurrency and are more easily amenable to induction proofs. If a proof fails, Salsa provides a *counterexample*. Unlike model checkers, however, the returned counterexample is a state or a state pair and not an execution sequence. Also, due to the incompleteness of induction, users must *validate* a returned counterexample. Salsa has the attributes of both a model checker and a theorem prover: It is automatic and provides counterexamples just like a model checker. Like a theorem prover, it uses decision procedures, can handle infinite state systems, and can use auxiliary lemmas to complete an analysis.

The design of Salsa was motivated by the need within the SCR Toolset [23] for more automation during consistency checking [24] and invariant checking [9,22]. Salsa achieves complete automation of proofs by its reliance on *decision procedures*, i.e., algorithms that establish the logical truth or falsity of formulae of *decidable* sub-theories, such as the fragment of arithmetic involving only integer linear constraints called Presburger arithmetic. Salsa's invariant checker consists of a tightly integrated set of decision procedures, each optimized to work within a particular domain. Currently, Salsa implements decision procedures for propositional logic, the theory of unordered enumerations, and integer linear arithmetic.

Although they are capable of checking more general properties (such as liveness), in practice model checkers are most often used to check invariant properties. The advantage of using Salsa over a standard model checker for this task is that Salsa can handle large (even infinite state) specifications that current day model checkers cannot analyze. This is due to the use of induction and the symbolic encoding of expressions involving integers as linear constraints. The primary disadvantage of Salsa (and proof by induction in general) is its incompleteness – a failed check does not necessarily imply that a formula is not an invariant because the returned state pair may not be reachable.

After some experimentation, we arrived at the following practical method for checking state and transition invariants using Salsa (see Figure 1): Initially apply Salsa. If Salsa returns *yes* then the property is an invariant of the system, and we are done. If Salsa returns *no*, then we examine the counterexample to determine whether the states corresponding to the counterexample are reachable in the system. If so, the property is false and we are done. However, if one concludes after this analysis that the counterexample states are unreachable, then one looks for *stronger invariants* to prove the property. Salsa currently includes a facility that allows users to include such auxiliary lemmas during invariant checking. There are promising algorithms for automatically deducing such invariants [5,6,11,26], although Salsa currently does not implement them.

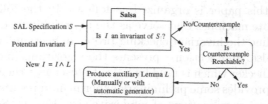

Fig. 1. Process for applying Salsa

Related Work. The use of SMV [28] and SPIN [25] on software specifications for consistency and invariant checking has been well documented [2,9,16,22]. SCR* [23] is a toolset that includes a *consistency checker* which uses a method based on semantic tableaux extended to handle simple constraints over the integers and reals. This tool has proved very useful in a number of practical case studies; however, the tool is unable to complete the checks on certain examples involving numbers. Systems that largely automate induction proofs by employing decision procedures include the Stanford Temporal Prover (STeP) [11]. Other tools that are built upon the interactive theorem prover PVS [30] include TAME (Timed Automata Modeling Environment) [3] and the tools of Graf et al. [21,32]. These tools are implemented as a set of special-purpose PVS strategies. The tool In-VeSt includes sophisticated algorithms for invariant generation and heuristics for invariant strengthening [5,6]. Also, if invariance cannot be established on a finite abstraction, an execution sequence is provided as a diagnostic. Validity checkers such as Mona [18], Mosel [31], and the Stanford Validity Checker (SVC) [4] are another class of systems that employ decision procedures for proving logical formulae. Although these tools do not directly check invariants, they may be used to discharge the verification conditions generated during an induction proof in a tool such as Salsa.

The idea of combining decision procedures for program verification dates back to the work of Shostak [33] and Nelson and Oppen [29]. The decision procedures of Salsa for both propositional logic and enumerated types are based on standard BDD algorithms. The integer constraint solver employs an automata-theoretic algorithm presented in [12], with extensions to handle negative numbers using ideas from [34]. Salsa's technique of combining BDD algorithms with constraint solvers was largely inspired by the approaches of [14] and [15] where, by incorporating constraint solvers into BDD-based fixpoint computation algorithms, verification of infinite state systems becomes a possibility. However, since the underlying algorithms of these systems are variants of the model checking algorithm for computing a fixpoint, we speculate that Salsa, due to its use of induction, can handle larger specifications than these systems. Also, the constraint solver of [14] is incomplete for integer linear arithmetic, whereas the one used by Salsa is complete. The system of [15], which uses an off-the-shelf backtracking solver that can be very inefficient in practice, can handle a class of non-linear constraints in addition to linear constraints.

The rest of this paper is organized as follows. In the following section we introduce the state machines that serve as the underlying models for SAL specifications and define the invariant checking problem. Section 3 describes the core algorithms of Salsa, and Section 4 presents the algorithms and heuristics of the unsatisfiability checker which is used by Salsa to discharge the verification conditions. Section 5 provides some preliminary experimental results of applying Salsa to several practical specifications of moderate size. Finally, Section 6 discusses ongoing work and future research.

2   Background

2.1   Model for System Behavior

The SCR Abstract Language (SAL), a specification language based on the SCR Formal Model [24], was designed to serve as an abstract interface to analysis tools such as theorem provers, model checkers, and consistency checkers. An example SCR specification in SAL is presented in Appendix A. Unlike concurrent algorithms or protocol descriptions, practical SAL specifications usually do not involve interleaving concurrency and are therefore more easily amenable to induction proofs.

A SAL specification may be translated into a state machine that models a system's behavior. We now introduce the state machine model for systems and the supporting machinery used in the paper. We define formulae in a simple constraint logic *(SCL)* by the following grammar:

$$
\begin{aligned}
\varPhi &:= C \mid X_b \mid \neg X_b \mid \varPhi \vee \varPhi \mid \varPhi \wedge \varPhi && \text{(simple formulae)} \\
C &:= C_i \mid C_e && \text{(constraints)} \\
C_e &:= X_e = Val_e \mid X_e \neq Val_e \mid X_e = Y_e \mid X_e \neq Y_e && \text{(enum. constraints)} \\
C_i &:= SUM \leq Val_i \mid SUM = Val_i \mid SUM \neq Val_i && \text{(integer constraints)} \\
SUM &:= Val_i \times X_i \mid SUM + SUM
\end{aligned}
$$

where X_b, X_e/Y_e, and X_i range over boolean, enumerated, and integer variables respectively. Similarly Val_b, Val_e, and Val_i respectively range over constants of the three types. We let $Vars(\varPhi)$ denote the free variables in $\varPhi$. Set $Vars(\varPhi)$ is partitioned by the three variable types: $Vars(\varPhi) = Vars_b(\varPhi) \cup Vars_e(\varPhi) \cup Vars_i(\varPhi)$. Note that SCL formulae will be interpreted in the context of either 1) a single state s that maps variable names to values or 2) a pair of states (s, s'), where s' is a successor of s. We adopt the convention that primed formulae and variable names (those ending in $'$) are evaluated in the "new state" whereas unprimed names are evaluated in the "old state." Formulae containing primed variables are called *two-state predicates* and those without primed variables are called *one-state predicates*.

Definition 1. A state machine Σ is a quadruple $\langle \mathcal{V}, \mathcal{S}, \theta, \rho \rangle$ where

- $\mathcal{V}$ is a set of variable names. This set is partitioned into *monitored variables* which denote environmental quantities the system observes; *controlled variables* which denote quantities in the environment that the system controls;

and *internal variables* which are updated by the system but not visible to the environment.

- $\mathcal{S}$ is the set of system states such that each state $s \in \mathcal{S}$ maps each $x \in \mathcal{V}$ to a value in its set of legal values. We write $x(s)$ to mean the value of variable x in state s, $\Phi_1(s)$ to mean the value of one-state predicate Φ_1 evaluated in s, and $\Phi_2(s, s')$ to mean the value of two-state predicate Φ_2 evaluated with values from s replacing unprimed variables and values from s' replacing primed variables.

- θ is a one-state SCL predicate defining the set of initial states.

- ρ is a two-state SCL predicate defining the transitions (execution steps) of Σ. A state s may evolve to a state s' if $\rho(s, s')$ is true.

  The transition relation ρ additionally includes environmental assumptions as well as assumptions introduced by users. For details, see [10].

2.2   The Invariant Checking Problem

Definition 2. Given a state machine $\Sigma = \langle \mathcal{V}, \mathcal{S}, \theta, \rho \rangle$, a state $s \in \mathcal{S}$ is *reachable* (denoted $Reachable_\Sigma(s)$) if and only if $\theta(s)$ or $\exists s_2 \in \mathcal{S} : Reachable_\Sigma(s_2) \wedge \rho(s_2, s)$

Definition 3. Given a state machine $\Sigma = \langle \mathcal{V}, \mathcal{S}, \theta, \rho \rangle$, a one-state SCL predicate Φ_1 is a *state invariant* of Σ if and only if

$$\forall s \in \mathcal{S} : Reachable_\Sigma(s) \Rightarrow \Phi_1(s)$$

A two-state SCL predicate Φ_2 is a *transition invariant* of Σ if and only if

$$\forall s, s' \in \mathcal{S} : (Reachable_\Sigma(s) \wedge \rho(s, s')) \Rightarrow \Phi_2(s, s')$$

The invariant checking problem : Given a state machine Σ and a one(two)-state predicate Φ, determine whether Φ is a state(transition) invariant.

3   The Invariant Checker

Theorem 1. Let $\Sigma = \langle \mathcal{V}, \mathcal{S}, \theta, \rho \rangle$, then Φ_1 is a state invariant of Σ if the following hold: 1) $\forall s \in \mathcal{S} : \theta(s) \Rightarrow \Phi_1(s)$ and 2) $\forall s, s' \in \mathcal{S} : \Phi_1(s) \wedge \rho(s, s') \Rightarrow \Phi_1(s')$

Proof: By induction on the number of steps of Σ to reach a state.

Theorem 2. Let $\Sigma = \langle \mathcal{V}, \mathcal{S}, \theta, \rho \rangle$, then Φ_2 is a transition invariant of Σ if the following holds:

$$\forall s, s' \in \mathcal{S} : \rho(s, s') \Rightarrow \Phi_2(s, s')$$

Proof: Follows directly from Definition 3.

3.1   The Invariant Checking Algorithms

Using Theorems 1 and 2 we check invariants of $\Sigma = \langle \mathcal{V}, \mathcal{S}, \theta, \rho \rangle$ as follows:

State Invariants. To determine if Φ_1 is a state invariant of Σ:

0. if $\neg\Phi_1$ is unsatisfiable then return *yes*.
1. if $\theta \wedge \neg\Phi_1$ is *not* unsatisfiable then return *no* and the satisfying state as counterexample.
2. if $\Phi_1 \wedge \rho \wedge \neg\Phi_1'$ is unsatisfiable then return *yes*.
   else return *no* and the satisfying state pair as counterexample.

Transition Invariants. To determine if Φ_2 is a transition invariant of Σ:

0. if $\neg\Phi_2$ is unsatisfiable then return *yes*.
1. if $\rho \wedge \neg\Phi_2$ is unsatisfiable then return *yes*.
   else return *no* and the satisfying state pair as counterexample.

These algorithms are sound but not complete – whenever Salsa returns *yes* the given formula is an invariant; however, a *no* answer with a counterexample (a state or a state pair) does not necessarily mean that the formula is not an invariant. Consequently, the user must validate that the counterexample is reachable[1]. Either there is a problem or additional theorems are used to "push through" the invariant. Of course, all added theorems should be proved as invariants by the user (either with Salsa or by some other means).

3.2   Optimizations

A naive application of the above algorithms to invariant checking will always fail, even for specifications of a moderate size. We perform several optimizations in Salsa to make invariant checking feasible. One important technique used extensively is to *cache* results as they are computed. In addition to the caching provided by BDD algorithms, we cache the results of calls to the integer constraint solver, the BDD encodings of components of the transition relation, etc.

To partition an unsatisfiability check into simpler sub-problems, we use a technique called *disjunctive partitioning* which corresponds to a case split in a standard proof. This approach takes advantage of the fact that a disjunction is unsatisfiable only if each of its disjuncts is unsatisfiable. The disjunctive form of the transition relation in SAL specifications has proven to be an effective basis for disjunctive partitioning.

The application of *abstraction* [9,22] is also very beneficial. We restrict ourselves to applying abstractions that are both sound and complete, by which we mean the following. Given a property Φ and a state machine Σ, an abstraction Σ_A is a sound and complete abstraction of Σ relative to Φ when Φ is an invariant of Σ_A if and only if Φ is an invariant of Σ. Currently, we apply what is termed "*Abstraction Method 1*" [8,9] that uses the set of variable names occurring in the predicate Φ and dataflow analysis to eliminate unneeded variables.

---

[1] The single state counterexample returned by step 1 of the algorithm for State Invariants (for a failed check of unsatisfiability of $\theta \wedge \neg\Phi_1$) is always a true counterexample.

4   The Unsatisfiability Checker

4.1   Overview

To discharge the verification conditions that arise during invariant checking, Salsa uses a routine that decides the unsatisfiability of SCL formulae. Both the problem of propositional unsatisfiability and the decision problem for integer linear arithmetic are NP-complete [20], and known algorithms for the latter problem have super-exponential worst case behavior [19]. The unsatisfiability checker uses a combination of binary decision diagrams and an integer constraint solver as a decision procedure for SCL formulae. Using the formula $x \leq 4 \wedge x = 7$ as an example we outline the algorithm (for specifics, see [10]). The initial step transforms a formula into one containing only logical connectives and boolean variables. This is done by assigning a fresh boolean variable to each integer constraint in the original formula. Fresh boolean variables are also introduced to encode expressions involving variables of enumerated type in the obvious way [10,28]. For the example, substituting a for $x \leq 4$ and b for $x = 7$ yields the formula $a \wedge b$. Next, a BDD for this formula (which encodes the propositional structure of the original formula) is constructed:

The next step brings in the information contained in the integer constraints. This is done by searching for paths from the root to "True", each path yielding a set of integer constraints. For the example, the only path from the root to "True" sets both a and b to true, which yields the set $\{x \leq 4, \; x = 7\}$. The final step is to determine whether each such set is infeasible (i.e., has no solution) using an integer constraint solver. If a set is feasible, this information is returned to the user as a counterexample. For the example, the (single) set of constraints is infeasible and the formula is unsatisfiable. We now describe the integer constraint solver in detail.

4.2   The Integer Constraint Solver

As an initial step, a set of integer constraints is partitioned into independent subsets. For example, the set of constraints $\{x < 4, x > 7, y < 10\}$ may be partitioned into $\{x < 4, x > 7\}$ and $\{y < 10\}$.

Definition 4. Constraints c_1 and c_2 are *independent* if $Vars(c_1) \cap Vars(c_2) = \emptyset$. The partition of a set of constraints $CS = \{c_1, ..., c_n\}$ into independent subsets (denoted $\Pi(CS)$) is defined as $\Pi(CS) = \{CS_1, ..., CS_m\}$ such that:

1. $\Pi(CS)$ partitions CS.
2. Constraints in different partitions are independent.
3. For each partition containing more than one constraint, every constraint in the partition depends on some other constraint in the partition.

To compute $\Pi(CS)$ Salsa uses a union-find algorithm that starts with each constraint in its own partition and iteratively merges partitions when they contain dependent constraints.

After partitioning a set of constraints into independent subsets, an integer constraint solver determines the feasibility of each independent subset. For a set of constraints, we may conclude that the whole set is infeasible if any independent subset is infeasible.

Salsa's constraint solver is a decision procedure that determines whether a set of integer constraints is infeasible, i.e., given $\{c_1, c_2, ..., c_n\}$ the solver checks whether $c_1 \wedge c_2 \wedge ... \wedge c_n$ is unsatisfiable. Note that the c_i are terms from the integer constraint fragment of SCL (defined in Section 2.1). Among several methods available for solving linear integer constraints, one possible approach is the use of automata theoretic methods. The idea, which dates back to Büchi in the early sixties [13], is to associate with each constraint an automaton accepting the solutions of the constraint. The feasibility of a set of constraints may then be computed by constructing a composite automaton (from the constraint automata for each c_i, $1 \leq i \leq n$) using the standard construction for automata intersection. Salsa's solver employs the algorithm of Boudet and Comon [12], extended to handle negative number based on ideas of Wolper [34]. We give an overview of the algorithm, for details see the above references.

Let us first examine how a constraint automaton may encode constraints over the natural numbers, and then extend this idea to automata for integer constraints. Let c be a constraint, let $Vars(c) = \{x_1, x_2, ..., x_n\}$, and let $c[y_1/x_1, y_2/x_2, ..., y_n/x_n]$ denote the result of substituting y_i for each x_i in c. We then define the *constraint automaton* for c, denoted CAut(c), such that the language of CAut(c) is $\{(y_1, ..., y_n) \in Int^n \mid c[y_1/x_1, ..., y_n/x_n]$ is true$\}$. Each number y_i is encoded in base two, so each y_i is a string in $\{0, 1\}^*$. The constraint automaton will recognize solutions to a constraint by simultaneously reading one bit for each of its free variables, i.e., the edges of the automaton will be labeled by elements of $\{0, 1\}^n$. For example, the satisfying assignments of "$x_1 + x_2 = 4$" are $\{(0, 4), (1, 3), (2, 2), (3, 1), (4, 0)\}$, so CAut($x_1 + x_2 = 4$) encodes this as shown in Figure 2.

We now explain how to construct a constraint automaton for a constraint c of the form $a_1 x_1 + a_2 x_2 + ... + a_n x_n = b$, where $a_1, a_2, ... a_n$, b are integer constants and $x_1, x_2, ... x_n$ are variables over the natural numbers. The resulting automaton will be of the form CAut(c) = $\langle S, E, St, Acc \rangle$ where $S \subseteq Integers$ is the set of states and $E \subseteq S \times \{0, 1\}^n \times S$ is the set of edges, $St \subseteq S$ is the set of start states, and $Acc \subseteq S$ is the set of accepting states. During construction we let S_{new} represent the set of states still to be processed. The construction proceeds backwards from the accepting state as follows.

(x_1, x_2)	Accepted string
(0,4)	0 0 0 1 0 0
(1,3)	0 1 1 1
(2,2)	1 0 1 0
(3,1)	1 1 0 1
(4,0)	1 0 0 0 0 0

Fig. 2. The constraint automaton encoding $x_1 + x_2 = 4$

1. Initialize both S_{new} and Acc to contain only b (the right hand side of the constraint) and initialize $S = E = St = \emptyset$.
2. Remove a state s from S_{new} for processing.
   (a) Add s to S. If $s = 0$ then also add s to St.
   (b) For each $\beta \in \{0,1\}^n$ where $\beta = \langle b_1, b_2, ..., b_n \rangle$
      let $\delta = s - (a_1 b_1 + a_2 b_2 + ... + a_n b_n)$ in
      if δ is even then
      - add edge $(\delta \text{ div } 2) \xrightarrow{\beta} s$ to E
      - if $(\delta \text{ div } 2) \notin (S \cup S_{new})$ then add $(\delta \text{ div } 2)$ to S_{new}

3. if $S_{new} = \emptyset$ then return $\langle S, E, St, Acc \rangle$ else goto 2.

Some simple modifications to the above algorithm extend it to handle negative numbers. For integer constraint c, the states of CAut(c) range over integers and we add a special state $\mathcal{I}$ that will encode the start state, thus $S \subseteq Int \cup \mathcal{I}$. Instead of the standard binary encoding employed for natural numbers the two's complement representation is used for integers. The above algorithm must also be modified to handle the sign bit of the two's complement notation via a special encoding for the start state ($\mathcal{I}$) and extra edges from $\mathcal{I}$. We do this by removing "if $s = 0$ then also add s to St" from 2(a) and adding the following to 2(b) above.

   if $s = (-a_1 b_1 - a_2 b_2 - ... - a_n b_n)$
   then add $\mathcal{I}$ to S and St and add edge $\mathcal{I} \xrightarrow{\beta} s$ to E.

The basic algorithm may also be changed to build constraint automata for constraints involving "$\neq$" and "$\leq$". For "$\neq$" the construction is exactly the same except that $Acc = S - b$, i.e., the accepting state becomes non-accepting and all others become accepting. For details of the slightly more complicated modifications for "$\leq$" see [10].

The constraint automaton for a set of constraints $CS = \{c_1, c_2, ..., c_n\}$, denoted CAut($CS$), is defined as CAut($CS$) = $\bigcap_{i=1}^{n}$ CAut(c_i). The automaton CAut(CS) is constructed *on the fly*, thereby avoiding the need to build each CAut(c_i). Let S_i denote the states of CAut(c_i), then the states of CAut(CS) are $S_{CS} \subseteq S_1 \times S_2 \times ... \times S_n$. An unsatisfiability check of CS then proceeds backwards from the accepting state and terminates with false when the initial state is reached or terminates with true if the automaton construction completes without reaching the start state.

5   Empirical Results

5.1   Motivation

Salsa was designed expressly for the problems of consistency checking and invariant checking SCR requirements specifications. More specifically, the consistency checker of the SCR Toolset [23] was unable to carry out certain checks, such as checks for unwanted nondeterminism called disjointness checks, especially on specifications containing expressions with numbers. We have also been using SPIN and SMV, and more recently TAME [3], to verify user formulated properties of SCR specifications. We compare Salsa with TAME/PVS to gain an insight into how well the Salsa approach performs in relation to that of a state-of-the-art theorem prover.

We compare Salsa with model checkers for the following reason. During the course of our experiments with SCR specifications we have discovered that for model checking to succeed on these specifications requires the application of abstraction, which currently requires user-direction but is automatable [9,22]. Further, SPIN and SMV are unable to provide a definitive answer for invariant checks on a number of examples, especially when they contain a large number of expressions with numbers [27]. Also, since several researchers are currently investigating the use of SPIN and SMV for invariant checking software specifications, it is our intention to demonstrate that Salsa affords a viable, perhaps more automated and cheaper, alternative to model checking. Whereas mechanical theorem provers are regarded as being difficult to use and therefore restricted to sophisticated users, model checking too is often misrepresented as fully automatic or "push button". Our intention is to demonstrate an approach to invariant checking that avoids both the ad hoc abstraction used in model checking and the sophistication required to apply mechanical theorem proving.

The specifications we use in our experiments were developed using the SCR Toolset. Since Salsa seems to work well on *all* of this limited set of examples, readers may express skepticism about the generality of our results – they may feel that there *must* be benchmarks for which the roles would be reversed. By using induction, abstract encodings for linear constraints, and application-specific heuristics, our experience is that the Salsa approach can in general be more efficient than fixpoint computation over a finite domain, i.e., model checking. However, Salsa has the disadvantage of not working in *all* cases, due to the associated problem of incompleteness.

Test Cases. These include a simplified specification of the control software for a nuclear power plant [24] (**safety-injection**), versions of the bomb-release component of the flight-control software of an attack aircraft [1] (**bomb-release-1 and bomb-release-2**), a simplified mode control panel for the Boeing 737 autopilot [7] (**autopilot**), a control system for home heating (**home-heating**), an automobile cruise control system (**cruise-control**), a navy application [27] (**navy**), the mode logic for the Operational Flight Program of an attack aircraft [1] (**a7-modes**), and a weapons control panel [22] (**wcp**).

5.2 Disjointness Checking

To evaluate the performance of Salsa, we checked the above specifications for disjointness errors (unwanted nondeterminism) and compared the results with the consistency checker of the SCR Toolset. The results of our experiments are shown in the table of Figure 3. **No auxiliary lemmas were used for any of the checks.** The column labeled "number of verification conditions" indicates how many invariant checks are required to establish disjointness for the corresponding entire specification. The number of BDD variables is an indicator of a specification's size, and the number of integer constraints correlates loosely with the degree to which integers are used in the specification. In these tables, symbol "∞_t" means that the corresponding system either ran out of memory or failed to terminate (over a weekend). The column labeled "number of failed VCs" shows the number of verification conditions that were not provable. Note: for the specification **a7-modes** Salsa reports more failed VCs than the SCR toolset because certain cases of overlap in table entries are misdiagnosed as disjointness errors when they should probably be warnings. For specification **cruise-control** Salsa establishes disjointness in three cases for which the SCR Toolset cannot. The tests were conducted on a PC running Linux with a 450 MHz Pentium II processor and 256 MBytes RAM.

Specification	Number of			Time (in seconds) to Check Disjointness		Number of Failed VCs	
	Verification Conditions	BDD Variables	Constraints	SCR Toolset	Salsa	SCR Toolset	Salsa
Specifications containing mostly booleans and enumerated types							
safety-injection	13	16	3	0.5	0.2	0	0
bomb-release-1	12	34	9	0.4	0.2	0	0
a7-modes	6171	158	3	145.9	68.9	110	152
Specifications containing mostly numerical variables							
home-heating	98	112	55	∞_t	4.8	n.a.	0
cruise-control	123	114	75	21.0	3.6	6	3
navy	397	147	102	390.1	198.2	0	0
bomb-release-2	339	319	230	∞_t	246.0	n.a.	11

Fig. 3. Results of Disjointness Checks

Figure 3 shows that for specifications containing mostly variables of boolean and enumerated type, both the SCR Toolset and Salsa can complete the analysis but Salsa is somewhat faster. For specifications containing mostly numerical variables, there were two specifications in which Salsa could perform the analysis but the SCR Toolset could not.

5.3   Checking Application Properties

To evaluate Salsa's performance on properties formulated by users, we compared the run times with the theorem prover TAME/PVS and the two popular model checkers SPIN [25] and SMV [28]. (We used SPIN Version 2.9.7 of April 18, 1997, SMV r2.4 of December 16, 1994, and PVS version 2.1 for our experiments.) The results are shown in Figure 4. Note that the PVS proof times do not include time for type checking, which can be substantial. We ran the experiments on a SPARC Ultra-2 running Solaris with a 296 MHz UltraSparc II processor and 262 MBytes RAM. All Salsa proofs were completely automatic, but for **property 304** of **wcp**, which had to be split into two verification conditions for Salsa to complete; the time indicated with an asterisk is the sum of the running times of the two sub-proofs. **All auxiliary lemmas were automatically generated** by the algorithm of [26] and proved as invariants by Salsa. Both SPIN and SMV ran out of memory (or ran indefinitely) when run on all examples other than **safety-injection**. This is probably because they contain a large number of numerical variables. Dashes ("-") in the SMV column indicate that we did not run SMV on these examples.

Specification	Number of Properties	Time (in seconds)				Properties Proved?	Auxiliary Lemmas Used?
		Salsa	SPIN	SMV	TAME/PVS		
safety-injection	4	0.8	36.0	155.0	68	Yes	Yes
bomb-release-1	2	1.3	∞_t	∞_t	30	Yes	No
autopilot	2	1.5	∞_t	∞_t	82	Yes	No
navy	7	396.0	∞_t	-	874	Yes	Yes
wcp	property 303	295.4	∞_t	-	∞_t	No	No
	property 304	923.3*	∞_t	-	19	No	No
	property 305	2.4	∞_t	-	8	No	No

Fig. 4. Results of Invariant Checks

6   Conclusions

In this paper, we show that the Salsa approach affords a useful alternative to model checking, especially for the analysis of descriptions of software. Mechanical theorem provers such as PVS are regarded as being too general and too expensive to use, requiring sophistication on the part of their users. Salsa provides the advantages of both mechanical theorem proving and model checking – it is automatic, easy to use, and provides counterexamples along the lines of model checkers. The counterexamples, however, are over two adjacent states and not entire execution sequences. The main advantage of our approach is that we are able to handle much larger specifications, even infinite state specifications, that current day model checkers cannot handle (without a prior application of abstraction).

The major disadvantage of the Salsa approach over conventional model checking is its incompleteness – a proof failure does not imply that the theorem does not hold. However, this is generally true of model checking too, because an initial application of model checking to a practical problem rarely succeeds – users of model checkers routinely apply abstractions (mostly manually and sometimes in ad-hoc ways) for model checking to proceed [9]. These abstractions are usually sound, but are often incomplete – consequently, if one model checks an incomplete abstraction of a problem, the entire process is incomplete. Model checking, however, remains very useful for *refuting* properties, i.e., as a debugging aid. As with Salsa, the resulting counterexample must be validated against the full specification.

We plan to extend Salsa to include decision procedures for the rationals, the congruence closure algorithm to reason about uninterpreted function symbols, and special-purpose theories such as for arrays and lists. We would also like to reason about quantifiers. We have designed Salsa to be general, i.e., to check a variety of state machine models for invariant properties. We plan on trying out the tool on state machine models other than SCR.

Acknowledgements

This project is funded by the Office of Naval Research. The work of Steve Sims was carried out at NRL under a contract from ONR. We thank Susanne Graf, Connie Heitmeyer, Ralph Jeffords, and the anonymous referees for their comments on previous drafts of this paper. Connie's very useful comments, her constructive criticism, and numerous suggestions for improvement greatly helped the presentation. Ralph was the first user of Salsa! We thank Myla Archer for data on the PVS proofs and Ralph for the mode invariants.

References

1. T. A. Alspaugh et al. Software requirements for the A-7E aircraft. Technical Report NRL-9194, Naval Research Laboratory, Wash., DC, 1992. 387
2. R. J. Anderson, P. Beame, et al. Model checking large software specifications. In *Proc. Fourth ACM FSE*, October 1996. 380
3. M. Archer, C. Heitmeyer, and S. Sims. TAME: A PVS interface to simplify proofs for automata models. In *Proc. User Interfaces for Theorem Provers*, Eindhoven, Netherlands, July 1998. Eindhoven University CS Technical Report. 380, 387
4. C. Barrett, D. Dill, and J. Levitt. Validity checking for combinations of theories with equality. In *Formal Methods In Computer-Aided Design*, volume 1166 of *LNCS*, pages 187–201, November 1996. 380
5. S. Bensalem and Y. Lakhnech. Automatic Generation of Invariants. *Formal Methods in Systems Design*, July 1998. 379, 380
6. S. Bensalem, Y. Lakhnech, and H. Saidi. Powerful techniques for the automatic generation of invariants. In *Conference on Computer Aided Verification CAV'96*, LNCS 1102, July 1996. 379, 380

7. R. Bharadwaj and C. Heitmeyer. Applying the SCR requirements method to a simple autopilot. In *Proc. Fourth NASA Langley Formal Methods Workshop (LFM97)*, NASA Langley Research Center, September 1997. 387

8. R. Bharadwaj and C. Heitmeyer. Verifying SCR requirements specifications using state exploration. In *1st ACM Workshop on Autom. Analysis of Software*, 1997. 383

9. R. Bharadwaj and C. Heitmeyer. Model checking complete requirements specifications using abstraction. *Journal of Automated Software Eng.*, January 1999. 378, 379, 380, 383, 387, 390, 393

10. R. Bharadwaj and S. Sims. Salsa: Combining decision procedures for fully-automatic verification. Technical report, Naval Research Laboratory, To appear. 382, 384, 386

11. N. Bjorner, A. Browne, M. Colon, B. Finkbeiner, Z. Manna, H. Sipma, and T. Uribe. Verifying temporal properties of reactive systems: A step tutorial. *Formal Methods in System Design*, 1999. 379, 380

12. A. Boudet and H. Comon. Diophantine equations, Presburger arithmetic and finite automata. In *Trees and Algebra in Programming – CAAP*, LNCS 1059, 1996. 380, 385

13. J. R. Büchi. On a decision method in restricted second order arithmetic. In *Proc. Int. Congress Logic, Methodology, and Philosophy of Science*, pages 1–11. Stanford University Press, 1960. 385

14. T. Bultan, R. Gerber, and C. League. Verifying systems with integer constraints and boolean predicates: A composite approach. Technical Report UMIACS-TR-97-62, University of Maryland, College Park, MD, August 1997. 380

15. W. Chan, R. Anderson, P. Beame, and D. Notkin. Combining constraint solving with symbolic model checking for a class of systems with non-linear constraints. In *Computer Aided Verification*, LNCS, pages 316–327, 1997. 380

16. William Chan, Richard J. Anderson, Paul Beame, Steve Burns, Francesmary Modugno, David Notkin, and Jon D. Reese. Model checking large software specifications. *IEEE Trans. on Softw. Eng.*, 24(7), July 1998. 380

17. E. M. Clarke, E. Emerson, and A. Sistla. Automatic verification of finite state concurrent systems using temporal logic specifications. *ACM Trans. on Prog. Lang. and Systems*, 8(2):244–263, April 1986. 378

18. J. Elgaard, N. Klarlund, and A. Moller. Mona 1.x: new techniques for ws1s and ws2s. In *Computer Aided Verification, CAV '98*, LNCS 1427, 1998. 380

19. Fischer and Rabin. Super-exponential complexity of Presburger arithmetic. In *Complexity of Computation: Proceedings of a Symposium in Applied Mathematics of the American Mathematical Society and the Society for Industrial and Applied Mathematics*, 1974. 384

20. M.R. Garey and D.S. Johnson. *Computers and Intractability: A guide to the theory of NP-Completeness*. W.H. Freeman and Company, 1979. 384

21. S. Graf and H. Saidi. Verifying invariants using theorem proving. In *Conference on Computer Aided Verification CAV'96*, LNCS 1102, Springer Verlag, 1996. 380

22. C. Heitmeyer, J. Kirby, B. Labaw, M. Archer, and R. Bharadwaj. Using abstraction and model checking to detect safety violations in requirements specifications. *IEEE Transactions on Software Engineering*, 24:927–947, November 1998. 379, 380, 383, 387

23. C. Heitmeyer, J. Kirby, B. Labaw, and R. Bharadwaj. SCR*: A toolset for specifying and analyzing software requirements. In *Proc. Computer-Aided Verification, 10th Annual Conf. (CAV'98)*, Vancouver, Canada, June 1998. 379, 380, 387

24. C. L. Heitmeyer, R. D. Jeffords, and B. G. Labaw. Automated consistency checking of requirements specifications. *ACM Transactions on Software Engineering and Methodology*, 5(3):231–261, July 1996. 379, 381, 387

25. G. J. Holzmann. The model checker SPIN. *IEEE Trans. on Softw. Eng.*, 23(5):279–295, May 1997. 380, 389

26. R. Jeffords and C. Heitmeyer. Automatic generation of state invariants from requirements specifications. In *Proc. Sixth ACM SIGSOFT Symp. on Foundations of Software Engineering*, November 1998. 379, 389

27. J. Kirby, Jr., M. Archer, and C. Heitmeyer. SCR: A practical approach to building a high assurance COMSEC system. In *Proceedings of the 15th Annual Computer Security Applications Conference (ACSAC '99)*, December 1999. 387

28. K. L. McMillan. *Symbolic Model Checking*. Kluwer Academic Publishers, 1993. 380, 384, 389

29. G. Nelson and D. C. Oppen. Simplification by cooperating decision procedures. *ACM Transactions on Programming Languages and Systems*, 1(2):245–257, 1979. 380

30. S. Owre, J. Rushby, N. Shankar, and F. von Henke. Formal verification for fault-tolerant architectures: Prolegomena to the design of PVS. *IEEE Transactions on Software Engineering*, 21(2):107–125, February 1995. 380

31. P.Kelb, T.Margaria, M.Mendler, and C.Gsottberger. Mosel: A flexible toolset for monadic second–order logic. In *Workshop on Tools and Algorithms for the Construction and Analysis of Systems (TACAS'97)*, volume 1217 of *(LNCS)*, pages 183–202, Heidelberg, Germany, March 1997. Springer–Verlag. 380

32. Y. Lakhnech S. Bensalem and S. Owre. InVeSt: A tool for the verification of invariants. In *Proc. Computer-Aided Verification, 10th Annual Conf. (CAV'98)*, Vancouver, Canada, June 1998. 380

33. Robert E. Shostak. Deciding combinations of theories. *JACM*, 31(1):1–12, January 1984. 380

34. P. Wolper and B. Boigelot. Verifying systems with infinite but regular state spaces. In *Computer Aided Verification – 10th Int'l. Conference*, LNCS 1427, 1998. 380, 385

A   SAL Specification of Safety Injection System

A module is the unit of specification in SAL and comprises variable declarations, assumptions and guarantees, and definitions. The `assumptions` section typically includes assumptions about the environment and previously proved invariants (lemmas). The required invariants of a module are specified in the `guarantees` section. The `definitions` section specifies updates to internal and controlled variables. A *one-state* definition, of the form var x = $rhs1$ (where $rhs1$ is a one-state SAL expression), defines the value of variable x in terms of the values of other variables *in the same state*. A two-state variable definition, of the form var x initially *init* := $rhs2$ (where $rhs2$ is a two-state SAL expression), requires the initial value of x to equal expression *init*; the value of x in the "new" state of each state transition is defined in terms of the values of variables in the "new" state *as well as* the "old" state. Expression @T(x) WHEN y is syntactic sugar for $\neg x \wedge x' \wedge y$ and @F(x) denotes @T(NOT x). A *conditional expression* consists of a sequence of branches "[] guard → expression", where the guards are boolean expressions, bracketed by the keywords "if" and "fi". In a given state, the value of a guarded expression is equivalent to the expression on the right hand side of the arrow whose associated guard is true. If more than one guard is true, the expression is nondeterministic. A conditional event expression (which is bracketed by the keywords "ev" and "ve") requires each guard to denote an *event*, where an event is a two-state expression that is true in a pair of states only if they differ in the value of at least one state variable.

We specify in SAL a simplified version of a control system for safety injection [9]. The system monitors water pressure and injects coolant into the reactor core when the pressure falls below a threshold. The system operator may override safety injection by pressing a "Block" button and may reset the system by pressing a "Reset" button. To specify the requirements of the control system, we use variables WaterPres, Block, and Reset to denote the monitored quantities and variable SafetyInjection to denote the controlled quantity. The specification includes a mode class Pressure, an abstract model of WaterPres, which has three modes: TooLow, Permitted, and High. It also includes a term Overridden and several conditions and events.

```
module sis
functions
  Low = 900; Permit = 1000;
monitored variables
  Block, Reset : {On, Off};
  WaterPres : int in [0,2000];
controlled variables
  SafetyInjection : {On, Off};
internal variables
  Overridden : bool;
  Pressure   : {TooLow, Permitted, High};

assumptions
  /* Mode invariant generated by the algorithm of Jeffords [26] */
  LemmaZ = (Overridden => Reset = Off and not (Pressure = High));
guarantees
  /* The following properties are true */
  Property1 = (Reset = On and  Pressure != High) =>  not Overridden;
  Property2 = (Reset = On and Pressure - TooLow) => SafetyInjection - On;
  /* The following properties are false */
  Property3 =(Block = Off and Pressure = TooLow) => SafetyInjection = On;
  Property4 =(@T(Pressure=TooLow) when Block=Off) => SafetyInjection'=On;

definitions
  var Overridden initially false :=
    ev
      [] @T(Pressure = High) -> false
      [] @T(Block = On) when (Reset = Off and Pressure != High) -> true
      [] @T(Pressure != High) or
         @T(Reset = On) when (Pressure != High) -> false
    ve
```

```
var Pressure initially TooLow :=
  case Pressure
    [] TooLow ->     ev [] @T(WaterPres >= Low) -> Permitted    ve
    [] Permitted ->  ev [] @T(WaterPres < Low) -> TooLow
                        [] @T(WaterPres >= Permit) -> High
                     ve
    [] High ->       ev [] @T(WaterPres < Permit) -> Permitted ve
  esac

var SafetyInjection =
  case Pressure
    [] High, Permitted -> if [] true  -> Off  [] false -> On fi
    [] TooLow -> if [] Overridden -> Off [] not Overridden -> On fi
  esac
end module
```

Fig. 5. SAL specification of Safety Injection System

Symbolic Model Checking of Probabilistic Processes Using MTBDDs and the Kronecker Representation

Luca de Alfaro[1], Marta Kwiatkowska[2]*, Gethin Norman[2]*, David Parker[2], and Roberto Segala[3]**

[1] Department of Electrical Engineering and Computing Science,
University of California at Berkeley
dealfaro@eecs.berkeley.edu
[2] University of Birmingham,
Birmingham B15 2TT, United Kingdom
{M.Z.Kwiatkowska,G.Norman,D.A.Parker}@cs.bham.ac.uk
[3] Dipartimento di Scienze dell'Informazione, Università di Bologna,
Mura Anteo Zamboni 7, 40127 Bologna, Italy
segala@cs.unibo.it

Abstract. This paper reports on experimental results with symbolic model checking of probabilistic processes based on Multi-Terminal Binary Decision Diagrams (MTBDDs). We consider concurrent probabilistic systems as models; these allow nondeterministic choice between probability distributions and are particularly well suited to modelling distributed systems with probabilistic behaviour, e.g. randomized consensus algorithms and probabilistic failures. As a specification formalism we use the probabilistic branching-time temporal logic PBTL which allows one to express properties such as "under any scheduling of nondeterministic choices, the probability of ϕ holding until ψ is true is *at least 0.78/at most 0.04*". We adapt the Kronecker representation of (Plateau 1985), which yields a very compact MTBDD encoding of the system. We implement an experimental model checker using the CUDD package and demonstrate that model construction and reachability-based model checking is possible in a matter of seconds for certain classes of systems consisting of up to 10^{30} states.

1 Introduction

There have been many advances in the BDD technology since BDDs were first introduced and applied to symbolic model checking [10,25]. There are several free and commercial BDD packages in existence, as well as a range of alternative techniques for efficient automatic verification. Model checking tools (to mention smv, SPIN, fdr2) are extensively used by industrial companies in the process of developing new designs for e.g. hardware circuits, network protocols, etc. More

---

* Supported in part by EPSRC grant GR/M04617.
** Supported in part by EPSRC grant GR/M13046.

S. Graf and M. Schwartzbach (Eds.): TACAS/ETAPS 2000, LNCS 1785, pp. 395–410, 2000.
© Springer-Verlag Berlin Heidelberg 2000

recently tremendous progress has been made with tools for the model checking of real-time systems, e.g. Uppaal [6].

One area that is lagging behind as far as experimental work is concerned, despite the fact that the fundamental verification algorithms have been known for over a decade [32,15,28], is model checking of *probabilistic* systems. This is particularly unsatisfactory since many systems currently being designed would benefit from probabilistic analysis performed *in addition to* the conventional, qualitative checks involving temporal logic formulas or reachability analysis available in established model checking tools. This includes not only quality of service properties such as "with probability 0.9 or greater, the system will respond to the request within time t", but also steady-state probability (until recently, see [17,4], separate from temporal logic model checking), which allows the computation of characteristics such as long-run average, resource utilization, etc.

In order to support efficient verification of probabilistic systems, BDD-based packages must allow a compact representation for sparse probability matrices. Such a representation, Multi-Terminal Binary Decision Diagrams (MTBDDs), was proposed in [14] along with some matrix algorithms. MTBDDs are also known as Algebraic Decision Diagrams (ADDs) [1] and are implemented in the Colorado University Decision Diagram (CUDD) package of Fabio Somenzi [31]. Based on [22], an MTBDD-based *symbolic* model checking procedure for purely probabilistic processes (state-labelled discrete Markov chains) for the logic PCTL of [22] (a probabilistic variant of CTL) was first presented in [3], and since extended to concurrent probabilistic systems in [2] (without implementation). Similarly, a symbolic model checking procedure for continuous time Markov chains is proposed in [4]. An alternative representation for Markov chains called Probabilistic Decision Graphs (PDGs) was introduced in [9], where early experimental results are also reported.

In this paper we consider *concurrent probabilistic systems* [5], based on Markov Decision Processes [7], similar to those of [32,8]. These are state-labelled systems which admit *nondeterministic choice* between discrete probability distributions on the successor states, and are particularly appropriate for the representation of randomized distributed algorithms, fault-tolerant and self-stabilising systems. The model checking procedure, first proposed in [15,8] for the case without fairness and extended to incorporate fairness constraints in [5,18], reduces to the computation of the *minimum/maximum* reachability probability. We can derive a set of *linear inequalities*, and maximize/minimize the sum of the components of the solution vector subject to the constraints given by the inequalities.

Multi-Terminal Binary Decision Diagrams [14] have the same structure as BDDs, except that terminals other than 0 and 1 are allowed. The similarity between the two types of diagrams means that many BDD operations generalise to the MTBDD case. MTBDDs are known to yield a compact and efficient representation for sparse matrices [14]. They share many positive features with BDDs: because they exploit *regularity* and *sharing*, they allow the representation of much larger matrices than standard sparse matrix representations. MTBDDs also combine well with BDDs in a shared environment, thus allowing *reacha-*

bility analysis via conversion to BDDs (which coincide with 0-1 MTBDDs) and conventional BDD reachability. However, MTBDDs also inherit negative BDD features: they are exponential in the worst case, very sensitive to variable ordering heuristics, and may be subject to a sudden, unpredictable, increase in size as the regularity of the structure is lost through performing operations on it. As a consequence, algorithms that *change* the structure of the matrix, such as Gaussian elimination for solving linear equations [1] or simplex for solving systems of linear inequalities [24], are significantly less efficient than state-of-the-art sparse matrix packages due to the loss of regularity. Iterative methods [21,23], on the other hand, which rely on matrix-by-vector multiplication without changing the matrix structure, perform better.

There has been very little work concerning MTBDD-based numerical linear algebra; a notable exception is the CUDD package [31], a free library of C routines which supports matrix multiplication in a shared BDD and MTBDD environment. In contrast, numerical analysis of Markov chains based on sparse matrices is much more advanced, particularly in the context of Stochastic Petri Nets. There, with the help of a Kronecker representation originally introduced by Brigitte Plateau [26], systems with millions of states can be analysed. The Kronecker representation applies to systems composed of parallel components; each component is represented as a set of (comparatively small) matrices, with the matrix of the full system defined as the reachable subspace of a Kronecker-algebraic expression (usually referred to as the *actual*, versus the *potential*, state space). Then one can avoid having to store the full size matrix by storing the component matrices instead and reformulating steady-state probability calculation in terms of the component matrices. Existing implementation work in this area includes tools such as SMART [11] and PEPS [27].

In this paper we adapt and extend the ideas of [3,2] in order to represent *concurrent probabilistic systems* in terms of MTBDDs. The differences with the corresponding work in numerical analysis of Markov chains are: we allow nondeterminism as well as probability; we work with probability matrices, not generator matrices of continuous time Markov chains; we generate the matrix in full, then perform BDD reachability analysis to obtain the actual state space; and we perform model checking against PBTL through a combination of reachability analysis and numerical approximation instead of steady-state probability calculation. The main contribution of the paper is threefold: (1) we implement an experimental symbolic model checker for PBTL [5] using MTBDDs; (2) we adapt the Kronecker representation of [26] and provide a translation into MTBDDs; and (3) we improve the model checking algorithm by incorporating the probability-1 precomputation step of [19].

2   Concurrent Probabilistic Systems

In this section, we briefly summarise our underlying model for concurrent probabilistic systems; the reader is referred to [5,2] for more details. Our model is based on "Markov decision processes", and is similar to "Concurrent Markov

Chains" of [32,16] and "simple deterministic automata" of [29]. Some familiarity with Markov chains and probability theory is assumed.

Concurrent probabilistic systems generalise ordinary Markov chains in that they allow a nondeterministic choice between possibly several probability distributions in a given state. Formally, a *concurrent probabilistic system* is a pair $\mathcal{S} = (S, Steps)$ where S is a finite set of states and $Steps$ a function which assigns to each state $s \in S$ a finite, non-empty set $Steps(s)$ of distributions on S. Elements of $Steps(s)$ are called *transitions*. Systems $\mathcal{S} = (S, Steps)$ such that $Steps(s)$ is a singleton set for each $s \in S$ are called *purely probabilistic* and coincide with discrete time Markov chains.

Paths in a concurrent probabilistic system arise by resolving both the nondeterministic and probabilistic choices. A *path* of the system $\mathcal{S} = (S, Steps)$ is a non-empty finite or infinite sequence $\pi = s_0 \xrightarrow{p_0} s_1 \xrightarrow{p_1} s_2 \xrightarrow{p_2} \cdots$ where $s_i \in S$, $p_i \in Steps(s_i)$ with $p_i(s_{i+1}) > 0$. We let $\pi(i)$ denote the ith state of the path π.

The selection of a probability distribution is made by an adversary (also known as a scheduler), a function mapping every finite path of the system onto one of the distributions in $Steps(s)$ where s is the last state of the path. Note we use *deterministic* adversaries, rather than randomized adversaries as in [8]. For an adversary A of a concurrent probabilistic system $\mathcal{S} = (S, Steps)$ we define $Path_{ful}^A$ to be the set of infinite paths corresponding to the choices of the adversary. In the standard way, we define the measure $Prob$ over infinite paths.

Since we allow nondeterministic choice between probability distributions, we may have to impose *fairness constraints* to ensure that liveness properties can be verified. In a distributed environment fairness corresponds to a requirement for each each concurrent component to progress whenever possible. Without fairness, certain liveness properties may trivially fail to hold in the presence of simultaneously enabled transitions of a concurrent component. An adversary is called *fair* if any choice of transitions that becomes enabled infinitely often along a computation path is taken infinitely often. The interested reader is referred to [5,20] for more information on the subject.

3   The Logic PBTL

In this section, based on [5,8], we recall the syntax and semantics of the probabilistic branching-time temporal logic PBTL. PBTL derives from CTL [13] and PCTL [22], borrowing the temporal operator $\mathcal{U}$ ("until") and the path quantifier $\exists$ from CTL, and the probabilistic operator $[\cdot]_{\sqsupseteq\lambda}$ from PCTL.

Let AP denote a finite set of atomic propositions. A *PBTL structure* is a tuple $(\mathcal{S}, AP, L)$ where $\mathcal{S} = (S, Steps)$ is a concurrent probabilistic system and $L : S \to 2^{AP}$ is a labelling function which assigns to each state $s \in S$ a set of atomic propositions. The syntax of PBTL is:

$$\phi ::= \texttt{true} \mid a \mid \phi_1 \wedge \phi_2 \mid \neg\phi \mid [\phi_1 \exists\mathcal{U} \phi_2]_{\sqsupseteq\lambda}$$

where a is an atomic proposition, $\lambda \in [0, 1]$, and $\sqsupseteq$ is either $\geq$ or $>$.

The branching time quantifier $\exists$ involves quantification over adversaries, meaning "there exists an adversary" of a given type. Note that to simplify this presentation, we have omitted the "bounded until", "next state" and "universal until" operators which can easily be added. The latter is defined similarly to the "existential until" operator included above. For a PBTL formula ϕ and set Adv of adversaries we define the satisfaction relation $s \models_{Adv} \phi$ inductively as follows:

$$s \models_{Adv} \textbf{true} \qquad \text{for all } s \in S$$
$$s \models_{Adv} a \qquad\qquad \Leftrightarrow a \in L(s)$$
$$s \models_{Adv} \phi_1 \wedge \phi_2 \qquad \Leftrightarrow s \models_{Adv} \phi_1 \text{ and } s \models_{Adv} \phi_2$$
$$s \models_{Adv} \neg\phi \qquad\quad\; \Leftrightarrow s \not\models_{Adv} \phi$$
$$s \models_{Adv} [\phi_1 \exists\mathcal{U} \phi_2]_{\sqsupseteq\lambda} \Leftrightarrow Prob(\{\pi \mid \pi \in Path_{ful}^A(s) \ \& \ \pi \models_{Adv} \phi_1 \, \mathcal{U} \, \phi_2\}) \sqsupseteq \lambda$$
$$\qquad\qquad\qquad\qquad \text{for some adversary } A \in Adv$$

$$\pi \models_{Adv} \phi_1 \, \mathcal{U} \, \phi_2 \qquad \Leftrightarrow \text{there exists } k \geq 0 \text{ such that } \pi(k) \models_{Adv} \phi_2$$
$$\text{and for all } j = 0, 1, \ldots, k-1, \ \pi(j) \models_{Adv} \phi_1$$

We denote satisfaction for *all* adversaries by $\models$ and satisfaction for *all fair* adversaries by $\models_{fair}$.

4   PBTL Model Checking

With the exception of "until" formulas and fairness, model checking for PBTL is straightforward, see [8,5]. It proceeds by induction on the parse tree of the formula, as in the case of CTL model checking [13].

We only consider existential "until" for reasons of space. To establish whether $s \models_{Adv} [\phi \exists\mathcal{U} \psi]_{\sqsupseteq\lambda}$, we calculate the *maximum probability*:

$$p_s^{\max}(\phi \, \mathcal{U} \, \psi) = \sup\{p_s^A(\phi \, \mathcal{U} \, \psi) \mid A \in Adv\}$$

where $p_s^A(\phi \, \mathcal{U} \, \psi) = Prob(\{\pi \mid \pi \in Path_{ful}^A(s) \ \& \ \pi \models \phi \, \mathcal{U} \, \psi\})$ and compare the result to the threshold λ, i.e. establish the inequality $p_s^{\max} \sqsupseteq \lambda$. First we introduce an operator on sets of states which will be used in the algorithm.

For $U_0, U_1 \subseteq S$, define $reachE(U_0, U_1) = \mu Z[H]$ as the least fixed point of the map $H : 2^S \to 2^S$, where:

$$H = \lambda x.(((x \in U_0) \wedge \exists p \in Steps(x) \, \exists y (p(y) > 0 \wedge y \in Z)) \vee (x \in U_1)).$$

The algorithm is shown in Figure 1. We use $\varepsilon = 10^{-6}$ as the termination criterion for the iteration in step 3. Observe that we compute *approximations* to the actual (minimum/maximum) probabilities from below to within ε. Alternatively, the values $p_s^{\max}(\phi \, \mathcal{U} \, \psi)$ can be calculated by reduction to linear optimization problems [8,5,2].

Fairness assumptions, which are necessary in order to verify liveness properties of concurrent probabilistic processes, for example "under any scheduling, process P will eventually enter a successful state with probability at least 0.7",

1. Compute the sets of states $Sat(\phi), Sat(\psi)$ that satisfy ϕ, ψ.
2. Let (a) $S^{\text{yes}} := Sat(\psi)$
        (b) $S^{>0} := reachE(Sat(\phi), S^{\text{yes}})$
        (c) $S^{\text{no}} := S \setminus S^{>0}$
        (d) $S^? := S \setminus (S^{\text{yes}} \cup S^{\text{no}})$
3. Set $p_s^{\max}(\phi \, \mathcal{U} \, \psi) = 1$ if $s \in S^{\text{yes}}$ and $p_s^{\max}(\phi \, \mathcal{U} \, \psi) = 0$ if $s \in S^{\text{no}}$.
   For $s \in S^?$, calculate $p_s^{\max}(\phi \, \mathcal{U} \, \psi)$ iteratively as the limit, as n tends to ∞, of the approximations $\langle x_{s,n} \rangle_{n \in \mathbb{N}}$, where $x_{s,0} = 0$ and for $n = 1, 2, \ldots$

$$x_{s,n} = \max \left\{ \sum_{t \in S^?} r(t) \cdot x_{t,n-1} + \sum_{t \in S^{\text{yes}}} r(t) \mid r \in Steps(s) \right\}.$$

4. Finally, let $Sat([\phi \, \exists\mathcal{U} \, \psi]_{\sqsupseteq \lambda}) := \{ s \in S \mid p_s^{\max}(\phi \, \mathcal{U} \, \psi) \sqsupseteq \lambda \}$.

Fig. 1. The Algorithm **EU**

can also be handled. This is possible via reduction of the model checking for $\models_{fair}$ to that for ordinary satisfaction $\models$ using results from [5,2].

For purely probabilistic systems, model checking of "until" reduces to a linear equation system in $|S^?|$ unknowns which can be solved either through a direct method such as Gaussian elimination, or iteratively via e.g. Jacobi or Gauss-Seidel iteration.

4.1   Probability-1 Precomputation Step

The model checking algorithm for "until" properties given below can be improved by pre-computing the set of *all* states from which the formula holds with maximal probability 1. The algorithm for this precomputation step is based on results of [15,16] and can be derived from that in [19] for computing the set of states that can reach a goal with probability 1. We have here adapted it to "until" formulas.

For any $Z_0, Z_1 \subseteq S$ let $Pre(Z_0, Z_1)$ be the set of states defined by:

$Pre(Z_0, Z_1) =$
    $\{ x \mid \exists p \in Steps(x)(\forall y(p(y) > 0 \rightarrow y \in Z_0) \wedge \exists y(p(y) > 0 \wedge y \in Z_1)) \}$.

Intuitively, $s \in Pre(Z_0, Z_1)$ if one can go from s to Z_1 with positive probability without leaving Z_0.

Theorem 1. *Let* $\mathcal{S} = (S, Steps)$ *be a concurrent probabilistic transition system,* $U_0, U_1 \subseteq S$ *subsets of states and* $prob1E(U_0, U_1)$ *be the set of states given by the solution to* $\nu Z_0 \mu Z_1 [G]$ *where*

$$G = \lambda x.((x \in U_1) \vee ((x \in U_0) \wedge x \in Pre(Z_0, Z_1))).$$

Then $s \in prob1E(U_0, U_1)$ if and only if from s, for some adversary, one reaches a state in U_1 via a path through states in U_0 with probability 1.

It follows from this theorem that we can strengthen the assignment to S^{yes} at step 2(a) of Algorithm **EU** to: $S^{yes} := prob1E(Sat(\phi), Sat(\psi))$. Hence, in cases of *qualitative* properties, i.e. properties which are required to hold with probability 1, no further computation of the probability vector will be required. In particular, this avoids potential difficulties with approximations.

4.2 Symbolic Model Checking

A symbolic method is obtained from the above procedure by representing the system and probability vector as MTBDDs, $Sat(\phi)$ as a BDD, and expressing the probability calculations as MTBDD/BDD operations (for more details see [3,2]). The operators $reachE(\cdot, \cdot)$ and $prob1E(\cdot, \cdot)$ can be expressed in terms of BDD fixed point computation with respect to the transition relation extracted from the MTBDD. The iterative calculation of the probability vector requires matrix-by-vector multiplication and the operation ABSTRACT(max).

5   Representing Probabilistic Processes with MTBDDs

MTBDDs were introduced in [14] as a generalisation of BDDs. Like BDDs, they take the form of a rooted directed acyclic graph, the nonterminal nodes of which are labelled with Boolean variables from an ordered set. Unlike BDDs however, the terminal nodes are labelled with values taken from a finite set D (usually a subset of the reals), not just 0 and 1. The operations on MTBDDs are derived from their BDD counter-parts, and include REDUCE, APPLY and ABSTRACT, see [1,14]. An MTBDD with n Boolean variables and terminals taken from the finite set D, can be considered as a map $f : \{0,1\}^n \to D$.

In [14] it is shown how to represent matrices in terms of MTBDDs. Consider a square $2^m \times 2^m$–matrix $\mathbf{A}$ with entries taken from D. Its elements a_{ij} can be viewed as the values of a function $f_{\mathbf{A}} : \{1, \ldots, 2^m\} \times \{1, \ldots, 2^m\} \to D$, where $f_{\mathbf{A}}(i, j) = a_{ij}$, mapping the position indices i, j to the matrix element a_{ij}. Using the standard encoding $c : \{0,1\}^m \to \{1, \ldots, 2^m\}$ of Boolean sequences of length m into the integers, this function may be interpreted as a Boolean function $f : \{0,1\}^{2m} \to D$ where $f(x, y) = f_A(c(x), c(y))$ for $x = (x_1, \ldots, x_m)$ and $y = (y_1, \ldots, y_m)$. We require the variables for the rows and columns to alternate, that is, use the MTBDD obtained from $f(x_1, y_1, x_2, y_2, \ldots, x_m, y_m)$. This convention imposes a recursive structure on the matrix from which efficient recursive algorithms for all standard matrix operations are derived [1,14].

Probability matrices are sparse, and thus can have a compact MTBDD representation. This compactness results from *sharing* of substructures, and increases with the regularity of the original matrix. Though in the worst case exponential, compared to sparse matrix representation and depending on the degree of regularity of the original matrix, MTBDDs can be much more space-efficient than sparse matrices. They also combine efficiently with BDDs.

Concurrent probabilistic transition systems with n states that enable at most l nondeterministic transitions each can be represented as a $nl \times n$ matrix, which can then be stored as an MTBDD. (For simplicity assume that n and l are powers of 2). Each row of the matrix represents a single nondeterministic choice, where the element in position $(i.k, j)$ represents the probability of reaching state j from state i in the kth transition that leaves from i.

Unfortunately, experimental evidence has shown that this simple MTBDD representation of concurrent probabilistic systems suffers from a disproportionately large number of internal nodes, due to the lack of regularity. Instead, we will adapt the *Kronecker representation* originally introduced for space-efficient storage of Markov processes as Stochastic Automata Networks [26].

5.1   A Modular Description Language for Probabilistic Processes

We propose a modular description language for concurrent probabilistic systems in an attempt to derive a more efficient MTBDD encoding. The system is considered as a composition of *modules*, acting concurrently, more specifically via the asynchronous parallel composition of probabilistic processes whose local transitions may be dependent on the global state of the system.

This model bears similarities to the Stochastic Automata Networks (SANs) of [26]. One difference between the two approaches is that we consider probabilistic, as opposed to stochastic processes. Secondly, SANs permit two types of process interaction: *synchronization* between components, and *functional transitions*, where the rate or probability with which one component makes a transition may depend on the state of another component. For simplicity, we discuss here only the latter type of interaction. Most importantly, the motivation is different: the fundamental idea with SANs is that since the transition matrix for the composed system is formulated as a Kronecker expression, only the small matrices which make up this expression need to be stored and explicit construction of the whole (often huge) transition matrix can be avoided. Although our aim is also to obtain a space efficient method of storage, we construct the whole matrix and use a Kronecker expression to derive an efficient MTBDD variable ordering.

We consider the system as a composition of n modules $M_1, \ldots, M_n$, each with a set of local variables Var_i. Each variable $x \in Var_i$ has a finite range of values, $range(x)$. The local state space S_i of module M_i is $\prod_{x \in Var_i} range(x)$. The global state space of the combined system is then $S = \prod_{i=1}^{n} S_i$.

Each module defines the transitions that it can make, depending on its current state and the state of the other modules in the system. The behaviour of a module M_i is given by a finite non-empty set L_i of tuples of the form (c, p), where $c = \wedge_{j=1}^{n} c_j$ is a conjunction of n variable constraints, c_j is a formula over Var_j and p is a probability distribution over S_i. Intuitively, c represents the condition under which transitions corresponding to the probability distribution p can be made. We can associate with a tuple $l = (c, p)$ the set of global states $S_l = \{s \in S \mid s \models c\}$ which satisfy the variable contraints. We require, for all modules M_i, that the sets S_l where $l \in L_i$ form a disjoint union of S.

We interpret the formal description of the behaviour of the modules as follows. If the global state of the system is $s = (s_1, \ldots, s_n)$ and $s \in S_l$ for a tuple $l = (c, p) \in L_i$ then the probability of module M_i moving from its current local state s_i to the local state t_i is $p(t_i)$. Hence, in each global state of the system, any of the n modules can make a move. The behaviour of each individual module is essentially that of a Markov chain. It is necessary to decide on some form of scheduling between the modules to define the behaviour of the composed system. We consider two possibilities: probabilistic and nondeterministic scheduling. In the former, each module has an equal probability of being scheduled, giving a Markov chain. In the latter, we allow a nondeterministic choice between modules, which gives a concurrent probabilistic system as described in Section 2.

Module M_1:
$(x = 0) \rightarrow \frac{1}{2} : (x' = 0) + \frac{1}{2} : (x' = 1)$
$(x = 1) \wedge (y \leq 1) \rightarrow (x' = 2)$
$(x = 1) \wedge (y = 2) \rightarrow (x' = 1)$
$(x = 2) \rightarrow \frac{1}{2} : (x' = 0) + \frac{1}{2} : (x' = 2)$
Module M_2:
$(y = 0) \rightarrow \frac{1}{2} : (y' = 0) + \frac{1}{2} : (y' = 1)$
$(y = 1) \wedge (x \leq 1) \rightarrow (y' = 2)$
$(y = 1) \wedge (x = 2) \rightarrow (y' = 1)$
$(y = 2) \rightarrow \frac{1}{2} : (y' = 0) + \frac{1}{2} : (y' = 2)$

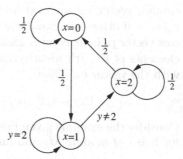

Fig. 2. (i) A system composed of two modules. (ii) Transition system of module M_1

Consider the example shown in Figure 2 of the modules M_1, M_2, with corresponding variable sets $Var_1 = \{x\}$ and $Var_2 = \{y\}$, where x and y have range $\{0, 1, 2\}$. Figure 2(i) shows a textual description of the modules. Each line corresponds to a tuple (c, p) where the condition c and the probability distribution p are separated by a $\rightarrow$ symbol. For example, in line 1 of module M_1, the condition is $(x = 0)$ and the distribution is $\frac{1}{2} : (x' = 0) + \frac{1}{2} : (x' = 1)$, where x' denotes the value of x in the state after the transition. Note $c = (x = 0)$ is in fact $c = c_1 \wedge c_2$ where $c_1 = (x = 0)$ and $c_2 = \text{true}$, i.e. there is no constraint on y.

5.2   A Kronecker Expression for the Modular Description

We now derive a Kronecker expression for the transition matrix of the composed system. As pointed out in [26], the transition matrix for the composition of n non-interacting stochastic automata can be written as:

$$\mathbf{Q} = \oplus_{i=1}^{n} \mathbf{L}_i = \sum_{i=1}^{n} \mathbf{Q}_i \text{ where } \mathbf{Q}_i = (\otimes_{j=1}^{i-1} \mathbf{I}_{n_j}) \otimes \mathbf{L}_i \otimes (\otimes_{j=i+1}^{n} \mathbf{I}_{n_j}).$$

In the above, $\mathbf{L}_i$ is the local transition matrix for component i, $\mathbf{I}_n$ the identity matrix of size n, and n_j the dimension of local matrix $\mathbf{L}_j$. We use the same basic construction here, but with *probability* matrices $\mathbf{P}_i$ for each module, rather than $\mathbf{Q}_i$. These local matrices are then combined through scheduling rather than simply summation. We also account for the fact that the behaviour of one module can depend on the state of another. As with functional transitions in SANs, this does not affect the overall structure of the Kronecker expression: some transitions are simply removed by zeroing out the relevant entry in the component matrix.

For a given module M_i, we want an expression for the corresponding transition matrix $\mathbf{P}_i$. Since $+$ distributes over $\otimes$, we can break the expression up into separate matrices $\mathbf{P}_{i,l}$, such that $\mathbf{P}_i = \sum_{l \in L_i} \mathbf{P}_{i,l}$. The restrictions on transitions are handled by zeroing out some entries of the identity matrices. We first convert the information from the module descriptions to vectors. For module M_i and line $l \in L_i$ where $l = (c, p)$ and $c = \wedge_{j=1}^n c_j$, we associate with each c_j the column vector $\mathbf{c}_j$, indexed over local states S_j, with $\mathbf{c}_j(s) = 1$ if $s \models c_j$ and $\mathbf{c}_j(s) = 0$ otherwise. Similarly, the probability distribution p is converted to a row vector $\mathbf{p}$, indexed over local states from S_i, with $\mathbf{p}(s) = p(s)$. The unwanted elements of the jth identity matrix are removed by a pointwise multiplication with the vector $\mathbf{c}_j$. Then:

$$\mathbf{P}_{i,l} = (\otimes_{j=1}^{i-1} \mathbf{c}_j \cdot \mathbf{I}_{n_j}) \otimes (\mathbf{c}_i \otimes \mathbf{p}) \otimes (\otimes_{j=i+1}^{n} \mathbf{c}_j \cdot \mathbf{I}_{n_j})$$

Consider the example given previously. We can write the matrices $\mathbf{P}_{1,1}$ and $\mathbf{P}_{2,2}$ for line 1 of module M_1 and line 2 of module M_2 respectively, as:

$$\mathbf{P}_{1,1} = \left(\begin{pmatrix} 1 \\ 0 \\ 0 \end{pmatrix} \otimes \left(\tfrac{1}{2} \tfrac{1}{2} 0 \right) \right) \otimes \left(\begin{pmatrix} 1 \\ 1 \\ 1 \end{pmatrix} \cdot \begin{pmatrix} 1 0 0 \\ 0 1 0 \\ 0 0 1 \end{pmatrix} \right) = \begin{pmatrix} \tfrac{1}{2} \tfrac{1}{2} 0 \\ 0 0 0 \\ 0 0 0 \end{pmatrix} \otimes \begin{pmatrix} 1 0 0 \\ 0 1 0 \\ 0 0 1 \end{pmatrix}$$

$$\mathbf{P}_{2,2} = \left(\begin{pmatrix} 1 \\ 1 \\ 0 \end{pmatrix} \cdot \begin{pmatrix} 1 0 0 \\ 0 1 0 \\ 0 0 1 \end{pmatrix} \right) \otimes \left(\begin{pmatrix} 0 \\ 1 \\ 0 \end{pmatrix} \otimes (0 0 1) \right) = \begin{pmatrix} 1 0 0 \\ 0 1 0 \\ 0 0 0 \end{pmatrix} \otimes \begin{pmatrix} 0 0 0 \\ 0 0 1 \\ 0 0 0 \end{pmatrix}$$

5.3   Module to MTBDD Translation

The construction of the transition matrix, as described above, can be derived directly from the syntax in Figure 2(i) by means of BDD and MTBDD operations. First, we encode all the module variables with Boolean variables. For convenience, we assume that the range of each variable, x, is a power of 2, i.e. $range(x) = \{0, \ldots, 2^k - 1\}$ for some k. Hence, x can be encoded with k Boolean variables $x_1, \ldots, x_k$, and x' with $x_1', \ldots, x_k'$. This gives a set of MTBDD row (unprimed) and column (primed) variables for each module variable in the system. The ordering of the modules in the textual description and of the module variables within them gives us an overall ordering for the Boolean variables in our MTBDDs. In our small example, we get $x_1 < x_1' < x_2 < x_2' < y_1 < y_1' < y_2 < y_2'$.

The column vectors $\mathbf{c}_j$, row vector $\mathbf{p}$ and identity matrices $\mathbf{I}_{n_j}$ can then be represented as MTBDDs, using the appropriate Boolean variables. The Kronecker product operation on matrices and vectors represented as MTBDDs can be performed using the APPLY($\times$) operator. The only precaution which must be taken is to ensure that the relative order of the MTBDD variables is correct. If the MTBDDs f and g represent the matrices F and G respectively and all the variables in f precede all those of g in the overall variable ordering then APPLY($\times, f, g$) gives the MTBDD for the matrix $F \otimes G$ which depends on the variables of both. Because we have ensured that our Boolean variables are grouped and ordered by module, the Kronecker expression can be computed easily with APPLY($\times$). Since pointwise multiplication is also carried using APPLY($\times$), the MTBDD expression for $\mathbf{P}_{i,l}$ is as shown below.

$$\mathbf{P}_{i,l} = \text{APPLY}(\times, \mathbf{c}_1, \mathbf{I}_{n_1}, \ldots, \mathbf{c}_{i-1}, \mathbf{I}_{n_{i-1}}, \mathbf{c}_i, \mathbf{p}, \mathbf{c}_{i+1}, \mathbf{I}_{n_{i+1}}, \ldots, \mathbf{c}_n, \mathbf{I}_{n_n}).$$

Since $\times$ is commutative and APPLY($\times, \mathbf{c}_1, \ldots, \mathbf{c}_n$) = $\mathbf{c}$, rearranging:

$$\mathbf{P}_{i,l} = \text{APPLY}(\times, \mathbf{c}, \mathbf{p}, \mathbf{I}_{n_1}, \ldots, \mathbf{I}_{n_{i-1}}, \mathbf{I}_{n_{i+1}}, \ldots, \mathbf{I}_{n_n}).$$

We then obtain $\mathbf{P}_i$ by summing the $\mathbf{P}_{i,l}$ for $l \in L_i$ using APPLY($+$). Finally, we compute the MTBDD $\mathbf{P}$ for the whole system. For probabilistic scheduling:

$$\mathbf{P} = \text{APPLY}(\times, \frac{1}{n}, \text{APPLY}(+, \mathbf{P}_1, \ldots, \mathbf{P}_n)).$$

For nondeterministic scheduling, we add MTBDD variables to encode the scheduler's choice: one variable, s_i, for each process, where $s_i = 1$ iff module M_i is scheduled. This variable can be inserted in the variable ordering next to the variables for M_i, to preserve regularity. Returning to our simple example, we would have the variable ordering $s_1 < x_1 < x_1' < x_2 < x_2' < s_2 < y_1 < y_1' < y_2 < y_2'$. The computation of $\mathbf{P}$ becomes:

$$\mathbf{P} = \text{APPLY}(+, \text{ITE}(s_1 = 1, \mathbf{P}_1, 0), \ldots, \text{ITE}(s_n = 1, \mathbf{P}_n, 0)).$$

where ITE($\cdot, \cdot, \cdot$) refers to the MTBDD operation IFTHENELSE($\cdot, \cdot, \cdot$).

The central observation of the paper is that if we convert each of the component matrices into an MTBDD using the Boolean variables and ordering given above, then this yields a very efficient state-space encoding through increase in regularity (for example, over the matrix obtained through breadth-first search[1]) and sharing. This complies with similar results in [23,30]. Moreover, Kronecker product and ordinary sum of two matrices are also very efficient as they respectively correspond to the MTBDD operations APPLY($\times$) and APPLY($+$).

6   Experimental Results

We have implemented an experimental symbolic model checking tool using the CUDD package [31]. This package provides support for BDDs and MTBDDs, together with matrix multiplication algorithms from [1,14].

---

[1] See www.cs.bham.ac.uk/~dxp/prism/ for MATLAB spy plots of matrices obtained via breadth-first search and Kronecker.

Our tool performs model checking for PBTL, with and without fairness. The MTBDD for a system of modules is automatically generated from its textual description using the translation described above. Forward reachability analysis is then performed to filter out the unreachable states.

To model check qualitative properties (typically 'with probability 1'), reachability analysis through fixed point computation suffices. Quantitative properties, however, require numerical computation. We work with double-precision floating point arithmetic, which is standard for numerical calculations. Our implementation relies on the matrix-by-vector multiplication obtained from the matrix-by-matrix multiplication algorithms supplied with the CUDD package. The model checking of unbounded "until" properties is through the Algorithm **EU**. For purely probabilistic processes we use Jacobi iteration, which has the following advantages: it is simple and numerically stable, relies only on the matrix-by-vector multiplication, and can deal with very large matrices (since it does not change the matrix representing the system). The limiting factor is thus the size of the probability vector (which can only be represented efficiently in MTBDDs if it has regularity).

We have tested our tool on several scalable examples from the literature, in particular the kanban problem [12] known from manufacturing and the randomized dining philosophers [28]. For more information see www.cs.bham.ac.uk/~dxp/prism/. Figures 3–6 show a summary of results for the dining philosophers model. The concurrent model corresponds to that presented in [28], whereas the probabilistic model corresponds to the same model with probabilistic scheduling. The tables give the MTBDD statistics, construction and model checking times in seconds of the liveness property in [28] (with fairness), performed on an Ultra 10 with 380MB.

The main observations we have made so far are as follows: (1) the variable ordering induced from the Kronecker representation results in very compact MTBDDs (see comparison of the number of internal nodes in breadth-first and Kronecker); (2) because of sharing, MTBDDs allow space-efficiency gains over conventional sparse matrices for certain systems; (3) the model construction is very fast, including the computation of the reachable subspace; (4) through use of probability-1 precomputation step, model checking of qualitative properties (with and without fairness) is very fast, and results in orders of magnitude speed-up; (5) performance of numerical calculation with MTBDDs is considerably worse than with sparse matrices, though MTBDDs can potentially handle larger matrices and vectors (e.g. up to 5 million) depending on their regularity.

7   Conclusion

We have demonstrated the feasibility of symbolic model checking for probabilistic processes using MTBDDs. In particular, the state encoding induced from the Kronecker representation allows us to verify qualitative properties of systems containing up to 10^{30} states in a matter of seconds. Moreover, model creation is

Model:	Breadth-first:		
	States:	NNZ:	Nodes:
phil 3	770	2,845	3,636
phil 4	7,070	34,125	30,358
phil 5	64,858	384,621	229,925

Model:	Kronecker:			After reachability:		
	States:	NNZ:	Nodes:	States	NNZ:	Nodes:
phil 3	1,331	4,654	647	770	2,845	873
phil 4	14,641	67,531	1,329	7,070	34,125	2,159
phil 5	161,051	919,656	2,388	64,858	384,621	3,977
phil 10	2.59×10^{10}	2.86×10^{11}	14,999	4.21×10^9	4.72×10^{10}	26,269
phil 20	6.73×10^{20}	1.43×10^{22}	174,077	1.77×10^{19}	3.81×10^{20}	291,760
phil 25	1.08×10^{26}	2.86×10^{26}	479,128	1.14×10^{24}	3.06×10^{25}	798,145

Fig. 3. Statistics for probabilistic models and their MTBDD representation

Model:	Breadth-first:		
	States:	NNZ:	Nodes:
phil 3	770	2,910	4,401
phil 4	7,070	35,620	41,670
phil 5	64,858	408,470	354,902

Model:	Kronecker:			After reachability		
	States:	NNZ:	Nodes:	States	NNZ:	Nodes:
phil 3	1,331	34,848	451	770	20,880	779
phil 4	14,641	1,022,208	669	7,070	511,232	1556
phil 5	161,051	2.81×10^7	887	64,858	1.17×10^7	2,178
phil 10	2.59×10^{10}	2.90×10^{14}	1,977	4.21×10^9	4.87×10^{13}	6,379
phil 20	6.73×10^{20}	1.54×10^{28}	4,157	1.77×10^{19}	4.19×10^{26}	14,429
phil 30	1.75×10^{31}	6.13×10^{41}	6,337	7.44×10^{28}	2.71×10^{39}	22,479

Fig. 4. Statistics for concurrent models and their MTBDD representation

very fast (typically seconds) due to the close correspondence between Kronecker product and APPLY($\times$), and efficiency of reachability analysis implemented as the usual BDD fixed point computation. Likewise, model checking of qualitative properties (expressed as 'with probability 1' PBTL formulas) is very fast. Many quantitative properties, however, are not handled efficiently by our present tool. This is due to poor efficiency of numerical computation, such as Jacobi iteration or simplex, compared to the corresponding sparse matrix implementation. The causes of this are a sudden loss of regularity of the probability vector due to explosion in the number of distinct values computed in the process of approximation (in the case of Jacobi) or fill-in of the tableau (in the case of simplex).

Future work will involve further development of the front end for our tool, comparison with the prototype tools of [4,9,12], and addressing the inefficiency of numerical calculations with MTBDDs.

Model:	Construction:	Reachability:		Model checking:	
	Time (s):	Time (s):	Iterations:	Time (s):	Iterations:
phil3	0.02	0.06	18	0.02	6
phil4	0.04	0.33	24	0.04	6
phil5	0.07	1.08	30	0.06	6
phil10	0.45	28.28	60	0.23	6
phil20	4.45	404.15	120	0.65	6
phil25	10.81	766.03	150	0.99	6

Fig. 5. Times for construction and model checking of probabilistic models

Model:	Construction:	Reachability:		Model checking:	
	Time (s):	Time (s):	Iterations:	Time (s):	Iterations:
phil3	0.02	0.07	18	0.02	6
phil4	0.03	0.35	24	0.04	6
phil5	0.05	1.00	30	0.07	6
phil10	0.24	27.03	60	0.22	6
phil20	1.45	389.56	120	0.49	6
phil30	4.10	5395.00	180	11.40	6

Fig. 6. Times for construction and model checking of concurrent models

Acknowledgements

The authors Kwiatkowska, Norman and Parker are members of the ARC project 1031 *Stochastic Modelling and Verification* funded by the British Council and DAAD. We also thank the anonymous referees for their helpful comments.

References

1. I. Bahar, E. Frohm, C. Gaona, G. Hachtel, E.Macii, A. Pardo, and F. Somenzi. Algebraic Decision Diagrams and their Applications. *Journal of Formal Methods in Systems Design*, 10(2/3):171–206, 1997. 396, 397, 401, 405
2. C. Baier. On algorithmic verification methods for probabilistic systems. Habilitation thesis, 1998. 396, 397, 399, 400, 401
3. C. Baier, E. Clarke, V. Hartonas-Garmhausen, M. Kwiatkowska, and M. Ryan. Symbolic model checking for probabilistic processes. In *Proceedings, 24th ICALP*, volume 1256 of *LNCS*, pages 430–440. Springer-Verlag, 1997. 396, 397, 401
4. C. Baier, J.-P. Katoen, and H. Hermanns. Approximate symbolic model checking of continuous-time Markov chains. In *CONCUR'99*, volume 1664 of *LNCS*, pages 146–161. Springer-Verlag, 1999. 396, 407
5. C. Baier and M. Kwiatkowska. Model checking for a probabilistic branching time logic with fairness. *Distributed Computing*, 11:125–155, 1998. 396, 397, 398, 399, 400
6. J. Bengtsson, K. G. Larsen, F. Larsson, P. Pettersson, W. Yi, and C. Weise. New generation of uppaal. In *Proceedings of the International Workshop on Software Tools for Technology Transfer*, Aalborg, Denmark, July 1998. 396

7. D. Bertsekas. *Dynamic Programming and Optimal Control.* Athena Scientific, 1995. 396
8. A. Bianco and L. de Alfaro. Model checking of probabilistic and nondeterministic systems. In *Proceedings, FST&TCS*, volume 1026 of *LNCS*, pages 499–513. Springer-Verlag, 1995. 396, 398, 399
9. M. Bozga and O. Maler. On the representation of probabilities over structured domains. In *Proc. CAV'99*, 1999. Available as Volume 1633 of *LNCS*. 396, 407
10. J. R. Burch, E. M. Clarke, K. L. McMillan, D. L. Dill, and J. Hwang. Symbolic model checking: 10^{20} states and beyond. In *LICS'90*, June 1990. 395
11. G. Ciardo and A. Miner. SMART: Simulation and markovian analyzer for reliability and timing. In *Tools Descriptions from PNPM'97*, pages 41–43, 1997. 397
12. G. Ciardo and A. Miner. A data structure for the efficient Kronecker solution of GSPNs. In *Proc. PNPM'99*, 1999. 406, 407
13. E. Clarke, E. Emerson, and A. Sistla. Automatic verification of finite state concurrent systems using temporal logic specifications: A practical approach. In *Proceedings, 10th Annual Symp. on Principles of Programming Languages*, 1983. 398, 399
14. E. Clarke, M. Fujita, P. McGeer, J.Yang, and X. Zhao. Multi-Terminal Binary Decision Diagrams: An Efficient Data Structure for Matrix Representation. In *International Workshop on Logic Synthesis*, 1993. 396, 401, 405
15. C. Courcoubetis and M. Yannakakis. Markov decision processes and regular events. In *Proc. ICALP'90*, volume 443 of *LNCS*, pages 336–349. Springer-Verlag, 1990. 396, 400
16. C. Courcoubetis and M. Yannakakis. The complexity of probabilistic verification. *Journal of the ACM*, 42(4):857–907, 1995. 398, 400
17. L. de Alfaro. How to specify and verify the long-run average behavior of probabilistic systems. In *Proc. LICS'98*, pages 454–465, 1998. 396
18. L. de Alfaro. Stochastic transition systems. In *Proc. CONCUR'98*, volume 1466 of *LNCS*. Springer-Verlag, 1998. 396
19. L. de Alfaro. Computing minimum and maximum reachability times in probabilistic systems. In *Proc. CONCUR'99*, volume 1664 of *LNCS*, 1999. 397, 400
20. L. de Alfaro. From fairness to chance. In *Proc. PROBMIV'98*, volume 21 of *ENTCS*. Elsevier, 1999. 398
21. G. Hachtel, E. Macii, A. Pardo, and F. Somenzi. Markovian Analysis of Large Finite State Machines. *IEEE Transactions on CAD*, 15(12):1479–1493, 1996. 397
22. H. Hansson and B. Jonsson. A logic for reasoning about time and probability. *Formal Aspects of Computing*, 6:512–535, 1994. 396, 398
23. H. Hermanns, J. Meyer-Kayser, and M. Siegle. Multi Terminal Binary Decision Diagrams to represent and analyse continuous time Markov chains. In *Proc. NSMC'99*, 1999. 397, 405
24. M. Kwiatkowska, G. Norman, D. Parker, and R. Segala. Symbolic model checking of concurrent probabilistic systems using MTBDDs and simplex. Technical Report CSR-99-1, University of Birmingham, 1999. 397
25. K. McMillan. *Symbolic Model Checking.* Kluwer Academic Publishers, 1993. 395
26. B. Plateau. On the Stochastic Structure of Parallelism and Synchronisation Models for Distributed Algorithms. In *Proc. 1985 ACM SIGMETRICS Conference on Measurement and Modeling of Computer Systems*, pages 147–153, May 1985. 397, 402, 403
27. B. Plateau, J. M. Fourneau, and K. H. Lee. PEPS: a package for solving complex Markov models of parallel systems. In R. Puigjaner and D. Potier, editors, *Modelling techniques and tools for computer performance evaluation*, 1988. 397

28. A. Pnueli and L. Zuck. Verification of multiprocess probabilistic protocols. *Distributed Computing*, 1:53–72, 1986. 396, 406
29. R. Segala. *Modelling and Verification of Randomized Distributed Real-Time Systems*. PhD thesis, MIT, 1995. 398
30. M. Siegle. Compact representation of large performability models based on extended BDDs. In *Fourth International Workshop on Performability Modeling of Computer and Communication Systems (PMCCS4)*, pages 77–80, 1998. 405
31. F. Somenzi. CUDD: CU decision diagram package. Public software, Colorado University, Boulder, 1997. 396, 397, 405
32. M. Vardi. Automatic verification of probabilistic concurrent finite-state programs. In *Proceedings, FOCS'85*, pages 327–338. IEEE Press, 1987. 396, 398

Symbolic Reachability Analysis
Based on SAT-Solvers

Parosh Aziz Abdulla[1], Per Bjesse[2], and Niklas Eén[2]

[1] Uppsala University and Prover Technology, Sweden
parosh@docs.uu.se
[2] Chalmers University of Technology, Sweden
{bjesse,een}@cs.chalmers.se

Abstract. The introduction of symbolic model checking using Binary Decision Diagrams (BDDs) has led to a substantial extension of the class of systems that can be algorithmically verified. Although BDDs have played a crucial role in this success, they have some well-known drawbacks, such as requiring an externally supplied variable ordering and causing space blowups in certain applications. In a parallel development, SAT-solving procedures, such as Stålmarck's method or the Davis-Putnam procedure, have been used successfully in verifying very large industrial systems. These efforts have recently attracted the attention of the model checking community resulting in the notion of *bounded model checking*. In this paper, we show how to adapt standard algorithms for symbolic reachability analysis to work with SAT-solvers. The key element of our contribution is the combination of an algorithm that removes quantifiers over propositional variables and a simple representation that allows reuse of subformulas. The result will in principle allow many existing BDD-based algorithms to work with SAT-solvers. We show that even with our relatively simple techniques it is possible to verify systems that are known to be hard for BDD-based model checkers.

1   Introduction

In recent years *model checking* [CES86,QS82] has been widely used for algorithmic verification of finite-state systems such as hardware circuits and communication protocols. In model checking, the specification of the system is formulated as a temporal logical formula, while the implementation is described as a finite-state transition system. Early model-checking algorithms suffered from *state explosion*, as the size of the state space grows exponentially with the number of components in the system. One way to reduce state explosion is to use *symbolic model checking* [BCMD92,McM93], where the transition relation is coded symbolically as a boolean expression, rather than explicitly as the edges of a graph. Symbolic model checking achieved its major breakthrough after the introduction of *Binary Decision Diagrams* (BDDs) [Bry86] as a data structure for representing boolean expressions in the model checking procedure. An important property of BDDs is that they are canonical. This allows for substantial

S. Graf and M. Schwartzbach (Eds.): TACAS/ETAPS 2000, LNCS 1785, pp. 411–425, 2000.

sub-expression sharing, often resulting in a compact representation. In addition, canonicity implies that satisfiability and validity of boolean expressions can be checked in constant time. However, the restrictions imposed by canonicity can in some cases lead to a space blowup, making memory a bottleneck in the application of BDD-based algorithms. There are examples of functions, for example multiplication, which do not allow sub-exponential BDD representations. Furthermore, the size of a BDD is dependent on the variable ordering which in many cases is hard to optimize, both automatically and by hand. BDD-based methods can typically handle systems with hundreds of boolean variables.

A related approach is to use satisfiability solvers, such as implementations of Stålmarck's method [Stå] and the Davis-Putnam procedure [Zha97]. These methods have already been used successfully for verifying industrial systems [SS00,Bor97,Bor98,SS90,GvVK95]. SAT-solvers enjoy several properties which make them attractive as a complement to BDDs in symbolic model checking. For instance, their performance is less sensitive to the size of the formulas, and they can in some cases handle propositional formulas with thousands of variables. Furthermore, SAT-solvers do not suffer from space explosion, and do not require an external variable ordering to be supplied. Finally, satisfiability solving is an NP-complete problem, whereas BDD-construction solves a #P-complete problem [Pap94] as it is possible to determine the number of models of a BDD in polynomial time. #P-complete problems are widely believed to be harder than NP-complete problems.

The aim of this work is to exploit the strength of SAT-solving procedures in order to increase the class of systems amenable to verification via the traditional symbolic methods. We consider modifications of two standard algorithms—forward and backward reachability analysis—where formulas are used to characterize sets of reachable states [Bje99]. In these algorithms we replace BDDs by satisfiability checkers such as the PROVER implementation of Stålmarck's method [Stå] or SATO [Zha97]. We also use a data structure which we call *Reduced Boolean Circuits* (RBCs) to represent formulas. RBCs avoid unnecessarily large representations through the reuse of subformulas, and allow for efficient storage and manipulation of formulas. The only operation of the reachability algorithms that does not carry over straightforwardly to this representation is quantification over propositional variables. Therefore, we provide a simple procedure for the removal of quantifiers, which gives adequate performance for the examples we have tried so far.

We have implemented a tool FIXIT [Eén99] based on our approach, and carried out a number of experiments. The performance of the tool indicates that even though we use simple techniques, our method can perform well in comparison to existing ones.

Related Work. *Bounded Model Checking* (BMC) [BCC+99,BCCZ99,BCRZ99] is the first approach in the literature to perform model checking using SAT-solvers. To check reachability, the BMC procedure searches for counterexamples (paths to undesirable states) by "unrolling" the transition relation k steps. The unrolling is described by a (quantifier-free) formula which characterizes the set of feasible paths through the transition relation with lengths smaller than or equal to k. The search can be terminated when the value of k is equal to the *diameter* of the system—the maximum length of all shortest path between states in the system. Although the diameter can be specified by a logical formula, its satisfiability is usually hard to check, making BMC incomplete in practice. Furthermore, for "deep" transition systems, formulas characterizing the set of reachable states may be much smaller than those characterizing witness paths. Since our method is based on encodings of sets of states, it may in some cases cope with systems which BMC fails to analyze as it generates formulas that are too large.

Our representation of formulas is closely related to *Binary Expression Diagrams* (BEDs) [AH97,HWA97]. In fact there are straightforward linear space translations back and forth between the representations. Consequently, RBCs share the good properties of BEDs, such as being exponentially more succinct than BDDs [AH97]. The main difference between our approach and the use of BEDs is the way in which satisfiability checking and existential quantification is handled. In [AH97], satisfiability of BEDs is checked through a translation to equivalent BDDs. Although many simplifications are performed at the BED level, converting to BDDs during a fixpoint iteration could cause degeneration into a standard BDD-based fixpoint iteration. In contrast, we check satisfiability by mapping RBCs back to formulas which are then fed to external SAT-solvers. In fact, the use of SAT-solvers can also be applied to BEDs, but this does not seem to have been explored so far. Furthermore, in the BED approach, existential quantification is either handled by introducing explicit quantification vertices, or by a special transformation that rewrites the representation into a form where naive expansion can be applied. We use a similar algorithm that also applies an extra inlining rule. The inlining rule is particularly effective in the case of backward reachability analysis, as it is always applicable to the generated formulas. To our knowledge, no results have been reported in the literature on applications of BEDs in symbolic model checking. We would like to emphasize that we view RBCs as a relatively simple representation of formulas, and not as a major contribution of this work.

2   Preliminaries

We verify systems described as synchronous circuits constructed from elementary combinational gates and unit delays—a simple, yet popular, model of computation. The unit delays are controlled by a global clock, and we place no restriction on the inputs to a circuit. The environment is free to behave in any fashion.

We define the *state-holding elements* of a circuit to be the primary inputs and the contents of the delays, and define a *valuation* to be an assignment of boolean values to the state-holding elements. The behaviour of a circuit is modelled as a state-transition graph where (1) each valuation is a state; (2) the initial states comprise all states that agree with the initial values of the delays; and (3) there

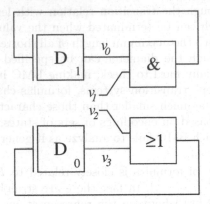

Fig. 1. A simple circuit built from combinational gates and delays

is a transition between two states if the circuit can move between the source state and the destination state in one clock cycle.

We construct a symbolic encoding of the transition graph in the standard manner. We assign every state-holding element a propositional state variable v_i, and make two copies of the set of state variables, $s = \{v_0, v_1, \ldots, v_k\}$ and $s' = \{v'_0, v'_1, \ldots, v'_k\}$. Given a circuit we can now generate two *characteristic formulas*. The first of the characteristic formulas, $Init(s) = \bigwedge_i v_i \leftrightarrow \phi_i$, defines the initial values of the state-holding elements. The second characteristic formula, $Tr(s, s') = \bigwedge_i v'_i \leftrightarrow \psi_i(s)$, defines the next-state values of state-holding elements in terms of the current-state values.

Example 1. The following formulas characterize the circuit in Figure 1:

$$Init = (v_0 \leftrightarrow \top) \wedge (v_3 \leftrightarrow \bot)$$
$$Tr = (v'_0 \leftrightarrow (v_0 \wedge v_1)) \ \wedge \ (v'_3 \leftrightarrow (v_2 \vee v_3))$$

We investigate the underlying state-transition graph by applying operations at the formula level. In doing so we make use of the following three facts. First, the relation between any points in a given circuit can be expressed as a propositional formula over the state-holding variables. Second, we can represent any set S of transition-graph states by a formula that is satisfied exactly by the states in S. Third, we can lift all standard set-level operations to operations on formulas (for example, set inclusion corresponds to formula-level implication and set nonemptiness checking to satisfiability solving, respectively).

3   Reachability Analysis

Given the characteristic formulas of a circuit and a formula $Bad(s)$, we define the *reachability problem* as that of checking whether it is possible to reach a state that satisfies $Bad(s)$ from an initial state. As an example, in the case of

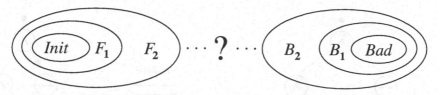

Fig. 2. The intuition behind the reachability algorithms

the circuit in Figure 1, we might be interested in whether the circuit could reach a state where the two delay elements output the same value (or equivalently, where the formula $v_0 \leftrightarrow v_3$ is satisfiable). We adapt two standard algorithms for performing reachability analysis. In *forward reachability* we compute a sequence of formulas $F_i(s)$ that characterize the set of states that the initial states can reach in i steps:

$$F_0(s) = Init$$
$$F_{i+1}(s') = toProp(\exists s. \; Tr(s, s') \land F_i(s)))$$

Each computation of F_{i+1} gives rise to a *Quantified Boolean Formula* (QBF), which we translate back to a pure propositional formula using an operation *toProp* (defined in in Section 5). We terminate the sequence generation if either (1) $F_n(s) \land Bad(s)$ is satisfiable: this means that a bad state is reachable; hence we answer the reachability problem positively; or (2) $\bigvee_{k=0}^{n} F_k(s) \rightarrow \bigvee_{k=0}^{n-1} F_k(s)$ holds: this implies that we have reached a fixpoint without encountering a bad state; consequently the answer to the reachability question is negative.

In *backward reachability* we instead compute a sequence of formulas $B_i(s)$ that characterize the set of states that can reach a bad state in i steps:

$$B_0(s) = Bad$$
$$B_{i+1}(s) = toProp(\exists s'. \; Tr(s, s') \land B_i(s')))$$

In a similar manner to forward reachability, we terminate the sequence generation if either (1) $B_n(s) \land Init(s)$ is satisfiable, or (2) $\bigvee_{k=0}^{n} B_k(s) \rightarrow \bigvee_{k=0}^{n-1} B_k(s)$ holds.

Figure 2 shows the intuition behind the algorithms. We remark that the two reachability methods can be combined by alternating between the computation of F_{i+1} and B_{i+1}. The generation can be terminated when either a fixpoint is reached in some direction, or when F_n and B_n intersect. However, we do not make use of hybrid analyses in this paper.

We need to address three nontrivial issues in an implementation of the adapted reachability algorithms. First, we must avoid the generation of unnecessarily large formula characterizations of the sets F_i and B_i—formulas are not a canonical representation. Second, we must define the operation *toProp* in such a way that it translates quantified boolean formulas to propositional logic without

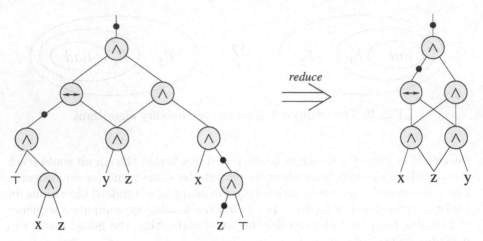

Fig. 3. A non-reduced *Boolean Circuit* and its reduced form

needlessly generating exponential results. Third, we must interface efficiently to external satisfiability solvers. The remainder of the paper explains our solutions, and evaluates the resulting reachability checker.

4 Representation of Formulas

Let **Bool** denote the set of booleans; **Vars** denote the set of propositional variables, including a special variable $\top$ for the constant *true*; and **Op** denote the set $\{\leftrightarrow, \wedge\}$.

We introduce the representation *Boolean Circuit* (BC) for propositional formulas. A BC is a directed acyclic graph, $(\mathbf{V}, \mathbf{E})$. The vertices $\mathbf{V}$ are partitioned into internal nodes, $\mathbf{V_I}$, and leaves, $\mathbf{V_L}$. The vertices and edges are given attributes as follows:

- Each internal vertex $v \in \mathbf{V_I}$ has three attributes: A binary operator $op(v) \in$ **Op**, and two edges $left(v), right(v) \in \mathbf{E}$.
- Each leaf $v \in \mathbf{V_L}$ has one attribute: $var(v) \in$ **Vars**.
- Each edge $e \in \mathbf{E}$ has two attributes: $sign(e) \in$ **Bool** and $target(e) \in \mathbf{V}$.

We observe that negation is coded into the edges of the graph, by the *sign* attribute. Furthermore, we identify *edges* with *subformulas*. In particular, the whole formula is identified with a special top-edge having no source vertex. The interpretation of an edge as a formula is given by the standard semantics of $\wedge, \leftrightarrow$ and $\neg$ by viewing the graph as a parse tree (with some common sub-expressions shared). Although $\wedge$ and $\neg$ are functionally complete, we choose to include $\leftrightarrow$ in the representation as it would otherwise require three binary connectives to express. Figure 3 shows an example of a BC.

A *Reduced Boolean Circuit* (RBC) is a BC satisfying the following properties:

```
reduce(AND, left ∈ RBC, right ∈ RBC)   reduce(EQUIV, left ∈ RBC, right ∈ RBC)
    if    (left = right)   return left        if    (left = right)   return ⊤
    elif  (left = ¬right)  return ⊥           elif  (left = ¬right)  return ⊥
    elif  (left = ⊤)       return right       elif  (left = ⊤)       return right
    elif  (right = ⊤)      return left        elif  (left = ⊥)       return ¬right
    elif  (left = ⊥)       return ⊥           elif  (right = ⊤)      return left
    elif  (right = ⊥)      return ⊥           elif  (right = ⊥)      return ¬left
    else                   return NIL         else                   return NIL


mk_Comp(op ∈ Op, left ∈ RBC, right ∈ RBC, sign ∈ Bool)
    result := reduce(op, left, right)
    if (result ≠ NIL)
        return id(result, sign)    – id returns result or ¬result depending on sign

    if (right < left)
        (left, right) := (right, left)    – Swap the values of left and right

    if (op = EQUIV)
        sign  := sign xor sign(left) xor sign(right)
        left  := unsigned(left)
        right := unsigned(right)

    result := lookup(RBC_env, (op, left, right))    – Look for vertex in environment
    if (result = NIL)
        result := insert(RBC_env, (op, left, right))
    return id(result, sign)
```

Fig. 4. Pseudo-code for creating a composite RBC from two existing RBCs

1. All common subformulas are shared so that no two vertices have identical attributes.
2. The constant ⊤ never occurs in an RBC, except for the single-vertex RBCs representing *true* or *false*.
3. The children of an internal vertex are syntactically distinct, $left(v) \neq right(v)$.
4. If $op(v) = \leftrightarrow$ then the edges to the children of v are unsigned.
5. For all vertices v, $left(v) < right(v)$, for some total order $<$ on BCs.

The purpose of these constraints is to identify as many equivalent formulas as possible, and thereby increase the amount of subformula sharing. For this reason we allow only one representation of $\neg(\phi \leftrightarrow \psi) \iff (\neg\phi \leftrightarrow \psi)$ (in 4 above), and $(\phi \wedge \psi) \iff (\psi \wedge \phi)$ (in 5 above).

The RBCs are created in an implicit environment, where all existing subformulas are tabulated. We use the environment to assure property (1). Figure 4 shows the only non-trivial constructor for RBCs, *mk_Comp*, which creates a composite RBC from two existing RBCs (we use $x \in \text{Vars}(\phi)$ to denote that x is a variable occurring in the formula ϕ). It should be noted that the above properties only takes constant time to maintain in *mk_Comp*.

5   Quantification

In the reachability algorithms we make use of the operation *toProp* to translate QBF formulas into equivalent propositional formulas. We reduce the translation of a set of existential quantifiers to the iterated removal of a single quantifier after we have chosen a quantification order. In the current implementation an arbitrary order is used, but we are evaluating more refined approaches.

Figure 5 presents the quantification algorithm of our implementation. By definition we have:

$$\exists x \, . \, \phi(x) \quad \Longleftrightarrow \quad \phi(\bot) \vee \phi(\top) \qquad (*)$$

The definition can be used to naively resolve the quantifiers, but this may yield an exponential blowup in representation size. To try to avoid this, we use the following well-known identities (applied from left to right) whenever possible:

Inlining:
$$\exists x \, . \, (x \leftrightarrow \psi) \wedge \phi(x) \quad \Longleftrightarrow \quad \phi(\psi) \qquad \qquad (\text{where } x \notin \mathrm{Vars}(\psi))$$

Scope Reduction:
$$\exists x \, . \, \phi(x) \wedge \psi \quad \Longleftrightarrow \quad (\exists x.\phi(x)) \wedge \psi \qquad (\text{where } x \notin \mathrm{Vars}(\psi))$$
$$\exists x \, . \, \phi(x) \vee \psi(x) \quad \Longleftrightarrow \quad (\exists x.\phi(x)) \vee (\exists x.\psi(x))$$

When applicable, *inlining* is an effective method of resolving quantifiers as it immediately removes all occurrences of the quantified variable x. The applicability of the transformation relies on the fact that the formulas occurring in reachability often have a structure that matches the rule. This is particularly true for backward reachability as the transition relation is a conjunction of next state variables defined in terms of current state variables $\bigwedge_i v_i' \leftrightarrow \psi_i(s)$.

The first step of the inlining algorithm temporarily changes the representation of the top-level conjunction. From the binary encoding of the RBC, we extract an equivalent set representation $\bigwedge \{\phi_0, \phi_1, \ldots, \phi_n\}$. If the set contains one or more elements of the form $x \leftrightarrow \psi$, the smallest such element is removed from the set and its right-hand side ψ is substituted for x in the remaining elements. The set is then re-encoded as an RBC.

If inlining is not applicable to the formula (and variable) at hand, the translator tries to apply the *scope reduction* rules as far as possible. This may result in a quantifier being pushed through an OR (represented as negated AND), in which case inlining may again be possible.

For subformulas where the scope can no longer be reduced, and where inlining is not applicable, we resort to *naive quantification* (*). Reducing the scope as much as possible before doing this will help prevent blowups. Sometimes the quantifiers can be pushed all the way to the leaves of the RBC, where they can be eliminated.

Throughout the quantification procedure, we may encounter the same subproblem more than once due to shared subformulas. For this reason we keep a table of the results obtained from all previously processed subformulas.

– *Global variable* processed *tabulates the results of the performed quantifications.*

quant_naive($\phi \in$ **RBC**, $x \in$ **Vars**)
   result = *subst*(ϕ, x, $\bot$) $\lor$ *subst*(ϕ, x, $\top$)
   insert(processed, ϕ, x, result)
   return result

quant_reduceScope($\phi \in$ **RBC**, $x \in$ **Vars**)
   if ($x \notin$ Vars(ϕ)) **return** ϕ
   if ($\phi = x$)   **return** $\top$

   result := *lookup*(processed, ϕ, x)
   if (result $\neq$ NIL)
      return result

   – *In the following ϕ must be composite and contain x:*
   if (ϕ_{op} = EQUIV)
      result := *quant_naive*(ϕ, x)
   elif (**not** ϕ_{sign}) – *Operator* AND, *unsigned*
      if   ($x \notin$ Vars(ϕ_{left})) result := ϕ_{left} $\land$ *quant_reduceScope*(ϕ_{right}, x)
      elif ($x \notin$ Vars(ϕ_{right})) result := *quant_reduceScope*(ϕ_{left}, x) $\land$ ϕ_{right}
      else   result := *quant_naive*(ϕ, x)
   else   – *Operator* AND, *signed ("OR")*
      result := *quant_inline*($\neg\phi_{left}$, x) $\lor$ *quant_inline*($\neg\phi_{right}$, x)

   insert(processed, ϕ, x, result)
   return result

quant_inline($\phi \in$ **RBC**, $x \in$ **Vars**)   – *"Main"*
     C := *collectConjuncts*(ϕ) – *Merge all binary* ANDs *at the top of ϕ into a*
                                        "big" conceptual conjunction (returned as a set).
     ψ := *findDef*(C, x)   –*Return the smallest formula ψ such that* ($x \leftrightarrow \psi$)
                                          is a member of C.

   if ($\psi \neq$ NIL)
      C' := $C \setminus (x \leftrightarrow \psi)$ – *Remove definition from C.*
      return *subst*(*makeConj*(C'), x, ψ)   – *makeConj builds an* RBC.
   else
      return *quant_reduceScope*(ϕ, x)

Fig. 5. Pseudo-code for performing existential quantification over one variable. By ϕ_{left} we denote *left*(*target*(ϕ)) etc. We use $\land$, $\lor$ as abbreviations for calls to *mk_Comp*.

6 Satisfiability

Given an RBC, we want to decide whether there exists a satisfying assignment for the corresponding formula by applying an external SAT-solver. The naive translation—unfold the graph to a tree and encode the tree as a formula—

has the drawback of removing sharing. We therefore use a mapping where each internal node in the representation is allocated a fresh variable. This variable is used in place of the subformula that corresponds to the internal node. The generated formula is the conjunction of all the definitions of internal nodes and the literal that defines the top edge.

Example 2. The right-hand RBC in Figure 3 is mapped to the following formula in which the i_k variables define internal RBC nodes:

$$(i_0 \leftrightarrow i_1 \wedge i_2)$$
$$\wedge (i_1 \leftrightarrow i_3 \leftrightarrow i_4)$$
$$\wedge (i_2 \leftrightarrow i_3 \wedge i_4)$$
$$\wedge (i_3 \leftrightarrow x \wedge z)$$
$$\wedge (i_4 \leftrightarrow z \wedge y)$$
$$\wedge \neg i_0$$

A formula resulting from the outlined translation is *not* equivalent to the original formula without sharing, but it will be satisfiable if and only if the original formula is satisfiable. Models for the original formula are obtained by discarding the values of internal variables.

7   Experimental Results

We have implemented a tool FIXIT [Eén99] for performing symbolic reachability analysis based on the ideas presented in this paper. The tool has a *fixpoint mode* in which it can perform both forward and backward reachability analysis, and an *unroll mode* where it searches for counterexamples in a similar manner to the BMC procedure. We have carried out preliminary experiments on three benchmarks: a *multiplier* and a *barrel shifter* (both from the BMC distribution), and a *swapper* (defined by the authors). The first two benchmarks are known to be hard for BDD-based methods.

In all the experiments, PROVER outperforms SATO, so we only present measurements made using PROVER. Furthermore, we only present time consumption. Memory consumption is much smaller than for BDD-based systems. Garbage collection has not yet been implemented in FIXIT, but the amount of simultaneously referenced memory peaks at about 5-6 MB in our experiments. We also know that the memory requirements of PROVER are relatively low (worst case quadratic in the formula size). The test results for FIXIT are compared with results obtained from VIS release 1.3, BMC version 1.0f and CADENCE SMV release 09-01-99.

The Multiplier. The example models a standard 16×16 bit shift-and-add multiplier, with an output result of 32 bits. Each output bit is individually verified against the C6288 combinational multiplier of the ISCAS'85 benchmarks by

Table 1. Experimental results for the multiplier

Bit	ᶠᴵˣᴵᵀFwd sec	ᶠᴵˣᴵᵀBwd sec	ᶠᴵˣᴵᵀUnroll sec	BMC sec	VIS sec	SMV sec
0	0.8	2.0	0.7	1.0	5.3	41.4
1	0.9	2.3	0.7	1.4	5.4	41.3
2	1.1	3.0	0.8	2.0	5.3	42.5
3	1.8	3.9	0.9	4.0	5.5	42.6
4	3.0	6.1	1.2	8.2	6.2	[>450 MB]
5	7.2	9.9	1.8	19.9	10.2	–
6	24.3	21.5	3.8	66.7	32.9	–
7	100.0	61.9	11.8	304.6	153.5	–
8	492.8	224.7	45.2	1733.7	[>450 MB]	–
9	2350.6	862.6	197.8	9970.8	–	–
10	11927.5	3271.0	862.8	54096.8	–	–
11	60824.6	13494.3	3838.0	–	–	–
12	–	50000.0	16425.8	–	–	–

checking that we cannot reach a state where the computation of the shift-and-add multiplier is completed, but where the selected result bit is not consistent with the corresponding output bit of the combinational circuit.

Table 1 presents the results for the multiplier. The SAT-based methods outperform both VIS and SMV. The unroll mode is a constant factor more efficient than the fixpoint mode. However, we were unable to prove the diameter of the system by the diameter formula generated by BMC, which means that the verification performed by the unroll method (and BMC) should be considered partial.

The Barrel Shifter. The barrel shifter rotates the contents of a register file R with one position in each step. The system also contains a fixed register file R_0, related to R in the following way: if two registers from R and R_0 have the same contents, then their neighbours also have the same contents. We constrain the initial states to have this property, and the objective is to prove that it holds throughout the reachable part of the state space. The width of the registers is $\log |R|$ bits, and we let the BMC tool prove that the diameter of the circuit is $|R|$.

Table 2 presents the results for the barrel shifter. No results are presented for VIS due to difficulties in describing the extra constraint on the initial state in the VIS input format.

The backward reachability mode of FIXIT outperforms SMV and BMC on this example. The reason for this is that the set of bad states is closed under the pre-image function, and hence FIXIT terminates after only one iteration. SMV is unable to build the BDDs characterising the circuits for larger problem instances. The BMC tool has to unfold the system all the way up to the diameter, producing very large formulas; in fact, the version of BMC that we used could

Table 2. Experimental results for the barrel shifter

$|R|$	ᴿᴵˣᴵᵀFwd sec	ᴿᴵˣᴵᵀBwd sec	ᴿᴵˣᴵᵀUnroll sec	BMC sec	Diam sec	SMV sec
2	1.7	0.1	0.1	0.0	0.0	0.0
3	2.3	0.1	0.1	0.0	0.0	0.1
4	3.0	0.1	0.2	0.0	0.0	0.1
5	42.4	0.2	0.3	0.1	0.1	44.2
6	848.9	0.2	0.5	0.3	0.1	[>450 MB]
7	5506.6	0.4	0.5	0.4	0.2	–
8	[>3 h]	0.5	1.0	1.2	0.3	–
9	–	0.8	1.6	2.4	0.6	–
10	–	1.1	2.3	8.6	0.8	–
11	–	1.5	2.3	3.3	1.1	–
12	–	2.3	4.1	25.6	1.5	–
13	–	2.6	3.9	7.1	2.0	–
14	–	3.2	7.8	80.1	2.6	–
15	–	3.7	8.6	75.1	3.5	–
16	–	4.3	12.1	150.0	4.4	–
17	–	6.7	11.0	34.6	7.9	–
18	–	8.7	30.5	?	?	–
19	–	9.2	15.6	?	?	–
20	–	13.5	49.1	?	?	–
... 30	–	51.4	452.1	?	?	–
... 40	–	230.5	2294.7	?	?	–
... 50	–	501.5	8763.3	?	?	–

not generate formulas for larger instances than size 17 (a size 17 formula is 2.2 MB large). The oscillating timing data for the SAT-based tools reflects the heuristic nature of the underlying SAT-solver.

The Swapper. N nodes, each capable of storing a single bit, are connected linearly:

$$\boxed{1}-\boxed{2}-\boxed{3}-\boxed{4}-\cdots-\boxed{N}$$

At each clock-cycle (at most) one pair of adjacent nodes may swap their values. From this setting we ask whether the single final state in which exactly the first $\lfloor N/2 \rfloor$ nodes are set to 1 is reachable from the single initial state in which exactly the last $\lfloor N/2 \rfloor$ nodes are set to 1. Table 3 shows the result of verifying this property.

Both VIS and SMV handle the example easily. FIXIT can handle sizes up to 14, but does not scale up as well as VIS and SMV, as the representations get too large. This illustrates the importance of maintaining a compact representation during deep reachability problems; something that is currently not done

Table 3. Experimental results for the swapper

N	FixIt Fwd sec	FixIt Bwd sec	FixIt Unroll sec	BMC sec	VIS sec	SMV sec
3	0.2	0.2	0.2	0.0	0.3	0.0
4	0.3	0.3	0.2	0.0	0.3	0.0
5	0.6	0.5	0.3	0.1	0.3	0.0
6	0.9	1.5	1.8	7.2	0.4	0.1
7	1.7	3.7	131.2	989.5	0.4	0.1
8	3.8	10.4	[>2 h]	[>2 h]	0.4	0.1
9	9.7	58.9	–	–	0.4	0.1
10	27.7	187.1	–	–	0.4	0.1
11	74.1	779.2	–	–	0.5	0.2
12	238.8	4643.2	–	–	0.6	0.2
13	726.8	[>2 h]	–	–	0.7	0.3
14	2685.7	–	–	–	0.7	0.4
15	[>2 h]	–	–	–	0.7	0.6
...						
20	–	–	–	–	1.6	7.9
...						
25	–	–	–	–	3.3	53.0
...						
30	–	–	–	–	15.1	263.0
...						
35	–	–	–	–	39.1	929.6
...						
40	–	–	–	–	89.9	2944.3

by FixIt. However, BMC does even worse, even though the problem is a strict search for an existing counterexample—something BMC is generally good at. This shows that fixpoint methods can be superior both for proving unreachability and detecting counterexamples for certain classes of systems.

8 Conclusions and Future Work

We have described an alternative approach to standard BDD-based symbolic model checking which we think can serve as a useful complement to existing techniques. We view our main contribution as showing that with relatively simple means it is possible to modify traditional algorithms for symbolic reachability analysis so that they work with SAT-procedures instead of BDDs. The resulting method gives surprisingly good results on some known hard problems.

SAT-solvers have several properties which make us believe that SAT-based model checking will become an interesting complement to BDD-based techniques. For example, in a proof system like Stålmarck's method, formula size does not play a decisive role in the hardness of satisfiability checking. This is particularly interesting since industrial applications often give rise to formulas which are extremely large in size, but not necessarily hard to prove.

There are several directions for future work. We are currently surveying simplification methods that can be used to maintain compact representations. One promising approach [AH97] is to improve the local reduction rules to span over multiple levels of the RBC graphs. We are also interested in exploiting the structure of big conjunctions and disjunctions, and in simplifying formulas using algorithms based on Stålmarck's notion of formula saturation [Bje99]. As for the representation itself, we are considering adding *if-then-else* and substitution nodes [HWA97]. Other ongoing work includes experiments with heuristics for choosing good quantification orderings.

In the longer term, we will continue to work on conversions of BDD-based algorithms. For example, we have already implemented a prototype model checker for general (fair) CTL formulas. Also, employing traditional BDD-based model checking techniques such as front simplification and approximate analysis are very likely to improve the efficiency of SAT-based model checking significantly.

Many important questions related to SAT-based model checking remain to be answered. For example, how should the user choose between bounded and fixpoint-based model checking? How can SAT-based approaches be combined with standard approaches to model checking?

Acknowledgements

The implementation of FIXIT was done as a Master's thesis at Prover Technology, Stockholm. Thanks to Purushothaman Iyer, Bengt Jonsson, Gordon Pace, Mary Sheeran and Gunnar Stålmarck for giving valuable feedback on earlier drafts.

This research was partially supported by TFR, the ASTEC competence center for advanced software technology, and the ARTES network for real-time research and graduate education in Sweden.

References

AH97.   H. R. Andersen and H. Hulgaard. Boolean expression diagrams. In *Proc. 12th IEEE Int. Symp. on Logic in Computer Science*, pages 88–98, 1997. 413, 424

BCC+99.   A. Biere, A. Cimatti, E. M. Clarke, M. Fujita, and Y. Zhu. Symbolic model checking using SAT procedures instead of BDDs. In *Design Automation Conference (DAC'99)*, 1999. 412

BCCZ99.   A. Biere, A. Cimatti, E. M. Clarke, and Y. Zhu. Symbolic model checking without BDDs. In *Proc. TACAS '98, 8th Int. Conf. on Tools and Algorithms for the Construction and Analysis of Systems*, 1999. 412

BCMD92.   J.R. Burch, E.M. Clarke, K.L. McMillan, and D.L. Dill. Symbolic model checking: 10^{20} states and beyond. *Information and Computation*, 98:142–170, 1992. 411

BCRZ99.   A. Biere, E. M. Clarke, R. Raimi, and Y. Zhu. Verifying safety properties of a PowerPC[tm] microprocessor using symbolic model checking without BDDs. In *Proc. 11th Int. Conf. on Computer Aided Verification*, 1999. 412

Bje99.   P. Bjesse. Symbolic model checking with sets of states represented as for-
             mulas. Technical Report CS-1999-100, Department of Computer Science,
             Chalmers technical university, March 1999. 412, 424
Bor97.   A. Borälv. The industrial success of verification tools based on Stålmarck's
             method. In *Proc. 9th Int. Conf. on Computer Aided Verification*, volume
             1254 of *Lecture Notes in Computer Science*, pages 7–10, 1997. 412
Bor98.   A. Borälv. Case study: Formal verification of a computerized railway inter-
             locking. *Formal Aspects of Computing*, 10(4):338–360, 1998. 412
Bry86.   R.E. Bryant. Graph-based algorithms for boolean function manipulation.
             IEEE Trans. on Computers, C-35(8):677–691, Aug. 1986. 411
CES86.   E.M. Clarke, E.A. Emerson, and A.P. Sistla. Automatic verification of
             finite-state concurrent systems using temporal logic specification. *ACM
             Trans. on Programming Languages and Systems*, 8(2):244–263, April 1986.
             411
Eén99.   N. Eén. Symbolic reachability analysis based on SAT-solvers. Master's
             thesis, Dept. of Computer Systems, Uppsala university, 1999. 412, 420
GvVK95.   J.F. Groote, S.F.M. van Vlijmen, and J.W.C. Koorn. The safety guaran-
             teeing system at station Hoorn-Kersenboogerd. In *COMPASS'95*, 1995.
             412
HWA97.   H. Hulgaard, P.F. Williams, and H.R. Andersen. Combinational logic-level
             verification using boolean expression diagrams. In *3rd International Work-
             shop on Applications of the Reed-Muller Expansion in Circuit Design*, 1997.
             413, 424
McM93.   K.L. McMillan. *Symbolic Model Checking*. Kluwer Academic Publishers,
             1993. 411
Pap94.   C. Papadimitriou. *Computational complexity*. Addison-Wesley, 1994. 412
QS82.   J.P. Queille and J. Sifakis. Specification and verification of concurrent
             systems in Cesar. In *5th International Symposium on Programming, Turin*,
             volume 137 of *Lecture Notes in Computer Science*, pages 337–352. Springer
             Verlag, 1982. 411
SS90.   G. Stålmarck and M. Säflund. Modelling and verifying systems and software
             in propositional logic. In *SAFECOMP'90*, pages 31–36. Pergamon Press,
             1990. 412
SS00.   M. Sheeran and G. Stålmarck. A tutorial on Stålmarck's method of propo-
             sitional proof. *Formal Methods In System Design*, 16(1), 2000. 412
Stå.   G. Stålmarck. A system for determining propositional logic theorems by
             applying values and rules to triplets that are generated from a formula.
             Swedish Patent No. 467 076 (approved 1992), US patent No. 5 276 897
             (1994), European Patent No. 0403 454 (1995). 412
Zha97.   H. Zhang. SATO: an efficient propositional prover. In *Proc. Int. Conference
             om Automated Deduction (CADE'97)*, volume 1249 of *LNAI*, pages 272–
             275. Springer Verlag, 1997. 412

Symbolic Representation of Upward-Closed Sets

Giorgio Delzanno[1] and Jean-François Raskin[2,3]

[1] Max-Planck-Institut für Informatik
Im Stadtwald, 66123 Saarbrücken, Germany
delzanno@mpi-sb.mpg.de

[2] Electrical Engineering and Computer Sciences, University of California at Berkeley
Berkeley, CA 94720-1770
jfr@eecs.berkeley.edu

[3] Département d'Informatique, Université Libre de Bruxelles
Blvd Du Triomphe, 1050 Bruxelles, Belgium

Abstract. The *control state reachability problem* is decidable for well-structured infinite-state systems like unbounded Petri Nets, Vector Addition Systems, Lossy Petri Nets, and Broadcast Protocols. An abstract algorithm that solves the problem is given in [AČJT96,FS99]. The algorithm computes the closure of the *predecessor* operator w.r.t. a given upward-closed set of target states. When applied to this class of verification problems, traditional (infinite-state) symbolic model checkers suffer from the *state explosion problem* even for very small examples. We provide BDD-like data structures to represent in a compact way collections of upwards closed sets over numerical domains. This way, we turn the abstract algorithm of [AČJT96,FS99] into a practical method. Preliminary experimental results indicate the potential usefulness of our method.

1 Introduction

In the last years many efforts have been made to extend the theoretical results and practical methods developed for finite-state systems [BCB+90] to systems with *infinite* state space (see e.g. [AČJT96,BM99,BW98,EFM99,FS99]). This class of systems comprises well-known examples like Vector Addition Systems [Min67], extensions of Petri Nets [Cia94,Ter94], Integral Relational Automata [Čer94], and more recent examples like Broadcast Protocols [EN98] and Lossy Petri Nets [BM99]. The *control state reachability problem* is decidable for all previous systems [AČJT96,BM99,EFM99,Fin90,FS99]. The abstract algorithm of [AČJT96,FS99] computes the closure of the *predecessor* operator w.r.t. a given upward-closed set of states. The algorithm can be used to check, e.g., invariant properties like *mutual exclusion* [DEP99] and *coverability for markings of Petri Nets* [AJKP98].

As in the finite-state case, the success of symbolic model checking for this class of problems depends on the data structures used as implicit representation of sets of states. Over numerical domains, upward-closed sets can be represented via a sub-class of integer arithmetic constraints (see e.g. [AČJT96,DEP99]). In this setting, the state-space generated by the algorithm of [AČJT96,FS99] can

S. Graf and M. Schwartzbach (Eds.): TACAS/ETAPS 2000, LNCS 1785, pp. 426–441, 2000.

be represented as a large *disjunction* of arithmetic constraints. In [DEP99], the authors tested constraint-based model checking methods over integers (based on a solver for Presburger arithmetic [BGP97]) and reals (based on polyhedra [HHW97]) on verification problems that can be expressed via upward-closed sets. Though the examples in [DEP99] would be considered of negligible size in finite-state model checking (e.g. 6 transitions and 10 variables, cf. [BCB+90]), the methods taken into consideration suffer from the state explosion problem[1]. Some of the experiments required (when terminating) execution times in the order of days. Based on these observations, it seems natural to look for BDD-like data structures to represent 'compactly' the generalization of boolean formulas we are interested in.

In this paper we propose a new symbolic representation for upward-closed sets based on the *sharing trees* of Zampuniéris and Le Charlier [ZL94]. Sharing trees are acyclic graphs used to represent large sets of tuples, e.g., of integer numbers. The intuition behind the choice of this data structure is the following. An upward-closed set U is determined by its finite set of generators (tuples of integers). Thus, we can represent the set U via a sharing tree whose paths correspond to its generators. This way, we managed to turn the abstract algorithm of [AČJT96,FS99] into a 'practical method' working on the examples studied in [DEP99,Ter94] in acceptable time cost.

Technically, our contributions are as follows. We introduce a logic (the logic $\mathcal{U}$) where collections of upward-closed sets can be represented as disjunctive formulas. $\mathcal{U}$-formulas are used for verification problems of infinite-state systems as boolean formulas are used for the finite-state case. We show that sharing trees can be used to obtain compact representations of $\mathcal{U}$-formulas (there exist a $\mathcal{U}$-formula that can be represented using a sharing tree whose size is logarithmic in the size of the formula). We show how basic operations on $\mathcal{U}$-formulas (e.g. conjunction and disjunction) can be implemented symbolically on the corresponding sharing trees. Sharing trees can be viewed as the BDDs for $\mathcal{U}$-formulas.

In practical cases (e.g., during the symbolic computation of the closure of the predecessor operator), sharing trees may still become very large. For this reason, we propose polynomial time algorithms that can be used to eliminate redundant paths. As we prove in the paper, the problem of removing all redundancies from a sharing tree representing a $\mathcal{U}$-formula is co-NP hard (in the size of the sharing tree). The same techniques can be used to give sufficient conditions for the subsumption test of sharing trees representing $\mathcal{U}$-formulas (i.e. for the termination test of the algorithm of [AČJT96]). The complete test is co-NP hard in the size of the sharing trees.

As an application of our method, we have implemented the algorithm of [AČJT96] in the case of Vector Addition Systems. The implementation makes use of the sharing tree library of [Zam97]. First experimental results indicate the potential usefulness of our method.

---

[1] One would say 'symbolic state explosion problem', in fact, the above cited methods operate on implicit representations of infinite sets of states.

Plan of the Paper. In Section 2, we define the logic $\mathcal{U}$. In Section 3, we introduce the symbolic representation of $\mathcal{U}$-formulas via sharing trees. In Section 4, we define simulation relations for nodes of sharing trees and discuss their application in the operations for $\mathcal{U}$-formulas. In Section 5, we define a symbolic model checking procedure for Vector Addition Systems. In Section 6, we present related work. In Section 7, we address some conclusions and future perspectives for our work.

The extended version of the paper (containing all proofs) is available as technical report MPI-1999-2-07 of Max-Planck-Institut für Informatik [DR99].

2   The Logic of Upward-Closed Sets

In this section we introduce the logic $\mathcal{U}$ that we use to define collections of upward-closed sets. Let $V = \{x_1, \ldots, x_k\}$ be a finite set of variables. The set of $\mathcal{U}$-formulas is defined by the following grammar.

$$\Phi ::= x_i \geq c \mid \Phi \wedge \Phi \mid \Phi \vee \Phi \mid \Phi[x_i + c/x_i],$$

where $c \in \mathbb{Z} \cup \{-\infty\}$. $\mathcal{U}$-formulas are interpreted over $\mathbb{Z}^k$. We use t to denote the valuation $\langle t_1, \ldots, t_k \rangle$, where $t_i \in \mathbb{Z}$ is the valuation for variable x_i. We consider the following order over tuples: $t \preccurlyeq t'$ iff $t_i \leq t'_i$ for $i : 1, \ldots, k$ ($-\infty \leq c$ for any $c \in \mathbb{Z}$). When restricted to positive values, $\preccurlyeq$ is a well-quasi ordering (see e.g. [AČJT96,FS99]). Given a tuple t, we define $t^\uparrow$ as the *upward-closed set* generated by t, namely, $t^\uparrow = \{ t' \mid t \preccurlyeq t' \}$. Satisfaction of a formula wrt. a valuation t is defined as follows:

- $t \models x_i \geq c$ iff $t_i \geq c$;
- $t \models \Phi_1 \wedge \Phi_2$ iff $t \models \Phi_1$ and $t \models \Phi_2$;
- $t \models \Phi_1 \vee \Phi_2$ iff $t \models \Phi_1$ or $t \models \Phi_2$;
- $t \models \Phi[x_i + c/x_i]$ iff $t' \models \Phi$ and t' is obtained from t replacing t_i with $t_i + c$.

The *denotation* of a formula Φ, namely $[\![\Phi]\!]$, is defined as the set of all evaluations t such that $t \models \Phi$. A formula Φ_1 is *subsumed* by a formula Φ_2, written $\Phi_1 \models \Phi_2$, if $[\![\Phi_1]\!] \subseteq [\![\Phi_2]\!]$. Two formulas are equivalent if their denotations coincide.

Note that, whenever we restrict the domain of interpretation of our formulas to *positive* integers (say $\mathbb{Z}_+$), the class of $\mathcal{U}$-formulas denotes all upward-closed sets, i.e., all sets $I \subseteq \mathbb{Z}_+^k$ such that if $t \in I$ then $t^\uparrow \subseteq I$.

All formulas can be reduced to *disjunctive formulas*, i.e., to formulas having the following form[2]:

$$\bigvee_{i \in I} (x_1 \geq c_{i,1} \wedge \ldots \wedge x_k \geq c_{i,k}).$$

Notation. In the rest of the paper we use Φ, Ψ, etc. to denote arbitrary $\mathcal{U}$-formulas, and ϕ, ψ, etc. to denote disjunctive formulas.
The set of *generators* of a disjunctive formula φ are defined as

---

[2] Adding formulas of the form $x_i \geq -\infty$ when necessary.

$$gen(\varphi) = \{ \ \langle c_1, \ldots, c_k \rangle \mid (x_1 \geq c_1 \wedge \ldots \wedge x_k \geq c_k) \text{ is a disjunct in } \varphi \ \}.$$

Thus, disjunctive formulas are in one-to-one correspondence with their set of generators modulo logical equivalences. The minimal elements (wrt. $\preccurlyeq$) of $gen(\varphi)$ are denoted by $min(\varphi)$. Note that $\llbracket \varphi \rrbracket = \bigcup_{t \in min(\varphi)} t^{\uparrow}$. We say that a disjunctive formula is in *normal form* whenever $gen(\varphi) = min(\varphi)$. As an example, consider the formula $\varphi = (x \geq 1 \wedge y \geq 2) \vee (x \geq 3 \wedge y \geq 1) \vee (x \geq 2 \wedge y \geq 0)$. Then, $gen(\varphi) = \{\langle 1, 2\rangle, \langle 3, 1\rangle, \langle 2, 0\rangle\}$, and $min(\varphi) = \{\langle 1, 2\rangle, \langle 2, 0\rangle\}$, i.e., φ is *not* in normal form.

2.1   Operations on Formulas in Disjunctive Form

Disjunction and Conjunction. Formulas in disjunctive form are closed under $\vee$. Furthermore, given the disjunctive formulas φ and ψ, the disjunctive formula for $\varphi \wedge \psi$ is defined as follows: $\bigvee_{t \in gen(\varphi), t' \in gen(\psi)} (x_1 \geq max(t_1, t_1') \wedge \ldots \wedge x_k \geq max(t_k, t_k'))$, i.e., $gen(\varphi \wedge \psi) = \{s \mid \exists t \in gen(\varphi), t' \in gen(\psi) \text{ and } s_i = max(t_i, t_i')\}$. Note that the resulting formula may not be in normal form.

Substitution. The formula $\varphi[x_i + c/x_i]$ is equivalent to the formula φ' obtained from φ by replacing every atom $x_i \geq d$ with $x_i \geq d - c$ ($-\infty - c = -\infty$ for any $c \in \mathbb{Z}$), i.e., $gen(\varphi[x_i + c/x_i]) = \{t' \mid t_i' + c = t_i, \ t_j' = t_j \ j \neq i, \ t \in gen(\varphi)\}$.

Satisfaction wrt. a tuple. Given a valuation t, we first note that $t \models \varphi$ iff there exists $t' \in gen(\varphi)$ such that $t' \preccurlyeq t$. Thus, checking $t \models \varphi$ can be done in time linear in the size of φ.

Subsumption. Let φ and ψ be in disjunctive form. We can check $\varphi \models \psi$ in time quadratic in the size of the formulas. In fact, $\varphi \models \psi$ holds iff for all $t \in gen(\varphi)$ there exists $t' \in gen(\psi)$ such that $t' \preccurlyeq t$.

It is important to remark that the subsumption test is much harder for *arbitrary* $\mathcal{U}$-formulas, as stated in the following theorem.

Theorem 1. Given two arbitrary $\mathcal{U}$-formulas Φ and Ψ, checking that $\Phi \models \Psi$ is co-NP complete in the size of the formulas.

Reduction in normal form. Given a disjunctive formula φ we can reduce it in normal form by eliminating all 'redundant' generators from $gen(\varphi)$, i.e., all $t \in gen(\varphi)$ such that there exists $t' \in gen(\varphi)$, $t \neq t'$, $t' \preccurlyeq t$. The reduction can be done in time quadratic in the size of φ.

All previous operations depend on the set of 'generators' of disjunctive formulas. In the following section we introduce a special data structure, called sharing tree [ZL94], for handling large sets of generators. We show how to use this data structure to represent and manipulate symbolically formulas of the logic $\mathcal{U}$.

3   Sharing Trees

In this paper we specialize the original definition of [ZL94] as follows. We call a k-sharing tree a rooted directed acyclic graph $(N, V, root, end, val, succ)$ where $N = \{root\} \cup N_1 \ldots \cup N_k \cup \{end\}$ is the finite set of *nodes*, (N_i is the set of nodes of *layer i* and, by convention, $N_0 = \{root\}$ and $N_{k+1} = \{end\}$), $val : N \rightsquigarrow \mathbb{Z} \cup \{\top, \bot\}$ is a labeling function for the nodes, and $succ : N \rightsquigarrow 2^N$ defines the successors of a node. Furthermore,

1. $val(n) = \top$ if and only if $n = root$;
2. $val(n) = \bot$ if and only if $n = end$;
3. $succ(end) = \emptyset$;
4. for $i : 0, \ldots, k$, forall $n \in N_i$, $succ(n) \subseteq N_{i+1}$ and $succ(n) \neq \emptyset$;
5. forall $n \in N$, forall $n_1, n_2 \in succ(n)$, if $n_1 \neq n_2$ then $val(n_1) \neq val(n_2)$.
6. for $i : 0, \ldots, k$, forall $n_1, n_2 \in N_i$ s.t. $n_1 \neq n_2$, if $val(n_1) = val(n_2)$ then $succ(n_1) \neq succ(n_2)$.

In other words, a k-sharing tree is an acyclic graph with root and terminal node such that: all nodes of layer i have successors in the layer $i+1$ (cond. 4); a node cannot have two successors with the same label (cond. 5); finally, two nodes with the same label in the same layer do not have the same set of successors (cond. 6). We say that S is a *pre-sharing* tree if it respects conditions (1)-(4) but possibly not (5) and (6).

Notation. In the rest of the paper we use $root^S$, N^S, $succ^S$ etc. to refer to the root, set of nodes, successor relation etc. of the sharing-tree S.

A path of a k-sharing tree is a sequence of nodes $\langle n_1, \ldots, n_m \rangle$ such that $n_{i+1} \in succ(n_i)$ $i : 1, \ldots, m$-1. Paths will represent tuples of size k of integer numbers. Formally, we use $elem(S)$ to denote the set of elements represented by the k-sharing tree S:

$$elem(S) = \{ \ \langle val(n_1), \ldots, val(n_k) \rangle \mid \langle \top, n_1, \ldots, n_k, \bot \rangle \text{ is a path of S } \}.$$

Condition 5 and 6 ensure the maximal sharing of prefixes and suffixes among the paths (elements) of the sharing tree. We define the 'size' of a sharing tree as the number of its *nodes* and *edges*. Note that the number of tuples in $elem(S)$ can be exponentially larger than the size of S. Given a node n of the i-th layer of a k-sharing tree S, the sub-(sharing)tree S_n rooted at n is the $k - i + 1$-sharing tree obtained as follows. We first isolate the graph rooted at n and consisting of all nodes reachable from n (this subgraph has $k - i + 1$ layers and a terminal node). Then, we add a layer with the single node $root$ and we set $succ(root) = \{n\}$. From the previous definition, $elem(S_n)$ consists of all tuples $\langle val(n), m_{i+1}, \ldots, m_k \rangle$ obtained from tuples $\langle m_1, \ldots, val(n), m_{i+1}, \ldots, m_k \rangle$ of $elem(S)$.

As shown in [ZL94], given a set of tuples F of size k, there exists a unique (modulo isomorphisms of graphs) sharing tree such that $elem(S) = F$. In the same paper the authors give algorithms for the basic set-operations on the set of elements represented by the sharing trees. The table in Fig. 1 gives the specifi-

Operation	Complexity
$elem(union(S,T)) = elem(S) \cup elem(T)$	$\mathcal{O}(max(edges(S), edges(T)) + Red)$
$elem(intersection(S,T)) = elem(S) \cap elem(T)$	$\mathcal{O}(min(edges(S), edges(T)) + Red)$
$member(\boldsymbol{t}, S)$ iff $\boldsymbol{t} \in elem(S)$	$\mathcal{O}(size(\boldsymbol{t}))$
$contained(S, T)$ iff $elem(S) \subseteq elem(T)$	$\mathcal{O}(edges(S))$
$is\_empty(S)$ iff $elem(S) = \emptyset$	$\mathcal{O}(const)$

Fig. 1. Operations on the sharing trees S and T: $edges(S)$=No.edges of S

cation and the complexity in terms of the size of sharing trees, for the operation we will consider in the rest of the paper: union, intersection, emptiness, containment, and equality test. In [ZL94], the authors show that the operations in Fig. 1 can be safely applied to pre-sharing trees that satisfy condition 5 only. The cost for intersection and union depends also on the cost Red in Fig. 1, of re-arranging condition 6. This task can be achieved using the algorithm presented in [ZL94] with cost quadratic in the number of nodes of the resulting sharing trees.

3.1 Symbolic Representation of $\mathcal{U}$-Formulas

We first show how to represent $\mathcal{U}$-formulas in disjunctive form, and then show how to define disjunction, conjunction, subsumption and reduction in normal form over the resulting data structure.

Let φ be a $\mathcal{U}$-formula in disjunctive form over $x_1, \ldots, x_k$. We define S_φ as the k-sharing tree such that $elem(S_\varphi) = gen(\varphi)$. The *denotation* of a k-sharing tree S is then defined as $[\![S]\!] = \bigcup_{t \in elem(S)} t^\uparrow$. Clearly, $[\![\varphi]\!] = [\![S_\varphi]\!]$. We say that S_φ is irredundant if φ is in normal form, i.e., there exists no $\boldsymbol{t} \subset clcm(S_\varphi)$ such that $\boldsymbol{t}' \preccurlyeq \boldsymbol{t}$ for $\boldsymbol{t}' \in elem(S_\varphi)$ distinct from $\boldsymbol{t}$. The following proposition explains the advantages of using sharing trees for representing $\mathcal{U}$-formulas.

Proposition 1. There exist a disjunctive formula in normal form φ such that the corresponding sharing tree S_φ has size (no. of nodes and arcs) logarithmic in the size of φ.

As an example, consider the $\mathcal{U}$-formula $\Phi = \bigvee_{i=1}^{m}(v_i \geq 1 \wedge w_i \geq 0) \vee (v_i \geq 0 \wedge w_i \geq 1)$. The corresponding disjunctive formulas φ (obtained by distributing $\wedge$) is $\bigvee_{c+d \geq 1} \bigwedge_{i=1}^{m}(v_i \geq c_i \wedge w_i \geq d_i)$ for $\boldsymbol{c}, \boldsymbol{d} \in \mathbb{Z}_+^m$. This formula has $\mathcal{O}(2^m)$ disjuncts. Also note that φ is in normal form. In contrast, the sharing tree S_φ shown in Fig. 2 has size logarithmic in φ and polynomial in Φ (each layer has two nodes and at most four arcs).

3.2 Symbolic Operations for $\mathcal{U}$-Formulas

In this section we show how operations on the disjunctive formulas φ and ψ can be defined symbolically on their representations S_φ and S_ψ. We use the term *symbolically* because the algorithms that we propose work directly on the graphs S_φ and S_ψ and not by enumerating the elements that they represent.

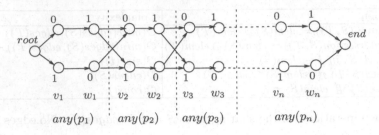

Fig. 2. Sharing tree for an exponential formula in DNF

Disjunction. Let S_φ and S_ψ be the k-sharing trees representing the formulas (in disjunctive form) φ and ψ. To build a sharing tree with $elem(S_{\varphi \vee \psi}) = gen(\varphi) \cup gen(\psi)$, we define $S_{\varphi \vee \psi}$ as $union(S_\varphi, S_\psi)$, where $union$ is the operation in Fig. 1. In [ZL94], it has been show that the size of the sharing-tree $S_{\varphi \vee \psi}$ is at most quadratic in the size of S_φ and S_ψ, and can be computed in time quadratic in the size of the input sharing-trees.

Conjunction. Given S_φ and S_ψ, we build $S_{\varphi \wedge \psi}$ as follows. We first define a pre-sharing tree P with the following components: (i) $N^P = \{root\} \cup N_1 \cup \ldots \cup N_k \cup \{end\}$ with $N_i = \{(n,m) \mid n \in N_i^{S_\varphi}, m \in N_i^{S_\psi}\}$ (i.e. a node in P correspond to a pair consisting of a node of S_φ and a node of S_ψ (at the same layer); (ii) $val^P((n,m)) = max(val^{S_\varphi}(n), val^{S_\psi}(m))$, and (iii) for all $(n,m) \in N_1 \cup \ldots \cup N_n$, we set $succ^P((n,m)) = \{(n',m') \mid n' \in succ^{S_\varphi}(n), m' \in succ^{S_\psi}(m)\}$, $succ^P(root) = N_1$, and for all $(n,m) \in N_k$ we set $succ^P((n,m)) = \{end\}$. We obtain the sharing-tree $S_{\varphi \wedge \psi}$ from P by enforcing conditions (5-6) of Section 3 with the algorithms proposed in [ZL94].

Substitution. Given the sharing tree S_φ we build a new sharing tree $S_{\varphi[x_i+c/x_i]}$ such that $elem(S_{\varphi[x_i+c/x_i]}) = gen(\varphi[x_i + c/x_i])$ as follows. $S_{\varphi[x_i+c/x_i]}$ has the same components as S_φ except from the valuation function: for every node $n \in N_i^{S_{\varphi[x_i+c/x_i]}}$ $val^{S_{\varphi[x_i+c/x_i]}}(n) = val^{S_\varphi}(n) - c$, and for every node $n \in N_j^{S_{\varphi[x_i+c/x_i]}}$, with $j \neq i$, $val^{S_{\varphi[x_i+c/x_i]}}(n) = val^{S_\varphi}(n)$. This way, we obtain a well-formed sharing tree. The complexity of the construction is linear in the number of nodes of S_φ, i.e., potentially logarithmic in the number of its elements.

Satisfaction wrt. a tuple. Checking that $t \models \varphi$ on the sharing tree S_φ has cost linear in the size of φ, i.e., following from Remark 1, possibly logarithmic in the size of φ. In fact, the following theorem holds.

Theorem 2. *Let S be a k-sharing tree and t be a vector of length k. We can check if t is subsumed by S in time linear in the number of edges of S.*

Subsumption. The subsumption problem is harder: the best possible algorithm for subsumption is exponential in the size of the trees, as shown by the following theorem.

Theorem 3. The subsumption problem for two (irredundant) k-sharing trees is co-NP complete in the size of the sharing trees.

Following from the previous result, the cost of checking subsumption may be exponential in the number of edges of the input sharing trees. The result follows from the fact that $\mathcal{U}$-formulas in disjunctive form can be represented compactly via sharing-tress.

Reduction in normal form. Let S_φ be the sharing tree associated to a disjunctive formula φ. We consider now the following problem: what is the complexity of computing the sharing-tree for the normal form of φ (i.e. the sharing-tree S such that $elem(S) = min(\varphi)$)? The following theorem shows that it is as hard as checking subsumption.

Theorem 4. Given a k-sharing tree S, computing the irredundant k-sharing tree S' such that $[\![S]\!] = [\![S']\!]$ is co-NP hard.

Let S_1 and S_2 be two k-sharing trees. Note that, if $elem(S_1) \subseteq elem(S_2)$ then $[\![S_1]\!] \subseteq [\![S_2]\!]$. Besides giving a sufficient condition for checking subsumption, the previous fact suggests a possible strategy to reduce the cost of the 'complete' test. We first compute $T = minus(S_1, S_2)$ (polynomial in the size of S_1, S_2) and then test $T \models S_2$ on the (possibly) smaller sharing tree T.

In the next section we give more interesting polynomial-time *sufficient conditions* for the subsumption test, based on a notion of *simulation* between nodes of k-sharing trees. We will see that this notion of simulation is also useful to reduce sharing-trees and "approximate" the reduction in normal form.

4   Simulations for Nodes of a k-Sharing Tree

In the previous section we have proved that the subsumption problem for two $\mathcal{U}$-formulas represented as sharing-trees and the computations of generators of the normal form of a $\mathcal{U}$-formula represented as a sharing-tree, are co-NP hard. In this section we will introduce 'approximations' of the subsumption relation that can be tested more efficiently. More precisely, given two nodes n and m of a sharing tree S we are looking for a relation $\frown_F$ such that: $n\frown_F m$ 'implies' $[\![S_n]\!] \subseteq [\![S_m]\!]$.

Definition 1 (Forward Simulation). Given two sharing tree S and T, let n be a node of the i-th layer of S, and m be a node of the i-th layer of T. We say that n is *simulated by* m, written $n\frown_F m$, if $val^S(n) \geq val^T(m)$ and for all $s \in succ^S(n)$ there exists $t \in succ^T(m)$ such that $s\frown_F t$.

Note that, if $S = T$ then the simulation relation is *reflexive* and *transitive*.

Let $father(n)$ be the set of fathers of a node n at layer i ($fathers(n) \subseteq N_{i-1}$). We define the backward simulation as follows:

Definition 2 (Backward simulation). Given two sharing tree S and T, let n be a node of the i-th layer of S, and m be a node of the i-th layer of T. We say that n is *backwards simulated by* m, written $n\frown_B m$, if $val^S(n) \geq val^T(m)$ and for all $s \in fathers^S(n)$ there exists $t \in fathers^T(m)$ such that $s\frown_B t$.

The following result (taken from [HHK95]) shows that the previous simulations can be computed efficiently.

Theorem 5 (From [HHK95]). The forward and backward simulation relations between the nodes of the sharing tree S and the nodes of the sharing tree T can be computed in $O(m \cdot n)$ where m is the sum of the number of nodes in S and in T, and n is the sum of the number of edges in S and in T.

In the rest of this section we will focus on properties and algorithms for the forward simulation. The results and algorithms can be reformulated for the backward simulations by replacing the successor relation with the father relation.

4.1 Properties of the Simulation

The following propositions relate subsumption and the simulation $\curvearrowright_F$.

Lemma 1. Given the sharing trees S and T, let S_n and T_m be the sub-sharing trees rooted at nodes n and m, respectively. If $n \curvearrowright_F m$ then $[\![S_n]\!] \subseteq [\![S_m]\!]$.

The converse does not hold (in accord with the co-NP hardness result for subsumption). As a counterexample, take the two trees in Fig. 3. The curly arrows represent the simulation relation between nodes of S and T. Note that none of the nodes of layer 2 in T simulates the single node of S at the same layer. However, the denotation of S are contained in that of T. In fact, $\langle 1, 1, 2, 0 \rangle \preccurlyeq \langle 1, 2, 2, 1 \rangle$ and $\langle 1, 0, 0, 2 \rangle \preccurlyeq \langle 1, 2, 1, 2 \rangle$. The following theorem follows from Lemma 1.

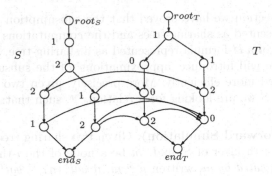

Fig. 3. The forward simulation is incomplete wrt. subsumption

Theorem 6. Let $root_S, end_S$ and $root_T, end_T$ be the root and terminal nodes of S and T, respectively. If $root_S \curvearrowright_F root_T$ then $[\![S]\!] \subseteq [\![T]\!]$. Symmetrically, if $end_S \curvearrowright_B end_T$ then $[\![S]\!] \subseteq [\![T]\!]$.

The previous theorem gives us sufficient conditions for testing subsumption.

4.2   Use of Simulations to Remove Redundancies

As for the subsumption test, the simulations we introduced in Section 4 can be used to 'approximate' the exact normalization procedure. For this purpose, we introduce a rule that allows us to exploit the information given from (one of) the simulation relation(s) in order to 'locally' remove edges of a sharing tree.

Definition 3 (Edge Removal). Given a sharing tree S with node N and successors $succ$, let us assume that for $n \in N$ there exist $s, t \in succ(n)$ $(s \neq t)$ such that $s \frown_F t$. Then, we define $remove(S, n)$ as the pre-sharing tree with successor relation $succ'$ obtained from S by setting $succ'(n) = succ(n) \setminus \{s\}$.

The following proposition states the 'correctness' of the previous rule.

Proposition 2. (1) S and $remove(S, n)$ have the same denotations, i.e., $\llbracket S \rrbracket \equiv \llbracket remove(S, n) \rrbracket$; (2) the simulation relation $\frown_F$ for S and $remove(S, n)$ coincides.

A possible strategy to apply Def. 3 consists of the 'on-the-fly' removal of edges during the computation of the simulation relation. Specifically, during a bottom-up traversal of the sharing tree, we first apply Rule 3 to every node of a layer, then compute the simulation relation for the nodes of the same layer, move to the next layer, and so on. The rule to remove edges is applied exhaustively at each step. In fact, given $s \in succ(n)$, let us assume that there exists $u, t \in succ(n)$ such that $u \frown_F s$, and $s' \frown_F t$. By transitivity, $u \frown_F t$ holds, as well, i.e., we can still remove u after having removed s. The pre-sharing tree $remove(S, n)$ may violate the condition 6 of the definition of sharing trees (Section 3). However, as already mentioned in the course of the paper, condition 6 can be restored using an algorithm proposed in [ZL94]. Similar algorithms can be defined for the *backward* simulation. It is important to note that, though an application of Rule 3 does not change the forward simulation (Fact (2) of Prop. 2), it may change the backward simulation (and, vice versa, the removal of edges according to the backward relation may change the forward simulation). As a consequence, we get better and better results iterating the application of the algorithm for removing edges for the backward-forward simulations. A simplified version of Rule 3 that requires only a local test for every node of a sharing tree is given as follows.

Definition 4 (Local Edge Removal). Given a sharing S tree with node N and successors $succ$, let assume that for $n \in N$ there exist $s, t \in succ(n)$ $(s \neq t)$ such that $val(s) \geq val(t)$ and $succ(s) \subseteq succ(t)$. Then, we define $local\_remove(S, n)$ as the pre-sharing tree with successor relation $succ'$ obtained from S by setting $succ'(n) = succ(n) \setminus \{s\}$.

Though less effective than Rule 3, Rule 4 can be paired with it in order to simplify the computation of the simulation. In the following section we show how to incorporate the previous ideas in a model checking procedure for an example of integer system.

5   Invariant Checking for Vector Addition Systems

A Vector Addition System (VAS) consists of n variables $x_1, \ldots, x_n$ ranging over positive integers, and m transition rules given as guarded command over the data variables. For every j, transition i contains a guard $x_j \geq c_{i,j}$ and an assignment $x_j := x_j + d_{i,j}$; if $d_{i,j} < 0$ then $c_{i,j} \geq d_{i,j}$. States are tuples of *positive* numbers and executions are sequences of tuples $t_0 t_1 \ldots t_i \ldots$ where t_{i+1} is obtained from t_i by applying (non-deterministically) one of the transition rules. The predecessor operator *pre* takes as input a set of states (tuples) F and returns the set of predecessors of F. Properties like *mutual exclusion* and *coverability* can be represented through upward-closed sets [AČJT96,DEP99]. Checking safety properties expressed as upward-closed set for Petri Nets is decidable using the following algorithm taken from [AČJT96]. Let F be an upward-closed set (denoting unsafe states). To test the safety property 'always $\neg(F)$' we compute symbolically the closure of the relation *pre*, say $pre^*(F)$, and then we check that the initial configuration is not part of the resulting set. From [AČJT96], $pre^*(F)$ is still an upward-closed set. The termination test is based on the containment relation, namely we stop the computation whenever $pre^{n+1}(F) \subseteq \bigcup_{i=0}^{n} pre^i(F)$.

U-Logic based Model Checking. Let φ_U a U-formula representing a collection of upward-closed set U. The predecessor relation for VAS can be represented as the following U-formula:

$$pre(\varphi_U) = \bigvee_{i=1,\ldots,m} (\varphi_i \ \wedge \ \varphi_U[x_1 + d_{i,1}/x_1] \ldots [x_k + d_{i,k}/x_k])$$

where $\varphi_i = x_1 \geq c_{i,1} \wedge \ldots \wedge x_n \geq c_{i,n}$. In other words, by using the results in the previous sections, starting from S_{φ_U} we can compute the sharing tree S_{pre^i} that represents $\bigvee_{k=0}^{i} pre^k(U)$. The termination test is implemented by the subsumption test for sharing trees. The algorithms based on the simulations that we described in this paper can be used for a weaker termination test and for removing redundancies from the intermediate results. We have define a prototype implementation for the algorithm using the library of [Zam97]. We discuss next some preliminary experimental results.

5.1   A Case-Study: The Table Manufacturing System

The *table manufacturing system* of Teruel [Ter94] is a production system modeled via a *weighted Petri Net* with 7 places and 6 transitions. The values of the weights on the transitions vary from 2 to 4. This Petri Net can be modeled using a VAS with 13 variables, 7 for the places and 6 extra variables, say $T_1, \ldots, T_6$, to keep track of the number of firings of each transition. As shown in [Ter94], all deadlock-free initial markings are exactly the predecessors of the set of states where the first transition is fired at least 3 times, and all the others are fired at least twice (i.e. $U = T_1 \geq 3 \ \wedge \ \bigwedge_{j>1} T_j \geq 2$). In [DEP99], different general purpose constraint-based checkers have been used to compute the set of predecessors via backward reachability. While other tools fail from terminate within

Example	NV	NR	NS	LR	FSR	ET	NE	Nodes	Ratio
Man. Sys.	13	6	24	no	—	39s	7563	4420	4%
Man. Sys.	13	6	24	yes	5	68s	727	1772	12%

Fig. 4. Flags: NV=No. Variable; NR=No. Rules; ET=Execution Time; LR=Use of local reduction; FSR=Frequency in the use of sim. reduction (__=not used); NS=No Steps; NE=No. of Elem. of the result sharing tree; Ratio=Nodes/(NV*NE)

1 day of execution, the tool based on the Omega library of Bultan, Gerber and Pugh's [BGP97] terminates after 19 hours and 50 minutes on a Sun Ultra Sparc, and the 'specialized' checker proposed in [DEP99] (see Sect. 6) terminates after 1090 seconds. Sharing trees allows us to dramatically speed up the computation. Our prototype implementation (based on the library of [Zam97]) terminates after 39 seconds on a Sun Ultra Sparc (see Fig. 4). In a first experiment we have not removed the redundancies from S_{pre^i}, whereas in a second experiment we have applied the reduction based on the forward simulation (every 5 steps) (see Fig 4). Simulation-based reduction (every 5 steps) allows us to reduce the set of states of a factor of ten (note: removing *all* redundancies yields 450 elements). Other examples are considered in the extended version of this paper [DR99].

6   Related Work

In [AČJT96], the authors introduce a symbolic representation (*constraint* system) for collections of upward-closed sets. Their representation corresponds to disjunctive $\mathcal{U}$-formulas. Traditional symbolic methods for handling linear constraints (e.g. polyhedra or Presburger arithmetics) suffer however from the state-explosion problem when applied to this type of 'constraints'. In [DEP99], a more efficient representation based on sequences of pairs *bitvector-constant* is proposed for representing the state-space of broadcast protocols, and, as special case, of VAS. In this paper we have shown how to obtain more compact and efficient representations via sharing trees.

In [Zam97,GGZ95], the authors apply sharing trees to represent the state-space of concurrent systems: a *state* is a *tuple* of values and a *set* of states is represented as a *sharing tree*. Note the difference with our approach. We represent a *set of states* via a *tuple*, and *collections of sets* of states via a *sharing tree*. The complexity issues are different when lifting the denotation to collections of sets of states (see Section 3). In [Zam97], Zampuniéris makes an accurate comparison between sharing trees and *binary decision diagrams* (BDDs) [Bry86]. When the aim is to represent tuples of (unbounded) integers (as in our case), the layered structure of sharing trees allows optimizations that seem more difficult using BDDs (or extensions like *multi-valued* DDs [SKM$^+$90] or *multi-terminal* DDs [CFZ96]).

Our approach shares some similarities with recent works on *interval decision diagrams* (IDDs) [ST99] and *clock decision diagrams* (CDDs) for timed automata [BLP⁺99]: all approaches make use of *acyclic* graphs to represent disjunctions of interval constraints. However, the use of simulations as abstractions for handling efficiently large disjunctions has not been considered in the other approaches. More experimentations are needed for a better comparison of all those methods. Finally, the PEP tool [Gra97] provides a BDD-based model checking method for Petri Nets (with a fixed-a-priori number of tokens) [Wim97]. We are not aware of BDDs-based representations for the 'constraints' we are interested in, e.g., for verification problems of Petri Nets with a possibly unbounded number of tokens.

7   Conclusions and Future Work

We have proposed a new symbolic representation for 'constraints', we called $\mathcal{U}$-formulas, that can be used in verification problems for infinite-state integer systems (e.g., coverability of Petri Nets). The representation is based on the sharing trees of Zampuniéris and Le Charlier. For our purposes, we lift the denotation of a sharing tree to the upward-closed set 'generated' by the tuples contained in the sharing tree. We have studied the theoretical complexity of the operations for sharing trees wrt. this denotation. Furthermore, we have given sufficient conditions for testing subsumption (co-NP hard for $\mathcal{U}$-formulas) we discover thanks to the view of $\mathcal{U}$-formulas as acyclic graphs. In fact, the conditions are based on simulations relations for nodes of sharing trees.

Though the termination test for the algorithm of [AČJT96] applied to collections of upward-closed sets ($\sim \mathcal{U}$-formulas $\sim$ sharing trees) may be very costly[3], testing for membership of the initial configuration (when it can be expressed with a conjunctive formula) can be done efficiently (Theorem 2). This gives us an effienct method to detect *violations* of safety properties.

The implementation is currently being optimized, but the preliminary experimental results are already promising. The type of optimizations we are interested in are: heuristics for finding 'good' orderings of variables; symbolic representation of the transition system (e.g. PADs [ST99]); partial order reductions (see e.g. [AJKP98] for an application to the coverability problem of Petri Nets). Finally, it would be interesting to extend our techniques to more general classes of constraints.

Acknowledgments. The authors would like to thank Jean-Marc Talbot, Andreas Podelski, and Witold Charatonik for fruitful discussions, and Denis Zampuniéris for having made the sharing tree library available for our experiments.

---

[3] Quadratic for disjunctive formulas, but disjunctive formulas suffers from the state explosion; exponential for sharing trees or arbitrary $\mathcal{U}$-formulas.

References

AČJT96.   P. A. Abdulla, K. Čerāns, B. Jonsson, and Y.-K. Tsay. General Decidability Theorems for Infinite-state Systems. In *Proceedings of the 11th Annual Symposium on Logic in Computer Science (LICS'96)*, pages 313–321. IEEE Computer Society Press, 1996. 426, 427, 428, 436, 437, 438

AJKP98.   P. A. Abdulla, B. Jonsson, M. Kindahl, and D. Peled. A General Approach to Partial Order Reductions in Symbolic Verification. In *Proceedings of the 10th Conference on Computer Aided Verification (CAV'98)*, volume 1427 of *LNCS*, pages 379–390. Springer, 1998. 426, 438

BLP+99.   G. Behrmann, K. G. Larsen, J. Pearson, C. Weise, and W. Yi. Efficient Timed Reachability Analysis Using Clock Difference Diagrams. In *Proceedings of the 11th Conference on Computer Aided Verification (CAV'99)*, volume 1633 of *LNCS*, pages 341–353. Springer 1999. 438

BW98.   B. Boigelot, P. Wolper. Verifying systems with infinite but regular state space. In *Proceedings of the 10th International Conference on Computer Aided Verification (CAV'98)*, volume 1427 of LNCS, pages 88–97. Springer, 1998. 426

BM99.   A. Bouajjani and R. Mayr. Model Checking Lossy Vector Addition Systems. In *Proceedings of the 16th Annual Symposium on Theoretical Aspects of Computer Science (STACS'99)*, volume 1563 of LNCS, pages 323–333. Springer, 1999. 426

Bry86.   R. E. Bryant. Graph-based Algorithms for Boolean Function Manipulation. *IEEE Transaction on Computers*, C-35(8):667-691, August, 1986. 437

BGP97.   T. Bultan, R. Gerber, and W. Pugh. Symbolic Model Checking of Infinite state Systems using Presburger Arithmetics. In *Proc. 9th Conf. on Computer Aided Verification (CAV'97)*, LNCS 1254, pages 400–411. Springer-Verlag, 1997. 427, 437

BCB⁺90.   J. R. Burch, E. M. Clarke, K. L. McMillan, D. L. Dill, and J. Hwang. Symbolic Model Checking: 10^{20} States and Beyond. In *Proceedings of the 5th IEEE Symposium on Logic in Computer Science*, pages 428-439. IEEE Computer Society Press, 1990. 426, 427

Čer94.   K. Čerāns. Deciding Properties of Integral Relational Automata. In *Proceedings of the International Conferences on Automata and Languages for Programming (ICALP 94)*, volume 820 of LNCS, pages 35-46. Springer, 1994. 426

Cia94.   G. Ciardo. Petri nets with marking-dependent arc multiplicity: properties and analysis. In *Proceedings of the 15th Int. Conf. on Application and Theory of Petri Nets 1994*, LNCS 815, pages 179–198. Springer-Verlag, 1994. 426

CFZ96.   E. Clarke, M. Fujita, and X. Zhao. Multi-terminal Binary Decision Diagrams and Hybrid Decision Diagrams. In *Representations of Discrete Functions*, pages 93-108. Kluwer Academic Publishers, 1996. 437

DEP99.   G. Delzanno, J. Esparza, and A. Podelski. Constraint-based Analysis of Broadcast Protocols. In *Proceedings of the Annual Conference of the European Association for Computer Science Logic (CSL'99)*, volume 1683 of LNCS, pag. 50–66. Springer, 1999. 426, 427, 436, 437

DP99.   G. Delzanno and A. Podelski, Model Checking in CLP. In W. R. Cleaveland, editor, *Proc. 5th Int. Con. on Tools and Algorithms for the Construction and Analysis of Systems (TACAS'99).*, LNCS 1579, pages 223–239. Springer-Verlag, 1999.

DR99.   G. Delzanno and J. F. Raskin. Symbolic Representation of Upward-
           Closed Sets. Technical report MPI-I-1999-2-007, Max-Planck-Institut für
           Informatik, November 1999. Available on the web at http://www.mpi-
           sb.mpg.de/units/ag2/. 428, 437

EN98.   E. A. Emerson and K. S. Namjoshi. On Model Checking for Non-
           deterministic Infinite-state Systems. In *Proceedings of the 13th Annual
           Symposium on Logic in Computer Science (LICS '98)*, pages 70–80. IEEE
           Computer Society Press, 1998. 426

EFM99.   J. Esparza, A. Finkel, and R. Mayr. On the Verification of Broadcast Proto-
           cols. In *Proceedings of the 14th Annual Symposium on Logic in Computer
           Science (LICS'99)*, pages 352–359. IEEE Computer Society Press, 1999.
           426

Fin90.   A. Finkel. Reduction and Covering of Infinite Reachability Trees. *Informa-
           tion and Computation* 89(2), pages 144–179. Academic Press, 1990. 426

FS99.   A. Finkel and P. Schnoebelen. Well-structured Transition Systems Every-
           where! *Theoretical Computer Science*, 1999. To appear. 426, 427, 428

GGZ95.   F. Gagnon, J.-Ch. Grégoire, and D. Zampuniéris. Sharing Trees for 'On-
           the-fly' Verification. In *Proceedings of the International Conference on
           Formal Description Techniques for Distributed Systems and Communica-
           tion Protocols (FORTE'95)*, 1995. 437

Gra97.   B. Grahlmann. The PEP Tool. In *Proceedings of the 9th Conference on
           Computer Aided Verification (CAV'97)*, volume 1254 of LNCS, pages 440–
           443. Springer, 1997. 438

HHK95.   M. R. Henzinger, T. A. Henzinger, P. K. Kopke. Computing Simulations
           on Finite and Infinite Graphs. In *Proceedings of the 36th Annual IEEE
           Symposium on Foundations of Computer Science (FOCS'95)*, pages 453–
           462. IEEE Society Press, 1995. 434

HHW97.   T. A. Henzinger, P.-H. Ho, and H. Wong-Toi. HYTECH: a Model Checker for
           Hybrid Systems. In *Proceedings of the 9th Conference on Computer Aided
           Verification (CAV'97)*, volume 1254 of *LNCS*, pages 460–463. Springer,
           1997. 427

McM93.   K. L. McMillan. *Symbolic Model Checking: An Approach to the State Ex-
           plosion Problem*. Kluwer Academic, 1993.

Min67.   N. M. Minsky. Finite and Infinite Machines. Prentice Hall, Englewood
           Cliffs, N.Y., 1967. 426

SKM⁺90.   A. Srinivasan, T. Kam, S. Malik, and R. K. Brayton. Algorithms for Dis-
           crete Functions Manipulation. In *Proceedings of the IEEE International
           Conference on Computer-Aided Design (ICCAD'90)*, 1990. 437

ST99.   K. Strehl, L. Thiele. Interval Diagram Techniques For Symbolic Model
           Checking of Petri Nets. In *Proceedings of the Design, Automation and Test
           in Europe Conference (DATE'99)*, pages 756–757, 1999. 438

Ter94.   E. Teruel. *Structure Theory of Weighted Place/Transition Net Systems:
           The Equal Conflict Hiatus*. Ph.D. Thesis, University of Zaragoza, 1994.
           426, 427, 436

Wim97.   G. Wimmel. A BDD-based Model Checker for the PEP Tool. Technical
           Report, University of Newcastle Upon Tyne, 1997. 438

Zam97.   D. Zampuniéris. The Sharing Tree Data Structure: Theory and Applica-
           tions in Formal Verification. PhD Thesis. Facultés Universitaires Notre-
           Dame de la Paix, Namur, Belgium, May 1997. 427, 436, 437

ZL94.   D. Zampuniéris, and B. Le Charlier. Efficient Handling of Large Sets of Tuples with Sharing Trees. In *Proceedings of the Data Compressions Conference (DCC'95)*, 1995.   427, 429, 430, 431, 432, 435

BDD vs. Constraint-Based Model Checking: An Experimental Evaluation for Asynchronous Concurrent Systems*

Tevfik Bultan

Department of Computer Science, University of California
Santa Barbara, CA 93106, USA
bultan@cs.ucsb.edu

Abstract. BDD-based symbolic model checking has been successful in verification of a wide range of systems. Recently, constraint-based approaches, which use arithmetic constraints as a symbolic representation, have been used in symbolic model checking of infinite-state systems. We argue that use of constraint-based model checking is not limited to infinite-state systems. It can also be used as an alternative to BDD-based model checking for systems with integer variables which have finite but large domains. In this paper we investigate the trade-offs between these two approaches experimentally. We compare the performance of BDD-based model checker SMV to the performance of our constraint-based model checker on verification of several asynchronous concurrent systems. The results indicate that constraint-based model checking is a viable option for verification of asynchronous concurrent systems with large integer domains.

1 Introduction

Model checking has been used in verification of diverse applications ranging from hardware protocols [McM93] to software specifications [CAB+98]. The success of model checking has been partially due to use of efficient data structures like Binary Decision Diagrams (BDDs) which can encode boolean functions in a highly compact format [Bry86]. The main idea in BDD-based *symbolic* model checking is to represent sets of system states and transitions as boolean logic formulas, and manipulate them efficiently using the BDD data structure [BCM+90].

An important property of the BDD data structure is that it supports operations such as intersection, union, complement, equivalence checking and existential quantifier elimination (used to implement relational image computations)—which also happen to be the main operations required for model checking. However, an efficient encoding for boolean domains may not be efficient for all variable types. For example, BDD-based model checkers can be very inefficient in representing arithmetic constraints [CAB+98].

---

* This work was supported in part by NSF grant CCR-9970976 and a University of California Regents' Junior Faculty Fellowship.

S. Graf and M. Schwartzbach (Eds.): TACAS/ETAPS 2000, LNCS 1785, pp. 441–456, 2000.

Another shortcoming of the BDD representation is its inability to encode infinite domains. Without abstraction, BDDs cannot be used for analyzing infinite-state systems—even those with just one unbounded integer. BDDs encode all underlying datatypes as boolean variables; hence all BDD-based model checkers inherently require the underlying types to be bounded.

Recently, arithmetic constraints have been used as a symbolic representation in model checking [AHH96,BGP97]. For example, HyTech, a symbolic model checker for hybrid systems, encodes real domains using linear constraints on real variables [AHH96]. We developed a model checker for integer based systems which uses Presburger arithmetic (integer arithmetic without multiplication) constraints as its underlying state representation [BGP97,BGP99]. Our model checker uses the Omega library [KMP+95] to manipulate Presburger arithmetic constraints. In [DP99] model checking queries are converted into constraint logic programs, and a CLP(R) library is used to verify concurrent systems by mapping integer variables to real domains.

Constraint representations allow verification of infinite-state systems since they can represent variables with infinite domains. There are algorithms for intersection, union, complement, equivalence checking and existential quantifier elimination for both real and integer constraint representations mentioned above. However model checking becomes undecidable for infinite-state systems. Hence the fixpoint computations are not guaranteed to converge. This problem is addressed using conservative approximation techniques [BGP99] which guarantee convergence but do not guarantee a definite answer, i.e., the model checker 1) may report that the property is verified, 2) provide a counter-example demonstrating violation of the property, or 3) report that the analysis is inconclusive.

Using arithmetic constraints one can also represent variables with finite domains. We just have to add additional constraints which show the range of values that an integer variable can take. An interesting issue is, then, comparing the performance of BDD-based model checking to constraint-based model checking for finite-state systems with integer variables.

In this paper we compare the performance of a BDD-based model checker (SMV [McM93]) and a constraint-based model checker (our model checker based on Omega library [BGP97,BGP99]) in verification of asynchronous concurrent systems with integer variables. On the extreme case where integer variables can take only two values, they can be treated as boolean variables and represented using BDDs. Using a constraint-representation would be very inefficient in such a case. On the other hand, although BDD-based model checkers are not capable of handling systems with unbounded integers, if the variables are restricted to a finite set of values, they can be represented using a set of boolean variables using a binary encoding. Our goal in this paper is to investigate the middle ground between these two extremes where the integer variables are neither unbounded nor have only two possible valuations.

We perceive efforts in constraint-based model checking as not only a way to solve infinite-state verification problems, but also as a way to deal with problems with large variable domains using formalisms that are more expressive than boolean logic formulas. However, because of the added expressive power, manipulation algorithms for these formalisms have higher complexity than corresponding algorithms for BDDs. These powerful algorithms may not be worthwhile to use for small domains because of their high complexity. On the other hand, for large domains their complexity maybe justified. The question is, when is the use of integer constraint representations justified instead of BDD encodings? In this paper we investigate this issue experimentally on verification of asynchronous concurrent systems.

The rest of the paper is organized as follows. We first discuss other related approaches to symbolic model checking in Sect. 2. In Sect. 3, we give a brief overview of symbolic model checking. After presenting the example concurrent systems in Sect. 4, we discuss the experimental results we obtained using BDD and constraint-based model checkers in Sect. 5. Finally, we present our conclusions and future directions.

2   Related Work

Another approach to infinite-state model checking is to use automata-based representations. Automata can be used to represent arithmetic constraints on unbounded integer variables [WB95,BKR96,KSA98]. An arithmetic constraint on k integer variables is represented by a k-track automata that accepts a string if it corresponds to a k-dimensional integer vector (in binary representation) that satisfies the corresponding arithmetic constraint. Again, since the automata representation supports the necessary operations, it can be used in symbolic model checking.

The constraint and automata-based representations provide two different ways of implementing model checking computations for systems with unbounded integer variables. In [SKR98] these two approaches are compared experimentally for reachability analysis of several concurrent systems. The results show no clear winner. On some problem instances the constraint representation is superior, on some others automata representation is. In automata-based representations, restricting variables to fixed finite domains ends up converting the automata representation to a model isomorphic to BDDs [KSA98]. Hence, for the experiments we conduct in this paper the automata-based representation is equivalent to BDD-based model checking.

Using a BDD-based model checker such as SMV [McM93] for checking systems with integer variables can easily result in inefficient encodings of arithmetic constraints [CAB+98]. It is pointed out both in [YMW97] and [CAB+98] that SMV can be very inefficient in constructing BDDs for integer variables. This inefficiency can be resolved for linear arithmetic constraints by using a better variable ordering as explained in [CAB+98]. For non-linear constraints, however, there is no efficient BDD representation [Bry86]. In [CABN97] SMV is augmented with a constraint solver for non-linear constraints. This technique is not applicable to the systems we analyze in this paper because of the restrictions put on the types of systems that can be analyzed.

Another approach to dealing with integer variables in BDD-based model checking is to use abstractions. In [CGL92], a conservative abstraction method is presented for model-checking infinite-state programs. The main idea is to produce a finite model of the program using a suitable abstraction technique (e.g., congruence modulo an integer, single-bit abstraction, symbolic abstraction), and then to check the property of interest on the abstraction. For systems such as the ones we analyze in this paper, finding a good abstraction maybe as difficult as proving the invariants of the system. On the other hand, automated abstractions such as the ones presented in [HKL+98] are not strong enough to eliminate the integer variables in the systems we analyze in this paper.

3 Symbolic Model Checking

In model checking, the system to be analyzed is represented as a transition system $TS = (S, I, R)$ with a set of states S, a set of initial states $I \subseteq S$, and a transition relation $R \subseteq S \times S$. The transition system model is never explicitly generated in symbolic model checking. For example, BDD-based model checkers represent transition relation R as a set of boolean logic formulas.

A popular temporal logic for specifying temporal properties of transition systems is Computation Tree Logic (CTL) [CES86] which consists of a set of temporal operators (the next-state operators EX and AX, the until operators EU and AU, the invariant operators EG and AG, and the eventuality operators EF and AF) for specifying temporal properties.

Our goal in model checking a system $TS = (S, I, R)$ and a temporal property p is (we use p to denote its truth set) : 1) either to prove that the system TS satisfies the property p by showing that $I \subseteq p$, or 2) to demonstrate a bug by finding a state $s \in I \cap \neg p$, and generating a counter-example path starting from s.

Assume that there exists a representation for sets of states which supports tests for equivalence and membership. Then, if we can represent the truth set of the temporal property p, and the set of initial states I using this representation, we can check the two conditions listed above. If the state space is finite, explicit state enumeration would be one such representation. Note that as the state space of a concurrent system grows, explicit state enumeration will become more expensive since the size of this representation is linearly related to the number of states in the set it represents. Unfortunately, state space of a concurrent system increases exponentially with the number of variables and concurrent components. This state space explosion problem makes a simple implementation of the explicit state enumeration infeasible.

Another approach is to use a *symbolic representation* for encoding sets of states. For example, a logic formula which is semantically interpreted as a set of states, can be used as a symbolic representation. Boolean logic formulas (stored using the BDD data structure) are the most common symbolic representation used in model checking [BCM+90]. Recently, we used Presburger arithmetic (integer arithmetic without multiplication) formulas for the same purpose [BGP97,BGP99].

Model checking procedures use state space exploration to compute the set of states which satisfy a temporal property. Fixpoints corresponding to truth sets of temporal formulas can be computed by iteratively aggregating states using pre-condition computations (which correspond to the next state operator EX). Temporal properties which require more than one fixpoint computation can be computed recursively starting from the inner fixpoints and propagating the partial results to the outer fixpoints.

All temporal properties in CTL can be expressed using boolean connectives, next state operator EX, and least fixpoints. For example, $\text{EF}p \equiv \mu x \cdot p \vee \text{EX } x$. The least fixpoint of a monotonic functional can be computed by starting from the bottom element (i.e., **false** $\equiv \emptyset$) and by iteratively applying the functional until a fixpoint is reached.

Assume that `Symbolic` is the data type used for encoding sets of states. In order to implement a symbolic model checker based on `Symbolic` data type we need the following procedures:

`Symbolic Not(Symbolic)` : Given an argument that represents a set $p \subseteq S$, it returns a representation for $S - p$.

`Symbolic And(Symbolic,Symbolic)` : Given two arguments representing two sets $p, q \subseteq S$, it returns a representation for $p \cap q$.

`Symbolic Or(Symbolic,Symbolic)` : Given two arguments representing two sets $p, q \subseteq S$, it returns a representation for $p \cup q$.

`Symbolic EX(Symbolic)` : Given an argument that represents a set $p \subseteq S$, it returns a representation for the set $\{s \mid \exists s' \cdot s' \in p \wedge (s, s') \in R\}$.

`Boolean Equivalent(Symbolic, Symbolic)` : Given two arguments representing two sets $p, q \subseteq S$, it returns **true** if $p \equiv q$, returns **false** otherwise.

Using the procedures described above, given a temporal formula, we can compute its truth set by computing the fixpoint that corresponds to that temporal formula.

The computation of the procedure EX involves computing a relational image. Given a set $p \subseteq S$ and a relation $X \subseteq S \times S$ we use X p to denote relational image of p under X, i.e., X p is defined as restricting the domain of X to set p, and returning the range of the result. Note that we can think of relation X as a functional $X : 2^S \rightarrow 2^S$. Then, X p denotes the application of the functional X to set p.

Let R^{-1} denote the inverse of the transition relation R. Then EX $p \equiv R^{-1}$ p, i.e., functional EX corresponds to the inverse of the transition relation R. Hence, we can compute the procedure EX using a relational image computation. Most model checkers represent transition relation R in a partitioned form to make the relational image computation more efficient [BCL91].

Any representation which is able to encode the set of initial states I and the set of atomic properties AP, and supports the above functionality can be used as a symbolic representation in a model checker. We call such a representation an *adequate language* for model checking [KMM+97]. For example, for finite-state systems, boolean logic would be one such representation. It is possible to implement procedures for negation, conjunction, disjunction and equivalence checking of boolean logic formulas. If we can represent the transition relation R as a boolean logic formula, then relational image computation R^{-1} p can be computed by conjuncting the formula representing R^{-1} and the formula representing p, and then eliminating the variables in the domain of the resulting relation using existential quantifier elimination. BDDs are an efficient data structure for representing boolean logic formulas, and they support all the functionality mentioned above [Bry86]. They have been successfully used for model checking [BCM+90,McM93]. However, they can not encode infinite variable domains.

Recently, we developed a model checker for systems with unbounded integer variables using Presburger arithmetic formulas as a symbolic representation [BGP97]. There are effective procedures for manipulating Presburger formulas which support the above functionality—for example Omega Library implements a set of such procedures [KMP+95]. We implemented a model checker using Omega Library as our symbolic manipulator. However, model checking computations become undecidable for infinite domains, i.e., the fixpoint computations corresponding to temporal properties may not always converge for infinite domains. We addressed this issue in [BGP99] using conservative approximations.

4   Example Concurrent Systems

The examples we use in this paper have the following characteristics: 1) they are all asynchronous concurrent systems, and 2) they all use shared integer variables to control their synchronization. We think this type of systems are especially suitable for constraint-based representations. Most of our examples are from [And91].

We represent each concurrent system with a set of events, where each event is considered atomic (Fig. 1). The state of a program is determined by the values of its data and control variables. If a variable v is used in an event, then the symbol v' denotes the new value of v after the action is taken. If v' is not mentioned in an event, then we assume that its value is not altered by that event. Each event specification defines a transition relation over the Cartesian product of the domains of the variables in the system. The transition relation of the overall concurrent system is defined as the union of the transition relations of all events in the system.

Bakery algorithm, shown in Fig. 1 for two processes, is a mutual exclusion algorithm. The algorithm we present above is the coarse grain solution [And91] which can be further refined to implement without fetch-and-add instructions.

In Fig. 1 we show a solution to sleeping barber problem [And91]. The barber allows a new customer into the shop with the event e_{next_1}. The customer gets a chair by calling the event $e_{haircut_1}$ (as long as their is an available chair). Then the barber starts the haircut with event e_{next_2}. When the haircut is finished the

---

Program: Bakery
Data Variables: a, b: positive integer
Control Variables: $pc_1 : \{T_1, W_1, C_1\}$, $pc_2 : \{T_2, W_2, C_2\}$
Initial Condition: $a = b = 0 \wedge pc_1 = T_1 \wedge pc_2 = T_2$
Events:
$e_{T_1} : pc_1 = T_1 \wedge pc_1' = W_1 \wedge a' = b + 1$
$e_{W_1} : pc_1 = W_1 \wedge (a < b \vee b = 0) \wedge pc_1' = C_1$
$e_{C_1} : pc_1 = C_1 \wedge pc_1' = T_1 \wedge a' = 0$
$e_{T_2} : pc_2 = T_2 \wedge pc_2' = W_2 \wedge b' = a + 1$
$e_{W_2} : pc_2 = W_2 \wedge (b < a \vee a = 0) \wedge pc_2' = C_2$
$e_{C_2} : pc_2 = C_2 \wedge pc_2' = T_2 \wedge b' = 0$

Program: Barber
Data Variables: $cinchair, cleave, bavail, bbusy, bdone$: positive integer
Control Variables: $pc_1 : \{1, 2\}$, $pc_2 : \{1, 2\}$ $pc_3 : \{1, 2\}$
Initial Condition: $cinchair = cleave = bavail = bbusy = bdone = 0$
$\wedge pc_1 = pc_2 = pc_3 = 1$
Events:
$e_{haircut_1} : pc_1 = 1 \wedge pc_1' = 2 \wedge cinchair < bavail \wedge cinchair' = cinchair + 1$
$e_{haircut_2} : pc_1 = 2 \wedge pc_1' = 1 \wedge cleave < bdone \wedge cleave' = cleave + 1$
$e_{next_1} \quad : pc_2 = 1 \wedge pc_2' = 2 \wedge bavail' = bavail + 1$
$e_{next_2} \quad : pc_2 = 2 \wedge pc_2' = 1 \wedge bbusy < cinchair \wedge bbusy' = bbusy + 1$
$e_{finish_1} : pc_3 = 1 \wedge pc_3' = 2 \wedge bdone < bbusy \wedge bdone' = bdone + 1$
$e_{finish_2} : pc_3 = 2 \wedge pc_3' = 1 \wedge bdone = cleave$

Program: Readers-Writers
Data Variables: nr, nw: positive integer
Initial Condition: $nr = nw = 0$
Events:
$e_{reader-enter} : nw = 0 \wedge nr' = nr + 1$
$e_{reader-exit} \;\; : nr > 0 \wedge nr' = nr - 1$
$e_{writer-enter} : nr = 0 \wedge nw = 0 \wedge nw' = nw + 1$
$e_{writer-exit} \;\; : nw > 0 \wedge nw' = nw - 1$

Program: Bounded-Buffer
Parameterized Constant: $size$: positive integer
Data Variables: $available, produced, consumed$: positive integer
Initial Condition: $produced = consumed = 0 \wedge available = size$
Events:
$e_{produce} \;\; : 0 < available \wedge produced' = produced + 1 \wedge available' = available - 1$
$e_{consume} : available < size \wedge consumed' = consumed + 1$
$\qquad\qquad \wedge available' = available + 1$

Program: Circular-Queue
Parameterized Constant: $size$: positive integer
Data Variables: $occupied, head, tail, produced, consumed$: positive integer
Initial Condition: $occupied = head = tail = produced = consumed = 0$
Events:
$e_{produce} \;\; : occupied < size \wedge occupied' = occupied + 1 \wedge produced' = produced + 1$
$\qquad\qquad \wedge (tail = size \wedge tail' = 0 \vee tail < size \wedge tail' = tail + 1)$
$e_{consume} : occupied > 0 \wedge occupied' = occupied - 1 \wedge consumed' = consumed + 1$
$\qquad\qquad \wedge (head = size \wedge head' = 0 \vee head < size \wedge head' = head + 1)$

Fig. 1. Example concurrent systems used in the experiments

barber executes e_{done_1}, and waits (e_{done_2}) till the customer leaves by executing the event $e_{haircut_2}$.

A well-known algorithm for readers-writers problem is also presented in Fig. 1. The invariant of the readers-writers problem states that at any time there would be either no writers accessing the database or no readers, and the number of writers should never be more than one.

Two algorithms given in Fig. 1 present bounded-buffer implementations. Both these systems have a parameterized constant *size* which specifies the size of the buffer. Since *size* is parameterized the systems given above should be correct for any value of *size*.

In Table 1 we list the invariants the systems presented above have to satisfy.

Table 1. List of problem instances used in the experiments

Problem Instance	Property
BAKERY	$AG(\neg(pc_1 = C_1 \wedge pc_2 = C_2))$
BARBER	$AG(cinchair \geq cleave \wedge bavail \geq bbusy \geq bdone$
	$\wedge\ cinchair \leq bavail \wedge bbusy \leq cinchair \wedge cleave \leq bdone)$
BARBER-1	$AG(cinchair \geq cleave \wedge bavail \geq bbusy \geq bdone)$
BARBER-2	$AG(cinchair \leq bavail \wedge bbusy \leq cinchair)$
BARBER-3	$AG(cleave \leq bdone)$
READERS-WRITERS	$AG((nr = 0 \vee nw = 0) \wedge nw \leq 1)$
BOUNDED-BUFFER	$AG(produced - consumed = size - available$
	$\wedge\ 0 \leq available \leq size)$
BOUNDED-BUFFER-1	$AG(produced - consumed = size - available)$
BOUNDED-BUFFER-2	$AG(0 \leq available \leq size)$
BOUNDED-BUFFER-3	$AG(0 \leq produced - consumed \leq size)$
CIRCULAR-QUEUE	$AG(0 \leq produced - consumed \leq size$
	$\wedge\ produced - consumed = occupied)$
CIRCULAR-QUEUE-1	$AG(0 \leq produced - consumed \leq size)$
CIRCULAR-QUEUE-2	$AG(produced - consumed = occupied)$

5   Experimental Evaluation

We translated the examples given in Fig. 1 to the SMV input language. For each concurrent process we used the **process** declaration in SMV which supports asynchronous composition. SMV converts all integer variables to a binary representation since it is a BDD-based model checker. We used an uninitialized variable that always preserves its value to represent the parameterized constant *size* in the bounded-buffer and circular-queue systems.

Our omega library based model checker accepts a Presburger arithmetic formula for each event in the input system. It forms the global transition relation by combining these formulas disjunctively. It uses asynchronous composition to combine two concurrent components. It is not efficient to map variables with small domains (such as program counters) to integer variables. So, for the examples with control variables we used control point partitioning to eliminate the control variables [BGP99].

To compare the performances of SMV and OMC (Omega library Model Checker) we assigned a finite domain to each integer variable. We generated 16 different instances for each concurrent system by restricting the integer variables to different ranges. We started with a range of $0 \leq i < 2^3$ for each integer variable i (which makes it possible to represent each variable i with 3 boolean variables in SMV) and increased it until $0 \leq i < 2^{26}$ (which requires 26 boolean variables for each integer variable).

In Figs. 2 and 3 we show the performances of both SMV and OMC in terms of execution time and memory usage. We ran all our experiments on an Intel Pentium III PC (500MHz, 128 MByte main memory) running Solaris. Each graph shows experiments on one concurrent system. Data points in each individual graph is generated by only changing the range of values that integer variables are allowed to take. The x axis in these graphs show the number of boolean variables required for the binary encoding of each integer variable (which ranged from 3 to 26 in our experiments). So, for each point in the graph, the range of each integer variable i in the concurrent system verified in that particular experiment is $0 \leq i < 2^x$.

In our initial experiments we observed that the execution time and the memory usage of SMV increases exponentially with the number of boolean variables required for the binary encoding of each integer variable (which corresponds to a linear increase in the size of the domains of the integer variables). This exponential increase can be observed in Figs. 2 and 3.

The worst-case complexity of the BDD representation is exponential in the number of boolean variables it represents. The exponential increase in execution time and memory usage of SMV is a realization of this worst-case complexity. However, as observed by Chan et al. [CAB+98] and Yang et al. [YMW97] this is because of the inefficient representation of integer variables in SMV and can be improved using a better variable ordering.

BDD representation is very sensitive to variable ordering [Bry86]. In SMV, given two integer variables i and j, all the boolean variables representing variable i either precede all the boolean variables representing j or vice versa. With such an ordering the BDD representing a constraint such as $i = j$ has exponential size in the number of boolean variables. However, if the order of boolean variables representing i and j are interleaved the same constraint has a linear BDD representation [CAB+98]. William Chan developed macros which generate such an interleaved order for SMV. Using his macros, we tested the SMV system again for the examples given in Fig. 1. As seen in Figs. 2 and 3, with this variable ordering the execution time and the memory usage of SMV increases linearly with the number of boolean variables required for the binary encoding of each integer variable (which corresponds to a logarithmic increase in the size of the domains of the integer variables).

For the examples shown in Figs. 2 and 3 the performance of OMC stays constant with respect to increasing variable domains. This is because of the fact that, for these examples, the size of the fixpoint iterates and the number of fix-point iterations stay constant with respect to increasing variable domains for the constraint-based model checker OMC. Note that, changing the maximum value that an integer variable can take from one integer constant to another integer constant does not increase the size of the constraint representation. Also, for the examples shown in Figures 2 and 3, the model checking procedure converges in a constant number of fixpoint iterations which is independent of the size of the domains of the variables. However, this may not always be the case. For example, for properties BOUNDED-BUFFER-3 and CIRCULAR-QUEUE-1 (Table 1) the number of fixpoint iterations depends on the size of the domain of the parameterized constant *size*.

Figure 2 shows the performances of SMV and OMC on verification of both two and three process implementations of the bakery algorithm with respect to the property BAKERY shown in Table 1. The performance of both SMV and OMC deteriorate significantly if the number of processes is increased. However, the cost of constraint-based model checking seems to increase more significantly compared to BDD-based model checking.

Based on Figs. 2 and 3 OMC outperforms SMV without interleaved variable ordering if the integer variables require more than 6 boolean variables to encode. If interleaved variable ordering [CAB+98] is used, for BAKERY with two processes and BARBER, the execution time of OMC is better than SMV if 18 and 14 boolean variables are used, respectively. The memory usage of OMC is always better than SMV in these cases. For the BAKERY with three processes SMV with interleaved variable ordering always outperforms OMC both in execution time and memory usage. For READERS-WRITERS, BOUNDED-BUFFER and CIRCULAR-QUEUE, OMC always outperforms SMV with interleaved variable ordering both in terms of execution time and memory usage.

Note that both bakery and barber algorithms given in Fig. 1 use variables with finite domains (pc_1, pc_2, pc_3). Presence of such variables increases the cost of the constraint based representation since OMC partitions the state space to eliminate them. We believe that this is why the relative performance of OMC is not as good for these examples as it is for readers-writers, bounded-buffer and circular-queue. A composite approach which combines the BDD and constraint-based representations can be used in such cases [BGL98].

In Table 2 we show the performance of SMV (with interleaved variable ordering) and OMC for the problem instances given in Table 1 where each integer variable i is restricted to the range $0 \leq i < 1024$ (we also restricted the parameterized constant *size* to $0 \leq size < 16$). For most of these instances SMV and OMC have comparable performances. However for the BAKERY the increase in execution time and memory usage of OMC with respect to increasing number of processes is significantly higher compared to SMV. For 4 processes OMC did not converge in one hour (we indicate this with ↑ in Table 2).

Another shortcoming of OMC is demonstrated in the verification of properties BOUNDED-BUFFER-3 and CIRCULAR-QUEUE-1 shown in Table 1. None of the fixpoint computations for these properties converged (in an hour) when we

Table 2. Experiments where each integer variable i is restricted to $0 \leq i < 1024$. In bounded-buffer and circular-queue instances the parameterized constant *size* is restricted to $0 \leq size < 16$ (↑ denotes that the fixpoint computations did not converge)

Problem Instance	SMV (with Chan's variable ordering)		OMC	
	Execution Time (seconds)	Memory Usage (Kbytes)	Execution Time (seconds)	Memory Usage (Kbytes)
BAKERY (2 processes)	0.12	1507	0.29	655
BAKERY (3 processes)	0.82	2228	7.32	12165
BAKERY (4 processes)	19.15	9110	↑	↑
BARBER	0.40	2425	0.55	1458
BARBER-1	0.53	2490	15.37	23101
BARBER-2	0.35	2228	0.29	926
BARBER-3	0.35	2228	0.15	655
READERS-WRITERS	0.03	1245	0.05	295
BOUNDED-BUFFER	0.28	2163	0.08	238
BOUNDED-BUFFER-1	0.27	2228	0.05	188
BOUNDED-BUFFER-2	0.26	2163	0.04	147
BOUNDED-BUFFER-3	163.30	3080	↑	↑
CIRCULAR-QUEUE	1.08	3408	0.10	377
CIRCULAR-QUEUE-1	1228.45	6357	↑	↑
CIRCULAR-QUEUE-2	1.04	3342	0.07	328

tried to verify them using OMC. This is the price we pay for using an expressive representation such as constraints which have higher worst case complexity than BDD manipulation. For the properties BOUNDED-BUFFER-3 and CIRCULAR-QUEUE-1, the number of fixpoint iterations depend on the size of the domain of the parameterized constant *size*. For these properties OMC does not converge even for the small domain $0 \leq size < 16$. Note that, for these cases BDD based model checking is not very efficient either (even with interleaved variable ordering). We think that for such cases using conservative approximation techniques would be helpful [BGP99].

6   Conclusions

The experimental results we obtained in this work suggests that constraint-based model checking can be more efficient than BDD-based model checking for verification of asynchronous concurrent systems with finite but large integer domains. This supports our view that constraint-based model checking is not limited to infinite-state systems but can also be useful for verification of systems with large integer domains.

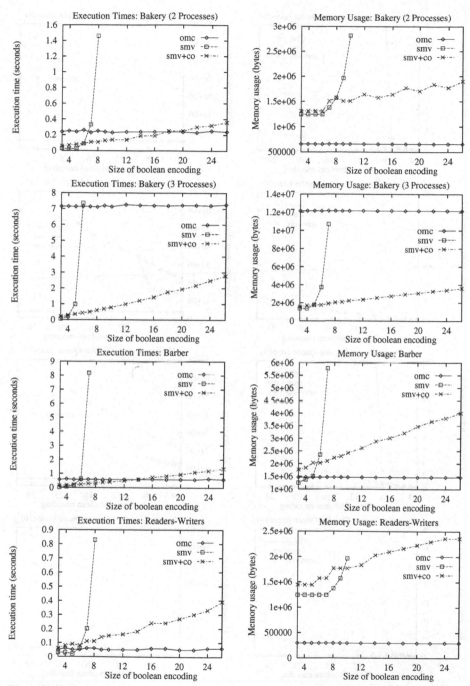

Fig. 2. Execution times and memory usage for OMC, SMV, and SMV with Chan's variable ordering (smv+co) in verification of BAKERY, BARBER and READERS-WRITERS

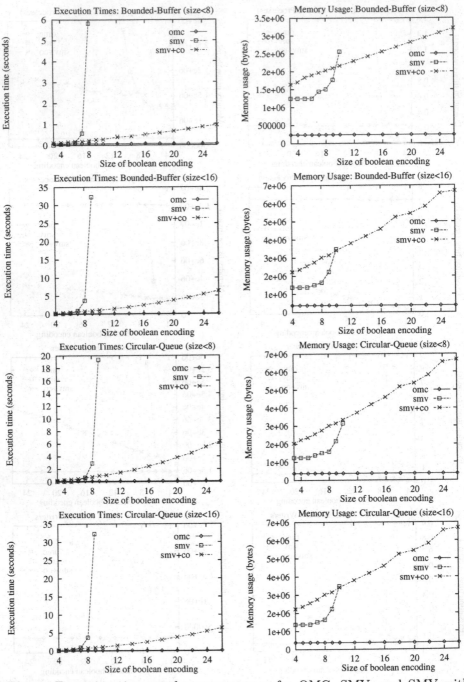

Fig. 3. Execution times and memory usage for OMC, SMV, and SMV with Chan's variable ordering (smv+co) in verification of BOUNDED-BUFFER and CIRCULAR-QUEUE

In the future we would like to compare the performance of constraint-based model checking with the performance of word-level model checking [CZ95]. We are also planning to investigate the performance of our composite model checking approach [BGL98] with respect to BDD-based representations.

We would also like to investigate the complexity analysis of both BDD and constraint-based model checking for the type of systems analyzed in this paper.

Acknowledgments

This work was significantly improved by William Chan who provided insightful comments for an earlier draft of this paper and allowed access to his macros for interleaved variable order generation for SMV. Tragically, few weeks after our correspondence William Chan was killed in an accident. His research contributions and friendship will be greatly missed by me and our research community.

References

AHH96.   R. Alur, T. A. Henzinger, and P. Ho. Automatic symbolic verification of embedded systems. *IEEE Transactions on Software Engineering*, 22(3):181–201, March 1996. 442

And91.   G. R. Andrews. *Concurrent Programming: Principles and Practice*. The Benjamin/Cummings Publishing Company, Redwood City, California, 1991. 446

BCL91.   J. R. Burch, E. M. Clarke, and D. E. Long. Symbolic model checking with partitioned transition relations. In *Proceedings of the International Conference on Very Large Scale Integration*, August 1991. 445

BCM+90.   J. R. Burch, E. M. Clarke, K. L. McMillan, D. L. Dill, and L. H. Hwang. Symbolic model checking: 10^{20} states and beyond. In *Proceedings of the 5th Annual IEEE Symposium on Logic in Computer Science*, pages 428–439, January 1990. 441, 444, 446

BGL98.   T. Bultan, R. Gerber, and C. League. Verifying systems with integer constraints and boolean predicates: A composite approach. In *Proceedings of the 1998 ACM SIGSOFT International Symposium on Software Testing and Analysis*, pages 113–123, March 1998. 450, 454

BGP97.   T. Bultan, R. Gerber, and W. Pugh. Symbolic model checking of infinite state systems using Presburger arithmetic. In O. Grumberg, editor, *Proceedings of the 9th International Conference on Computer Aided Verification*, volume 1254 of *Lecture Notes in Computer Science*, pages 400–411. Springer, June 1997. 442, 445, 446

BGP99.   T. Bultan, R. Gerber, and W. Pugh. Model-checking concurrent systems with unbounded integer variables: Symbolic representations, approximations, and experimental results. *ACM Transactions on Programming Languages and Systems*, 21(4):747–789, July 1999. 442, 445, 446, 449, 451

BKR96.   M. Biehl, N. Klarlund, and T. Rauhe. Mona: Decidable arithmetic in practice. In *Proceedings of Formal Techniques in Real-Time and Fault-Tolerant Systems, 4th International Symposium*, volume 1135 of *Lecture Notes in Computer Science*. Springer, 1996. 443

Bry86.   R. E. Bryant. Graph-based algorithms for boolean function manipulation. *IEEE Transactions on Computers*, 35(8):677–691, 1986. 441, 443, 446, 449

CAB+98.   W. Chan, R. J. Anderson, P. Beame, S. Burns, F. Modugno, D. Notkin, and J. D. Reese. Model checking large software specifications. *IEEE Transactions on Software Engineering*, 24(7):498–520, July 1998. 441, 443, 449, 450

CABN97.   W. Chan, R. J. Anderson, P. Beame, and D. Notkin. Combining constraint solving and symbolic model checking for a class of systems with non-linear constraints. In O. Grumberg, editor, *Proceedings of the 9th International Conference on Computer Aided Verification*, volume 1254 of *Lecture Notes in Computer Science*, pages 316–327. Springer, June 1997. 443

CES86.   E. M. Clarke, E. A. Emerson, and A. P. Sistla. Automatic verification of finite-state concurrent systems using temporal logic specifications. *ACM Transactions on Programming Languages and Systems*, 8(2):244–263, April 1986. 444

CGL92.   E. M. Clarke, O. Grumberg, and D. E. Long. Model checking and abstraction. In *Proceedings of the 18th Annual ACM Symposium on Principles of Programming Languages*, pages 343–354, 1992. 444

CZ95.   E. Clarke and X. Zhao. Word level symbolic model checking: A new approach for verifying arithmetic circuits. Technical Report CMU-CS-95-161, School of Computer Science, Carnegie Mellon University, May 1995. 454

DP99.   G. Delzanno and A. Podelski. Model checking in CLP. In Rance Cleaveland, editor, *Proceedings of the 5th International Conference on Tools and Algorithms for the Construction and Analysis of Systems*, volume 1579 of *Lecture Notes in Computer Science*, pages 223–239. Springer, March 1999. 442

HKL+98.   C. L. Heitmeyer, J. Kirby, B. Labaw, M. Archer, and R. Bharadwaj. Using abstraction and model checking to detect safety violations in requirements specifications. *IEEE Transactions on Software Engineering*, 24(11):927–948, November 1998. 444

KMM+97.   Y. Kesten, O. Maler, M. Marcus, A. Pnueli, and E. Shahar. Symbolic model checking with rich assertional languages. In O. Grumberg, editor, *Proceedings of the 9th International Conference on Computer Aided Verification*, volume 1254 of *Lecture Notes in Computer Science*, pages 400–411. Springer, June 1997. 446

KMP+95.   W. Kelly, V. Maslov, W. Pugh, E. Rosser, T. Shpeisman, and D. Wonnacott. The Omega library interface guide. Technical Report CS-TR-3445, Department of Computer Science, University of Maryland, College Park, March 1995. 442, 446

KSA98.   J. H. Kukula, T. R. Shiple, and A. Aziz. Implicit state enumeration for FSMs with datapaths. In *Proceedings of Formal Methods in Computer-Aided Design*, 1998. 443

McM93.   K. L. McMillan. *Symbolic model checking*. Kluwer Academic Publishers, Massachusetts, 1993. 441, 442, 443, 446

SKR98.   T. R. Shiple, J. H. Kukula, and R. K. Ranjan. A comparison of Presburger engines for EFSM reachability. In *Proceedings of the 10th International Conference on Computer-Aided Verification*, 1998. 443

WB95.   P. Wolper and B. Boigelot. An automata-theoretic approach to Presburger arithmetic constraints. In *Proceedings of the Static Analysis Symposium*, September 1995. 443

YMW97.   J. Yang, A. K. Mok, and F. Wang. Symbolic model checking for event-driven real-time systems. *ACM Transactions on Programming Languages and Systems*, 19(2):386–412, March 1997.   443, 449

Tool-Based Specification of Visual Languages and Graphic Editors

Magnus Niemann and Roswitha Bardohl

Department of Computer Science
Technische Universität Berlin
{maggi,rosi}@cs.tu-berlin.de

Abstract In this contribution we introduce GENGED, an environment which is used to interactively specify and generate syntax-directed editors for visual languages.

In analogy to textual languages a visual language is specified by both, an alphabet and a grammar. Hence, the GENGED environment provides an Alphabet Editor and a Grammar Editor, respectively. The grammar rules defined using the Grammar Editor specify not only language-generating rules but additionally the editing commands of the Graphic Editor for the specific visual language. The language-specific Graphic Editor then can be used in various environments to allow for syntax-directed drawing of diagrams.

1 Introduction

Visual languages are everywhere! Since often a graphical description of a problem or a model provides more readability and takes less space than a textual one, diagrams are used to visualize complex facts. To support the communication within larger communities, diagrams need some syntax and semantics to be understood by all members. In analogy to textual languages (natural but also formal ones) we can summarize syntactical and even semantical information in diagrams.

The graphical capabilities of today's computer systems permit the construction of diagrams completely with a computer, like it is done in architecture and electrical engineering. Nowadays, diagrams are additionally used in computer science for modeling and programming of complex systems. Such diagrams concern *visual languages*. It depends on the purpose of the visual language whether it is called *visual modeling language* or *visual programming language*. Visual modeling languages used for software engineering are, e.g., the Unified Modeling Language (UML) [Rat98] and statecharts [Har87]. Without a doubt, there are needs for editors to draw diagrams in those languages. Furthermore, in order to state about software quality and correctness it is important to draw *correct*[1] diagrams.

---

[1] Diagrams can be *correct* with respect to some formal specification.

S. Graf and M. Schwartzbach (Eds.): TACAS/ETAPS 2000, LNCS 1785, pp. 456–470, 2000.
© Springer-Verlag Berlin Heidelberg 2000

The problem with existing tools and editors for, e.g., software development (Rational Rose, Statemate, etc.) and also with so-called visual programming environments (Visual Basic, Delphi, etc.) is that the visual means are tightly integrated in the visual environment. Re-implementation is necessary whenever the concepts of a visual language or the basic visual means change. The GENGED environment [Bar00,BNS00] on the other hand permits the easy and interactive definition of arbitrary Graphic Editors for visual languages[2].

There are two major ways to build an editor for a visual language according to some specification: The first way is to take a simple graphical editor with which some kind of diagrams based on graphical primitives (like line, rectangle, circle etc.) can be drawn. This can be either some existing vector graphics editor or a slightly modified editor adapted to the symbols we use in our language. To check for syntactical correctness of a drawn diagram we will have to do some scanning- and parsing-like operations on the diagram according to a graphical syntax given in some way. We will denote those editors as *freehand editors*. The second way is to provide the user drawing a diagram with only the operations (insert a symbol, remove a symbol) with which he or she is "forced" to draw syntactically correct diagrams. That circumvents the syntax checking but adds more restriction to the user of such an editor. These editors will be called *syntax-directed editors*.

The path we choose in the GENGED environment is the second one, i.e., we consider syntax-directed editors. We do this because we can provide the designer of a visual language with powerful means to write grammars – in analogy to formal language grammars – with which we then generate a Graphic Editor for this language. So our environment can be used to specify existing visual languages like graph-like class diagrams occurring in the UML or box-like Nassi-Shneiderman diagrams [NS73], but also to construct completely new visual languages from scratch.

This presentation is built as follows: We start by giving an informal definition about the concepts of visual language specifications underlying the GENGED environment in section 2. For illustrational reasons we use some features of the well-known visual language of class diagrams [Rat98]. In section 3 we introduce the GENGED environment which is elucidated by screenshots. Some related approaches concerned in generating editors from visual language definitions will be mentioned in section 4. Concluding remarks will be made in section 5.

2   Concepts of Visual Language Specifications

When we take a closer look on two-dimensional diagrams following a certain specification there are two major parts we have to consider. On one hand we have some graphical *symbols* like classes or associations in an UML class diagram (see fig. 1 (a)). On the other hand there are spatial *relations* such that a symbol

[2] Research is partially supported by the German Research Council (DFG), and the ESPRIT Basic Research Working Group APPLIGRAPH

458   Magnus Niemann and Roswitha Bardohl

must be aligned with another one or, more precisely, that an association arrow must start at the border of a class symbol (see fig. 1 (b)).

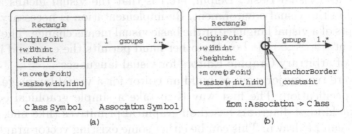

Figure1. Symbols (a) and connections (b) of class diagrams

In formal textual languages, relations between symbols like "follows" are not described explicitly in an alphabet. However, in analogy to formal languages, for a visual language we first need an *alphabet* over which sentences, namely diagrams, can be constructed. In the GENGED approach, an alphabet keeps all the information about the graphical symbols and furthermore, the possible relations between symbols. We will denote those relations as *connections* because we consider not only spatial relations like the `anchorBorder` constraint in figure 1 (b) but additionally the corresponding underlying structural relationships `from: Association → Class`. These structural relationships are used to express the *logical* meaning of a diagram. E.g., according to the UML specification, it is not allowed that an association symbol is "dangling" as illustrated in figure 1 (b). The end of the association arrow has to be connected with a class symbol, too. In order to avoid such *incorrect* constellations, a second structural relationship like `to: Association → Class` has to be defined together with suitable spatial relations. Both connections (`from`, `to`) then ensure that an association symbol is always connected with class symbols.

It is not sufficient to construct diagrams from an alphabet only. And additionally, it is not sufficient to generate a specific Graphic Editor where one can arbitrarily insert and remove symbols and connections. In this case there will be diagrams with illegal syntactical constellations. Like in formal languages, we have to give some *rules* to define insertion and deletion of symbols and implicitly the corresponding connections. The rules together with a *start diagram* (which is analogous to a start sentence in formal languages) form a *grammar*. The grammar rules are used as editing operations on the start diagram[3] – so we will not only give language-generating rules, but also editing rules allowing for changing or deleting symbols and connections in a language-specific Graphic Editor.

The alphabet and the grammar of a visual language establishes a visual language specification over that diagrams can be edited. These concepts are based on the well-established theory of algebraic graph transformation that is fully described in [Bar00]. In the following we do informally explain these concepts which are implemented in the GENGED environment.

---

[3] In fact this will be done in the GENGED environment later on.

2.1   The Alphabet

An alphabet comprises a set of symbols and a set of connections. From the graphical point of view, symbols are expressed by sets of graphical *primitives*, and connections are expressed by sets of graphical *constraints*.

Primitives Graphical *primitives* are simple graphics like lines, rectangles, circles, etc. They all have a location in a two-dimensional space and some properties like width, height, color, starting point etc.

Constraints Graphical *constraints* denote spatial relations between graphics. One constraint may concern to one or more graphics. A constraint is given by a set of equations and inequalities over the graphic's properties. Some examples for constraints are given in figure 2. A *graphically correct* diagram is a diagram where all constraints are satisfied. So we have to make sure that the symbol's properties like size and location are chosen in a way that the corresponding constraints are satisfied. This can be achieved using a constraint solver.

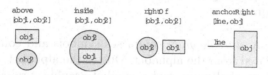

Figure2. Constraint examples

Symbols A symbol consists of a certain symbol name and a symbol graphic. This graphic is a grouping of several graphical *primitives*. The grouping is defined by graphical constraints like that of figure 2. Nevertheless, each symbol graphic consists of a box enclosing the corresponding primitives. This box can be treated like a common graphical primitive.

Connections A *connection* is defined between two symbols with respect to the symbol names and the symbol graphics. According to the symbol names it is a directed connection where one symbol name is in the source and the other one is in the target of the connection (see fig. 1 (b)). Note that due to the underlying theory [Bar00] the insertion of a directed connection on the instance level requires for a symbol that is in the source of the connection the presence of a symbol that is in the target such that the connection is correctly defined. We will call this property "structural correctness". In addition to a directed connection, according to the structural relationship a connection is defined by a set of constraints between the involved symbol graphics.

Data Attributes Some symbols need attributes we cannot handle in a purely graphical way. Such attributes are e.g., class names or association cardinalities as shown in figure 1. Data attributes can be strings, integers, lists or any other well-defined[4] datatype. Every data type has a set of operations (like `append`: `StringList String` → `StringList`) which can be used to code attribute changes (renaming, increasing counters and the like) into our rules. This goes beyond the capabilities of graphic editors which allow only the use and the simple renaming of strings. Nevertheless, each datatype must have a certain layout that depends on the specific datatype. For strings, e.g., the layout information includes text size and text font.

2.2   The Grammar

With the means to describe the graphical structure of diagrams we will now add the concepts used to construct syntactically correct diagrams. This is made possible by the grammar that is based on the language-specific alphabet. The grammar is defined by a start diagram and a set of rules. The rules are not restricted to be context-free; they are context-sensitive and may be enhanced with some application conditions. Moreover, the rules define the editing commands of the aimed Graphic Editor that is generated from the visual language specification consisting of an alphabet and a grammar. These rules can be applied to a given start diagram.

Start diagram A *start diagram* comprises symbols and connections that are uniquely instantiated from the alphabet. Due to the alphabet, each symbol consists of a certain symbol name and a symbol graphic, probably some symbol constraints. Each connection is defined by a directed connection between the involved symbol names and some constraints between the corresponding symbol graphics.

Rules and Rule Application A visual language *rule* consists mainly of a left hand side (LHS) and a right hand side (RHS). A mapping of symbols from the LHS to the RHS (see upper part of fig. 3) indicates that the mapped symbols are preserved when the rule is applied to a given diagram. The connections are mapped implicitly.

Applying a rule to a given diagram, the symbols of the LHS have to be mapped to the symbols of the diagram we want to transform. This mapping is called *match*. The connections are mapped implicitly if there are some. This implicit mapping is called "match completion".

The RHS of a rule contains another diagram comprising all the elements which persist through the transformation (namely those which are mapped from the left to the right) and all elements which are added through the transformation. The elements (symbols and connections) which appear in the LHS but not in the RHS will be deleted from the diagram where the rule is applied to.

Figure 3 illustrates the application of the rule that allows for the insertion of an association symbol. The two class symbols of its LHS are mapped to the

---

[4] Well-defined in GENGED means that the attribute can be handled like a "black box" which can be drawn somewhere in the diagram.

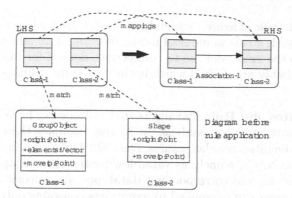

Figure3. Example rule `InsertAssociation` and its application to a diagram

class symbols of the diagram. Due to the mappings, the transformation process inserts the association symbol between these two class symbols. Note that it is also conceivable to map both class symbols of the rule's LHS to one class symbol of the diagram.

Negative Application Conditions Rules like that of figure 3 are sometimes not sufficient to describe the complete syntax of a visual language and the editing commands of the aimed Graphic Editor. Therefore, rules can be enhanced with *negative application conditions* (NACs) expressing that some constellations must not occur in the diagram where the rule is applied to. So one of our rules consists of a LHS, a RHS, a mapping from the LHS to the RHS and a (possibly empty) set of NACs, each one with a mapping from the LHS into the NAC diagram. The mappings into the NACs deliver the connection for the conditions.

In order to illustrate NACs let us have a look to figure 4 showing the rule for deleting a class symbol. This rule is enhanced with two NACs stating that the class symbol that is to be deleted is not connected with an association symbol, neither by the structural **from** connection nor by the **to** connection. For the application of a rule with NACs, we have to check whether one of the NACs can be satisfied after matching the LHS' elements to a diagram. If this is the case, the application will not take place.

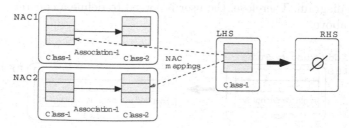

Figure4. Rule with negative application conditions

Assuming the rule of figure 4 without any NACs. We have to mention that the application of such a rule would lead to the deletion of all adherent association symbols due to the `from` and the `to` connections defined for the alphabet. This behavior is probably not desired which is the reason for defining the NACS.

Data Attributes and Rule Parameters Until now we have presented rules without data attributes for symbols, so in the examples there have been no association cardinalities nor class names. *Data attributes* may appear in the LHS, RHS and in the NACs, namely as variables, constants or complex expressions that are defined for the corresponding datatypes. In contrast to the rules, a diagram where rules can be applied to, comprises constants only.

Rule parameters allow for the external definition of data attributes. A rule parameter consists usually of a variable and a datatype. The rule is applied with user-defined values for the rule parameters. Then, the variables take the role of matched variables, i.e., they are matched with a constant. One example is given by figure 5 showing the rule for the insertion of a class symbol. The rule comprises a rule parameter with the variable *cn* of type *String*. This variable occurs in the NAC as well as in the RHS of the rule. Applying this rule, the user is asked to define a class name for the variable that is substituted by the name. Hence, the NAC states that the class symbol with this name must not be existent in the diagram where the rule is applied to.

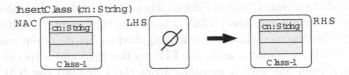

Figure5. Rule for inserting a class name

An example for complex expressions is given by figure 6. Each class symbol comprises a method list (modeled by the datatype *StringList*) that is connected to the lower rectangle of a class symbol. The rule that allows for adding a method to the method list of a class symbol is given by figure 6. It contains a variable for the user-defined method in its rule parameter. In its LHS the variable for the method list is illustrated together with the datatype. This variable together with the rule parameter variable are part of the available operation *add* denoted in the RHS of the rule. The operation is executed when the rule is to be applied to a given diagram. Therefore, the user is forced to define a concrete method as described above.

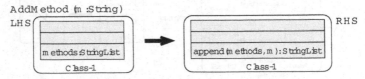

Figure6. Rule for adding methods to the method list

Until now we have suggested the most important concepts for visual language specifications and editing of diagrams. These concepts are implemented in the GENGED environment that is explained in the following section.

3   The GenGEd Environment

The GENGED environment comprises two major components: the *Alphabet Editor* and the *Grammar Editor* (see fig. 7), each editor corresponds to the respective part of the visual language, namely the alphabet and the grammar. To assure the graphically correct drawing of diagrams both editors use the constraint solver PARCON [Gri96]. The transformation of diagrams via rule application is done by the graph transformation system AGG [TER99].

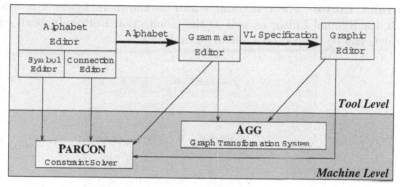

Figure7. Overview about the GENGED environment

Simply speaking, the specification of a Graphic Editor for a visual language using GENGED works like this:

1. We define the symbols and connections of a specific visual language using the Alphabet Editor.
2. The final alphabet is taken as an input to the Grammar Editor which then generates simple insertion/deletion rules. Those rules are to be used (in the notion of editor commands) to construct more complex visual language rules and to define a start diagram for the visual language.
3. The final visual language specification, consisting of the alphabet, the visual language rules and the start diagram, are then fed into a parameterized Graphic Editor. The user-defined editing commands of this editor ("insert", "delete" etc.) are built from the grammar rules.

The GENGED environment is implemented in Java, also is the AGG system. Because the PARCON constraint solver – implemented in Objective-C – is only available for Linux and Solaris, GENGED runs only on these two platforms. A prototype is available for download at

http://cs.tu-berlin.de/~genged.

3.1   The Alphabet Editor

The *Alphabet Editor* is a bundling of two minor editors – the *Symbol Editor* (see fig. 9) and the *Connection Editor* (see fig. 10). The Alphabet and Connection Editors feature the usual GUI elements like a menu and toolbar to add symbols, data attributes, connections and constraints and a statusbar to display various useful information. The appearance of the editors is the same: on the left side there is a structure display of the objects we work on showing primitives and constraints. On the right there is a graphical display of the selected symbol or connection. This graphical display is already constraint-based, so each added constraint will be checked for solvability and will be visualized immediately after creation. Both editors use a further subcomponent, the *Constraint Editor*.

Constraint Editor   The constraint editor as shown in figure 8 is available in both, the Symbol Editor as well as the Connection Editor. In both editors, constraints can be defined on arbitrary primitives.

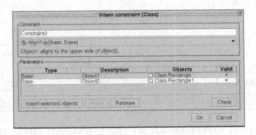

Figure8. The Constraint Editor

The constraint solver PARCON that is used for constraint solving permits only the definition of very low level constraints. We have enhanced these constraints by a *high-level constraint language* (HLCL). This language features extensibility, types over the graphical primitives and built-in definitions for user dialogs. Here is an example for an **above**-Constraint taken from the extendable HLC database:

```
constraint Above(Base a, Base b) {
  Dialog(a, "English", "Object1");
  Dialog(a, "Deutsch", "Objekt1");
  Dialog(b, "English", "Object2");
  Dialog(b, "Deutsch", "Objekt2");
  Description("English", "Object1 lies above object2.");
  Description("Deutsch", "Objekt1 liegt \"{u}ber Objekt2.");
  a.lt.y < b.lt.y - a.h; }
```

The graphical attributes of the primitives being part of the constraint (width, height, x/y-location, etc.) can be accessed using a path notation. The HLCL is easily editable and extendable by editing a simple text file.

All constraints we define in one of the GENGED Alphabet Editors are immediately applied to the symbol(s). When the user scales or moves single objects in the display all constraints are automatically solved, which leads possibly to a new arrangement of the whole graphic in the display. Constraints which are unsolvable will be marked for overworking.

Symbol Editor The Symbol Editor is shown in figure 9. It works similar to well-known vector graphic editors except that the grouping of symbols is handled as described in section 2 – using constraints to connect the primitives in a graphic. Implemented primitives available are lines, polylines, bezier curves, rectangles, ellipses, images (GIF/JPEG), text, invisible boxes (which can serve as placeholders) and connection points which can be used to define complex connections in the Connection Editor. The primitives' properties like color, line width or text properties can be edited.

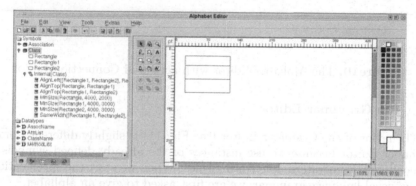

Figure9. The Alphabet Editor with activated Symbol Editor

Data attributes appear as independent graphical objects. From the constraint view they are just "boxes with something in it". Each datatype is implemented by a unique Java class. Similar to a JavaBean, the datatype class has to provide methods for drawing the attributes and for changing the properties (like text font, text size or, for a list of strings, the arrangement of text elements) either interactively (using an editing dialog) or by calling a changing method. Other methods can be used to build complex Java expressions which will be evaluated during rule application (see section 3.2).

Currently implemented are the classes `StringDT`, `StringListDT`, `IntegerDT` and `FloatDT`. Using the given interface for datatype classes and the existing implementations as templates, the designer of a visual language may add own datatype classes.

Connection Editor Concerning the constraint definitions, the Connection Editor as illustrated in figure 10 works in just the same way as the Symbol Editor.

In contrast to the Symbol Editor, we can select any two symbols as source and target of the connection that is to be defined. Again the Constraint Editor is used to define constraints between the primitives of the involved symbol graphics. Note that the connection according to the structural relationship connects two symbols (namely the symbol names). In contrast to the concepts, in the current implementation the connection constraints can be defined between the primitives only, and not between the boxes enclosing the symbol graphics.

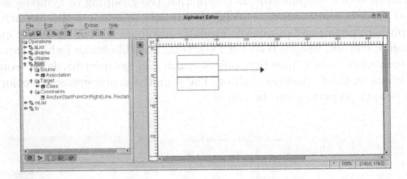

Figure10. The Alphabet Editor with activated Connection Editor

3.2   The Grammar Editor

The behavior of the Grammar Editor (see Fig. 11) is slightly different from the Alphabet Editor because we use instances of the already defined symbols and connections to generate simple editing rules. When we start the specification of a new visual language grammar, we are first asked to give an alphabet.

Simple Rules and Structural Correctness From the alphabet, some simple rules are generated that are the editing commands of the grammar editor. These rules reflect the structure of the alphabet in the sense that they are "structurally correct". This property has been described in section 2 when we talked about connections. This means that on the one hand every single rule diagram is structurally correct and that on the other hand every rule does a "'structurally correct"' transformation, i.e. correct diagrams are transformed into correct diagrams. An example for a generated rule `InsertAssociation` is given in figure 3. Note that some of these automatically generated rules may be already a rule of the intended grammar.

Data Attributes and Rule Parameters For the data attribute part of the visual language specification we have means to define rule parameters as well as to define and change the expressions for the transformation of datatypes. Because of the data attributes belonging to Java classes, the attribute expressions depicted in section 2 are in fact Java expressions which are evaluated to get an object of the corresponding data attribute class. For example, the expression on the right hand side in figure 6 will look like this: `methods.append(m)`. Applying this rule to a given diagram, the user is first asked to match the class symbol of the rule's LHS to one class symbol in the diagram. Then, the editor window for the data attribute `StringDT` (the rule parameter) will pop up. When the user has given a value for the parameter, the expression on the RHS will be evaluated during transformation. In this example, the user-defined method is added to the method list of the class symbol.

The Graphical User Interface The Grammar Editor is shown in figure 11. On the left hand side there is a structure view of the grammar which contains all the names of the automatically generated rules, the start diagram and the rules we build using the Grammar Editor. The names of NACs which may occur in a rule are written below the rule names. On the right hand side we have two parts: The upper part shows the LHS and RHS of a rule which will be used for transformation. The NACs (selected in the structure view) can be displayed, too. The lower part is the *work display*: Here we built the LHS and RHS (or LHS and a NAC respectively) of a new rule, add mappings between the two rule sides and edit the rule parameters.

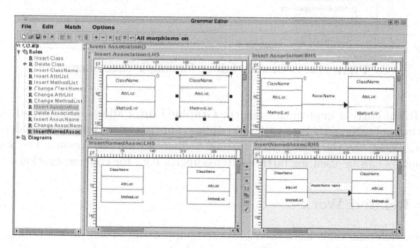

Figure11. The Grammar Editor

There are two toolbars: The main toolbar (below the menu) is used to add and delete rules and NACs and to provide save/load and other main functionality. Furthermore, the main toolbar is used to define a match from the rule which is to be applied onto one of the work diagrams and to trigger the transformation. The smaller toolbar (in the work display) provides functionality to add/remove mappings in the work rule and to edit the rule parameters.

Because the graphical displays which are used in the Grammar Editor are derived from those in the Alphabet Editor, they provide constraint solving, moving and scaling of symbols and also single graphical primitives in the same fashion.

3.3   Generating a Graphic Editor

The final step is to export a set of rules and a start diagram into a visual language grammar[5]. Then, the Graphic Editor that is a parameterized editor takes this grammar and uses the grammar rules to provide the language-specific editing commands. The Graphic Editor for our simple class diagram language is is illustrated in figure 12.

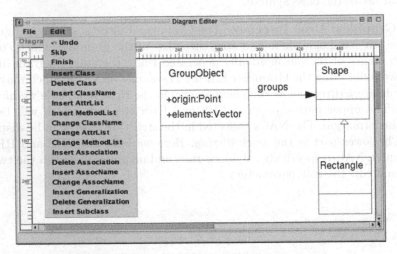

Figure12. A Graphic Editor for simple class diagrams

In the current implementation, the Graphic Editor allows for syntax-directed editing only. Nevertheless, each edited diagram comprises two levels of description. These are the *logical* structure of a diagram and its layout. The logical structure can be used for further extensions as, e.g., for code generation.

4   Related Work

Many different tools have been proposed supporting visual programming. The reader is referred to [Shu88,Cha90,BGL95] giving a broad overview. However, most existing tools are developed for specific application purposes. Moreover, the tools allow for visual programming and not for modeling languages like GENGED. This means that the visual means are tightly integrated with the corresponding programming environment. In contrast to such environments, GENGED is a generic framework based on a user-defined visual alphabet and a grammar.

The purpose of GENGED is the visual definition of visual languages. From the definition a language-specific Graphic Editor is generated. Some other

---

[5] The alphabet is added automatically, so in fact we export a visual language *specification*.

approaches with the same purpose are to mention. These are e.g., PROGRES [SWZ99], DIAGEN [MV95], and VLCC [CODL95]. We have to mention that a comparison between GENGED, PROGRESand DIAGEN according to the underlying theory as well as the tools is given in [BTMS99]. A brief summary is given below.

PROGRES is a graph-based framework allowing for programming with rules and for the generation of prototypes. The PROGRES environment offers assistance for creating, analyzing, compiling, and debugging graph transformation specifications. Outside the PROGRES environment such a specification can be executed in a stand-alone prototype. In PROGRES, visual languages can be specified using the visual means of graphs. It is not possible to specify a visual language under consideration of the appearances of symbols as it can be done using GENGED.

DIAGEN is a diagram editor generator. The input of the generator is a textual specification of a visual language. In general, visual statements are difficult to describe textually because of their graphical structure. This is due to the fact that multi-dimensional representations have to be coded into one-dimensional strings. Moreover, the DIAGEN approach is concerned with a restricted kind of context-sensitive grammars. Hence, the class diagram language, e.g., cannot be specified using the DIAGEN approach [BTMS99].

G.Costagliola et al. introduced the VLCC-environment [CODL95] supporting the visual definition of visual languages, too. A symbol editor can be used to define terminal and non-terminal symbols. The defined symbols are then available within a production editor allowing the definition of context-free positional grammar rules. In contrast, we use grammars which are not restricted to be context-free.

5 Summary

In this contribution we informally introduced visual languages as they can be defined using the GENGED environment. Similar to textual languages, a visual language is defined by an alphabet and a grammar. Correspondingly, the GENGED environment comprises an Alphabet Editor and a Grammar Editor. These editors as well as a generated Graphic Editor are described. An in-depth description of the design and the implementation of the environment can be found in [Sch99] and [Nie99], the underlying theory is depicted in [Bar00].

Despite the prototypical character of the environment, there are several case studies. These are restricted kinds of visual languages like statecharts, class diagrams, sequence diagrams and Nassi-Shneiderman diagrams. Some more are yet to come. Thereby, we investigate how to integrate several visual languages similar to the UML in order to generate not only a Graphic Editor but a visual environment. Future work is concerned with a major overhaul of the Grammar Editor, simplifying the rule definition. Another idea is to change the generated Graphic Editor into a JavaBean, thus providing other tools (e.g., the AGG system) with a generic graphic display and making the underlying structure of a diagram accessible. We are also planning to allow for more freedom in diagram editing, combining syntax-directed and freehand editing. The latter one is concerned with parsing.

References

Bar00.   R. Bardohl. *Visual Definition of Visual Languages based on Algebraic Graph Transformation.* PhD thesis, Technische Universität Berlin, Berlin, 2000. 457, 458, 459, 469

BGL95.   Margaret M. Burnett, Adele Goldberg, and Ted G. Lewis, editors. *Visual Object-Oriented Programming: Concepts and Environments.* Manning Publications Co., Greenwich, 1995. 468

BNS00.   R. Bardohl, M. Niemann, and M. Schwarze. GENGED – A Development Environment for Visual Languages. In *Application of Graph Transformations with Industrial Relevance*, LNCS. Springer, 2000. 457

BTMS99.   R. Bardohl, G. Taentzer, M. Minas, and A. Schürr. Application of Graph Transformation to Visual Languages. In *[Roz99]*. 1999. 469

Cha90.   Shi-Kuo Chang, editor. *Principles of Visual Programming Systems.* International Editions. Prentice Hall, Englewood Cliffs, NJ, 1990. 468

CODL95.   G. Costagliola, S. Orefice, and A. De Lucia. Automatic Generation of Visual Programming Environments. *IEEE Computer*, 28(3):56–66, March 1995. 469

Gri96.   P. Griebel. *ParCon - Paralleles Lösen von grafischen Constraints.* PhD thesis, Paderborn University, February 1996. 463

Har87.   D. Harel. Statecharts: A visual formalism for complex systems. *Science of Computer Programming*, 8:231–274, 1987. 456

MV95.   M. Minas and G. Viehstaedt. Diagen: A generator for diagram editors providing direct manipulation and execution of diagrams. In *Proc. IEEE Symposium on Visual Languages*, pages 203–210, 1995. 469

Nie99.   M. Niemann. Konzeption und Implementierung eines generischen Grammatikeditors für visuelle Sprachen. Master's thesis, Technische Universität Berlin, 1999. 469

NS73.   I. Nassi and B. Shneiderman. Flowchart techniques for structured programming. *SIGPLAN Notices*, 8(8), 1973. 457

Rat98.   Rational Software Corporation. UML – Unified Modeling Language. Technical report, Rational Software Corporation, 2800 San Tomas Expressway, Santa Clara, CA 95051-0951, 1998. http://www.rational.com/uml. 456, 457

Roz99.   G. Rozenberg, editor. *Handbook of Graph Grammars and Computing by Graph Transformations, Volume 2: Applications, Languages and Tools.* World Scientific Publishing, Singapore, 1999. 470

Sch99.   M. Schwarze. Konzeption und Implementierung eines generischen Alphabeteditors für visuelle Sprachen. Master's thesis, Technische Universität Berlin, 1999. 469

Shu88.   N.C. Shu, editor. *Visual Programming.* Van Nostrand Reinhold, New York, 1988. 468

SWZ99.   A. Schürr, A.J. Winter, and A. Zündorf. The PROGRES Approach: Language and Tool Environment. In *[Roz99]*. 1999. 469

TER99.   G. Taentzer, C. Ermel, and M. Rudolf. The AGG Approach: Language and Tool Environment. In *[Roz99]*. 1999. 463

VIP: A Visual Editor and Compiler for v-Promela*

Moataz Kamel[1] and Stefan Leue[2]

[1] Department of Electrical and Computer Engineering, University of Waterloo
Waterloo, Ontario N2L 3G1, Canada
m2kamel@uwaterloo.ca
http://fee.uwaterloo.ca/~m2kamel
[2] Institut für Informatik
Albert-Ludwigs-Universität Freiburg
D-79110 Freiburg, Germany
http://www.informatik.uni-freiburg.de/~leue
leue@informatik.uni-freiburg.de

Abstract. We describe the *Visual Interface to* PROMELA (VIP) tool
that we have recently implemented. VIP supports the visual editing and
maintenance of v-Promela models. v-Promela is a visual, object-oriented
extension to PROMELA, the input language to the SPIN model checker.
We introduce the v-Promela notation as supported by the VIP editor,
discuss PROMELA code generation, and describe the process of property
validation for the resulting models. Our discussion centers around two
case studies, a call processing system and the CORBA GIOP protocol.

1 Introduction

As Davis argues in [2], a significant return of investment can be expected when
investing resources into the early stages of the software design cycle: in particular,
fixing design flaws at the requirements stage can be 200 times less expensive
than fixing them at the maintenance stage. Even corrections at the architectural
design stage can be 50 times more cost efficient than at the maintenance stage.
The inherent complexity of concurrent real-time systems makes it necessary
to employ mechanized, formally supported methods to analyze early life-cycle
artifacts. In this context the main questions to be answered are whether the
requirements are consistent and correct with the intended behavior of the system,
and whether the system's design correctly implements the requirements.

It has been shown that state-based modeling and automatic model checking
is an effective tool for answering these questions for concurrent reactive systems.
Recent advances in model checking research have made verification based on
state space exploration more feasible for realistic software problems [6,7]. However, the introduction of formal methods in the software engineering process is

---

* The work documented in this paper was largely performed while the second author
was with the University of Waterloo. We are currently working on a public release
version of the VIP tool, interested parties are requested to contact the authors.

S. Graf and M. Schwartzbach (Eds.): TACAS/ETAPS 2000, LNCS 1785, pp. 471–486, 2000.
© Springer-Verlag Berlin Heidelberg 2000

often hampered by textual interfaces laden with mathematical notations. Visual formalisms, on the other hand, appear to enjoy broad acceptance in engineering practice.

With the ever increasing complexity of concurrent, reactive systems that continue to be designed, the requirements and high-level design models are becoming sizeable artifacts themselves. In order to facilitate the model development process, we propose the alignment of the modeling language of a state-of-the art formal analysis tool with the state of the art visual, object-oriented hierarchical notations used in current software development. This has the benefit of fostering maintainability and evolvability of these models while increasing the chances that the models actually express the intentions of the designers and increasing the acceptance of formal analysis in the practical software engineering community.

In this paper we present the prototype of a graphical user interface-based tool called the *Visual Interface for Promela* (VIP) that we have developed. VIP supports a visual language called v-Promela which is the graphical extension of PROMELA, the input language for the model checker SPIN [8]. The tool provides graphical editing capabilities for v-Promela models and generates standard PROMELA code from the graphical representation. In the process of describing VIP we also show how modeling of complex real-time systems for the purpose of formal analysis can be based on a state-of-the art visual object-oriented notation, and that efficient tool support can be provided.

Related Work. VIP supports visual modeling using v-Promela. The v-Promela notation has first been described in [13] and [5]. The design of v-Promela was guided by a number of desiderata. First, we desired to use PROMELA/SPIN validation technology without any changes to the existing model checker. Hence every feature of v-Promela had to be compilable into Promela. Next, we were interested in a visual notation that would capture both structural and behavioral modeling aspects. We were also interested in providing hierarchical modeling and object-oriented concepts. Finally, we have attempted to comply as far as possible with existing or emerging software design methodology standards for concurrent real-time systems. As a consequence, the v-Promela notation inherited largely from the UML-RT notation [16]. UML-RT, which evolved from the ROOM notation [15], is supported by an industrial-strength case tool (ROSE-RT) and is expected to be a prominent player in the real-time systems domain in coming years. Some of the syntactic as well as some of the semantic aspects of UML-RT are not completely specified at this time. The authors of UML-RT suggest that these missing aspects can be derived from the definitions of the syntax and semantics of ROOM as given in [15]. The development of the VIP tool is described in more detail in [10] which also discusses some modifications of the original v-Promela proposal.

Organization of the Paper. In Section 2 we describe the architecture of the VIP tool, and we illustrate the use of VIP in Section 3 through an example. In Section 4 we discuss the v-Promela compiler implemented in VIP. In Section 5 we show how to perform property validation in the context of our approach. Finally, in Section 6 we discuss further issues related to the implementation of VIP, and we conclude in Section 7.

2   VIP Architecture

To support the editing and maintenance of v-Promela models we have developed the VIP (*Visual Interface to Promela*) tool. Figure 1 illustrates the functional architecture of VIP. We will describe the functionality of the VIP editor in the following section. The edited v-Promela models are compiled into Promela code by VIP, and the resulting Promela models can be validated by the SPIN model checker. SPIN error traces can then be re-interpreted in the context of the original v-Promela model. Currently, the re-interpretation has to be done manually. To store v-Promela models, we currently use JAVA class serialization. The use of this feature of the JAVA Development Toolkit saved considerable development time, however, to allow better future expandability we are currently working on implementing storage and retrieval functionality based on XML [17] schema definitions and an XML parser.

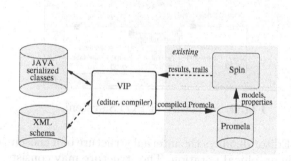

Fig. 1. VIP tool architecture.   **Fig. 2.** POTS Model editor.

3   Modeling in VIP

In this Section we describe the main features of the VIP graphical user interface. As a running example we use a simplified *Plain Old Telephony System* (POTS) call processing problem. The example consists of two User processes and two PhoneHandler processes contained in the environment of the POTS system. [1]

---

[1] In order to obtain models that can be translated into Promela all v-Promela models must be closed systems. Therefore, the environment behavior must be modeled as part of the system.

The **User** processes represent the behavior of the telephones which communicate with **PhoneHandler** processes which represent the call processing software inside the switch. The **PhoneHandler** processes are responsible for responding to events from the **User** processes as well as communicating with other **PhoneHandlers** in order to establish a voice connection.

3.1   Structural Modeling

Model Editor. The Model Editor is the starting point for creating v-Promela models. It allows the user to define the basic elements of a v-Promela model: capsule classes, protocol classes, and data classes. From the model editor the user can open editors for each one of the above mentioned basic elements. From the model editor, the user can also save the model or generate Promela code. Figure 2 illustrates the model editor for the POTS example. It specifies three capsule classes, three protocol classes, and a data class.

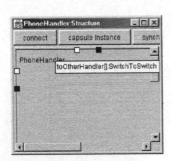

Fig. 3.   **PhoneHandler** capsule structure.

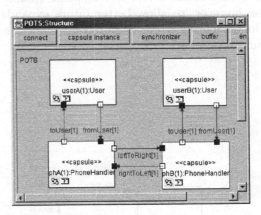

Fig. 4. Structure of POTS system.

Structure Editor The Structure Editor displays the internal structure of a chosen capsule class using the v-Promela graphical notation. The structure may consist of other capsule instances, buffers, synchronizers, ports, and connectors. Changes to the structure of the capsule class are automatically reflected in other views that contain an instance of the capsule class.

Figure 4 represents the POTS system structure. Concurrent objects are called *capsules* in accordance with the UML-RT terminology. The POTS system consists of a high-level capsule class called **POTS**. It is decomposed into four contained capsules as indicated by the capsule references in Figure 4. None of the contained capsule classes is further refined. However, Figure 3 illustrates the internal structure definition of the **PhoneHandler** capsule class. The black and white boxes at the border of the capsule denote in and outbound **ports**, respectively. Ports represent message passing interfaces for capsules. In contrast to v-Promela where ports are either uni- or bi-directional, all ports in VIP are uni-directional. Incorporating bi-directional ports into VIP is part of future improvements which are in-progress. The type of a port is a protocol class, see below for a discussion of their definition. Ports need to be connected to ports in other capsule instances to enable messages to be exchanged. *Connectors*, as indicated by the labeled arrows in Figure 4, are used to establish connections between ports. The connector label shows the name of the connector and the message buffering capacity of the connector within brackets. Only ports of identical type can be connected, and a connector must join an out-port to an in-port.

A capsule instance can have an associated replication factor that is greater or equal to 1. The replication factor specifies the number of capsule instances that will be generated at instantiation time. For simplicity of presentation all capsule instances in the POTS example have a replication factor of 1.

Fig. 5. Protocol class definition for POTS model.

Protocol Classes. A Protocol class consists of a name and a list of message classes. Each message class has a name which identifies the message type and an associated message body type. Figure 5 illustrates the protocol class definition for the POTS example. The names of the protocol classes as well as the message class names are indicative of signals passed in a telephone switch.

Fig. 6. Dataclass definition and usage in protocol class definitions.

Data Classes. Figure 6 illustrates the definition of data classes in VIP based on the available Promela data types. If a data class is mapped onto a basic

Promela data type it merely serves as an alias for that type. However, a data class definition can also take advantage of the `typedef` construct in Promela. Figure 6 shows the definition of the data class `subscriber_number` as a record consisting of a short integer field `area_code` and an integer field `phone_number`. Compared to the data type capabilities of languages like UML-RT the v-Promela possibilities are rather limited. However, this restriction is necessary to allow exhaustive model-checking by SPIN. The right side of Figure 6 shows how a data class definition is used to define a message body type. The `dialdigit` message of the `UserToSwitch` protocol is defined to have a message body type of `subscriber_number`.

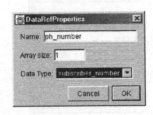

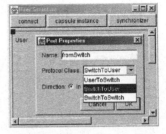

Fig. 7. Data object definition.

Fig. 8. Defining ports based on protocol class definitions.

Data Objects. Data objects are instances of data classes that can be used in expressions. They are defined as attributes of capsule classes. Figure 7 illustrates the definition of a data object `ph_number` within the `User` capsule class as an instance of the `subscriber_number` data class. A data object may also be defined to be an array.

Buffers and Synchronizers. UML-RT is very rigid in the way that it allows inter-process communication to happen. Communication between processes takes place exclusively through point-to-point message exchanges via ports. In contrast, Promela allows arbitrary sets of processes to share channels or to synchronize via rendez-vous channels. In order to permit the more general modeling approach that Promela makes possible, v-Promela introduces the concepts of *buffers* and *synchronizers*. These concepts have been used in the CORBA GIOP example that is described in Section 5 and we have used them to model producer-consumer problems as well as semaphores.

3.2 Behavior Modeling

Behavior in v-Promela is modeled using hierarchical, communicating extended finite state machines.

Hierarchical State-Machines. The behavior editor in VIP allows for editing the
state machine associated with a capsule class. In the POTS example, only the
User and PhoneHandler capsules have state machines associated with them, as
illustrated in Figures 9 and 10. The top-level state of any state machine has the
name TOP. To illustrate the hierarchical nature of state machines in VIP, the
refinement of the await_digit state of Figure 9 is shown in Figure 10. It should
be noted that in the current implementation of VIP we consider two states with
identical name labels to denote different states. We use various icons inside the
state symbols to express attributes of the states. As an example, the circle in the
lower left corner of the idle state in Figure 9 indicates that this state has been
marked as a valid end state, and the icons in the await_digit state indicate
that this state has a refinement and that entry code has been defined for it.

Circled X and E symbols indicate exit and entry points for multi-level transitions, respectively. Typical for the use of hierarchical state machines is the
occurrence of *chained* and *group* transitions. For instance, if the PhoneHandler
capsule is in any state contained within the await_digit state this state may
be exited if the transition labeled onhook_ in its super state executes. v-Promela
and VIP allow for explicit return or return to history semantics for hierarchical
state machines. If an entry point is not connected to a contained state, the return to history semantics will be chosen in the event of an incoming transition.
Otherwise, the explicit return to a contained state is indicated by an arrow from
the entry point to the contained target state.

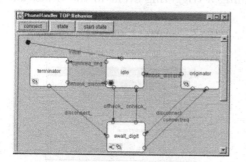

Fig. 9. PhoneHandler TOP state.

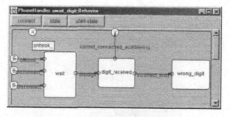

Fig. 10. PhoneHandler
TOP:await_digit state.

Transition code. The labels on the state transitions in the previous state transition diagrams have no executable semantics, they are merely used to identify
the transition and to enhance readability of the state machine model. To attach
enabling conditions and executable code to a state machine transition we open
the transition's property editor, as shown in Figures 11 and 12. There are two
formats for specifying transition code. Figure 11 shows the UML style of defining transition code. The code consists first of an *event* specification which in our
implementation consists of the reception of a message from a port. In the editor
we use pull-down menus that allow the user first to select a port from which the

message is to be received, and second to select a message type from the list of all messages that are allowable for the selected port. A *guard* can be specified as a side-effect free Promela expression. The chosen semantics is that only if the specified message is receivable and the guard is true will the transition be taken. The *action* can be an arbitrary Promela code fragment and will typically contain a send statement for a message. Care has to be taken that the code specified here is always executable and does not contain internal control flow loops. The current version of VIP does not parse the action code and hence it is the responsibility of the modeler to ensure that the code is meaningful. The second format, illustrated in Figure 12 shows the more liberal way of defining a transition. Unlike UML-RT, v-Promela transitions can be triggered by the executability of any Promela statement, in this case a boolean expression specified in the event clause. If the event clause evaluates to true then the action part will be executed. In this example a message of type busytone is sent to the port toUser.

As illustrated in Figure 13, state entry and exit code will be executed whenever a state is entered or exited, respectively. In our example this means that from whichever state we enter the await_digit state we will apply a dialtone signal to the user. This has bearing on the format in which transition code is specified. It could be argued that transition code could be specified by simply allowing an arbitrary Promela statement to be attached to a transition. However, exit code should be executed prior to executing the transition code, which would be impossible if we were not distinguishing a triggering event in the transition code.

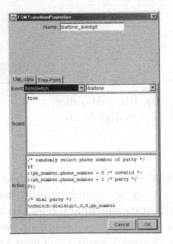

Fig. 11. Promela code in action portion of transition definition.

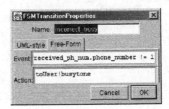

Fig. 12. Free-form transition definition.

Fig. 13. Entry code definition.

4   The VIP Compiler

The basic principles of the Promela code generation are that capsules are mapped onto proctypes, protocols onto `mtype` declarations, and that ports with their connectors as well as buffers and synchronizers are mapped onto channel declarations. Message bodies are implemented as record structures (`typedefs` in Promela parlance) with one field for every message type that the protocol comprises. Data objects are mapped onto PROMELA variables. For a more extensive discussion we refer to [14,5,10].

Ports. Ports form part of the interface to capsule classes. Accordingly, the VIP compiler generates ports as channel type parameters in the parameter list of the corresponding capsule class proctype. On instantiation of a proctype, the VIP compiler generates the proper arguments to bind the correct connectors to the ports. For instance, in the POTS example the `POTS` proctype contains a channel declaration of the form `chan toUser2105717128 = [1] of SwitchToUser` [2]. The definition of the `User` proctype declares two ports (from-Switch and toSwitch): `proctype User(chan fromSwitch, toSwitch )`. In the body of the POTS proctype, the User proctype is instantiated and its ports are bound by the code `run User( toUser2105717128, fromUser2016588168 )`. This scheme has the desirable property that ports can be referenced within the proctype without regard for which channel may be connected to it.

State Machine Encoding. The v-Promela control states could be implemented in two ways: a) by using Promela variables, or b) by using Promela control state labels and `goto` statements. Measurements documented in [10] suggest that, while the state vector size for both variants is identical, the state space size for variant a) is about twice the size for variant b). We therefore implemented variant b) in VIP. The state name label is chosen such that it starts with the state name in the v-Promela model and the VIP compiler adds a numeric sequence to disambiguate states with identical v-Promela names.

Transition Code. The code generated for transitions specified in the UML style starts with checking whether the specified message reception event is available by polling the relevant channel. The result is conjoined with the evaluation of the guard which yields the transition's enabling condition. The firing of the transition will cause the sequential execution of the following code fragments: first the message reception is performed, next the exit code of the current state, then the action code associated with the transition, followed by entry code for the new state and finally the `goto` into the successor control state. Promela does not allow polling the state of synchronous rendez-vous channels. Therefore, in such cases the first part of the transition code consists only of the rendez-vous communication, and any specified guard will be ignored. Figure 14 illustrates

---

[2] The VIP compiler disambiguates element names by concatenating a unique identifier to the name.

this mechanism for the offhook transition from the idle state of Figure 9. To enhance comprehensibility of the code, the compiler automatically inserts meaningful comments even if no entry or exit code has been specified. Note that the transition modeled here is a chained multi-level transition from the idle state into the wait sub-state contained in the await_digit state (c.f. Figure 10), and that the entry code defined for await_digit, i.e., toUser!dialtone is executed during this transition.

```
if
idle1723158139:
:: fromUser?[offhook] && true->
   fromUser?UserToSwitch_msg;
   /* exit idle */
   /* action offhook_ */
   /* entry await_digit */
   toUser!dialtone;
   /* entry wait */
   goto wait2091208315
...
fi
```

```
if
/* correct_connectreq_audiblering */
:: received_ph_num.phone_number == 1->
   /* exit digit_received */
   /* action
   correct_connectreq_audiblering */
   toOtherHandler!connectreq;
   toUser!audiblering;
   /* exit await_digit */
   /* action connectreq */
   /* entry originator */
   /* action untitled */
   /* entry party_ringing */
   goto party_ringing1956295048
```

Fig. 14. Transition code for UML-style.

Fig. 15. Transition code for free-form chained transition

Figure 15 illustrates the generated code for the VIP free form format for transition code specification. In this case the enabling condition is specified by an equality test on the value of a variable. The example also illustrates a chained transition, i.e., one that crosses nesting levels in the hierarchical state machine. All relevant entry and exit code specified along the transition chain is inlined into the transition code which, in certain cases, allows it to be processed as one atomic action[3].

Priority Schemes for Group Transitions. The implementation of group transitions depends on the priority model the user wishes to adopt. Three possible transition priority schemes are possible. In the first scheme, higher-level (group) transitions could take priority over lower-level transitions. Alternatively, lower-level transitions could take priority over higher-level transitions. Finally, both high and low-level transitions can be given equal priority. In VIP, all three priority schemes have implemented with the user having control over which scheme is used. Equal priority is the default in VIP. It is implemented simply by combining both high-level and low-level transition code as separate conditions in the same

---

[3] Promela allows non-blocking statements to be grouped into an atomic clause which can improve model checking efficiency.

```
ringing62399654:
{if
:: fromUser?[offhook] ...
fi } unless {
if
:: fromUser?[onhook]...
:: fromOtherHandler?[disconnect] ...
fi}
```

```
ringing62399654:
{if
:: fromUser?[onhook] ...
:: fromOtherHandler?[disconnect] ...
fi } unless {
if
:: fromUser?[offhook] ...
fi}
```

Fig. 16. Priority on grouptransition   **Fig. 17.** Priority on local transition

```
ringing2063158907:
if
:: fromUser?[offhook] ...
:: fromUser?[onhook] ...
:: fromOtherHandler?[disconnect] ...
fi
```

Fig. 18. Transition code with equal priority

`if ... fi` statement as illustrated in Figure 18. Promela semantics dictate that multiple enabled conditions in an `if` statement are chosen non-deterministically resulting in equal priority among alternatives. The other two priority schemes are implemented using the Promela `{A}unless{B}` construct which pre-empts statements in A if the statement in B becomes executable. The first priority scheme is implemented by placing high-level transition code in B and low-level code in A. The second scheme implements the reverse. Figures 16 and 17 illustrate both of these schemes. Note that only the non-pre-emptive scheme complies with the *run-to-completion* semantics of UML-RT as described in [15].

5 Property Validation

Property validation of VIP-synthesized models currently relies on using the SPIN model checker to analyze the generated Promela models. The interpretation of the validation results that SPIN produces in the context of the v-Promela model currently relies on manual interpretation. We discuss two validation case studies using VIP-generated Promela code.

Validation of POTS. The previously presented POTS model was designed with the intention of revealing most of the significant features of v-Promela as supported by VIP. As a consequence, little attention was paid to developing a flawless model of POTS. The described POTS model is not free of deadlock. We have labeled the `idle` state in the `PhoneHandler` process and the `on_hook` state in the `User` process as end-states and an end-state check in SPIN easily shows a trace that terminates with one process an invalid end-state. This is mainly due to the fact that we have not synchronized the User and PhoneHandler interactions. Thus, the User can repeatedly generate offhook and onhook event sequences that will eventually fill up the channel to the PhoneHandler. Also, call processing software is rarely "live", i.e., it only satisfies trivial liveness properties. A progress test in SPIN easily shows offhook and onhook cycles that do not imply system progress.

We therefore decided to answer the question of whether our POTS model was at all capable of doing it's very raison d'être, namely to connect two phones. In order to show that such a scenario exists, we formulate the converse property (namely, that the scenario does not exist) and hope that SPIN would refute the claim by showing us a trail to the contrary. The property we seek to prove is: "there exists a scenario in which both PhoneHandler processes are in the respective conversation states." The converse of the property is: "it is never the case that, at the same time, one PhoneHandler process reaches the conversation state for an originator and the other reaches the conversation state for a terminator." This property is represented by the LTL formula: !<>(p && q) where p and q are defined in SPIN by the state propositions:

    #define p (PhoneHandler[2]@conversation_orig1985130888)
    #define q (PhoneHandler[3]@conversation_term2034323067)

These expressions are referred to as *remote references* in Promela parlance. The expression PhoneHandler[2]@conversation_orig1985130888 is a boolean expression that evaluates to true if the process named PhoneHandler with process id equal to 2 is at the control state labeled conversation_orig1985130888.

Shortly after running the model checker on the above claim, an error trace was found. As expected, the error trace that SPIN found showed a scenario in which both Phone Handler processes were in the respective conversation states. The validation required matching appr. 448,000 states, 680,000 transitions and 45.5 MByte of memory.

Validation of CORBA GIOP. In a previous work we modeled and formally validated the Common Object Request Broker Architecture (CORBA) *General Inter-ORB Protocol (GIOP)* [4] using PROMELA/SPIN validation technology [11]. In that work, a hand-built model of GIOP was developed and validated in Promela. Subsequently, a v-Promela model of GIOP was created using the VIP tool. The v-Promela model of GIOP has the equivalent functionality of the scaled-down, hand-built model that was validated in [11]. It comprises two User, two Server, one GIOPClient and two GIOPAgent processes. The model structure is shown in Figure 19. Behavior of the various capsules is defined using non-hierarchical v-Promela state machines.

Certain limitations of the VIP tool caused difficulty in expressing the structure of the model in a natural way. For example, replication of capsule instances was not implemented in the tool at the time the experiments were run and therefore, multiple instances of capsules had to be explicitly shown in the model. Similarly, replicated ports and channels were also not available in the tool and thus, buffers were used to emulate the desired communication structure.

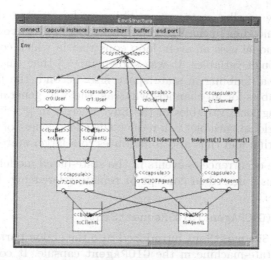

Fig. 19. Structure of the v-Promela GIOP model.

In the v-Promela model of GIOP, messages destined to the `GIOPClient` from either of the `User` processes are merged into a single buffer called `toClientU`. Similarly, messages destined for the `GIOPClient` from either of the `GIOPAgent` processes are merged into a buffer called `toClientL`. In the opposite direction, the `GIOPClient` may send messages to the `User` or `GIOPAgent` by placing them in the `toUser` and `toAgentL` buffers respectively. The messages are tagged with the Promela process id (pid) of the receiving process which only receives messages that contain its pid as a tag.

Table 1. Verification of safety and progress properties of hand-built versus automatically generated code.

Model	Property	State vector	Depth	States	Transitions	Memory usage
hand-built	safety	244 byte	119	77,261	92,566	17.697 Mb
VIP	safety	256 byte	171	8,704	13,236	4.590 Mb
hand-built	progress	248 byte	229	237,157	534,157	49.032 Mb
VIP	progress	260 byte	223	13,641	36,376	5.819 Mb

A basic safety properties verification run was carried out on the two models. This checked for invalid end-states and assertion violations. Equivalent assertions were placed in both models to check for invalid conditions such as reception of a `Reply` when no `Request` was outstanding. Also, end-state labels were placed in both models to identify valid end-states in each process. To validate progress properties a progress label was inserted into the models where the `User` process reaches the `UReplyRecvd` state. Both models ran with no violations on the safety as well as the progress properties. The results are shown in Table 1. As can be seen, the VIP generated code, although it required a larger state vector, resulted in a significantly smaller state space. This can be attributed to two factors. First, the state encoding of the VIP generated model uses goto statements while the hand-built model uses an event loop construct in which control states were represented through variables. It was shown in [10] that this difference alone can account for a doubling in state space size. Second, the hand-built model uses global variables for all channels whereas, the VIP generated code declares channels as being local variables of the Env process. In [10] it was also shown that the use of global variables can reduce the effectiveness of the partial order reduction algorithm and thus also contributes to a larger state space.

To model the occurrence of events in the state-based model checker SPIN we used the previously described concept of remote referencing. For example, the remote reference:

```
#define p (GIOPAgent[5]@SRequestSent)
```

refers to a label SRequestSent introduced into the action part of the transition code within a state-machine in the GIOPAgent capsule. It corresponds to the state after the SRequest message has been sent.

For the hand-built GIOP model, ten high-level requirements (HLR) were formulated and verified in [11]. Of the ten requirements, two were explicitly checked on the VIP generated code for the GIOP model. Some other requirements were checked implicitly through the use of assertions. All requirements that were checked were exhaustively verified successfully on the VIP generated model. This serves to confirm that the required behaviors present in the hand-built model are also present in the VIP model and that the VIP-generated code does not cause a prohibitive state space size penalty.

6   VIP Implementation

VIP was implemented in the Java programming language using Sun Microsystem's freely available *Java Development Toolkit* version 1.2. This allowed us to achieve a highly portable tool while leveraging Java's extensive GUI support. In developing VIP we adhered to a strict model-view separation which has enhanced flexibility and reuse in the design. To achieve maintainability, a quintessential requirement in the academic environment in which VIP was built, all class structures have been documented in UML. The graphical editors used in VIP are based on a separately developed component called Nexus. Other components such as windows and dialog boxes are based on standard Java class libraries.

As discussed in [10], VIP contains a set of approximately 30 well-formedness rules, the majority of which are checked whenever a model component is changed as a result of changes in the view. An example rule is that *"... a connector can only connect Ports that are protocol compatible..."*

7 Conclusions

We introduced the VIP tool which permits the creation and editing of v-Promela models as well as the compilation of these models into Promela code. We showed that the resulting models are analyzable using standard SPIN model checking technology.

The current version of VIP supports many features of v-Promela. A major thrust in research and development effort will be needed to develop VIP into a comprehensive CASE tool for requirements and high-level design. First, the aspect of property specification is currently not supported very strongly. We hope that an incorporation of ideas stemming from the temporal logic specification pattern approach [3] and from graphical interval logics [12] will facilitate the specification of requirements. We will also design ways of relieving the user from having to build hooks inside the synthesized Promela code, for example by introducing labels, by allowing property formulae to refer to states and variables in the v-Promela model. Next, we plan to feed the SPIN validation results back into the VIP environment including an animation of simulation and error traces inside VIP[4]. We also intend to explore linking the v-Promela models to other model checking tools by suitable intermediate representations as for instance the IF representation [1]. The question of the different priority schemes for implementing transition code has highlighted the need for parametric semantics in order to remain compatible with other modeling tools and methods. We plan, in particular, to develop a set of semantic options that will allow analyzing models which have semantics identical to UML-RT. Finally, some concepts from v-Promela such as structural and behavioral inheritance as well as data object scoping have not yet been implemented and we plan to add these as well.

We hope that by reconciling an industrial standard visual modeling language like UML-RT with the input language of a model checker, and by providing suitable tool support we can contribute to increasing the acceptance of formal methods in the practical software engineering community.

Acknowledgements

The Nexus component that VIP uses was jointly developed with Christopher Trudeau.

References

1. M. Bozga, L. Ghirvu, S. Graf, L. Mounier, and J. Sifakis. The Intermediate Representation IF: Syntax and semantics. Technical report, Vérimag, Grenoble, 1999. 485

2. A. M. Davis. *Software Requirements: Objects, Functions and States.* Prentice Hall, Upper Saddle River, New Jersey, USA, 1993. 471

---

[4] The feasibility of this has been demonstrated quite convincingly in [9]

3. Matthew B. Dwyer, George S. Avrunin, and James C. Corbett. Property Specification Patterns for Finite State Verification. In *Proceedings of the 2nd Workshop on Formal Methods in Software Practice*, March 1998. For access to the patterns catalog see URL http://www.cis.ksu.edu/~dwyer/spec-patterns.html. 485

4. Object Management Group. The Common Object Request Broker: Architecture and Specification. Revision 2.1, August 1997. 482

5. G. J. Holzmann and S. Leue. Towards v-Promala, a visual, object-oriented interface for Xspin. Unpublished manuscript, 1998. 472, 479

6. G. J. Holzmann and Margaret H. Smith. A practical method for the verification of event-driven software. In *Proc. ICSE99*, pages 597–607, Los Angeles, CA, USA, May 1999. invited. 471

7. G. J. Holzmann and Margaret H. Smith. Software model checking. In *Proc. FORTE/PSTV 1999*, pages 597–607, Beijing, China, October 1999. Kluwer. invited. 471

8. G.J. Holzmann. The model checker Spin. *IEEE Trans. on Software Engineering*, 23(5):279–295, May 1997. Special issue on Formal Methods in Software Practice. 472

9. W. Janssen, R. Mateescu, S Mauw, P. Fennema, and P. van der Stappen. Model checking for managers. In *Theoretical and Practical Aspects of SPIN Model Checking, Proceedings of the 5th and 6th International SPIN Workshops*, volume 1680 of *Lecture Notes in Computer Science*, pages 92–107. Springer Verlag, September 1999. 485

10. M. Kamel. On the visual modeling and verification of concurrent systems. Master's thesis, University of Waterloo, 1999. Available from URL http://fee.uwaterloo.ca/~m2kamel/research/thesis.ps. 472, 479, 484

11. M. Kamel and S. Leue. Formalization and Validation of the General Inter-ORB Protocol (GIOP) using Promela and Spin. *Software Tools for Technology Transfer*, 1999. To appear. 482, 484

12. G. Kutty, Y. S. Ramakrishna, L. E. Moser, L. K. Dillon, and P. M. Melliar-Smith. A graphical interval logic toolset for verifying concurrent systems. In C. Courcoubetis, editor, *Computer Aided Verification, 5th International Conference, CAV'93*, volume 697 of *Lecture Notes in Computer Science*, pages 138–153. Springer Verlag, 1993. 485

13. S. Leue and G. Holzmann. v-Promela: A Visual, Object-Oriented Language for SPIN. In *Proceedings of the 2nd IEEE Symposium on Object-Oriented Real-Time Distributed Computing (ISORC'99), Saint Malo, France*, pages 14 – 23. IEEE Computer Society Press, May 1999. 472

14. S. Leue and G. Holzmann. v-Promela: A Visual, Object-Oriented Language for SPIN. In *Proceedings of the 2nd IEEE Symposium on Object-Oriented Real-Time Distributed Computing ISORC'99*, pages 14–23. IEEE Computer Society, May 1999. 479

15. B. Selic, G. Gullekson, and P.T. Ward. *Real-Time Object-Oriented Modelling*. John Wiley & Sons, Inc., 1994. 472, 481

16. B. Selic and J. Rumbaugh. Using UML for modeling complex real-time systems. http://www.objectime.com, March 1998. 472

17. W3C. Extensible Markup Language (XML) - W3C Recommendation. http://www.w3.org/TR/REC-xml, February 1998. 473

A Comparison of Two Verification Methods for Speculative Instruction Execution*

Tamarah Arons and Amir Pnueli

The John von Neumann Minerva Center for Verification of Reactive Systems,
Weizmann Institute of Science, Rehovot, Israel
{tamarah,amir}@wisdom.weizmann.ac.il

Abstract. In this paper we describe and compare two methodologies for verifying the correctness of a speculative out-of-order execution system with interrupts. Both methods are deductive (we use PVS) and are based on refinement. The first proof is by direct refinement to a sequential system; the second proof combines refinement with induction over the number of retirement buffer slots.

1 Introduction

Modern out-of-order super-scalar microprocessors use dynamic scheduling to increase the number of instructions executed per cycle. These processors maintain a fixed-size window into the instruction stream, analyzing the instructions in the window to determine which can be executed out of order to improve performance. Branch prediction and register renaming are employed in order to keep the window full, while result-buffering techniques maintain the in-order-execution model required by the architecture.

In this paper we discuss two *refinement*-based proofs of the correctness of such processors. Our model is based on the Tomasulo algorithm in [13,4] and [6], with modifications for in-order-retirement and speculative instruction prediction adapted from [5]. This paper is a continuation of the work on out-of-order execution presented in [4,2] and [10]. We extend the methodology of these papers to deal with exceptions and speculative instruction execution, while also presenting a new, inductive, methodology. Both proofs have been verified using the PVS [9] theorem prover[1].

In the first proof, which we refer to as the *direct* proof, we use a top-down methodology to generate and prove the system invariants needed to prove that our speculative system refines a sequential system. Starting with the final invariant to be proved, this methodology allows the user to systematically generate and prove all other necessary invariants.

In the second proof we combine *refinement* and *induction*. Under the premise that the more similar two systems are the easier it should be to prove refinement between them, we use induction to generate two refinement proofs between

---

* Research supported in part by a grant from the German-Israel bi-national GIF foundation and a gift from Intel.
[1] The PVS files are available at http://www.wisdom.weizmann.ac.il/~tamarah

S. Graf and M. Schwartzbach (Eds.): TACAS/ETAPS 2000, LNCS 1785, pp. 487–502, 2000.

similar systems. Noting that the number of instructions which are in progress in an out-of-order system is limited to the number of retirement buffer slots, we first show that a speculative system which has only one buffer slot (and thus functions sequentially) refines a sequential system, and then, that a system with $B+1$ buffer slots refines one with B slots. The base case thus deals only with the differences in data structures, while in the induction step we focus on the effect of the greater measure of 'out-of-order'ness allowed by one additional buffer slot.

Due to the enormous differences between sequential and speculative systems it is not immediately obvious how the first may refine the second. However, it is easy to anticipate that a system may refine another with one more retirement buffer. Thus, our intuition was that the inductive proof would prove to be simpler than the direct one. However, this proved not to be the case. While the run-time of the direct-proof is somewhat longer than that of the inductive proof, the inductive proof required far more intricate human interaction, taking far more person-time. We believe that not only was the inductive proof more complex in this case, but that using induction will frequently complicate refinement proofs. This evaluation is discussed in the final section of the paper.

While there is a lot of work in the field of out-of-order executions, not much has been published on speculative execution. It is unclear whether, or how, techniques used for out-of-order execution can be applied to speculative instruction execution. Candidate techniques which have been used to verify out-or-order execution include the completion function approach [7], incremental flushing [12], compositional model checking [8], and techniques combining model checking with uninterpreted functions [3].

A speculative system is verified in [11]. This system is more complex than ours, including memory operations, but the proof is specific to one configuration. An intermediate model comprising a table of history variables is used to verify the system in ACL2. Our proofs have the advantage of being independent of the system configuration and of not requiring an intermediate abstraction.

2   Refinement between Systems

Refinement is the comparison of an *abstract system* $S_A = \langle V_A, \Theta_A, \rho_A \rangle$ and a *concrete system* $S_C = \langle V_C, \Theta_C, \rho_C \rangle$ where V is the set of system variables, Θ defines the initial conditions of the systems, and ρ, the transition relation, defines how the system progresses from one state to another. The abstract system serves as a *specification* capturing all the acceptable correct computations of the concrete system. Correctness of the concrete system is established by proving that every computation of S_C corresponds to some computation of S_A.

The correspondence between the two systems is with respect to *observation functions* $\mathcal{O}_A$ and $\mathcal{O}_C$. Intuitively, these are the features of the two systems which are considered significant for the comparison. For example, in instruction execution systems one would expect the register file to be included in the observation functions while internal data structures might not be.

Given a concrete system $S_C = \langle V_C, \Theta_C, \rho_C \rangle$ with observation function $\mathcal{O}_C$, and an abstract system $S_A = \langle V_A, \Theta_A, \rho_A \rangle$ with observation function $\mathcal{O}_A$, such that $V_C \cap V_A = \emptyset$, we define an *superposition system*

$$S_S = \langle V_C \cup V_A, \Theta_C \wedge \Theta_A, \rho_C \wedge \rho_A^* \rangle$$

where $\rho_A^*(V_C, V_C', V_A, V_A')$ may refer to all variables in $V_C \cup V_A$ in their primed and unprimed versions.

The intention of the superposition system S_S is that it emulates the joint behavior of S_C and S_A in a way that allows any previously admissible step of S_C and matches it with an S_A-step. Thus, $\rho_C \wedge \rho_A^*$ should not exclude any possible S_C-step, but may select among the possible S_A-steps one that matches the S_C-step. Intuitively, ρ_A^* is a modification of ρ_A taking as parameters V_C and V_C' in order to choose a ρ_A-successor matching the S_C-step. We further require that the projection of an S_S-computation onto V_A is a legal computation of S_A.

In any superposition system S_S satisfying the above requirements the problem of showing that $S_C \sqsubseteq S_A$ is reduced to the problem of showing that $\mathcal{O}_C = \mathcal{O}_A$ is an invariant of S_S. However, to do so it may be useful, or necessary, to prove a stronger invariant, $\alpha(V_C, V_A)$ of the superposition system.

We formalize this as refinement rule REF:

$$
\begin{array}{l}
\textbf{R1. } \alpha \wedge \rho_C \longrightarrow \exists V_A' : \rho_A^* \\
\textbf{R2. } \rho_A^* \longrightarrow \rho_A \\
\textbf{R3. } S_S \models \Box\, \alpha \\
\textbf{R4. } \alpha \longrightarrow \mathcal{O}_C = \mathcal{O}_A \\
\hline
S_C \sqsubseteq S_A
\end{array}
$$

That is, S_A refines S_C if using ρ_A^* a legal (R2) computation of S_S can be generated (R1) such that $\mathcal{O}_C$ always equals $\mathcal{O}_A$ (R3, R4).

3   The Reference Model: System SEQ

In this section we present system SEQ which is to serve as a reference model. System SEQ executes in a strictly sequential manner an input program which may contain branches and instructions generating interrupts. It accepts one parameter, R, the number of registers.

An uninterpreted function, *prog*, from *PC_RANGE* to instructions defines the program to be executed. Each instruction has an *operation*, a *target* and two *source* operands. In addition, a *branch target* field stores the target address of branches. A program counter, *pc*, points to the next instruction in *prog*. A register file *reg* records the current values of each register.

At each step, system SEQ either delays, in which case no change is made in the system, or executes the instruction pointed to by *pc*. If the instruction execution generates an interrupt, the program counter is updated to point to the relevant interrupt handler address. In the case of branches, the branch is evaluated and the program counter updated to the branch target if the branch is taken. The *do_op* and *do_branch* functions are used to compute the value of the instruction (*do_branch* returns "1" if a branch is to be taken, "0" otherwise). This value is stored in the target register (if any), and the program counter is updated to point to the next instruction.

4   The Out-Of-Order Design: System DES

In this section we briefly describe our algorithm for speculative out-of-order data-driven instruction execution with in-order-retirement. Our definitions are based on the descriptions in [6,4] and [5].

Instructions flow from the instruction queue to the retirement buffer, where they assume their places in the queue for retirement, and the dispatch buffer, where they await availability of their source operands and a free execution unit. Branch instructions are *predicted* at dispatch time and the program counter updated accordingly. Once both operands are available execution of the instruction can be initiated by the appropriate functional unit. As in system SEQ, the instruction value is calculated by the *do_op* and *do_branch* functions. During execution an *internal interrupt* can be generated, in which case a flag is set in the retirement buffer slot. Results are written back to the retirement and dispatch buffers. Once an instruction reaches the head of the retirement queue it is checked for an internal interrupt or branch misprediction before being retired. If an interrupt was generated the program-counter is updated to the appropriate interrupt handler address and the dispatch and retirement buffers are flushed. If no interrupt was generated the system checks branches for mispredictions. Mispredictions result in the program counter being updated to the instruction which should follow the branch, while dispatch and retirement buffers are flushed. Instructions which generated neither interrupts nor incorrect predictions can be retired, updating the register file with the instruction result.

The data structures of system DES are illustrated in Fig. 1. The shaded fields are auxiliary variables which have been added to our model in order to simplify the proofs. Auxiliary variables are only updated and copied from one record to another and thus do not affect the flow of control. The two proofs use different auxiliary variables, the unified set of which are shown in the diagrams for completeness. The *numinst* variable counts the number of instructions retired so far and is used in synchronizing the two sequential and speculative systems.

The functionality of system DES can be divided into three subsystems:

- DISPATCH: This module dispatches instructions in program order.
- EXECUTE: This module executes and writes back instructions.
- RETIRE: This module retires the slot at the head of the retirement buffer.

While only one instruction is dispatched or retired per cycle, module EXECUTE is parameterized by the number of functional units: when this module is invoked, each functional unit in the system may execute and write-back a result. Multiple instructions may be executed and written back in each cycle.

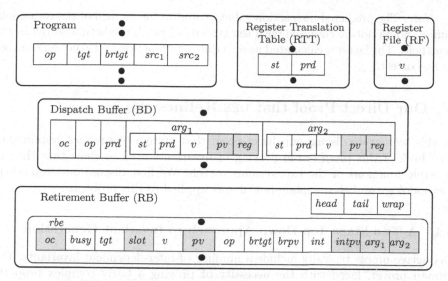

Fig. 1. Data structures for DES

In practice these three subsystems operate concurrently. That is, in the same cycle all three can be invoked simultaneously. Any concurrent execution of the three subsystems is equivalent to a three-step sequential execution of the subsystems in which each subsystem is executed once. We therefore consider each of the three systems separately, ignoring the possible interaction between them.

A note on the retirement buffer The retirement buffer, RB, is the central data structure in the system. It stores instructions in dispatch order until their retirement, ensuring that retirement is in-order. The buffer contains a circular array rbe of retirement buffer entries. This array is treated as a queue, with the oldest entry being "popped" off during retirement, while dispatched instructions are "pushed" onto the end of the queue. The pointers $head$ and $tail$ point to the head of the queue and the next free slot, respectively.

The use of predicted values The inductive proof utilizes the auxiliary predicted value fields. Every value field v in the system is paired with an auxiliary predicted value pv field, while the interrupt field int in the retirement buffer slots is matched with an interrupt predict field, $intpv$.

When an instruction is dispatched its predicted values are calculated. The predicted value of arithmetic operations are calculated by applying the instruction operation to the predicted values of its operands.

The generation of interrupts and taking of branches are decided by the uninterpreted functions $interrupt$ and do_branch, respectively, whose parameters are available at dispatch time. The same functions and parameters are used to predict whether an interrupt will be taken ($intpv$) and the predicted value (pv) of a branch instruction. Both predictions are trivially correct.

Note: The predicted instruction value, stored in the *pv* field of the retirement buffer should not be confused with the system's branch prediction stored in the *brpv* field. The latter is calculated using a different function and is not guaranteed to be correct.

5   Our Direct Proof that DES Refines SEQ

In this section we discuss our direct proof that system DES refines system SEQ. The bulk of this proof is the proving of invariants used to show that the observable functions of the two systems match. We first discuss our 'top-down' methodology and then explain how it was applied to this problem.

5.1   A Two Stage Top-Down Approach to Invariant Generation

Deductive proofs typically include a number of inter-dependent invariants. The human prover, faced with the necessity of proving a fairly complex property may be uncertain how to begin. We define a simple two stage procedure which we believe provides a framework for proving such invariants in a systematic manner. We note that while only the second step of this procedure is 'top-down' the dominance of this step leads us to call the whole procedure 'top-down'.

1. Formulate, and prove, a set of simple invariants of the data structures and the model. These invariants can be chosen with little or no consideration of the invariant to be ultimately proved. Good candidate properties for this step are simple properties of data-structures or relationships between two data structures. Properties chosen in this step are typically sufficiently simple that they are not dependent on any other properties.
2. Attempt to prove the final correctness invariant using the invariants proved in step one. Should the proof reach a step from which one cannot progress, analyze the situation, define one or more properties which would allow the proof to progress and attempt to prove these properties.

The purpose of the first step is threefold. Firstly, it is likely to expose simple errors in the model, should they exist. It is frequently the case that in writing up the model in the PVS description language an error was made, often a very simple one such as using an incorrect index for an array. Such errors may cause the proof of even simple invariants to fail, and the simpler the proof which fails the easier it is to locate the problem in the model. Secondly, the construction of incorrect properties reflects user misunderstanding. Discovering why such properties are incorrect helps the user comprehend the model more completely. Thirdly, even if these properties were not formulated with the final invariant in mind, they will almost certainly be useful in its proof.

In the second step constant progress is made towards the conclusion of the proof. When the proof fails, and it is expected to, it is generally due to the necessity of proving another invariant first. The second step thus incrementally reveals the "hidden" properties on which the desired invariant is dependent, generating a string of properties to be proved invariant. The recursive proving of invariants should conclude after a few iterations, allowing the model to be proved correct.

The balance between the two steps is variable. The greater the number of invariants proved in the first step the less frequently the proofs of the second step will fail due to missing properties or simple errors in the model. However, there is no need to worry about too few, or "missing" invariants in the first step. All invariants needed in the proof will be revealed in the second step and can be proved at this point. While invariants proved in the first step will typically be useful, they are not strictly necessary.

The framework described is very flexible, but, we believe, firm enough to provide structure and direction to the proof.

5.2   System DES refines system SEQ

Auxiliary variables used: The auxiliary variables used in this proof are the *reg* field in the operand structures, and the *oc* and *arg* fields of the retirement buffers.

Both SEQ and DES have program counters called *pc* and counters *numinst* counting the number of instructions which have been completed. We will term the variables in SEQ pc_a and $numinst_a$ and those in DES pc_c and $numinst_c$.

For ρ_A^*, we restrict ρ_A by modifying the *delay* variable such that SEQ delays when the two systems have completed the same number of instructions:

$$delay := (numinst_a = numinst_c)$$

The system invariant, α, is simply the conjunction of the single system invariants and the equality $\mathcal{O}_C = \mathcal{O}_A$, with the observation functions defined as:

$$\mathcal{O}_C : (RF, numinst_c, \textbf{if} \quad RB.head = RB.tail \wedge \neg RB.wrap$$
$$\textbf{then} \ pc_c \ \textbf{else} \ RB.rbe[RB.head].pc \ )$$
$$\mathcal{O}_A : (reg, numinst_a, pc_a)$$

Thus, the register files of the two systems always agree. When the retirement buffer is empty the program counters also agree. Otherwise, the program counter of the next instruction to be retired matches the program counter of SEQ.

Proving premises R1, R2 and R4 of the refinement rule is easy, the difficult part is in proving that $\mathcal{O}_C = \mathcal{O}_A$ is an invariant of the system. To do this we must prove that both machines compute the same value for each instruction, and modify the program counter identically. Since both the value and the program counter are influenced by taking an interrupt, we must also show that an instruction generates an interrupt in system DES if and only if it does so in SEQ.

5.3   Invariants Used in Proving the Refinement

In the first stage we prove simple properties of the system, for example, lemmas relating to the structure of the retirement buffer (e.g. if *tail* and *head* point to the same slot then the retirement buffer is full if *wrap* is true, empty otherwise).

We consider now the second stage of the proof. We start by trying to prove that the value in the head retirement buffer slot is the value calculated by SEQ for the given instruction. This property is quickly formalized and divided into four properties. The first states that the value in the head slot is the value that would be obtained by applying the *do_op* or *do_branch* functions to the values in the operand registers:

$$\phi_1 : RB.rbe[RB.head].oc \wedge \neg RB.rbe[RB.head].busy \longrightarrow$$
$$RB.rbe[RB.head].v =$$
$$\quad \textbf{if} \quad type\_op(RB.rbe[RB.head].op) = \textbf{branch}$$
$$\quad \textbf{then} \; do\_branch(RB.rbe[RB.head].pc,$$
$$\qquad\qquad iss\_before(numinst, RB, RB.head))$$
$$\quad \textbf{else} \; do\_op(RB.rbe[RB.head].op,$$
$$\qquad\qquad RF[RB.rbe[RB.head].arg[1].reg],$$
$$\qquad\qquad RF[RB.rbe[RB.head].arg[2].reg])$$

However, this invariant is insufficient: the values stored in fields of *rbe* must be matched to counterparts in SEQ to allow us to prove that the computed values are correct. This relationship is asserted by showing that the operation, register, target and branch target fields in the retirement buffer match those in the program used by both systems. We must also prove that the two systems use the same criteria to generate interrupts, and will thus generate interrupts at the same time. Lastly, it is necessary that the program counters in the two systems match, if not they will execute different instructions. Whereas in a purely sequential program the updating of the program counter is trivial, once branches are considered the relation between the instruction indices of two instructions that complete one after the next may vary and the correspondence between the program counters is more complicated.

Of these properties, the relationship between the retirement buffer and the program, and the matching interrupt generation are simple to prove while property ϕ_1 is the most difficult. We concentrate on the proof of this property.

Property ϕ_1 is, intuitively, stating two phenomena – firstly, that the result of the instruction is that obtained from the operands used, and secondly, that the values of these operands can now be found in the register file. This second property, operand correctness, depends primarily on operands with "retired" status having values matching those in the register file:

$$\phi_2 : RB.rbe[rb].oc \wedge RB.rbe[rb].arg[j].st = \textbf{retire} \longrightarrow$$
$$RB.rbe[rb].arg[j].v = RF[RB.rbe[rb].arg[j].reg] \wedge$$
$$\forall rb' \; RB.rbe[rb'].oc \wedge RB.rbe[rb'].tgt = RB.rbe[rb].arg[j].reg \longrightarrow$$
$$rb = rb' \vee preceed(rb, rb', RB)$$

where $preceed(rb, rb', RB)$ is true iff both retirement buffer slots are occupied and slot rb precedes slot rb' in the queue of slots waiting for retirement.

The need to prove that there is no preceding retirement buffer slot targeting the operand registers is crucial: should such a slot exist it would, on retiring, over-write the values in the register file, invalidating any correspondence between the retirement buffer slot operand fields and the register file.

Property ϕ_2, in turn, depends on the value in operand fields matching the closest preceding slot targeting the operand register, when such a slot exists. Property ϕ_3 asserts that while the operand status is **write_b** (the operand value has been written back but the instruction has not yet been retired) such a slot does exist, and its value matches that in the operand fields. In order to prove that there is no slot targeting the registers matching retired operands, as required in ϕ_2, it is necessary now to prove a parallel property: there is no slot targeting the operand register between the instruction slot and the slot pointed to by the operand fields.

In order to prove the invariance of ϕ_3 it is necessary to define an invariant, ϕ_4, defining similar properties for busy operands.

Proving the invariance of ϕ_2, ϕ_3, and ϕ_4 is the most difficult part of the direct proof. Intuitively, these properties assert the correctness of the relationship between instructions and their operands, that instructions always use the value calculated for the operand by the last preceding instruction writing to the operand register. These dependency relations are one of the difficulties of out-of-order executions, and it is unsurprising that proving that they hold is the crux of our correctness proof.

We proved a total of 23 invariants in our proof, many of which were simple technical results, such as proving that if the *head* and *tail* pointers of the retirement buffer are equal then the buffer is either full or empty. We omit further details of these invariants.

6   An Inductive Proof of Refinement

There is an enormous difference between an out-of-order system in which many instructions progress simultaneously and a simple sequential system. Whereas in the direct approach we prove a correspondence between these diverse systems, the inductive approach is based on the premise that it will be easier to prove a number of smaller refinements between systems which are more similar. This approach requires more user effort in defining the multiple refinement relations, an investment which simplifies the invariants which need to be proved.

We have performed induction on the number of slots in the retirement buffer. In the base case, where there is only one slot, the out-of-order machine will operate sequentially as only one instruction can be in progress. The inductive step involves proving that machine DES(B+1) with $B+1$ slots refines one with B slots (denoted DES(B)). The difference between these two machines is intuitively far less than that between an out-of-order system and a sequential one.

The invariants needed to prove the refinement relations were proved using the top-down approach detailed previously. In fact, many of the properties needed were proved as part of the direct proof.

Auxiliary variables used: The predicted value fields in the dispatch and retirement buffers are used, as are the *oc* and *slot* fields of the retirement buffer.

6.1   Base Case: DES(1) Refines SEQ(R)

We consider DES(1), an implementation of DES with only one retirement buffer slot. As was the case of the direct proof, we synchronize the two systems at retirement time by setting the delay variable exactly when the *numinst* variables of the two systems agree. Details of this straightforward proof are omitted.

6.2   The Inductive Step: DES(B+1) Refines DES(B)

We show that a system with $B + 1$ retirement buffer slots refines one with B slots. We have chosen to synchronize at instruction dispatch time.

There are two difficulties here: Firstly, DES(B+1) can store $B + 1$ issued but incomplete instructions whereas DES(B) cannot; secondly, even when the two systems contain the same number of occupied retirement buffer slots, their positions will be different since as soon as the *head* pointer wraps the *head* pointers of the two systems will differ. This technical problem complicates the proof which we therefore divided into two stages. We first prove that DES(B+1) refines $DES_f(B+1)$, a system with $B + 1$ slots in which there is always at least one free slot. We then show that $DES_f(B+1)$ refines DES(B). That is, the first proof proves that a system functioning with one fewer slot refines DES(B), without considering mismatched slot positions, a problem delayed to the second proof.

DES(B+1)**refines** DES_f(B+1): We run the two systems in parallel, synchronizing at instruction issue. As long as there is at least one free slot in DES(B+1), all the data structures in the two systems are identical. We consider the case of an instruction being issued into the last free retirement buffer slot of DES(B+1).

We cannot issue the instruction in system $DES_f(B+1)$ as this system will not allow all $B + 1$ slots to be occupied simultaneously. We free the slot at the head of the retirement buffer (that pointed to by *head*) and then issue the instruction.

We consider first the case of the *head* slot containing an executed instruction (the *busy* flag is *false*) which is not a mispredicted branch, nor generates an interrupt. This instruction is retired, after which system $DES_f(B+1)$ issues the new instruction. The register files of the two systems are equal except that the value of the target register of the head slot is updated in DES(B+1) with the value found in the head slot in $DES_f(B+1)$.

However, it may be the case that no value is yet available in the *head* slot as the instruction has not yet been executed. In this case the instruction is stored in the dispatch buffer pointed to by the auxiliary *slot* field of the retirement buffer entry. Any operands of the instructions depended on values of previous instructions, all of which have been retired, and so the instruction will have available operands and can be executed. After execution, the instruction can be retired and the new instruction issued.

The fact that DES(B+1) does not have any value for the instruction makes matching the two systems more difficult. The new value in the register file (assuming that the retired instruction had a target register) of $DES_f(B+1)$ is not found anywhere in the DES(B+1) system. This problem has been overcome by using *predicted values*. The value which has been calculated and retired should be the same value that will be calculated and retired for the instruction at the head of RB. We formalize this by predicting the value of all instructions at dispatch time, and later prove that these predictions are correct. We can then assert that

> The predicted value of the head retirement buffer slot in DES(B+1) equals that found in the the r'th register of the register file of $DES_f(B+1)$, where r is the target index stored in the head slot of DES(B+1).

Similarly, dispatch buffer operand values which are now written back in system $DES_f(B+1)$ match the predicted values for these operands in system DES(B+1).

The final case is that of instructions which either generate interrupts or are mispredicted branches. We use predicted values to assert that when the slot at the head of the retirement buffer in DES(B+1) is retired, an interrupt will be generated or a branch misprediction discovered.

Once system DES(B+1) retires the head slot all data structures of the two systems will again match. Until this retirement occurs, DES(B+1) cannot issue another instruction (it has no free slots) but can execute and write back instructions stored in the dispatch buffer.

Values are predicted correctly In this subsection we sketch our proof that values are predicted correctly.

We would like to prove that value finally obtained for a field matches its predicted value:

$$\psi_1 : \forall s : [1..Z], j : [1..2]. \quad DB[s].oc \wedge DB[s].arg[j].st \neq \textbf{busy} \longrightarrow$$
$$DB[s].arg[j].v = DB[s].arg[j].pv$$
$$\wedge \ \forall b : [1..B]. \ \ RB.rbe.[b].oc \wedge \neg RB.rbe[b].busy \longrightarrow$$
$$RB.rbe[b].v = RB.rbe[b].pv \ \wedge \ RB.rbe[b].int = RB.rbe[b].intpv$$

The proof is inductive. The base case is the state before the start of execution. Since all dispatch and retirement slots are unoccupied property ψ_1 holds trivially.

Assume that ψ_1 holds at the current state. The next state is obtained by either issuing, executing, or retiring an instruction. These three cases are considered separately.

Consider a data instruction issued into dispatch buffer s and retirement buffer slot *tail*. The busy flag of retirement buffer slot *tail* is set to true, and thus there is no constraint on its predicted values. Each of the two operands s_i of s are looked up in the RTT. If the RTT entry for s_i is not busy, the value in $RF[s_i]$ is copied to both the value and predicted value fields of the dispatch buffer. Else, the status, value and predicted value fields are copied from the retirement buffer slot pointed to by the RTT. If the status of the retirement buffer slot is not **busy** then, by the induction hypothesis, its value and predicted values agree. Otherwise, the operand status is set to **busy** and there is no requirement that its value and predicted values agree. Thus, in all cases, if the operand status is not **busy**, its value and predicted value will agree.

We next assume that instruction I is executed and written back. We consider first a data instruction. Both of its operands are available and are not busy and thus, by the induction hypothesis, their value and predicted value fields agree. The value of the instruction is calculated by applying the instruction operation to the value of the operands. As the predicted value was obtained by applying the operation to the predicted value of the operands, the value and predicted values for the instruction will agree. Thus, when the instruction value is written back to any operand fields waiting for it, and to the instruction retirement slot, it will match the predicted value field in these data structures.

Interrupt generation and the predicted values of branches are both decided by the same functions, with the same parameters, as were used to predict the interrupt or the instruction value when the instruction was dispatched. This prediction is trivially correct.

Lastly, we consider instruction retirement. The only value or predicted value fields modified are the value fields in the register file (which have no predicted values). It is easy to prove that ψ_1 continues to hold.

This completes the inductive step. This proof, like all others, has been rigorously proved in the PVS theorem prover. □

Completing the proof of refinement We would like to use the refinement rule of section 2. However, this rule requires that the abstract machine, progress one step with each step of the concrete machine, while we need the abstract system, $DES_f(B+1)$, to progress up to three steps with each step of $DES(B+1)$.

To overcome this problem we follow Abadi and Lamport [1] in using auxiliary variables to introduce stuttering into the system. We add an auxiliary variable *stutter* to $DES(B+1)$ to derive system $DES_s(B+1)$. Intuitively, *stutter* is the minimum number of idling steps that the system must take before taking a non-idling step. When an instruction is dispatched into the $B+1$'st slot of $DES(B+1)$ *stutter* is set so as to force $DES(B+1)$ to idle while $DES_f(B+1)$ performs all the necessary actions to retire the *head* slot before dispatching the new instruction. The transition relation is modified so as to idle, decrementing *stutter*, if it is non-zero.

The proof sketched above allows us to show that the stuttering system $DES_s(B+1)$ refines $DES_f(B+1)$. To complete the proof that $DES(B+1)$ refines $DES_f(B+1)$ we must show that $DES(B+1)$ refines $DES_s(B+1)$.

Abadi and Lamport describe formally under which conditions a stuttering system refines a non-stuttering one. Our system fulfills these requirements and so $DES(B+1)$ refines $DES_s(B+1)$ and therefore $DES(B+1)$ refines $DES_f(B+1)$.

DES$_f$(B+1) **refines** DES(B): System DES$_f$(B+1) has one more slot than DES(B), but as it can never fill all its slots simultaneously, the two systems function as if they have the same number (B) of slots. The difference in the size of the buffer does, however, affect the values of the *head* and *tail* pointers – after the retirement buffer has wrapped these values no longer agree in the two systems. Similarly, any producer fields, whether in the dispatch buffer or register translation table, do not agree for the two systems, and while each retirement buffer entry in system DES$_f$(B+1) has a matching entry in DES(B) its slot index differs.

A mapping, *map*, is defined from slot indices in DES$_f$(B+1) to those in DES(B). The two systems are run in parallel, both issuing, executing and retiring instructions simultaneously. All data structures in the two systems are identical, modulo the *map* function.

Refinement is thus intuitively simple: ρ_A^* is ρ_A with the non-deterministic choices made as they were in system DES$_f$(B+1). As our observation functions we take the register files of the two systems. Since the register files do not mention retirement slot indices, these are identical at all stages.

7   Liveness Properties

Our system is highly non-deterministic and each of the three sub-instructions (dispatch, execute or retire) can cause the system to idle instead of progressing. There is thus no guarantee that any instruction will ever complete.

However, he have proved that it is always *possible* for the system to progress. That is, there is always at least one instruction in the system which can either be dispatched, executed or retired.

8   Conclusion: Comparing the Two Proofs

In this paper we have shown that both the direct, top-down approach, and an inductive methodology are applicable to proving the correctness of our speculative instruction execution model. We note that we used the top-down approach in proving invariants in the inductive proof, too. The two approaches are not mutually exclusive, however using induction modifies the structure of the proof enormously. In this section we compare the two approaches.

We found that, perhaps counter-intuitively, the inductive proof was far more difficult to construct than the direct proof: it was far easier to prove refinement between a speculative and a sequential system than between two speculative systems where one has one more retirement buffer slot.

Most of the complexity of the inductive proof was in proving that DES$_f$(B+1) refines DES(B+1). The data structures in the two systems are 'almost' the same, but we found it necessary to define *precisely* how they differ, in all circumstances. For example, the dispatch buffers are the same unless DES$_f$(B+1) has retired one instruction more than DES(B). In this case the dispatch buffer of DES$_f$(B+1) will be empty if the retired instruction generated a flush. Otherwise, the value of the retired instruction may be available in operand fields in $\text{DES}_f(\text{B}+1)$ but not in the corresponding fields in $\text{DES}(\text{B}+1)$. All the cases sketched in subsection 6.2 had to be rigorously examined and formalized. The invariant α of the superposition system details the differences between *each* data structure of the two systems.

In contrast, in the direct proof the comparison between the abstract and concrete systems involves only the observables, and the internal data structures (dispatch buffer, etc) of the speculative machine are not matched with any in the sequential system. The speculative system is designed so that externally its speculative, out-of-order character is hidden and the register file presents an in-order view of instruction execution. Since we synchronize at retirement time we can compare the register files and not the internal data structures, utilizing the external 'in-order' behavior of the speculative machine so that neither speculation nor out-of-order execution is overtly verified in the refinement proof. Instead, a number of extra invariants of the speculative system were needed to show that it, indeed, behaves 'correctly' – that instruction values are calculated correctly and that the correct instructions are flushed when mispredictions occur. In particular, the instruction-operand relationship expressed by ϕ_2, ϕ_3 and ϕ_4 is used for the purpose of showing that instruction values are correctly calculated. These invariants have trivial counterparts in the base case of the inductive proof, and no counterparts in the inductive step. When we are performing a comparison between two speculative systems these properties hold in both systems and need not be expressed explicitly.

Thus, the different structures of the two proofs resulted in different types of difficulty. In the direct proof the emphasis was on proving single system invariants, in the inductive proof on proving properties of the superposition system. While proving system invariants can be tedious and time consuming, it required less user effort than the complicated, if faster running, refinement analyses in the inductive proof. That single system invariants were easier to formulate than those of the superposition system is reasonable since the the relationship between two systems is potentially more complex than the complexity of each system individually. Since human effort, rather than run-time, is the more limiting factor in deductive proofs of this type, we consider the slower, yet simpler, direct proof to be the more efficient and evaluate the top-down methodology as the one more appropriate for this problem.

Our conclusion is that more important than the similarity of the systems between which we prove refinement is the *complexity* of the two systems and the *granularity* of the comparison between them.

In the inductive proof both the abstract and concrete systems are of similar complexity; in the direct proof the abstract system is far simpler. The complexity of the abstract system contributes directly to the complexity of the refinement proof. Both the definition of the refinement relation and its proof are dependent on the complexity of both systems. For example, in proving premise R1 of the refinement rule we generate for each concrete step a matching transition in the abstract system. In the direct proof the simplicity of SEQ makes this trivial, in the inductive proof it is more difficult.

The granularity of the comparison is crucial: When the comparison is fine grain it is reasonable that defining it correctly, and then proving it invariant, will be a process requiring a similarly detailed understanding of the systems. When the comparison is coarser much of the complexity is shifted from properties of the superposition system to properties of the individual systems, which, we believe, tend to be simpler to formalize.

When using induction one compares two relatively similar systems. Intuitively, this suggests that a fine grain comparison will often be necessary, as it is only in a detailed examination of the systems that a meaningful comparison can be made. The similarity of the systems seems to be, in this case, detrimental rather than beneficent, implying both a complex abstract system and a fine grain comparison.

The balance between the complexity of the additional single system invariants needed in a direct proof and the complexity of the inductive comparison will, of course, differ from problem to problem. However, it is our contention that not only was the inductive methodology inappropriate for our refinement, but that the difficulties we encountered will often occur when combining induction and refinement: Induction inherently suggests that the abstract system will be of complexity similar to that of the concrete system, with the differences between them small and thus apparent only in a fine grain comparison.

References

1. M. Abadi and L. Lamport. The existence of refinement mappings. *Theoretical Computer Science* 82(2):253–284, May 1991. 498
2. T. Arons and A. Pnueli. Verifying Tomasulo's algorithm by refinement. *Proceedings of the 12'th VLSI design conference*, 1999. 487
3. S. Berezin, A. Biere, E. Clarke and Y. Zhu. Combining symbolic model checking with uninterpreted functions for out-or-order processor verification. *FMCAD'98*:369–386, Palo Alto, 1998. 488
4. W. Damm and A. Pnueli. Verifying out-of-order executions. *CHARME'97*:23–47, Montreal, 1997. Chapmann & Hall. 487, 490
5. Gwennap L. Intel's p6 uses decoupled superscalar design. *Microprocessor Report*, 9(2):9–15, 1995. 487, 490
6. J.L. Hennessy and D.A. Patterson. *Computer Architecture: A Quantitative Approach*. Morgan Kaufmann Publishers Inc., 1996. 487, 490
7. R. Hosabett, G. Gopalakrishnan and M. Srivas. A proof of correctness of a processor implementing Tomasulo's algorithm without a reorder buffer. *CHARME' 99*. 488
8. K.L. McMillan. Verification of an implementation of Tomasulo's algorithm by compositional model checking. *CAV'98*:110–121, 1998. 488
9. S. Owre, J.M. Rushby, N. Shankar, and M.K. Srivas. A tutorial on using PVS for hardware verification. *Proceedings of the Second Conference on Theorem Provers in Circuit Design*:167–188. FZI Publication, Universität Karlsruhe, 1994. 487
10. A. Pnueli, T. Arons. Verification of Data-Insensitive Circuits: An In-Order-Retirement Case Study. *FMCAD'98*:351–368, Palo Alto, 1998. 487

11. J. Sawada and Jr. W.A. Hunt. Processor verification with precise exceptions and speculative execution flushing. *CAV'98*:135–146, Vancouver, 1998. 488
12. J.U. Skakkebaek, R.B. Jones, and D.L. Dill. Formal verification of out-of-order execution using incremental flushing. *CAV'98*:pp 98–110, Vancouver, 1998. 488
13. R.M. Tomasulo. An efficient algorithm for exploiting multiple arithmetic units. *IBM J. of Research and Development*, 11(1):25–33, 1967. 487

Partial Order Reductions
for Security Protocol Verification*

Edmund Clarke[1], Somesh Jha[1], and Will Marrero[1]

Department of Computer Science, Carnegie Mellon University,
Pittsburgh, PA 15213.
{emc,sjha,marrero}@cs.cmu.edu

Abstract. In this paper we explore partial order reduction that make
the task of verifying cryptographic protocols more efficient. These reduction techniques have been implemented in our tool BRUTUS. Although
we have implemented several reduction techniques in our tool BRUTUS,
due to space restrictions in this paper we only focus on partial order reductions. Partial order reductions have proved very useful in the domain
of model checking reactive systems. These reductions are not directly
applicable in our context because of additional complications caused by
tracking knowledge of various agents. We present partial order reductions
in the context of verifying security protocols and prove their correctness.
Experimental results showing the benefits of this reduction technique are
also presented.

Keywords: Model checking, partial order reductions, and security.

1   Introduction

Due to the rapid growth of such entities as "the Internet" and "the World Wide
Web", computer security has recently become a very popular topic. As more
and more people gain access to these shared resources, and as more services are
offered, the importance of being able to provide security guarantees becomes
paramount. Typically, these guarantees are provided by means of security protocols that make use of encryption. Several researchers have proposed techniques
to analyze these protocols in an attempt to find errors or to prove them correct.
There are three basic approaches for verifying such protocols.

One of the first attempts at formalizing the notion of a correct protocol was
the Logic of Authentication, more commonly known as the BAN logic [BAN90].
This logic proved useful in analyzing security protocols. Kindred and Wing
helped to automate the use of this logic by developing a theory generator for

* This research is sponsored by the National Science Foundation (NSF) under Grant
  No. CCR-9505472 and the Defense Advanced Research Projects Agency (DARPA)
  under Contract No. DABT63-96-C-0071. Any opinions, findings and conclusions or
  recommendations expressed in this material are those of the author(s) and do not
  necessarily reflect the views of NSF, DARPA, or the United States Government.

S. Graf and M. Schwartzbach (Eds.): TACAS/ETAPS 2000, LNCS 1785, pp. 503–518, 2000.
© Springer-Verlag Berlin Heidelberg 2000

it [KW97]. However, one of the drawbacks of the logic is the lack of a formal model with which to define the semantics of the logic.

There has been much work recently on formal models for security protocols. A number of researchers have used general purpose model checkers to verify authentication protocols [Low97,MMS97,Ros96]. In all these cases, the users must specify the "bad traces" and check to see if any of them are valid traces of the model. In [CJM98], we describe a special purpose model checking tool for verifying authentication protocols which has a built-in adversary that can construct new messages when trying to subvert a protocol.

Bella and Paulson have used theorem proving to verify authentication protocols [BP97]. Their method requires that one express the set of all possible traces by providing a set of rules that describe how to extend a valid trace. Using the same syntax, one then describes the relationships between events that must hold true of correct traces, and Isabelle tries to prove that all valid traces are also correct traces. A theorem proving type approach is also taken by [Mea96].

Model checking based techniques for verifying security protocols suffer from the well known *state explosion problem*, i.e., the state space of the system grows exponentially in the number of components. In the domain of model checking of reactive systems there are numerous techniques for reducing the state space of the system. One such important technique is *partial order reduction*. This technique does not directly apply to our framework because we explicitly keep track of knowledge of various agents and because our logic can refer to this knowledge in a meaningful way.

Partial order reduction allows one to prune the set of traces of a system by reducing the number of inter-leavings to be considered. For example, if the system is insensitive to permuting two actions α and β, then one can consider only one interleaving (say $\alpha\beta$) and ignore the other interleaving ($\beta\alpha$) while exploring the system. This kind of reduction has proved valuable in verifying reactive systems [GPS96,Pel96,Val91]. In this paper we present partial order reduction technique as it applies to the verification of security protocols. The proof of correctness is also presented. Due to space limitations, proofs of various results are not presented, but the general structure of the proof of correctness is clearly described. The framework for our proof is fairly general so that other researchers working in this area can also use it.

The rest of this paper is organized as follows: In Section 2 we review the most common way in which messages are modelled when verifying security protocols. Sections 3 and 4 describe the computation model which we use to provide the semantics for the logic. This model is closely based on our tool, BRUTUS. The syntax and semantics of a logic capable of expressing properties of authentication and electronic commerce protocols are described in Section 5. Partial order reductions are described in Section 6. Experimental results are presented in Section 7. Related and future work are discussed in Sections 8 and 9.

2   Messages

Typically, messages exchanged during the run of a protocol are constructed from smaller sub-messages using pairing and encryption. The smallest such sub-messages (i.e. those which contain no sub-messages themselves) are called *atomic messages*. There are four kinds of *atomic messages*.

- *Keys* are used to encrypt messages. Keys have the property that every key k has an inverse k^{-1} such that for all messages m, $\{\{m\}_k\}_{k^{-1}} = m$. (Note that for symmetric key cryptography the decryption key is the same as the encryption key, so $k = k^{-1}$.)
- *Principal names* are used to refer to the participants in a protocol.
- *Nonces* can be thought of as randomly generated numbers. The intuition is that no one can predict the value of a nonce; therefore, any message containing a nonce can be assumed to have been generated after the nonce was generated. (It is not an "old" message.)
- *Data* plays no role in how the protocol works but is intended to be communicated between the principals.

Let $\mathcal{A}$ denote the space of *atomic messages*. The set of all messages $\mathcal{M}$ over some set of atomic messages $\mathcal{A}$ is inductively defined as follows:

- If $a \in \mathcal{A}$ then $a \in \mathcal{M}$. (Any *atomic message* is a message.)
- If $m_1 \in \mathcal{M}$ and $m_2 \in \mathcal{M}$ then $m_1 \cdot m_2 \in \mathcal{M}$. (Two messages can be paired together to form a new message.)
- If $m \in \mathcal{M}$ and key $k \in \mathcal{A}$ then $\{m\}_k \in \mathcal{M}$. (A message m can be encrypted with key k to form a new message.)

We would also like to generalize the notion of messages to *message templates*. A message template can be thought of as a message containing one or more message variables. To extend messages to message templates we add the following to the inductive definition of messages:

- If v is a message variable, then $v \in \mathcal{M}$.

Since all keys have inverses, we always take advantage of the following reduction: $\{\{m\}_k\}_{k^{-1}} = m$. It is also important to note that we make the following *perfect encryption* assumption: the only way to generate $\{m\}_k$ is from m and k. In other words, for all messages m, m_1, and m_2 and keys k, $\{m\}_k \neq m_1 \cdot m_2$, and $\{m\}_k = \{m'\}_{k'} \Rightarrow m = m' \wedge k = k'$.

We also need to consider how new messages can be created from already known messages by encryption, decryption, pairing (concatenation), and projection. The following rules capture this relationship by defining how a message can be derived from some initial set of messages I.

1. If $m \in I$ then $I \vdash m$.
2. If $I \vdash m_1$ and $I \vdash m_2$ then $I \vdash m_1 \cdot m_2$. (**pairing**)

3. If $I \vdash m_1 \cdot m_2$ then $I \vdash m_1$ and $I \vdash m_2$. (**projection**)
4. If $I \vdash m$ and $I \vdash k$ for key k, then $I \vdash \{m\}_k$. (**encryption**)
5. If $I \vdash \{m\}_k$ and $I \vdash k^{-1}$ then $I \vdash m$. (**decryption**)

This defines the most common derivability relation used to model the capabilities of the adversary in the literature. Given some base set of messages I, we denote all the messages that can be derived from I as $\overline{I}$, the *closure* of I under the rules above. For example, if I_0 is some finite set of messages overheard by the adversary, then $\overline{I_0}$ represents the set of all messages known to the adversary. In general, $\overline{I}$ is infinite, but researchers have taken advantage of the fact that one need not actually compute $\overline{I}$. Once we describe the semantics of our logic, it will be clear that it suffices to check whether $m \in \overline{I}$ for some finite number of messages m. However, checking whether $m \in \overline{I}$ must still be decidable. For a detailed discussion of this question, see [CJM98].

3   The Model

We model a protocol by the asynchronous composition of a set of named communicating processes which model the honest agents and the adversary. We would like to model an insecure and lossy communication medium, in which a principal has no guarantees about the origin of a message, and where the adversary is free to eavesdrop on all communications. Therefore, in the model, we insist that all communications go through the adversary. In other words, all messages sent are intercepted by the adversary and all messages received by honest agents are actually sent by the adversary. In addition, in an attempt to subvert the protocol, the adversary is allowed to create new messages from the information it gains by eavesdropping. The adversary is also allowed to participate in the sessions as an honest agent.

In order to make the model finite, we must place a bound on the number of sessions that a principal may attempt. A session will be modelled as an instance of a principals role in the protocol. Each session is a separate copy or execution of a principal and consists of a single sequence of actions that make up that agent's role in the protocol, along with all the variable bindings and knowledge acquired during the execution [1]. An agent can have multiple sessions, but each session is executed once. When we combine these with a single session of the adversary, we get the entire model of the protocol.

Each session of an honest principal is modelled as a 5-tuple $\langle N, S, B, I, P \rangle$ where:

- $N \in$ *names* is the name of the principal.
- S is the unique *ID* for this session.
- B: *vars*$(N) \to \mathcal{M}$ is a set of bindings for *vars*(N), the set of variables appearing in principal N, which are bound for a particular session as it receives messages.

---

[1] Principal and agent will be used synonymously throughout the paper

- $I \subseteq \mathcal{M}$ is the set of messages known to the principal of this session.
- P is a process description (similar in style to CSP) given as a sequence of actions to be performed. These actions include the pre-defined actions **send** and **receive**, as well as user defined internal actions such as **commit** and **debit**.

The model of the adversary, Ω, is similar to that of an honest agent or principal; however, the adversary is not bound to follow the protocol and so it does not make sense to include either a sequence of actions P_Ω or a set of bindings B_Ω for the adversary. Instead, at any time, the adversary can receive any message or it can send any message it can generate from its set of known messages I_Ω. The global model is then simply the asynchronous composition of the models for each session, including the one corresponding to the adversary.

4 Actions

The actions allowed during the execution of a protocol include the two predefined actions **send** and **receive** as well as possibly some user defined actions. The model makes transitions between global states as a result of actions executed by the sessions. More formally, we define a transition relation $\rightarrow \ \subseteq \Sigma \times S \times A \times \mathcal{M} \times \Sigma$ where Σ is the set of global states, S again is the set of session IDs, A is the set of action names (which includes **send** and **receive**), and $\mathcal{M}$ is the set of all possible messages. We will use the notation $\sigma \xrightarrow{s \cdot a \cdot m} \sigma'$ in place of $(\sigma, s, a, m, \sigma') \in \ \rightarrow$ when it is more convenient. In the definitions below, we will denote the adversary's session as $\Omega - \langle N_\Omega, S_\Omega, \phi, I_\Omega, \emptyset \rangle$ and the sessions corresponding to the honest agents as $\Psi_i = \langle N_i, S_i, B_i, I_i, P_i \rangle$. We will use $\sigma = \langle \Omega, \Psi_1, \ldots, \Psi_n \rangle$ to denote the global state before the transition and $\sigma' = \langle \Omega', \Psi_1', \ldots, \Psi_n' \rangle$ to denote the global state after the transition. In addition, we will use the notation $\hat{B}$ to denote the obvious extension of a set of bindings B from the domain of variables to the domain of message templates. In other words, $\hat{B}(m)$ is the result of substituting $B(v)$ for every occurrence of v in the message template m for all the variables v appearing in m.

- $\sigma \xrightarrow{s \cdot \textbf{send} \cdot m} \sigma'$

  A session with ID s can send message m in global state σ and the new global state is σ' if and only if
  1. $I_{\Omega'} = I_\Omega \cup m$. (The adversary adds m to the set of messages it knows.)
  2. There is a session $\Psi_i = \langle N_i, s, B_i, I_i, \textbf{send}(s\text{-}msg).P_i' \rangle$ in σ such that in σ', $\Psi_i' = \langle N_i, s, B_i, I_i, P_i' \rangle$ and $m = \hat{B}_i(s\text{-}msg)$. (There is a session that is ready to send message m.)
  3. $\Psi_j = \Psi_j'$ for all $j \neq i$. (All other sessions remain unchanged.)
- $\sigma \xrightarrow{s \cdot \textbf{receive} \cdot m} \sigma'$

  A session with ID s can receive message m in global state σ and the new global state is σ' if and only if
  1. $m \in \overline{I_\Omega}$. (The adversary can generate the message m.)

2. There is a session $\Psi_i = \langle N_i, s, B_i, I_i, \mathbf{receive}(r\text{-}msg).P_i' \rangle$ in σ such that in σ', $\Psi_i' = \langle N_i, s, B_i', I_i', P_i' \rangle$, $I_i' = I_i \cup m$, and B_i' is the smallest extension of B_i such that $\hat{B}'_i(r\text{-}msg) = m$. (There is a session ready to receive a message of the form of m and its bindings are updated correctly in the next state.)

3. $\Psi_j = \Psi_j'$ for all $j \neq i$. (All other sessions remain unchanged.)

$- \sigma \xrightarrow{s \cdot \mathbf{Act} \cdot m} \sigma'$

A session with ID s can perform some user defined internal action $\mathbf{Act}$ with argument m in global state σ and the new global state is σ' if and only if

1. There is a session $\Psi_i = \langle N_i, s, B_i, I_i, \mathbf{Act}(msg).P_i' \rangle$ in σ such that in σ', $\Psi_i' = \langle N_i, s, B_i, I_i, P_i' \rangle$ and $m = \hat{B}_i(msg)$. (There is a session s that is ready to perform action $\mathbf{Act}$ with argument m.)

2. $\Psi_j = \Psi_j'$ for all $j \neq i$. (All other sessions remain unchanged).

Notice that internal actions are purely symbolic, i.e., there is no semantics associated with these actions.

Each possible execution of the model corresponds to a *trace*, a finite, alternating sequence of global states and actions $\pi = \sigma_0 \alpha_1 \sigma_1 \alpha_2 \cdots \alpha_n \sigma_n$ for some $n \in \mathbb{N}$, such that $\sigma_{i-1} \xrightarrow{\alpha_i} \sigma_i$ for $0 < i \leq n$ for the transition relation $\rightarrow$ just defined. Actually, technically speaking α_i belongs to the set $S \times A \times M$, but abusing the notation slightly we will refer to α_i as an action.

5 Logic

In order to specify the requirements or the desired properties of the protocol, we will use a first order logic where quantifiers range over the finite set of instances in a model. In addition, the logic will include the past-time modal operator so that we can talk about things that happened in the history of a particular protocol run or trace. The atomic propositions of the logic will allow us to refer to the bindings of variables in the model, to actions that occur during execution of the protocol, and to the knowledge of the different agents participating in the protocol. We will begin with the syntax of the logic, followed by the formal semantics.

5.1 Syntax

As stated above, we will use a first order logic where quantifiers range over the finite set of instances. The atomic propositions are used to characterize states, actions, and knowledge in the model. The arguments to the atomic propositions are terms expressing instances or messages. We begin by a formal description of terms.

- If S is a instance ID, then S is an instance term.
- If s is an instance variable, then s is an instance term.

- If M is a message, then M is a message term.
- If m is a message variable, then m is a message term.
- If s is an instance term, then $pr(s)$ represents the principal that is executing instance s.
- If s is an instance term and m is a message variable, then $s.m$ is a message term representing the binding of m in the instance s.
- If m_1 and m_2 are message terms, then $m_1 \cdot m_2$ is a message term.
- If m_1 and m_2 are message terms, then $\{m_1\}_{m_2}$ is a message term. Note that here we implicitly assume that m_2 is of atomic type key.

As in standard first order logic, atomic propositions are constructed from terms using relation symbols. The predefined relation symbols are "=" and "**Knows**". The user can also define other relation symbols which would correspond to user defined actions in the model. The syntax for atomic propositions is as follows: (All relation symbols are used in the infix notation.)

- If m_1 and m_2 are message terms, then $m_1 = m_2$ is an atomic proposition. Examples of this atomic proposition would be checking if a customer and merchant agree on the price of a purchase ($C_0.price = M_0.price$), or to check if a particular instance of A believes it's authenticating with B ($A_0.partner = B$).
- If s is an instance term and m is a message term, then s **Knows** m is an atomic proposition which intuitively means that instance s knows the message m. This proposition can be used to check if the adversary has compromised the session key (Ω **Knows** K)
- If s is an instance term, m is a message term, and **Act** is a user defined action, then s **Act** m is an atomic proposition which intuitively means that instance s performed action **Act** with message m as an argument. For example, this could be used to check if a customer C_0 has committed to a transaction with identifier TID (C_0**commit** TID).

Finally, *well-formed formulas* (or *wffs* for short) are built up from atomic propositions with the usual connectives from first-order and modal logic.

- if f is an atomic proposition, then f is a wff.
- if f is a wff, then $\neg f$ is a wff.
- if f_1 and f_2 are wffs, then $f_1 \wedge f_2$ is a wff.
- if f is a wff and s is an instance variable, then $\exists s.f$ is a wff.
- if f is a wff, then $\Diamond_P f$ is a wff.

The formula $\exists s.f$ has the intent that there exists some instance s_0 such that f is true when you substitute s_0 for s in f while $\Diamond_P f$ is supposed to mean that at some point in the past, f was true. We also use the following common shorthands:

- $f_1 \vee f_2 \equiv \neg(\neg f_1 \wedge \neg f_2)$
- $f_1 \rightarrow f_2 \equiv \neg f_1 \vee f_2$

- $f_1 \leftrightarrow f_2 \equiv f_1 \rightarrow f_2 \wedge f_2 \rightarrow f_1$
- $\forall s.f \equiv \neg \exists s.\neg f$ (For all instances, s_0, f is true when you substitute s_0 for s.)
- $\Box_P f \equiv \neg \Diamond_P \neg f$ (At all points in the past, f was true.)

The formula $\forall s.f$ is supposed to mean that for any instance s_0, f is true when you substitute s_0 for s in f while $\Box_P f$ is supposed to mean that at all points in the past, f was true.

5.2 Semantics

Next we provide semantics to the logic just presented. These semantics will be given in terms of the formal model presented in Section 3. Again, we begin with the terms of the logic.

- An instance ID S refers to the instance with that ID.
- An instance variable s ranges over all the instances corresponding to the honest agents in the model.
- An atomic message M is an atomic message in the model.
- A message variable v varies over messages in the model and can be defined as a binding variable in a particular principal.
- The function pr maps an instance ID to a principal name. If s is an instance ID, then $pr(s)$ is the principal executing the instance with ID s.
- We use "." as a scoping operator. If s is an instance term and v is a message variable, then $s.v$ refers to the variable v bound in the instance s. The interpretation $\sigma(s.v)$ of $s.v$ in a particular state σ is $B_s(v)$, the value bound to the variable v in instance s in state σ.
- Message terms can be concatenated using "·" just as messages are concatenated.
- Similarly a message term m_1 can be encrypted with another message term m_2 just as messages are encrypted in the model.

The wffs of the logic will be interpreted over the traces of a particular model. Recall that a trace consists of a finite, alternating sequence of states and actions $\pi = \sigma_0 \alpha_1 \sigma_1 \ldots \sigma_n$. Length of a trace π is denoted by $length(\pi)$. We give the semantics of wffs in our model via a recursive definition of the satisfaction relation $\models$. We will write $\langle \pi, i \rangle \models f$ to mean that the i-th state in π satisfies the formula f. We begin with atomic propositions.

- $\langle \pi, i \rangle \models m_1 = m_2$ iff $\sigma_i(m_1) = \sigma_i(m_2)$. Thus the formula $m_1 = m_2$ is true in a state if the interpretations of m_1 and m_2 are equal. In other words, two message terms are equal in a state if after applying the appropriate substitutions to the variables appearing in the message terms, the resulting messages are equal.
- The formula $\langle \pi, i \rangle \models s$ **Knows** m iff $\sigma_i(m) \in \overline{I_j}$ for some instance Ψ_j in σ_i such that $S_j = s$ (the instance ID of Ψ_j is s). In other words, the formula s **Knows** m is true in a state if the instance with ID s can derive message m from its known set of messages in that state. Ω **Knows** m is true if the adversary Ω knows message m (recall that Ω denotes the adversary).

- $\langle \pi, i \rangle \models s$ **Act** m for some user defined action **Act** iff $\alpha_i = s \cdot$ **Act** $\cdot m$. In other words, the formula $(s$ **Act** $m)$ is true in a state if the transition taken to enter the current state was one in which instance s took action **Act** with argument m.

The extension of the satisfaction relation to the logical connectives is the same as for standard first order logic. We use the notation $f[s_0\backslash s]$ to denote the result of substituting every free occurrence of the instance variable s in f with the instance ID s_0.

- $\langle \pi, i \rangle \models \neg f$ iff $\langle \pi, i \rangle \not\models f$.
- $\langle \pi, i \rangle \models f_1 \wedge f_2$ iff $\langle \pi, i \rangle \models f_1$ and $\langle \pi, i \rangle \models f_2$
- $\langle \pi, i \rangle \models \exists s.f$ iff there exists a honest instance s_0 in the model such that $\langle \pi, i \rangle \models f[s_0\backslash s]$.
- $\langle \pi, i \rangle \models \Diamond_P f$ iff there exists a $0 \leq j \leq i$ such that $\langle \pi, j \rangle \models f$ In other words, the formula $\Diamond_P f$ is true in a state of a trace π if the formula f is true in any state of the trace up to and including the current state.

A formula f is said to be true in a trace π (denoted as $\pi \models f$) iff f is true in *every state* of the trace π.

5.3   Specification Examples

For the sake of concreteness, we now include examples of some of the properties we have checked using BRUTUS and how they are specified in our logic. For the sake of clarity, we break the specification into two parts. The first part (referred to as ϕ_H) expresses properties about honest agents. The second part (referred to as ϕ_Ω) pertains to the adversary. Hence, the entire specification ϕ is simply $\phi_H \wedge \phi_\Omega$.

Payment Authorization. For the secure payment 1KP protocol [BGH+95], we wish to show that whenever the customer's account is debited, the customer must have authorized that debit. For this we simply choose ϕ_H to be

$$\forall A_0 \cdot (pr(A_0) = A) \wedge (A_0 \text{ debit } (A_0.\text{CC} \cdot A_0.\text{price})) \to$$

$$\exists C_0.(pr(C_0) = C) \wedge (A_0.\text{CC} = C_0.\text{CC}) \wedge \Diamond_P(C_0 \text{ auth } A_0.\text{price})$$

This formula states that for all sessions A_0, if A_0 is a session being executed

by the authority A, and A_0 debits the credit card account $A_0.\text{CC}$ by $A_0.\text{price}$, then there exists a session C_0 being executed by the customer C with that same credit card number that authorized a debit of that amount. Since in this case we do not refer to the adversary, we let $\phi_\Omega = \mathbf{true}$.

Privacy. The 1KP protocol should not reveal information about the transaction. In other words, only the appropriate principals should know the order information. For this we choose ϕ_H to be

$$\forall S_0 . \forall C_0 . (pr(C_0) = C) \land (S_0 \textbf{ Knows } C_0.DESC) \rightarrow$$
$$(pr(S_0) = C \lor pr(S_0) = M)$$

This formula states that for all sessions S_0, if S_0 knows the customer's description $(C_0.DESC)$ of the transaction, then S_0 is a session being executed by either the customer or the merchant. We will also need to make sure that the adversary does not know the information, so we choose ϕ_Ω to be

$$\forall C_0 . (pr(C_0) = C) \rightarrow \neg(\Omega \textbf{ Knows } C_0.DESC)$$

Non-repudiation. We may want to check that a principal cannot deny knowledge of a particular value (a key or nonce). For instance, in the Needham-Schroeder authentication protocol [NS78], we may want to make sure that whenever A ends a session with B, B must know the nonce created by A. Note, that this is a somewhat weak notion of non-repudiation. A may not be able to prove B's knowledge of A's nonce. Indeed, A may not even be able to convince itself that B knows the nonce. We are simply checking that there is no trace in which B does not know the nonce. For this specification we choose ϕ_H to be

$$\forall S_0 . \forall T_0. \ S_0 \textbf{ end } \ pr(T_0) \rightarrow (T_0 \textbf{ Knows } S_0.Nonce)$$

This formula states that for all pairs of sessions S_0 and T_0, if S_0 ends a session with T_0, then T_0 knows the nonce generated by S_0. We choose $\phi_\Omega = \textbf{true}$.

5.4   An Ordering on Traces

We introduce an ordering on traces that will aid us in proving the correctness of partial order reductions. Throughout this sub-section assume that we are given a specification ϕ. Since the number of sessions is finite, we can assume that the specification is quantifier free (see the equations given below).

$$\exists s.f \ = \ \lor_{i=1}^n f[s_i \backslash s]$$
$$\forall s.f \ = \ \land_{i=1}^n f[s_i \backslash s]$$

In the equations given above we have assumed that there are n honest sessions with session IDs $s_1, \cdots, s_n$. We also assume that the negations are pushed down to the innermost level. A quantifier free formula where the negation has been pushed to the innermost level is said to be in *negation normal form*. Let AP_H be the set of atomic formulas corresponding to honest sessions that appear in the specification (see subsection 5.1). Similarly, let AP_Ω be the set of atomic formulas pertaining to the adversary that appear in the specification. A specification is called *admissible* if it is in negation normal form and the atomic formulas in AP_Ω appear negated. From here on, assume that formulas are constructed using the set of atomic formula $AP_H \cup AP_\Omega$, and are admissible. We let $\mathcal{CF}$ be the class of normal and admissible formula built using the atomic formula in the set $AP_H \cup AP_\Omega$.

Notice that the truth of a specification ϕ on a trace π is completely determined by the values of the atomic propositions in the set AP_H and the adversary's knowledge (the set of messages known to the adversary) at each state of the trace π. Adversary's knowledge determines the truth of the atomic formula in the set AP_Ω. Assume that for each state σ we are given the set of atomic propositions true in that state and the knowledge of the adversary. $L(\sigma) \subseteq 2^{AP_H}$ is the labelling function which indicates whether an atomic proposition in AP_H is true in the state σ or not ($p \in L(\sigma)$ means that the atomic proposition p is true in the state σ). Knowledge of the adversary in state σ is denoted by $I_\Omega(\sigma)$, or equivalently the set of messages known to the adversary in the state σ is $I_\Omega(\sigma)$. We introduce a partial order between traces, which will help us to prove the correctness of our reduction techniques.

Definition 1. A trace π_1 is *greater than* a trace π_2 (denoted by $\pi_1 \succeq \pi_2$) iff there exists partitions $\{A_1, \cdots, A_m\}$ and $\{B_1, \cdots, B_m\}$ of the two traces π_1 and π_2 such that the following conditions hold:

- There exists $0 = a_0 < a_1 < a_2 < \cdots < a_m = length(\pi_1)$ such that $A_k = \{\langle \pi_1, a_{k-1} + 1 \rangle, \cdots, \langle \pi_1, a_k \rangle\}$, or in other words A_k represents the sub-trace starting at index $a_{k-1} + 1$ and ending at a_k.
- A symmetric condition holds for the partition $\{B_1, \cdots, B_m\}$ of the trace π_2 with indices $0 = b_0 < b_1 < b_2 < \cdots < b_m = length(\pi_2)$.
- For two states in the corresponding partitions A_k and B_k ($1 \leq k \leq m$) the labelling of atomic propositions in AP_H is identical and adversary's knowledge in *every* state of A_k is greater than in the last state of B_k. Since knowledge of the adversary is monotonic along a trace (adversary never forgets anything), this also implies that the adversary's knowledge in an arbitrary state of A_k is more than the knowledge in all states of B_k. More precisely, the following conditions hold:

$$\forall s \in A_k \forall s' \in B_k (L(s) = L(s'))$$
$$\forall s \in A_k (I_\Omega(s) \supseteq I_\Omega(\langle \pi_2, b_k \rangle))$$

Informally, the lemma given below states that if $\pi_1 \succeq \pi_2$ the correctness of an admissible specification in π_1 implies its correctness in π_2.

Lemma 1. Given two traces π_1, π_2 such that $\pi_1 \succeq \pi_2$ and an admissible specification ϕ, $\pi_1 \models \phi$ implies that $\pi_2 \models \phi$. In other words, the partial order $\succeq$ is monotonic with respect to the satisfaction relation $\models$.

6   Partial Order Reduction

Partial order reductions reduce the search space by ignoring redundant interleavings. The theory of partial order reductions is well developed in the context of verification of reactive systems [GPS96,Pel96,Val91]. Reductions presented in this section are very heavily influenced by traditional partial order reduction techniques. However, since we are working with a very specific model and logic, the theory is simplified and different. We present the theory as it applies to our setting.

Throughout this section assume that we are given a specification ϕ that is admissible. Recall that AP_H is the set of atomic propositions pertaining to the honest agents and AP_Ω is the set of atomic propositions referring to the adversary. An internal action **Act** is called *invisible* if and only if it does not appear in the specification ϕ, or in other words **Act** is not referred to by the atomic formulas in the set AP_H. Next we describe transformations on traces.

Permuting invisible internal actions (Rule 1)
Consider a trace $\pi = \sigma_0\alpha_1\sigma_1\ldots\sigma_n$. If there exists a sequence of transitions $\sigma_i\alpha_{i+1}\sigma_{i+1}\alpha_{i+2}$, such that α_{i+2} is an invisible internal action, and actions α_{i+1} and α_{i+2} do not belong to the same session, then we can permute the actions to get a new trace given below:

$$\sigma_0\alpha_1\sigma_1\ldots\sigma_i\alpha_{i+2}\sigma'_{i+1}\alpha_{i+1}\ldots\sigma_n$$

Permuting sends (Rule 2)
This operation allows one to permute two consecutive **send** actions if they belong to different sessions.

Moving send before receives (Rule 3)
If a **receive** or an internal action **Act** appears before a **send** in a trace and these actions belong to different sessions, then this operation allows us to move the **send** action before the **receive** or the internal action **Act**.

We call the set of transformations just described *allowable operations* on a trace. Suppose we obtain a trace π' by applying one of the *allowable operations* to the trace π, then we say that $\pi \Rightarrow \pi'$. The reflexive transitive closure of $\Rightarrow$ is denoted by $\Rightarrow^*$. The following lemma is crucial in proving correctness of the partial order reduction.

Lemma 2. *Consider two traces π and π' such that $\pi \Rightarrow \pi'$. In this case $\pi \preceq \pi'$.*

Using Lemmas 2 and 1, the proof of the following lemma is transparent (note that $\pi \preceq \pi'$).

Lemma 3. *Assume that we are given a specification ϕ. If there are two traces π and π' such that $\pi \Rightarrow^* \pi'$, then $\pi' \models \phi$ implies that $\pi \models \phi$, or equivalently $\pi \not\models \phi$ implies that $\pi' \not\models \phi$.*

The basic algorithm for verifying whether a protocol satisfies a specification works by exploring the state space starting from the initial state using depth-first search. As soon as we reach a state where the specification is false, we report an error. If the depth-first search procedure terminates without reporting an error, the protocol is correct. In the ensuing discussion we will focus on the depth-first search algorithm. In the description of the algorithms we do not show book-keeping details such as reporting an error or checking whether a state has been visited or not. Algorithm $\mathcal{A}$ given in Figure 1 performs the depth-first search starting from state s. The predicate $en(s, \alpha)$ is true if action α is enabled in the state s, i.e., action α can be executed from the state s. The set of enabled actions $EN(s)$ in a state s is $\{\, \alpha \mid en(s, \alpha)\,\}$. Algorithm $\mathcal{A}_{\mathcal{PO}}$ (shown in Figure 2) is the modified depth-first search procedure with partial-order reductions. The set of actions $ample(EN(s))$ is defined as follows:

- If $EN(s)$ contains an invisible internal action , then $ample(EN(s))$ is an arbitrary invisible action $\{\mathbf{Act}\}$ picked from $EN(s)$.
- Suppose $EN(s)$ does not contain an invisible internal action, but does contain a **send** action. In this case $ample(EN(s))$ is an arbitrary **send** action picked from the set $EN(s)$.
- If $EN(s)$ does not contain an invisible internal action or a **send** action, $ample(EN(s))$ is equal to $EN(s)$

Theorem 1 proves the correctness of the partial order reduction. Notice that the reduced algorithm $\mathcal{A}_{\mathcal{PO}}$ explores fewer traces than the algorithm $\mathcal{A}$. Theorem 1 basically states that every trace considered by the exhaustive algorithm $\mathcal{A}$ can be transformed into a trace considered by the reduced algorithm $\mathcal{A}_{\mathcal{PO}}$ using allowable operations described earlier.

```
1  funct dfs(s)
2     EN (s) = { α | en(s,α) }
3     foreach α ∈ EN (s)
4        do dfs(α(s))
```

Fig. 1. Depth first search algorithm $\mathcal{A}$

```
1  funct dfs(s)
2     EN (s) = { α | en(s,α) }
3     foreach α ∈ ample(EN(s))
4        do dfs(α(s))
```

Fig. 2. Modified depth first search algorithm $\mathcal{A}_{\mathcal{PO}}$

Theorem 1. *For every trace π considered by the algorithm $\mathcal{A}$, algorithm $\mathcal{A}_{\mathcal{PO}}$ considers a trace π' such that $\pi \Rightarrow^* \pi'$.*

Using this theorem along with other results proved earlier, subsequent discussion shows that the algorithm with partial order reduction will discover an incorrect trace if and only if the full algorithm $\mathcal{A}$ will discover an incorrect trace. Suppose the protocol we are verifying is incorrect. In this case algorithm $\mathcal{A}$, being exhaustive in nature, will consider a trace π such that $\pi \not\models \phi$. Using Theorem 1 we can deduce that the reduced algorithm $\mathcal{A}_{\mathcal{PO}}$ considers a trace π' such that $\pi \Rightarrow^* \pi'$. Using Lemma 3 we obtain that $\pi' \not\models \phi$. Therefore, if the protocol is incorrect, the reduced algorithm will detect it. Since the reduced algorithm only executes a subset of actions enabled from a state, it only considers a subset of the entire set of traces. This means that if the reduced algorithm finds an incorrect trace, the protocol is incorrect. Hence the protocol is *correct if and only the reduced algorithm* $\mathcal{A}_{PO}$ *does not find an incorrect trace*. Therefore, the reduced algorithm $\mathcal{A}_{PO}$ can be safely used.

7   Experimental Results

The table shown in Figure 3 summarizes the results of applying partial reductions to a few protocols. We examined the 1KP secure payment protocol [BGH+95], the Needham-Schroeder public key protocol [NS78], and the Wide-Mouthed Frog protocol [BAN90,Sch96]. Columns 2 and 3 give the number of initiator and responder sessions used in the model. The other columns give the number of states encountered during state space traversal using exhaustive search and search with partial order reductions. The entries with an "X" represents computations that were aborted after a day of computation (over 700,000,000 states).

Fig. 3. Table of results

protocol	init	resp	none	partial order
1KP	1	1	17,905,267	906,307
N-S	1	1	1,208	146
N-S	1	2	1,227,415	6,503
WMF	3	3	X	1,286,074

8   Related Work

As mentioned in the introduction, there are several research efforts that have applied existing model checkers to the verification of security protocols. Our model checker is especially built to check properties of cryptographic and electronic commerce protocols. For example, we explicitly keep track of the knowledge for each agent and our logic can refer to the knowledge of various agents. However, because we extend the system state to keep track of knowledge, the correctness of various reduction techniques in the domain of traditional model checking cannot be directly applied. Here we developed the theory of partial order reductions for the verification of cryptographic and electronic commerce protocols. A reduction similar to partial order reduction appears in [SS98]. In [SS98] authors use Murϕ to verify cryptographic protocols. The connection to partial order reductions was not made in [SS98] and the set of reductions considered in [SS98] are more restrictive than the ones considered here. Moreover, the arguments presented in [SS98] only apply to a restrictive logic. Arguments presented in this paper are much more precise and apply to a much richer logic.

9   Conclusion

In this paper we presented a logic for specifying properties of security protocols. In this context, we also presented partial order reduction techniques. Experimental results clearly indicate that this reduction technique significantly reduces the size of the state space. In the future, we want to test our ideas on larger protocols. Currently, internal actions do not have any semantics associated with them. In the future we also want to add semantics to internal actions, e.g., the **debit** action will actually debit the customer's account.

Acknowledgements

Darrell Kindred, Juergen Dingel, and Helmult Veith provided very helpful comments that enhanced the overall quality of the paper.

References

BAN90. Michael Burrows, Martín Abadi, and Roger Needham. A logic of authentication. *ACM Transactions on Computer Systems*, 8(1):18–36, February 1990. 503, 516

BGH+95. M. Bellare, J. Garay, R. Hauser, A. Herberg, H. Krawczyk, M. Steiner, G. Tsudik, and M. Waidner. *i*KP - a family of secure electronic payment protocols. In *Proceedings of the 1st USENIX Workshop on Electronic Commerce*, July 1995. 511, 516

BP97. G. Bella and L. C. Paulson. Using isabelle to prove properties of the kerberos authentication system. In *DIMACS Workshop on Design and Formal Verification of Security Protocols*, 1997. 504

CJM98. E. M. Clarke, S. Jha, and W. Marrero. Using state space exploration and a natural deduction style message derivation engine to verify security protocols. In *Proceedings of the IFIP Working Conference on Programming Concepts and Methods (PROCOMET)*, 1998. 504, 506

GPS96. Patrice Godefroid, Doron Peled, and Mark Staskauskas. Using partial order methods in the formal validation of industrial concurrent programs. In *ISSTA'96, International Symposium on Software Testing and Analysis*, pages 261–269, San Diego, California, USA, 1996. ACM Press. 504, 513

KW97. D. Kindred and J. M. Wing. Closing the idealization gap with theory generation. In *DIMACS Workshop on Design and Formal Verification of Security Protocols*, 1997. 504

Low97. G. Lowe. Casper: A compiler for the analysis of security protocols. In *Proceedings of the 1997 IEEE Computer Society Symposium on Research in Security and Privacy*, pages 18–30, 1997. 504

Mea96. C. Meadows. Language generation and verification in the NRL protocol analyzer. In *Proceedings of the 9th Computer Security Foundations Workshop*. IEEE Computer Society Press, 1996. 504

MMS97. J. C. Mitchell, M. Mitchell, and U. Stern. Automated analysis of cryptographic protocols using murφ. In *Proceedings of the 1997 IEEE Symposium on Security and Privacy*. IEEE Computer Society Press, 1997. 504

518   Edmund Clarke et al.

NS78.   R. Needham and M. Schroeder. Using encryption for authentication in large
          networks of computers. *Communications of the ACM*, 21(12):993–999, 1978.
          512, 516
Pel96.   Doron Peled. Combining partial order reductions with on-the-fly model-
          checking. *Journal of Formal Methods in Systems Design*, 8 (1):39–64, 1996.
          also appeared in 6th International Conference on Computer Aided Verifica-
          tion 1994, Stanford CA, USA, LNCS 818, Springer-Verlag, 377-390.   504,
          513
Ros96.   A. W. Roscoe. Intensional specifications of security protocols. In *9th Com-
          puter Security Foundations Workshop*, 1996.   504
Sch96.   B. Schneier. *Applied Cryptography*. John Wiley & Sons, Inc., second edition,
          1996.   516
SS98.   V. Shmatikov and U. Stern. Efficient finite-state analysis for large secu-
          rity protocols. In *Proceedings of the 1998 Computer Security Foundations
          Workshop*. IEEE Computer Society Press, June 1998.   516
Val91.   A. Valmari. Stubborn sets of colored petri nets. In *Proceedings of the 12th
          International Conference on Application and Theory of Petri Nets*, pages
          102–121, Gjern, Denmark, 1991.   504, 513

Model Checking Security Protocols Using a Logic of Belief

Massimo Benerecetti[1] and Fausto Giunchiglia[1,2]

[1] DISA - University of Trento,
Via Inama 5, 38050 Trento, Italy
[2] IRST - Istituto Trentino di Cultura,
38050 Povo, Trento, Italy
{bene,fausto}@cs.unitn.it

Abstract. In this paper we show how model checking can be used for the verification of security protocols using a logic of belief. We model principals as processes able to have beliefs. The idea underlying the approach is to treat separately the temporal evolution and the belief aspects of principals. Therefore, when we consider the temporal evolution, belief formulae are treated as atomic propositions; while the fact that principal A has beliefs about another principal B is modeled as the fact that A has access to a representation of B as a process. As a motivating example, we use the framework proposed to formalize the Andrew protocol.

1   Introduction

In this paper we show how model checking (see, e.g., [5,6]) can be used for the verification of security protocols using a logic of belief (see [3] for an example of the use of a belief logic in security applications). Our approach allows us to reuse with almost no variations all the technology and tools developed in model checking.

Model checking allows us to verify concurrent reactive finite state *processes*. We model *principals* participating to a protocol session as (concurrent reactive finite state) processes able to have beliefs. The specification of a principal has therefore two orthogonal aspects: a temporal aspect and a belief aspect. The key idea underlying our approach is to keep these two aspects separated. In practice things work as follows:

- when we consider the temporal evolution of a principal we treat belief atoms (namely, atomic formulae expressing belief) as atomic propositions. The fact that these formulae talk about beliefs is not taken into consideration.
- We deal with beliefs as follows. The fact that principal a_1 has beliefs about another principal a_2 is modeled as the fact that a_1 has access to a representation of a_2 as a process. Then, any time it needs to verify the truth value of some belief atom about a_2, e.g., $B_2\phi$, a_1 simply tests whether, e.g., ϕ holds in its (appropriate) representation of a_2. Beliefs are essentially used to control the "jumping" among processes. This operation is iterated in the obvious way in case of nested beliefs.

S. Graf and M. Schwartzbach (Eds.): TACAS/ETAPS 2000, LNCS 1785, pp. 519–534, 2000.

The paper is structured as follows. In Section 2 we describe a well known protocol, the Andrew protocol, as a motivating example. Section 3 presents the theoretical framework we employ (called MultiAgent Finite State Machines). The description is given incrementally over the standard model checking notions. In particular, we adopt CTL [5] as the propositional temporal logic used to state temporal specifications. Section 4 shows how the Andrew protocol can be formalized in our framework. Section 5 describes the model checking procedure we propose, while Section 6 illustrates how the algorithm described in Section 5 works in verifying a property of the Andrew protocol. Finally, some conclusions are drawn.

2   The Andrew Protocol

In this section we briefly recall a simple authentication protocol, known as the Andrew protocol, which has been proved to be vulnerable to various attacks (see, e.g., [3]). The protocol involves two principals, A and B, which share a secret key K_{ab}, and carry out a handshake to authenticate each other. The ultimate goal of the protocol is to exchange a new secret session key K'_{ab} between A and B. B is intended to be the key server, while A is the recipient.

We use standard notation, and present the version of the protocol proposed in [3]. N_i denotes a nonce (a fresh message) newly created by principal i for the current session; K_{ij} is a shared key between principals i and j; $\{M\}_{K_{ij}}$ denotes a message M encrypted with the key K_{ij}; M_1, M_2 is the message resulting from the concatenation of the two messages M_1 and M_2; while $i \rightarrow j : M$ denotes the fact that principal i sends the message M to principal j. The Andrew protocol can be formulated as follows:

$$
\begin{array}{llll}
1 & A \rightarrow B & : & \{N_a\}_{K_{ab}} \\
2 & B \rightarrow A & : & \{N_a, N_b\}_{K_{ab}} \\
3 & A \rightarrow B & : & \{N_b\}_{K_{ab}} \\
4 & B \rightarrow A & : & \{K'_{ab}, N'_b\}_{K_{ab}}
\end{array}
$$

Intuitively, the protocol works as follows: with message 1, A sends B the (fresh) nonce N_a encrypted with the key K_{ab}, which is supposed to be a good key. The goal of this message is to request authentication from B. With message 2, B sends back to A the nonce N_a concatenated with a newly created nonce N_b, both encrypted. At this point, since B must have decrypted message 1 to be able to generate message 2, A knows that it is talking with B. Then, in message 3, A sends back to B N_b encrypted. This allows B to conclude that it is actually talking to A (as it must have decrypted message 2 to obtain N_b and generate message 3). The two principals are now authenticated. Finally with message 4, B sends A the new session key K'_{ab} together with a new nonce N'_b encrypted with the shared key. The final message is the one subject to attacks. Indeed, in message 4 there is nothing that A can recognize as fresh. An intruder might send A an old message, possibly containing a compromised key.

The kind of analysis we're interested in is based on the idea, originally proposed in [3] (but see also [1]), of studying how messages sent and received during a protocol session by a trusted party may affect its beliefs about the other parties. In the present case, one might want to prove the following property: after message 4 has been received by A, A (respectively B) believes that the new key is a good key between A and B. Another property is that after message 4, A (respectively B) believes that B (respectively A) believes that the new key is a good key for communication between A and B. As pointed out in [3], the second property is stronger than the first, as it ensures that both principals believe that the protocol ended correctly and that they both possess a good session key. It turns out that neither of the properties above can be attained by principal A.

3   Multiagent Finite State Machines

Principals engaged in an authentication session can be modeled as finite state processes. We build the notion of principal (agent) incrementally over the notion of process. Suppose we have a set I of principals. Each principal is seen as a process having beliefs about (itself and) other principals. We adopt the usual syntax for beliefs: $B_i\phi$ means that principal i believes ϕ, and ϕ is a belief of i. B_i is the belief operator for i.

The idea is to associate to each (level of) nesting of belief operators a process evolving over time. Therefore, let $B = \{B_1, ..., B_n\}$, where each index $1, ..., n \in I$ corresponds to a principal. The set B^* denotes the set of finite strings of elements of B, i.e., strings of the form $B_1, ..., B_n$ with $B_l \subset B$. We call any $\alpha \in B^*$, a *view*. Each view in B^* corresponds to a possible nesting of belief operators. We also allow for the empty string, ϵ. Figure 1 depicts the general structure of the views. The intuition is that ϵ represents the view of an external observer (e.g., the designer) which, from the outside, "sees" the behavior of the overall protocol. To each nesting of belief operators we associate a view of the corresponding principal. Intuitively, in Figure 1, the beliefs of principal 1 correspond to the view B_1 and can be modeled by a process playing 1's role. The beliefs that 1 has about (the behavior of) principal 2 correspond to the view B_1B_2 and can be modeled by a process playing 2's role in (1's view of) the protocol. Things work in the same way for the beliefs of 2 and the beliefs that 2 can have about 1.

We associate a language $\mathcal{L}_\alpha$ to each view $\alpha \in B^*$. Intuitively, each $\mathcal{L}_\alpha$ is the language used to express what is true (and false) of the process of view α. We employ the logic CTL, a well known propositional branching-time temporal logic widely used in formal verification [5]. For each α, let P_α be a set of propositional atoms. Each P_α allows for the definition of a different language, called a Multi-Agent Temporal Logic (MATL) language (on P_α). A MATL language $\mathcal{L}_\alpha$ on P_α is the smallest CTL language containing the set of propositional atoms P_α and the belief atoms $B_i\phi$, for any formula ϕ of $\mathcal{L}_{\alpha B_i}$. In particular, $\mathcal{L}_\epsilon$ is used to speak about the whole protocol. The language $\mathcal{L}_{B_i}$ is the language adopted to represent i's beliefs. The language $\mathcal{L}_{B_iB_j}$ is used to specify i's beliefs about j's beliefs, and so on. For instance, the formula $\mathsf{AG}\,(p \supset B_i\neg q) \in \mathcal{L}_\epsilon$, (denoted by

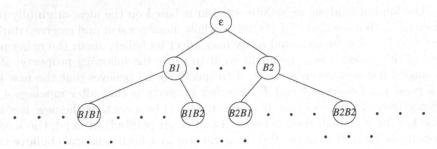

Fig. 1. A set of views

$\epsilon : \text{AG}\,(p \supset B_i\neg q)$), intuitively means that in every future state, if p is true then principal i believes q is false. Given a family $\{P_\alpha\}$ of sets of propositional atoms, the family of MATL languages on $\{P_\alpha\}$ is the family of CTL languages $\{\mathcal{L}_\alpha\}$.

We are interested in extending CTL model checking to the model checking of belief formulae. In model checking, finite state processes are modeled as finite state machines. A *finite state machine* (FSM) is a tuple $f = \langle S, J, R, L \rangle$, where S is a finite set of states, $J \subseteq S$ is the set of *initial states*, the transition relation R is a total binary relation on S, and $L : S \rightarrow \mathcal{P}(P)$ is a *labelling function*, which associates to each state $s \in S$ the set $L(s)$ of propositional atoms true at s. Our solution is to extend the notion of FSM to that of *MultiAgent Finite State Machine (MAFSM)*, where, roughly speaking, a MAFSM is a finite set of FSMs.

A first step in this direction is to restrict ourselves to a finite number of views α. Let B^n denote a finite subset of B^* obtained by taking the views in any finite subtree of B^* rooted at ϵ. This restriction is not enough, as a finite set of views still allows for an infinite number of belief atoms. Even if we had a finite number of processes we would not be able to model them as FSMs. This problem can be solved introducing the notion of *explicit belief atoms* as a finite subset of the set of belief atoms. Explicit belief atoms are the only belief atoms which are explicitly represented in a FSM.

Formally, if $\mathcal{L}_\alpha$ is a MATL language of view α, then for each belief operator B_i, the set $Expl(B_i, \alpha)$ of *explicit belief atoms* of B_i for α is a (possibly empty) *finite* subset of the belief atoms of $\mathcal{L}_\alpha$. We have the following:

Definition 1. *Let $\{\mathcal{L}_\alpha\}$ be a family of MATL languages on $\{P_\alpha\}$. A MultiAgent Finite State Machine (MAFSM) $F = \{F_\alpha\}$ for $\{\mathcal{L}_\alpha\}$ is a recursive total function such that:*

1. *$F_\epsilon \neq \emptyset$;*
2. *for all views $\alpha \in B^n \subset B^*$ with B^n finite, it associates with α a finite set F_α of FSMs on the MATL language on the following atoms: P_α and , for every principal i, $Expl(B_i, \alpha)$;*
3. *for all the views $\alpha \in B^* \setminus B^n$, $F_\alpha = \emptyset$.*

where $B^* \setminus B^n$ denotes the difference between B^* and B^n, namely the set of all views not contained in B^n.

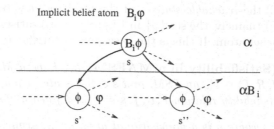

Fig. 2. Explicit belief atoms and satisfiability

The first condition ensures that the protocol specification is not empty; the second allows us to deal, in each view, with finite sets of FSMs; and the third restricts us to a finite number of views. In general, there may be more than one FSM associated with each view. This allows for situations in which a view can be only partially specified, and consequently there can be more than one process modeling that view. If it is completely specified, a view contains only one FSM.

Given the notion of MAFSM, the next step is to give a notion of satisfiability in a MAFSM. We start from the notion of satisfiability of CTL formulae in an FSM at a state (defined as in CTL structures). Since FSMs are built on the propositional and explicit belief atoms of a view, to assess satisfiability of the propositional and explicit belief atoms (and the CTL formulae build out of them) we do not need to use the machinery associated with belief operators. However, this machinery is needed in order to deal with the (infinite) number of belief atoms which are not memorized anywhere in MAFSM.

Let $Impl(B_i, \alpha)$, the set of *implicit belief atoms* of a view α, be the (infinite) subset of all belief atoms of $\mathcal{L}_\alpha$ which are not explicit belief atoms, i.e., $Impl(B_i, \alpha) = \{B_i\phi \in \mathcal{L}_\alpha \setminus Expl(B_i, \alpha)\}$. The idea is to use the information explicitly contained in the labelling function of each state s of a FSM f of a view α to assess the truth value of the implicit belief atoms at a state s. Figure 2 illustrates the underlying intuition. Intuitively, the principal modeled by FSM f (in view α), when in state s, ascribes to principal i the explicit belief atoms of the form $B_i\phi$ true at s. This means that the FMSs of view αB_i, which model the beliefs of i, must be in any of the states (s' and s'' in Figure 2) in which the formulae ϕ, occurring as arguments of the explicit belief atoms, are true. This motivates the following definition. Let $ArgExpl(B_i, \alpha, s)$ be defined as follows:

$$ArgExpl(B_i, \alpha, s) = \{\phi \in \mathcal{L}_{\alpha B_i} \mid B_i\phi \in L(s) \cap Expl(B_i, \alpha)\}$$

$ArgExpl(B_i, \alpha, s)$ consists of all the formulae $\phi \in \mathcal{L}_{\alpha B_i}$ such that the explicit belief atom $B_i\phi$ is true at state s (i.e., it belongs to the labelling function of s). The set $ArgExpl(B_i, \alpha, s)$ contains the formulae which identify the states in which the FSMs in view αB_i can be, whenever the process in view α is in state s.

We are now ready to define the notion of satisfiability of implicit belief atoms. Let $B_i\psi$ be an implicit belief atom of a view α. For each state s of a FSM of α, we can compute $ArgExpl(B_i, \alpha, s)$. As shown in Figure 2, we just need to check whether all the *reachable states* [1] of the FSMs of view αB_i, which satisfy $ArgExpl(B_i, \alpha, s)$ (namely, the set $\{\phi\}$ in Figure 2), also satisfy the argument ψ of the implicit belief atom. If this is the case, then s satisfies $B_i\psi$.

Definition 2. (Satisfiability in a MAFSM) *Let F be a MAFSM, α a view in B^*, $f = \langle S, J, R, L \rangle \in F_\alpha$ an FSM, and $s \in S$ a state. Then, for any formula ϕ of $\mathcal{L}_\alpha$, the satisfiability relation $F, \alpha, f, s \models \phi$ is defined as follows:*

1. *$F, \alpha, f, s \models p$, where p is a propositional atom or an explicit belief atom: the same as FSM satisfiability;*
2. *satisfiability of propositional connectives and CTL operators: the same as FSM satisfiability;*
3. *$F, \alpha, f, s \models B_i\psi$, where $B_i\psi$ is an implicit belief atom, iff for all $f' \in F_{\alpha B_i}$ and s' reachable state of the FSM f', $F, \alpha B_i, f', s' \models \bigwedge ArgExpl(B_i, \alpha, s) \supset \psi$.*

We have furthermore:

4. *for every $s \in J$, $F, \alpha, f \models \phi$ iff $F, \alpha, f, s \models \phi$;*
5. *$F, \alpha \models \phi$ iff for all $f \in F_\alpha$, $F, \alpha, f \models \phi$;*
6. *$F \models \alpha : \phi$ iff $F, \alpha \models \phi$.*

In the definition of satisfiability above, Item 3 is the crucial step. The formula $\bigwedge ArgExpl(B_i, \alpha, s)$ is the conjunction of all the elements of $ArgExpl(B_i, \alpha, s)$.[2] Item 4 states that a FSM satisfies a formula if this formula is satisfied in all its initial states. Item 5 states that a formula is satisfied in a view if it is satisfied by all the FSMs of that view. Finally, Item 6 states that a labeled formula $\alpha : \phi$ is satisfied if ϕ is satisfied in the view corresponding to the label.

4   Modeling the Andrew Protocol Using MAFSMs

As described in Section 3, a MAFSM can be constructed out of the following elements: the structure of the views; the atomic propositions of each view and how they vary over time; the choice of explicit belief atoms of each view and how they vary over time; and the specification of the initial states for the FSMs in each view. In this section we present a MAFSM-based model of the Andrew protocol, thus providing, in turn, all these elements. For lack of space, we give only a partial description, emphasizing those elements of the model which are relevant to illustrate our approach.

In the MAFSM modeling the Andrew protocol there is only one FSM per view. Indeed, the processes associated to the all the views can be completely

---

[1] A state s of a FSM is said to be reachable if there is a path leading from an initial state of the FSM to state s.

[2] Item 3 gives to belief operators the same strength as modal $K(m)$, where m is the number of principals. In particular, we have that if $\Gamma \supset \phi$ is a theorem in a view then $B_i\Gamma \supset B_i\phi$ is a theorem in the (appropriate) view above, where $B_i\Gamma$ is the set $\{B_i\phi \mid \phi \in \Gamma\}$.

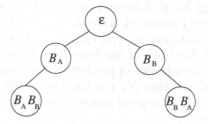

Fig. 3. The set of views of the Andrew protocol (Section 2)

specified, starting from the protocol specification given in Section 2. In the presentation below, we give the FSM specifications using the input language of the model checker NuSMV [4].

The structure of the views. The Andrew protocol involves two principals, A and B. Therefore, we have $I = \{A, B\}$. We model each principal as having beliefs about the other. Since, for the sake of the example, we do not need to model beliefs that a principal has about itself, we will need only to consider, besides the external view ϵ, the views of A and B, the view A has about B and the view B has about A. Therefore, $B^n = \{\epsilon, B_A, B_B, B_A B_B, B_B B_A\}$. Figure 3 shows the resulting situation. ϵ (the external observer) is modeled as a process which "sees" all the messages sent and received by the principals. B_A and $B_B B_A$ model the behavior of principal A, while views B_B and $B_A B_B$ model the behavior of principal B.

The set of atomic propositions P_α. In each view, we need to model a principal sending a message to another principal and/or receiving a message, as well as the properties the principal attributes to the (sub)messages it receives or sends. In particular, a (sub)message can be fresh and a key can be a good key for secret communication between the two principals. Each view has its own set of atomic propositions, reflecting the atomic properties of interest about its associated process. Since B_A and $B_B B_A$ model the same principal, we associate to both of them the same set of atomic propositions. Similarly for the views B_B and $B_A B_B$. For what concerns the views B_A and $B_A B_B$ in the Andrew protocol, we can consider the following set of atomic propositions:

$$P_{B_A} = \left\{ \begin{array}{l} send_B\, N_a\_K_{ab}, \\ rec\, N_a\_N_b\_K_{ab}, \\ send_B\, N_b\_K_{ab}, \\ rec\, K'_{ab}\_N'_b\_K_{ab}, \\ fresh\, N_a, \\ fresh\, K'_{ab}\_N'_b\_K_{ab}, \\ shk\, K'_{ab} \\ \dots \end{array} \right\} \qquad P_{B_A B_B} = \left\{ \begin{array}{l} rec\, N_a\_K_{ab}, \\ send_A\, N_a\_N_b\_K_{ab}, \\ send_A\, K'_{ab}\_N'_b\_K_{ab}, \\ fresh\, N_b, \\ fresh\, K'_{ab}\_N'_b\_K_{ab}, \\ shk\, K'_{ab} \\ \dots \end{array} \right\}$$

where the variables of the form $rec\, M$ or $send_B\, M$ (where M is a message of the Andrew protocol) are called *message variables* and represent the act of receiving M, and sending M to B, respectively. For instance, $rec\,N_a\_N_b\_K_{ab}$ and $send_B\,N_a\_K_{ab}$ in view $_{BA}$ represent A receiving $\{N_a, N_b\}_{K_{ab}}$ (message 2 in the Andrew protocol), and A sending $\{N_a\}_{K_{ab}}$ to B (message 3 in the Andrew protocol), respectively. Variables of the form $fresh\,M$ or $shk\,M$ are called *freshness variables*, and express freshness properties of (sub)messages. For instance, $fresh\,N_a$ in view $_{BA}$ means that N_a is a fresh (sub)message, while $shk\,K'_{ab}$ expresses the fact that K'_{ab} is a good shared key between A and B. For what concerns view ϵ, we set:

$$P_\epsilon = \left\{ \begin{array}{l} send_{B,A}\,K'_{ab}\_N'_b\_K_{ab}, \\ rec_A\,K'_{ab}\_N'_b\_K_{ab}, \\ ... \end{array} \right\}$$

where the variables for the sent messages (e.g., $send_{B,A}\,K'_{ab}\_N'_b\_K_{ab}$) are labeled (in subscript) with both the sender (B) and the intended receiver (A), while those of received messages (e.g., $rec_A\,K'_{ab}\_N'_b\_K_{ab}$) are labeled only with the actual receiver (A). With respect to the other views, the additional subscripts for both *send* and *rec* reflect the fact that ϵ knows who sends a message to whom and who receives what message.

Evolution of message variables. To specify the evolution of variables in a view we use the *next()* operator of the NuSMV input language. The *next* operator allows us to specify the next value of a variable in each state, possibly depending on its value in the current state. Since all variables are of type boolean, the possible values are T (for true) and F (for false). We report below the definitions of the next state value for some message variables in the language of view $_{BA}$, modeling the behavior of (the beliefs of) A. [3]

$_{BA}$
1 $next(send_B\,N_a\_K_{ab}) :=$ *case*
　　　　　　　$!send_B\,N_a\_K_{ab} : \{T,F\}$;
　　　　　　　$1 : send_B\,N_a\_K_{ab}$;
　　　　　　esac;
2 $next(rec\,K'_{ab}\_N'_b\_K_{ab}) :=$ *case*
　　　　　　　$send_B\,N_b\_K_{ab}$ & $!rec\,K'_{ab}\_N'_b\_K_{ab}: \{T,F\}$;
　　　　　　　$1 : rec\,K'_{ab}\_N'_b\_K_{ab}$;
　　　　　　esac;

Statement 1 contains a case statement, whose first clause ($!send_B\,N_a\_K_{ab} : \{T, F\}$) contains a precondition on the left-hand side and the next value on the right-hand side. The precondition is the negation of a message variable and is true when $send_B\,N_a\_K_{ab}$ is false, that is if message $N_a\_K_{ab}$ has not been sent to B yet . The next value is a set of values ($\{T, F\}$). This intuitively means that the first message of the Andrew protocol ($\{N_a\}_{K_{ab}}$) may or may not be sent (i.e., $send_B\,N_a\_K_{ab}$ may nondeterministically take value T or F) in the next state, if it has not been sent yet in the current state. The second item is the "default" clause, and it is taken if the precondition in the first clause does

---

[3] The label $_{BA}$ at the top of a block of statements means that the block belongs to the specification of view $_{BA}$, and similarly for the other views.

not apply. The result of this clause is that $send_B N_a\_K_{ab}$ keeps, in the next state, its current value. In Statement 2, the precondition of the first clause (i.e., $send_B N_b\_K_{ab}$ & $!rec\ K'_{ab}\_N'_b\_K_{ab}$) is a conjunction of two boolean expressions. The first expression means that $\{N_b\}_{K_{ab}}$ has been already sent to B, and the second means that $\{K'_{ab}, N'_b\}_{K_{ab}}$ has not been received yet. The next value again is the nondeterministic choice between values T and F (the message is received or not). The messages in each session of the Andrew protocol are supposed to be sent and received following the order reported in Section 2. Therefore, for each message variable, the preconditions in the next statement checks whether the previous message (and therefore all the previous messages) involving the current principal (A in the case of view B_A), has been already conveyed or not. The default clause is similar to that of Statement 1. The specification of the evolution of the other message variables in the other views is specified in a similar way.

Evolution of freshness variables. In any path of states of a view, freshness variables for (sub)messages originated by that principal always keep their initial values. In the Andrew protocol, this is the case for N_a in view B_A (and also $B_B B_A$), as expressed by the *next* statements below, and N_b in views B_B and $B_A B_B$.

B_A
3 $next(fresh\ N_a) := fresh\ N_a;$

Statement 3 simply says that $fresh\ N_a$ keeps the current value in the next state. Similar statements are made also for $fresh\ N_b$, $fresh\ N'_b$ and $shk\ K'_{ab}$ (which are messages originated by B) in the views modeling B.

On the other hand, a principal can attain freshness of the messages it has not originated itself, only after it receives (possibly other) messages which contain them. Therefore, freshness variables of a message M not originated by a principal may change their value (e.g., from false to true) only when the principal has received a message containing M. After the last message of the session has been conveyed, the freshness variables of M keep their current value (no new information can be gained by the principal). Moreover, once it becomes true, a freshness variable remains stable. All of the above intuitions are specified as follows:

B_A
4 $next(shk\ K'_{ab}) := case$
    $!shk\ K'_{ab}$ & $!rec\ K'_{ab}\_N'_b\_K_{ab} : \{T,F\};$
    $1 : shk\ K'_{ab}\ ;$
   $esac;$
5 $next(fresh\ K'_{ab}\_N'_b\_K_{ab}) := case$
    $!fresh\ K'_{ab}\_N'_b\_K_{ab}$ & $!rec\ K'_{ab}\_N'_b\_K_{ab} : \{T,F\};$
    $1 : fresh\ K'_{ab}\_N'_b\_K_{ab};$
   $esac;$

Statement 4 and 5 are very similar in form. As to statement 4, the precondition in the first clause of the case statement is a conjunction ($!shk\ K'_{ab}$ & $!rec\ K'_{ab}\_N'_b\_K_{ab}$) of two negations (meaning respectively that "K'_{ab} is not known to be a good shared key", and that the "$\{K'_{ab}, N'_b\}_{K_{ab}}$ has not been received yet"). If this condition is true, the nondeterministic choice on the left-hand side of the clause is taken. The "default" clause leaves the value of the variable in the next state unchanged. Statement 5 checks, in the first clause of the case statement, if the conjunction in the precondition ($!fresh\ K'_{ab}\_N'_b\_K_{ab}$ & $!rec\ K'_a b\_N'_b\_K_{ab}$) is true ($\{K'_{ab}, N'_b\}_{K_{ab}}$ is not known to be fresh, and it has not been received yet), and in this case chooses nondeterministically the next value of the variable.

Clearly Statements 4 and 5 are very general and do not allow us to model appropriately the freshness of (sub)messages. Indeed, additional constraints are needed. Following the BAN logic approach, there are a number of properties of messages, which relate their freshness to that of their components. For instance, a principal can conclude that a message is fresh from the freshness of one of its components. This is the case for $\{N_a\}_{K_{ab}}$, which is known to be fresh whenever N_a is known to be.[4] NuSMV allows for specifying constraints on the admissible (reachable) states by means of invariants, which are boolean formulae that must hold in every reachable state. The following invariant statement captures a relevant constraint on some freshness variables:

B_A
6 $INVAR\ (fresh\ K'_{ab}\ |\ fresh\ N'_b)\ \&\ rec\ K'_{ab}\_N'_b\_K_{ab} \leftrightarrow fresh\ K'_{ab}\_N'_b\_K_{ab}$

Invariant 6 is an equivalence ($\leftrightarrow$) whose left-hand side is a conjunction. The disjunction in the left conjunct ($fresh\ K'_{ab}\ |\ fresh\ N'_b$) means that K'_{ab} or N'_b is fresh; the second conjunct is meant to be true when the message $\{K'_{ab}, N'_b\}_{K_{ab}}$ has been received. Intuitively, it states that A can consider (the encrypted message) $\{K'_{ab}, N'_b\}_{K_{ab}}$ fresh (right-hand side of the equivalence) if and only if it has received the message (second conjunct on the left-hand side) and either of its components is fresh (first conjunct on the left-hand side). Similar invariants must be added for each message received by the principal.

View $_{B_A}B_B$ can be specified in a similar way. Some additional statements must be added, though, reflecting the role of principal B. Indeed, the Andrew protocol assumes that B is the key server (see Section 2). Therefore, B is supposed to generate and send a good shared key in message 4, whenever it believes that $\{K'_{ab}, N'_b\}_{K_{ab}}$ is fresh. Remember that we have a variable for the freshness of the last message of the protocol (namely, $fresh\ K'_{ab}\_N'_b\_K_{ab}$), and a variable for K'_{ab} being a good key ($shk\ K'_{ab}$). Then we can specify the above invariant as an implication:

$B_A B_B$
7 $INVAR\ fresh\ K'_{ab}\_N'_b\_K_{ab} \rightarrow shk\ K'_{ab}$

---

[4] For (sub)messages which are not originated by the principal, usually BAN-like logics substitute the notion of freshness with that of recentness. A message is then considered recently conveyed by another principal, if it is part of a fresh message encrypted with a secret key, shared with that principal. The difference between these two concepts is not relevant for the present paper.

Explicit belief atoms of a view. We need now to choose the explicit belief atoms of each view. In general, the choice of the appropriate set of explicit belief atoms of (the views in) a MAFSM depends on what kind of aspects of the protocol one wants to analyze, and on what kind of properties need to be verified. In the case of authentication protocols, principals can only gain information carried by the messages they receive. In BAN-like logics the freshness of the received messages is based on their form, and it is a basic property to be attained by a principal. We choose, therefore, the following belief atoms as explicit beliefs atoms: the beliefs about other principals having sent or received a given message, and the beliefs about the freshness of messages. In our case, we have:

$$Expl(B_A, \epsilon) = \left\{ \begin{array}{l} B_A\,rec\ K'_{ab}\_N'_b\_K_{ab}, \\ B_A\,fresh\ N_a \\ \ldots \end{array} \right\} \quad Expl(B_B, B_A) = \left\{ \begin{array}{l} B_B\,send_A\ K'_{ab}\_N'_b\_K_{ab}, \\ B_B\,fresh\ K'_{ab}\_N'_b\_K_{ab} \\ \ldots \end{array} \right\}$$

where, for instance, $B_A\,fresh\ N_a$ in ϵ intuitively means that A believes that N_a is a fresh nonce; while $B_B\,send_A\ K'_{ab}\_N'_b\_K_{ab}$ in B_A expresses the fact that A believes that B believes that it has sent $\{K'_{ab}, N'_b\}_{K_{ab}}$ to A. There are no explicit belief atoms in $B_B B_A$ and $B_A B_B$, as they have no beliefs atoms at all in their language. Indeed, the example we are considering does not need to model more than two nesting of the belief operators.

Evolution of explicit belief atoms. Variables representing explicit belief atoms are supposed to vary similarly to freshness variables. In particular, as long as there are still messages to be received by a principal of a view, explicit belief atoms of that view are free to change value from F to T. Once the last message of the protocol has been received, no new belief can be attained, and explicit belief atoms keep their value, thereafter. Again, once they become true, they remain stable. The following statement specifies how the value of $B_B\,send_A\ N_a\_N_b\_K_{ab}$ may vary in B_A:

B_A
8 $next(B_B\,send_A\ N_a\_N_b\_K_{ab}) := case$
                $!B_B\,send_A\ N_a\_N_b\_K_{ab}\ \&\ !rec\ K'_{ab}\_N'_b\_K_{ab} : \{T,F\};$
                $1 : B_B\,send_A\ N_a\_N_b\_K_{ab};$
      $esac;$

Very similar statements can be added for all the explicit beliefs in all views. Similarly to freshness variables, additional constraints, in the form of state invariants, on reachable states need to be added for explicit beliefs atoms. In particular we report below some relevant ones for the Andrew protocol. All these invariants can be seen as encodings of standard properties holding in BAN-like logics.

B_A
9 $INVAR\ rec\ K'_{ab}\_N'_b\_K_{ab} \rightarrow B_B\,send_A\ K'_{ab}\_N'_b\_K_{ab}$
10 $INVAR\ fresh\ K'_{ab}\_N'_b\_K_{ab} \rightarrow B_B\,fresh\ K'_{ab}\_N'_b\_K_{ab}$

Both invariants are implications. Intuitively, Invariant 9 states that if it receives the message $\{K'_{ab}, N'_b\}_{K_{ab}}$ (left-had side of the implication) then A ascribes to B the belief that B has sent that message to A (right-hand side of the implication).

Invariant 10 states that if it can conclude that $\{K'_{ab}, N'_b\}_{K_{ab}}$ is fresh, then A also ascribes to B the same belief.

Initial states of a view. Finally, we have to set the initial states of the FSM in each view. They can be specified as a boolean formula which identifies all and only the admissible initial states of the FSM. Following the BAN logic tradition, we want to model a single session of the Andrew protocol and study what beliefs each principal can attain at the end of the session. A protocol session starts with no message sent or received. Thus, the process in each view starts with the value of all the message variables set to false. Since no message has been received yet, freshness variables of messages not originated by a principal are set to false as well. All the other variables can take nondeterministically the value T or F in the initial states. The following specification in view B_A formalises these intuitions for the Andrew protocol:

B_A
INIT !send$_B$ N_a_K_{ab} &
    !rec N_a_N_b_K_{ab} &
    !send$_B$ N_b_K_{ab} &
    !rec K'_{ab}_N'_b_K_{ab} &
    !fresh K'_{ab}_N'_b_K_{ab} &
    !shk K'_{ab}
    ...

All the other views can be specified in a similar way.

5   Model Checking a MAFSM

The basic operation of a standard CTL model checking algorithm is to extend the labelling function of an FSM (which considers only propositional atoms) to all the sub-formulae of the formula being model checked. Let us call Extended FSM (or, simply, FSM when the context makes clear what we mean) the result of this operation. The generation of an extended FSM relies on the fact that the labelling function explicitly defines the truth value of all atoms. The problem is that in the FSMs of a MAFSM the labelling function is not defined on implicit belief atoms, whose truth value is therefore left undefined; and we need to know the truth values of the implicit belief atoms occurring in the formula to be model checked. The definition of satisfiability in a MAFSM (Item 3 in Definition 2) tells us how to solve this problem.

The crucial observation is that $ArgExpl(B_i, \alpha, s)$, in Item 3 of Definition 2, is generated from the formulae in $Expl(B_i, \alpha)$ and the labelling functions of the FSMs in α; $ArgExpl(B_i, \alpha, s)$ is a finite set; and it only depends on the MAFSM specified (thus independent of the formula to be model checked). For each belief operator B_i, C_{B_i} is called the *(MAFSM) compatibility relation* of B_i, and it is a relation defined as follows. Let $ex \subseteq Expl(B_i, \alpha)$ be a subset of the explicit belief atoms of a view α. Then:

$$C_{B_i}(\alpha, ex) = \left\{ \langle f', s' \rangle \mid f' \in F_{\alpha B_i}, s' \text{ a reachable state of } f' \text{ and } \atop F, \alpha B_i, f', s' \models \{\phi \mid B_i\phi \in ex\} \right\}$$

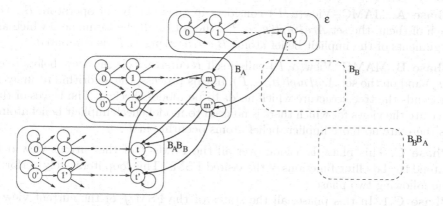

Fig. 4. Some FSMs for the Andrew Protocol

Starting from a view α and a subset of explicit belief atoms ex of α, $C_{B_i}(\alpha, ex)$
collects all the FSMs f' and reachable states s' of f' (in the view αB_i) which
satisfy the arguments of the explicit belief atoms ex (formally: $\{\phi \mid B_i\phi \in ex\}$).
Intuitively, $C_{B_i}(\alpha, ex)$ contains all the pairs $\langle f', s'\rangle$ of view αB_i, in which the
process associated to view αB_i can be, whenever the process modeling view α is
in a state that satisfies all the explicit belief atoms in ex.

It can be easily seen that, for f' a FSM of view αB_i, s' any reachable state
of f', and s a state of a FSM of view α:

$$\langle f', s'\rangle \subset C_{B_i}(\alpha, L(s) \cap Expl(B_i, \alpha)) \text{ iff } F, \alpha B_i, f', s' \models \bigwedge ArgExpl(B_i, \alpha, s)$$

where $L(s) \cap Expl(B_i, \alpha)$ is the set of explicit belief atoms true at state s. Hence,
the following holds:

$$F, \alpha, f, s \models B_i\phi \text{ iff for all } \langle f', s'\rangle \in C_{B_i}(\alpha, L(s) \cap Expl(B_i, \alpha)), F, \alpha B_i, f', s' \models \phi \tag{1}$$

where $B_i\phi$ is any implicit belief atom.

Figure 4 represents the underlying intuition on the MAFSM for the Andrew
protocol. The relation $C_{B_i}(\alpha, L(s) \cap Expl(B_i, \alpha))$ is depicted as arrows connecting
states of adjacent views. Let us consider view ϵ. When the process associated to
ϵ is in state n, the external observer believes that principal A, modeled by view
B_A, can be in any one of the states m and m' of the FSM of that view, which
are compatible with state n. The states of view B_A are completely identified by
the explicit beliefs of ϵ true at state n. Therefore, ϵ believes $B_i\phi$ in state n if
and only if each state of B_A, in which ϵ believes A to be (i.e., states m and m'
in Figure 4), satisfies ϕ. Given a state s' of a FSM f' of view αB_i, we say
that s' is *compatible* with a state s of a FSM of view α if the pair $\langle f', s'\rangle$ belongs
to $C_{B_i}(\alpha, L(s) \cap Expl(B_i, \alpha))$.

The model checking algorithm MAMC$-$View(α, Γ) (see [2] for a complete
description and a proof of correctness) takes two arguments: a view α, and a set
of MATL formulae $\Gamma \subset \mathcal{L}_\alpha$. MAMC$-$View$(\alpha, \Gamma)$ performs the following phases:

Phase A. MAMC−View(α, Γ) considers in turn the belief operators B_i. For each of them, the set $ArgImpl(B_i, \alpha, \Gamma)$, the set of all the formulae ϕ which are arguments of the implicit belief atoms $B_i\phi$ occurring in Γ, is computed.

Phase B. MAMC−View(α, Γ) calls itself recursively on the view below (e.g., αB_i) and on the set $ArgImpl(B_i, \alpha, \Gamma)$. In this process, the algorithm recursively descends the tree structure which needs to be model checked. The leaves of this tree are the views for which there is no need to model check implicit belief atoms, as there are no more implicit belief atoms occuring in Γ.

Phase C. This phase is a loop over all the FSMs f of the current view α to extend the labelling functions of the visited FSMs. This loop iteratively performs the following two phases:

Phase C.1. In this phase, all the states of the FSM f of the current view α where the algorithm is, are labeled with the implicit belief atoms. This phase is executed only if there occur implicit belief atoms in the input formulae. The labelling of states of f is computed according to definition of satisfiability of implicit belief atoms in a MAFSM. Therefore, for each reachable state s of f, the set $L(s) \cap Expl(B_i, \alpha)$ is computed. Then, the algorithm computes the implicit belief atoms occurring in Γ which can be added to the labelling function of s. That is, for each implicit belief atom $B_i\phi$, $B_i\phi$ is added to $L(s)$ if ϕ is satisfied by all the pairs $\langle f', s' \rangle$ belonging to the compatibility relation $C_{B_i}(\alpha, L(s) \cap Expl(B_i, \alpha))$.

Phase C.2. This phase simply calls a standard CTL model checking algorithm on the FSM f of the current view. Indeed, at this point every state s in the current FSM f is labeled (by phase C.1) with all the atoms (i.e, propositional atoms, explicit and implicit belief atoms) occurring in the input formulae.

Notice that in phase C.2 we can employ any model checker (in our case NuSMV) as a black box.

6   Model Checking the Andrew Protocol

In this section, we show how the model checking algorithm described in Section 5 works, trying to check a desired property of the Andrew protocol of Section 2. Let us consider the following property (from Section 2): A believes that B believes that K'_{ab} is a good shared key, any time it receives the last message of the Andrew protocol. This property can be written as the following MATL formula in view ϵ:

$$\epsilon : \mathsf{AG}\,(rec_A\,K'_{ab}\text{-}N'_b\text{-}K_{ab} \wedge B_A\,\mathit{fresh}\,N_a \rightarrow B_A\,B_B\,shk\,K'_{ab}) \qquad (2)$$

where the (sub)formula $B_A\,B_B\,shk\,K'_{ab}$ is an implicit belief atom.

Phase A and B. We only have to consider the belief operator B_A. We construct the set $ArgImpl(B_B, \epsilon, \Gamma) = \{B_B\,shk\,K'_{ab}\}$. Since $B_B\,shk\,K'_{ab}$ is an implicit belief atom of ϵ, MAMC−View$(\epsilon, \{\mathsf{AG}\,(rec_A\,K'_{ab}\text{-}N'_b\text{-}K_{ab} \wedge B_A\,\mathit{fresh}\,N_a \rightarrow B_A B_B\,shk\,K'_{ab})\})$ calls itself recursively on view B_A and $\{B_B\,shk\,K'_{ab}\}$ (calling MAMC−View$(B_A, \{B_B\,shk\,K'_{ab}\})$). In view B_A, we need to consider the operator B_B and to compute $ArgImpl(B_B, B_A, \{B_B\,shk\,K'_{ab}\}) = \{shk\,K'_{ab}\}$.

$MAMC-View(_{BA}, \{B_B\ shk\ K'_{ab}\})$ descends to view $_{BABB}$ (calling $MAMC-View(_{BABB}, \{shk\ K'_{ab}\})$). Phase B is not performed in view $_{BABB}$ as no implicit beliefs occur in the input formulae (namely, $\{shk\ K'_{ab}\}$).

Phases C.1 and C.2 at $_{BABB}$. The only formula to check in this view is the atomic formula $shk\ K'_{ab}$. The FSM of this view already contains the information about its truth value in each state (see Section 4). Therefore, both phases end immediately.

Phase C.1 at $_{BA}$. The FSM f of this view is labeled with the implicit belief atom $B_B\ shk\ K'_{ab}$. For each reachable state s of f and each pair $\langle f', s' \rangle \in C_{B_B}(_{BA}, L(s)\ \cap\ Expl(_{BB}, _{BA}))$, the intersection of $ArgImpl(_{BB}, _{BA}, \{B_B\ shk\ K'_{ab}\}) = \{shk\ K'_{ab}\}$ and $L(s')$ is computed. This gives either the empty set (meaning that $shk\ K'_{ab}$ is not true in s') or $\{shk\ K'_{ab}\}$ itself (meaning that $shk\ K'_{ab}$ is true in s'). The final step consists in adding to $L(s)$ the implicit belief atom $B_B\ shk\ K'_{ab}$, if every state of f', compatible with s, satisfies $shk\ K'_{ab}$. It turns out that the states of $_{BA}$ satisfying that implicit belief are those which satisfy $rec\ K'_{ab}\_N'_b\_K_{ab}$ (A has received message 4) and $fresh\ K'_{ab}\_N'_b\_K_{ab}$ (message 4 is known by A to be fresh). All those states also satisfy the explicit belief atom $B_B\ fresh\ K'_{ab}\_N'_b\_K_{ab}$ (by Invariant 10), and are therefore compatible only with those states of view $_{BABB}$ where $fresh\ K'_{ab}\_N'_b\_K_{ab}$ is true. Notice that there can be a reachable state of $_{BA}$ where $rec\ K'_{ab}\_N'_b\_K_{ab}$ and $fresh\ N_a$ are both true but $fresh\ K'_{ab}\_N'_b\_K_{ab}$ is false. This is possible, as nothing in message 4 is recognisable by A as fresh. As a consequence, there is a reachable state of view $_{BA}$, which does not satisfy $B_B\ fresh\ K'_{ab}\_N'_b\_K_{ab}$ either. Let the state m of view $_{BA}$ in Figure 4 be one such state. Therefore, state m satisfies $rec\ K'_{ab}\_N'_b\_K_{ab}$ and $fresh\ N_a$ but not $B_B\ shk\ K'_{ab}$.

Phase C.2 at view $_{BA}$. Once again, the formula to check is atomic (though an implicit belief atom). Therefore, this phase ends immediately.

Phase C.1 at ϵ. We have now to process the implicit belief $B_A\ B_B\ shk\ K'_{ab}$. It performs similar steps as in phase C.1 for view $_{BA}$. It turns out that there is (at least) a reachable state in the FSM of ϵ which does not satisfy this implicit belief. Indeed, as we have pointed out above, there is a state of view $_{BA}$ (state m in Figure 4) which does not satisfy $B_B\ shk\ K'_{ab}$ but satisfies both $fresh\ N_a$ and $rec\ K'_{ab}\_N'_b\_K_{ab}$. Let us assume that state n in ϵ (see Figure 4) satisfies $B_A\ fresh\ N_a$ and $rec_A\ K'_{ab}\_N'_b\_K_{ab}$ but does not satisfy the explicit belief atom $B_A\ fresh\ K'_{ab}\_N'_b\_K_{ab}$. n is actually a reachable state of the FSM of ϵ. Since n satisfies $rec_A\ K'_{ab}\_N'_b\_K_{ab}$, by an invariant of ϵ similar to Invariant 9, n also satisfies $B_A\ rec_A\ K'_{ab}\_N'_b\_K_{ab}$. Since n does not satisfy the belief atom $B_A\ fresh\ K'_{ab}\_N'_b\_K_{ab}$, the explicit belief atoms true at n are not enough to rule out the compatibility with state m in $_{BA}$ (see again Figure 4). Indeed, m does not satisfy $fresh\ K'_{ab}\_N'_b\_K_{ab}$, therefore, it belongs to the compatibility relation $C_{B_A}(\epsilon, L(n) \cap Expl(_{BA}, \epsilon))$. State m, as we know, does not satisfy $B_B\ shk\ K'_{ab}$. As a consequence of (1), state n of ϵ does not satisfy $B_A\ B_B\ shk\ K'_{ab}$.

Phase C.2 at ϵ. Here the usual CTL model checking algorithm on the formula (2) is called. As expected, the final answer is negative since, from phase C.1 in ϵ, there are reachable states satisfying $rec_A K'_{ab} \_N'_b \_K_{ab} \wedge B_A \, fresh \, N_a$ but not $B_A \, B_B \, shk \, K'_{ab}$.

7   Conclusion

In this paper we have described a model-checking based verification procedure for security protocols employing a logic of belief. Our approach allows us to reuse the technology and tools developed in model checking.

To model beliefs in security protocols, we have defined the notion of Multi-agent Finite State Machine as an extension of the usual notion of Finite State Machine. Then, we have described a model checking algorithm which allows us to verify formulae containing belief (sub)formulae in a MAFSM. Finally, we have formalized within this framework a well known security protocol, the Andrew protocol.

References

1. M. Abadi and M. Tuttle. A semantics for a logic of authentication. In *Proceedings of the 10th Annual ACM Symposium on Principles of Distributed Computing*, pages 201–216, 1991. 521
2. M. Benerecetti, F. Giunchiglia, and L. Serafini. Model Checking Multiagent Systems. *Journal of Logic and Computation, Special Issue on Computational & Logical Aspects of Multi-Agent Systems*, 8(3):401–423, 1998. Also IRST-Technical Report 9708-07, IRST, Trento, Italy. 531
3. M. Burrows, M. Abadi, and R. M. Needham. A logic of authentication. *ACM Transactions on Computer Systems*, 8(1):18–36, 1990. 519, 520, 521
4. A. Cimatti, E. Clarke, F. Giunchiglia, and M. Roveri. Nusmv: a new symbolic model verifier. In *Proceedings of the International Conference on Computer-Aided Verification (CAV'99)Trento, Italy. July 1999.* 525
5. E. Clarke, O. Grumberg, and D. Long. Model Checking. In *Proceedings of the International Summer School on Deductive Program Design*, Marktoberdorf, Germany, 1994. 519, 520, 521
6. K.L. McMillan. Symbolic Model Checking. Kluwer Academic, 1993. 519

A Formal Specification and Validation of a Critical System in Presence of Byzantine Errors*

S. Gnesi[1], D. Latella[2], G. Lenzini[1],
C. Abbaneo[3], A. Amendola[3], and P. Marmo[3]

[1] Istituto Elaborazione dell'Informazione – CNR
{gnesi,lenzini}@iei.pi.cnr.it
[2] CNUCE – CNR
d.latella@cnuce.cnr.it
[3] Ansaldobreda Segnalamento Ferroviario
{cabbaneo,amendola, marmo}@asf.atr.ansaldo.it

Abstract. This paper describes an experience in formal specification and fault tolerant behavior validation of a railway critical system. The work, performed in the context of a real industrial project, had the following main targets: (a) to validate specific safety properties in the presence of byzantine system components or of some hardware temporary faults; (b) to design a formal model of a critical railway system at a right level of abstraction so that could be possible to verify certain safety properties and at the same time to use the model to simulate the system. For the model specification we used the PROMELA language, while the verification was performed using the SPIN model checker. Safety properties were specified by means of both assertions and temporal logic formulae. To make the problem of validation tractable in the SPIN environment, we used ad hoc abstraction techniques.

Keywords: safety critical systems, formal verifications, fault tolerant behavior, linear temporal logic, model checking.

1 Introduction

In the area of industrial processes, the use of Formal Methods (FM) to check safety critical components is in evident increase. Due to the high integration of information technology in the quite total amount of control systems, safety request is becoming more and more pressing. However some other important factors induce industries to use FM. First of all, the interest in discovering as many errors as possible before entering in the production phase; in fact, during this stage the cost of correction per error increases enormously (see [16] for a good statistical study). Moreover, governments and international institutions require industries to conform to international standards (*e.g.*, EN 50128 CENELEC

---

* This work was supported in part by the CNR project "Strumenti Automatici per la Verifica Formale nel Progetto di Sistemi Software"

S. Graf and M. Schwartzbach (Eds.): TACAS/ETAPS 2000, LNCS 1785, pp. 535–549, 2000.
© Springer-Verlag Berlin Heidelberg 2000

Railways Applications [20], or IEC 65108 [13]) where FM are strongly suggested for validation and verification analysis.

In the last decade many industries, like the Ansaldobreda Segnalamento Ferroviario, started pilot projects (e.g., the ones documented in [8,15,18,2]) directed to evaluate the impact of FM on their production costs. Within Ansaldobreda Segnalamento Ferroviario encouraging results [1,3] - using CCS process algebras, with properties expressed in CTL and verified in the JACK environment - have shown how, for railway control systems, could be possible to formalize significant models and to perform verification in the model checking [7,21,4] approaches. Similar studies, using different formalisms (e.g., [9] used VCL* and μCRL to model a station vital processor and propositional logic to specify properties then verified in ASF+SDF), seem to confirm this positive trend. A recent thesis in [6], formally supports how railway systems share important robustness and locality properties, that distinguish them from most hardware systems and make them easily checkable in symbolic model checking and Stålmarck checking.

In this paper we describe the principal results of a real project jointly carried out by Ansaldobreda Segnalamento Ferroviario and CNR Institutes - IEI, CNUCE and CPR - of Pisa. The project consisted in designing a formal model of a critical control system called *Computerized Central Apparatus*, and successively in verifying specific safety properties under the hypothesis of *byzantine* faults. In this context, byzantine is to be intended as it was in Lamport et al. [14], where a byzantine component can arbitrarily fail in running its algorithm. In addition, other fault tolerant properties were verified under a weaker definition of byzantine fault, where a consistent behavior has been required. Industrial choices in Ansaldobreda suggested the use of the PROMELA [11] specification language, and of the SPIN [12] model checker.

The paper is organized as follows: in Section 2, we briefly and informally describe the system and all its component units; in Section 3 we recall the most important features of PROMELA and SPIN; in Section 4 we explain the PROMELA specification used as formal model, and how we described, in PROMELA, communication time-out and byzantine behavior; in Section 5 we discuss some abstraction and implementation techniques we used to contain the state explosion problem; in Section 6 we report some significant result of the verification phase, where a subtle and erroneous situation, due to the byzantine behavior of a module, was discovered; finally in Section 7 we conclude with some consideration on the whole experience.

2   System Description

The application we studied is a safety software within Safety Nucleus, which is part of a control system called *Computerized Central Apparatus* (ACC)[1] produced by Ansaldobreda Segnalamento Ferroviario [17]. The ACC is a highly programmable centralized control system for railway stations. It plays a critical

---

[1] "Apparato Centrale a Calcolatore", in Italian.

role in a wider railway signaling system, which is a very complex distributed architecture designed to manage a large railway network. Each node in the network is devoted to the control of a medium-large railway station, or a line section with small stations, or a complete low traffic line with a simple interlocking logic.

The ACC architecture (see Figure 1) consists in two sub-systems that independently perform *management* and *vital* functions. **Management functions,**

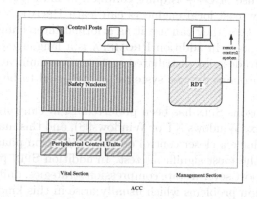

Fig. 1. The Computerized Central Apparatus architecture and its environment

run by a sub-section called Recording, Diagnosis and data Transmission (RDT), consists in auxiliary tasks, such as data recording, diagnostic management and remote control interface. **Vital functions** are reserved to control train movements and wayside equipment, and generally safe-critical procedures. This section of ACC is composed by a *Safety Nucleus* (SN), *Peripheral Control Units* (PCUs) and *Control Posts* (CPs).

Due to the critical characteristic of the vital section of ACC, particular attention has been paid to design fault tolerant mechanisms aimed to avoid that non-predictable (temporary or permanent) faults might compromise the correct operation of the system. To guarantee a trustable level of robustness many components have been replicated and consistency control tests have been inserted into the algorithm defining the behavior of the system. The **Safety Nucleus** is specifically designed for these control and safety purposes. It is interposed between CPs, from which an human operator can digit commands, and the PCUs that, in turn, execute them. Those commands are considered *critical* because their execution takes effect to critical machineries such as railway semaphores, rail points, or crossing levels. The SN has the principal aim to safely deliver the commands to the PCUs in case of faults in some hardware components. It is based on a triple modular redundancy configuration of computers which independently run different versions of the same application program.

Peripheral Control Units are designed to execute critical operation and to directly command physical devices. **Control Posts** are formed by input/output interfaces and by terminal by with an human operator compose a request or a command. Control Posts will not be considered in this study.

3 PROMELA and SPIN

Industrial choices within Ansaldobreda Segnalamento Ferroviario induced us to use PROMELA (Process Meta Language) [11] as specification language and SPIN as model checker environments. The fact that PROMELA is an imperative language with variables, with a C-like syntax makes it quite appreciated in industrial environment: the use of C++ is quite common in industrial development, and then with very low cost local engineers can learn PROMELA syntax and informal semantics, so that they can use it as a formal interchange language in the model refinement step. In addition PROMELA is a language of general applicability introduced to describe distributed systems, communication protocols and, in general, asynchronous process systems and resorted to be quite appropriate for our project.

For similar reasons SPIN has been preferred. SPIN can run on different platforms (Unix, Linux, Windows NT or Windows98), and this makes it possible, for the industries to have a closer control on the verification phase; for example by running some of the most significant test. In addition SPIN performs on-the-fly analysis, and support several state compression strategies, quite useful in dealing with state explosion problems which usually arise in this kind of work.

A PROMELA specification consists in one or more *process templates* (called also *proctype*) and in at least one process instantiation. The language is extended with non-deterministic constructs and with communication primitives, *send* and *receive*, using a weakly recalling Dijkstra's guarded command language notation [5] and Hoare's language CSP [10]. Processes can communicate via rendezvous, or via asynchronous message passing through buffered channels or shared memory. In addition any running process can instantiate further asynchronous processes using process templates.

SPIN [12] is an efficient formal verification tool for checking the logical consistence of a specification given in PROMELA. SPIN translates each PROMELA process template given in input, into a finite automaton. A global automaton of a system behavior is obtained by the interleaving product (referred as the *space state*) of all the automata of the processes composing the system. SPIN accepts correctness claims specified either in the syntax of standard Linear Temporal Logic (LTL) [19], or as process invariants (using assertions) expressing base *safety* and *liveness* properties[2].

4 Formalization

In this section we describe the PROMELA model of the vital section of ACC, and the PROMELA models used to formalize time-out expiring and byzantine faults[3]. We used four PROMELA processes for the SN, and a PROMELA process for each

---

[2] Further information about PROMELA and SPIN can be found at the official SPIN URL http://plan9.bell-labs.com/netlib/spin/whatispin.html.

[3] The detailed specification is property of Ansaldobreda Segnalamento Ferroviario. We describe here, with permission, just what is needed to understand this work.

PCUs[4]. In the following with safety nucleus (lowercase) we mean the PROMELA model of the SN and with peripheral units (lowercase) the one of the PCUs.

4.1   The Safety Nucleus Model

A scheme of the safety nucleus processes and of the channels among them is reported in Figure 2. We want to underline:

1. the three identical *central processes*, called *module* A, B, and C, implementing the triple modular redundancy;
2. a special process called *exclusion logic*, devoted to checking the consistency of the three modules, and able to disconnect each of them if necessary;
3. the *interconnections* among the modules, between the modules and the exclusion logic, and between the modules and the PCUs;
4. the PCUs, here represented as a black box, composed by n control units.

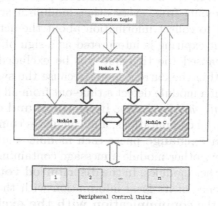

Fig. 2. The PROMELA processes with which we modeled the SN and the relative connections

The **modules** A, B, and C are designed for: (a) collecting global information on the system state, composed by the local states of each modules, by the state of the peripheral units and busses; (b) performing local computation taking care of the information collected and composing commands to be sent to the peripheral units. The three modules can communicate each other via symmetric channels; each module is further connected, via symmetric channels, with the exclusion logic and, via a double bus, with the peripheral units.

The behavior of a module is composed by a repeated sequence of *phases*, formally described with the following pseudo-code[5]:

---

[4] in the work we considered only two of such devices.
[5] n is the number of peripheral units

```
loop
1. * <synchronization>
2.   <command elaboration>
3. * <data exchange with the other modules>
4.   <distributed voting>
5. * <communication to exclusion logic>
{ communication with the PCUs }
        for i = 1 to n do
        6.1   if <is my turn> the
        6.2 *   <synchronization>
        6.3 *   <send command to the PCUs>
        6.4 *   <receive acknowledge from the PCUs>
        endfor
endloop
```

During each phase a central module runs local computations or communicates with other components of the system (we have pointed out these phases with an *). In particular, in the **synchronization** phase each module sends to and receives (with time-out) from every other module a synchronization message. This phase is used to collect information about the activity state of the other modules: a time-out expiring is interpreted as a sign of the non activeness, and the module that caused the time-out will be excluded from any successively communication within the current loop. Because the system is expected to run at least 2 out of 3, if a module detect a time-out from all the other modules, then it commutes in a *safe shutdown state*. In the **command elaboration** phase each module performs local computations, and calculates commands to be sent to the PCUs. In the **data exchange** phase each module sends to and receives (with time-out) from every other module a message containing information about the local state of the other modules. In the **distributed voting** phase, each module checks the consistency of its local information with the one received from the other modules. In the **communication with the exclusion logic**, the result of this test is sent to the exclusion logic which, after having analyzed all the results, can disconnect a module considered potentially faulty. Successively, in the **communication with the PCUs**, a module communicates (with time-out) with the PCUs, following a particular circular protocol. At each loop only two modules are able to communicate their command to the PCUs: a distributed procedure assures a cyclic selection of the modules communicating with the periphery and a cyclic use of the busses, also in case of faults.

4.2   The Peripheral Units Model

A scheme of the *peripheral units* its processes and of the channels connecting them to the safety nucleus is reported in Figure 3. We can identify:

- a process for each unit;
- the interconnection (a double bus) between the units and each of the module of safety nucleus, here represented as a black box.

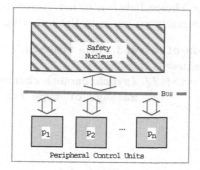

Fig. 3. The PROMELA processes with which we modeled the Peripheral Control Units and their connections with the safety nucleus

In the real system each peripheral unit is composed by two computers in configuration 2 out-of 2, that we modeled by a single process. Its behavior can be summarized with the following pseudo-code:

```
loop
  {communication with the safety nucleus}
parallel for i=1 to 2 do
      <computer[i] receives a command from a module
          and sends acknowledgements in reply>
    endfor
endloop
```

Informally each computer waits for a command, and then returns an acknowledgement back to all the modules.

4.3   Other Formalization Issues

The PROMELA model given so far describes the correct behavior of the system, but to complete the specification phase we needed to formalize also:

- a time-out expiring in the communications;
- a byzantine behavior of a module of the system.
- an arbitrary temporary fault in some system units.

Time-Out Expiring. In the ACC most communications are with time-out. Since PROMELA does not deal with time, we had to abstract from any definition of it. To simulate a communication with time-out we defined a particular *empty* message, whose presence in a channel must be interpreted, by the receiver, as absence of any message it was waiting for, an than as a time-out expiring in a receive action[6]. In addition, wherever we had a **send** action we indeed introduced

---

[6] Formally the *empty* message is defined as follows: supposing the type of a channel was the tuple $(t_1, t_2, \ldots t_k)$, the *empty* message is the tuple $(EMPTY)^k$, where $EMPTY$ is a specific non-null integer constant.

a non deterministic choice between either transmitting the "real" message or transmitting the *empty* message, as in the following PROMELA pseudo-code[7]:

```
/* implementation of a send with time-out  */
define EMPTY <value>
chan c = [0] of <t>; // (synchronous) channel of type <t>
<t> msg;              // message of type <t>

[...]

if
:: true -> c!msg    // send the real message
:: true -> c!EMPTY  // send the empty message
fi;
```

Consequently a **receive** action needs to discern, depending on the content of the message, if a time-out has been expired or if the receiving has been successfully executed. Formally [8]:

```
/* implementation of a receive with time-out  */
c?x ->
    if
    :: (x == EMPTY)  -> <time-out failure>
    :: else          -> <success>
    fi;
```

Modeling a Byzantine Behavior. In order to model a situation in which the failure in one module of the safety nucleus, may cause conflicting information to be sent to the other modules, we need to develop a model of a byzantine behavior. In this context, byzantine behavior is to be intended as it was in Lamport et al. interpretation [14], and precisely:

1. all loyal modules run the same algorithm, and in particular correctly send all messages as specified in the algorithm of Section 4.1 ;
2. a byzantine module runs the same algorithm of a loyal module, but it can arbitrarily fail in executing it, and in particular it may send wrong messages, or send a message delayed respect to a synchronization, or send no message at all.

In this interpretation of byzantine behavior, we have focused the attention on communication events. We have supposed that an arbitrary fault in the procedure will be visible, to the environment, only when the unit tries to communicate.

---

[7] We remind that in Promela, if ::*guard*₁ -> x ::*guard*₂ -> y fi is a guarded non-deterministic choice between x and y, and c!x is a send operation on the channel c, of the variable, or value, x.

[8] We remind that, in Promela, c?x is a receive operation from the channel c, of a value locally memorized into the variable x.

A consequence of this assumption is that an arbitrary fault is modeled as a *communication error*, and precisely as either a communication of a corrupted message, or as a delayed communication, or as no communication at all. To generate corrupted messages, we have supposed to have a function $corrupt() : T \longrightarrow T$, for each message type T, used to compromise the contents of a message[9]. Then a byzantine behavior can be modeled as in the following PROMELA code:

```
/* implementation of a send with byzantine failure */
define EMPTY <value>
chan c = [0] of <t>;
<t> msg;

[...]

if
:: true -> c!msg      // send the corrected message
:: true -> c!EMPTY    // send the empty message (i.e., no messages)
:: true -> c!corrupt(msg) // send the corrupted message
fi;
```

Modeling a Temporary Faulty Component. Besides modeling a byzantine behavior of a central module, we were interested in some other arbitrary faults in:

1. one or both busses connecting SN to PCUs;
2. one or both computers of one or both peripheral units.

In this case we were interested in formalizing faults that were persistent for at least one loop. This could be interpreted as a weaker byzantine behavior definition, in which we wanted to model an arbitrary fault in a component of the system, under the assumption that it behaves consistently (within a loop) when interacting with the other components.

This weaker byzantine fault has been implemented as in the following pseudo-code, relative to the PCU formalization:

```
loop
0.1 <decide the state of each of the two busses>
0.2 <decide the state of each of the two computers>

{communication with the safety nucleus}
   parallel for  i=1  to  2  do
```

---

[9] Possible instantiation for the *corrupt()* are: (a) if the type T is the boolean type, the *not()* function; (b) if the type T is the integer type, supposing that *EMPTY* is a non-null integer value, the *corrupt()* function can be any integer valued function such that $corrupt(n) = EMPTY$ iff $n = EMPTY$ (to avoid semantic ambiguities from the *EMPTY* value and a corrupted message).

```
            <computer[i] receives a command from a module
      [*]      and EVENTUALLY sends acknowledgements in reply>
         endfor
endloop
```

With "decide the state", we mean a preliminary setting of the functional state either of the busses or of the computers of the peripheral unit. In case of state "fault" every communication via the faulty bus or coming from the faulty computer, until the end of the loop, results in a time-out .

5   Abstraction and Implementation Strategies

The complexity of the model of ACC, more critic respect to state dimension than the other SN components, forced us to introduce *modularity* techniques to cope with the state explosion problem. We proceeded in the following ways:

1. by fisically separating the implementation of each phase composing the ACC behavior, with the intention to use them as building blocks In other words we planned to develop the phases in separate files, to be included in main file representing the whole ACC model;
2. by implementing each building block representing a *communication* phase, i.e. the ones where the three modules exchange a message, in a *correct* and in a *byzantine* version;
3. by implementing each building block representing a correct or a byzantine communication phase in a *concrete* and in an *abstract* version.

In the byzantine (versus the correct) version, we modified communication primitives as described in Section 8. In this way we: (a) could take under control the state dimension growing of the whole model by inserting a byzantine phase, which introduces more non determinism than a correct phase, at a time; (b) could test the robustness of the system in presence of some particular byzantine phases and not in presence of a widely distributed, quite less realistic, byzantine behavior.

In the concrete (versus the abstract) version, we modeled the communication without fixing, a priori, any ordering of the send/receive events. That is what happens in the real system. On the contrary, in the abstract version we impose a total order on those events. For example, we decided that the module A sends and receives first from B and then from C, that the module B first receives and sends to A and then sends and receives from C, and finally that the module C first receives from A and from B and then sends to A and to B. Note that the correct and the concrete, respect to the byzantine and the abstract implementations, have different impact on the state space. In fact: (a) the correct version has less not determinism, as least in our implementation of byzantine communication error; (b) forcing a total order on the send/receive eliminates all the non determinism in the external communication events. Inserting either the concrete or the abstract version of a particular phase in the whole model of ACC, we could obtain a set models of different abstraction level (see Figure 4).

While planning a modular model, we had tried to maintain an acceptable degree of *scalability*. In this case scalability is referred of abstract versus the concrete implementations and respect to certain properties decided in accordance with Ansaldobreda Segnalamento Ferroviario. Those properties express fundamental, known a priori, invariants on the communication phases among internal modules composing the ACC. Relatively to the local knowledge of each module, these properties can be informally described as:

(P1) before starting a communication phase, at least two out of three modules are active;

(P2) after a communication phase, each module has sent a message to all the other active modules;

(P3) after a communication phase, in receiving from all the other active module, a module has either received a message, or detected a time-out expiring;

(P4) after a communication phase, if a module has detect a time-out in receiving from all the other active modules, it commutes in a safe shutdown state.

Those properties, expressed as assertions on the code, was verified using the tool SPIN, and resulted satisfied on both the concrete and abstract models.

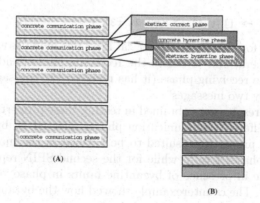

Fig. 4. The framework in which we developed abstract/concrete and byzantine/correct model (A). An example of instantiation of the model (B)

6   Formal Verification

We checked safety properties by varying the number of the byzantine phases inserted in the model. In addition, whenever the state dimension started to become problematic for our computational resources, we preferred the abstract to the concrete implementation of some, or all, the phases. In this way we executed a wide set of verification runs.

In the following we list only some of the more significant properties checked and their formalization as LTL formulae:

(F1) If two modules agree in recognizing something wrong in a third module, that module will be in the future disconnected.

```
[] (p1 -> [] (q1 -> <> r1) )
```

In the previous formula p1 stands for "the module A recognizes something wrong in C", q1 stands for "the module B recognizes something wrong in C" and r1 "C is disconnected".

(F2) When two or more modules are active, then a peripheral units is in a receiving state infinitely often and when it is in this state it effectively receives from two different modules.

```
([] p2) -> ( ([] <> q2) && [] ( q2 -> (<> r2 && t2) ) )
```

In the previous formula p2 stands for "at least two modules are active", q2 stands for "the peripheral unit is before the receiving phase" and r2 "the peripheral unit is after the receiving phase" and t2 "the senders of the two messages are different".

(F3) When two or more modules are active, if a peripheral units receives messages then it receives exactly two messages.

```
([] p3) -> [] ( q3 -> (r3 && t3) )
```

In the previous formula p3 stands for "at least two modules are active", q3 stands for "the peripheral unit is before the receiving phase" and r3 "the peripheral unit is after the receiving phase (it has received two messages)" and t3 "it has received exactly two messages".

Interesting results were obtained in testing these properties on a model of the system with different communication phases affected by byzantine faults. The first and third properties resulted to be verified in the model with the byzantine faults in phases 1 to 5, while for the second SPIN reported an interesting counterexample in presence of byzantine faults in phase "communication with the periphery". The counterexample showed how the byzantine module can maliciously induce the other two modules in erroneous deduction on the global state and consequently to wrongly execute the communication protocol with the peripheral control units.

Most verifications, due to the high state space size required the use of both the two optimization strategies native in SPIN: the MA e COLLAPSE methods, which respectively use a minimized version of the Büchi Automata and a compressed representation of the state vector. As an example we report in the following the SPIN output relative to the verification to property (F2):

```
for p.o. reduction to be valid the never claim must be stutter-closed
(never claims generated from LTL formulae are stutter-closed)
pan: acceptance cycle (at depth 2342)
pan: wrote mainltl.c.trail
```

```
(Spin Version 3.2.3 -- 1 August 1998)
Warning: Search not completed
        + Partial Order Reduction
        + Compression
        + Graph Encoding (-DMA=180)

Full statespace search for:
        never-claim           +
        assertion violations  + (if within scope of claim)
        acceptance   cycles   + (fairness disabled)
        invalid endstates     - (disabled by never-claim)

State-vector 196 byte, depth reached 2345, errors: 1
     990 states, stored
     699 states, matched
    1689 transitions (= stored+matched)
     256 atomic steps
hash conflicts: 0 (resolved)
(max size 2^19 states)
```

7   Conclusions

The project described in this paper consisted in verifying certain safety properties on a model of a safety-critical control system in presence of byzantine behavior of one of its components. The real system has been validated also by Ansaldobreda Segnalamento Ferroviario, and errors we found confirmed the ones discovered with traditional techniques. The importance of developing a formal model, however stood in its great flexibility and in its high expandibility. In fact, during this project itself the model has been enriched, respect to the first requirements, or modified in some its procedures.

On the basis of this project an assessment on the application of the tool we used to support formal specification and verification process has been done. For what concerns the language PROMELA, we already underlined its suitability and expressivity power in describing this type of distributed system. The only disadvantage we found was the missing of any automatic management of termination of processes, that obliged us to model ad hoc time-out expiring as an active communication with heavy repercussion on the state dimension. In fact, we needed to explicitly formalize the shut-down behavior of a module as a module that does not anything but participating in all the communications by sending *EMPTY* messages to cause time-out.

Regarding the tool SPIN the most important fact to be underlined is related to strategies against the state explosion problem. In particular, the use of a minimized automaton encoding technique (MA) combined with the state compression option (COLLAPSE) resorted to be quite useful in helping with out-of memory problems, but at the cost of a very long execution time.

As an example, in Figure 5 we have reported a quite significative representative data, respect to all the other we obtained, concerning a verification run on a 256 Mbyte RAM Pentium II - Linux Suse 5.3 - for a system model whose complete description required 348 bytes per state; in the figure memory and time resources have been compared using, respectively, the COLLAPSE (for which we had an out-of-memory termination, with the longest depth-first search path contained 15125 transitions from the initial state) and the COLLAPSE + MA options (for which we have successully terminated the verification, with longest depth-first search of 15916).

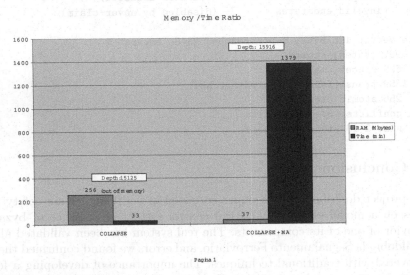

Fig. 5. The Memory/Time ratio using collapse and graph encoding reducing memory techniques

References

1. C. Bernardeschi, A. Fantechi, S. Gnesi, S. Larosa, G. Mongardi, and D. Romano. A Formal Verification Environment for Railway Signaling System Design. *Formal Methods in System Design*, 2(12):139–161, 1998. 536
2. A. Borälv. A Fully Automated Approach for Proving Safety Properties in Interlocking Software Using Automatic Theorem-Proving. In *Proceedings of the 2nd International ERCIM Workshop on Formal Methods Industrial Critical Systems*, 1997. 536
3. A. Cimatti, F. Giunchiglia, G. Mongardi, D. Romano, F. Torielli, and P. Traverso. Formal Verification of a Railway Interlocking System using Model Checking. *Formal Aspect of Computing*, 10(4):361–380, 1998. 536
4. E. M. Clarke, E. A. Emerson, and A. P. Sistla. Automatic Verification of Finite-State Concurrent Systems Using Temporal Logic Specification. *ACM Transaction on Programming Languages and Systems*, 8:244–263, 1986. 536

5. E. W. Dijkstra. Guarded Commands, Non-Determinacy and a Calculus for The Derivation of Programs. *ACM SIGPLAN Notices*, 10(6):2–14, June 1975. 538
6. Cindy Eisner. Using Symbolic Model Checking to Verify the Railway Stations of Hoorn-Keersenboogerd and Heerhugowaard. In *Proceedings of CHARME '99*, 1999. 536
7. E.M. Clarke and E.A. Emerson. Design and Synthesis of Synchronization Skeletons using Branching Time Temporal Logic. In D. Kozen, editor, *Proceedings of the Workshop on Logics of Programs*, volume 131 of *Lecture Notes in Computer Science*, pages 52–71, Yorktown Heights, New York, 1981. Springer-Verlag. 536
8. W. J. Fokkink. Safey Criteria for Hoorn-Keersenboogerd Railway Station. Technical Report Preprint Series 135, Utrecht, 1995. 536
9. J. F. Groote, S. F. M. van Vlijemn, and J. W. C. Koorn. The Safety Guaranteeing System at Station Hoorn-Kersenboogerd in Propositional Logic. In *Proceedings of 10th Annual Conference on Computer Assurance (COMPASS'95)*, pages 57–68, 1995. 536
10. C. A. R. Hoare. *Communicating Sequential Processes*. Prantice-Hall International, 1991. 538
11. G. J. Holzmann. *Design and Validation of Computer Protocols*. Prentice Hall, 1991. 536, 538
12. G. J. Holzmann. The Model Checker SPIN. *IEEE Transaction on Software Engineering*, 5(23):279–295, 1997. 536, 538
13. IEC 61508 IEC. Functional safety of electrical/electronic/programmable electronic safety-related systems. 536
14. L. Lamport, R. Shostak, and M. Pease. The Byzantine Generals Problem. *ACM Transaction on Programming Languages and Systems*, 4(3):382–401, 1982. 536, 542
15. P. G. Larsen, J. Fitzgerald, and T. Brookers. Applying Formal Specification in Industry. *IEEE Software*, 13(7):48–56, 1996. 536
16. P. Liggersmeyer, M. Rothfelder, M. Rettelbach, and T. Ackermann. Qualitätssincherung Software-basierter Technischer Systeme - Problembereiche und Lösungsänsatze. *Informatik Spektrum*, 21:249–258, 1998. in German. 535
17. G. Mongardi. *Dependable Computing for Railway Control System*, chapter 3. Springer-Verlag, 1993. 536
18. M. J. Morely. Safety-Level Communication in Railway Interlockings. *Science of Communication*, 29:147–170, 1997. 536
19. A. Pnueli. The temporal logic of programs. In *Proceedings of the 18th IEEE Symposium on the Foundations of Computer Science (FOCS-77)*, pages 46–57, Providence, Rhode Island, 1977. IEEE, IEEE Computer Society Press. 538
20. pr EN 50128 CENELEC. Railways Applications: Software for Railway Control and Protection Systems. 536
21. J. P. Queille and J. Sifakis. Specification and Verification of Concurrent Systems in CESAR. In *Proceedings of 5th International Symposium on Programming*, Lecture Notes in Computer Science, Vol. 137, pages 337–371. SV, Berlin/New York, 1982. 536

Author Index